Explorations in
CORE MATH
for Common Core Grade 8

HOUGHTON MIFFLIN HARCOURT

Cover photo credit: © Comstock/Getty Images

Printed in the U.S.A.

ISBN 978-0-547-87576-7

6 7 8 9 10   0982   21 20 19 18 17 16 15 14 13

4500425934   B C D E F G

Table of Contents Grade 8

COMMON CORE

▶ Chapter 1   Rational Numbers

		Chapter Overview... 1
CC.8.NS.1	1-1	Rational Numbers.................................... 5
PREP FOR CC.8.EE.7b	1-2	Multiplying Rational Numbers 11
PREP FOR CC.8.EE.7b	1-3	Dividing Rational Numbers 15
PREP FOR CC.8.EE.7b	1-4	Adding and Subtracting with Unlike Denominators 19
CC.8.EE.7b	1-5	Solving Equations with Rational Numbers 23
CC.8.EE.7b	1-6	Solving Two-Step Equations 29
		Problem Solving Connections 35
		Performance Task.................................. 39
		Assessment Readiness 41

▶ Chapter 2   Graphs and Functions

		Chapter Overview... 43
PREP FOR CC.8.EE.8	2-1	Ordered Pairs 47
PREP FOR CC.8.SP.1	2-2	Graphing on a Coordinate Plane 51
CC.8.F.5	2-3	Interpreting Graphs.................................. 55
CC.8.F.1	2-4	Functions.. 61
CC.8.F.4	2-5	Equations, Tables, and Graphs........................ 67
		Problem Solving Connections 71
		Performance Task.................................. 75
		Assessment Readiness 77

© Houghton Mifflin Harcourt Publishing Company

▶ Chapter 3   Exponents and Roots

Chapter Overview		. . . .	**79**
CC.8.EE.1	**3-1**	Integer Exponents	83
CC.8.EE.1	**3-2**	Properties of Exponents.	87
CC.8.EE.3	**3-3**	Scientific Notation	93
CC.8.EE.4	**3-4**	Operating with Scientific Notation.	99
CC.8.EE.2	**3-5**	Squares and Square Roots	105
CC.8.NS.2	**3-6**	Estimating Square Roots	111
CC.8.NS.1	**3-7**	The Real Numbers	117
CC.8.G.7	**3-8**	The Pythagorean Theorem	121
CC.8.G.6	**3-9**	Applying the Pythagorean Theorem and Its Converse	127
		Problem Solving Connections	131
		Performance Task.	135
		Assessment Readiness	137

▶ Chapter 4   Ratios, Proportions, and Similarity

Chapter Overview		. . . .	**139**
PREP FOR CC.8.EE.5	**4-1**	Ratios, Rates, and Unit Rates.	143
PREP FOR CC.8.EE.5	**4-2**	Solving Proportions	147
CC.8.G.5	**4-3**	Similar Figures	151
CC.8.G.3	**4-4**	Dilations	157
		Problem Solving Connections	163
		Performance Task	167
		Assessment Readiness	169

© Houghton Mifflin Harcourt Publishing Company

Chapter 5 Geometric Relationships

Chapter Overview **171**

PREP FOR **CC.8.G.1**   **5-1** Angle Relationships 175

CC.8.G.5   **5-2** Parallel and Perpendicular Lines 179

CC.8.G.5   **5-3** Triangles 185

PREP FOR **CC.8.G.3**   **5-4** Coordinate Geometry 191

PREP FOR **CC.8.G.2**   **5-5** Congruence 195

CC.8.G.3   **5-6** Transformations 199

CC.8.G.1   **5-7** Similarity and Congruence Transformations 205

CC.8.G.2   **5-8** Identifying Combined Transformations 209

            Problem Solving Connections 217

            Performance Task 221

            Assessment Readiness 223

Chapter 6 Measurement and Geometry

Chapter Overview **225**

PREP FOR **CC.8.G.9**   **6-1** Circles 229

CC.8.G.9   **6-2** Volume of Prisms and Cylinders 235

CC.8.G.9   **6-3** Volume of Pyramids and Cones 239

CC.8.G.9   **6-4** Spheres 243

            Problem Solving Connections 247

            Performance Task 251

            Assessment Readiness 253

Chapter 7   Multi-Step Equations

Chapter Overview. **255**

PREP FOR **CC.8.EE.7**   **7-1** Simplifying Algebraic Expressions. 259

CC.8.EE.7b   **7-2** Solving Multi-Step Equations 265

CC.8.EE.7   **7-3** Solving Equations with Variables on Both Sides 271

CC.8.EE.8   **7-4** Systems of Equations. 277

        Problem Solving Connections 283

        Performance Task. 287

        Assessment Readiness 289

Chapter 8   Graphing Lines

Chapter Overview. **291**

CC.8.F.4   **8-1** Graphing Linear Equations 295

CC.8.EE.6   **8-2** Slope of a Line 299

CC.8.F.4   **8-3** Using Slopes and Intercepts. 305

CC.8.F.4   **8-4** Point-Slope Form 313

CC.8.EE.5   **8-5** Direct Variation 317

CC.8.EE.8   **8-6** Solving Systems of Linear Equations by Graphing. 321

        Problem Solving Connections 327

        Performance Task. 331

        Assessment Readiness 333

► Chapter 9 Data, Prediction, and Linear Functions

Chapter Overview. **335**

CC.8.SP.1	9-1	Scatter Plots	339
CC.8.SP.3	9-2	Linear Best Fit Models	345
CC.8.SP.4	Ext	Patterns in Two-Way Tables	351
CC.8.F.3	9-3	Linear Functions	355
CC.8.F.2	9-4	Comparing Multiple Representations.	361
		Problem Solving Connections	367
		Performance Task.	371
		Assessment Readiness	373

Learning the Standards for Mathematical Practice

The Common Core State Standards include eight Standards for Mathematical Practice. Here's how *Explorations in Core Math Grade 8* helps you learn those standards as you master the Standards for Mathematical Content.

1 Make sense of problems and persevere in solving them.

In *Explorations in Core Math Grade 8*, you will work through Explores and Examples that present a solution pathway for you to follow. You are asked questions along the way so that you gain an understanding of the solution process, and then you will apply what you've learned in the Try This and Practice for the lesson.

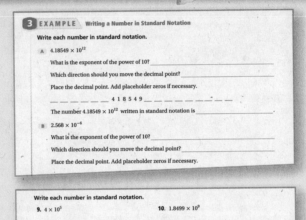

3 EXAMPLE   Writing a Number in Standard Notation

Write each number in standard notation.

A 4.18549×10^{12}

What is the exponent of the power of 10? _____

Which direction should you move the decimal point? _____

Place the decimal point. Add placeholder zeros if necessary.

_ _ _ _ _ _ _ 4 1 8 5 4 9 _ _ _ _ _ _ _._ _

The number 4.18549×10^{12} written in standard notation is _____.

B 2.568×10^{-6}

What is the exponent of the power of 10? _____

Which direction should you move the decimal point? _____

Place the decimal point. Add placeholder zeros if necessary.

Write each number in standard notation.

9. 4×10^5 | **10.** 1.8499×10^9

11. 8.3×10^{-4} | **12.** 3.582×10^{-6}

2 Reason abstractly and quantitatively.

When you solve a real-world problem in *Explorations in Core Math Grade 8*, learn to represent the situation symbolically by translating the problem into a mathematical expression or equation. You will use these mathematical models to solve the problem and then state your answer in terms of the problem context. You will reflect on the solution process in order to check your answer for reasonableness and to draw conclusions.

1 EXPLORE   Solving Equations by Combining Like Terms

A soccer club spent $97.50 on trophies from a custom trophy company. The cost of manufacturing *x* custom trophies is $18.50 for the setup cost, plus $12.50 per trophy. To ship the trophies, the company charges a standard fee of $4 per order plus $2.50 per trophy. How many trophies did the soccer club order?

A Write an expression representing the **cost of manufacturing**.

Setup cost + Cost for *x* trophies

+ 12.50*x*

B Write an expression representing the **cost of shipping**.

Standard fee + Cost for *x* trophies

+

C Write an equation that can be solved to find the number of trophies the soccer club ordered.

Cost of manufacturing + Cost of shipping = Club's total cost

+ =

D Solve your equation for *x*.

REFLECT

1. How can you check your answer?

_____
_____

③ Construct viable arguments and critique the reasoning of others.

Throughout *Explorations in Core Math Grade 8* you will be asked to make conjectures, construct a mathematical argument, explain your reasoning, and justify your conclusions. Reflect questions offer opportunities for cooperative learning and class discussion. You will have additional opportunities to critique reasoning in Error Analysis problems.

> **2b. Conjecture** Do you think that the value of r in the point $(1, r)$ is always the unit rate for any situation? Explain.
> _____
> _____
> _____

> **7. Error Analysis** A student claims that the equation $y = 7$ is not a linear equation because it does not have the form $y = mx + b$. Do you agree or disagree? Why?
> _____
> _____

④ Model with mathematics.

Explorations in Core Math Grade 8 presents problems in a variety of contexts such as as science, business, and everyday life. You will use mathematical models such as expressions, equations, tables, and graphs to represent the information in the problem and to solve the problem. Then you will interpret your results in the problem context.

> **2 EXPLORE** Comparing a Table and an Equation
>
> Josh and Maggie buy MP3 files from different music download services. With both services, the monthly charge is a linear function of the number of songs downloaded. The cost at Josh's service is described by $y = 0.50x + 10$ where y is the cost in dollars and x is the number of songs downloaded.
>
> | Cost of MP3s at Maggie's Music Service | | | | |
> |---|---|---|---|---|
> | Songs, x | 5 | 10 | 15 | 20 | 25 |
> | Cost ($), y | 4.95 | 9.90 | 14.85 | 19.80 | 24.75 |
>
> **A** Find the unit rate of each function.
>
> Josh: _____   Maggie: _____
>
> **B** Which function has the greater rate of change? What does that mean in this context?
>
> **C** Write an equation in slope-intercept form to describe the cost at Maggie's music service.
>
> $y = mx + b$
>
> $\underline{\quad} = \underline{\quad} \cdot \underline{\quad} + b$ Substitute for y, m, and b.
>
> $\underline{\quad} = \underline{\quad} + b$ Subtract the number that is added to b from both sides.
>
> $\underline{\quad} = b$
>
> $y = \underline{\quad} x + \underline{\quad}$
>
> **D** Describe each service's cost in words using the meanings of the slopes and y-intercepts.
> _____
>
> **REFLECT**

© Houghton Mifflin Harcourt Publishing Company

⑤ Use appropriate tools strategically.

You will use a variety of tools in *Explorations in Core Math Grade 8,* including manipulatives, paper and pencil, and technology. You might use manipulatives to develop concepts, paper and pencil to practice skills, and technology (such as graphing calculators, spreadsheets, or geometry software) to investigate more complicated mathematical ideas.

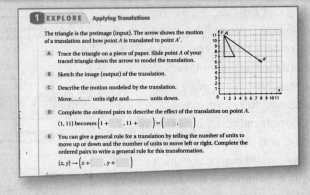

1 EXPLORE   Applying Translations

The triangle is the preimage (input). The arrow shows the motion of a translation and how point A is translated to point A'.

A Trace the triangle on a piece of paper. Slide point A of your traced triangle down the arrow to model the translation.

B Sketch the image (output) of the translation.

C Describe the motion modeled by the translation.

Move _____ units right and _____ units down.

D Complete the ordered pairs to describe the effect of the translation on point A.

$(1, 11)$ becomes $\left(1 + , 11 + \right) = \left(, \right)$

E You can give a general rule for a translation by telling the number of units to move up or down and the number of units to move left or right. Complete the ordered pairs to write a general rule for this transformation.

$(x, y) \rightarrow \left(x + , y + \right)$

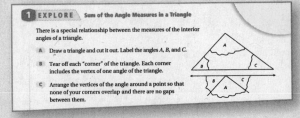

1 EXPLORE   Sum of the Angle Measures in a Triangle

There is a special relationship between the measures of the interior angles of a triangle.

A Draw a triangle and cut it out. Label the angles A, B, and C.

B Tear off each "corner" of the triangle. Each corner includes the vertex of one angle of the triangle.

C Arrange the vertices of the angle around a point so that none of your corners overlap and there are no gaps between them.

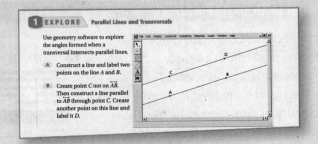

1 EXPLORE   Parallel Lines and Transversals

Use geometry software to explore the angles formed when a transversal intersects parallel lines.

A Construct a line and label two points on the line A and B.

B Create point C not on $\overleftrightarrow{AB}$. Then construct a line parallel to $\overleftrightarrow{AB}$ through point C. Create another point on this line and label it D.

⑥ Attend to precision.

Precision refers not only to the correctness of arithmetic calculations, algebraic manipulations, and geometric reasoning but also to the proper use of mathematical language, symbols, and units to communicate mathematical ideas. Throughout *Explorations in Core Math Grade 8* you will demonstrate your skills in these areas when you are asked to calculate, describe, show, explain, prove, and predict.

REFLECT

4a. Scientists captured and released a whale shark that weighed about 6×10^5 units. Circle the best choice for the units this measurement is given in: ounces /pounds /tons .

4b. Explain how you chose a unit of measurement in **4a.**

_____

_____

2c. Use your answers to **2a** and **2b** to explain whey there is only one cube root of a positive number.

_____

_____

_____

⑦ Look for and make use of structure.

⑧ Look for and express regularity in repeated reasoning.

In *Explorations in Core Math Grade 8,* you will look for patterns or regularity in mathematical structures such as expressions, equations, operations, geometric figures, and diagrams. You will use these patterns to generalize beyond a specific case and to make connections between related problems.

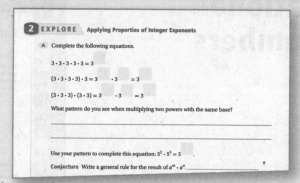

2 EXPLORE Applying Properties of Integer Exponents

A Complete the following equations.

$3 \cdot 3 \cdot 3 \cdot 3 \cdot 3 = 3$

$(3 \cdot 3 \cdot 3 \cdot 3) \cdot 3 = 3 \quad \cdot 3 \quad = 3$

$(3 \cdot 3 \cdot 3) \cdot (3 \cdot 3) = 3 \quad \cdot 3 \quad = 3$

What pattern do you see when multiplying two powers with the same base?

_____

_____

Use your pattern to complete this equation: $5^2 \cdot 5^5 = 5$.

Conjecture Write a general rule for the result of $a^m \cdot a^n$. _____

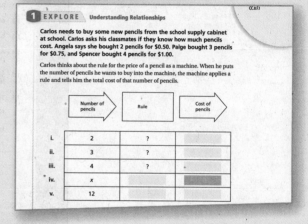

1 EXPLORE Understanding Relationships   CC.8.F.1

Carlos needs to buy some new pencils from the school supply cabinet at school. Carlos asks his classmates if they know how much pencils cost. Angela says she bought 2 pencils for $0.50. Paige bought 3 pencils for $0.75, and Spencer bought 4 pencils for $1.00.

Carlos thinks about the rule for the price of a pencil as a machine. When he puts the number of pencils he wants to buy into the machine, the machine applies a rule and tells him the total cost of that number of pencils.

	Number of pencils	Rule	Cost of pencils
i.	2	?	
ii.	3	?	
iii.	4	?	
iv.	x		
v.	12		

CHAPTER 1

Rational Numbers

CHAPTER 1

CHAPTER 1

Rational Numbers

Chapter Focus

You will write rational numbers as decimals and fractions. You will multiply and divide rational numbers. The sums and differences of fractions with unlike denominators will be found using common denominators. Finally, you will solve equations containing rational numbers.

Chapter at a Glance

COMMON CORE

Lesson	Standards for Mathematical Content
1-1 Rational Numbers	CC.8.NS.1
1-2 Multiplying Rational Numbers	PREP FOR CC.8.EE.7b
1-3 Dividing Rational Numbers	PREP FOR CC.8.EE.7b
1-4 Adding and Subtracting with Unlike Denominators	PREP FOR CC.8.EE.7b
1-5 Solving Equations with Rational Numbers	CC.8.EE.7b
1-6 Solving Two-Step Equations	CC.8.EE.7b
Problem Solving Connections	
Performance Task	
Assessment Readiness	

COMMON CORE
PROFESIONAL
DEVELOPMENT **CC.8.NS.1**

In Grade 7, students used long division to distinguish between repeating and terminating decimals. Building on this work, students in Grade 8 distinguish between rational and irrational numbers. Students recognize that the decimal equivalent of a fraction will either terminate or repeat. Students using patterns or algebraic reasoning will convert repeating decimals into their fraction equivalents.

Unpacking the Standards

Understanding the standards and the vocabulary terms in the standards will help you know exactly what you are expected to learn in this chapter.

COMMON CORE **CC.8.NS.1**

Understand informally that every number has a decimal expansion; the rational numbers are those with decimal expansions that terminate in 0s or eventually repeat. Know that other numbers are called irrational.

Key Vocabulary

rational number *(número racional)* Any number that can be expressed as a ratio of two integers.

irrational number *(número irracional)* A number that cannot be expressed as a ratio of two integers or as a repeating or terminating decimal.

What It Means to You

You will learn the definition of an irrational number. You will write rational numbers as decimals.

EXAMPLE

Write each fraction as a decimal. Then determine if the numbers are rational.

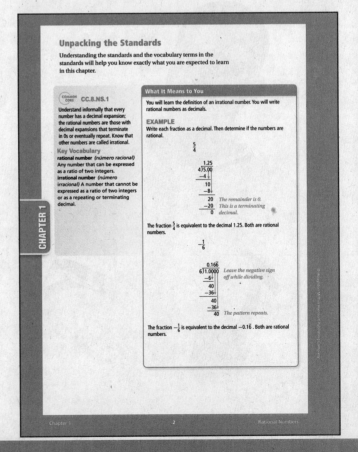

$\dfrac{5}{4}$

The remainder is 0. This is a terminating decimal.

The fraction $\frac{5}{4}$ is equivalent to the decimal 1.25. Both are rational numbers.

$-\dfrac{1}{6}$

Leave the negative sign off while dividing.

The pattern repeats.

The fraction $-\frac{1}{6}$ is equivalent to the decimal $-0.1\overline{6}$. Both are rational numbers.

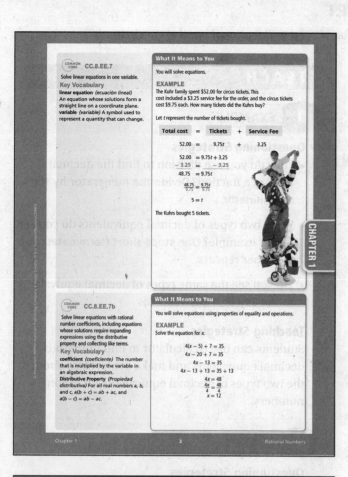

COMMON CORE CC.8.EE.7

Solve linear equations in one variable.

Key Vocabulary

linear equation *(ecuación lineal)* An equation whose solutions form a straight line on a coordinate plane.
variable *(variable)* A symbol used to represent a quantity that can change.

What It Means to You

You will solve equations.

EXAMPLE

The Kuhr family spent $52.00 for circus tickets. This cost included a $3.25 service fee for the order, and the circus tickets cost $9.75 each. How many tickets did the Kuhrs buy?

Let *t* represent the number of tickets bought.

Total cost	=	Tickets	+	Service Fee
52.00	=	9.75t	+	3.25

$$52.00 = 9.75t + 3.25$$
$$-3.25 \qquad -3.25$$
$$48.75 = 9.75t$$
$$\frac{48.75}{9.75} = \frac{9.75t}{9.75}$$
$$5 = t$$

The Kuhrs bought 5 tickets.

COMMON CORE CC.8.EE.7b

Solve linear equations with rational number coefficients, including equations whose solutions require expanding expressions using the distributive property and collecting like terms.

Key Vocabulary

coefficient *(coeficiente)* The number that is multiplied by the variable in an algebraic expression.
Distributive Property *(Propiedad distributiva)* For all real numbers a, b, and c, a(b + c) = ab + ac, and a(b − c) = ab − ac.

What It Means to You

You will solve equations using properties of equality and operations.

EXAMPLE

Solve the equation for x.

$$4(x - 5) + 7 = 35$$
$$4x - 20 + 7 = 35$$
$$4x - 13 = 35$$
$$4x - 13 + 13 = 35 + 13$$
$$4x = 48$$
$$\frac{4x}{4} = \frac{48}{4}$$
$$x = 12$$

Chapter 1   3   Rational Numbers

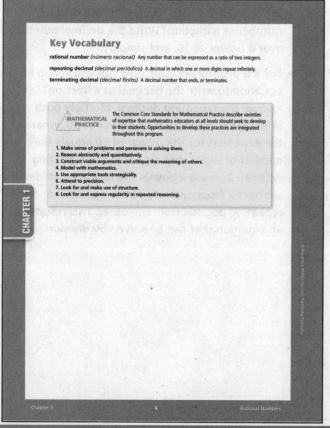

Key Vocabulary

rational number *(número racional)* Any number that can be expressed as a ratio of two integers.
repeating decimal *(decimal periódico)* A decimal in which one or more digits repeat infinitely.
terminating decimal *(decimal finito)* A decimal number that ends, or terminates.

MATHEMATICAL PRACTICE   The Common Core Standards for Mathematical Practice describe varieties of expertise that mathematics educators at all levels should seek to develop in their students. Opportunities to develop these practices are integrated throughout this program.

1. Make sense of problems and persevere in solving them.
2. Reason abstractly and quantitatively.
3. Construct viable arguments and critique the reasoning of others.
4. Model with mathematics.
5. Use appropriate tools strategically.
6. Attend to precision.
7. Look for and make use of structure.
8. Look for and express regularity in repeated reasoning.

Chapter 1   4   Rational Numbers

COMMON CORE PROFESIONAL DEVELOPMENT CC.8.EE.7

Based on work with multi-step equations in Grade 7, students in Grade 8 have the tools to solve one-variable equations with variables on both sides of the equals sign. Students understand that the solution to the equation is the value(s) of the variable which make a true equality when substituted back into the equation. In Grade 8, equations will include rational numbers, the Distributive Property, and combining like terms.

Rational Numbers
Going Deeper

Essential question: *How do you write rational numbers as decimals and as fractions?*

COMMON
CORE Standards for
Mathematical Content

CC.8.NS.1 Know that numbers that are not rational are called irrational. Understand informally that every number has a decimal expansion; for rational numbers show that the decimal expansion repeats eventually, and convert a decimal expansion which repeats eventually into a rational number.

Materials
Scientific calculator

Vocabulary
rational number
terminating decimal
repeating decimal

Math Background
Real numbers consist of rational numbers and irrational numbers. A rational number can be written as a ratio a to b for integers a and b, where $b \neq 0$. Irrational numbers such as π and $\sqrt{7}$ cannot be expressed as a rational number. Every real number can be expressed in decimal form. Rational numbers have decimal equivalents that terminate or repeat a pattern. Irrational numbers have decimal equivalents that neither terminate nor repeat a pattern. They must be approximated in decimal form.

INTRODUCE

Connect to prior learning by asking students how to convert fractions into decimals. Ask students what the decimal equivalent is for $\frac{1}{2}$. They should easily be able to answer 0.5. Tell students that in this lesson they will write rational numbers as decimals and fractions.

TEACH

1 EXAMPLE

Questioning Strategies

- How do you use division to find the decimal form of a fraction? **Divide the numerator by the denominator.**

- What two types of decimal equivalents do you see in this example? **One stops short (terminates) and the other repeats.**

- Do you see the same types of decimal equivalents in the Try This answers? **Yes**

Teaching Strategies
Students can use a calculator to find numerous decimal equivalents and make conjectures about the two types of decimal equivalents for rational numbers.

2 EXAMPLE

Questioning Strategies

- What is the first step when writing a decimal number as a fraction? **Write the decimal number over a power of 10, and simplify.**

- For a repeating decimal, how can you set up an equation to write the decimal as a fraction? **Let** *x* **equal the repeating decimal. Multiply both sides of the equation by a power of 10, where the exponent for the power of 10 equals the number of digits that repeat in the repeating decimal. Because** *x* **equals the repeating decimal, subtract** *x* **from one side of the equation and the repeating decimal from the other. This results in an equation that can be solved by division.**

Name_____ Class_____ Date_____

1-1

Rational Numbers
Going Deeper

Essential question: *How do you write rational numbers as decimals and as fractions?*

A **rational number** is a number that can be written as a ratio in the form $\frac{a}{b}$, where a and b are integers and b is not 0.

CC.8.NS.1

1 EXAMPLE Writing Fractions as Decimals

Write each fraction as a decimal.

A $\frac{1}{4}$

```
        0.2 5
  4)1.0 0
    −8
      2 0
    − 20
        0
```

$\frac{1}{4} = 0.25$

Remember that the fraction bar means "divided by." Divide the numerator by the denominator.

Divide until the remainder is 0, adding zeros after the decimal point in the dividend as needed.

B $\frac{1}{3}$

```
        0.3 33
  3)1.0 0 0
    − 9
      10
    − 9
      10
    − 9
      1
```

Will this division ever end in a remainder of 0? Explain.

No; the same pattern keeps repeating.

Describe the quotient.

0.33333…; the digit 3 repeats indefinitely.

When a decimal has one or more digits that repeat indefinitely, write the decimal with a bar over the repeating digit(s).

$\frac{1}{3} = 0.\overline{3}$

TRY THIS!

Write each fraction as a decimal.

1a. $\frac{5}{11}$ **1b.** $\frac{1}{8}$ **1c.** $\frac{4}{5}$

$0.\overline{45}$ 0.125 0.8

REFLECT

1c. How do you write $1\frac{1}{4}$ as a decimal?

1.25

1d. How do you write $2\frac{1}{3}$ as a decimal?

$2.\overline{3}$

The examples in **1** show the two kinds of decimals that represent rational numbers.

• After the decimal point, there may be a finite number of digits. This is called a **terminating decimal**. 0.25 is a **terminating decimal**.

• After the decimal point, there may be a block of one or more digits that are not all zero that repeat indefinitely. This is called a repeating decimal. $0.\overline{3}$ is a **repeating decimal**.

Every rational number can be written as a terminating decimal or a repeating decimal.

CC.8.NS.1

2 EXAMPLE Writing Decimals as Fractions

Write each decimal as a fraction in simplest form.

A 0.825

The decimal 0.825 means "825 thousandths." Write this as a fraction.

$$\frac{825}{1000}$$

Then simplify the fraction.

$$\frac{825 \div 25}{1000 \div 25} = \frac{33}{40}$$

$$0.825 = \frac{33}{40}$$

© Houghton Mifflin Harcourt Publishing Company

Avoid Common Errors

Students may automatically assume that 100 is the power of 10 to use when converting a repeating decimal into a fraction. Remind students to count the number of decimal places that repeat in order to determine the power of 10 to use.

MATHEMATICAL PRACTICE **Highlighting the Standards**

This Example is an opportunity to address Standard 2 (Reason abstractly and quantitatively). Students are asked to think of numbers abstractly when converting repeating decimals to fractions. By using a variable to represent a repeating decimal, students write an equation and use abstract methods and representations to solve for the same variable in fraction form.

CLOSE

Essential Question

How do you write rational numbers as decimals and as fractions?

Possible answer: To change a rational number to a fraction, divide the numerator by the denominator. If a rational number changes to a terminating decimal, write the decimal as a fraction over a power of 10 and simplify. If the rational number changes to a repeating decimal, write an equation where x equals the repeating decimal, and use properties to solve so that the result is a fraction.

Summarize

Have students explain in their own words how to write rational numbers as fractions and as decimals. Have them support their statements with examples.

PRACTICE

Where skills are taught	Where skills are practiced
1 EXAMPLE	EXS. 1–6, 13–19, 21–22, 24–26
2 EXAMPLE	EXS. 7–12, 20, 23

B $0.\overline{37}$

Let $x = 0.\overline{37}$. $0.\overline{37}$ has ___2___ repeating digits, so multiply each side of the equation $x = 0.\overline{37}$ by 10^2, or ___100___.

Because $x = 0.\overline{37}$, you can subtract x from one side and $0.\overline{37}$ from the other.

To solve for x, divide both sides of the equation by ___99___. Then simplify if necessary.

$x = 0.\overline{37}$

$(100)x = (100) \, 0.\overline{37}$

$100x = 37.\overline{37}$

$\underline{-x \quad - 0.\overline{37}}$

$99x = 37$

$\dfrac{99x}{99} = \dfrac{37}{99}$

$x = \dfrac{37}{99}$

$0.\overline{37} = \dfrac{37}{99}$

REFLECT

2a. How do you know that 0.825 and $0.\overline{37}$ can be written as fractions?

0.825 is a terminating decimal and $0.\overline{37}$ is a repeating decimal. Therefore both are rational numbers and can be written in the form $\frac{a}{b}$.

TRY THIS!

Write each decimal as a fraction in simplest form.

2b. 0.12 ___$\frac{3}{25}$___ **2c.** $0.\overline{57}$ ___$\frac{19}{33}$___ **2d.** 1.4 ___$1\frac{2}{5}$___

PRACTICE

Write each fraction as a decimal.

1. $\frac{7}{8}$
0.875

2. $\frac{2}{3}$
$0.\overline{6}$

3. $2\frac{4}{5}$
2.8

4. $\frac{23}{24}$
$0.958\overline{3}$

5. $\frac{17}{20}$
0.85

6. $\frac{18}{25}$
0.72

Write each decimal as a fraction in simplest form.

7. $7.\overline{4}$ ___$7\frac{4}{9}$___ **8.** 0.56 ___$\frac{14}{25}$___ **9.** 0.45 ___$\frac{9}{20}$___

10. $0.\overline{93}$ ___$\frac{31}{33}$___ **11.** $0.5\overline{4}$ ___$\frac{6}{11}$___ **12.** 6.02 ___$6\frac{1}{50}$___

Compare. Write <, >, or =.

13. $\frac{4}{7}$ > $\frac{3}{8}$ **14.** $\frac{3}{4}$ = 0.75 **15.** 0.35 > $\frac{1}{3}$

16. $0.\overline{5}$ = $\frac{5}{9}$ **17.** 1.5 < $1\frac{3}{5}$ **18.** $\frac{2}{3}$ < 0.67

19. A $\frac{5}{16}$-inch-long bolt is used in a machine. What is the length of the bolt written as a decimal?

0.3125 in.

20. The average width of a robin's egg is about 0.015 meter. Write this length as a fraction in simplest form.

$\frac{3}{200}$ m

21. The weight of an object on the moon is $\frac{1}{6}$ its weight on Earth. Write $\frac{1}{6}$ as a decimal.

$0.1\overline{6}$

22. Oxygen makes up about $\frac{3}{5}$ of the human body. Write $\frac{3}{5}$ as a decimal.

0.6

23. On a test, Jerry answered 52 out of 60 questions correctly. What portion of Jerry's answers was correct? Write your answer as a decimal.

$0.8\overline{6}$

24. Write $\frac{1}{9}$ and $\frac{2}{9}$ as decimals. Use the results to predict the decimal equivalent of $\frac{8}{9}$.

$0.\overline{1}; 0.\overline{2}; 0.\overline{8}$

25. The decimal equivalent of $\frac{1}{25}$ is 0.04, and the decimal equivalent of $\frac{2}{25}$ is 0.08. Without dividing, find the decimal equivalent of $\frac{6}{25}$. Explain how you found your answer.

0.24; $\frac{6}{25}$ is 6 times $\frac{1}{25}$, so I multiplied 6 times 0.04.

26. **Conjecture** A number that is not rational is called an irrational number. When written as a decimal, an irrational number is not a terminating decimal or a repeating decimal.

Assign these pages to help your students practice and apply important lesson concepts. For additional exercises, see the Student Edition.

Answers

Additional Practice

1. $\frac{2}{3}$

2. $\frac{1}{2}$

3. $\frac{1}{4}$

4. $\frac{1}{4}$

5. $\frac{3}{8}$

6. $\frac{1}{12}$

7. $\frac{2}{9}$

8. $\frac{1}{6}$

9. $\frac{18}{25}$

10. $\frac{29}{500}$

11. $\frac{45}{99}$

12. $2\frac{1}{10}$

13. $\frac{9}{250}$

14. $\frac{7}{9}$

15. $2\frac{61}{200}$

16. $\frac{4}{625}$

17. $\frac{31}{99}$

18. $6\frac{19}{20}$

19. $\frac{2}{125}$

20. $\frac{1}{2000}$

21. 0.125

22. $2.\overline{6}$

23. $0.9\overline{3}$

24. 3.2

25. 0.6875

26. $0.\overline{7}$

27. 0.8

28. 1.24

29. Possible answer: $\frac{5}{24}$

Problem Solving

1.

Decimal	Decimal	Decimal
0.25	0.171875	0.09375
0.234375	0.15625	0.078125
0.21875	0.140625	0.0625
0.203125	0.125	
0.1875	0.109375	

2. Terminating decimals

3. D

4. H

5. D

6. F

7. A

Name_____ Class_____ Date_____ **1-1**

Additional Practice

Simplify.

1. $\frac{6}{9}$　　　2. $\frac{48}{96}$　　　3. $\frac{13}{52}$　　　4. $\frac{7}{28}$

5. $\frac{15}{40}$　　　6. $\frac{4}{48}$　　　7. $\frac{14}{63}$　　　8. $\frac{12}{72}$

Write each decimal as a fraction in simplest form.

9. 0.72　　　10. 0.058　　　11. $0.\overline{45}$　　　12. 2.1

13. 0.036　　　14. $0.\overline{7}$　　　15. 2.305　　　16. 0.0064

17. $0.\overline{31}$　　　18. 6.95　　　19. 0.016　　　20. 0.0005

Write each fraction as a decimal.

21. $\frac{1}{8}$　　　22. $\frac{8}{3}$　　　23. $\frac{14}{15}$　　　24. $\frac{16}{5}$

25. $\frac{11}{16}$　　　26. $\frac{7}{9}$　　　27. $\frac{4}{5}$　　　28. $\frac{31}{25}$

29. Write a fraction that cannot be simplified that has 24 as its denominator.

© Houghton Mifflin Harcourt Publishing Company

Chapter 1　　　　　9　　　　Practice and Problem Solving

Problem Solving

Write the correct answer.

1. Fill in the table below which shows the sizes of drill bits in a set.

2. Do the drill bit sizes convert to repeating or terminating decimals?

_____

13-Piece Drill Bit Set

Fraction	Decimal	Fraction	Decimal	Fraction	Decimal
$\frac{1}{4}$"		$\frac{11}{64}$"		$\frac{3}{32}$"	
$\frac{15}{64}$"		$\frac{5}{32}$"		$\frac{5}{64}$"	
$\frac{7}{32}$"		$\frac{9}{64}$"		$\frac{1}{16}$"	
$\frac{13}{64}$"		$\frac{1}{8}$"			
$\frac{3}{16}$"		$\frac{7}{64}$"			

Use the table at the right that lists the world's smallest nations. Choose the letter for the best answer.

3. What is the area of Vatican City expressed as a fraction in simplest form?

　A $\frac{8}{50}$　　C $\frac{17}{1000}$
　B $\frac{4}{25}$　　D $\frac{17}{100}$

Three of the World's Smallest Nations

Nation	Area (square miles)
Vatican City	0.17
Monaco	0.75
Nauru	8.2

4. What is the area of Monaco expressed as a fraction in simplest form?

　F $\frac{75}{100}$　　H $\frac{3}{4}$
　G $\frac{15}{20}$　　J $\frac{2}{3}$

5. What is the area of Nauru expressed as a mixed number?

　A $8\frac{1}{50}$　　C $8\frac{2}{100}$
　B $8\frac{2}{50}$　　D $8\frac{1}{5}$

6. The average annual precipitation in Miami, FL is 57.55 inches. Express 57.55 as a mixed number.

　F $57\frac{11}{20}$　　H $57\frac{5}{100}$
　G $57\frac{55}{1000}$　　J $57\frac{1}{20}$

7. The average annual precipitation in Norfolk, VA is 45.22 inches. Express 45.22 as a mixed number.

　A $45\frac{11}{50}$　　C $45\frac{11}{20}$
　B $45\frac{22}{1000}$　　D $45\frac{1}{5}$

© Houghton Mifflin Harcourt Publishing Company

Chapter 1　　　　　10　　　　Practice and Problem Solving

© Houghton Mifflin Harcourt Publishing Company

Multiplying Rational Numbers
Going Deeper

Essential question: How do you multiply rational numbers?

COMMON CORE **Standards for Mathematical Content**

Prep for CC.8.EE.7b Solve linear equations with rational number coefficients, including equations whose solutions require expanding expressions using the distributive property and collecting like terms.

Math Background

Multiplying decimals is similar to multiplying whole numbers, except for the additional step of correctly placing the decimal point in the product. Likewise, multiplying mixed numbers is similar to multiplying improper fractions using $\frac{a}{b} \cdot \frac{c}{d} = \frac{ac}{bd}$, except for the additional step of rewriting mixed numbers as improper fractions.

INTRODUCE

Connect to prior learning of rational numbers. Review that rational numbers include positive and negative fractions and decimals—any number that can be expressed as a ratio of two integers (with the denominator being nonzero). You may want to remind students that whole numbers can be written as fractions with a denominator of 1. Then review rewriting mixed numbers as improper fractions.

TEACH

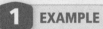 **EXAMPLE**

Questioning Strategies

* What word in the problem indicates multiplication? **of**

* Do you need to count the number of decimal places in whole numbers? **No, because a whole number has 0 decimal places and it will not change where the decimal point will be placed.**

Differentiated Instruction

Clarify that "decimal places" refers to the places to the right of the decimal point: tenths, hundredths, thousandths, etc.

2 **EXAMPLE**

Questioning Strategies

* What do you need to do to each mixed number to apply the rule $\frac{a}{b} \cdot \frac{c}{d} = \frac{ac}{bd}$? **Rewrite the mixed numbers as improper fractions.**

> **MATHEMATICAL PRACTICE** **Highlighting the Standards**
>
> This Lesson is an opportunity to address Standard 7 (Look for and make use of structure). Students are asked to multiply decimals in Example 1 and to multiply mixed numbers in Example 2. Both procedures involve applying previously learned rules for multiplying whole numbers and for multiplying fractions.

CLOSE

Essential Question

How do you multiply rational numbers?
Possible answer: For decimals, first multiply as if the factors were whole numbers. Then count and add the number of decimal places in the factors to find the number of decimal places in the product. For fractions, write each mixed number as an improper fraction. Then multiply the numerators and multiply the denominators of the fractions. Simplify as needed.

PRACTICE

Where skills are taught	Where skills are practiced
1 EXAMPLE	EXS. 1–2
2 EXAMPLE	EXS. 3–6

Name _____ Class _____ Date _____

1-2

Multiplying Rational Numbers
Going Deeper

Essential question: *How do you multiply rational numbers?*

video tutor

CC.8.EE.7b

1 EXAMPLE Multiplying Decimals

Pat's mom bought a new car for $19,055. After a year, its value depreciated to 0.8 of its original value. What was the value of the car after one year?

Multiply 0.8 × $19,055 to solve the problem.

Step 1: Multiply as you would with whole numbers.

$$\begin{array}{r} 19,055 \\ \times\ \ \ 08 \\ \hline 152440 \end{array}$$

Step 2: Count the number of decimal places in each factor. Mark off the *same number* of decimal places in the product.

$$\begin{array}{r} 19,055 \leftarrow 0 \text{ decimal places} \\ \times\ \ 0.8 \leftarrow 1 \text{ decimal place} \\ \hline 15244.0 \leftarrow 0 + 1 = 1 \text{ decimal place} \end{array}$$

After one year, Pat's mom's car had a value of $15,244 .

REFLECT

1a. You can use estimation to check that your answer is reasonable. Round $19,055 to its greatest place value.

$19,055 ≈ $20,000

0.8 × $20,000 = $16,000

Is the answer reasonable? Explain.

Yes. $16,000 is close to $15,244, so the answer is reasonable.

1b. Why is rounding to the greatest place value an effective strategy for checking the solution to the car's value problem?

Sample answer: Rounding to the greatest place value allows you to change only

one factor and to use a multiplication pattern to compute the estimate mentally.

TRY THIS!

1c. Anya's $25,000 salary was multiplied by a factor of 1.25. What is her new salary?

$31,250

Chapter 1   11   Lesson 2

CC.8.EE.7b

2 EXAMPLE Multiplying Fractions

The evening temperature is decreasing at a rate of $1\frac{1}{2}$°F per hour. What will the change in temperature be in $4\frac{1}{2}$ hours, to the nearest whole degree?

Multiply the rational numbers $-1\frac{1}{2}$ and $4\frac{1}{2}$.

Step 1: Rename any mixed numbers as fractions greater than one.

$$-1\frac{1}{2} \times 4\frac{1}{2} = -\frac{3}{2} \times \frac{9}{2}$$

Step 2: Multiply numerators and denominators. Simplify, if possible, and round the answer to the nearest whole degree.

$$-1\frac{1}{2} \times 4\frac{1}{2} = -\frac{27}{4} = -6\frac{3}{4} \quad \rightarrow \quad -7$$

After $4\frac{1}{2}$ hours, the temperature change will be about −7 °F.

REFLECT

2. Is your answer reasonable? How can you tell?

Possible answer: Round the first factor to −2 and the second to 4.

4(−2) = −8, so −7 is reasonable.

PRACTICE

Solve. Use estimation to check that your answers make sense.

1. What is the area of a classroom measuring 40 feet by 22.5 feet?

900 ft²

2. What is the price of 1.8 lb of ground turkey priced at $4.30 per pound?

$7.74

3. For $\frac{1}{4}$ hour, Sam climbs down a mountain at a rate of 188 feet per hour. What integer describes his change in altitude?

−47

4. Fancy cat food is selling for $1.75 per pound. What will $2\frac{1}{2}$ pounds cost? Give your answer to the nearest cent.

$4.38

5. Elena earns $10/hour at her job. When she works more than 20 hours in 1 week, she is paid one and one-half times her normal rate. What does she earn in a week that she works 25 hours?

$275

6. One-half of the students in Richard's science class are girls. One-third of the girls in the class have blond hair. If 10 girls do not have blond hair, how many students are in Richard's science class?

30

Chapter 1   12   Lesson 2

Assign these pages to help your students practice and apply important lesson concepts. For additional exercises, see the Student Edition.

Answers

Additional Practice

1. 6
2. -3
3. $-7\frac{1}{2}$
4. $3\frac{1}{2}$
5. $-\frac{4}{27}$
6. $\frac{7}{18}$
7. $-\frac{1}{8}$
8. $\frac{3}{22}$
9. $-\frac{3}{16}$
10. $-\frac{9}{25}$
11. $-\frac{2}{17}$
12. $-\frac{3}{10}$
13. $-8\frac{2}{3}$
14. $1\frac{1}{32}$
15. $2\frac{2}{15}$
16. $-2\frac{1}{12}$
17. 10.4
18. 0.0212
19. 27.3
20. -16.26
21. -0.0924
22. -3.9
23. 3.485
24. -50.4
25. -0.75
26. 5.168
27. -0.9
28. 0.12
29. $180

Problem Solving

1. 252 births
2. 6,120 deaths
3. 362,880 births
4. $2\frac{1}{10}$ births
5. $1\frac{1}{20}$ births
6. B
7. F
8. C

Additional Practice

Multiply. Write each answer in simplest form.

1. $8\left(\dfrac{3}{4}\right)$

2. $-6\left(\dfrac{9}{18}\right)$

3. $-9\left(\dfrac{5}{6}\right)$

4. $-6\left(-\dfrac{7}{12}\right)$

5. $-\dfrac{5}{18}\left(\dfrac{8}{15}\right)$

6. $\dfrac{7}{12}\left(\dfrac{14}{21}\right)$

7. $-\dfrac{1}{9}\left(\dfrac{27}{24}\right)$

8. $-\dfrac{1}{11}\left(\dfrac{3}{2}\right)$

9. $\dfrac{7}{20}\left(-\dfrac{15}{28}\right)$

10. $\dfrac{16}{25}\left(-\dfrac{18}{32}\right)$

11. $\dfrac{1}{9}\left(-\dfrac{18}{17}\right)$

12. $\dfrac{17}{20}\left(-\dfrac{12}{34}\right)$

13. $-4\left(2\dfrac{1}{6}\right)$

14. $\dfrac{3}{4}\left(1\dfrac{3}{8}\right)$

15. $3\dfrac{1}{5}\left(\dfrac{2}{3}\right)$

16. $-\dfrac{5}{6}\left(2\dfrac{1}{2}\right)$

Multiply.

17. $-2(-5.2)$

18. $0.53(0.04)$

19. $(-7)(-3.9)$

20. $-2(8.13)$

21. $0.02(-4.62)$

22. $0.5(-7.8)$

23. $(-0.41)(-8.5)$

24. $(-8)(6.3)$

25. $15(-0.05)$

26. $(-3.04)(-1.7)$

27. $10(-0.09)$

28. $(-0.8)(-0.15)$

29. Travis painted for $6\dfrac{2}{3}$ hours. He received $27 an hour for his work. How much was Travis paid for doing this painting job?

_____

Problem Solving

Use the table at the right.

1. What was the average number of births per minute in 2001?

_____

2. What was the average number of deaths per hour in 2001?

_____

3. What was the average number of births per day in 2001?

_____

4. What was the average number of births in $\dfrac{1}{2}$ of a second in 2001?

_____

5. What was the average number of births in $\dfrac{1}{4}$ of a second in 2001?

_____

Average World Births and Deaths per Second in 2001

Births	$4\dfrac{1}{5}$
Deaths	1.7

Use the table below. During exercise, the target heart rate is 0.5–0.75 of the maximum heart rate. Choose the letter for the best answer.

6. What is the target heart rate range for a 14 year old?

A 7–10.5

B 103–154.5

C 145–166

D 206–255

Age	Maximum Heart Rate
13	207
14	206
15	205
20	200
25	195

Source: American Heart Association

7. What is the target heart rate range for a 20 year old?

F 100–150

G 125–175

H 150–200

J 200–250

8. What is the target heart rate range for a 25 year old?

A 25–75

B 85–125

C 97.5–146.25

D 195–250

Dividing Rational Numbers
Going Deeper

Essential question: *How do you divide rational numbers?*

Standards for Mathematical Content

Prep for CC.8.EE.7b Solve linear equations with rational number coefficients, including equations whose solutions require expanding expressions using the distributive property and collecting like terms.

Prerequisites
Reciprocals
Divisors
Dividends
Quotients

Math Background
Dividing decimals is similar to dividing whole numbers, except for the additional step of correctly placing the decimal point in the quotient. Some students have trouble translating from horizontal form to the 'division house' form: $a \div b \rightarrow b\overline{)a}$.

Dividing by a nonzero fraction is the same as multiplying by the reciprocal of that fraction. The reciprocal of $\frac{c}{d}$ is $\frac{d}{c}$. So the rule for dividing fractions is $\frac{a}{b} \div \frac{c}{d} = \frac{a}{b} \cdot \frac{d}{c}$.

INTRODUCE

Use the Example 1 application of salmon swimming against the current to introduce the lesson. Point out that dividing decimals is similar to multiplying decimals in that you need to be aware of the placement of the decimal point. Point out that students can use multiplication to check that their decimal division is indeed correct.

TEACH

1 EXAMPLE

Questioning Strategies
- How can you check to make sure you placed the decimal point correctly? **Possible answer: Check your answer by multiplying 0.025 times 24 which gives 0.6.**

2 EXAMPLE

Questioning Strategies
- How do you find the reciprocal of a fraction? **Exchange the numerator and the denominator.**
- When dividing by a fraction, how do you use reciprocals? **Instead of dividing by the fraction, multiply by its reciprocal.**

> MATHEMATICAL
> PRACTICE
> **Highlighting the Standards**
>
> This Example is an opportunity to address Standard 7 (Look for and make use of structure). Students perform fraction division by: changing division by a fraction to multiplication by its reciprocal, and writing the product as a mixed number.

CLOSE

Essential Question
How do you divide rational numbers?
Possible answer: For decimals, first put the decimal point in the quotient and divide as with whole numbers. Bring down additional zeros as needed. For fractions, write any mixed numbers as improper fractions. Then change division by a fraction into multiplication by the reciprocal.

PRACTICE

Where skills are taught	Where skills are practiced
1 EXAMPLE	EXS. 1, 3, 6
2 EXAMPLE	EXS. 2, 4, 5, 7, 8

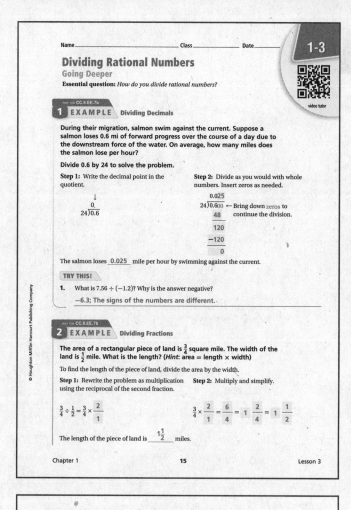

Name _____ Class _____ Date _____

1-3

Dividing Rational Numbers
Going Deeper

Essential question: *How do you divide rational numbers?*

video tutor

PREP FOR CC.8.EE.7b

1 E X A M P L E Dividing Decimals

During their migration, salmon swim against the current. Suppose a salmon loses 0.6 mi of forward progress over the course of a day due to the downstream force of the water. On average, how many miles does the salmon lose per hour?

Divide 0.6 by 24 to solve the problem.

Step 1: Write the decimal point in the quotient.

$$24\overline{)0.6}$$

Step 2: Divide as you would with whole numbers. Insert zeros as needed.

$$
\begin{array}{r}
0.025 \\
24\overline{)0.600} \\
\underline{48} \\
120 \\
\underline{-120} \\
0
\end{array}
$$

← Bring down zeros to continue the division.

The salmon loses __0.025__ mile per hour by swimming against the current.

TRY THIS!

1. What is $7.56 \div (-1.2)$? Why is the answer negative?

   −6.3; The signs of the numbers are different.

PREP FOR CC.8.EE.7b

2 E X A M P L E Dividing Fractions

The area of a rectangular piece of land is $\frac{3}{4}$ square mile. The width of the land is $\frac{1}{2}$ mile. What is the length? (*Hint*: area = length × width)

To find the length of the piece of land, divide the area by the width.

Step 1: Rewrite the problem as multiplication using the reciprocal of the second fraction.

$$\frac{3}{4} \div \frac{1}{2} = \frac{3}{4} \times \frac{2}{1}$$

Step 2: Multiply and simplify.

$$\frac{3}{4} \times \frac{2}{1} = \frac{6}{4} = 1\frac{2}{4} = 1\frac{1}{2}$$

The length of the piece of land is __$1\frac{1}{2}$__ miles.

REFLECT

2a. How can you check your answer?

   Multiply the length by the width.

TRY THIS!

2b. What is $-15 \div \left(-1\frac{1}{2}\right)$?

   10

P R A C T I C E

Solve. Check that your answers make sense.

1. What is $-24.3 \div (-4.5)$?

   5.4

2. What is $\frac{4}{9} \div \frac{-4}{9}$?

   −1

3. The width of a classroom is 28.5 ft. Its area is 1,182.75 ft². What is its length?

   41.5 ft

4. How many beads with a diameter of $1\frac{1}{2}$ cm are needed to make a bracelet 18 cm long?

   12

5. Halle is hiking down into a canyon. She descends 3,000 feet in $1\frac{3}{4}$ hours. To the nearest foot, what number shows her descent per hour?

   −1,714 ft

6. Doug spent $52 on 35 pounds of dog food. To the nearest cent, what is the price per pound?

   $1.49

7. Cal's Cabs charges $4 for the first mile and $0.40 for each additional one-fifth mile. Al pays $7 for his ride. How far was the ride?

   $2\frac{1}{2}$ miles

8. Alex earns $12 an hour at his job. When he works more than 40 hours in 1 week, he is paid one and one-third his normal rate. How many hours does he work in a week in which he earns $576? Explain how you arrived at your answer.

   46; students can write that 40 • $12 is $480, and that they first found the difference between 576 and 480, and then divided it by $1\frac{1}{3}$ (12), or 16.

© Houghton Mifflin Harcourt Publishing Company

Assign these pages to help your students practice and apply important lesson concepts. For additional exercises, see the Student Edition.

Answers

Additional Practice

1. $\frac{2}{3}$ 2. $-\frac{5}{6}$

3. 2 4. $-2\frac{1}{2}$

5. $\frac{11}{15}$ 6. $-1\frac{3}{4}$

7. 4 8. $-\frac{5}{6}$

9. $-\frac{1}{40}$ 10. $-\frac{5}{72}$

11. 4 12. $-\frac{3}{20}$

13. 48.7 14. 54

15. 158 16. 24.4

17. 145.6 18. 99.2

19. 610 20. 70.9

21. 410 22. 694

23. 52.8 24. 1378

25. 150 26. 360

27. -7.65 28. 7 servings

Problem Solving

1. 0.005 hour   2. 0.006 hour

3. 0.009 hour   4. 1.471 hours

5. 1.667 hours   6. A

7. G   8. D

9. F

1-3

Additional Practice

Divide. Write each answer in simplest form.

1. $\frac{1}{5} \div \frac{3}{10}$

2. $-\frac{5}{8} \div \frac{3}{4}$

3. $\frac{1}{4} \div \frac{1}{8}$

4. $-\frac{2}{3} \div \frac{4}{15}$

5. $1\frac{2}{9} \div 1\frac{2}{3}$

6. $-\frac{7}{10} \div \left(\frac{2}{5}\right)$

7. $\frac{6}{11} \div \frac{3}{22}$

8. $\frac{4}{9} \div \left(-\frac{8}{15}\right)$

9. $\frac{3}{8} \div -15$

10. $-\frac{5}{6} \div 12$

11. $6\frac{1}{2} \div 1\frac{5}{8}$

12. $-\frac{9}{10} \div 6$

Find each quotient.

13. $24.35 \div 0.5$

14. $2.16 \div 0.04$

15. $3.16 \div 0.02$

16. $7.32 \div 0.3$

17. $87.36 \div 0.6$

18. $79.36 \div 0.8$

19. $4.27 \div 0.007$

20. $63.81 \div 0.9$

21. $1.23 \div 0.003$

22. $62.46 \div 0.09$

23. $21.12 \div 0.4$

24. $82.68 \div 0.06$

Evaluate each expression for the given value of the variable.

25. $\frac{18}{x}$ for $x = 0.12$

26. $\frac{10.8}{x}$ for $x = 0.03$

27. $\frac{9.18}{x}$ for $x = -1.2$

28. A can of fruit contains $3\frac{1}{2}$ cups of fruit. The suggested serving size is $\frac{1}{2}$ cup. How many servings are in the can of fruit?

Problem Solving

Use the table at the right that shows the maximum speed over a quarter mile of different animals. Find the time it takes each animal to travel one-quarter mile at top speed. Round to the nearest thousandth.

1. Quarter horse

_____

2. Greyhound

_____

3. Human

_____

4. Giant tortoise

_____

Maximum Speeds of Animals

Animal	Speed (mph)
Quarter horse	47.50
Greyhound	39.35
Human	27.89
Giant tortoise	0.17
Three-toed sloth	0.15

5. Three-toed sloth

Choose the letter for the best answer.

6. A piece of ribbon is $1\frac{7}{8}$ inches long. If the ribbon is going to be divided into 15 pieces, how long should each piece be?

A $\frac{1}{8}$ in.   C $\frac{2}{3}$ in.

B $\frac{1}{15}$ in.   D $28\frac{1}{8}$ in.

7. The recorded rainfall for each day of a week was 0 in., $\frac{1}{4}$ in., $\frac{3}{4}$ in., 1 in., 0 in., $1\frac{1}{4}$ in., $1\frac{1}{4}$ in. What was the average rainfall per day?

F $\frac{9}{10}$ in.   H $\frac{7}{8}$ in.

G $\frac{9}{14}$ in.   J $4\frac{1}{2}$ in.

8. A drill bit that is $\frac{7}{32}$ in. means that the hole the bit makes has a diameter of $\frac{7}{32}$ in. Since the radius is half of the diameter, what is the radius of a hole drilled by a $\frac{7}{32}$ in. bit?

A $\frac{14}{32}$ in.   C $\frac{9}{16}$ in.

B $\frac{7}{32}$ in.   D $\frac{7}{64}$ in.

9. A serving of a certain kind of cereal is $\frac{2}{3}$ cup. There are 12 cups of cereal in the box. How many servings of cereal are in the box?

F 18

G 15

H 8

J 6

Adding and Subtracting with Unlike Denominators
Going Deeper

Essential question: *How do you add and subtract fractions with unlike denominators?*

COMMON CORE **Standards for Mathematical Content**

Prep for CC.8.EE.7b Solve linear equations with rational number coefficients, including equations whose solutions require expanding expressions using the distributive property and collecting like terms.

Prerequisites

Least common denominator (LCD)

Math Background

To add or subtract fractions, the fractions must have the same denominator, known as a *common denominator*. The product of the denominators will always give a common denominator, but it may not be the *least common denominator* (LCD). The LCD is the smallest denominator that is common to both fractions, and using it to add or subtract fractions may save the step of simplifying the sum or difference.

INTRODUCE

Connect to prior learning of adding and subtracting fractions with like denominators. Emphasize that the sum or difference of the original expression is not changed when fractions with unlike denominators are replaced by equivalent fractions with like denominators. As needed, review how to find the LCD (Least Common Denominator) of two fractions.

TEACH

1 EXAMPLE

Questioning Strategies

- What number is multiplied times each fraction to obtain equivalent fractions with the same denominator? **Forms of 1, or $\frac{4}{4}$ and $\frac{5}{5}$**

- How do you add fractions with common denominators? **Add the numerators and keep the denominator unchanged. Then simplify.**

Differentiated Instruction

Inform students that the prefix *un-* means *not*, and *un*like denominators means denominators that are *not* the same. Circle the unlike denominators in the Example and emphasize that they need to be the same. Consider showing the additional step of the addition (or subtraction) of the numerators over the common denominator, such as $\frac{11+10}{20}$ for the last step.

CLOSE

Essential Question

How do you add and subtract fractions with unlike denominators?

Possible answer: Rewrite each fraction using a common denominator. Then add or subtract numerators, keep the denominator the same, and simplify as needed.

Summarize

Have students write the steps for adding or subtracting fractions with *like* denominators. Then have them revise the steps for *unlike* denominators, as shown below in blue.

Adding or Subtracting Fractions with Unlike Denominators

1. **Rewrite fractions using a common denominator.**

2̶. Add or subtract numerators, keeping the denominator unchanged.

3̶. Simplify as needed.

PRACTICE

Where skills are taught	Where skills are practiced
1 EXAMPLE	EXS. 1–4

Name_____ Class_____ Date_____

Adding and Subtracting with Unlike Denominators
Going Deeper

Essential question: *How do you add and subtract fractions with unlike denominators?*

PREV USE CC.8.EE.7b

1 EXAMPLE   Adding and Subtracting Fractions

Jorge took his dog Gracie on a walk. They walked $\frac{4}{5}$ mile north, a tenth of a mile east, a quarter-mile south, another $\frac{3}{4}$ mile east, and then half a mile north. There they stopped to rest. How far north of their beginning point did they stop?

Compute $\left(\frac{4}{5} - \frac{1}{4}\right) + \frac{1}{2}$ to solve the problem.

Step 1: Perform the subtraction.

$\frac{4}{5} - \frac{1}{4}$ *Find a common denominator: 5(4) =* **20** .

$\frac{4}{5}\left(\frac{4}{4}\right) - \frac{1}{4}\left(\frac{5}{5}\right)$ *Multiply each fraction by a fraction equivalent to 1.*

$\frac{16}{20} - \frac{5}{20} = \frac{11}{20}$ *Rewrite with the common denominator.*

Step 2: Perform the addition.

$\frac{11}{20} + \frac{1}{2}$ *Find a common denominator:* **20** .

$\frac{11}{20} + \frac{1}{2}\left(\frac{10}{10}\right)$ *Multiply $\frac{1}{2}$ by a fraction equivalent to 1.*

$\frac{11}{20} + \frac{10}{20} = \frac{21}{20}$ *Rewrite with the common denominator.*

$\frac{21}{20} = 1\frac{1}{20}$ *Simplify.*

Jorge and Gracie were ____$1\frac{1}{20}$____ miles north of where they started when they rested.

REFLECT

1a. You used the least common denominator of 5, 4, and 2 to rename the fractions. Why isn't 10 the LCD of 5, 4, and 2?

   10 is not divisible by 4.

1b. When you add or subtract fractions with unlike denominators you can use a common denominator, not just the LCD, to compute. What is a quick way to find a common denominator for any two fractions? *But*, what is a benefit of finding and using the LCD?

   Multiply their denominators; the product will be a common denominator. By using the LCD, simplifying the sum or difference becomes easier because you'll be dividing smaller numbers.

TRY THIS!

1c. Gina bought 4 yards of fabric and used $2\frac{3}{4}$ yards of it. How much fabric did she *not* use? How much more will she need to make a scarf that requires $1\frac{2}{3}$ yards of fabric?

   $1\frac{1}{4}$ yd; $\frac{5}{12}$ yd

1d. Leyla has $3\frac{3}{4}$ ounces of flour in a cup. She uses $2\frac{5}{9}$ ounces to cook dinner. She spills a quarter-ounce. How much flour does she have left?

   $\frac{17}{18}$ oz

PRACTICE

Solve.

1. Cheng fenced in three sides of his backyard. How much fencing did he use?

   $35\frac{3}{8}$ yd

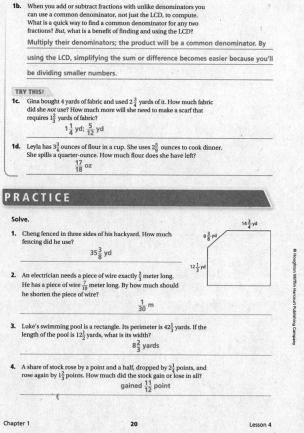

2. An electrician needs a piece of wire exactly $\frac{2}{3}$ meter long. He has a piece of wire $\frac{7}{10}$ meter long. By how much should he shorten the piece of wire?

   $\frac{1}{30}$ m

3. Luke's swimming pool is a rectangle. Its perimeter is $42\frac{1}{3}$ yards. If the length of the pool is $12\frac{1}{2}$ yards, what is its width?

   $8\frac{2}{3}$ yards

4. A share of stock rose by a point and a half, dropped by $2\frac{1}{4}$ points, and rose again by $1\frac{2}{3}$ points. How much did the stock gain or lose in all?

   gained $\frac{11}{12}$ point

© Houghton Mifflin Harcourt Publishing Company

Assign these pages to help your students practice and apply important lesson concepts. For additional exercises, see the Student Edition.

Answers

Additional Practice

1. $1\frac{1}{6}$

2. $\frac{14}{15}$

3. $\frac{5}{12}$

4. $-\frac{1}{18}$

5. $-\frac{5}{16}$

6. $1\frac{11}{18}$

7. $\frac{5}{8}$

8. $\frac{11}{24}$

9. $6\frac{7}{24}$

10. $3\frac{5}{18}$

11. $2\frac{1}{15}$

12. $-\frac{11}{12}$

13. $4\frac{7}{9}$

14. $7\frac{1}{4}$

15. $4\frac{5}{6}$

16. $-1\frac{9}{10}$

17. $4\frac{5}{24}$

18. $-\frac{1}{15}$

19. $\frac{9}{70}$

20. $-\frac{13}{24}$

21. $-\frac{7}{12}$

22. $\frac{1}{5}$

23. $19\frac{5}{12}$ h

Problem Solving

1. $102\frac{3}{8}$ inches

2. $53\frac{7}{8}$ inches

3. $\frac{7}{8}$ cup

4. $7\frac{2}{5}$ inches

5. D

6. H

Additional Practice

Add or subtract.

1. $\frac{2}{3} + \frac{1}{2}$

2. $\frac{3}{5} + \frac{1}{3}$

3. $\frac{3}{4} - \frac{1}{3}$

4. $\frac{1}{2} - \frac{5}{9}$

5. $\frac{5}{16} - \frac{5}{8}$

6. $\frac{7}{9} + \frac{5}{6}$

7. $\frac{7}{8} - \frac{1}{4}$

8. $\frac{5}{8} - \frac{3}{8}$

9. $2\frac{7}{8} + 3\frac{5}{12}$

10. $1\frac{2}{9} + 2\frac{1}{18}$

11. $3\frac{2}{3} - 1\frac{3}{5}$

12. $1\frac{5}{6} + \left(-2\frac{3}{4}\right)$

13. $8\frac{1}{3} - 3\frac{5}{9}$

14. $5\frac{1}{3} + 1\frac{11}{12}$

15. $7\frac{1}{4} + \left(-2\frac{5}{12}\right)$

16. $5\frac{2}{5} - 7\frac{3}{10}$

Evaluate each expression for the given value of the variable.

17. $2\frac{3}{8} + x$ for $x = 1\frac{5}{6}$

18. $x - \frac{2}{5}$ for $x = \frac{1}{3}$

19. $x - \frac{3}{10}$ for $x = \frac{3}{7}$

20. $1\frac{5}{8} + x$ for $x = -2\frac{1}{6}$

21. $x - \frac{3}{4}$ for $x = \frac{1}{6}$

22. $x - \frac{3}{10}$ for $x = \frac{1}{2}$

23. Ana worked $6\frac{1}{2}$ h on Monday, $5\frac{3}{4}$ h on Tuesday and $7\frac{1}{6}$ h on Friday. How many total hours did she work these three days?

_____

Problem Solving

Write the correct answer.

1. Nick Hysong of the United States won the Olympic gold medal in the pole vault in 2000 with a jump of 19 ft $4\frac{1}{4}$ inches, or $232\frac{1}{4}$ inches. In 1900, Irving Baxter of the United States won the pole vault with a jump of 10 ft $9\frac{7}{8}$ inches, or $129\frac{7}{8}$ inches. How much higher did Hysong vault than Baxter?

2. In the 2000 Summer Olympics, Ivan Pedroso of Cuba won the Long jump with a jump of 28 ft $\frac{3}{4}$ inches, or $336\frac{3}{4}$ inches. Alvin Kraenzlein of the United States won the long jump in 1900 with a jump of 23 ft $6\frac{7}{8}$ inches, or $282\frac{7}{8}$ inches. How much farther did Pedroso jump than Kraenzlein?

3. A recipe calls for $\frac{1}{8}$ cup of sugar and $\frac{3}{4}$ cup of brown sugar. How much total sugar is added to the recipe?

4. The average snowfall in Norfolk, VA for January is $2\frac{3}{5}$ inches, February $2\frac{9}{10}$ inches, March 1 inch, and December $\frac{9}{10}$ inches. If these are the only months it typically snows, what is the average snowfall per year?

Use the table at the right that shows the average snowfall per month in Vail, Colorado.

5. What is the average annual snowfall in Vail, Colorado?

A $15\frac{13}{20}$ in.   C $187\frac{1}{10}$ in.

B 153 in.   D $187\frac{4}{5}$ in.

6. The peak of the skiing season is from December through March. What is the average snowfall for this period?

F $30\frac{19}{20}$ in.   H $123\frac{4}{5}$ in.

G $123\frac{3}{5}$ in.   J 127 in.

Average Snowfall in Vail, CO

Month	Snowfall (in.)	Month	Snowfall (in.)
Jan	$36\frac{7}{10}$	July	0
Feb	$35\frac{7}{10}$	August	0
March	$25\frac{2}{5}$	Sept	1
April	$21\frac{1}{5}$	Oct	$7\frac{4}{5}$
May	4	Nov	$29\frac{7}{10}$
June	$\frac{3}{10}$	Dec	26

Solving Equations with Rational Numbers
Going Deeper

Essential question: *How do you solve equations that contain rational numbers?*

COMMON CORE Standards for Mathematical Content

CC.8.EE.7b Solve linear equations with rational number coefficients, including equations whose solutions require expanding expressions using the distributive property and collecting like terms.

Prerequisites

Equations

Solutions

Properties of Equality

Math Background

An *equation* is one expression set equal to another expression. An *algebraic equation* is an equation with one or more variables. The *solution* (or solutions) to an algebraic equation are the values of the variable that make the equation true. To *solve* an algebraic equation, isolate the variable on one side of the equal sign. You do this by writing a series of *equivalent equations*—equations that have the same solution (or solutions)—using inverse operations, which is allowed by the *properties of equality*. The properties of equality can be generalized as: "Whatever you do to one side of an equation, you must do to the other side." There is one restriction to this statement: division by zero is not allowed, because it is undefined.

INTRODUCE

Begin by discussing the differences between *expressions* and *equations*. Students *simplified* expressions in previous lessons, and now they will *solve* equations. As needed, clarify that an equation includes two expressions and an equal sign. Then guide students in identifying the solution as an equivalent equation in which the variable is isolated on one side of the equation. Remind students how they can isolate the variable by applying the same inverse operation to both sides of the equation.

TEACH

1 EXAMPLE

Questioning Strategies

- What operation would you use to undo the operation on the side with the variable? **subtraction**

- How can you estimate the cost for the shorts? $53 - 20 = 33$, **which is very close to the answer of $32.95.**

Avoid Common Errors

Have students circle the variable and identify the operation that is performed on that variable. Ask them to then identify the corresponding inverse operation that will isolate the variable. This strategy can be helpful for equations that use more than one property of equality.

2 EXAMPLE

Questioning Strategies

- How do you decide which operation to use? **Identify which operation is used on the variable and apply the inverse operation.**

- Could you apply the subtraction property of equality to solve this equation? **Yes, by subtracting** $-\frac{2}{3}$.

Differentiated Instruction

Review how fractions with unlike denominators cannot be added unless they have the same denominator. Then have students describe how they would rename each fraction, by multiplying each fraction by a form of 1 that gives the common denominator of 6.

© Houghton Mifflin Harcourt Publishing Company

Name_____ Class_____ Date_____

1-5

Solving Equations with Rational Numbers
Going Deeper

Essential question: *How do you solve equations that contain rational numbers?*

Recall that to solve an equation you need to find a value for the variable that makes the equation true. This value is the solution.

Using the properties of equality helps you solve equations containing rational numbers.

CC.8.EE.7b

1 EXAMPLE Using the Subtraction Property of Equality

Rebecca spent a total of $52.90 at the clothing store. She bought two things: a T-shirt for $19.95 and a pair of shorts. What did the shorts cost her?

You can write and solve an equation to solve the problem.

$c + \$19.95 = \$52.90$ *Write the equation. Let c = cost for a pair of shorts.*

$c + 19.95 = 52.90$ *Use the subtraction property of equality to isolate the variable.*
$\underline{-19.95 \quad -19.95}$ *Subtract the same number from both sides of the equation.*
$c \qquad = 32.95$

The shorts cost $\underline{\$32.95}$.

TRY THIS!

1a. Two suitcases together weigh 82 pounds. One weighs 28.25 pounds. Write two equations you can use to find the weight of the other suitcase: one with decimals and one with fractions.
$n + 28.25 = 82; \ n + 28\frac{1}{4} = 82$

1b. Explain how you can use the subtraction property of equality to solve the equation you wrote in 1a.
Subtract 28.25 or $28\frac{1}{4}$ from both sides of the equation to

isolate the variable *n*.

1c. What is the solution to the equation? To the problem?
$n = 53.75$ lb or $53\frac{3}{4}$ lb; the suitcase weighs 53.75 or $53\frac{3}{4}$ lb

© Houghton Mifflin Harcourt Publishing Company

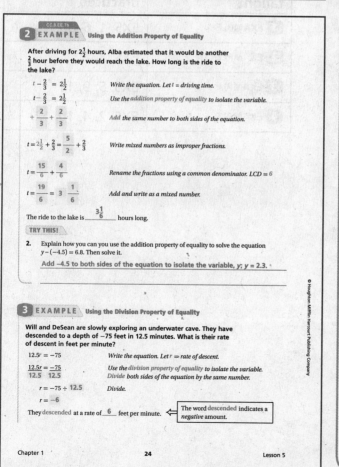

CC.8.EE.7b

2 EXAMPLE Using the Addition Property of Equality

After driving for $2\frac{1}{2}$ hours, Alba estimated that it would be another $\frac{2}{3}$ hour before they would reach the lake. How long is the ride to the lake?

$t - \frac{2}{3} = 2\frac{1}{2}$ *Write the equation. Let t = driving time.*

$t - \frac{2}{3} = 2\frac{1}{2}$ *Use the addition property of equality to isolate the variable.*
$+\frac{2}{3} \quad +\frac{2}{3}$ *Add the same number to both sides of the equation.*

$t = 2\frac{1}{2} + \frac{2}{3} = \frac{5}{2} + \frac{2}{3}$ *Write mixed numbers as improper fractions.*

$t = \frac{15}{6} + \frac{4}{6}$ *Rename the fractions using a common denominator. LCD = 6*

$t = \frac{19}{6} = 3\frac{1}{6}$ *Add and write as a mixed number.*

The ride to the lake is $\underline{3\frac{1}{6}}$ hours long.

TRY THIS!

2. Explain how you can you use the addition property of equality to solve the equation $y - (-4.5) = 6.8$. Then solve it.
Add –4.5 to both sides of the equation to isolate the variable, *y*; y = 2.3.

3 EXAMPLE Using the Division Property of Equality

Will and DeSean are slowly exploring an underwater cave. They have descended to a depth of −75 feet in 12.5 minutes. What is their rate of descent in feet per minute?

$12.5r = -75$ *Write the equation. Let r = rate of descent.*

$\dfrac{12.5r}{12.5} = \dfrac{-75}{12.5}$ *Use the division property of equality to isolate the variable.*
Divide both sides of the equation by the same number.

$r = -75 \div 12.5$ *Divide.*

$r = -6$

They descended at a rate of $\underline{6}$ feet per minute.

> The word descended indicates a *negative* amount.

© Houghton Mifflin Harcourt Publishing Company

Questioning Strategies

- What does the variable r represent? The rate of descent in feet per minute.

- What would you *multiply* the equation $12.5r = -75$ by to isolate the variable? The reciprocal of 12.5, or $\frac{1}{12.5}$.

Differentiated Instruction

As needed, clarify that the negative sign describes the direction of the motion as down. In the answer statement, the word 'descended' gives the direction so the rate is 6. This is similar to a *loss* of $10, which is represented by -10.

4 EXAMPLE

Questioning Strategies

- Which operation is needed to undo what is done to the variable? multiplication

- Could you use division to undo what is done to the variable? Yes, but you would need to divide by $\frac{1}{4}$.

MATHEMATICAL PRACTICE | **Highlighting the Standards**

This Lesson is an opportunity to address Standard 2 (Reason abstractly and quantitatively). Students are asked to solve one-step equations with fractions and decimals by applying the properties of equality. They will learn to identify and apply the appropriate property of equality for a given explicit, real-world situation.

CLOSE

Essential Question

How do you solve equations that contain rational numbers?

Possible answer: Identify what operation has been performed on the variable and apply the inverse operation to both sides of the equation.

Summarize

Have students write four equations, each solved by applying a different property of equality. You may have students use the same two positive integers so that students can focus on the solution method, as shown.

$$
\begin{array}{ll}
x - 2 = 5 & x + 2 = 5 \\
\underline{+2 \quad +2} & \underline{-2 \quad -2} \\
x \quad\;\; = 7 & x \quad\;\; = 3
\end{array}
$$

$$
\begin{array}{ll}
\frac{x}{2} = 5 & 2x = 5 \\
(2)\,\frac{x}{2} = 5(2) & \frac{2x}{2} = \frac{5}{2} \\
x = 10 & x = \frac{5}{2}
\end{array}
$$

PRACTICE

Where skills are taught	Where skills are practiced
1 EXAMPLE	EXS. 1, 6–8
2 EXAMPLE	EXS. 3
3 EXAMPLE	EXS. 5, 9, 11
4 EXAMPLE	EXS. 2, 4, 10, 12

TRY THIS!

3. Explain how you can you use the division property of equality to solve the equation $\frac{-2}{3}n = 16$. Then solve the equation.

Divide both sides of the equation by $\frac{-2}{3}$, which means to multiply

by its reciprocal, $\frac{-3}{2}$; $n = -24$.

4 EXAMPLE CC.8.EE.7b **Using the Multiplication Property of Equality**

A stock that Carmen purchased lost, on average, $3.75 per share each week. If she held the stock for 4 weeks, what was her total loss, per share?

$$\frac{m}{4} = -3.75 \qquad \text{Write the equation. Let } m = \text{total stock loss.}$$

$$\frac{m}{4} \times \frac{4}{1} = \frac{-3.75}{1} \times \frac{4}{1} \qquad \text{Use the } \textit{multiplication property of equality} \text{ to isolate the variable. Multiply both sides of the equation by the same number.}$$

$$m = \frac{-3.75}{1} \times \frac{4}{1} \qquad \text{Multiply.}$$

$$m = -15$$

The total loss was __$15__ per share. ← The word loss indicates a *negative* amount.

TRY THIS!

4a. Explain how you can you use the multiplication property of equality to solve the equation $\frac{w}{-2.25} = -12$. Then solve the equation.

Multiply both sides of the equation by -2.25; $w = 27$

REFLECT

4b. How are multiplication and division related? How can you use that relationship to solve equations involving these operations?

They are inverse operations; one "undoes" the other.

PRACTICE

Tell which property of equality you would use to solve each equation.

1. $n + (-6.5) = 14.7$
   subtraction

2. $\frac{p}{0.3} = 1.5$
   multiplication

3. $b - 1\frac{5}{8} = \frac{-4}{5}$
   addition

4. $\frac{r}{-4} = 2$
   multiplication

5. $-3t = 24$
   division

6. $y + 5 = \frac{3}{5}$
   subtraction

Solve by writing and solving an equation.

7. Jacob purchased a DVD player online. He paid $25.95 less than the price of the same item at a local store: $159. What did Jacob pay for his DVD player?

$p + $25.95 = 159; $p = 133.05; he paid $133.05

8. Anna is $3\frac{1}{2}$ years older than her sister and 8 years younger than her brother. If Anna's brother is 19, how old is her sister?

$s + 3\frac{1}{2} = 19 - 8$; $7\frac{1}{2}$ years old

9. Jan and Mica are rock climbing in Yosemite National Park. Mica has descended 400 feet, which is 2.5 times as far as Jan has come down. What rational number expresses the change, in feet, of Jan's elevation?

$2.5j = -400$; -160

10. Anita and Miguel are deep sea diving off the coast of Mexico. Anita has dived to a depth of -6.5 meters. This is two-thirds as deep as Miguel's current depth. What rational number identifies Miguel's location beneath the ocean surface?

$\frac{2}{3}x = -6.5$; -9.75 m or $-9\frac{3}{4}$ m

11. **Error Analysis** Ivan says that the solution to the equation $6n = -19.2$ is -13.2. What is his mistake?

He subtracted 6 from both sides of the equation rather than dividing both sides by 6.

12. **Error Analysis** Kita estimates that the solution to the equation $4\frac{5}{6}y = 18$ is about $4\frac{1}{2}$. Is she right? Explain.

No; $4\frac{5}{6}$ rounds to 5, and $18 \div 5$ is less than, not greater than, 4.

Assign these pages to help your students practice and apply important lesson concepts. For additional exercises, see the Student Edition.

Answers

Additional Practice

1. $x = 5.39$

2. $y = 15.54$

3. $w = 125$

4. $a = 74.21$

5. $x = 12.35$

6. $d = 85.68$

7. $m = -1.7$

8. $n = -3.56$

9. $x = -38.772$

10. $x = \dfrac{1}{3}$

11. $y = -1\dfrac{1}{2}$

12. $d = 1\dfrac{1}{2}$

13. $x = \dfrac{1}{14}$

14. $x = 3\dfrac{4}{7}$

15. $a = -1\dfrac{11}{16}$

16. 7 cups of flour and $3\dfrac{3}{4}$ cups of sugar

17. 19.5 mi

Problem Solving

1. $5\dfrac{1}{4}$ feet

2. 31 pieces

3. $2.45

4. -252.87 ºC

5. C

6. G

7. A

8. G

© Houghton Mifflin Harcourt Publishing Company

Name _____ Class _____ Date _____ **1-5**

Additional Practice

Solve.

1. $x + 6.8 = 12.19$

2. $y - 10.24 = 5.3$

3. $0.05w = 6.25$

4. $\dfrac{a}{9.05} = 8.2$

5. $-12.41 + x = -0.06$

6. $\dfrac{d}{-8.4} = -10.2$

7. $-2.89 = 1.7m$

8. $n - 8.09 = -11.65$

9. $\dfrac{x}{5.4} = -7.18$

10. $\dfrac{7}{9} + x = 1\dfrac{1}{9}$

11. $\dfrac{6}{11}y = -\dfrac{18}{22}$

12. $\dfrac{7}{10}d = \dfrac{21}{20}$

13. $x - \left(-\dfrac{9}{14}\right) = \dfrac{5}{7}$

14. $x - \dfrac{15}{21} = 2\dfrac{6}{7}$

15. $-\dfrac{8}{15}a = \dfrac{9}{10}$

16. A recipe calls for $2\dfrac{1}{3}$ cups of flour and $1\dfrac{1}{4}$ cups of sugar. If the recipe is tripled, how much flour and sugar will be needed?

17. Daniel filled the gas tank in his car with 14.6 gal of gas. He then drove 284.7 mi before needing to fill up his tank with gas again. How many miles did the car get to a gallon of gasoline?

Chapter 1   **27**   Practice and Problem Solving

Problem Solving

Write the correct answer.

1. In the last 150 years, the average height of people in industrialized nations has increased by $\dfrac{1}{3}$ foot. Today, American men have an average height of $5\dfrac{7}{12}$ feet. What was the average height of American men 150 years ago?

2. Jaime has a length of ribbon that is $23\dfrac{1}{2}$ in. long. If she plans to cut the ribbon into pieces that are $\dfrac{3}{4}$ in. long, into how many pieces can she cut the ribbon? (She cannot use partial pieces.)

3. Todd's restaurant bill for dinner was $15.55. After he left a tip, he spent a total of $18.00 on dinner. How much money did Todd leave for a tip?

4. The difference between the boiling point and melting point of Hydrogen is 6.47 °C. The melting point of Hydrogen is −259.34 °C. What is the boiling point of Hydrogen?

Choose the letter for the best answer.

5. In 2005, a sprinter won the gold medal in the 100-m dash in with a time of 9.85 seconds. His time was 0.95 seconds faster than the winner in the 100-m dash in 1900. What was winner's time in 1900?

  A 8.95 seconds

  B 10.65 seconds

  C 10.80 seconds

  D 11.20 seconds

6. The balance in Susan's checking account was $245.35. After the bank deposited interest into the account, her balance went to $248.02. How much interest did the bank pay Susan?

  F $1.01

  G $2.67

  H $3.95

  J $493.37

7. After a morning shower, there was $\dfrac{17}{100}$ in. of rain in the rain gauge. It rained again an hour later and the rain gauge showed $\dfrac{1}{4}$ in. of rain. How much did it rain the second time?

  A $\dfrac{2}{25}$ in.   C $\dfrac{21}{50}$ in.

  B $\dfrac{1}{6}$ in.   D $\dfrac{3}{8}$ in.

8. Two-third of John's savings account is being saved for his college education. If $2500 of his savings is for his college education, how much money in total is in his savings account?

  F $1666.67   H $4250.83

  G $3750   J $5000

Chapter 1   **28**   Practice and Problem Solving

Solving Two-Step Equations
Going Deeper

Essential question: *How do you solve equations that contain multiple operations?*

© Houghton Mifflin Harcourt Publishing Company

COMMON CORE **Standards for Mathematical Content**

CC.8.EE.7b Solve linear equations with rational number coefficients, including equations whose solutions require expanding expressions using the distributive property and collecting like terms.

Prerequisites
Order of operations

Math Background
Two-step equations involve two distinct operations: addition or subtraction for one step and multiplication or division for the other step. The goal in solving two-step equations is the same as for solving any equation: to isolate the variable on one side of the equation by applying inverse operations. It is often easier to solve a two-step equation by adding or subtracting *before* multiplying or dividing—which is the reverse of the order of operations.

INTRODUCE

Begin by discussing what a two-step equation is: an equation that contains two operations. Have students guess how many operations they will need to undo to solve a *two*-step equation. (Two!) Then point out that when an equation involves two operations, they will need to decide which inverse operation to apply first, which depends on the equation that they are solving. However, it is generally easier to solve a two-step equation if students add or subtract before they multiply or divide. Point out that this is the *reverse* order of the Order of Operations: Add or subtract first, then multiply or divide.

TEACH

1 EXAMPLE

Questioning Strategies
- What would happen if you first divided both sides of the equation by 7.5? This is mathematically acceptable; however, it would create awkward numbers for the second step.

- What does the variable represent in the equation? The number of weeks it takes Remy to have $500 in his savings account.

TRY THIS

As needed, spend time helping students write the algebraic equation that describes the situation in Try This 1b. Ask students to identify what operation is indicated by 10° warmer. They should recognize the operation as *addition*.

Differentiated Instruction
Have students write a description that requires 2 or more steps like how they get from the math classroom to the gym or lunch room. Then have students write a description of how they would travel from the gym or lunch room back to math class. Use this activity to illustrate how the steps involved are reversed (left becomes right, etc.) and backward (first becomes last, etc.). Then connect this to solving a two-step equation in the reverse order and using the inverse operations from the operations involved.

Name_____ Class_____ Date_____

1-6

Solving Two-Step Equations
Going Deeper

Essential question: *How do you solve equations that contain multiple operations?*

To solve an equation containing more than one operation applied to the variable, you typically *undo the operations* in *reverse* order. You undo addition and subtraction *before* you undo multiplication and division.

CC.8.EE.7b

1 EXAMPLE Solving a Two-Step Equation Containing Decimals

Remy has $447.50 in a savings account. Each week he deposits $7.50 from his earnings at his after-school job into the account. In how many weeks will Remy have $500 in his savings account?

A Write a two-step equation to represent the situation.

Let w = number of weeks Remy makes deposits.

$7.50w + 447.50 = 500$

B Use a table to help you solve the equation.

First, list the operations in the equation *by the order in which they are applied* to the variable. Then, undo the operations in the equation in the *reverse* order.

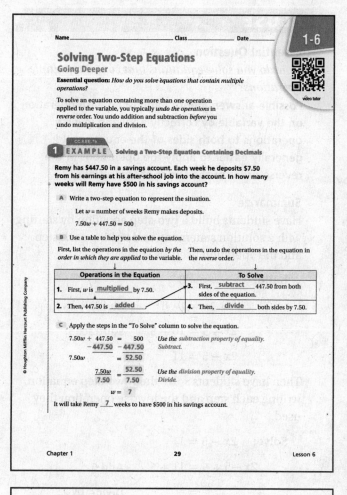

Operations in the Equation	To Solve
1. First, w is __multiplied__ by 7.50.	3. First, __subtract__ 447.50 from both sides of the equation.
2. Then, 447.50 is __added__.	4. Then, __divide__ both sides by 7.50.

C Apply the steps in the "To Solve" column to solve the equation.

$$7.50w + 447.50 = 500$$
$$\underline{-447.50 \quad -447.50}$$ *Use the* subtraction property of equality. *Subtract.*
$$7.50w \quad = 52.50$$

$$\frac{7.50w}{7.50} = \frac{52.50}{7.50}$$ *Use the* division property of equality. *Divide.*

$$w = 7$$

It will take Remy __7__ weeks to have $500 in his savings account.

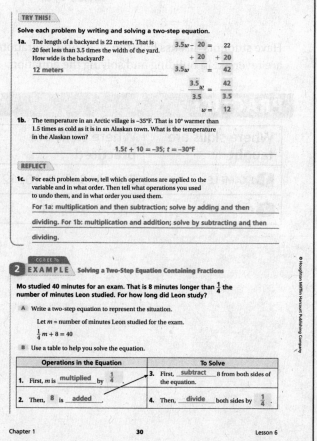

TRY THIS!

Solve each problem by writing and solving a two-step equation.

1a. The length of a backyard is 22 meters. That is 20 feet less than 3.5 times the width of the yard. How wide is the backyard?

___12 meters___

$$3.5w - 20 = 22$$
$$\underline{+20 \quad +20}$$
$$3.5w \quad = 42$$
$$\frac{3.5w}{3.5} = \frac{42}{3.5}$$
$$w = 12$$

1b. The temperature in an Arctic village is –35°F. That is 10° warmer than 1.5 times as cold as it is in an Alaskan town. What is the temperature in the Alaskan town?

$$1.5t + 10 = -35; \quad t = -30°F$$

REFLECT

1c. For each problem above, tell which operations are applied to the variable and in what order. Then tell what operations you used to undo them, and in what order you used them.

For 1a: multiplication and then subtraction; solve by adding and then

dividing. For 1b: multiplication and addition; solve by subtracting and then

dividing.

CC.8.EE.7b

2 EXAMPLE Solving a Two-Step Equation Containing Fractions

Mo studied 40 minutes for an exam. That is 8 minutes longer than $\frac{1}{4}$ the number of minutes Leon studied. For how long did Leon study?

A Write a two-step equation to represent the situation.

Let m = number of minutes Leon studied for the exam.

$$\frac{1}{4}m + 8 = 40$$

B Use a table to help you solve the equation.

Operations in the Equation	To Solve
1. First, m is __multiplied__ by $\frac{1}{4}$.	3. First, __subtract__ 8 from both sides of the equation.
2. Then, 8 is __added__.	4. Then, __divide__ both sides by $\frac{1}{4}$.

© Houghton Mifflin Harcourt Publishing Company

Questioning Strategies

- What can you do to check that your solution is correct? **Substitute it for the variable in the original equation and verify that the resulting number equation is true.**

- When checking your solution, in what order do you perform the simplification? **the order of operations: multiplication or division followed by addition or subtraction**

- Does it make sense that Leon studied more than Mo? **Yes, because Mo studied 8 minutes more than $\frac{1}{4}$ as long as Leon.**

TRY THIS

As needed, help students write the equation that describes the problem situation in Try This 2b. Guide students to first define the variable. Then direct them to identify what they need to find to answer the question. Some students will say the number of push-ups. Ask them to specify *whose* push-ups they are looking for: Avi's push-ups.

MATHEMATICAL PRACTICE   **Highlighting the Standards**

This Lesson is an opportunity to address Standard 2 (Reason abstractly and quantitatively). Students are asked to solve two-step equations with fractions and decimals by applying the properties of equality. Students then practice writing and solving two-step equations for real-world situations by using, generally, the reverse order of operations.

CLOSE

Essential Question

How do you solve equations that contain multiple operations?

Possible answer: Identify and undo each operation on the variable by correctly applying inverse operations to both sides of the equation. It is generally easier to apply the operations in the reverse order of the Order of Operations.

Summarize

Have students build a two-step equation by starting with a solution statement, and writing each step and the operation used, as shown.

Build: $x = 8$

$2x = 2 \cdot 8$ **Multiply** by 2.

$2x - 5 = 16 - 5$ **Subtract** 5.

$2x - 5 = 11$

Then have students solve their two-step equation, writing each step and the inverse operation they used.

Solve: $2x - 5 = 11$

$2x - 5 + 5 = 11 + 5$ **Add** 5.

$\frac{2x}{2} = \frac{16}{2}$ **Divide** by 2.

$x = 8$

Have students discuss how the steps and operations are reversed in building and solving the equation.

PRACTICE

Where skills are taught	Where skills are practiced
1 EXAMPLE	EXS. 1, 3–6, 9–10, 12
2 EXAMPLE	EXS. 2, 7–8, 11

C Apply the steps in the "To Solve" column to solve the equation.

$$\frac{1}{4}m + 8 = 40$$ *Use the* subtraction property of equality *to isolate the variable.*
$$\underline{\quad -8 \quad\quad -8\quad}$$ *Subtract the same number from both sides of the equation.*
$$\frac{1}{4}m = 32$$

$$\frac{4}{1} \times \frac{1}{4}m = 32 \times \frac{4}{1}$$ *Use the* multiplication property of equality *to isolate the variable.*
$$m = 128$$ *Multiply both sides of the equation by the same number.*

Leon studied for __128__ minutes.

TRY THIS!

Solve each problem by writing and solving an equation.

2a. Leonard sold 15 tickets to his band's concert. That is 5 fewer than half of the number Vera sold. How many tickets did Vera sell?

___40 tickets___

$$\frac{1}{2}n - 5 = 15$$
$$\underline{\quad +5 \quad +5\quad}$$
$$\frac{1}{2}n = 20$$

2b. Dimitri did 18 push-ups. That is 12 more than one-fifth the number Avi did. How many push-ups did Avi do?

$$\frac{p}{5} + 12 = 18; \ p = 30 \text{ push-ups}$$

$$\left(\frac{2}{1}\right)\frac{1}{2}n = 20\left(\frac{2}{1}\right)$$

$$n = 40$$

REFLECT

2c. For each problem above, tell *which operations* are applied to the variable and *in what order*. Then tell what operations you used to undo them, and in what order you used them.

For 2a: multiplication and then subtraction; solve by adding and then dividing.

For 2b: division and then addition; solve by subtracting and then multiplying.

PRACTICE

Tell which operations you will use and in which order you will use them to solve each equation.

1. $4.5n + 22 = 50$ subtraction, then division

2. $2\frac{3}{4}y - 6 = 10$ addition, then division

3. $25.5 = 2x + 2.75$ subtraction, then division

Pedro runs a pedicab business that charges customers for rides through the park and around the city. The advertisement shows Pedro's prices.

> **Go with Pedro's Pedicabs!**
> **Low, Low Prices! Friendly Drivers! Comfy Seats!**
> **$30 for first hour**
> **$7.50 for each additional 15 minutes**
> **$2.50 for blanket rental**
> **NO CHARGE for driver's jokes!**
> **Tipping appreciated ↑↑**
> "...the best ride of my life!" Andy, from Dallas, TX

4. What is the cost of a 2-hour pedicab ride with Pedro's Pedicabs?
___$60___

5. What is the total price of a 2.25-hour drive with a tip of $15?
___$82.50___

6. The Suarez family took a pedicab ride with Pedro's Pedicabs. With a blanket rental and a $10 tip, the price of their ride came to $57.50. How long was their ride?
___1.5 hours___

7. Elden took a ride for $1\frac{3}{4}$ hours. He gave a $10 tip. Marla's ride was a half-hour longer than Elden's. She left no tip. Whose ride cost more? How much more?
___Marla's; $5.00 more___

Solve by writing and solving an equation.

8. If you add 8 to a number divided by 5, the sum is 8. What is the number?
___0___

9. Fred is 3 years more than two and one-half times his sister's age. If Fred is 18, how old is his sister?
___6 years old___

10. Five dollars more than half the price of a sweater is equal to $40.39. What is the full price of the sweater?
___$70.78___

11. Four bags of dry dog food plus 8.5 pounds of dry cat food weigh 17.5 pounds in all. How many pounds does each bag of dog food weigh?
___2.25 lb___

12. Make a Conjecture You know that one way to solve the equation $2n - 8 = 2.8$ is to undo operations applied to the variable:
- First add 8 to both sides to undo the subtraction of 8.
- Then divide both sides by 2 to undo the multiplication by 2.

What other method can you think of to solve this two-step equation?
Possible answer: divide each term by 2, and then solve the one-step

equation $n - 4 = 1.4$

Assign these pages to help your students practice and apply important lesson concepts. For additional exercises, see the Student Edition.

Answers

Additional Practice

1. $x = $ # of uniforms;

   $1762 = 598 + 24.25x;$

   $1762 - 598;$

   $= 598 - 598 + 24.25x;$

   $1164 = 24.25x;$

   $\dfrac{1164}{24.25} = \dfrac{24.25x}{24.25};$

   $48 = x$

2. $x = $ # of laps

   $4 = \dfrac{3}{4} + \dfrac{1}{4}x + \dfrac{3}{4}$

   $4 - \dfrac{6}{4} = \dfrac{6}{4} - \dfrac{6}{4} + \dfrac{1}{4}x$

   $\dfrac{5}{2} = \dfrac{1}{4}x$

   $4\left(\dfrac{5}{2}\right) = \left(\dfrac{1}{4}x\right)4$

   $10 = x$

3. $a = 31$ 　　4. $x = -10$

5. $y = -14$ 　　6. $k = 55$

7. $x = 4$ 　　8. $x = -14$

9. $n = 15$ 　　10. $a = -1$

11. $x = 3$ 　　12. $r = -6.1$

13. $w = -4$ 　　14. $r = -1.22$

15. 31 minutes 　　16. 11

Problem Solving

1. 201 min 　　2. 184 min

3. 200 min 　　4. Plan A

5. Plan B 　　6. B

7. J 　　8. A

9. F

Name_____ Class_____ Date_____ **1-6**

Additional Practice

1. The school purchased baseball equipment and uniforms for a total cost of $1762. The equipment costs $598 and the uniforms were $24.25 each. How many uniforms did the school purchase?

_____

_____

_____

_____

2. Carla runs 4 miles every day. She jogs from home to the school track, which is $\frac{3}{4}$ mile away. She then runs laps around the $\frac{1}{4}$-mile track. Carla then jogs home. How many laps does she run at the school?

_____

_____

_____

_____

_____

Solve.

3. $\frac{a+5}{3} = 12$

4. $\frac{x+2}{4} = -2$

5. $\frac{y-4}{6} = -3$

6. $\frac{k+1}{8} = 7$

7. $0.5x - 6 = -4$

8. $\frac{x}{2} + 3 = -4$

9. $\frac{1}{5}n + 3 = 6$

10. $2a - 7 = -9$

11. $\frac{3x-1}{4} = 2$

12. $-7.8 = 4.4 + 2r$

13. $\frac{-4w+5}{-3} = -7$

14. $1.3 - 5r = 7.4$

15. A phone call costs $0.58 for the first 3 minutes and $0.15 for each additional minute. If the total charge for the call was $4.78, how many minutes was the call?

_____

16. Seventeen less than four times a number is twenty-seven. Find the number.

_____

Problem Solving

The chart below describes three different long-distance calling plans. Jamie has budgeted $20 per month for long-distance calls. Write the correct answer.

1. How many minutes will Jamie be able to use per month with plan A? Round to the nearest minute.

_____

Plan	Monthly Access Fee	Charge per minute
A	$3.95	$0.08
B	$8.95	$0.06
C	$0	$0.10

2. How many minutes will Jamie be able to use per month with plan B? Round to the nearest minute.

_____

3. How many minutes will Jamie be able to use per month with plan C? Round to the nearest minute.

_____

4. Which plan is the best deal for Jamie's budget?

_____

5. Nolan has budgeted $50 per month for long distance. Which plan is the best deal for Nolan's budget?

_____

The table describes three different car loans that Susana can get to finance her new car. The total column gives the amount she will end up paying for the car including the down payment and the payments with interest. Choose the letter for the best answer.

6. How much will Susana pay each month with loan A?

A $252.04   C $330.35

B $297.02   D $353.68

Loan	Down Payment	Number of Months	Total
A	$2000	60	$19,821.20
B	$1000	48	$19,390.72
C	$0	60	$20,197.20

7. How much will Susana pay each month with loan B?

F $300.85   H $323.17

G $306.50   J $383.14

8. How much will Susana pay each month with loan C?

A $336.62   C $369.95

B $352.28   D $420.78

9. Which loan will give Susana the smallest monthly payment?

F Loan A   H Loan C

G Loan B   J They are equal

Problem Solving Connections
The Plot Thickens

COMMON CORE **Standards for Mathematical Content**

CC.8.NS.1 Know that numbers that are not rational are called irrational. Understand informally that every number has a decimal expansion; for rational numbers show that the decimal expansion repeats eventually, and convert a decimal expansion which repeats eventually into a rational number.

CC.8.EE.7 Solve linear equations in one variable.

CC.8.EE.7b Solve linear equations with rational number coefficients, including equations whose solutions require expanding expressions using the distributive property and collecting like terms.

INTRODUCE

Begin by asking students if they have ever worked in a school garden or community garden. Ask them to consider some of the things that would have to be done when setting up a new plot in a garden. In particular, ask students to name some of the costs associated with setting up a plot. Students might mention the cost of building materials for flower beds, the cost of fencing, the cost of soil, and/or the cost of seeds and plants. Tell the class that they will have a chance to use what they have learned about rational numbers and equations to solve a multi-step problem about a new plot in a school garden.

TEACH

1 Find the Cost of the Fence

Questioning Strategies

- What is the perimeter of a figure? **It is the distance around the figure.**
- How do you find the perimeter of a rectangle that has length l and width w? $l + l + w + w$, **or use the formula** $P = 2l + 2w$.
- How can you use estimation to check that the perimeter you found is reasonable? **The length is about 12 feet and the width is about 9 feet, so the perimeter should be close to** $2 \cdot 12 + 2 \cdot 9 = 42$ **ft.**

- How can you tell whether a number is rational or irrational? **If the decimal form of the number terminates or repeats, the number is rational. Otherwise, it is irrational.**

Differentiated Instruction

You may wish to have groups of students work together to find the perimeter the garden plot. In this case, consider having different groups use different met hods. For example, two groups might calculate $8\frac{3}{4} + 12\frac{1}{8} + 8\frac{3}{4} + 12\frac{1}{8}$, two groups might calculate $2\left(8\frac{3}{4}\right) + 2\left(12\frac{1}{8}\right)$, and two groups might calculate $2\left(8\frac{3}{4} + 12\frac{1}{8}\right)$. Have representatives of each group share their results. Then lead a brief discussion to compare the pros and cons of each method.

2 Find the Cost of the Beds

Questioning Strategies

- What should you do to set up an equation to determine the width of each bed? **Use the fact that 2 times the width of each bed plus 3 times the width of a path must equal the total width of the garden plot.**
- How can you check your solution? **Possible answer: Check that the sum of the widths of the two beds and the three paths is $8\frac{3}{4}$ ft.**
- In part D, what operation should you use to find the number of boards that will be needed? **division**
- After you divide, should you round the quotient up or down? Why? **Round up; you cannot buy a fraction of a board.**

© Houghton Mifflin Harcourt Publishing Company

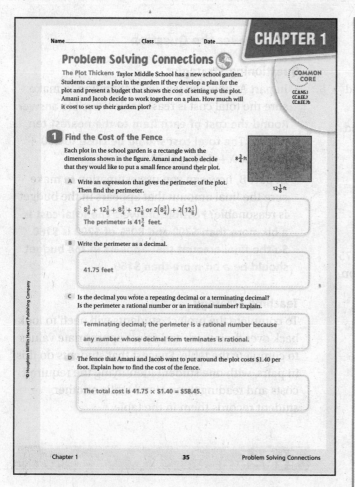

Name _____ Class _____ Date _____

CHAPTER 1

Problem Solving Connections

The Plot Thickens Taylor Middle School has a new school garden. Students can get a plot in the garden if they develop a plan for the plot and present a budget that shows the cost of setting up the plot. Amani and Jacob decide to work together on a plan. How much will it cost to set up their garden plot?

COMMON CORE
CC.8.NS.1
CC.8.EE.7
CC.8.EE.7b

1 Find the Cost of the Fence

Each plot in the school garden is a rectangle with the dimensions shown in the figure. Amani and Jacob decide that they would like to put a small fence around their plot.

$8\frac{3}{4}$ ft

$12\frac{1}{8}$ ft

A Write an expression that gives the perimeter of the plot. Then find the perimeter.

$8\frac{3}{4} + 12\frac{1}{8} + 8\frac{3}{4} + 12\frac{1}{8}$ or $2\left(8\frac{3}{4}\right) + 2\left(12\frac{1}{8}\right)$

The perimeter is $41\frac{3}{4}$ feet.

B Write the perimeter as a decimal.

41.75 feet

C Is the decimal you wrote a repeating decimal or a terminating decimal? Is the perimeter a rational number or an irrational number? Explain.

Terminating decimal; the perimeter is a rational number because any number whose decimal form terminates is rational.

D The fence that Amani and Jacob want to put around the plot costs $1.40 per foot. Explain how to find the cost of the fence.

The total cost is 41.75 × $1.40 = $58.45.

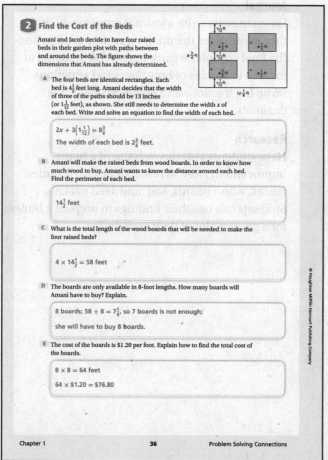

2 Find the Cost of the Beds

Amani and Jacob decide to have four raised beds in their garden plot with paths between and around the beds. The figure shows the dimensions that Amani has already determined.

$8\frac{3}{4}$ ft

$1\frac{1}{12}$ ft
$4\frac{1}{2}$ ft
x

$12\frac{1}{8}$ ft

A The four beds are identical rectangles. Each bed is $4\frac{1}{2}$ feet long. Amani decides that the width of three of the paths should be 13 inches (or $1\frac{1}{12}$ feet), as shown. She still needs to determine the width x of each bed. Write and solve an equation to find the width of each bed.

$2x + 3\left(1\frac{1}{12}\right) = 8\frac{3}{4}$

The width of each bed is $2\frac{3}{4}$ feet.

B Amani will make the raised beds from wood boards. In order to know how much wood to buy, Amani wants to know the distance around each bed. Find the perimeter of each bed.

$14\frac{1}{2}$ feet

C What is the total length of the wood boards that will be needed to make the four raised beds?

$4 × 14\frac{1}{2} = 58$ feet

D The boards are only available in 8-foot lengths. How many boards will Amani have to buy? Explain.

8 boards; $58 ÷ 8 = 7\frac{1}{4}$, so 7 boards is not enough; she will have to buy 8 boards.

E The cost of the boards is $1.20 per foot. Explain how to find the total cost of the boards.

$8 × 8 = 64$ feet

$64 × $1.20 = 76.80

3 Find the Cost of the Soil

Questioning Strategies
- What units do you use for the length, width, and height of a raised bed? **feet**
- What units do you use for the volume of a raised bed? **cubic feet**
- Why do you need to know the volume of the beds? **The volume tells you how much soil the beds will hold.**

Avoid Common Errors
Students might solve the equation $3h - 0.25 = 2.75$ by subtracting 0.25 from both sides of the equation. Remind students that they should isolate the variable by undoing the operations in the reverse order. On the left side of the equation, the variable h is multiplied by 3 and then 0.25 is subtracted from the result. To undo these operations in the reverse order, students should add 0.25 to both sides and then divide by 3.

4 Find the Cost of the Seeds

Questioning Strategies
- Assuming each packet of seeds costs p dollars, what expression gives the remaining balance on Amani's gift card after she buys 9 packets of seeds? **10 − 9p**
- What is the first step in solving the equation $10 - 9p = -11.15$? **Subtract 10 from both sides of the equation.**
- What is the next step? **Divide both sides of the equation by −9.**
- Do you expect the solution of the equation to be positive or negative? Why? **Positive; the price of a packet of seeds must be greater than 0.**

5 Answer the Question

Questioning Strategies
- In part A, how can you use estimation to make sure the total cost is reasonable? **Possible answer: Round the cost of each item to the nearest ten dollars. The total cost should be close to $60 + $80 + $80 + $10 = $230.**
- In part B, how can you use estimation to make sure the final amount that appears in the budget is reasonable? **Possible answer: The total cost is a bit more than $200 and 80% of $200 is $160. So the final amount that appears in the budget should be a bit more than $160.**

Teaching Strategy
To complete the project, students will need to look back over their work and select appropriate values to complete the table. Suggest that students do this in pairs, with one student identifying the required costs and reading them aloud while another student records them in the table.

CLOSE

Journal
Have students write a journal entry in which they summarize the main steps they used to find the final cost of the garden plot. Ask students to include examples of how they used equations involving fractions and equations involving decimals.

Research
Have students visit the web site of a home-improvement store to research prices of garden fences, wood boards, soil, and seed packets. Students can use their findings to prepare a budget for a garden plot of their own design.

3 Find the Cost of the Soil

Next, Jacob wants to calculate the amount of soil that will be needed to fill the four raised beds and the total cost of the soil.

A   Three times the height of each bed is 0.25 feet more than the width of the bed. Write and solve an equation to find the height *h* of each bed.

$3h - 0.25 = 2.75; h = 1$
The height is 1 foot.

B   Complete the figure of one of the raised beds by filling in the dimensions. Write all dimensions as decimals.

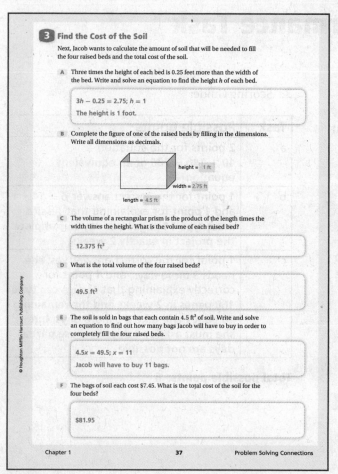

height = 1 ft
width = 2.75 ft
length = 4.5 ft

C   The volume of a rectangular prism is the product of the length times the width times the height. What is the volume of each raised bed?

12.375 ft³

D   What is the total volume of the four raised beds?

49.5 ft³

E   The soil is sold in bags that each contain 4.5 ft³ of soil. Write and solve an equation to find out how many bags Jacob will have to buy in order to completely fill the four raised beds.

$4.5x = 49.5; x = 11$
Jacob will have to buy 11 bags.

F   The bags of soil each cost $7.45. What is the total cost of the soil for the four beds?

$81.95

4 Find the Cost of the Seeds

Amani has a $10 gift card for a gardening store. She plans use her gift card to order some packets of seeds at the store's web site.

A   The web site allows users to enter the number of packets of seeds they wish to purchase and find out the remaining balance on their gift card. Amani decides that she and Jacob need 9 packets of seeds. She enters this amount on the web site and sees the result at right. What does the negative card balance represent?

Value of gift card:	$10
Enter number of packets of seeds	9
Card balance:	−$11.15

The cost of 9 packets exceeds the value of the gift card by $11.15.

B   Suppose each packet of seeds costs *p* dollars. Write and solve an equation to find the cost of a packet of seeds.

$10 - 9p = -11.15; p = 2.35.$
A packet of seeds costs $2.35.

C   Amani decides she will use her gift card to buy the packets of seeds. She and Jacob will include the balance (the amount of money not covered by the gift card) in their budget. How much will they include in the budget?

$11.15

5 Answer the Question

Amani and Jacob are ready to prepare their budget for their garden plot.

A   Look back at your work to complete the table.

Amani and Jacob's Budget	
Item	Total Cost
Fence for perimeter of garden plot	$58.45
Wood boards for raised beds	$76.80
Soil for raised beds	$81.95
Seed packets	$11.15
TOTAL	$228.35

B   Amani and Jacob learn that a community organization will pay for 20% of the total cost of each garden plot. This means Amani and Jacob only need to ask for 80% of their total cost when they present their budget. Multiply the total cost by 0.8 to find the final amount that will appear in their budget.

$182.68

This page provides students with the opportunity to apply concepts from the Common Core in real-world problem situations. There are three different levels of performance tasks:

⭐ **Novice:** These are short word problems that require students to apply the math they have learned in straightforward, real-world situations.

⭐⭐ **Apprentice:** These are more involved problems that guide students step-by-step through more complex tasks. These exercises include more complicated reasoning, writing, and open-ended elements.

⭐⭐⭐ **Expert:** These are open-ended, non-routine problems that, instead of stepping the students through, asks them to choose their own methods for solving and justify their answers and reasoning.

Sample answers

1. **a.** $m = 9$, or 9 minutes
   b. No, she will get $m = 10$; 0.6 is a terminating decimal while $\frac{2}{3} = 0.\overline{6}$ is a repeating decimal.

2. **a.** $1808 + 24s = 2000$
   b.
   $$1808 + 24s = 2000$$
   $$1808 + 24s - 1808 = 2000 - 1808$$
   $$\frac{24s}{24} = \frac{192}{24}$$
   $$s = 8$$

   It will take Bill 8 weeks to reach 2,000 songs.

3. Scoring Guide:

Task	Possible points
a	**2 points** for the equation $10 + 14p = 206$ or an equivalent equation
b	**1 point** for the correct answer $p = 14$, and **1 point** for explaining that Jessica must type 14 pages per day to complete the project in exactly 2 weeks.
c	**1 point** for the correct answer yes, she needs 3 more days, and **1 point** for correctly explaining that Jessica can type 168 pages in 2 weeks and the remaining 28 pages will take $2\frac{1}{3}$ more days, but she must ask for 3 days because partial days are not possible.

Total possible points: 6

Name _____ Class _____ Date _____

Performance Task

COMMON CORE

CC.8.NS.1
CC.8.EE.7
CC.8.EE.7b

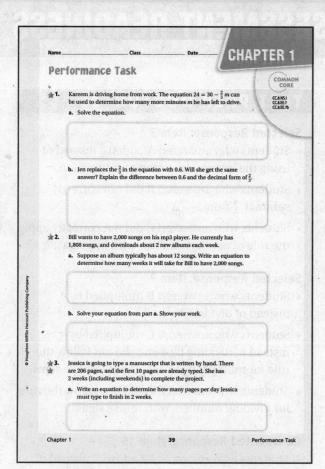

⭐ **1.** Kareem is driving home from work. The equation $24 = 30 - \frac{2}{3}m$ can be used to determine how many more minutes m he has left to drive.

    a. Solve the equation.

    b. Jen replaces the $\frac{2}{3}$ in the equation with 0.6. Will she get the same answer? Explain the difference between 0.6 and the decimal form of $\frac{2}{3}$.

⭐ **2.** Bill wants to have 2,000 songs on his mp3 player. He currently has 1,808 songs, and downloads about 2 new albums each week.

    a. Suppose an album typically has about 12 songs. Write an equation to determine how many weeks it will take for Bill to have 2,000 songs.

    b. Solve your equation from part **a**. Show your work.

⭐⭐ **3.** Jessica is going to type a manuscript that is written by hand. There are 206 pages, and the first 10 pages are already typed. She has 2 weeks (including weekends) to complete the project.

    a. Write an equation to determine how many pages per day Jessica must type to finish in 2 weeks.

© Houghton Mifflin Harcourt Publishing Company

---

    b. Solve your equation from part **a**. Explain what the solution means.

    c. Jessica can type 12 pages per day. Should she ask for an extension to complete the project? If so, how many days does she need? She cannot ask for a part of a day as an extension. Explain your answer.

⭐⭐⭐ **4.** Fred is taking an online test. To pass, he must answer $\frac{7}{10}$ of the questions correctly. There are 120 multiple-choice questions on the test. After answering 45 questions, Fred has gotten 21 correct.

    a. Write and solve an equation to determine how many more questions Fred must answer correctly to pass the test.

    b. What fraction of the questions has Fred gotten right so far? What fraction must he get right from now on to pass the test? Is it likely he will pass? Explain your reasoning.

© Houghton Mifflin Harcourt Publishing Company

---

4. Scoring Guide:

Task	Possible points
a	**1 point** for the equation $\frac{21+x}{120} = \frac{7}{10}$ or equivalent and **1 point** for the solution 63 questions.
b	**1 point** for correctly answering Fred has gotten $\frac{21}{45} = \frac{7}{15}$ of the questions right so far, **1 point** for correctly answering that he needs to get $\frac{63}{120-45} = \frac{63}{75} = \frac{21}{25}$ of the remaining questions correct, **1 point** for answering that passing the test is unlikely, and **1 point** for explaining that so far Fred has gotten less than half of the questions answered correct, and he needs to get much more than half of the rest of the questions correct to pass.

Total possible points: 6

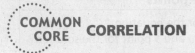
COMMON
CORE **CORRELATION**

Standard	Items
CC.8.EE.7	1, 3, 8, 11
CC.8.EE.7b	2, 4–7, 9–10, 11-17

TEST PREP DOCTOR ⊕

Selected Response: Item 3
- Students who answered **A** added $\frac{4}{5}$ instead of using the inverse operation of subtraction.
- Students who answered **B** did not correctly subtract $\frac{4}{5}$ from $-\frac{1}{10}$.
- Students who answered **C** did not correctly apply the rule of adding numbers with like signs.

Selected Response: Item 7
- Students who answered **B** multiplied by 4 instead of dividing by 4.
- Students who answered **C** multiplied by 4 instead of dividing by 4 and did not follow the rule for multiplying numbers with unlike signs.
- Students who answered **D** did not follow the rule for dividing numbers with unlike signs.

Constructed Response: Item 16
- Students who answered **22** added 7 instead of subtracting 7.
- Students who answered **9** incorrectly subtracted 7 from 15.

© Houghton Mifflin Harcourt Publishing Company

CHAPTER 1 COMMON CORE ASSESSMENT READINESS

Name _____ Class _____ Date _____

SELECTED RESPONSE

1. Solve $\frac{z}{9} + 5 = 10$.

  A. $z = 14$ **C.** $z = 135$

  B. $z = 85$ **(D.)** $z = 45$

2. Solve $3 + 5z = -12$.

  (F.) $z = -3$ **H.** $z = 1$

  G. $z = -15$ **J.** $z = -1.8$

3. Solve $y + \frac{4}{5} = -\frac{1}{10}$. Make sure your answer is in simplest form.

  A. $y = \frac{7}{10}$ **C.** $y = \frac{9}{10}$

  B. $y = -\frac{7}{10}$ **(D.)** $y = -\frac{9}{10}$

4. What is the value for m for this equation: $3m - 6.8 = 31$?

  F. 8.06   **H.** 37.8

  (G.) 12.6   **J.** 40.8

5. Solve $3.7a + 4.4 = -40$.

  A. $a = -11$ **C.** $a = -13$

  B. $a = -2$ **(D.)** $a = -12$

6. Solve $5 = \frac{1}{2}m + 3$.

  F. $m = 1\frac{1}{2}$ **H.** $m = 6$

  (G.) $m = 4$ **J.** $m = 10$

7. Solve $4b = -\frac{2}{3}$.

  (A.) $b = -\frac{1}{6}$ **C.** $b = \frac{8}{3}$

  B. $b = -\frac{8}{3}$ **D.** $b = \frac{1}{6}$

8. Solve $m - 13.5 = -16.5$.

  F. $m = 3$ **H.** $m = -29$

  (G.) $m = -3$ **J.** $m = 29$

9. Solve $-\frac{5}{6}w = -\frac{3}{5}$.

  (A.) $w = \frac{18}{25}$ **C.** $w = \frac{17}{60}$

  B. $w = \frac{50}{39}$ **D.** $w = \frac{7}{30}$

10. Solve $-1.7p = 3.4$.

  F. $p = -5.78$ **H.** $p = -8$

  G. $p = -0.5$ **(J.)** $p = -2$

11. Solve $7 = \frac{1}{2}m + 9$.

  A. $m = -1\frac{1}{2}$ **C.** $m = 46$

  (B.) $m = -4$ **D.** $m = -10$

12. Solve $\frac{1}{2}y + 10 = -25$.

  (F.) $y = -70$ **H.** $y = -30$

  G. $y = -35$ **J.** $y = 70$

13. Your class earned $110.00 Saturday afternoon by washing cars to raise money for a class trip. This is $\frac{1}{4}$ of the money needed for the trip. What is the total amount needed?

  A. $114.00

  B. $27.50

  C. $106.00

  (D.) $440.00

CONSTRUCTED RESPONSE

14. A group of friends share a large popcorn at the movies. It costs $3.15 to buy it and $0.85 for each refill. If they spent $7.40, how many times did the group of friends refill their popcorn? Show your work.

$$0.85x + 3.15 = 7.40$$
$$\underline{-3.15 = 3.15}$$
$$0.85x = 4.25$$
$$x = 5$$

15. John has picked 40 apples, which is $\frac{1}{3}$ of the amount his grandmother uses to make applesauce. How many apples does she use to make applesauce? Show your work.

$$\frac{1}{3} \cdot x = 40$$
$$3 \cdot \frac{1}{3} \cdot x = 40 \cdot 3$$
$$x = 120$$

16. If you can find the number of bones the dog buried in the backyard this week as compared to last week by using the equation $b + 7 = 15$, then did the dog bury 22 bones, 8 bones, or 9 bones this week?

The dog buried 8 bones this week.

_____

_____

17. By dividing the number of houses in Antonio's subdivision by 4 and adding 15, you can find the number of houses in Hector's subdivision. If Hector has 47 houses in his subdivision, how many houses are in Antonio's subdivision? Show your work.

$$\frac{a}{4} + 15 = 47$$
$$\frac{a}{4} + 15 - 15 = 47 - 15$$
$$\frac{a}{4} = 32$$
$$4 \cdot \frac{a}{4} = 32 \cdot 4$$
$$a = 128$$

CHAPTER 2

Graphs and Functions

CHAPTER 2

COMMON CORE
**PROFESIONAL
DEVELOPMENT** **CC.8.F.5**

Given a verbal description of a situation involving the relationship between two quantities, students will model the situation with a graph. Given a graph modeling a situation involving the relationship between two quantities, students will give a verbal description of the situation. The relationship between the two quantities will be functional.

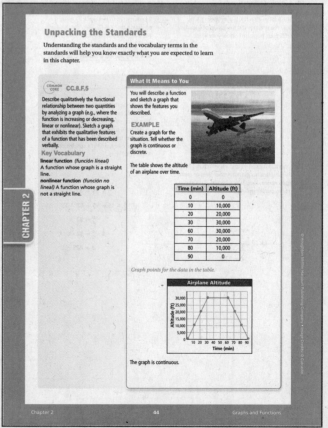

CHAPTER 2

Graphs and Functions

Chapter Focus

You will determine whether an ordered pair is a solution of an equation. You will locate and name points in the coordinate plane. You will also describe a relationship given a graph and sketch a graph given a description. A function is a rule that assigns exactly one output to each input. You will represent a function with a table or graph. Finally, you will use equations, tables, and graphs to represent relationships between two variables.

Chapter at a Glance

COMMON CORE

Lesson		Standards for Mathematical Content
2-1	Ordered Pairs	PREP FOR CC.8.EE.8
2-2	Graphing on a Coordinate Plane	PREP FOR CC.8.SP.1
2-3	Interpreting Graphs	CC.8.F.5
2-4	Functions	CC.8.F.1
2-5	Equations, Tables, and Graphs	CC.8.F.4
	Problem Solving Connections	
	Performance Task	
	Assessment Readiness	

Unpacking the Standards

Understanding the standards and the vocabulary terms in the standards will help you know exactly what you are expected to learn in this chapter.

COMMON CORE **CC.8.F.5**

Describe qualitatively the functional relationship between two quantities by analyzing a graph (e.g., where the function is increasing or decreasing, linear or nonlinear). Sketch a graph that exhibits the qualitative features of a function that has been described verbally.

Key Vocabulary

linear function *(función lineal)* A function whose graph is a straight line.

nonlinear function *(función no lineal)* A function whose graph is not a straight line.

What It Means to You

You will describe a function and sketch a graph that shows the features you described.

EXAMPLE

Create a graph for the situation. Tell whether the graph is continuous or discrete.

The table shows the altitude of an airplane over time.

Time (min)	Altitude (ft)
0	0
10	10,000
20	20,000
30	30,000
60	30,000
70	20,000
80	10,000
90	0

Graph points for the data in the table.

Airplane Altitude

The graph is continuous.

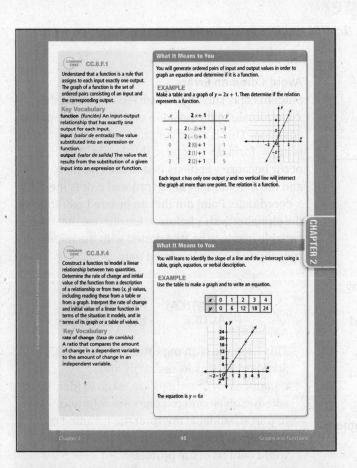

CC.8.F.1

Understand that a function is a rule that assigns to each input exactly one output. The graph of a function is the set of ordered pairs consisting of an input and the corresponding output.

Key Vocabulary

function *(función)* An input-output relationship that has exactly one output for each input.

input *(valor de entrada)* The value substituted into an expression or function.

output *(valor de salida)* The value that results from the substitution of a given input into an expression or function.

What It Means to You

You will generate ordered pairs of input and output values in order to graph an equation and determine if it is a function.

EXAMPLE

Make a table and a graph of $y = 2x + 1$. Then determine if the relation represents a function.

x	$2x + 1$	y
−2	2(−2) + 1	−3
−1	2(−1) + 1	−1
0	2(0) + 1	1
1	2(1) + 1	3
2	2(2) + 1	5

Each input x has only one output y and no vertical line will intersect the graph at more than one point. The relation is a function.

CC.8.F.4

Construct a function to model a linear relationship between two quantities. Determine the rate of change and initial value of the function from a description of a relationship or from two (x, y) values, including reading these from a table or from a graph. Interpret the rate of change and initial value of a linear function in terms of the situation it models, and in terms of its graph or a table of values.

Key Vocabulary

rate of change *(tasa de cambio)* A ratio that compares the amount of change in a dependent variable to the amount of change in an independent variable.

What It Means to You

You will learn to identify the slope of a line and the y-intercept using a table, graph, equation, or verbal description.

EXAMPLE

Use the table to make a graph and to write an equation.

x	0	1	2	3	4
y	0	6	12	18	24

The equation is $y = 6x$

CHAPTER 2

COMMON CORE PROFESIONAL DEVELOPMENT

Using equations, graphs, and tables, students will distinguish between functions and non-functions. Non-functions occur where there is more than one y-value associated with any x-value. In Grade 8, students are not expected to use the function notation $f(x)$.

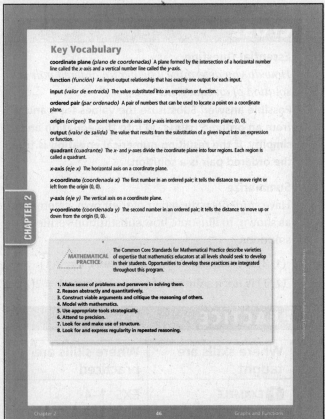

Key Vocabulary

coordinate plane *(plano de coordenadas)* A plane formed by the intersection of a horizontal number line called the x-axis and a vertical number line called the y-axis.

function *(función)* An input-output relationship that has exactly one output for each input.

input *(valor de entrada)* The value substituted into an expression or function.

ordered pair *(par ordenado)* A pair of numbers that can be used to locate a point on a coordinate plane.

origin *(origen)* The point where the x-axis and y-axis intersect on the coordinate plane; (0, 0).

output *(valor de salida)* The value that results from the substitution of a given input into an expression or function.

quadrant *(cuadrante)* The x- and y-axes divide the coordinate plane into four regions. Each region is called a quadrant.

x-axis *(eje x)* The horizontal axis on a coordinate plane.

x-coordinate *(coordenada x)* The first number in an ordered pair; it tells the distance to move right or left from the origin (0, 0).

y-axis *(eje y)* The vertical axis on a coordinate plane.

y-coordinate *(coordenada y)* The second number in an ordered pair; it tells the distance to move up or down from the origin (0, 0).

MATHEMATICAL PRACTICE

The Common Core Standards for Mathematical Practice describe varieties of expertise that mathematics educators at all levels should seek to develop in their students. Opportunities to develop these practices are integrated throughout this program.

1. Make sense of problems and persevere in solving them.
2. Reason abstractly and quantitatively.
3. Construct viable arguments and critique the reasoning of others.
4. Model with mathematics.
5. Use appropriate tools strategically.
6. Attend to precision.
7. Look for and make use of structure.
8. Look for and express regularity in repeated reasoning.

CHAPTER 2

Ordered Pairs
Going Deeper

Essential question: *How do you determine whether an ordered pair is a solution of an equation?*

COMMON CORE **Standards for Mathematical Content**

Prep for CC.8.EE.8 Analyze and solve pairs of simultaneous linear equations.

Vocabulary
ordered pair

Prerequisites
Solutions

Math Background
In a two-variable equation such as $y = 2x + 5$, any ordered pair (x, y) that makes the equation true is a solution of the equation. To find if an ordered pair is a solution, substitute its numbers into the equation and simplify. If the equation is true, the ordered pair is a solution. More than one ordered pair can be a solution of a two-variable linear equation like $y = 2x + 5$. In fact, it has an infinite number of ordered-pair solutions. This will become clear when students graph lines.

INTRODUCE

Connect to prior learning by asking students to give examples of one-variable equations and their solutions. Discuss how a number value can be substituted for the variable to determine if that number is a solution to the equation. Point out that equations can also have two variables, and the solutions to two-variable equations will require two numbers, or a *pair* of numbers.

TEACH

1 EXAMPLE

Questioning Strategies
- Can more than one ordered pair be a solution to an equation? Yes, a two-variable equation can have many ordered pair solutions.
- Is an ordered pair a solution if the simplified equation is $0 = 0$? Yes, because $0 = 0$ is a true equation.

Avoid Common Errors
Students may substitute incorrectly, putting the x-coordinate in the position of the y-variable of the equation. This is more common when the equation is in $y =$ form, as is done in this lesson. This may occur because y appears first in the equation, and the first number in the ordered pair is the x-coordinate. Point out that an ordered pair follows the alphabet with x before y. Emphasize that each variable needs to be substituted with the matching coordinate from the ordered pair.

MATHEMATICAL PRACTICE | **Highlighting the Standards**

This Example is an opportunity to address Standard 2 (Reason abstractly and quantitatively). Students are asked to identify whether given ordered pairs are solutions. In part **B**, students interpret the meaning of an ordered pair solution in terms of the real-world context of the problem.

CLOSE

Essential Question
How do you determine whether an ordered pair is a solution of an equation?
Possible answer: Substitute the values for x and y from an ordered pair (x, y) into the equation and simplify. If the resulting numerical equation is true, the ordered pair is a solution.

Summarize
Have students write a pair of their own statements, as shown, to illustrate how substitution verifies solutions.

$(1, 2)$ is a solution of $y = 2x$ because $2 = 2(1)$.

$(2, 1)$ is *not* a solution of $y = 2x$ because $1 \neq 2(2)$.

PRACTICE

Where skills are taught	Where skills are practiced
1 EXAMPLE	EXS. 1–4

2-1

Name_____ Class_____ Date_____

Ordered Pairs
Going Deeper

Essential question: *How do you determine whether an ordered pair is a solution of an equation?*

An **ordered pair** (x, y) can be used to write a solution for a two-variable equation such as $y = 10x - 15$. The *order* in an *ordered pair* is important.

$$(3, 15)$$
x-value *y*-value

1 EXAMPLE CC.8.EE.8 Identifying an Ordered Pair as a Solution

A group of students is washing cars to raise money. They spend $15 on soap and charge $10 for each car *x*. The equation for the profit *y* is $y = 10x - 15$.

A Determine whether each ordered pair is a solution of $y = 10x - 15$.
Complete the following by substituting the correct values for each variable.

$(5, 35)$	$(20, 195)$	$(50, 485)$
$y = 10x - 15$	$y = 10x - 15$	$y = 10x - 15$
$35 \overset{?}{=} 10(5) - 15$	$195 \overset{?}{=} 10(20) - 15$	$485 \overset{?}{=} 10(50) - 15$
$35 \overset{?}{=} 50 - 15$	$195 \overset{?}{=} 200 - 15$	$485 \overset{?}{=} 500 - 15$
$35 = 35$	$195 \neq 185$	$485 = 485$

Circle the correct answer.

$(5, 35)$ **is** / is not a solution of $y = 10x - 15$.

$(20, 195)$ is / **is not** a solution of $y = 10x - 15$.

$(50, 485)$ **is** / is not a solution of $y = 10x - 15$.

B What does the ordered pair $(50, 485)$ mean in this situation?

50 represents the number of cars washed and 485 represents the profit made

in dollars.

The ordered pair (x, y) represents (number of ___cars___, ___profit___ in $).

TRY THIS!

Determine whether each ordered pair is a solution of $y = 10x - 15$.

1a. $(5, 25)$ **1b.** $(10, 75)$ **1c.** $(25, 235)$

No   No   Yes

Chapter 2   47   Lesson 1

REFLECT

1d. Error Analysis A student claims that the ordered pair $(10, 5)$ is a solution of the equation $y = 21 - 2x$. Do you agree or disagree? Why?

Disagree; by substituting the values 10 and 5 for *x* and *y*, respectively, we find

that $5 \neq 21 - 20$.

PRACTICE

Complete each table of solutions.

1. The temperature *y* in Albany, NY, is 6°F colder than the temperature *x* in New York City. This situation is represented by the equation $y = x - 6$.

x	$x - 6$	y	(x, y)
56	$56 - 6$	50	$(56, 50)$
48	$48 - 6$	42	$(48, 42)$
44	$44 - 6$	38	$(44, 38)$
41	$41 - 6$	35	$(41, 35)$

Is $(60, 54)$ a solution to $y = x - 6$? What does the ordered pair represent in this situation?

Yes. 60°F represents the temperature

in New York City and 54°F represents

the temperature in Albany.

2. Nate scored *x* number of 2-point baskets and *y* number of 1-point free throws. He scored 18 points in all. This situation is represented by the equation $y = 18 - 2x$.

x	$18 - 2x$	y	(x, y)
3	$18 - 2(3)$	12	$(3, 12)$
4	$18 - 2(4)$	10	$(4, 10)$
5	$18 - 2(5)$	8	$(5, 8)$
10	$18 - 2(10)$	-2	$(10, -2)$

Is $(10, -2)$ a solution to $y = 18 - 2x$? What does the ordered pair represent in this situation and does it make sense?

Yes. 10 represents the number of

2-point baskets and -2 represents

the number of 1-point baskets. You

cannot have a negative number of

baskets so it does not make sense.

3. Nina bought a frozen yogurt for $1.40. She paid with *x* quarters and *y* dimes. Write an equation that represents the situation. Then find all ordered pair solutions that make sense for the problem.

$1.40 = 0.25x + 0.1y$; $(0, 14)$, $(2, 9)$, $(4, 4)$

4. Create an equation that has $(3, 5)$ as a solution. Then give a possible scenario for your equation.

Possible answer: $y = x + 2$. Yves is 2 years older than Xavier.

Chapter 2   48   Lesson 1

Assign these pages to help your students practice and apply important lesson concepts. For additional exercises, see the Student Edition.

Answers

Additional Practice

1. no		**2.** yes	
3. yes		**4.** no	
5. yes		**6.** yes	
7. no		**8.** yes	

9.

x	x + 5	y	(x, y)
0	0 + 5	5	(0, 5)
1	1 + 5	6	(1, 6)
2	2 + 5	7	(2, 7)
3	3 + 5	8	(3, 8)
4	4 + 5	9	(4, 9)

10.

x	3x + 1	y	(x, y)
1	3(1) + 1	4	(1, 4)
2	3(2) + 1	7	(2, 7)
3	3(3) + 1	10	(3, 10)
4	3(4) + 1	13	(4, 13)
5	3(5) + 1	16	(5, 16)

11.

x	2x + 6	y	(x, y)
0	2(0) + 6	6	(0, 6)
1	2(1) + 6	8	(1, 8)
2	2(2) + 6	10	(2, 10)
3	2(3) + 6	12	(3, 12)
4	2(4) + 6	14	(4, 14)

12.

x	4x − 2	y	(x, y)
2	4(2) − 2	6	(2, 6)
4	4(4) − 2	14	(4, 14)
6	4(6) − 2	22	(6, 22)
8	4(8) − 2	30	(8, 30)
10	4(10) − 2	38	(10, 38)

13. $220

Problem Solving

1. (1990, 20.2)	**2.** (2020, 28.9)
3. (30, 86)	**4.** (22, 71.6)
5. C	**6.** G
7. A	**8.** H

Name_____ Class_____ Date_____

2-1

Additional Practice

Determine whether each ordered pair is a solution of $y = 4 + 2x$.

1. (1, 1)   2. (2, 8)   3. (0, 4)   4. (8, 2)

_____   _____   _____   _____

Determine whether each ordered pair is a solution of $y = 3x - 2$.

5. (1, 1)   6. (3, 7)   7. (5, 15)   8. (6, 16)

_____   _____   _____   _____

Use the given values to complete the table of solutions.

9. $y = x + 5$ for $x = 0, 1, 2, 3, 4$

x	x + 5	y	(x, y)
0			
1			
2			
3			
4			

10. $y = 3x + 1$ for $x = 1, 2, 3, 4, 5$

x	3x + 1	y	(x, y)
1			
2			
3			
4			
5			

11. $y = 2x + 6$ for $x = 0, 1, 2, 3, 4$

x	2x + 6	y	(x, y)
0			
1			
2			
3			
4			

12. $y = 4x - 2$ for $x = 2, 4, 6, 8, 10$

x	4x - 2	y	(x, y)
2			
4			
6			
8			
10			

13. Alexis opened a savings account with a $120 deposit. Each week she will put $20 into the account. The equation that gives the total amount t in her account is $t = 120 + 20w$, where w is the number of weeks since she opened the account. How much money will Alexis have in her savings account after 5 weeks?

_____

Problem Solving

Use the table at the right for Exercises 1–2.

1. Write the ordered pair that shows the average miles per gallon in 1990.

_____

2. The data can be approximated by the equation $m = 0.30887x - 595$ where m is the average miles per gallon and x is the year. Use the equation to find an ordered pair (x, m) that shows the estimated miles per gallon in the year 2020.

Average Miles per Gallon

Year	Miles per Gallon
1970	13.5
1980	15.9
1990	20.2
1995	21.1
1996	21.2
1997	21.5

For Exercises 3–4 use the equation $F = 1.8C + 32$, which relates Fahrenheit temperatures F to Celsius temperatures C.

3. Write ordered pair (C, F) that shows the Celsius equivalent of 86 °F.

4. Write ordered pair (C, F) that shows the Fahrenheit equivalent of 22 °C.

Choose the letter for the best answer.

5. A taxi charges a $2.50 flat fee plus $0.30 per mile. Use an equation for taxi fare t in terms of miles m. Which ordered pair (m, t) shows the taxi fare for a 23-mile cab ride?

  A (23, 6.90)   C (23, 9.40)

  B (23, 18.50)   D (23, 64.40)

6. The perimeter p of a square is four times the length of a side s, or $p = 4s$. Which ordered pair (s, p) shows the perimeter for a square that has sides that are 5 in.?

  F (5, 1.25)   H (5, 9)

  G (5, 20)   J (5, 25)

7. Maria pays a monthly fee of $3.95 plus $0.10 per minute for long-distance calls. Use an equation for the phone bill p in terms of the number of minutes m. Which ordered pair (m, p) shows the phone bill for 120 minutes?

  A (120, 15.95)   C (120, 28.30)

  B (120, 474.10)   D (120, 486.00)

8. Tickets to a baseball game cost $12 each, plus $2 each for transportation. Use an equation for the cost c of going to the game in terms of the number of people p. Which ordered pair (p, c) shows the cost for 6 people?

  F (6, 74)   H (6, 84)

  G (6, 96)   J (6, 102)

Graphing on a Coordinate Plane
Going Deeper

Essential question: *How do you locate and name points in the coordinate plane?*

 COMMON CORE

Standards for Mathematical Content

Prep for CC.8.SP.1 Construct and interpret scatter plots for bivariate measurement data to investigate patterns of association between two quantities. ...

Vocabulary

coordinate plane   *x*-axis   *y*-axis

quadrants   origin   *x*-coordinate

y-coordinate

Prerequisites

Ordered pairs

Solutions

Math Background

Any location on the coordinate plane can be described by an ordered pair (*x*, *y*) of coordinates. Ordered pairs are ordered: the first number of the pair (*x*-coordinate) describes a point's location to the left or right of the origin and the second number (*y*-coordinate) describes a point's location up or down.

INTRODUCE

Connect to prior learning by drawing a horizontal number line and discussing how a point on the line is identified by one number: negative numbers are left of 0 and positive numbers are right of 0. Then draw a vertical number line. Show that identifying a point now involves two numbers: one for left or right, and another for up or down. Show how the ordered pairs (+, +), (−, +), (−, −), and (+, −) describe the location of points in each of the four quadrants.

TEACH

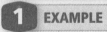 **1 EXAMPLE**

Questioning Strategies

• Are (2, 0) and (−2, 0) the same point? **No, they both are on the *x*-axis but they lie on different sides of the origin.**

• How many distinct ordered pairs are formed by the directions right or left and up or down? **four: (right, up), (left, up), (right, down), and (left, down) and they each correspond with one of the quadrants**

⋮ MATHEMATICAL PRACTICE   **Highlighting the Standards**

This Example is an opportunity to address Standard 6 (Attend to precision). Students are asked to graph and name points in the coordinate plane. In the Reflect questions, students extend graphing ordered pairs to include points that have fractional coordinates and points that lie on an axis instead of in the four quadrants.

CLOSE

Essential Question

How do you locate and name points in the coordinate plane?
Possible answer: The first number in an ordered pair (*x*, *y*) is the location of the point to the right or left of the origin. The second number is the location of the point up or down.

Summarize

Have students sketch their own coordinate plane with a point in each quadrant. Label the points as well as vocabulary terms including: coordinate plane, *x*-axis, *y*-axis, origin, and for one point label its *x*-coordinate and *y*-coordinate.

PRACTICE

Where skills are taught	Where skills are practiced
1 EXAMPLE	EXS. 1–8

Name_____ Class_____ Date_____

2-2

Graphing on a Coordinate Plane
Going Deeper

Essential question: *How do you locate and name points in the coordinate plane?*

The **coordinate plane** is formed by two number lines: the **x-axis**, which is a horizontal number line, and the **y-axis**, a vertical number line. These axes intersect at right angles to divide the plane into four **quadrants**.

The point where the two axes intersect is the **origin** and labeled by the ordered pair (0, 0). In an ordered pair (x, y), the first number is the **x-coordinate**. It tells how many units to move **right** or **left**. The **y-coordinate** tells how many units to move **up** or **down**.

Move **up** or **down**

(x, y)

Move **right** or **left**

PREP FOR CC.8.SP.1

1 EXAMPLE Graphing Points in the Coordinate Plane

An air traffic operator stationed at (0, 0) reports airplane *A* at (4, 3), which represents 4 miles east and 3 miles north of her location. She spots airplane *B* at (−3, −2), or 3 miles west and 2 miles south, and airplane *C* at (5.5, −2), or 5.5 miles east and 2 miles south. Graph the location of each airplane.

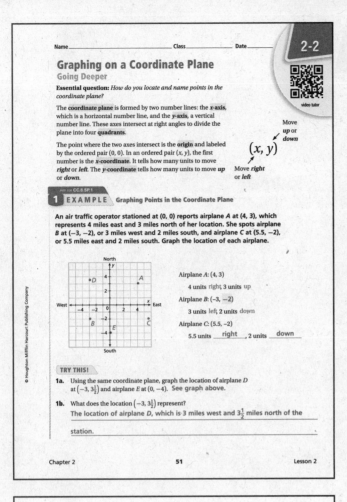

Airplane *A*: (4, 3)

    4 units right, 3 units up

Airplane *B*: (−3, −2)

    3 units left, 2 units down

Airplane *C*: (5.5, −2)

    5.5 units __right__, 2 units __down__

TRY THIS!

1a. Using the same coordinate plane, graph the location of airplane *D* at $\left(-3, 3\frac{1}{2}\right)$ and airplane *E* at (0, −4). See graph above.

1b. What does the location $\left(-3, 3\frac{1}{2}\right)$ represent?

The location of airplane *D*, which is 3 miles west and $3\frac{1}{2}$ miles north of the

station.

Chapter 2　　51　　Lesson 2

REFLECT

1c. How far is airplane *B* from airplane *D*? How can you use the coordinate plane to determine this distance?

$5\frac{1}{2}$ miles; Possible answer: Find the vertical difference between *B*(−3, −2) and

$D\left(-3, 3\frac{1}{2}\right)$ by subtracting their *y*-coordinates.

1d. What do you know when an ordered pair has the same *x*- and *y*-coordinate?

Possible answer: The number of units right (or left) is the same as the number

of units up (or down). The point is located in quadrant I or quadrant III.

PRACTICE

Use the coordinate plane for 1–8.

Write an ordered pair to represent each location. Then graph ordered pairs not shown on the coordinate plane.

1. The public library is located at *M*.

    M(3.5 , 3)

2. The fire station is located at *N*.

    N(5 , 0)

3. Ben, Carlos, and Deena live in a house located at the origin.

    O(0 , 0)

4. From home, Ben walks 2 blocks east, turns and walks 4.5 blocks south, and stops.

    B(2 , −4.5)

5. Carlos starts from home, walks 4.5 blocks north, walks west for 2.5 blocks, and then stops.

    C(−2.5 , 4.5)

6. Deena walks 4 blocks west from home, turns and walks 4.5 blocks south, and then stops.

    D(−4 , −4.5)

This coordinate plane represents a neighborhood measured in blocks.

7. How far from Ben is Deena at the end of their walks? 6 blocks

8. There is a pizza restaurant halfway between Deena's location and Ben's location. What are the coordinates of the restaurant? How far will they each have to walk to meet there?

(−1, −4.5); they will each have to walk 3 blocks.

Chapter 2　　52　　Lesson 2

Assign these pages to help your students practice and apply important lesson concepts. For additional exercises, see the Student Edition.

Answers

Additional Practice

1. $(-2, -3)$; III   **2.** $(-6, 3)$; II

3. $(8, -3)$; IV   **4.** $(5, -4)$; IV

5. $(-4, 4)$; II   **6.** $(1, -8)$; IV

7. $(3, 8)$; I   **8.** $(-5, -6)$; III

9–14.

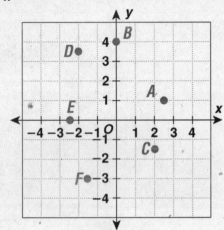

15. 16   **16.** 14

17. 10   **18.** 4

Problem Solving

1. Check students' graphs.

2. rectangle

3. 16 units

4. 15 square units

5. Check students' graphs.

6. square

7. 24 units

8. 36 square units

9. D

10. B

11. B

12. C

Additional Practice

Give the coordinates and quadrant of each point.

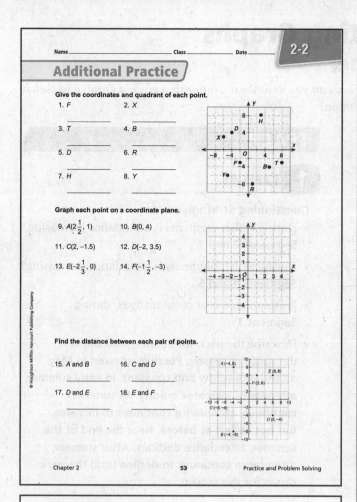

1. F _____
2. X _____
3. T _____
4. B _____
5. D _____
6. R _____
7. H _____
8. Y _____

Graph each point on a coordinate plane.

9. $A(2\frac{1}{2}, 1)$
10. $B(0, 4)$
11. $C(2, -1.5)$
12. $D(-2, 3.5)$
13. $E(-2\frac{1}{3}, 0)$
14. $F(-1\frac{1}{2}, -3)$

Find the distance between each pair of points.

15. A and B _____
16. C and D _____
17. D and E _____
18. E and F _____

Problem Solving

Graph the points to answer each question.

1. Graph the points $(-4, 1)$, $(-4, -2)$, $(1, 1)$, and $(1, -2)$.

2. What type of quadrilateral do the vertices form?

_____

3. What is the perimeter of the figure?

_____

4. What is the area of the figure?

_____

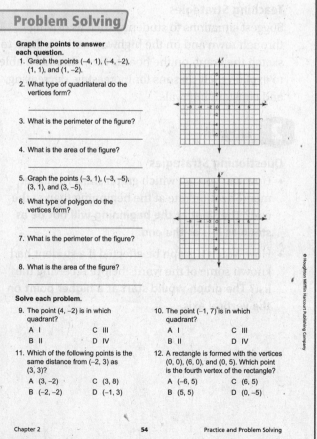

5. Graph the points $(-3, 1)$, $(-3, -5)$, $(3, 1)$, and $(3, -5)$.

6. What type of polygon do the vertices form?

_____

7. What is the perimeter of the figure?

_____

8. What is the area of the figure?

_____

Solve each problem.

9. The point $(4, -2)$ is in which quadrant?

   A I   C III
   B II   D IV

10. The point $(-1, 7)$ is in which quadrant?

    A I   C III
    B II   D IV

11. Which of the following points is the same distance from $(-2, 3)$ as $(3, 3)$?

    A $(3, -2)$ C $(3, 8)$
    B $(-2, -2)$ D $(-1, 3)$

12. A rectangle is formed with the vertices $(0, 0)$, $(6, 0)$, and $(0, 5)$. Which point is the fourth vertex of the rectangle?

    A $(-6, 5)$ C $(6, 5)$
    B $(5, 5)$ D $(0, -5)$

Interpreting Graphs
Going Deeper

Essential question: *How can you describe a relationship given a graph and sketch a graph given a description?*

COMMON **Standards for**
CORE **Mathematical Content**

CC.8.F.5 Describe qualitatively the functional relationship between two quantities by analyzing a graph (e.g., where the function is increasing or decreasing, linear or nonlinear). Sketch a graph that exhibits the qualitative features of a function that has been described verbally.

Prerequisites

Functions

Graphing functions

Math Background

The graph of a function describes a function visually so you can get a lot of information at a glance. From a graph, you can identify intervals where a function is increasing, decreasing, or constant. From left to right, when the graph:

- slants upward, the function is increasing;
- slants downward, it is decreasing; and
- is horizontal, it is constant.

A linear function increases or decreases at a constant rate. If a function is curved, then its rate of change is variable. You can approximate the rate of change at any point in the domain by sketching a line tangent to the curve. The slope of the tangent line is the rate of change of the function's graph at the tangent point.

INTRODUCE

A function's graph gives lots of information at a glance. When using a function to model a real-world situation, the graph can help you understand the situation. Tell students they will learn to analyze function relationships by looking at the graph of the function.

TEACH

1 EXPLORE

Questioning Strategies

- During which segments is attendance increasing? **Segments 2 and 3**
- During which segments is attendance decreasing? **Segments 4 and 5**
- Is attendance ever constant? **yes, during Segment 1**
- Describe the park attendance pattern over the summer season. **Possible answer: In May, attendance is low and constant. In early summer, attendance increases quickly. As summer continues, attendance continues to increase, but not as fast as before. Near the end of the summer, attendance declines. After summer, attendance continues to decline until the park closes for the season.**

Teaching Strategies

Suggest situations to students, such as driving through town and on the highway, and ask them to sketch the graph on the board. They should be able to explain their reasons for increasing, decreasing, and constant intervals.

2 EXPLORE

Questioning Strategies

- How can you tell which graph shows a slower memorization rate at the beginning than at the end? **The slant at the beginning will not be as steep as it is at the end.**
- How would a graph be affected if a student had known some of the words before receiving the list? **The graph would start at a higher point on the vertical axis.**

Name_____ Class_____ Date_____

2-3

video tutor

Interpreting Graphs
Going Deeper

Essential question: *How can you describe a relationship given a graph and sketch a graph given a description?*

CC.8.F.5

1 EXPLORE Interpreting Graphs

A roller coaster park is open from May to October each year. The graph shows the number of park visitors over its season.

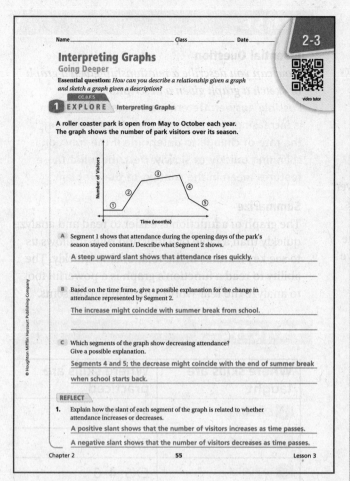

A Segment 1 shows that attendance during the opening days of the park's season stayed constant. Describe what Segment 2 shows.

A steep upward slant shows that attendance rises quickly.

_____

B Based on the time frame, give a possible explanation for the change in attendance represented by Segment 2.

The increase might coincide with summer break from school.

_____

C Which segments of the graph show decreasing attendance? Give a possible explanation.

Segments 4 and 5; the decrease might coincide with the end of summer break

when school starts back.

REFLECT

1. Explain how the slant of each segment of the graph is related to whether attendance increases or decreases.

A positive slant shows that the number of visitors increases as time passes.

A negative slant shows that the number of visitors decreases as time passes.

CC.8.F.5

2 EXPLORE Matching Graphs to Situations

Grace, Jet, and Mike are studying 100 words for a spelling bee.

- Grace started by learning many words each day, but then learned fewer and fewer words each day.
- Jet learned the same number of words each day.
- Mike started by learning only a few words each day, but then learned a greater number of words each day.

Match each student's study progress with the correct graph.

A — Time (days) — Number of Words Learned — Jet
B — Time (days) — Number of Words Learned — Mike
C — Time (days) — Number of Words Learned — Grace

A Describe the progress represented by Graph A.

Graph A shows a constant rate. This means the student learned the same

number of words each day.

_____

B Describe the progress represented by Graph B.

Graph B begins with a shallow curve and gets steeper over time. This means

the student learned a small number of words at first, and then learned more

and more words toward the end.

C Describe the progress represented by Graph C.

Graph C begins with a steep curve that gets more and more shallow. This

means the student learned many words a day at first, and then learned fewer

and fewer words toward the end.

D Determine which graph represents each student's study progress and write the students' names under the appropriate graphs.

REFLECT

2. What would it mean if one of the graphs slanted downward from left to right?
A student forgot words that he or she had already learned.

Questioning Strategies

Can the graphs for the math tutoring situation vary or is there exactly one correct answer? The graph will be the same for the first week and the rate of increase may vary according to each student's interpretation of the words "gradually increases."

Teaching Strategies

Have students work in groups to create graphs given descriptions of real-world situations. Have groups present their graphs on the board and discuss how the graphs are alike and different. Discuss the information that would be needed in order to have exactly one correct graph for the situation.

MATHEMATICAL PRACTICE **Highlighting the Standards**

This Explore is an opportunity to address Standard 3 (Construct viable arguments and critique the reasoning of others). By comparing their graphs to those of others, students will gain insight into the different reasonings of other students. They will learn to distinguish between mistakes in reasoning and differences in interpretation. By explaining their own reasoning, students will learn to construct convincing arguments.

CLOSE

Essential Question

How can you describe a relationship given a graph or sketch a graph given a description?
Possible answer: Determine where the function is increasing, decreasing, or constant. Analyze the rate of change to determine if the function is changing quickly or slowly. Describe what these features mean in the context of the problem.

Summarize

The graph of a function is easier to read and analyze quickly than a table or a function rule. It allows us to see key features of the relationship quickly. The ability to read a function's graph is a powerful tool to analyze the real-world situation it represents.

PRACTICE

Where skills are taught	Where skills are practiced
1 EXPLORE	EXS. 1–3
2 EXPLORE	EXS. 4–6
3 EXPLORE	EXS. 4–6

3 EXPLORE CC.8.F.5 Sketching a Graph for a Situation

Mrs. Sutton provides free math tutoring to her students every day after school. No one comes to tutoring sessions during the first week of school. Over the next two weeks, use of the tutoring service gradually increases.

A Sketch a graph showing the number of students who use the tutoring service over the first three weeks of school.

Sample answer:

B Mrs. Sutton's students are told that they will have a math test at the end of the fifth week of school. How do you think this will affect the number of students who come to tutoring?

Sample answer: More students might come to tutoring right before the test.

After the test, the number of students might decrease.

C Considering your answer to **B**, sketch a graph showing the number of students who might use the tutoring service over the first six weeks of school.

Sample answer:

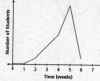

REFLECT

3a. Suppose Mrs. Sutton offered bonus credit to students who came to tutoring sessions. How do you think this would affect the number of students who come to tutoring?

Sample answer: More students might come to tutoring each week.

3b. How would your answer to **3a** affect the graph?

Sample answer: The graph would shift upward because more students would

participate. Overall, trends would stay the same.

PRACTICE

In a lab environment, colonies of bacteria follow a predictable pattern of growth. The graph shows this growth over time.

1. During which phase is growth slowest? During which phase is growth fastest? Explain.

Slowest growth: Phase 1; the curve is

increasing, but not very steep. Fastest

growth: Phase 2; the curve is increasing

and steeper than Phase 1.

Bacterial Growth Curve

2. What is happening to the population during Phase 3?

The graph is almost horizontal.

The population is stable (not increasing or

decreasing).

3. What is happening to the population during Phase 4?

The graph is decreasing, so the number

of microbes is decreasing.

A woodland area on an island contains a population of foxes. The graph describes the changes in the fox population over time.

4. What is happening to the fox population before time *t*?

The population is decreasing at first, but

begins to increase again.

Fox Population

5. At time *t*, a conservation organization moves a large group of foxes to the island. Sketch a graph to show how this action might affect the population on the island after time *t*.

6. At some point after time *t*, a forest fire destroys part of the woodland area on the island. Describe how your graph from problem **5** might change.

Fox Population

The graph would show a steep decline at the point

that represents the fire. Then as the forest regrows, the gradual increasing and

decreasing pattern would resume.

Assign these pages to help your students practice and apply important lesson concepts. For additional exercises, see the Student Edition.

Answers

Additional Practice

1. Dog 2

2. Dog 3

3. Exercise 2 (Dog 3)

4. Exercise 1 (Dog 2)

5.

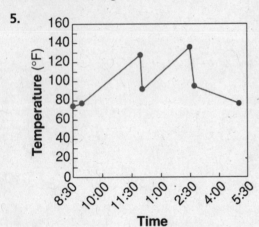

Problem Solving

1. Students' graphs should be labeled "Speed" on the y-axis and "Time" on the x-axis. Ryan's speed is constant until he begins to run. His speed increases, and then remains constant for about 10 minutes. Then his speed decreases, and again remains constant at a slower speed until he stops. At this point his speed is 0.

2. Students' graphs should be labeled "Speed" on the y-axis and "Time" on the x-axis. Susanna's speed increases as she begins to run, and then remains constant for about 10 minutes while she is running. Her speed then drops to 0 while she talks. Her speed then increases again as she begins to run, and remains constant. As she approaches home, her speed decreases until she stops. At this point her speed is 0.

3. Students' graphs should be labeled "Speed" on the y-axis and "Time" on the x-axis. Mark's speed is 0 until he starts walking. His speed increases, remains constant while he walks, and then increases again as he begins to run. His speed is constant while running. As he approaches home, his speed decreases until he stops. At this point his speed is 0.

4. A

5. D

6. H

7. C

8. G

Additional Practice

The table gives the speed of three dogs in mi/h at the given times. Tell which dog corresponds to each situation described below.

Time	5:00	5:01	5:02	5:03	5:04
Dog 1	0	1	12	0	0
Dog 2	5	23	4	0	0
Dog 3	14	0	18	2	9

1. Leshaan walks his dog. Then he lets the dog off the leash and it runs around the yard. Then they go into the house and the dog stands eating from his dog dish and drinking from his water bowl. _____

2. Luke's dog is chasing its tail. Then it stops and pants. The dog then runs to the backyard fence and walks along the fence, barking at a neighbor. Then it runs to Luke at the back door. _____

Tell which graph corresponds to each situation in Exercises 1–2.

3.

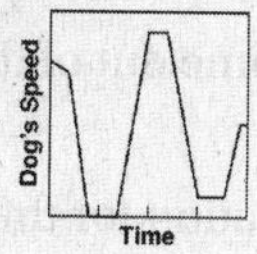

4.

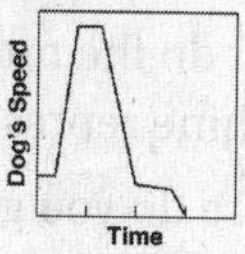

5. Create a graph that illustrates the temperature inside the car.

Location	Temperature on Arrival	Temperature on Departure
Home	—	74° at 8:30
Summer job	77° at 9:00	128° at 12:05
Pool	92° at 12:15	136° at 2:30
Library	95° at 2:40	77° at 5:10

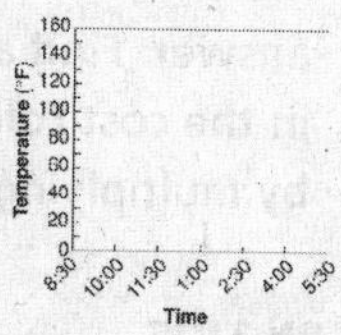

Problem Solving

Sketch a graph that illustrates each situation.

1. Ryan walks for several blocks, and then he begins to run. After running for 10 minutes, he walks for several blocks and then stops.

2. Susanna starts running. After 10 minutes, she sees a friend and stops to talk. When she leaves her friend, she runs home and stops.

3. Mark stands on the porch and talks to a friend. Then he starts walking home. Part way home he decides to run the rest of the way, and he doesn't stop until he gets home.

The graph represents the height of water in a bathtub over time. Choose the correct letter.

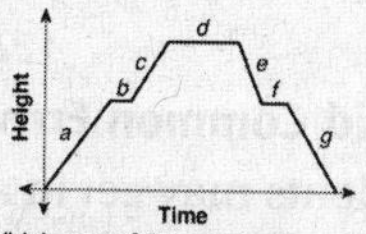

4. Which part of the graph best represents the tub being filled with water?

A a   C c
B d   D g

5. Which part of the graph shows the tub being drained of water?

A c   C d
B e   D g

6. Which part of the graph shows someone soaking in the tub?

F b   H d
G e   J f

7. Which part of the graph shows when someone gets into the tub?

A a   C c
B e   D f

8. Which parts of the graph show when the water level is not changing in the tub?

F a, b, c   H b, d, g
G b, d, f   J c, e, f

Functions
Going Deeper

Essential question: *How do you represent a function with a table or graph?*

COMMON CORE **Standards for Mathematical Content**

CC.8.F.1 Understand that a function is a rule that assigns to each input exactly one output. The graph of a function is the set of ordered pairs consisting of an input and the corresponding output.

Vocabulary

input

output

function

Prerequisites

Graphing equations

Math Background

A function is a relationship between two variables such that any input value corresponds to *exactly* one output value. In the graph of a function, the input variable is represented by the *x*-axis (horizontal) and the output variable is represented by the *y*-axis (vertical). Any letters can be used for the input and output variables, but without context, variables *x* and *y* are typically used.

INTRODUCE

Real-world examples that are relevant to students are the best way to engage them as you introduce functions. There are many relationships in students' lives that can be modeled by functions. For example, ask students whether the amount of sleep they get the night before a test will affect their performance on the test. Ask about other things that might impact their performance on a test, such as the amount of time spent studying.

TEACH

1 EXPLORE

Questioning Strategies

- What do the numbers that go into the machine represent? pencils
- What do the numbers that come out of the machine represent? cost
- Where do you get the information for the first three rows of the table? It is given in the problem.
- How can you tell what the rule is? Possible answer: Find a pattern in the consecutive values in the cost column, adding 0.25. Test it as a rule by multiplying 0.25 by the number of pencils.

TRY THIS

Students used patterns in the table to find the rule in the Explore. In the Try This, students are asked to use number sense and inverse operations to find a rule.

MATHEMATICAL PRACTICE | **Highlighting the Standards**

This Example is an opportunity to address Standard 4 (Model with mathematics). Students are asked to write equations that describe the relationship between given quantities. To extend the application of this standard, ask students to suggest other situations in real life that can be described with equations and/or tables.

Avoid Common Errors

Students may get in a rush and think they know the rule from looking at only the first one or two pairs of corresponding values in a table. Remind them that it must work for all the values, and encourage them to verify that their rule holds for all known values.

Functions
Going Deeper

Essential question: *How do you represent a function with a table or graph?*

2-4

video tutor

CC.8.F.1

1 EXPLORE Understanding Relationships

Carlos needs to buy some new pencils from the school supply cabinet at school. Carlos asks his classmates if they know how much pencils cost. Angela says she bought 2 pencils for $0.50. Paige bought 3 pencils for $0.75, and Spencer bought 4 pencils for $1.00.

Carlos thinks about the rule for the price of a pencil as a machine. When he puts the number of pencils he wants to buy into the machine, the machine applies a rule and tells him the total cost of that number of pencils.

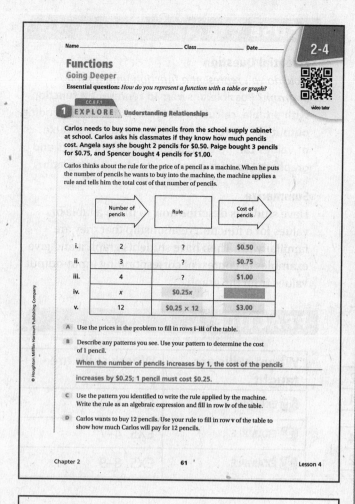

	Number of pencils	Rule	Cost of pencils
i.	2	?	$0.50
ii.	3	?	$0.75
iii.	4	?	$1.00
iv.	x	$0.25x	
v.	12	$0.25 × 12	$3.00

A Use the prices in the problem to fill in rows **i–iii** of the table.

B Describe any patterns you see. Use your pattern to determine the cost of 1 pencil.

When the number of pencils increases by 1, the cost of the pencils

increases by $0.25; 1 pencil must cost $0.25.

C Use the pattern you identified to write the rule applied by the machine. Write the rule as an algebraic expression and fill in row **iv** of the table.

D Carlos wants to buy 12 pencils. Use your rule to fill in row **v** of the table to show how much Carlos will pay for 12 pencils.

TRY THIS!

There are 6 pencil-top erasers in 2 packages of erasers. There are 9 erasers in 3 packages.

1a. Write a rule in words for the number of packages Carlos needs to buy to get *x* erasers. Then write the rule as an algebraic expression.

Divide the number of erasers by 3; $\frac{x}{3}$

1b. How many packages does Carlos need to buy to get 18 erasers?

$\frac{18}{3} = 6$ packages

REFLECT

1c. How can you decide what operation to use in your rule?

If the results of applying the rule are greater than the numbers put in

the machine, the rule may use addition or multiplication. If the results

are smaller, the rule may use subtraction or division.

The rules in **1** are functions, and the machines are function machines. The value that is put into a function machine is the **input**. The result after applying the function machine's rule is the **output**. A **function** is a rule that assigns exactly one output to each input.

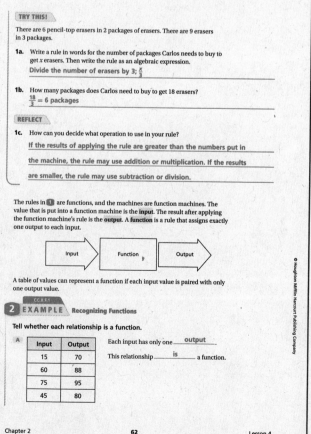

A table of values can represent a function if each input value is paired with only one output value.

CC.8.F.1

2 EXAMPLE Recognizing Functions

Tell whether each relationship is a function.

A

Input	Output
15	70
60	88
75	95
45	80

Each input has only one ___output___.

This relationship ___is___ a function.

Questioning Strategies

- In part A, what is the output for the input value of 15? **70**

- Can the input value of 15 have any other corresponding output value? **not if the relationship is a function**

- In part B, what is the output value for the input 14? **There are two corresponding outputs: 60 and 57.**

- How can you tell that the table in part B represents a relationship that is *not* a function? **There are two different output values that correspond to one single input value.**

Teaching Strategies

Point out that a function *can* have two different inputs that both have the same output.

Function:	Input	−2	−1	0	1	2
	Output	4	2	0	2	4

Not a Function:	Input	4	2	0	2	4
	Output	−2	−1	0	1	2

3 EXAMPLE

Questioning Strategies

- What does the middle column of the table display? **the substitution of input values into the function rule**

- Where do the ordered pairs come from? **They are the input and output values, respectively.**

- What is the difference between what the points on the graph represent and what the line through them represents? **Points represent specific input-output values. The line represents all possible input-output values.**

- What do the arrowheads on a line represent? **The relationship continues.**

Differentiated Instruction

Use kinesthetic strategies and cooperative learning by having students work in groups at the board.

CLOSE

Essential Question

How do you represent a function with a table or graph? **Possible answer: To represent a function with a table, calculate and record the corresponding output values for different input values. A table of values can be translated into ordered pairs and graphed. Look for a pattern to sketch the graph.**

Summarize

Have students describe how to make a table of values for a function relationship that they are familiar with. Then have students graph it and give examples in context of corresponding input-output values from the graph.

PRACTICE

Where skills are taught	Where skills are practiced
1 EXPLORE	EXS. 1–3
2 EXAMPLE	EXS. 4–7
3 EXAMPLE	EXS. 8–9

B

Input	Output
14	60
13	55
14	57
15	52

The input ___14___ has more than one output.

This relationship ___is not___ a function.

The input values (x) and output values (y) of a function can be displayed in a table or written as ordered pairs (x, y). These ordered pairs can be graphed in the coordinate plane to show a graph of the function.

Some function rules can be written as equations such as $y = 2x$. By substituting values for x, you can generate corresponding y-values. The ordered pairs (x, y) are solutions of the equation.

3 EXAMPLE CC.8.F.1 Graphing a Function

Graph the function $y = 2x + 3$.

Create a table of values.

x	2x + 3	y
−4	2(−4) + 3	−5
−1	2(−1) + 3	1
0	2(0) + 3	3
2	2(2) + 3	7
3	2(3) + 3	9

Write ordered pairs.

(x, y)
(−4, −5)
(−1, 1)
(0, 3)
(2, 7)
(3, 9)

Graph the ordered pairs.

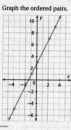

Draw a line through the points to represent all the possible x-values and their corresponding y-values.

PRACTICE

Fill in each table. In the row with x as the input, write a rule as an algebraic expression for the output. Then complete the last row of the table using the rule.

1.

Input	Output
Tickets	Cost ($)
2	40
5	100
7	140
8	160
x	20x
10	200

2.

Input	Output
Minutes	Pages Read
2	1
10	5
20	10
30	15
x	$\frac{x}{2}$
60	30

3.

Input	Output
Muffins	Cost ($)
1	2.25
3	6.75
6	13.50
12	27.00
x	2.25x
18	40.50

Tell whether each relationship is a function.

4.

Input	6	7	8	7	9
Output	75	80	87	88	95

___not a function___

5.

Input	1	2	3	4	5
Output	4	8	12	16	20

___function___

6. (1, 3), (2, 5), (3, 0), (4, −1), (5, 5)

___function___

7. (2, 7), (6, 4), (0, 3), (2, 6), (1, 5)

___not a function___

Graph each function on the coordinate plane.

8. $y = -2x$

9. $y = x - 3$

Assign these pages to help your students practice and apply important lesson concepts. For additional exercises, see the Student Edition.

Answers

Additional Practice

1.

x	$-2x + 5$	y
−2	$-2(-2) + 5$	9
−1	$-2(-1) + 5$	7
0	$-2(0) + 5$	5
1	$-2(1) + 5$	3
2	$-2(2) + 5$	1

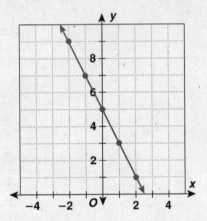

2.

x	$x - 2$	y
−2	$-2 - 2$	−4
−1	$-1 - 2$	−3
0	$0 - 2$	−2
1	$1 - 2$	−1
2	$2 - 2$	0

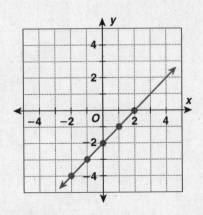

3. yes   **4.** no

5. yes   **6.** no

Problem Solving

1.

x	20x	y
0	20(0)	0
1	20(1)	20
2	20(2)	40
3	20(3)	60

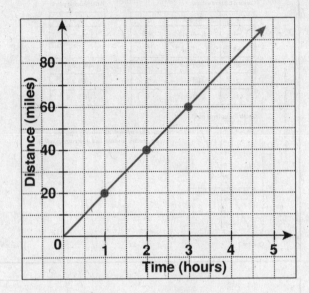

2. Yes   **3.** 80 miles

4. 30 miles   **5.** 2.5 hours

6. B   **7.** G

2-4

Name_____ Class_____ Date_____

Additional Practice

Complete the table and graph each function.

1. $y = -2x + 5$

x	−2x + 5	y
−2		
−1		
0		
1		
2		

2. $y = x - 2$

x	x − 2	y
−2		
−1		
0		
1		
2		

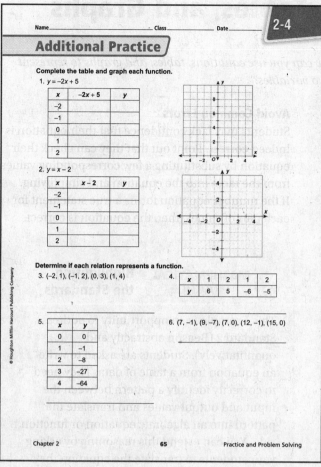

Determine if each relation represents a function.

3. (−2, 1), (−1, 2), (0, 3), (1, 4)

4.
x	1	2	1	2
y	6	5	−6	−5

5.
x	y
0	0
1	−1
2	−8
3	−27
4	−64

6. (7, −1), (9, −7), (7, 0), (12, −1), (15, 0)

Problem Solving

A cyclist rides at an average speed of 20 miles per hour. The equation $y = 20x$ shows the distance, y, the cyclist travels in x hours.

1. Make a table for the equation and graph the equation at the right.

x	20x	y
0		
1		
2		
3		

2. Is the relationship between the time and the distance the cyclist rides a function?

3. If the cyclist continues to ride at the same rate, about how far will the cyclist ride in 4 hours?

4. About how far does the cyclist ride in 1.5 hours?

5. If the cyclist has ridden 50 miles, about how long has the cyclist been riding?

The cost of renting a jet-ski at a lake is represented by the equation $f(x) = 25x + 100$ where x is the number of hours and $f(x)$ is the cost including an hourly rate and a deposit. Choose the letter for the best answer.

6. How much does it cost to rent the jet-ski for 5 hours?

   A $125
   B $225
   C $385
   D $525

7. If the cost to rent the jet-ski is $300, for how many hours is the jet-ski rented?

   F 6 hours
   G 8 hours
   H 12 hours
   J 16 hours

Equations, Tables, and Graphs
Going Deeper

Essential question: *How can you use equations, tables, and graphs to represent relationships between two variables?*

© Houghton Mifflin Harcourt Publishing Company

Standards for Mathematical Content

CC.8.F.4 Construct a function to model a linear relationship between two quantities...

Prerequisites
Ordered pairs
Equations

Math Background
The relationship between two variables can be represented by an equation (algebraic), a table (numeric), and a graph. Although each format can represent the same relationship, they each have advantages. For example, the equation allows you to quickly find an ordered pair for any given value of a variable, the graph visually shows the relationship between successive ordered pairs, and the table gives exact values.

INTRODUCE

Connect to prior learning on translating words (verbal descriptions) into equations (function rules). Remind student that they used equations to make tables and graphs. Point out that they will now also move in the opposite direction to write equations from tables.

TEACH

1 EXAMPLE

Questioning Strategies
- Who works more hours after school, and how many more hours do they work each day?
  Each day Leon works 2 hours more than Lisa.
- When graphing an ordered pair, what does the first number tell you? What does the second number tell you? **How many places to the right or left of the origin you move. How many places up or down from the origin you move.**

Avoid Common Errors
Students may lack confidence that their equation is indeed correct. Point out that they can check their equation by substituting a few corresponding values from the table into the equation and simplifying. If the number equation forms a true statement for each pair of values, then the equation is correct.

MATHEMATICAL PRACTICE | **Highlighting the Standards**

This Example is an opportunity to address Standard 2 (Reason abstractly and quantitatively). Students are asked to write an equation from a table of data. They need to correctly identify a pattern between the input and output values and translate the pattern into an algebraic equation or function rule. You can extend this reasoning by asking your students to translate the equation they wrote into a verbal description (words) for the problem context.

CLOSE

Essential Question
How can you use equations, tables, and graphs to represent relationships between two variables?
Possible answer: You can translate between equations, tables, and graphs to represent the same relationship.

Summarize
Have students write an equation and make a table and graph for their own real-world scenarios. Have students identify one representation that they prefer for their scenario, and justify their choice.

PRACTICE

Where skills are taught	Where skills are practiced
1 EXAMPLE	EXS. 1–5

Name_____ Class_____ Date_____

2-5

[video tutor]

Equations, Tables, and Graphs
Going Deeper

Essential question: How can you use equations, tables, and graphs to represent relationships between two variables?

CC.8.F.4

1 EXAMPLE Generating Different Representations of Data

Lisa and Leon work after school at their uncle's store. The table shows the hours Lisa worked x and the hours Leon worked y each week for a month.

Lisa, x	3	4	6	8
Leon, y	5	6	8	10

A Write an equation from the data in the table.

Compare each output value with its corresponding input value.

Lisa, x	3	4	6	8	← input values
Leon, y	5	6	8	10	← output values

$$5 - 3 = 2 \quad 6 - 4 = 2 \quad 8 - 6 = 2 \quad 10 - 8 = 2$$

For each hour Lisa worked, Leon worked __2__ more hours.

The equation is Leon = Lisa + 2.

$$y = x + 2$$

B Make a graph of the data.

Write the input and output values as ordered pairs.

x	y	(x, y)
3	5	(3, 5)
4	6	(4, 6)
6	8	(6, 8)
8	10	(8, 10)

Hours Leon Worked vs. Hours Lisa Worked

Then plot the ordered pairs and connect the points with a line.

TRY THIS!

1a. Write an equation from the data in the table. Then write the input and output values as ordered pairs.

$y = 3x$

x	0	1	2	3
y	0	3	6	9
(x, y)	(0, 0)	(1, 3)	(2, 6)	(3, 9)

REFLECT

1b. How can you use the graph to predict the number of hours Leon will work when Lisa works 10 hours?

Possible answer: On the x-axis, find the number of hours that Lisa works. Then find the y-coordinate of the line at that point. So, when Lisa works 10 hours, Leon will work 12.

PRACTICE

Complete each table to write an equation. Use the same grid to graph each equation.

1.

x	0	1	3	5
y	4	5	7	9
(x, y)	(0, 4)	(1, 5)	(3, 7)	(5, 9)

$y = x + 4$

2.

x	0	−1	−2	−3
y	0	2	4	6
(x, y)	(0, 0)	(−1, 2)	(−2, 4)	(−3, 6)

$y = -2x$

3. Lupe is walking in a walkathon. The distance she walks is represented by the equation $d = 1.5h$, where h is the number of hours she walks and 1.5 is how many miles she walks in an hour. Make a table and sketch a graph of the data.

h	0	2	4	6
d	0	3	6	9
(h, d)	(0, 0)	(2, 3)	(4, 6)	(6, 9)

$d = 1.5h$

4. Conjecture Why did you not graph the equation $d = 1.5h$ in Quadrant IV?

Lupe could not walk a negative distance.

5. Over 5 days, the temperatures in Chicago, in °F, were 0, −2, −3, −1, and 2. On those same days, the temperatures in Detroit were three degrees warmer. Write an equation and sketch a graph of the data.

$y = x + 3$

© Houghton Mifflin Harcourt Publishing Company

Assign these pages to help your students practice and apply important lesson concepts. For additional exercises, see the Student Edition.

Answers

Additional Practice

1.

m	20m	g
0	20(0)	0
1	20(1)	20
2	20(2)	40
3	20(3)	60
4	20(4)	80

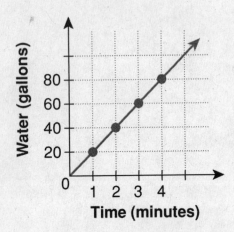

2. $y = x + 4$

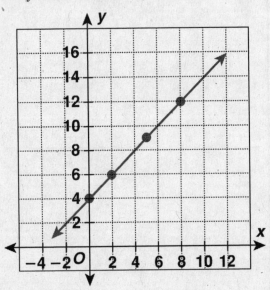

3.

x	0	1	2	3	4
y	0	3	6	9	12

$y = 3x$

Problem Solving

1. 35 gallons   **2.** 25 gallons

3. 5 min   **4.** 7 min

5. D   **6.** F

7. A

2-5

Additional Practice

Name_____ Class_____ Date_____

1. The amount of water in a tank being filled is represented by the equation $g = 20m$, where g is the number of gallons in the tank after m minutes. Complete the table and sketch a graph of the equation.

m	20m	g
0		
1		
2		
3		
4		

2. Use the table to make a graph and to write an equation.

x	0	2	5	8	12
y	4	6	9	12	16

3. Use the graph to make a table and to write an equation.

x					
y					

Chapter 2   69   Practice and Problem Solving

Problem Solving

Use the graph to answer Exercises 1–4. An aquarium tank is being drained. The graph shows the number of gallons of water, q, in the tank after m minutes. Write the correct answer.

1. How many gallons of water are in the tank before it is drained?

_____

2. How many gallons of water are left in the tank after 2 minutes?

_____

3. How long does it take until there are 10 gallons of water left in the tank?

_____

4. How long does it take to drain the tank?

_____

Use the graph to answer Exercises 5–7. The graph shows the distance, d, a hiker can hike in h hours. Choose the letter of the best answer.

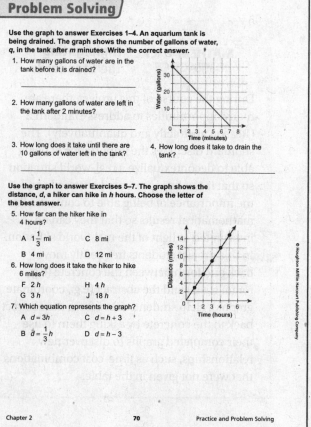

5. How far can the hiker hike in 4 hours?

A $1\frac{1}{3}$ mi   C 8 mi

B 4 mi   D 12 mi

6. How long does it take the hiker to hike 6 miles?

F 2 h   H 4 h

G 3 h   J 18 h

7. Which equation represents the graph?

A $d = 3h$ C $d = h + 3$

B $d = \frac{1}{3}h$ D $d = h - 3$

Chapter 2   70   Practice and Problem Solving

© Houghton Mifflin Harcourt Publishing Company

COMMON CORE **Standards for Mathematical Content**

CC.8.F.1 Understand that a function is a rule that assigns to each input exactly one output. The graph of a function is the set of ordered pairs consisting of an input and the corresponding output.

CC.8.F.4 Construct a function to model a linear relationship between two quantities. ...

CC.8.F.5 Describe qualitatively the functional relationship between two quantities by analyzing a graph (e.g., where the function is increasing or decreasing, linear or nonlinear). Sketch a graph that exhibits the qualitative features of a function that has been described verbally.

INTRODUCE

Ask students if they have ever rented inline skates, ice skates, a bicycle, or other sports equipment. Ask students to explain how the price of the rental was calculated. Point out that many sports shops rent equipment by the hour, and that there is often a flat fee as well as an hourly rate. Tell students that this project will give them a chance to use tables, equations, and graphs to do some detective work about three shops that rent inline skates.

TEACH

 Compare Rental Data

Questioning Strategies
- Is it possible to tell the number of daily rentals from these graphs? Why or why not? No; there is no scale marked on the vertical axis.
- What does a horizontal segment mean in these graphs? The number of daily rentals is not changing.
- What does the steepness of a segment tell you? It tells you whether the number of daily rentals is changing rapidly (a steep segment) or slowly (a less steep segment).

- What must be true about the graph when the number of daily rentals is 0? The graph must lie on the x-axis.

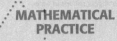 **Analyze Pricing at Shop A**

Questioning Strategies
- What patterns do you see in the table? The cost is always 2.5 times the number of hours; the cost increases by $2.50 as you move from one column to the next.
- In this situation, which values are the input values? Which values are the output values? Input: number of hours; output: cost
- In part F, how do you use the table to write the ordered pairs? In each column of the table, use the x-value (number of hours) as the first value in the ordered pair and the y-value (cost of rental) as the second value in the ordered pair.
- Why do you only draw this graph in the first quadrant of the coordinate plane? The number of hours and the cost must both be nonnegative.

MATHEMATICAL PRACTICE **Highlighting the Standards**

During the course of this project, there are many opportunities to address Standard 2 (Reason abstractly and quantitatively). The standard discusses the importance of being able to decontextualize a real-world situation so that it can be represented abstractly and the importance of being able to contextualize mathematical results so that they can be interpreted in light of the real-world situation. In this project students frequently move back and forth between the concrete (e.g., rental costs) and the abstract (e.g., coordinate graphs). Help students move from the abstract back to the concrete by asking them to use their completed graphs to discover new relationships, such as time-cost combinations that were not given in the table.

Name_____ Class_____ Date_____

Problem Solving Connections

Which Is Which? Sonia is writing an article about places to rent inline skates in her town. She collected data about Wheel World, Super Skates, and Roller Rentals. Unfortunately, the names of the skate shops got separated from the data. How can Sonia use her notes to match the names to the data?

COMMON CORE
CC.8.F.1
CC.8.F.4
CC.8.F.5

1 Compare Rental Data

Sonia calls the skate shops A, B, and C until she figures out which is which. She starts by looking at graphs that show the number of daily rentals over the course of a year (January through December).

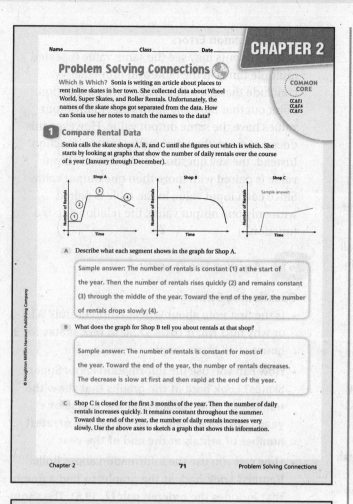

A Describe what each segment shows in the graph for Shop A.

Sample answer: The number of rentals is constant (1) at the start of the year. Then the number of rentals rises quickly (2) and remains constant (3) through the middle of the year. Toward the end of the year, the number of rentals drops slowly (4).

B What does the graph for Shop B tell you about rentals at that shop?

Sample answer: The number of rentals is constant for most of the year. Toward the end of the year, the number of rentals decreases. The decrease is slow at first and then rapid at the end of the year.

C Shop C is closed for the first 3 months of the year. Then the number of daily rentals increases quickly. It remains constant throughout the summer. Toward the end of the year, the number of daily rentals increases very slowly. Use the above axes to sketch a graph that shows this information.

© Houghton Mifflin Harcourt Publishing Company

2 Analyze Pricing at Shop A

Sonia looks through her notes and finds a table that gives information about the cost of inline skate rentals at Shop A.

A Look for patterns to complete the table.

Number of Hours, x	2	3	4	5	6
Cost of Rental, y	$5.00	$7.50	$10.00	$12.50	$15.00

B What is the cost of renting inline skates for 1 hour?

$2.50

C Write an equation that gives the cost y of renting skates for x hours.

$y = 2.50x$

D Is the ordered pair (8, 20) a solution of the equation? Why or why not?

Yes; substitute $x = 8$ and $y = 20$ in the equation.
$20 \stackrel{?}{=} 2.50(8)$
$20 = 20$

E What does the ordered pair (8, 20) represent in this situation?

The cost of renting skates for 8 hours is $20.

F Write the values from the above table as ordered pairs.

(2, 5), (3, 7.5), (4, 10), (5, 12.5), and (6, 15)

G Plot the ordered pairs on the coordinate plane to help you graph the equation. Then describe the graph.

The graph is a straight line that passes through the origin.

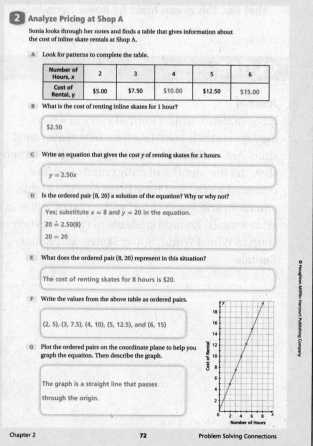

© Houghton Mifflin Harcourt Publishing Company

© Houghton Mifflin Harcourt Publishing Company

Analyze Pricing at Shop B

Questioning Strategies

- How do you use the given equation to find the cost of renting skates for 1 hour at Shop B? **Substitute $x = 1$ in the equation; $y = 1.50(1) + 3 = \$4.50$.**

- What patterns do you see in the completed table? **Possible answer: The cost increases by $1.50 as you move from one column to the next.**

- Do you expect the point (2, 8) to lie on your graph? Why or why not? **No; the graph shows all ordered pairs that are solutions of the equation. Since (2, 8) is not a solution of the equation, it will not lie on the graph.**

Technology

You may wish to have students graph the functions $y = 2.5x$ and $y = 1.5x + 3$ on their graphing calculators. By doing so, students can also view a table that shows values for both functions. This makes it easy to compare the functions and ask "what if" questions. For instance, you might ask students whether Shop A or Shop B is a better deal when renting skates for 9 hours. Scrolling down the table and comparing the appropriate y-values shows that Shop B is a better deal ($16.50 versus $22.50).

 Analyze Pricing at Shop C

Questioning Strategies

- What do you notice about this table? **The cost of a rental is always $7.50, no matter the number of hours.**

- What do you need to do in order to decide whether the relationship is a function? **Check to see if each input value is paired with only one output value.**

- What is true about all the ordered pairs for this function? **The y-value in every ordered pair is 7.5.**

- What equation gives the cost y of renting inline skates for x hours at Shop C? **$y = 7.50$**

Avoid Common Errors

Some students may see the same value repeated multiple times in the table and immediately conclude that the relationship is not a function. Point out that the table shows that many input values have the same output value. However, this does not mean the relationship is not a function. Instead, the key question is whether any input value is paired with more than one output value. Since each input value in the table is paired with only one output value, the relationship is a function.

 Answer the Question

Questioning Strategies

- Is the first note about Wheel World useful? Why or why not? **No; it costs $7.50 to rent skates for 3 hours at all three shops.**

- How can you use the information about Super Skates? **Look back at the graphs that show the number of daily rentals over the course of a year. Look for a graph that shows the greatest number of rentals at the end of the year.**

- How can you use the information about Roller Rentals? **Look back at the graphs to find a graph that includes the ordered pair (7, 13.5). The shop that has this graph must be Roller Rentals.**

CLOSE

Journal

Have students write a journal entry in which they create their own data for a new skate rental shop. Ask students to sketch and describe a graph showing the number of daily rentals over the course of a year, and have them provide a table, equation, and graph showing the cost of inline skate rentals. Remind students to compare their shop to Wheel World, Super Skates, and Roller Rentals.

3 Analyze Pricing at Shop B

Sonia's notes also include some information about pricing at Shop B. At this shop, the cost y of renting inline skates for x hours is given by $y = 1.50x + 3$.

A Is the ordered pair (2, 8) a solution of the equation? Why or why not?

No; substitute $x = 2$ and $y = 8$ in the equation.

$8 \stackrel{?}{=} 1.50(2) + 3$

$8 \stackrel{?}{=} 3 + 3$

$8 \neq 6$

B Complete the table of values.

Number of Hours, x	1	2	3	4	5
Cost of Rental, y	\$4.50	\$6	\$7.50	\$9	\$10.50

C Write the values from the table as ordered pairs.

(1, 4.5), (2, 6), (3, 7.5), (4, 9), and (5, 10.5)

D Plot the ordered pairs on the coordinate plane to help you graph the equation. Then describe the graph.

The graph is a straight line that does not pass through the origin.

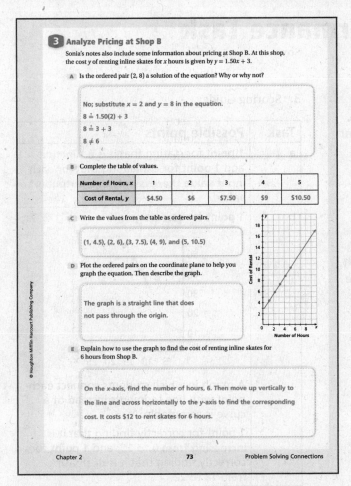

E Explain how to use the graph to find the cost of renting inline skates for 6 hours from Shop B.

On the x-axis, find the number of hours, 6. Then move up vertically to the line and across horizontally to the y-axis to find the corresponding cost. It costs \$12 to rent skates for 6 hours.

4 Analyze Pricing at Shop C

Sonia's notes include this table that gives the price of renting inline skates at Shop C.

Number of Hours, x	Cost of Rental, y
1	\$7.50
2	\$7.50
3	\$7.50
4	\$7.50
5	\$7.50

A Is the relationship shown in the table a function? Why or why not?

Yes; each input value (number of hours) is paired with only one output value (cost).

B Make a graph that shows the cost of renting inline skates at Shop C. Then describe the graph.

The graph is a horizontal straight line.

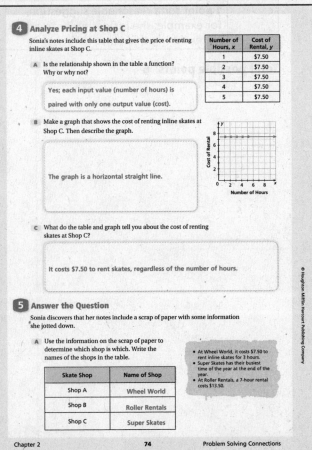

C What do the table and graph tell you about the cost of renting skates at Shop C?

It costs \$7.50 to rent skates, regardless of the number of hours.

5 Answer the Question

Sonia discovers that her notes include a scrap of paper with some information she jotted down.

A Use the information on the scrap of paper to determine which shop is which. Write the names of the shops in the table.

- At Wheel World, it costs \$7.50 to rent inline skates for 3 hours.
- Super Skates has their busiest time of the year at the end of the year.
- At Roller Rentals, a 7-hour rental costs \$13.50.

Skate Shop	Name of Shop
Shop A	Wheel World
Shop B	Roller Rentals
Shop C	Super Skates

This page provides students with the opportunity to apply concepts from the Common Core in real-world problem situations. There are three different levels of performance tasks:

⭐ Novice: These are short word problems that require students to apply the math they have learned in straightforward, real-world situations.

⭐⭐ Apprentice: These are more involved problems that guide students step-by-step through more complex tasks. These exercises include more complicated reasoning, writing, and open-ended elements.

⭐⭐⭐ Expert: These are open-ended, non-routine problems that, instead of stepping the students through, asks them to choose their own methods for solving and justify their answers and reasoning.

Sample answers

1. Tericho makes more money, by $0.30 per hour.

2. $y = 8.95x + 25$; $114.50

3. Scoring Guide:

Task	Possible points
a	**1 point** for stating that it is a function and **1 point** for explaining that for each input value there is only one output value.
b	**1 point** for correct graph: A graph in which students connect each point with line segments instead of a curve is acceptable. **1 point** for correctly finding that it is increasing from 0 to 15, and **1 point** for correctly finding that it is decreasing from 18 to 22.
c	**1 point** for a reasonable suggestion, for example: she is floating or treading water during this time.

Total possible points: 6

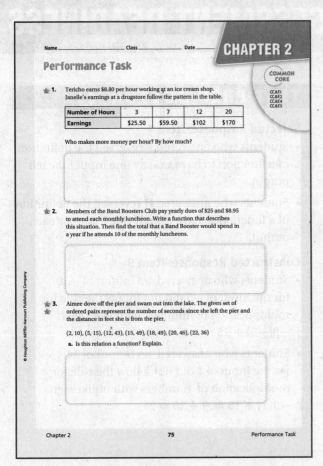

CHAPTER 2

Performance Task

COMMON CORE
CC.8.F.1
CC.8.F.2
CC.8.F.4
CC.8.F.5

⭐ 1. Tericho earns $8.80 per hour working at an ice cream shop. Janelle's earnings at a drugstore follow the pattern in the table.

Number of Hours	3	7	12	20
Earnings	$25.50	$59.50	$102	$170

Who makes more money per hour? By how much?

⭐ 2. Members of the Band Boosters Club pay yearly dues of $25 and $8.95 to attend each monthly luncheon. Write a function that describes this situation. Then find the total that a Band Booster would spend in a year if he attends 10 of the monthly luncheons.

⭐⭐ 3. Aimee dove off the pier and swam out into the lake. The given set of ordered pairs represent the number of seconds since she left the pier and the distance in feet she is from the pier.

(2, 10), (5, 15), (12, 43), (15, 49), (18, 49), (20, 46), (22, 36)

a. Is this relation a function? Explain.

4. Scoring Guide:

Task	Possible points
a	**1 point** for correctly writing a function $d = 60t$ with t as the time in hours and d as the distance in miles (OR equivalent function), and **2 points** for correctly calculating 3:27 AM as the departure time from Portland
b	**1 point** for noting that the departure time in part a is not acceptable, and **2 points** for choosing a departure time that is acceptable and calculating the arrival time, for example: A train leaving at 10 PM would get Susanna to Los Angeles at 2:03 PM the day of the game.

Total possible points: 6

---

b. Graph the ordered pairs and connect them with line segments. Where is the graph increasing? Where is it decreasing?

c. What might Aimee be doing between 15 and 18 seconds after she leaves the pier?

⭐⭐⭐ 4. A train travels at an average speed of 60 miles per hour from Portland to Los Angeles, a distance of 963 miles. Susanna is taking the train to Los Angeles to see a football game. The game is at 8 PM and it takes her 30 minutes to get from the train station to her seat in the stadium.

a. By what time does the train need to leave Portland for Susanna to arrive in time? As part of your answer, write a function that describes the situation.

b. Susanna does not want to leave Portland later than 10 PM or earlier than 6 AM. Does the train in part a meet her requirements? If not, give a new departure time that would allow her to still get to the game on time, and find the arrival time of that train.

COMMON CORE CORRELATION

Standard	Items
CC.8.F.1	3–6, 9–10
CC.8.F.4	10
CC.8.F.5	1–2, 7–8

TEST PREP DOCTOR ➕

Selected Response: Item 4

- Students who answered **F** reversed the definition of a function to have exactly one input for each output.

- Students who answered **H** reversed the definition of a function to have exactly one input for each output.

Constructed Response: Item 9

- Students who answered an output of -30 for the input of -5 did not follow the rule for multiplication of numbers with like signs $-9(-5) + 15 = -45 + 15 = -30$

- Students who answered an output of 24 for the input of 1 did not follow the rule for multiplication of numbers with unlike signs. $-9(1) + 15 = 9 + 15 = 24$

CHAPTER 2 COMMON CORE ASSESSMENT READINESS

Name _____ Class _____ Date _____

SELECTED RESPONSE

1. Gloria drives her daughter to school in the morning and then comes back home. She stays home until she has to go to pick up her daughter from school, and then they both return home again. Which graph best shows the situation?

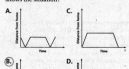

A.

C.

B.

D.

2. Which situation is best represented by the graph?

F. A swimmer starts at a steady pace, slows down to a stop, and then starts up swimming again, but at a slower pace than when she first started.

G. After a ball is thrown into the air, it falls back to the ground and bounces.

H. An airplane starts slowly on the runway, and then quickly takes off before finding a nice cruising speed.

J. A car starts on flat ground and drives quickly up a hill, and then it keeps driving.

3. Determine if the relation represents a function.

x	y
0	−5
1	−1
2	3
3	6

A. The relation is a function.

B. The relation is not a function.

4. The data in the table below form a function. What values in the table would change the relation to NOT be a function?

x	y
4	9
6	1
0	2
−2	7
−8	10

F. (1, 9)

G. (−3, 7)

H. (9, 4)

J. (6, 5)

5. Choose the equation that is represented by the data in the table.

b	c
−1	5
0	6
1	7
2	8

A. $b = c + 4$ **C.** $c = b − 4$

B. $c = b − 6$ **D.** $c = b + 6$

© Houghton Mifflin Harcourt Publishing Company

---

6. Which table is a function table for $y = −3x + 3$?

F.
x	−3	0	3	6	9
y	−2	−1	0	1	2

G.
x	−2	−1	0	1	2
y	9	6	3	0	−3

H.
x	−2	−1	0	1	2
y	−3	0	3	6	9

J.
x	9	6	3	0	−3
y	−2	−1	0	1	2

CONSTRUCTED RESPONSE

7. Robert starts walking on a flat surface. He goes up a gradual incline until he reaches its peak, and then he immediately starts down a gradual decline. After reaching the bottom of the decline, he continues walking on a flat surface. Make a graph of elevation versus time to demonstrate this situation. Explain your graph.

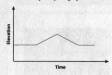

The graph starts with a horizontal

line and rises as Robert goes up. The

graph comes to a point when he

reaches the peak, and then decreases

as he goes down. It ends with a

horizontal line.

8. Write a statement that best tells the story of the graph.

Possible answer: The train slows

down steadily to a stop.

9. Find the output for each input.

Input	Rule	Output
x	−9x + 15	y
−5	−9(−5) + 15	60
1	−9(1) + 15	6
3	−9(3) + 15	−12

10. Gasoline is pumped at a rate of 3 gallons per minute into a container that already has 4 gallons inside. Write a linear function that describes the amount of gas in the container over time. Then make a graph to show the amount of gas in the container over the first 5 minutes.

$y = 3x + 4$

Input	Rule	Output
x	3x + 4	y
0	3(0) + 4	4
4	3(4) + 4	.16
5	3(5) + 4	19

© Houghton Mifflin Harcourt Publishing Company

CHAPTER 3

Exponents and Roots

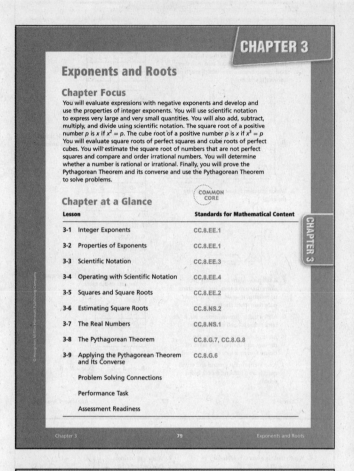

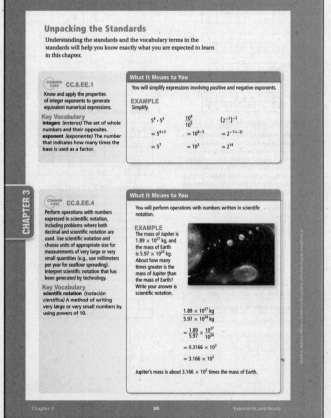

COMMON CORE PROFESIONAL DEVELOPMENT **CC.8.EE.1**

In Grade 8, students add the properties of integer exponents to their list of rules for transforming expressions. Since Grade 5, students have been expressing whole number powers of 10 with exponential notation. For whole numbers a and b, they have expressed the pattern seen in the number of zeros when powers of 10 are multiplied as in $10^a \cdot 10^b = 10^{a+b}$. In Grade 8, expanding this rule to integer exponents leads to the definition of the powers with 0 and negative exponents.

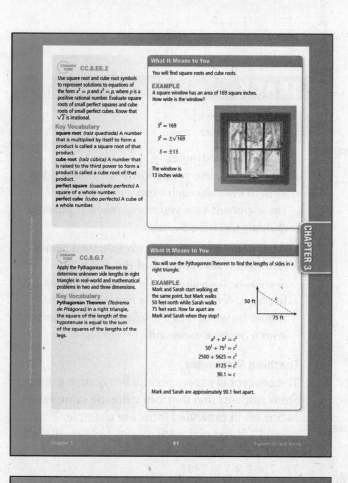

CC.8.EE.2

Use square root and cube root symbols to represent solutions to equations of the form $x^2 = p$ and $x^3 = p$, where p is a positive rational number. Evaluate square roots of small perfect squares and cube roots of small perfect cubes. Know that $\sqrt{2}$ is irrational.

Key Vocabulary

square root *(raíz quadrada)* A number that is multiplied by itself to form a product is called a square root of that product.

cube root *(raíz cúbica)* A number that is raised to the third power to form a product is called a cube root of that product.

perfect square *(cuadrado perfecto)* A square of a whole number.

perfect cube *(cubo perfecto)* A cube of a whole number.

What It Means to You

You will find square roots and cube roots.

EXAMPLE

A square window has an area of 169 square inches. How wide is the window?

$$S^2 = 169$$
$$S^2 = \pm\sqrt{169}$$
$$S = \pm13$$

The window is 13 inches wide.

CC.8.G.7

Apply the Pythagorean Theorem to determine unknown side lengths in right triangles in real-world and mathematical problems in two and three dimensions.

Key Vocabulary

Pythagorean Theorem *(Teorema de Pitágoras)* In a right triangle, the square of the length of the hypotenuse is equal to the sum of the squares of the lengths of the legs.

What It Means to You

You will use the Pythagorean Theorem to find the lengths of sides in a right triangle.

EXAMPLE

Mark and Sarah start walking at the same point, but Mark walks 50 feet north while Sarah walks 75 feet east. How far apart are Mark and Sarah when they stop?

$$a^2 + b^2 = c^2$$
$$50^2 + 75^2 = c^2$$
$$2500 + 5625 = c^2$$
$$8125 = c^2$$
$$90.1 \approx c$$

Mark and Sarah are approximately 90.1 feet apart.

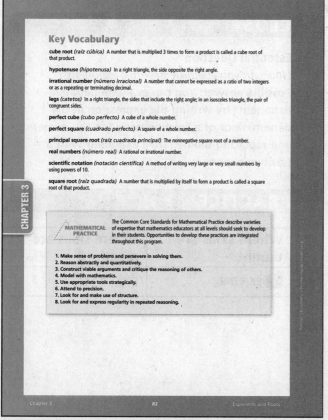

Key Vocabulary

cube root *(raíz cúbica)* A number that is multiplied 3 times to form a product is called a cube root of that product.

hypotenuse *(hipotenusa)* In a right triangle, the side opposite the right angle.

irrational number *(número irracional)* A number that cannot be expressed as a ratio of two integers or as a repeating or terminating decimal.

legs *(catetos)* In a right triangle, the sides that include the right angle; in an isosceles triangle, the pair of congruent sides.

perfect cube *(cubo perfecto)* A cube of a whole number.

perfect square *(cuadrado perfecto)* A square of a whole number.

principal square root *(raíz cuadrada principal)* The nonnegative square root of a number.

real numbers *(número real)* A rational or irrational number.

scientific notation *(notación científica)* A method of writing very large or very small numbers by using powers of 10.

square root *(raíz quadrada)* A number that is multiplied by itself to form a product is called a square root of that product.

MATHEMATICAL PRACTICE

The Common Core Standards for Mathematical Practice describe varieties of expertise that mathematics educators at all levels should seek to develop in their students. Opportunities to develop these practices are integrated throughout this program.

1. Make sense of problems and persevere in solving them.
2. Reason abstractly and quantitatively.
3. Construct viable arguments and critique the reasoning of others.
4. Model with mathematics.
5. Use appropriate tools strategically.
6. Attend to precision.
7. Look for and make use of structure.
8. Look for and express regularity in repeated reasoning.

COMMON CORE PROFESIONAL DEVELOPMENT **CC.8.EE.2**

In Grade 8, students begin working with square roots and cube roots. Students do not learn the properties of rational exponents until high school. They recognize that squaring a number and taking the square root of a number are inverse operations and that cubing a number and taking the cube root of a number are inverse operations. By using this inverse operation students solve equations containing square or cube numbers. These equations may include rational numbers where both the numerator and denominator are perfect squares or perfect cubes. Students will recognize that non-perfect squares and non-perfect cubes are irrational.

CHAPTER 3

Integer Exponents
Reasoning

Essential question: *How can you evaluate negative exponents?*

COMMON CORE Standards for Mathematical Content

CC.8.EE.1 Know and apply the properties of integer exponents to generate equivalent numerical expressions.

Prerequisites
base
exponent
order of operations

Math Background
A number written in exponential form has base *a* raised to an exponent *b* in the form a^b, with *b* also sometimes referred to as a *power*. Exponents are a shorthand version for writing numbers. For example, the expanded form of 3 raised to the 4th power is written as $3 \times 3 \times 3 \times 3$. Using an exponent, this is written as 3^4. The base is 3. The exponent is 4 because the base is multiplied 4 times by itself.

INTRODUCE

Connect to prior learning by asking students to give examples of numbers written with exponents such as 3^2 and 2^3. Explain to students that exponential form is like an abbreviation. For example, it is much easier to write 2^5 than it is to write $2 \times 2 \times 2 \times 2 \times 2$. Tell students that in this lesson they will examine patterns of integer exponents.

TEACH

1 **EXPLORE**

Questioning Strategies
- How can you use your knowledge of expanded form to evaluate each exponential number? **The exponent tells you the number of times to multiply the base by itself.**

- What pattern can you use to evaluate negative exponents? **As the value of the exponent decreases, the value of the power is divided by the base. A number with a negative exponent should be written as the inverse of the number with a positive exponent.**

Teaching Strategies
The concept of exponents can be confusing at first. Show students that they can write the same values as powers in expanded form. For example, 7^4 is called "7 raised to the 4th power" or "7 multiplied by itself 4 times". This can be written as $7 \times 7 \times 7 \times 7 = 2401$.

CLOSE

Essential Question
How can you evaluate negative exponents?
Possible answer: You can evaluate negative exponents by writing the expression in the denominator of a fraction with 1 in the numerator and replacing the negative exponent with a positive exponent.

PRACTICE

Where skills are taught	Where skills are practiced
1 EXPLORE	EXS. 1–16

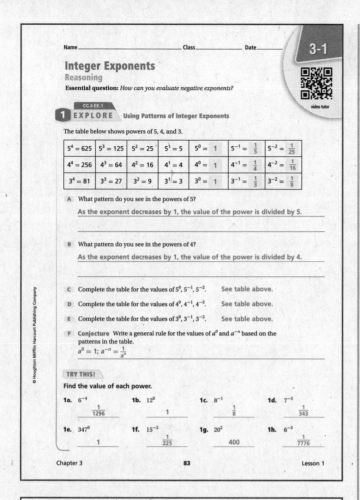

Name_____ Class_____ Date_____

Integer Exponents
Reasoning
Essential question: *How can you evaluate negative exponents?*

3-1

video tutor

1 EXPLORE CC.8.EE.1 **Using Patterns of Integer Exponents**

The table below shows powers of 5, 4, and 3.

$5^4 = 625$	$5^3 = 125$	$5^2 = 25$	$5^1 = 5$	$5^0 = 1$	$5^{-1} = \frac{1}{5}$	$5^{-2} = \frac{1}{25}$
$4^4 = 256$	$4^3 = 64$	$4^2 = 16$	$4^1 = 4$	$4^0 = 1$	$4^{-1} = \frac{1}{4}$	$4^{-2} = \frac{1}{16}$
$3^4 = 81$	$3^3 = 27$	$3^2 = 9$	$3^1 = 3$	$3^0 = 1$	$3^{-1} = \frac{1}{3}$	$3^{-2} = \frac{1}{9}$

A What pattern do you see in the powers of 5?

As the exponent decreases by 1, the value of the power is divided by 5.

_____

B What pattern do you see in the powers of 4?

As the exponent decreases by 1, the value of the power is divided by 4.

_____

C Complete the table for the values of $5^0, 5^{-1}, 5^{-2}$.   See table above.

D Complete the table for the values of $4^0, 4^{-1}, 4^{-2}$.   See table above.

E Complete the table for the values of $3^0, 3^{-1}, 3^{-2}$.   See table above.

F **Conjecture** Write a general rule for the values of a^0 and a^{-n} based on the patterns in the table.

$a^0 = 1; a^{-n} = \frac{1}{a^n}$

TRY THIS!

Find the value of each power.

1a. 6^{-4}
$\frac{1}{1296}$

1b. 12^0
1

1c. 8^{-1}
$\frac{1}{8}$

1d. 7^{-3}
$\frac{1}{343}$

1e. 347^0
1

1f. 15^{-2}
$\frac{1}{225}$

1g. 20^2
400

1h. 6^{-5}
$\frac{1}{7776}$

© Houghton Mifflin Harcourt Publishing Company

PRACTICE

Find the value of each power.

1. 10^{-4}
$\frac{1}{10,000}$

2. 2^{-5}
$\frac{1}{32}$

3. n^{-2}
$\frac{1}{n^2}$

Simplify each expression. Write in decimal form.

4. $(10 \cdot 10)^{-1}$
0.01

5. $10 + (10 \cdot 10)^{-3}$
10.000001

Simplify each expression.

6. $(9 - 5)^{-1}$
$\frac{1}{4}$

7. $(3 \cdot 3)^{-2}$
$\frac{1}{81}$

8. $12 + (4 \cdot 10^0)$
16

9. $25 - \left(\frac{9}{10} + 10^{-1}\right)$
24

10. $(5^2 - 3^2) \cdot 8^0$
16

11. $3^{-2} + 4^{-1} \cdot 3^0$
$\frac{13}{36}$

Solve.

12. An *ohm* is a unit of electrical resistance. Erin measures the resistance of a resistor. She finds it to be $\frac{1}{10^4}$ ohms. How can you write this resistance using negative exponents?

10^{-4}

13. An *amp* is a unit for measuring electrical current. Luis orders a 10^{-3} amp fuse to replace one that has blown. How can you write this number of amps in decimal *and* fraction form?

$0.001; \frac{1}{1,000}$

Polonium is a highly radioactive chemical element that has a half-life of about 140 days. This means that one half of a given amount of the element decays in that time. Write each amount as a negative exponent and as a fraction.

14. How much polonium remains after 140 days?

$2^{-1}, \frac{1}{2}$

15. How much polonium remains after 560 days?

$2^{-4}, \frac{1}{16}$

16. **Conjecture** Examine some positive numbers and their reciprocals, such as 3 and $\frac{1}{3}$. As numbers increase, what happens to their reciprocals?

As positive numbers increase, their reciprocals get smaller and get

closer to zero.

© Houghton Mifflin Harcourt Publishing Company

Assign these pages to help your students practice and apply important lesson concepts. For additional exercises, see the Student Edition.

Answers

Additional Practice

1. 0.001
2. 1000
3. 0.00001
4. 0.01
5. 1
6. 10,000
7. 10
8. 100,000
9. $\dfrac{1}{36}$
10. $\dfrac{1}{729}$
11. $\dfrac{1}{32}$
12. $\dfrac{1}{81}$
13. $\dfrac{1}{12}$
14. $\dfrac{1}{216}$
15. $9\dfrac{1}{2}$
16. $16\dfrac{1}{9}$
17. $6\dfrac{1}{16}$
18. $\dfrac{1}{2}$
19. $1\dfrac{4}{9}$
20. 2
21. $\dfrac{1}{1000}$
22. 1,000,000

Problem Solving

1. 10,000,000
2. 0.0000001
3. 1,000,000
4. 0.000001
5. D
6. H
7. C
8. G

© Houghton Mifflin Harcourt Publishing Company

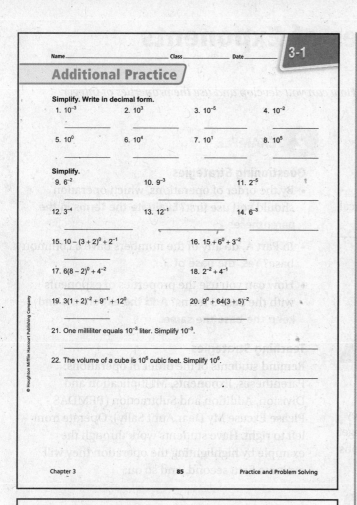

Name_____ Class_____ Date_____ **3-1**

Additional Practice

Simplify. Write in decimal form.

1. 10^{-3} 2. 10^3 3. 10^{-5} 4. 10^{-2}

_____   _____   _____   _____

5. 10^0 6. 10^4 7. 10^1 8. 10^5

_____   _____   _____   _____

Simplify.

9. 6^{-2} 10. 9^{-3} 11. 2^{-5}

_____   _____   _____

12. 3^{-4} 13. 12^{-1} 14. 6^{-3}

_____   _____   _____

15. $10 - (3 + 2)^0 + 2^{-1}$ 16. $15 + 6^0 + 3^{-2}$

_____   _____

17. $6(8 - 2)^0 + 4^{-2}$ 18. $2^{-2} + 4^{-1}$

_____   _____

19. $3(1 + 2)^{-2} + 9^{-1} + 12^0$ 20. $9^0 + 64(3 + 5)^{-2}$

_____   _____

21. One milliliter equals 10^{-3} liter. Simplify 10^{-3}.

_____

22. The volume of a cube is 10^6 cubic feet. Simplify 10^6.

_____

Chapter 3   85   Practice and Problem Solving

Problem Solving

Write the correct answer.

1. The weight of 10^7 dust particles is 1 gram. Simplify 10^7.

_____

2. The weight of one dust particle is 10^{-7} gram. Simplify 10^{-7}.

_____

3. As of 2001, only 10^6 rural homes in the United States had broadband Internet access. Simplify 10^6.

_____

4. Atomic clocks measure time in microseconds. A microsecond is 10^{-6} second. Simplify 10^{-6}.

_____

Choose the letter for the best answer.

5. The diameter of the nucleus of an atom is about 10^{-15} meter. Simplify 10^{-15}.

A 0.0000000000001

B 0.00000000000001

C 0.0000000000000001

D 0.000000000000001

6. The diameter of the nucleus of an atom is 0.000001 nanometer. How many nanometers is the diameter of the nucleus of an atom?

F $(-10)^5$

G $(-10)^6$

H 10^{-6}

J 10^{-5}

7. A ruby-throated hummingbird weighs about 3^{-2} ounce. Simplify 3^{-2}.

A -9

B -6

C $\frac{1}{9}$

D $\frac{1}{6}$

8. A ruby-throated hummingbird breathes 2×5^3 times per minute while at rest. Simplify this amount.

F 1,000

G 250

H 125

J 30

Chapter 3   86   Practice and Problem Solving

Properties of Exponents
Reasoning

Essential question: *How can you develop and use the properties of integer exponents?*

COMMON CORE **Standards for Mathematical Content**

CC.8.EE.1 Know and apply the properties of integer exponents to generate equivalent numerical expressions.

Prerequisites
base
exponent
order of operations

INTRODUCE

Connect to prior learning by reviewing the Commutative and Associative Properties of Multiplication. Tell students that in this lesson they will examine patterns and learn properties of integer exponents. Using these properties makes operations with numbers in exponential form more efficient.

TEACH

1 EXPLORE

Questioning Strategies
- In each property what happens to the base? **The base stays the same.**

- In Part B, in what order must you subtract the exponents? **The bottom exponent is subtracted from the top exponent.**

Avoid Common Errors
Students may confuse the Product Rule of Exponents $a^m \cdot a^n$ with the Power Rule of Exponents $(a^m)^n$. Remind them to add exponents for $a^m \cdot a^n$, and multiply exponents for $(a^m)^n$. If they forget, remind them to write the rule again.

2 EXAMPLE

Questioning Strategies
- By the order of operations, which operation should you use first? **Evaluate the terms in the parentheses.**

- In Part A, do any of the numbers have a common base? **Yes, the base of 3.**

- How can you use the properties of exponents with the base 3 terms? **Add the exponents and keep the base the same.**

Teaching Strategies
Remind students of the order of operations: Parentheses, Exponents, Multiplication and Division, Addition and Subtraction (PEMDAS - Please Excuse My Dear Aunt Sally). Operate from left to right. Have students work through the example by highlighting the operation they will evaluate first, second, and so on.

MATHEMATICAL PRACTICE **Highlighting the Standards**

This Example is an opportunity to address Standard 7 (Look for and make use of structure). Students are asked to identify patterns in integer exponents. Students use this pattern of behavior in values involving integer exponents to identify the structure of integer exponents, and summarize those patterns of behavior with properties. Students apply the properties of exponents to evaluate exponents and to simplify more complex expressions involving integer exponents.

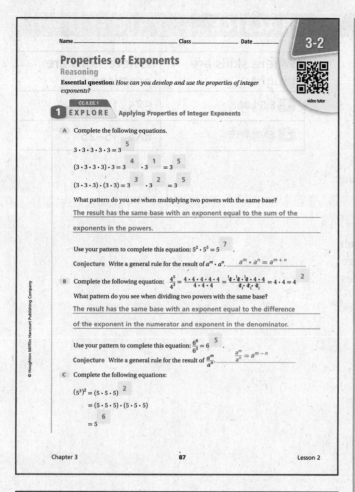

Name_____ Class_____ Date_____

3-2

Properties of Exponents
Reasoning

Essential question: *How can you develop and use the properties of integer exponents?*

CC.8.EE.1

1 EXPLORE Applying Properties of Integer Exponents

A Complete the following equations.

$3 \cdot 3 \cdot 3 \cdot 3 \cdot 3 = 3^{\boxed{5}}$

$(3 \cdot 3 \cdot 3 \cdot 3) \cdot 3 = 3^{\boxed{4}} \cdot 3^{\boxed{1}} = 3^{\boxed{5}}$

$(3 \cdot 3 \cdot 3) \cdot (3 \cdot 3) = 3^{\boxed{3}} \cdot 3^{\boxed{2}} = 3^{\boxed{5}}$

What pattern do you see when multiplying two powers with the same base?

The result has the same base with an exponent equal to the sum of the exponents in the powers.

Use your pattern to complete this equation: $5^2 \cdot 5^5 = 5^{\boxed{7}}$

Conjecture Write a general rule for the result of $a^m \cdot a^n$. $a^m \cdot a^n = a^{m+n}$

B Complete the following equation: $\frac{4^5}{4^3} = \frac{4 \cdot 4 \cdot 4 \cdot 4 \cdot 4}{4 \cdot 4 \cdot 4} = \frac{\cancel{4} \cdot \cancel{4} \cdot \cancel{4} \cdot 4 \cdot 4}{\cancel{4} \cdot \cancel{4} \cdot \cancel{4}} = 4 \cdot 4 = 4^{\boxed{2}}$

What pattern do you see when dividing two powers with the same base?

The result has the same base with an exponent equal to the difference of the exponent in the numerator and exponent in the denominator.

Use your pattern to complete this equation: $\frac{6^8}{6^3} = 6^{\boxed{5}}$

Conjecture Write a general rule for the result of $\frac{a^m}{a^n}$. $\frac{a^m}{a^n} = a^{m-n}$

C Complete the following equations:

$(5^3)^2 = (5 \cdot 5 \cdot 5)^{\boxed{2}}$

$\quad = (5 \cdot 5 \cdot 5) \cdot (5 \cdot 5 \cdot 5)$

$\quad = 5^{\boxed{6}}$

Chapter 3   87   Lesson 2

© Houghton Mifflin Harcourt Publishing Company

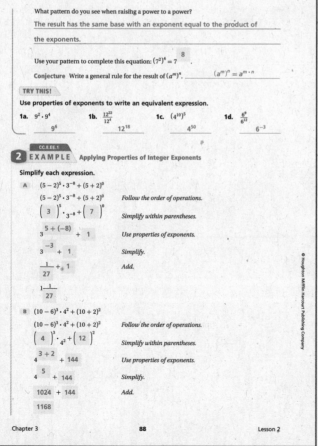

What pattern do you see when raising a power to a power?

The result has the same base with an exponent equal to the product of the exponents.

Use your pattern to complete this equation: $(7^2)^4 = 7^{\boxed{8}}$.

Conjecture Write a general rule for the result of $(a^m)^n$. $(a^m)^n = a^{m \cdot n}$

TRY THIS!

Use properties of exponents to write an equivalent expression.

1a. $9^2 \cdot 9^4$
9^6

1b. $\frac{12^{22}}{12^4}$
12^{18}

1c. $(4^{10})^5$
4^{50}

1d. $\frac{6^9}{6^{12}}$
6^{-3}

CC.8.EE.1

2 EXAMPLE Applying Properties of Integer Exponents

Simplify each expression.

A $(5-2)^5 \cdot 3^{-8} + (5+2)^0$

$(5-2)^5 \cdot 3^{-8} + (5+2)^0$ *Follow the order of operations.*

$\left(\boxed{3}\right)^5 \cdot 3^{-8} + \left(\boxed{7}\right)^0$ *Simplify within parentheses.*

$3^{5+(-8)} + 1$ *Use properties of exponents.*

$3^{-3} + 1$ *Simplify.*

$\frac{1}{27} + 1$ *Add.*

$1\frac{1}{27}$

B $(10-6)^3 \cdot 4^2 + (10+2)^2$

$(10-6)^3 \cdot 4^2 + (10+2)^2$ *Follow the order of operations.*

$\left(\boxed{4}\right)^3 \cdot 4^2 + \left(\boxed{12}\right)^2$ *Simplify within parentheses.*

$4^{3+2} + 144$ *Use properties of exponents.*

$4^5 + 144$ *Simplify.*

$1024 + 144$ *Add.*

1168

Chapter 3   88   Lesson 2

© Houghton Mifflin Harcourt Publishing Company

Essential Question

How can you develop and use the properties of integer exponents?

Possible answer: You can use the properties of integer exponents as a shorthand method of evaluating exponents and simplifying expressions using the order of operations. The Product Rule is $a^m \cdot a^n = a^{m+n}$, the Quotient Rule is $\frac{a^m}{a^n} = a^{m-n}$, and the Power Rule is $(a^m)^n = a^{m \times n}$.

Summarize

Have students answer the following prompt in their journals: How can you use expanded form to prove the properties of integer exponents? Give examples to justify your answer.

Where skills are taught	Where skills are practiced
1 EXPLORE	EXS. 1–14
2 EXAMPLE	EXS. 15–25

TRY THIS!

Simplify each expression.

2a. $\dfrac{[(6-1)^2]^2}{(3+2)^3}$ ___5___

2b. $(2^2)^3 - (10-6)^3 \cdot 4^{-5}$ $63\frac{15}{16}$

PRACTICE

Complete each table.

1.

Product of Powers	Write the Factors	Write as a Single Power
$2^2 \cdot 2^4$	$(2 \cdot 2)(2 \cdot 2 \cdot 2 \cdot 2) = 2 \cdot 2 \cdot 2 \cdot 2 \cdot 2 \cdot 2$	2^6
$4^4 \cdot 4^3$	$(4 \bullet 4 \bullet 4 \bullet 4)(4 \bullet 4 \bullet 4) = 4 \bullet 4 \bullet 4 \bullet 4 \bullet 4 \bullet 4 \bullet 4$	4^7
$5^1 \cdot 5^4$	$(5)(5 \cdot 5 \cdot 5 \cdot 5) = 5 \cdot 5 \cdot 5 \cdot 5 \cdot 5$	5^5

2.

Quotient of Powers	Write the Factors	Write as a Single Power
$\dfrac{3^5}{3^2}$	$\dfrac{3 \cdot 3 \cdot 3 \cdot \cancel{3} \cdot \cancel{3}}{\cancel{3} \cdot \cancel{3}}$	3^3
$\dfrac{5^4}{5^1}$	$\dfrac{5 \cdot 5 \cdot 5 \cdot \cancel{5}}{\cancel{5}}$	5^3
$\dfrac{4^4}{4^6}$	$\dfrac{\cancel{4} \cdot \cancel{4} \cdot \cancel{4} \cdot \cancel{4}}{4 \cdot 4 \cdot \cancel{4} \cdot \cancel{4} \cdot \cancel{4} \cdot \cancel{4}}$	4^{-2} or $\frac{1}{16}$

Use properties of integers to write an equivalent expression.

3. $15^2 \cdot 15^{-5}$ ___15^{-3}___

4. $\dfrac{20^{10}}{20^7}$ ___20^3___

5. $\dfrac{14^4}{14^9}$ ___14^{-5}___

6. $(8^4)^{12}$ ___8^{48}___

7. $(12^{-5})^3$ ___12^{-15}___

8. $4^{-3} \cdot 4^{-21}$ ___4^{-24}___

9. $m \cdot m^4$ ___m^5___

10. $\dfrac{r^5}{r^2}$ ___r^3___

11. $(a^3)^{-3}$ ___a^{-9}___

Chapter 3   89   Lesson 2

© Houghton Mifflin Harcourt Publishing Company

Find the missing exponent.

12. $b^{\boxed{6}} \cdot b^2 = b^8$

13. $\dfrac{x^5}{x^{\boxed{7}}} = x^{-2}$

14. $\left(n^{\boxed{0}}\right)^4 = n^0$

Simplify each expression.

15. $3 \cdot (3^2)^2 + (8-4)^{-3}$ ___$243\frac{1}{64}$___

16. $[(5+1)^2 \div 3] - 9^0$ ___11___

17. $\dfrac{(6-2^2)^1}{(5-4)^6}$ ___-2___

18. $\dfrac{[(4-1)^2]^0}{(2+1)^2}$ ___$\frac{1}{9}$___

19. $(2+4)^2 + 8^{-6} \times (12-4)^{10}$ ___$6^2 + 8^4$___

20. $(3^3)^2 \times \left(\dfrac{(5-2)^3}{3^4}\right) + (10-4)^2 \times 6^{10}$ ___$3^5 + 6^{12}$___

21. There are $2^5 + 3^2$ games in half a full NBA season. How many games are in a full NBA season?

___82___

22. From Earth, it is about 22^4 miles to the moon and about 9.3×10^7 to the sun. About how much farther is it to the sun than to the moon?

___about 92,765,744 mi___

23. **Error Analysis** A student simplified the expression $\dfrac{4^3}{16^3}$ as $\dfrac{1}{4}$. Do you agree with the student? Justify your answer.

No; $\dfrac{4^3}{16^3} = \dfrac{4 \times 4 \times 4}{(4 \times 4) \times (4 \times 4) \times (4 \times 4)} = \dfrac{1}{4 \times 4 \times 4} = \dfrac{1}{64}$.

24. Find the values of $x^5 \cdot x^{-3}$ and $\dfrac{x^5}{x^3}$. What do you notice about the two values? Explain why your results make sense based on the properties you learned in this lesson.

x^2; x^2; You can write $\dfrac{x^5}{x^3}$ as $x^5 \cdot \dfrac{1}{x^3}$ which is equal to $x^5 \cdot x^{-3}$.

25. **Reasoning** Eric says that you can find the product of $2^4 \cdot 3^3$ by combining the exponents and then multiplying. Is he right? Explain.

No; you only can multiply by combining exponents when the bases are the same, and here they are not.

© Houghton Mifflin Harcourt Publishing Company

Chapter 3   90   Lesson 2

Chapter 3   **90**   Lesson 2

Assign these pages to help your students practice and apply important lesson concepts. For additional exercises, see the Student Edition.

Answers

Additional Practice

1. 10^{12}
2. x^{17}
3. 14^{16}
4. 12^{14}
5. y^{22}
6. 15^{23}
7. 11^{30}
8. a^{13}
9. 12^{7}
10. 11^{4}
11. x^{-5}
12. 16^{8}
13. 17^{17}
14. 14^{-2}
15. 23^{8}
16. a^{5}
17. 6^{8}
18. 2^{-12}
19. 3^{-5}
20. y^{10}
21. 9^{-6}
22. 10^{0}
23. x^{-8}
24. 5^{0}
25. w^{9}
26. d^{13}
27. 15^{15}
28. 6^{2}
29. $x^{15} \cdot x^{10} = x^{25}$

Problem Solving

1. 2^{12} fruit flies
2. 8^{11} bacteria
3. 13 hr
4. 3^{12} cm^3
5. D
6. F
7. D
8. H

Name_____ Class_____ Date_____ **3-2**

Additional Practice

Multiply. Write the product as one power.

1. $10^5 \cdot 10^7$ _____

2. $x^9 \cdot x^8$ _____

3. $14^7 \cdot 14^9$ _____

4. $12^6 \cdot 12^8$ _____

5. $y^{12} \cdot y^{10}$ _____

6. $15^9 \cdot 15^{14}$ _____

7. $11^{20} \cdot 11^{10}$ _____

8. $a^6 \cdot a^7$ _____

Divide. Write the quotient as one power.

9. $\dfrac{12^9}{12^2}$

10. $\dfrac{11^{12}}{11^8}$

11. $\dfrac{x^5}{x^{10}}$

12. $\dfrac{16^{10}}{16^2}$

13. $\dfrac{17^{19}}{17^2}$

14. $\dfrac{14^{13}}{14^{15}}$

15. $\dfrac{23^{17}}{23^9}$

16. $\dfrac{a^{12}}{a^7}$

Simplify.

17. $(6^2)^4$

18. $(2^4)^{-3}$

19. $(3^5)^{-1}$

20. $(y^5)^2$

21. $(9^{-2})^3$

22. $(10^0)^3$

23. $(x^4)^{-2}$

24. $(5^{-2})^{0}$

Write the product or quotient as one power.

25. $\dfrac{w^{12}}{w^3}$

26. $d^8 \cdot d^5$

27. $15^5 \cdot 15^{10}$

28. Jefferson High School has a student body of 6^4 students. Each class has approximately 6^2 students. How many classes does the school have? Write the answer as one power.

29. Write the expression for a number used as a factor fifteen times being multiplied by a number used as a factor ten times. Then, write the product as one power.

Problem Solving

Write each answer as a power.

1. Cindy separated her fruit flies into equal groups. She estimates that there are 2^{10} fruit flies in each of 2^2 jars. How many fruit flies does Cindy have in all?

2. Suppose a researcher tests a new method of pasteurization on a strain of bacteria in his laboratory. If the bacteria are killed at a rate of 8^9 per sec, how many bacteria would be killed after 8^2 sec?

3. A satellite orbits the earth at about 13^4 km per hour. How long would it take to complete 24 orbits, which is a distance of about 13^5 km?

4. The side of a cube is 3^4 centimeters long. What is the volume of the cube? (Hint: $V = s^3$.)

Use the table to answer Exercises 5–6. The table describes the number of people involved at each level of a pyramid scheme. In a pyramid scheme each individual recruits so many others to participate who in turn recruit others, and so on. Choose the letter of the best answer.

5. Using exponents, how many people will be involved at level 6?

   A 6^6 C 5^5

   B 6^5 D 5^6

6. How many times as many people will be involved at level 6 than at level 2?

   F 5^4 H 5^5

   G 5^3 J 5^6

Pyramid Scheme
Each person recruits 5 others.

Level	Total Number of People
1	5
2	5^2
3	5^3
4	5^4

7. There are 10^3 ways to make a 3-digit combination, but there are 10^6 ways to make a 6-digit combination. How many times more ways are there to make a 6-digit combination than a 3-digit combination?

   A 5^{10} C 2^5

   B 2^{10} D 10^3

8. After 3 hours, a bacteria colony has $(25^3)^3$ bacteria present. How many bacteria are in the colony?

   F 25^1 H 25^9

   G 25^6 J 25^{33}

Scientific Notation
Going Deeper

Essential question: *How can you use scientific notation to express very large and very small quantities?*

COMMON CORE **Standards for Mathematical Content**

CC.8.EE.3 Use numbers expressed in the form of a single digit times an integer power of 10 to estimate very large or very small quantities, and to express how much larger or smaller one is than the other.

Vocabulary
scientific notation

Prerequisites
Properties of exponents of integers

Math Background
Scientific notation is a method used to express very large and very small numbers in terms of a decimal number between 1 and 10 (including 1, but not 10) multiplied by a power of 10. For example, in scientific notation 85,488 equals 8.5488×10^4 and 0.0783 equals 7.83×10^{-2}. The power of 10 indicates the number of places that the decimal will move to equal the number in standard notation. In scientific notation, numbers greater than 1 are expressed with a positive exponent, and numbers less than 1 are expressed with a negative exponent.

INTRODUCE

Connect to prior learning by reviewing powers of 10 with students. Explain that powers of 10 are used in scientific notation to express extremely large or extremely small numbers, such as those used in science. Tell students that they will convert numbers in standard notation to scientific notation and vice versa.

TEACH

1 EXPLORE

Questioning Strategies

- For each number, where would you relocate the decimal point to create an integer greater than or equal to 1 and less than 10? **For 250,000 between 2 and 5; for 41,200 between 4 and 1; for 133.25 between 1 and the first 3; for 0.95 between 9 and 5.**

- Why does only the minnow have a negative exponent of 10? **The number of pounds is less than 1.**

Differentiated Instruction

Visual and kinesthetic learners may benefit from a hands-on approach to the numbers. For 250,000, write each digit in the number on a separate index card. Create one index card containing a decimal point. Spread the numbers on the floor. Have students physically walk the decimal point card to its new location and count the number of places the decimal point moves as they walk. Repeat this process for the other numbers.

2 EXAMPLE

Questioning Strategies

- Where would you relocate the decimal point to create an integer greater than or equal to 1 and less than 10? **Move the decimal point between the 6 and 8 to create 6.88.**

- How many decimal places are between the original decimal point and the new location of the decimal point? **9**

Teaching Strategies

Have students draw an arc between each decimal place to indicate they have moved the decimal point. For example:

$$6.880000000$$

© Houghton Mifflin Harcourt Publishing Company

Name_____ Class_____ Date_____

3-3

Scientific Notation
Going Deeper

Essential question: *How can you use scientific notation to express very large and very small quantities?*

Scientific notation is a method of expressing very large and very small numbers as a product of a number greater than or equal to 1 and less than 10, and a power of 10.

CC.8.EE.3

1 EXPLORE Using Scientific Notation

The weights of various sea creatures are shown in the table. You can write the weights in scientific notation.

Sea Creature	Blue Whale	Whale Shark	Eel	Minnow
Weight (lb)	250,000	41,200	133.25	0.95

Write the weight of the blue whale in scientific notation.

A Move the decimal point in 250,000 to the left as many places as necessary to find a number that is greater than or equal to 1 and less than 10.

What number did you find? _____ 2.5 _____

B Divide 250,000 by your answer to **A** . Write your answer as a power of 10.

_____ 100,000; 10^5 _____

C Combine your answers to **A** and **B** to represent 250,000.

$250,000 = 2.5 \times 10^5$

Write the weight of the minnow in scientific notation.

D Move the decimal point in 0.95 to the right as many places as necessary to find a number that is greater than or equal to 1 and less than 10.

What number did you find? _____ 9.5 _____

E Divide 0.95 by your answer to **D** . Write your answer as a power of 10.

_____ 0.1 or $\frac{1}{10}$; 10^{-1} _____

F Combine your answers to **D** and **E** to represent 0.95.

$0.95 = 9.5 \times 10^{-1}$

REFLECT

1a. What do you notice about the sign of the exponent for weights greater than one pound?

The exponent is positive for a weight greater than one pound.

1b. What do you notice about the sign of the exponent for weights less than one pound?

The exponent is negative for a weight less than one pound.

To translate between standard notation and scientific notation, you can count the number of places the decimal point moves.

Writing Numbers in Scientific Notation		
When the number is greater than or equal to 1, use a positive exponent.	$84,000 = 8.4 \times 10^4$	*The decimal point moves 4 places.*
When the number is less than 1, use a negative exponent.	$0.0783 = 7.83 \times 10^{-2}$	*The decimal point moves 2 places.*

CC.8.EE.3

2 EXAMPLE Writing a Number in Scientific Notation

An estimate of the world population in 2010 was 6,880,000,000. Write the world's population in scientific notation.

To write 6,880,000,000 in scientific notation, move the decimal point as many places as necessary to find a number that is greater than or equal to 1 and less than 10.

Place the decimal point: 6.8 8 0 0 0 0 0 0 0

Which direction did you move the decimal point? _____ left _____

What number did you find? _____ 6.88 _____

How many places did you move the decimal point? _____ 9 _____

When 6,880,000,000 is written in scientific notation, should the exponent of the power of 10 be positive or negative? Explain.

Positive; you multiply 6.88 by a power of 10 greater than 1 to get 6,880,000,000.

The world's population, 6,880,000,000, written in scientific notation is

6.88×10^9

To translate between scientific notation and standard notation, you can move the decimal point the number of places indicated by the exponent in the power of 10. When the exponent is positive, move the decimal point to the right. When the exponent is negative, move the decimal point to the left.

Questioning Strategies

- What is the power of 10? **The power of 10 is 12 in Part A and −6 in Part B.**

- What does the sign of the power of 10 tell you when moving the decimal point? **For positive powers of 10, move the decimal point to the right. For negative powers of 10, move the decimal point to the left.**

- What place holder do you use after you run out of numbers when moving the decimal point? **Use zeroes as place holders.**

Avoid Common Errors

Remind students that positive powers of 10 always move the decimal point to the right when converting from scientific notation to standard notation. Negative powers of 10 always move the decimal point to the left.

4 EXAMPLE

Questioning Strategies

- What is the integer part of each number? **The integers are 4 and 2.**

- How can you use the properties of integer exponents to compare the powers of 10 for the given numbers? **Use the quotient rule:**
$$\frac{10^4}{10^2} = 10^{4-2} = 10^2 = 100.$$

Teaching Strategies

To reinforce the connection between standard and scientific notation, have students write each weight in standard notation, divide, and then write the answer in scientific notation.

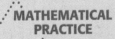 **Highlighting the Standards**

This Example is an opportunity to address Standard 2 (Model with mathematics). Students are asked to model very large and very small numbers using scientific notation. They will connect scientific notation with rules of exponents.

CLOSE

Essential Question

How can you use scientific notation to express very large and very small quantities?

Possible answer: Scientific notation expresses very large and very small numbers in terms of a decimal number between 1 and 10 multiplied by a power of 10. To determine the power of 10, simply count the number of decimal places between the original decimal point and the location of the decimal point in the decimal number. Numbers larger than 1 will have a positive exponent. Numbers smaller than 1 will have a negative exponent.

Summarize

Have students answer the following prompt in their journals: What are examples of very large and very small numbers that you encounter in everyday life? How would you write these numbers using scientific notation?

PRACTICE

Where skills are taught	Where skills are practiced
1 EXPLORE	EXS. 1–8
2 EXAMPLE	EXS. 1–8
3 EXAMPLE	EXS. 9–16
4 EXAMPLE	EXS. 17–22

3 EXAMPLE — CC.8.EE.3 — Writing a Number in Standard Notation

Write each number in standard notation.

A 4.18549×10^{12}

What is the exponent of the power of 10? _____ 12 _____

Which direction should you move the decimal point? _____ right _____

Place the decimal point. Add placeholder zeros if necessary.

_ _ _ _ _ _ 4 1 8 5 4 9 0 0 0 0 0 0 0 . _ _

The number 4.18549×10^{12} written in standard notation is _____ 4,185,490,000,000 _____.

B 2.568×10^{-6}

What is the exponent of the power of 10? _____ −6 _____

Which direction should you move the decimal point? _____ left _____

Place the decimal point. Add placeholder zeros if necessary.

_ _ _ 0 . 0 0 0 0 0 2 5 6 8 _ _ _ _ _

The number 2.568×10^{-6} written in standard notation is _____ 0.000002568 _____.

4 EXAMPLE — CC.8.EE.3 — Comparing Numbers in Scientific Notation

The approximate weight of a whale shark is 4×10^4 pounds. The approximate weight of a common dolphin is 2×10^2 pounds. How many times as great as the weight of the whale shark is the weight of the dolphin?

First compare the values between 1 and 10.

The 4 in 4×10^4 is _____ 2 _____ times as great as the 2 in 2×10^2.

Next compare the powers of 10.

10^4 is _____ 100 _____ times as great as 10^2.

Circle the most reasonable answer.

The weight of the whale shark is 2 / 20 / (200) / 2000 times as great as the weight of the dolphin.

REFLECT

4a. Scientists captured and released a whale shark that weighed about 6×10^5 units. Circle the best choice for the units this measurement is given in: (ounces) / pounds / tons.

4b. Explain how you chose a unit of measurement in 4a.

4×10^4 is 40,000 and 6×10^5 is 600,000; 6×10^5 is about 15 times 4×10^4

and I know that there are 16 ounces in 1 pound, so it makes sense that the

measurement would be in ounces.

PRACTICE

Write each number in scientific notation.

1. 58,927
   5.8927×10^4

2. 1,304,000,000
   1.304×10^9

3. 0.000487
   4.87×10^{-4}

4. 0.000028
   2.8×10^{-5}

5. 0.000059
   5.9×10^{-5}

6. 6,730,000
   6.73×10^6

7. 13,300
   1.33×10^4

8. 0.0417
   4.17×10^{-2}

Write each number in standard notation.

9. 4×10^5
   400,000

10. 1.8499×10^9
    1,849,900,000

11. 8.3×10^{-4}
    0.00083

12. 3.582×10^{-6}
    0.000003582

13. 2.97×10^{-2}
    0.0297

14. 6.41×10^3
    6,410

15. 8.456×10^7
    84,560,000

16. 9.06×10^{-5}
    0.0000906

Circle the correct answer.

17. 8×10^5 is 2 / 20 / 200 / (2,000) times as great as 4×10^2.

18. 9×10^{10} is 30 / 300 / (3,000) / 30,000 times as great as 3×10^7.

19. 4×10^{-5} is 0.02 / (0.2) / 2 / 20 times as great as 2×10^{-4}.

20. 4×10^{-12} is 0.00001 / (0.0001) / 10 / 1000 times as great as 4×10^{-8}.

21. The mass of a proton is about 1.7×10^{-24} g. The mass of a neutron is about the same as a proton. The nucleus of an atom of carbon has 6 protons and 6 neutrons. The mass of the nucleus is about 2×10^{-26} units. Circle the best choice for the units this measurement is given in: g / (kg) / tons.

22. The air distance between Los Angeles, California, and New York City, New York, is about 3.9×10^3 units. Circle the best choice for the units this measurement is given in: cm / m / (km).

Assign these pages to help your students practice and apply important lesson concepts. For additional exercises, see the Student Edition.

Answers

Additional Practice

1. 254
2. 0.067
3. 1140
4. 0.38
5. 0.00753
6. 56,000
7. 910,000
8. 0.000608
9. 859,000
10. 3,331,000
11. 0.00721
12. 0.000588
13. 7.5×10^7
14. 2.08×10^2
15. 9.071×10^5
16. 5.6×10^1
17. 9.3×10^{-2}
18. 6.0×10^{-5}
19. 8.52×10^{-3}
20. 5.05×10^{-2}
21. 3.007×10^{-3}
22. 5.226×10^3
23. 4.0×10^{-2}
24. 9.8856×10^4
25. 7.7812×10^8
26. the hair

Problem Solving

1. 1.5×10^{12}
2. 1,000,000,000
3. 2×10^{-8} m
4. 0.002
5. B
6. G
7. A
8. F
9. D

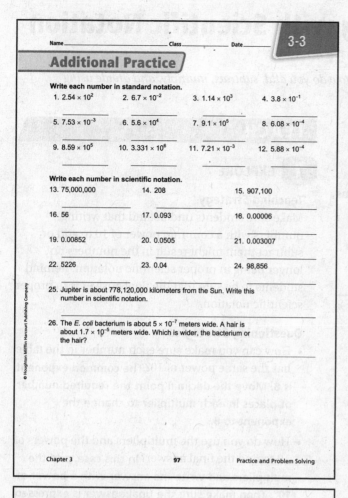

Name_____ Class_____ Date_____ **3-3**

Additional Practice

Write each number in standard notation.

1. 2.54×10^2 2. 6.7×10^{-2} 3. 1.14×10^3 4. 3.8×10^{-1}

_____   _____   _____   _____

5. 7.53×10^{-3} 6. 5.6×10^4 7. 9.1×10^5 8. 6.08×10^{-4}

_____   _____   _____   _____

9. 8.59×10^5 10. 3.331×10^6 11. 7.21×10^{-3} 12. 5.88×10^{-4}

_____   _____   _____   _____

Write each number in scientific notation.

13. 75,000,000   14. 208   15. 907,100

_____   _____   _____

16. 56   17. 0.093   18. 0.00006

_____   _____   _____

19. 0.00852   20. 0.0505   21. 0.003007

_____   _____   _____

22. 5226   23. 0.04   24. 98,856

_____   _____   _____

25. Jupiter is about 778,120,000 kilometers from the Sun. Write this number in scientific notation.

_____

26. The *E. coli* bacterium is about 5×10^{-7} meters wide. A hair is about 1.7×10^{-5} meters wide. Which is wider, the bacterium or the hair?

_____

Chapter 3   97   Practice and Problem Solving

Problem Solving

Write the correct answer.

1. In June 2001, the Intel Corporation announced that they could produce a silicon transistor that could switch on and off 1.5 trillion times a second. Express the speed of the transistor in scientific notation.

2. With this transistor, computers will be able to do 1×10^9 calculations in the time it takes to blink your eye. Express the number of calculations using standard notation.

3. The elements in this fast transistor are 20 nanometers long. A nanometer is one-billionth of a meter. Express the length of an element in the transistor in meters using scientific notation.

4. The length of the elements in the transistor can also be compared to the width of a human hair. The length of an element is 2×10^{-3} times smaller than the width of a human hair. Express 2×10^{-3} in standard notation.

Use the table to answer Exercises 5–9. Choose the best answer.

5. Express a light-year in miles using scientific notation.

  A 58.8×10^{11} C 588×10^{10}
  B 5.88×10^{12} D 5.88×10^{-13}

6. How many miles is it from Earth to the star Sirius?

  F 4.705×10^{12} H 7.35×10^{12}
  G 4.704×10^{13} J 7.35×10^{11}

7. How many miles is it from Earth to the star Canopus?

  A 3.822×10^{15} C 3.822×10^{14}
  B 1.230×10^{15} D 1.230×10^{14}

8. How many miles is it from Earth to the star Alpha Centauri?

  F 2.352×10^{13} H 2.352×10^{14}
  G 5.92×10^{13} J 5.92×10^{14}

Distance From Earth To Stars
Light-Year = 5,880,000,000,000 mi.

Star	Constellation	Distance (light-years)
Sirius	Canis Major	8
Canopus	Carina	650
Alpha Centauri	Centaurus	4
Vega	Lyra	23

9. How many miles is it from Earth to the star Vega?

  A 6.11×10^{13} C 6.11×10^{14}
  B 1.3524×10^{13} D 1.3524×10^{14}

Chapter 3   98   Practice and Problem Solving

3-4 Operating with Scientific Notation
Going Deeper

Essential question: *How do you add, subtract, multiply, and divide using scientific notation?*

COMMON CORE Standards for Mathematical Content

CC.8.EE.4 Perform operations with numbers expressed in scientific notation, including problems where both a decimal and scientific notation are used. Use scientific notation and choose units of appropriate size for measurements of very large or very small quantities. Interpret scientific notation that has been generated by technology.

Materials
Scientific calculator

Prerequisites
Properties of exponents
Scientific notation

Math Background
The properties of exponents are used when performing operations with numbers in scientific notation:

1. Product Rule: $a^m \cdot a^n = a^{m+n}$
   example: $5^3 \cdot 5^{-2} = 5^{3+(-2)} = 5^1$

2. Quotient Rule: $\frac{a^m}{a^n} = a^{m-n}$
   example: $\frac{5^3}{5^{-2}} = 5^{3-(-2)} = 5^5$

3. Power Rule: $(a^m)^n = a^{m \times n}$
   example: $(5^3)^{-2} = 5^{3 \cdot -2} = 5^{-6}$

INTRODUCE

Connect to prior learning by asking students to give examples of numbers written in standard notation and scientific notation. Discuss with students how tedious operations on very large numbers such as 1,408,582,895 and 20,855,392,858 can be. Tell students that they will perform operations by hand as well as by using a calculator on very large and very small numbers expressed in scientific notation.

TEACH

1 EXPLORE

Teaching Strategy
Make sure students understand that writing numbers with a common power of 10 to add or subtract them might result in the numbers no longer being in proper scientific notation. Remind students to be sure that the final answer is in proper scientific notation.

Questioning Strategies
- How can you make sure each number in the table has the same power of 10? **The common exponent is 8. Move the decimal point the required number of places in each multiplier to change the exponent to 8.**
- How do you use the multipliers and the powers of 10 to find the final answer? **In this case, add the multipliers and write the answer with a power of 10^8. Then make sure the final answer is expressed in proper scientific notation.**
- What is another way to add the numbers? **Rewrite each number in standard notation, find the sum, and then rewrite the answer in scientific notation.**

2 EXPLORE

Questioning Strategies
- In order to compare the numbers, must both the measurements be in the same or different notations? **To compare the numbers they must be in the same format.**
- What do you do with the multipliers? **Divide 2.025 by 2.25.**
- How can you use properties of exponents to divide the powers of 10? **Subtract the bottom exponent from the top exponent.**

TRY THIS

To multiply using scientific notation, students should multiply the multipliers, then use the product rule to add the powers of 10. Finally, write the answer in scientific notation.

Name _____ Class _____ Date _____

3-4

video tutor

Operating with Scientific Notation
Going Deeper

Essential question: *How do you add, subtract, multiply, and divide using scientific notation?*

CC.8.EE.4

1 **EXPLORE** Adding and Subtracting with Scientific Notation

The table below shows the population of the three largest countries in North America. Find the total population of the three countries.

Country	United States	Canada	Mexico
Population	3.1×10^8	3.38×10^7	1.1×10^8

Method 1:

A First write each population with the same power of 10.

United States: 3.1×10^8

Canada: 0.338×10^8

Mexico: 1.1×10^8

B Add the multipliers for each population. $3.1 + 0.338 + 1.1 = 4.538$

C Write the final answer in scientific notation. _____ 4.538×10^8

Method 2:

D First write each number in standard notation.

United States: 310,000,000

Canada: 33,800,000

Mexico: 110,000,000

E Find the sum of the numbers in standard notation.

$310,000,000 + 33,800,000 + 110,000,000 = 453,800,000$

F Write the answer in scientific notation. _____ 4.538×10^8

TRY THIS!

1a. Using the population table above, how many more people live in Mexico than in Canada?

$$1.1 \times 10^8 - 3.38 \times 10^7 = 1.1 \times 10^8 - 0.338 \times 10^8$$
$$= 0.762 \times 10^8$$
$$= 7.62 \times 10^7$$

© Houghton Mifflin Harcourt Publishing Company

CC.8.EE.4

2 **EXPLORE** Multiplying and Dividing with Scientific Notation

When the sun makes an orbit around the center of the Milky Way, it travels 2.025×10^{14} kilometers. The orbit takes 225 million years. At what rate does the Sun travel around the Milky Way? Write your answer in scientific notation.

A Set up a division problem to represent the situation.

$$\text{Rate} = \frac{\text{Distance}}{\text{Time}}$$

$$\text{Rate} = \frac{2.025 \times 10^{14} \text{ kilometers}}{225{,}000{,}000 \text{ years}}$$

B Write 225 million years in scientific notation. _____ 2.25×10^8

C Write the expression for rate with years in scientific notation.

$$\text{Rate} = \frac{2.025 \times 10^{14} \text{ kilometers}}{2.25 \times 10^8 \text{ years}}$$

D Find the quotient by dividing the multipliers.

$2.025 \div 2.25 = 0.9$

E Use the laws of exponents to divide the powers of 10.

$$\frac{10^{14}}{10^8} = 10^{14-8} = 10^6$$

F Combine the answers from D and E to write the rate in scientific notation.

$0.9 \times 10^6 = 9.0 \times 10^5$ km per year

TRY THIS!

2a. Light from the Sun travels at a speed of 1.86×10^5 miles per second. It takes sunlight about 4.8×10^3 seconds to reach Saturn. Find the approximate distance from the Sun to Saturn. Write your answer in scientific notation.

$d = rt$

$$= \left(1.86 \times 10^5 \right) \left(4.8 \times 10^3 \right)$$

$$= \left(1.86 \right)(4.8) \times \left(10^5 \right)(10^3)$$

$$= 8.928 \times 10^{5+3}$$

$$= 8.928 \times 10^8 \text{ miles}$$

© Houghton Mifflin Harcourt Publishing Company

Questioning Strategies

- What does "E" mean on your calculator? This refers to the power of 10. For example, "E9" means $\times 10^9$.

Avoid Common Errors

Students may try to use the "ENTER" key after each addend. Remind students that when they use the "E" key, the calculator will use the properties of integer exponents and correct order of operations.

MATHEMATICAL PRACTICE — Highlighting the Standards

This Example is an opportunity to address Standard 5 (Use appropriate tools strategically.). When using pen and paper, students will apply properties of integer exponents when performing operations with numbers in scientific notation. When using technology, students will use calculators to input and perform operations on numbers in scientific notation.

CLOSE

Essential Question

How do you add, subtract, multiply, and divide using scientific notation?

Possible answer: If powers are the same, you can add or subtract the multipliers of numbers in scientific notation and keep the same power. You can multiply or divide the multipliers of each number and use properties of integer exponents for the powers. You can also convert numbers to standard notation, perform the operation, and then convert the result to scientific notation. Lastly, you can use a calculator.

Summarize

Have students answer the following prompt in their journals: Explain how properties of integer exponents are used to operate with numbers in scientific notation.

PRACTICE

Where skills are taught	Where skills are practiced
1 EXPLORE	EXS. 1–6
2 EXPLORE	EXS. 7–10
3 EXAMPLE	EXS. 11–17

On many scientific calculators, you can enter numbers in scientific notation by using a function labeled "ee" or "EE". Usually, the letter "E" takes the place of "×10". So, the number 4.1×10^9 would appear as 4.1E9 on the calculator.

3 EXAMPLE CC.8.EE.4 **Scientific Notation on a Calculator**

The table below shows the approximate populations for the three continents with the greatest populations. What is the total population of these three continents? Use your calculator to find the answer.

Continent	Asia	Africa	Europe
Population	4.1×10^9	1.0×10^9	7.28×10^8

Find $4.1 \times 10^9 + 1.0 \times 10^9 + 7.28 \times 10^8$.

Enter 4.1E9 + 1E ▢9 + 7.28 E ▢8 on your calculator.

Write the results from your calculator. _____5,828,000,000 or 5.828E9_____

Write this number in scientific notation. _____5.828×10^9_____

The total population of the three continents is _____5.828×10^9_____ people.

TRY THIS!

Write each number using calculator notation.

3a. 7.5×10^5
_____7.5E5_____

3b. 3×10^{-7}
_____3E−7_____

3c. 2.7×10^{13}
_____2.7E13_____

Write each number using scientific notation.

3d. 4.5E−1
_____4.5×10^{-1}_____

3e. 5.6E12
_____5.6×10^{12}_____

3f. 6.98E−8
_____6.98×10^{-8}_____

PRACTICE

Add or subtract. Write your answer in scientific notation.

1. $3.2 \times 10^5 + 4.9 \times 10^8$
_____4.9032×10^8_____

2. $4.378 \times 10^{12} + 7.701 \times 10^7$
_____$4.37807701 \times 10^{12}$_____

3. $2.3 \times 10^8 - 2.12 \times 10^3$
_____2.2999788×10^8_____

4. $4.55 \times 10^{15} - 7.4 \times 10^{11}$
_____4.54926×10^{15}_____

5. $6.35 \times 10^3 + 1.65 \times 10^6$
_____1.65635×10^6_____

6. $5 \times 10^3 - 1.23 \times 10^2$
_____4.877×10^3_____

Multiply or divide. Write your answer in scientific notation.

7. $(1.8 \times 10^9)(6.78 \times 10^{12})$
_____1.2204×10^{22}_____

8. $(5.092 \times 10^{21})(3.38 \times 10^6)$
_____1.721096×10^{28}_____

9. $\dfrac{8.4 \times 10^{21}}{4.2 \times 10^{14}}$
_____2.0×10^7_____

10. $\dfrac{3.46 \times 10^{17}}{2 \times 10^9}$
_____1.73×10^8_____

11. A newborn baby has about 26,000,000,000 cells. An adult has about 1.9×10^3 times as many cells as a newborn. About how many cells does an adult have? Write your answer in scientific notation.

_____4.94×10^{13} cells_____

12. The edge of a cube measures 3.5×10^{-2} meters. What is the volume of the cube in cubic meters? Write your answer in scientific notation.

_____4.2875×10^{-5} cubic meters_____

13. The smallest state in the United States is Rhode Island with a land area of about 2.9×10^{10} square feet. The largest state is Alaska whose land area is about 5.5×10^2 as great as the land area of Rhode Island. What is the land area of Alaska in square feet? Write your answer in scientific notation.

_____1.595×10^{13} ft^2_____

14. Astronomers estimate that the diameter of the Andromeda galaxy is approximately 2.2×10^5 light-years. A light-year is the distance light travels in a vacuum in 1 year. One light-year is approximately 5.9×10^{12} miles. What is the diameter of the Andromeda galaxy in miles? Write your answer in scientific notation.

_____1.298×10^{18} miles_____

The table below shows the approximate populations of three countries.

Country	China	France	Australia
Population	1.33×10^9	6.48×10^7	2.15×10^7

15. How many more people live in France than in Australia? Write your answer in scientific notation.

_____4.33×10^7 people_____

16. The area of Australia is about 2.95×10^6 square miles. What is the approximate average number of people per square mile in Australia?

_____about 7 people per square mile_____

17. What is the ratio of the population of China to the population of France? What does this mean?

_____20.52; there are about 20 people in China for every 1 person in France._____

Notes

Assign these pages to help your students practice and apply important lesson concepts. For additional exercises, see the Student Edition.

Answers

Additional Practice

1. 6.634×10^5 sq mi

2. 6.220×10^0 times

3. $\$5.368 \times 10^9$

4. 6.6×10^8 times

5. 2.7075×10^8 cu yd

Problem Solving

1. 2.33×10^3 times

2. 1.61×10^{10} mi

3. 3.533×10^6 sq mi

4. $\$4.07 \times 10^9$

5. A

6. G

7. B

8. J

Additional Practice

Write your answer in scientific notation.

1. Rhode Island is the smallest state. It has an area of approximately 1.55×10^3 square miles. Alaska is the largest state. The area of Alaska is 4.28×10^2 times greater than the area of Rhode Island.

   What is the approximate area of Alaska in square miles? _____

2. In 2008, the total trade between the United States and Japan was 2.04×10^{11}. The total trade between the U.S. and Australia was 3.28×10^{10}.

   How many times greater was the trade with Japan than the trade with Australia? _____

3. Between 2008 and 2009, Americans spent 8.48×10^8 on baby food. During the same period, Americans spent 4.52×10^9 on ice cream.

   How much did Americans spend altogether on ice cream and baby food between 2008 and 2009? _____

4. Wrangell-St. Elias National Park in Alaska is the largest national park. It includes approximately 1.32×10^7 acres. Thaddeus Kosciuszcko National Memorial in Pennsylvania is the smallest national park. It is located on approximately 2.0×10^{-2} acres.

   How many times greater is the area of Wrangell-St. Alias National Park than Thaddeus Kosciuszcko National Memorial? _____

5. Approximately 3.25×10^6 cubic yards of material were used to build Boulder Dam on the Arizona-Nevada border. The New Cornelia Tailings Dam in Arizona used 2.74×10^8 cubic yards of material.

   How many more cubic yards of material were used to build the Cornelia Tailings Dam than Boulder Dam? _____

Problem Solving

Write your answer in scientific notation.

1. The top speed of a garden snail is 3.0×10^{-2} miles per hour. The top speed of a cheetah is 7.0×10^1. How many times greater is the speed of the cheetah than the garden snail?

   _____

2. The speed of light is approximately 1.86×10^5 miles per second. How many miles will light travel in a 24-hour day?

   _____

3. The total area for the 50 U.S. states and Washington, D.C. is 3.79×10^6 square miles. Of that, 2.57×10^5 square miles are water. The rest of the area is land. How many square miles is the land area?

   _____

4. In 2008, Americans spent 3.8×10^9 on bottled water and 2.7×10^8 on coffee. How much did Americans spend altogether on bottled water and coffee?

   _____

Choose the letter for the best answer.

5. The all-time top grossing U.S. movie, *Titanic*, made 6.008×10^8. In 2008, *Dark Knight* was the top grossing movie at 5.309×10^8. How much did Titanic and Dark Knight gross in all?

   A 1.13×10^9

   B 3.19×10^8

   C 6.99×10^8

   D 8.84×10^9

6. A large department store chain employs 1.8×10^6 people. The average annual wage for the employees is 2.1×10^4. How much does the chain pay in employee wages each year?

   F 3.00×10^2

   G 3.78×10^{10}

   H 3.90×10^{24}

   J 8.57×10^{10}

7. Gary measures a paramecium and an ant. The paramecium is 4.2×10^{-4} meter long, and the ant is 3.8×10^{-3} meter long. How much longer, in meters, is the ant than the paramecium?

   A 4.00×10^{-2} C 3.82×10^{-3}

   B 3.38×10^{-3} D 4.22×10^{-3}

8. The average radius of Jupiter is 4.34×10^4 miles. The average radius of the Sun is 4.32×10^5. How many times greater is the average radius of the sun?

   F 1.00×10^1

   G 2.00×10^3

   H 4.75×10^1

   J 9.95×10^0

Squares and Square Roots
Extension: Cube Roots

Essential question: *How do you evaluate square roots and cube roots?*

© Houghton Mifflin Harcourt Publishing Company

COMMON CORE Standards for Mathematical Content

CC.8.EE.2 Use square root and cube root symbols to represent solutions to equations of the form $x^2 = p$ and $x^3 = p$, where p is a positive rational number. Evaluate square roots of small perfect squares and cube roots of small perfect cubes. ... Know that $\sqrt{2}$ is irrational ...

Vocabulary

square root

principal square root

perfect square

cube root

perfect cube

Prerequisites

Evaluating exponents

Math Background

The square root of a positive number, p, is $\pm x$ if $x^2 = p$. There are two square roots for every positive number. The $\sqrt{}$ indicates the principal square root. When a number is a perfect square, its square roots are integers. For example, 25 is a perfect square; the square root of 25 is ± 5 because $(5)(5) = 25$ and $(-5)(-5) = 25$.

INTRODUCE

Connect to prior learning by asking students to give examples of numbers written in exponential notation such as 5^2 and 10^3. Remind students that they can evaluate these exponents by multiplying the base times itself the number of times indicated by the exponent. For example, $5^2 = 5 \cdot 5 = 25$ and $10^3 = 10 \cdot 10 \cdot 10 = 1000$. Tell students that in this lesson they will work in the reverse order: finding square roots and cube roots. For example, instead of finding 5^2 they will find $\sqrt{25}$ and, instead of finding 10^3 they will find $\sqrt[3]{1000}$.

TEACH

1 EXPLORE

Questioning Strategies

- What method can you use to find the relationship between the side length and the total number of tiles? **The side length squared equals the total number of tiles.**

- How can you use square root to describe the relationship between the total number of tiles and the number of tiles along one side of the figure? **The total number of tiles is a perfect square. The square root of the total number of tiles is the number of tiles along one side of the figure.**

- In this case, why does only one square root make sense? **Only the positive square root makes sense because a length cannot be negative.**

TRY THIS

Students may have difficulty finding the square root of a fraction. For 1b, encourage them to think "What fraction multiplied by itself is $\frac{1}{16}$? In the numerator, 1 times 1 is 1; in the denominator, 4 times 4 is 16. So, the square root of $\frac{1}{16}$ must be $\frac{1}{4}$."

2 EXPLORE

Questioning Strategies

- What is the relationship between the side length of the cube and total number of unit cubes that form the cube? **The total number of unit cubes is equal to the cube of the number of unit cubes along one side of the shape.**

- How can you use the cube root sign to represent the number of unit cubes along one side? **The cube root of the total number of unit cubes equals the number of unit cubes along one side.**

TRY THIS

Students may have difficulty finding the cube root of a fraction. For 2e, encourage them to think "What fraction used as a factor three times is $\frac{1}{8}$? In the numerator, 1 times 1 times 1 is 1; in the denominator, 2 times 2 times 2 is 8. So, the cube root of $\frac{1}{8}$ must be $\frac{1}{2}$."

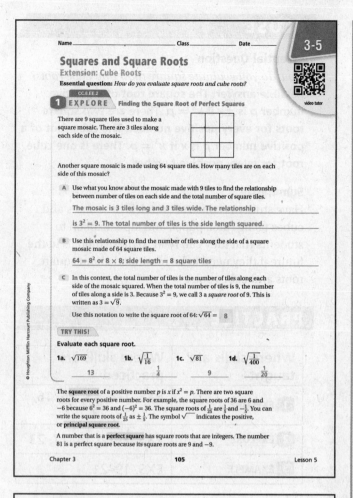

Name_____ Class_____ Date_____

3-5

Squares and Square Roots

Extension: Cube Roots

Essential question: *How do you evaluate square roots and cube roots?*

video tutor

1 EXPLORE CC.8.EE.2   Finding the Square Root of Perfect Squares

There are 9 square tiles used to make a square mosaic. There are 3 tiles along each side of the mosaic.

Another square mosaic is made using 64 square tiles. How many tiles are on each side of this mosaic?

A Use what you know about the mosaic made with 9 tiles to find the relationship between number of tiles on each side and the total number of square tiles.

The mosaic is 3 tiles long and 3 tiles wide. The relationship

is $3^2 = 9$. The total number of tiles is the side length squared.

B Use this relationship to find the number of tiles along the side of a square mosaic made of 64 square tiles.

$64 = 8^2$ or 8×8; side length $= 8$ square tiles

C In this context, the total number of tiles is the number of tiles along each side of the mosaic squared. When the total number of tiles is 9, the number of tiles along a side is 3. Because $3^2 = 9$, we call 3 a *square root* of 9. This is written as $3 = \sqrt{9}$.

Use this notation to write the square root of 64: $\sqrt{64} = $ 8

TRY THIS!

Evaluate each square root.

1a. $\sqrt{169}$
13

1b. $\sqrt{\frac{1}{16}}$
$\frac{1}{4}$

1c. $\sqrt{81}$
9

1d. $\sqrt{\frac{1}{400}}$
$\frac{1}{20}$

The **square root** of a positive number p is x if $x^2 = p$. There are two square roots for every positive number. For example, the square roots of 36 are 6 and -6 because $6^2 = 36$ and $(-6)^2 = 36$. The square roots of $\frac{1}{25}$ are $\frac{1}{5}$ and $-\frac{1}{5}$. You can write the square roots of $\frac{1}{25}$ as $\pm\frac{1}{5}$. The symbol $\sqrt{}$ indicates the positive, or **principal square root.**

A number that is a **perfect square** has square roots that are integers. The number 81 is a perfect square because its square roots are 9 and -9.

Chapter 3   105   Lesson 5

2 EXPLORE CC.8.EE.2   Finding the Cube Root

A cube shaped toy is made of 27 small cubes. There are 3 cubes along each edge of the toy.

Another cube shaped toy is made using 8 small cubes. How many small cubes are on each edge of this toy?

A Use what you know about the toy made with 27 small cubes to find the relationship between number of cubes on each edge and the total number of cubes.

The toy is 3 cubes long, 3 cubes wide, and 3 cubes tall. The

relationship is $3^3 = 27$. The total number of small cubes is the

side length cubed.

B Use this relationship to find the number of small cubes along each edge of a toy made of 8 small cubes.

$8 = 2^3$ or $2 \times 2 \times 2$. Side length $= 2$ small cubes.

C In this situation, the total number of small cubes is the number of small cubes along each edge of the toy cube. When the total number of small cubes is 27, the number of small cubes along each edge is 3. Because $3^3 = 27$, we call 3 a *cube root* of 27. This is written as $\sqrt[3]{27} = 3$.

Use this notation to write the cube root of 8: $\sqrt[3]{8} = $ 2

REFLECT

2a. The product of 3 equal positive factors is (positive) / negative.

2b. The product of 3 equal negative factors is positive / (negative).

2c. Use your answers to **2a** and **2b** to explain when there is only one cube root of a positive number.

For the product of 3 equal factors to be positive, the factors must

be positive.

TRY THIS!

Evaluate each cube root.

2d. $\sqrt[3]{125}$
5

2e. $\sqrt[3]{\frac{1}{8}}$
$\frac{1}{2}$

2f. $\sqrt[3]{1000}$
10

2g. $\sqrt[3]{\frac{1}{343}}$
$\frac{1}{7}$

Chapter 3   106   Lesson 5

© Houghton Mifflin Harcourt Publishing Company

Questioning Strategies

- How many square roots of 121 are there? **Two**

- How do you solve $121 = x^2$? **Find the principal square root of 121, which is 11, and give the answer both positive and negative signs.**

- How many cube roots are there for 729? **One**

- How do you solve $729 = x^3$? **Find the principal cube root of 729, which is 9. Because 729 is positive, the cube root can only be positive.**

Avoid Common Errors

Students may be tempted to find two cube roots since they found two square roots. Review how signed numbers in multiplication work for three factors. A cube root of a positive number can't be negative because $(-)(-)(-) = (-)$.

MATHEMATICAL PRACTICE **Highlighting the Standards**

This Example is an opportunity to address Standard 4 (Model with mathematics). Students are asked to identify the relationships between side length and total number of tiles or cubes in square or cube models. Students use the models to analyze their answers for reasonability, realizing that answers representing distance or length cannot be negative.

CLOSE

Essential Question

How do you evaluate square roots and cube roots?
Possible answer: The square root of a positive number p is $\pm x$ if $x^2 = p$. There are two square roots for every positive number. The cube root of a positive number p is x if $x^3 = p$. There is one cube root for every positive number.

Summarize

Have students construct models of squares and cubes using ruler, paper, and tape. Explain to students that they can refer to these models in the future if they need to be reminded about square roots and cube roots.

PRACTICE

Where skills are taught	Where skills are practiced
1 EXPLORE	EXS. 1–6, 13, 15, 16, 18, 22
2 EXPLORE	EXS. 7–12, 14, 17, 23
3 EXAMPLE	EXS. 19–21

The **cube root** of a positive number p is x if $x^3 = p$. There is one cube root for every positive number. For example, the cube root of 8 is 2 because $2^3 = 8$. The cube root of $\frac{1}{27}$ is $\frac{1}{3}$ because $\left(\frac{1}{3}\right)^3 = \frac{1}{27}$. The symbol $\sqrt[3]{}$ indicates the cube root. A number that is a **perfect cube** has a cube root that is an integer. The number 125 is a perfect cube because its cube root is 5.

3 EXAMPLE Solving Equations Using Square Roots and Cube Roots

Solve each equation for x.

A $x^2 = 121$

$\sqrt{x^2} = \sqrt{121}$ *Solve for x by taking the square root of both sides.*

$x = \sqrt{121}$ *Think: What number squared equals 121?*

$x = \pm\ \underline{11}$ *Use ± to show both square roots.*

The solutions are __11__ and __−11__.

B $x^2 = \frac{16}{169}$

$\sqrt{x^2} = \sqrt{\frac{16}{169}}$ *Solve for x by taking the square root of both sides.*

$x = \sqrt{\frac{16}{169}}$ *Think: What number squared equals $\frac{16}{169}$?*

$x = \pm\ \dfrac{4}{13}$ *Use ± to show both square roots.*

The solutions are $\frac{4}{13}$ and $\frac{4}{13}$.

C $729 = x^3$

$\sqrt[3]{729} = \sqrt[3]{x^3}$ *Solve for x by taking the cube root of both sides.*

$\sqrt[3]{729} = x$ *Think: What number cubed equals 729?*

$\boxed{9} = x$

The solution is __9__.

D $x^3 = \frac{8}{125}$

$\sqrt[3]{x^3} = \sqrt[3]{\frac{8}{125}}$ *Solve for x by taking the cube root of both sides.*

$x = \sqrt[3]{\frac{8}{125}}$ *Think: What number cubed equals $\frac{8}{125}$?*

$x = \dfrac{2}{5}$

The solution is $\frac{2}{5}$.

© Houghton Mifflin Harcourt Publishing Company

PRACTICE

Find the square roots of each number.

1. 144 __±12__   2. 256 __±16__   3. $\frac{1}{81}$ __$\pm\frac{1}{9}$__

4. $\frac{49}{900}$ __$\pm\frac{7}{30}$__   5. 400 __±20__   6. $\frac{1}{100}$ __$\pm\frac{1}{10}$__

Find the cube root of each number.

7. 216 __6__   8. 8000 __20__   9. $\frac{27}{125}$ __$\frac{3}{5}$__

10. $\frac{1}{27}$ __$\frac{1}{3}$__   11. $\frac{27}{64}$ __$\frac{3}{4}$__   12. 512 __8__

Simplify each expression.

13. $\sqrt{16} + \sqrt{25}$ __9__   14. $\sqrt[3]{125} + 10$ __15__   15. $\sqrt{25} + 10$ __15__

16. $8 - \sqrt{64}$ __0__   17. $\sqrt[3]{\frac{16}{2}} + 1$ __3__   18. $\sqrt{\frac{16}{4}} + \sqrt{4}$ __4__

19. The foyer of Ann's house is a square with an area of 36 square feet. What is the length of each side of the foyer?

__6 feet__

20. A chessboard has 32 black squares and 32 white squares arranged in a square. How many squares are along each side of the chessboard?

__8 squares__

21. A cubic aquarium holds 27 cubic feet of water. What is the length of each edge of the cube?

__3 feet__

22. **Reasoning** How can you check your answer when you find the square root(s) of a number?

__Multiply the square root by itself. The product should be the number you__

__started with.__

23. **Reasoning** Can you arrange 12 small squares to make a larger square? Can you arrange 20 small cubes to make a larger cube? Explain how this relates to perfect squares and perfect cubes.

__No; 12 is not a perfect square. No; 20 is not a perfect cube.__

© Houghton Mifflin Harcourt Publishing Company

ADDITIONAL PRACTICE

Assign these pages to help your students practice and apply important lesson concepts. For additional exercises, see the Student Edition.

Answers

Additional Practice

1. $6, -6$
2. $9, -9$
3. $7, -7$
4. $10, -10$
5. $8, -8$
6. $11, -11$
7. $5, -5$
8. $12, -12$
9. 9
10. $\dfrac{1}{8}$
11. 2
12. 7
13. $\dfrac{2}{3}$
14. $\dfrac{1}{11}$
15. 4
16. $\dfrac{3}{10}$
17. 9
18. 30
19. 5
20. 3
21. 755 ft
22. 25 in.

Problem Solving

1. 42 feet
2. 38 feet
3. 9 squares
4. Bedroom three
5. D
6. G
7. D
8. H

3-5

Additional Practice

Name_____ Class_____ Date_____

Find the square roots of each number.

1. 36   2. 81   3. 49   4. 100

5. 64   6. 121   7. 25   8. 144

Find the cube root of each number.

9. 729   10. $\frac{1}{512}$ 11. 8   12. 343

13. $\frac{8}{27}$ 14. $\frac{1}{1331}$ 15. 64   16. $\frac{27}{1000}$

Simplify each expression.

17. $\sqrt{100-19}$

18. $36-\sqrt{36}$

19. $\sqrt{100}-\sqrt{25}$

20. $\sqrt{\frac{25}{4}}+\frac{1}{2}$

The Pyramids of Egypt are often called the first wonder of the world. This group of pyramids consists of Menkaura, Khufu, and Khafra. The largest of these is Khufu, sometimes called Cheops. During this time in history, each monarch had his own pyramid built to bury his mummified body. Cheops was a king of Egypt in the early 26th century B.C. His pyramid's original height is estimated to have been 482 ft. It is now approximately 450 ft. The estimated completion date of this structure was 2660 B.C.

21. If the area of the square base of Cheops' pyramid is 570,025 ft^2, what is the length of one of the sides of the ancient structure? (Hint: $A = s^2$)

_____

22. If a replica of the pyramid were built with a base area of 625 in^2, what would be the length of each side?

_____

Problem Solving

Write the correct answer.

1. For college wrestling competitions, the NCAA requires that the wrestling mat be a square with an area of 1764 square feet. What is the length of each side of the wrestling mat?

2. For high school wrestling competitions, the wrestling mat must be a square with an area of 1444 square feet. What is the length of each side of the wrestling mat?

3. The Japanese art of origami requires folding square pieces of paper. Elena begins with a large sheet of square paper that is 169 square inches. How many squares can she cut out of the paper that are 4 inches on each side?

4. When the James family moved into a new house they had a square area rug that was 132 square feet. In their new house, there are three bedrooms. Bedroom one is 11 feet by 11 feet. Bedroom two is 10 feet by 12 feet and bedroom three is 13 feet by 13 feet. In which bedroom will the rug fit?

Choose the letter for the best answer.

5. A square picture frame measures 36 inches on each side. The actual wood trim is 2 inches wide. The photograph in the frame is surrounded by a bronze mat that measures 5 inches. What is the maximum area of the photograph?

A 841 sq. inches
B 900 sq. inches
C 1156 sq. inches
D 484 sq. inches

6. To create a square patchwork quilt wall hanging, square pieces of material are sewn together to form a larger square. Which number of smaller squares can be used to create a square patchwork quilt wall hanging?

F 35 squares   H 84 squares
G 64 squares   J 125 squares

7. A can of paint claims that one can will cover 400 square feet. If you painted a square with the can of paint, how long would it be on each side?

A 200 feet   C 25 feet
B 65 feet   D 20 feet

8. A box of tile contains 12 square tiles. If you tile the largest possible square area using whole tiles, how many tiles will you have left from the box?

F 9   H 3
G 6   J 0

Estimating Square Roots
Connect: Irrational Numbers

Essential question: *How do you estimate and compare irrational numbers?*

COMMON CORE **Standards for Mathematical Content**

CC.8.EE.2 … Use square root and cube root symbols to represent solutions to equations of the form $x^2 = p$ and $x^3 = p$, where p is a positive rational number. Evaluate square roots of small perfect squares and cube roots of small perfect cubes… Know that $\sqrt{2}$ is irrational.

CC.8.NS.2 Use rational approximations of irrational numbers to compare the size of irrational numbers, locate them approximately on a number line diagram, and estimate the value of expressions (e.g., π^2).

Vocabulary
irrational numbers

Prerequisites
Rational numbers

Math Background
You can estimate irrational numbers that are written as square roots of non-perfect squares by using square roots of perfect squares as a reference. For example, because $\sqrt{4} < \sqrt{5} < \sqrt{9}$, you know that $2 < \sqrt{5} < 3$. For a closer estimation, find the square of selected test points between 2 and 3. For example, $2.2^2 = 4.84$ and $2.3^2 = 5.29$, so the answer must be between 2.2 and 2.3. Then try 2.21 and 2.25, and so on. So, $\sqrt{5} \approx 2.236$.

INTRODUCE

Connect to prior learning by asking students to give examples of the square roots of perfect squares. Tell students that in this lesson they will approximate the square roots of numbers that are not perfect squares using estimation and a number line.

TEACH

1 EXPLORE

Questioning Strategies
- What perfect square roots are near $\sqrt{2}$? **Perfect squares near $\sqrt{2}$ include $\sqrt{1}$ and $\sqrt{4}$, which equal 1 and 2, respectively.**
- How can you use the number line to estimate $\sqrt{2}$? **The number line displays a range in which $\sqrt{2}$ will fall. This allows you to choose helpful test points that hone in on a good estimate.**

MATHEMATICAL PRACTICE Highlighting the Standards

This Example is an opportunity to address Standard 8 (regularity in repeated reasoning). Students use number sense to place rational and irrational numbers together on a number line. To estimate irrational numbers, students apply previously learned properties of exponents, square roots, and rational number operations to reason through the process of refining their estimates of irrational numbers.

---

2 EXAMPLE

Questioning Strategies
- How can you find the sum of an irrational number and a rational number? **Find an estimate for the irrational number and add it to the rational number.**

Teaching Strategies
Use cooperative learning to help students improve their estimation skills. Students can try to predict what the correct inequality symbol will be. Then students can split up in pairs to estimate the value of each expression. Setting up teams and allowing them to compete with points in this type of estimation game might add some fun to the tedium of so much computation.

3-6

Name_____ Class_____ Date_____

Estimating Square Roots
Connect: Irrational Numbers

Essential question: *How do you estimate and compare irrational numbers?*

video tutor

Irrational numbers are numbers that are not rational. In other words, they cannot be written in the form $\frac{a}{b}$, where a and b are integers and $b \neq 0$. Square roots of integers that are not perfect squares are irrational. Other special numbers, like π, are also irrational.

CC.8.NS.2
1 EXPLORE Estimating Irrational Numbers

Estimate the value of $\sqrt{2}$.

A Since 2 is not a perfect square, $\sqrt{2}$ is irrational.

To estimate $\sqrt{2}$, first find two consecutive perfect squares that 2 is between. Complete the inequality by writing these perfect squares in the boxes.

$1 < 2 < 4$

Now take the square root of each number.

$\sqrt{1} < \sqrt{2} < \sqrt{4}$

Simplify the square roots of perfect squares.

$1 < \sqrt{2} < 2$

$\sqrt{2}$ is between 1 and 2 . $\sqrt{2} \approx 1.5$

Estimate that $\sqrt{2} \approx 1.5$.

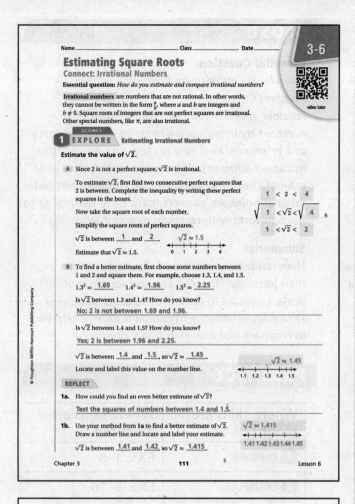

B To find a better estimate, first choose some numbers between 1 and 2 and square them. For example, choose 1.3, 1.4, and 1.5.

$1.3^2 = 1.69$ $1.4^2 = 1.96$ $1.5^2 = 2.25$

Is $\sqrt{2}$ between 1.3 and 1.4? How do you know?

No; 2 is not between 1.69 and 1.96.

Is $\sqrt{2}$ between 1.4 and 1.5? How do you know?

Yes; 2 is between 1.96 and 2.25.

$\sqrt{2}$ is between 1.4 and 1.5 , so $\sqrt{2} \approx 1.45$.

Locate and label this value on the number line.

$\sqrt{2} \approx 1.45$

1.1 1.2 1.3 1.4 1.5

REFLECT

1a. How could you find an even better estimate of $\sqrt{2}$?

Test the squares of numbers between 1.4 and 1.5.

1b. Use your method from **1a** to find a better estimate of $\sqrt{2}$. Draw a number line and locate and label your estimate.

$\sqrt{2} \approx 1.415$

$\sqrt{2}$ is between 1.41 and 1.42 , so $\sqrt{2} \approx 1.415$

1.41 1.42 1.43 1.44 1.45

© Houghton Mifflin Harcourt Publishing Company

Chapter 3   111   Lesson 6

TRY THIS!

1c. Estimate the value of $\sqrt{7}$ to the nearest hundredth. Draw a number line and locate and label your estimate.

$\sqrt{7} \approx 2.65$

2.5 2.6 2.7 2.8 2.9

$\sqrt{7}$ is between 2.6 and 2.7 , so $\sqrt{7} \approx 2.65$

CC.8.NS.2
2 EXAMPLE Comparing Irrational Numbers

Compare. Write <, >, or =.

A $\sqrt{3} + 5$ ⬤ $3 + \sqrt{5}$

First approximate $\sqrt{3}$ to the nearest tenth.

$\sqrt{3}$ is between 1 and 2 , so $\sqrt{3} \approx 1.5$

Next approximate $\sqrt{5}$ to the nearest tenth.

$\sqrt{5}$ is between 2 and 3 , so $\sqrt{5} \approx 2.5$

Then use your approximations to simplify the expressions.

$\sqrt{3} + 5$ ⬤ $3 + \sqrt{5}$

$1.5 + 5$ ⬤ $3 + 2.5$ *Substitute your approximations.*

$6.5 > 5.5$ *Simplify, then compare.*

So, $\sqrt{3} + 5 > 3 + \sqrt{5}$

B $\sqrt{10} + 2$ ⬤ $10 + \sqrt{2}$

First approximate $\sqrt{10}$ to the nearest tenth.

$\sqrt{10}$ is between 3 and 4 , so $\sqrt{10} \approx 3.5$

Next approximate $\sqrt{2}$ to the nearest tenth.

$\sqrt{2}$ is between 1 and 2 , so $\sqrt{2} \approx 1.5$

Then use your approximations to simplify the expressions.

$\sqrt{10} + 2$ ⬤ $10 + \sqrt{2}$

$3.5 + 2$ ⬤ $10 + 1.5$ *Substitute your approximations.*

$5.5 < 11.5$ *Simplify, then compare.*

So, $\sqrt{10} + 2 < 10 + \sqrt{2}$

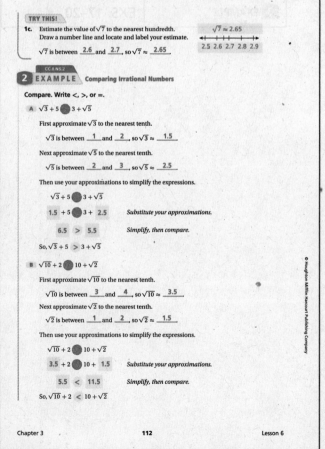

© Houghton Mifflin Harcourt Publishing Company

Chapter 3   112   Lesson 6

© Houghton Mifflin Harcourt Publishing Company

Questioning Strategies

- How do you express all the numbers so that you can compare them? Write fractions as decimals and write irrational numbers as approximate decimal numbers.

- Why do you need a better estimate than 1.5 for $\sqrt{3}$ in this example? Because one of the numbers to compare is equal to 1.5, we need an estimate for $\sqrt{3}$ that can tell us whether $\sqrt{3}$ is less than or greater than 1.5.

Technology

Students can use a graphing calculator to order real numbers. Have students enter each number into a list and sort the list.

Essential Question

How do you estimate and compare irrational numbers?

Possible answer: You can estimate irrational numbers by using square roots of perfect squares as a reference. Find two perfect squares that the irrational number falls between, then refine your estimate with trial and error. To compare and order rational numbers, convert them all to decimal or to fraction form with common denominators.

Summarize

Have students answer the following prompts in their journals: How can you use square roots of perfect squares to estimate irrational numbers? How does estimating irrational numbers help you to compare and order irrational numbers?

PRACTICE

Where skills are taught	Where skills are practiced
1 EXPLORE	EXS. 1–8
2 EXAMPLE	EXS. 9–16
3 EXAMPLE	EXS. 17–20

TRY THIS!

Compare. Write <, >, or =.

2a. $\sqrt{2} + 4$ **>** $2 + \sqrt{4}$ **2b.** $\sqrt{12} + 6$ **<** $12 + \sqrt{6}$

3 EXAMPLE   CC.8.NS.2   Ordering Irrational Numbers

Order $\sqrt{3}$, π, and 1.5 from least to greatest.

First approximate $\sqrt{3}$ to the nearest tenth.

$\sqrt{3}$ is between __1__ and __2__, so $\sqrt{3} \approx$ __1.5__.

You need to find a better estimate for $\sqrt{3}$ so you can compare it to 1.5.
Approximate $\sqrt{3}$ to the nearest hundredth.

$\sqrt{3}$ is between __1.7__ and __1.8__, so $\sqrt{3} \approx$ __1.75__.

An approximate value of π is 3.14.

Plot $\sqrt{3}$, π, and 1.5 on a number line.

Read the numbers from left to right to place them in order from least to greatest.
From least to greatest, the numbers are __1.5__, __$\sqrt{3}$__, __π__.

TRY THIS!

Order the numbers from least to greatest.

3a. $\sqrt{5}$, 2.5, $\sqrt{3}$ $\sqrt{3}, \sqrt{5}, 2.5$

3b. π^2, 10, $\sqrt{75}$ $\sqrt{75}, \pi^2, 10$

© Houghton Mifflin Harcourt Publishing Company

PRACTICE

Approximate each irrational number to the nearest hundredth without using a calculator.

1. $\sqrt{34}$

__5.85__

2. $\sqrt{82}$

__9.05__

3. $\sqrt{45}$

__6.75__

4. $\sqrt{104}$

__10.15__

5. $\sqrt{71}$

__8.45__

6. $\sqrt{19}$

__4.35__

7. $\sqrt{24}$

__4.85__

8. $\sqrt{41}$

__6.45__

Compare. Write <, >, or =.

9. $\sqrt{3} + 2$ **<** $\sqrt{2} + 3$

10. $\sqrt{11} + 15$ **>** $\sqrt{15} + 11$

11. $\sqrt{6} + 5$ **<** $6 + \sqrt{5}$

12. $\sqrt{9} + 3$ **<** $9 + \sqrt{3}$

13. $\sqrt{15} - 3$ **>** $-2 + \sqrt{5}$

14. $10 - \sqrt{8}$ **<** $12 - \sqrt{2}$

15. $\sqrt{7} + 1$ **>** $\sqrt{10} - 1$

16. $\sqrt{12} + 3$ **>** $3 + \sqrt{11}$

Order the numbers from least to greatest.

17. $\sqrt{7}, \frac{\sqrt{8}}{2}, 2$

$\frac{\sqrt{8}}{2}, 2, \sqrt{7}$

18. $\sqrt{10}, \pi, 3.5$

$\pi, \sqrt{10}, 3.5$

19. $1.5, \frac{\sqrt{12}}{3}, \sqrt{3}$

$\frac{\sqrt{12}}{3}, 1.5, \sqrt{3}$

20. $2\sqrt{7}, \sqrt{24}, 2\pi$

$\sqrt{24}, 2\sqrt{7}, 2\pi$

© Houghton Mifflin Harcourt Publishing Company

Assign these pages to help your students practice and apply important lesson concepts. For additional exercises, see the Student Edition.

Answers

Additional Practice

1. 2 and 3; 6 is between 4 and 9

2. 4 and 5; 20 is between 16 and 25

3. 5 and 6; 28 is between 25 and 36

4. 6 and 7; 44 is between 36 and 49

5. 5 and 6; 31 is between 25 and 36

6. 7 and 8; 52 is between 49 and 64

7. 8.37 cm   8. 7.94

9. 4.24   10. 9.33

11. 17.86   12. >

13. <   14. >

15. =   16. $\frac{\sqrt{35}}{2}, 4, \sqrt{20}$

17. $\sqrt{32}, 2\pi, 3\sqrt{5}$ 18. $2.5, \sqrt{8}, \pi$

19. $\frac{\sqrt{17}}{3}, \pi, \sqrt{11}$

Problem Solving

1. 336 km   2. 281 km

3. 5 km   4. at most 226 km

5. C   6. F

7. D   8. G

Name_____ Class_____ Date_____

Additional Practice

Each square root is between two consecutive integers. Name the integers. Explain your answer.

1. $\sqrt{6}$ _____

2. $\sqrt{20}$ _____

3. $\sqrt{28}$ _____

4. $\sqrt{44}$ _____

5. $\sqrt{31}$ _____

6. $\sqrt{52}$ _____

7. The area of a square piece of cardboard is 70 cm². What is the approximate length of each side of the cardboard?

_____

Approximate each irrational number to the nearest hundredth without using a calculator.

8. $\sqrt{63}$ _____

9. $\sqrt{18}$ _____

10. $\sqrt{87}$ _____

11. $\sqrt{319}$ _____

Compare. Write <, >, or =.

12. $7 + \sqrt{3}$ ☐ $\sqrt{7} + 3$

13. $\sqrt{12} - 2$ ☐ $12 - \sqrt{2}$

14. $\sqrt{10} + 5$ ☐ $10 - \sqrt{5}$

15. $-3 + \sqrt{15}$ ☐ $\sqrt{15} - 3$

Order the numbers from least to greatest.

16. $\sqrt{20}$, 4, $\dfrac{\sqrt{35}}{2}$

17. 2π, $\sqrt{32}$, $3\sqrt{5}$

18. 2.5, π, $\sqrt{8}$

19. $\sqrt{11}$, $\dfrac{\sqrt{17}}{3}$, π

Problem Solving

The distance to the horizon can be found using the formula $d = 112.88\sqrt{h}$ where d is the distance in kilometers and h is the number of kilometers from the ground. Round your answer to the nearest kilometer.

1. How far is it to the horizon when you are standing on the top of Mt. Everest, a height of 8.85 km?

_____

2. Find the distance to the horizon from the top of Mt. McKinley, Alaska, a height of 6.194 km.

_____

3. How far is it to the horizon if you are standing on the ground and your eyes are 2 m above the ground?

_____

4. Mauna Kea is an extinct volcano on Hawaii that is about 4 km tall. You should be able to see the top of Mauna Kea when you are how far away?

_____

You can find the approximate speed of a vehicle that leaves skid marks before it stops. The formulas $S = 5.5\sqrt{0.7L}$ and $S = 5.5\sqrt{0.8L}$, where S is the speed in miles per hour and L is the length of the skid marks in feet, will give the minimum and maximum speeds that the vehicle was traveling before the brakes were applied. Round to the nearest mile per hour.

5. A vehicle leaves a skid mark of 40 feet before stopping. What was the approximate speed of the vehicle before it stopped?

A 25–35 mi/h   C 29–31 mi/h
B 28–32 mi/h   D 68–70 mi/h

6. A vehicle leaves a skid mark of 100 feet before stopping. What was the approximate speed of the vehicle before it stopped?

F 46–49 mi/h   H 62–64 mi/h
G 50–55 mi/h   J 70–73 mi/h

7. A vehicle leaves a skid mark of 150 feet before stopping. What was the approximate speed of the vehicle before it stopped?

A 50–55 mi/h   C 55–70 mi/h
B 53–58 mi/h   D 56–60 mi/h

8. A vehicle leaves a skid mark of 200 feet before stopping. What was the approximate speed of the vehicle before it stopped?

F 60–63 mi/h   H 72–78 mi/h
G 65–70 mi/h   J 80–90 mi/h

3-7

The Real Numbers
Going Deeper

Essential question: *How can you tell whether a number is rational or irrational?*

COMMON CORE **Standards for Mathematical Content**

CC.8.NS.1 Know that numbers that are not rational are called irrational. Understand informally that every number has a decimal expansion; for rational numbers show that the decimal expansion repeats eventually, and convert a decimal expansion which repeats eventually into a rational number.

Vocabulary

irrational number

real numbers

Prerequisites

Rational numbers

Integers

Decimals

Math Background

A rational number can be stated in the form a/b where a is an integer and b is any nonzero integer. When rational numbers are expressed as decimals, the digits either terminate ($\frac{1}{2} = 0.5$) or repeat ($\frac{1}{3} = 0.333...$). An irrational number like π cannot be expressed as a ratio of integers, and as a decimal π is non-terminating and non-repeating.

INTRODUCE

Have students suggest names that describe sets of numbers such as even, odd, positive, negative, prime, and square numbers (1, 4, 9, 16, 25, ...). You may want to point out that you are not presenting any new numbers in this lesson—students have worked with an irrational number in *pi*—but they are learning how each set of numbers is related.

TEACH

1 EXAMPLE

Questioning Strategies

• What name would change if you replace 3 with −3? **Only the classification negative integer would change to whole number and natural number.**

• Can a number belong to more than one set? **Yes, a number can belong to more than one number set; for example, 0.3 is both real and rational.**

Differentiated Instruction

Discuss the non-mathematical meaning of *irrational* as thinking, talking, or acting *without* reason, mental clarity, or sound judgment. Explain that the prefix *ir-* means "not" for words starting with *r*. Ask for examples of words that use this prefix, such as irregular, irrelevant, irresponsible, irreligious, etc. Conclude by stating the mathematical meaning of irrational means *not* rational.

CLOSE

Essential Question

How can you tell whether a number is rational or irrational? **Possible answer: A rational number is any number that can be written as a ratio of integers, where the divisor is not zero, while an irrational number is a decimal that neither terminates nor repeats.**

Summarize

Have students make their own Venn diagram to reinforce how the number sets are related. Students can include examples for each number type.

PRACTICE

Where skills are taught	Where skills are practiced
1 EXAMPLE	EXS. 1–14

Name_____ Class_____ Date_____

3-7

video tutor

The Real Numbers
Going Deeper

Essential question: *How can you tell whether a number is rational or irrational?*

Recall that a *rational number* is any number that can be expressed as the quotient of two integers where the divisor is not zero. All rational numbers can be written as fractions or as decimals that either terminate or repeat, such as −1.5 and 9.106106106....

An **irrational number** can only be written as a decimal that neither terminates nor repeats. If a whole number is not a perfect square, then its square root is an irrational number.

All rational and irrational numbers together make up the set of **real numbers**.

CC.8.NS.1

1 EXAMPLE Classifying Real Numbers

Write all names that apply to the number −3.

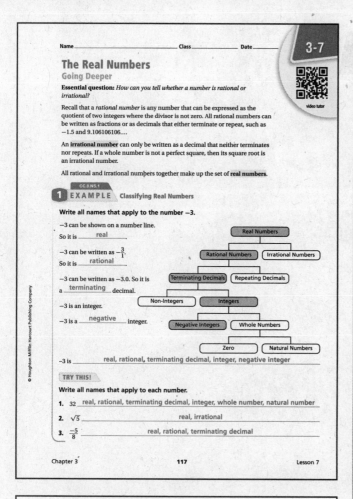

−3 can be shown on a number line.
So it is ____real____.

−3 can be written as $-\frac{3}{1}$.
So it is ___rational___.

−3 can be written as −3.0. So it is a ___terminating___ decimal.

−3 is an integer.

−3 is a ___negative___ integer.

−3 is ___real, rational, terminating decimal, integer, negative integer___

TRY THIS!

Write all names that apply to each number.

1. 32 ___real, rational, terminating decimal, integer, whole number, natural number___

2. $\sqrt{5}$ ___real, irrational___

3. $-\frac{5}{8}$ ___real, rational, terminating decimal___

Chapter 3   **117**   Lesson 7

PRACTICE

Write all names that apply to each number.

1. 41 ___real, rational, terminating decimal, integer, whole number, natural number___

2. 9.020020002... ___real, irrational___

3. −12 ___real, rational, terminating decimal, integer, negative integer___

4. $\sqrt{25}$ ___real, rational, terminating decimal, integer, whole number, natural number___

Is the statement *true* or *false*? Give a reason or an example to support your answer.

5. All rational numbers are real numbers.
   ___true; definition of real numbers___

6. All integers are real numbers.
   ___true; all integers are rational numbers___

7. All irrational numbers are real numbers.
   ___true; definition of real numbers___

8. All real numbers are integers.
   ___false; $\frac{2}{3}$ is not an integer___

9. The fraction $\frac{22}{7}$ is often used to approximate the irrational number π. So, $\frac{22}{7}$ is also an irrational number.
   ___false; it is rational because it can be expressed as the quotient of two integers___

10. All negative numbers are rational numbers.
    ___false; −7.616616661... is an irrational number___

Write *sometimes true, always true,* or *never true*. Give a reason or an example to support your answer.

11. Whole numbers are rational numbers.
    ___always true; each can be written as a fraction or terminating decimal___

12. Terminating decimals are irrational numbers.
    ___never true; every irrational number is non-terminating and non-repeating___

13. Negative numbers are integers.
    ___sometimes true; −4 is an integer, while −2.5 is not___

14. **Error Analysis** Derek says that the number 4.05005005... is a rational number because it has a pattern. What do you think?
    ___He is wrong; there is a pattern, but it is neither a terminating nor a repeating___
    ___pattern. The number is irrational.___

Chapter 3   **118**   Lesson 7

Assign these pages to help your students practice and apply important lesson concepts. For additional exercises, see the Student Edition.

Answers

Additional Practice

1. rational; real
2. irrational; real
3. natural; whole; integer; rational; real
4. irrational; real
5. integer; rational; real
6. rational; real
7. irrational
8. not real
9. not real
10. rational
11. rational
12. rational
13. irrational
14. rational
15. sample answer: $7\frac{7}{10}$
16. sample answer: 6.48
17. sample answer: $\frac{22}{25}$
18. sample answer: 0
19. sample answer: $-\sqrt{\frac{22}{7}}$
20. sample answer: $\frac{2}{0}$

Problem Solving

1. Possible answer: $\sqrt{31}$
2. Possible answer: $\frac{31}{10}$
3. Possible answer: $\frac{5}{2}$
4. Possible answer: $\sqrt{43}$
5. B
6. H
7. D
8. G

3-7

Name_____ Class_____ Date_____

Additional Practice

Write all names that apply to each number.

1. $-\dfrac{7}{8}$

2. $\sqrt{0.15}$

3. $\sqrt{\dfrac{18}{2}}$

_____ _____ _____

4. $\sqrt{45}$

5. -25

6. -6.75

_____ _____ _____

State if the number is rational, irrational, or not a real number.

7. $\sqrt{14}$

8. $\sqrt{-16}$

9. $\dfrac{6.2}{0}$

10. $\sqrt{49}$

_____ _____ _____ _____

11. $\dfrac{7}{20}$

12. $-\sqrt{81}$

13. $\sqrt{\dfrac{7}{9}}$

14. -1.3

_____ _____ _____ _____

Find a real number between each pair of numbers.

15. $7\dfrac{3}{5}$ and $7\dfrac{4}{5}$

16. 6.45 and $\dfrac{13}{2}$

17. $\dfrac{7}{8}$ and $\dfrac{9}{10}$

_____ _____ _____

18. Give an example of a rational number between $-\sqrt{4}$ and $\sqrt{4}$

_____

19. Give an example of an irrational number less than 0.

_____

20. Give an example of a number that is not real.

_____

Problem Solving

Write the correct answer.

1. Twin primes are prime numbers that differ by 2. Find an irrational number between twin primes 5 and 7.

_____

2. Rounded to the nearest ten-thousandth, $\pi = 3.1416$. Find a rational number between 3 and π.

_____

3. One famous irrational number is e. Rounded to the nearest ten-thousandth e is 2.7183. Find a rational number that is between 2 and e.

_____

4. Perfect numbers are those for which the divisors of the number sum to the number itself. The number 6 is a perfect number because $1 + 2 + 3 = 6$. The number 28 is also a perfect number. Find an irrational number between 6 and 28.

_____

Choose the letter for the best answer.

5. Which is a rational number?

A the length of a side of a square with area 2 cm²

B the length of a side of a square with area 4 cm²

C a non-terminating decimal

D the square root of a prime number

6. Which is an irrational number?

F a number that can be expressed as a fraction

G the length of a side of a square with area 4 cm²

H the length of a side of a square with area 2 cm²

J the square root of a negative number

7. Which is an integer?

A the number half-way between 6 and 7

B the average rainfall for the week if it rained 0.5 in., 2.3 in., 0 in., 0 in., 0 in., 0.2 in., 0.75 in. during the week

C the money in an account if the balance was $213.00 and $21.87 was deposited

D the net yardage after plays that resulted in a 15 yard loss, 10 yard gain, 6 yard gain and 5 yard loss

8. Which is a whole number?

F the number half-way between 6 and 7

G the total amount of sugar in a recipe that calls for $\dfrac{1}{4}$ cup of brown sugar and $\dfrac{3}{4}$ cup of granulated sugar

H the money in an account if the balance was $213.00 and $21.87 was deposited

J the net yardage after plays that resulted in a 15 yard loss, 10 yard gain, 6 yard gain and 5 yard loss

The Pythagorean Theorem
Extension: In Three Dimensions

Essential question: *How can you use the Pythagorean Theorem to solve problems?*

Standards for Mathematical Content

CC.8.G.7 Apply the Pythagorean Theorem to determine unknown side lengths in right triangles in real-world and mathematical problems in two and three dimensions.

CC.8.G.8 Apply the Pythagorean Theorem to find the distance between two points in a coordinate system.

Vocabulary

legs

hypotenuse

Prerequisites

Properties of right triangles

Simplifying square roots

Math Background

The Pythagorean Theorem states that in a right triangle with legs a and b and hypotenuse c, the relationship between side lengths is:

$$a^2 + b^2 = c^2$$

Using the Pythagorean Theorem, you can find the length of any side of a right triangle when given the length of the two other sides. Students will substitute values in the Pythagorean Theorem and solve for the unknown length. The relationship can also be rewritten as follows:

$$c = \sqrt{a^2 + b^2} \quad \text{or} \quad b = \sqrt{c^2 - a^2} \quad \text{or} \quad a = \sqrt{c^2 - b^2}$$

INTRODUCE

Review with students the properties of a right triangle, including the Pythagorean Theorem. Allow students to practice using the Pythagorean Theorem with lengths of a right triangle to practice working with square roots. Tell students that in this lesson, they will use this relationship between sides of a right triangle to solve real-world problems.

TEACH

1 EXAMPLE

Questioning Strategies

- In part A, which side length is missing? **hypotenuse**

- What do you know about the length of the hypotenuse in comparison with the lengths of the legs? **The hypotenuse is the longest side.**

- In part B, which side length is missing? **longer leg**

Teaching Strategies

Point out to students that in part A, before taking the square root of both sides, the variable c is already alone on one side of the equation. However in part B, they will need to subtract one of the terms from both sides to get the variable alone on one side of the equation before using square roots.

2 EXAMPLE

Questioning Strategies

- How is 1 unit represented on the coordinate grid? **The side length of one square grid on the coordinate grid represents 1 unit.**

- How can you estimate $\sqrt{34}$? **Find the closest perfect squares greater than and less than 34, and write the inequality $\sqrt{25} < \sqrt{34} < \sqrt{36}$. Now you can estimate $\sqrt{34}$ to be between 5 and 6, and closer to 6.**

Technology

Have students practice estimating square roots and checking their estimates with a calculator. You might want to let students play a contest-style game to see who can estimate square roots to the nearest tenth the most accurately and most often, checking with a calculator.

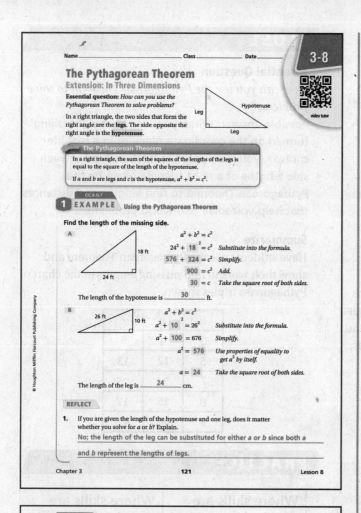

Name_____ Class_____ Date_____

3-8

video tutor

The Pythagorean Theorem

Extension: In Three Dimensions

Essential question: *How can you use the Pythagorean Theorem to solve problems?*

In a right triangle, the two sides that form the right angle are the **legs**. The side opposite the right angle is the **hypotenuse**.

Leg — Hypotenuse — Leg

> **The Pythagorean Theorem**
>
> In a right triangle, the sum of the squares of the lengths of the legs is equal to the square of the length of the hypotenuse.
>
> If a and b are legs and c is the hypotenuse, $a^2 + b^2 = c^2$.

CC.8.G.7
1 EXAMPLE Using the Pythagorean Theorem

Find the length of the missing side.

A

18 ft, 24 ft

$$a^2 + b^2 = c^2$$
$$24^2 + 18^2 = c^2 \quad \textit{Substitute into the formula.}$$
$$576 + 324 = c^2 \quad \textit{Simplify.}$$
$$900 = c^2 \quad \textit{Add.}$$
$$30 = c \quad \textit{Take the square root of both sides.}$$

The length of the hypotenuse is ___30___ ft.

B

26 ft, 10 ft

$$a^2 + b^2 = c^2$$
$$a^2 + 10^2 = 26^2 \quad \textit{Substitute into the formula.}$$
$$a^2 + 100 = 676 \quad \textit{Simplify.}$$
$$a^2 = 576 \quad \textit{Use properties of equality to get } a^2 \textit{ by itself.}$$
$$a = 24 \quad \textit{Take the square root of both sides.}$$

The length of the leg is ___24___ cm.

REFLECT

1. If you are given the length of the hypotenuse and one leg, does it matter whether you solve for a or b? Explain.

   No; the length of the leg can be substituted for either a or b since both a

   and b represent the lengths of legs.

Chapter 3   121   Lesson 8

© Houghton Mifflin Harcourt Publishing Company

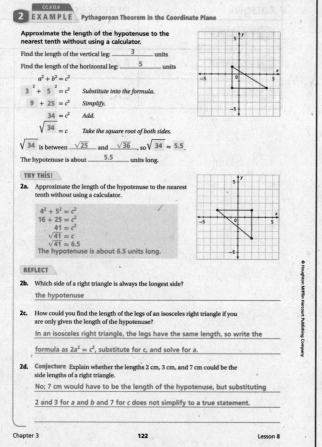

CC.8.G.8
2 EXAMPLE Pythagorean Theorem in the Coordinate Plane

Approximate the length of the hypotenuse to the nearest tenth without using a calculator.

Find the length of the vertical leg: ___3___ units

Find the length of the horizontal leg: ___5___ units

$$a^2 + b^2 = c^2$$
$$3^2 + 5^2 = c^2 \quad \textit{Substitute into the formula.}$$
$$9 + 25 = c^2 \quad \textit{Simplify.}$$
$$34 = c^2 \quad \textit{Add.}$$
$$\sqrt{34} = c \quad \textit{Take the square root of both sides.}$$

$\sqrt{34}$ is between ___$\sqrt{25}$___ and ___$\sqrt{36}$___, so $\sqrt{34} \approx 5.5$.

The hypotenuse is about ___5.5___ units long.

TRY THIS!

2a. Approximate the length of the hypotenuse to the nearest tenth without using a calculator.

$$4^2 + 5^2 = c^2$$
$$16 + 25 = c^2$$
$$41 = c^2$$
$$\sqrt{41} = c$$
$$\sqrt{41} \approx 6.5$$
The hypotenuse is about 6.5 units long.

REFLECT

2b. Which side of a right triangle is always the longest side?

   the hypotenuse

2c. How could you find the length of the legs of an isosceles right triangle if you are only given the length of the hypotenuse?

   In an isosceles right triangle, the legs have the same length, so write the

   formula as $2a^2 = c^2$, substitute for c, and solve for a.

2d. **Conjecture** Explain whether the lengths 2 cm, 3 cm, and 7 cm could be the side lengths of a right triangle.

   No; 7 cm would have to be the length of the hypotenuse, but substituting

   2 and 3 for a and b and 7 for c does not simplify to a true statement.

Chapter 3   122   Lesson 8

© Houghton Mifflin Harcourt Publishing Company

Questioning Strategies

- How do you find the diagonal length along the bottom of the box? **Use the length and width of the bottom rectangle as the lengths of the legs, and the diagonal as the hypotenuse.**

- How can you find the diagonal length from a bottom corner to the opposite top corner? **Use the diagonal length along the bottom box as the length of the longer leg and the height as the other leg.**

Teaching Strategies

Have students practice identifying the legs and hypotenuse of a right triangle in various positions in different settings. You may include right triangles in a variety of orientations drawn on the board and right triangles found in three-dimensional figures, such as prisms.

MATHEMATICAL PRACTICE — Highlighting the Standards

This example is an opportunity to address Standard 2 (Reason abstractly and quantitatively). Students must reason abstractly to identify right triangles in three-dimensional figures in a real-world setting, such as in a box. Students reason quantitatively when they apply the Pythagorean Theorem and solve equations to find lengths within a box in order to answer real-world questions.

CLOSE

Essential Question

How can you use the Pythagorean Theorem to solve problems?

Possible answer: When you identify a right triangle formed on the coordinate plane or in a real-life context, you can apply the relationship between side lengths of a right triangle given by the Pythagorean Theorem to find lengths and distances that help you solve real-world problems.

Summarize

Have students use the Pythagorean Theorem and show their work to find missing lengths in the chart of Pythagorean triples shown.

a	b	c
3	4	5
5	12	13
7	24	25
8	15	17
9	40	41

PRACTICE

Where skills are taught	Where skills are practiced
1 EXAMPLE	EXS. 1–2
2 EXAMPLE	EXS. 3–6
3 EXAMPLE	EX. 7

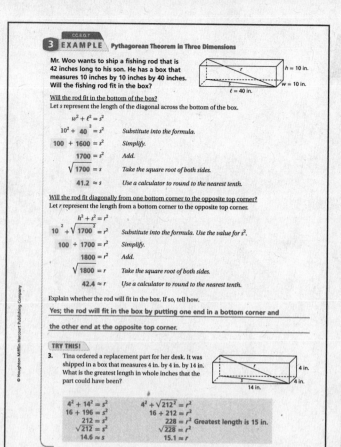

3 EXAMPLE CC.8.G.7 **Pythagorean Theorem in Three Dimensions**

Mr. Woo wants to ship a fishing rod that is 42 inches long to his son. He has a box that measures 10 inches by 10 inches by 40 inches. Will the fishing rod fit in the box?

$h = 10$ in.
$w = 10$ in.
$\ell = 40$ in.

Will the rod fit in the bottom of the box?
Let s represent the length of the diagonal across the bottom of the box.

$$w^2 + \ell^2 = s^2$$
$10^2 + 40^2 = s^2$ Substitute into the formula.
$100 + 1600 = s^2$ Simplify.
$1700 = s^2$ Add.
$\sqrt{1700} = s$ Take the square root of both sides.
$41.2 \approx s$ Use a calculator to round to the nearest tenth.

Will the rod fit diagonally from one bottom corner to the opposite top corner?
Let r represent the length from a bottom corner to the opposite top corner.

$$h^2 + s^2 = r^2$$
$10^2 + \sqrt{1700}^2 = r^2$ Substitute into the formula. Use the value for s^2.
$100 + 1700 = r^2$ Simplify.
$1800 = r^2$ Add.
$\sqrt{1800} = r$ Take the square root of both sides.
$42.4 \approx r$ Use a calculator to round to the nearest tenth.

Explain whether the rod will fit in the box. If so, tell how.

Yes; the rod will fit in the box by putting one end in a bottom corner and
the other end at the opposite top corner.

TRY THIS!

3. Tina ordered a replacement part for her desk. It was shipped in a box that measures 4 in. by 4 in. by 14 in. What is the greatest length in whole inches that the part could have been?

r
4 in.
14 in.
4 in.

$4^2 + 14^2 = s^2$ $4^2 + \sqrt{212}^2 = r^2$
$16 + 196 = s^2$ $16 + 212 = r^2$
$212 = s^2$ $228 = r^2$ Greatest length is 15 in.
$\sqrt{212} = s^2$ $\sqrt{228} = r^2$
$14.6 \approx s$ $15.1 \approx r$

Chapter 3   123   Lesson 8

PRACTICE

Find the length of the missing side. Approximate square roots of non-perfect squares to the nearest tenth without using a calculator.

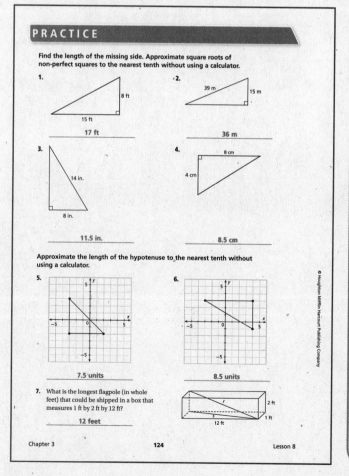

1.
8 ft
15 ft

_17 ft_

2.
39 m   15 m

_36 m_

3.
14 in.
8 in.

_11.5 in._

4.
8 cm
4 cm

_8.5 cm_

Approximate the length of the hypotenuse to the nearest tenth without using a calculator.

5.

7.5 units

6.

8.5 units

7. What is the longest flagpole (in whole feet) that could be shipped in a box that measures 1 ft by 2 ft by 12 ft?

12 feet

r
2 ft
12 ft
1 ft

Chapter 3   124   Lesson 8

Assign these pages to help your students practice and apply important lesson concepts. For additional exercises, see the Student Edition.

Answers

Additional Practice

1. 13
2. 10.5
3. 51
4. 13.4
5. 20
6. 18.2
7. 17 mi
8. 8.5

Problem Solving

1. 20.9 m
2. 11.7 ft
3. 127.3 ft
4. 128.2 yd
5. C
6. H
7. A
8. G

Name_____ Class_____ Date_____ **3-8**

Additional Practice

Find the length of the missing side. Round your answers to the nearest tenth if neccessary.

1. c / 12, B 5 C, A

2. 8.4, c, C 6.3 B, A

3. c / 45, A 24 C, B

4. 18, a, A 12 C, B

5. b, 29, A, 21 B

6. A b C, 23, 14, B

7. A glider flies 8 miles south from the airport and then 15 miles east. Then it flies in a straight line back to the airport. What was the distance of the glider's last leg back to the airport?

_____

8. Approximate the length of the hypotenuse to the nearest tenth without using a calculator.

_____

Problem Solving

Write the correct answer. Round to the nearest tenth.

1. A utility pole 10 m high is supported by two guy wires. Each guy wire is anchored 3 m from the base of the pole. How many meters of wire are needed for the guy wires?

2. A 12 foot-ladder is resting against a wall. The base of the ladder is 2.5 feet from the base of the wall. How high up the wall will the ladder reach?

3. The base-path of a baseball diamond forms a square. If it is 90 ft from home to first, how far does the catcher have to throw to catch someone stealing second base?

4. A football field is 100 yards with 10 yards at each end for the end zones. The field is 45 yards wide. Find the length of the diagonal of the entire field, including the end zones.

Choose the letter for the best answer.

5. The frame of a kite is made from two strips of wood, one 27 inches long, and one 18 inches long. What must the perimeter of the kite be? Round to the nearest tenth.

A 18.8 in.   C 65.7 in.
B 32.8 in.   D 131.2 in.

6. The glass for a picture window is 8 feet wide. The door it must pass through is 3 feet wide. How tall must the door be for the glass to pass through the door? Round to the nearest tenth.

F 3.3 ft   H 7.4 ft
G 6.7 ft   J 8.5 ft

7. A television screen measures approximately 15.5 in. high and 19.5 in. wide. A television is advertised by giving the approximate length of the diagonal of its screen. How should this television be advertised?

A 25 in.   C 12 in.
B 21 in.   D 6 in.

8. To meet federal guidelines, a wheelchair ramp that is constructed to rise 1 foot off the ground must extend 12 feet along the ground. How long will the ramp be? Round to the nearest tenth.

F 11.9 ft   H 13.2 ft
G 12.0 ft   J 15.0 ft

Applying the Pythagorean Theorem and Its Converse
Modeling

Essential question: How can you prove the Pythagorean Theorem and its converse?

© Houghton Mifflin Harcourt Publishing Company

Standards for Mathematical Content

CC.8.G.6 Explain a proof of the Pythagorean Theorem and its converse.

Prerequisites
Pythagorean Theorem

Math Background
The proof of the Pythagorean Theorem in this lesson is a hands-on approach and does not require knowledge of algebra. You can also use algebra to prove the Pythagorean Theorem as follows:

The area of the large square is $(a + b)^2$. The area of each triangle is $\frac{1}{2}ab$.

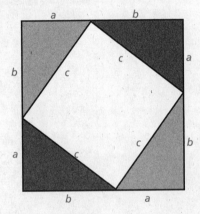

To find the area of the inner square, subtract the area of the four triangles from the area of the larger square:

$$(a + b)^2 - 4\left(\frac{1}{2}ab\right)$$
$$= a^2 + 2ab + b^2 - 2ab$$
$$= a^2 + b^2$$

Therefore, $c^2 = a^2 + b^2$.

INTRODUCE

In this lesson, you will develop a proof of the Pythagorean Theorem, which states: "If a triangle is a right triangle, then $a^2 + b^2 = c^2$." You will also consider the converse of the Pythagorean Theorem, which states "If $a^2 + b^2 = c^2$, then the triangle is a right triangle," and determine whether the converse is true.

TEACH

1 EXPLORE

Questioning Strategies
- What variable is used for the side lengths of the inner square? Why? *c*; because the sides of the inner square form the hypotenuses of the right triangles.

2 EXPLORE

Questioning Strategies
- Although you may be convinced that the converse is true, have you proved it? Explain. No, because we did not try all possibilities nor prove that it must be true for all possibilities.
- A mathematical proof shows that a statement is true for all cases without any exceptions. Do you think your experiment with grid paper is a proof of the converse of the Pythagorean Theorem? Explain. Students should note that they have only shown that a few cases are true and have not proven that there are no exceptions.

MATHEMATICAL PRACTICE — **Highlighting the Standards**

This Explore is an opportunity to address Standard 3 (Construct viable arguments and critique the reasoning of others). Students are constructing a proof, and they discuss which conclusions are valid and which are not.

CLOSE

Essential Question
How can you prove the Pythagorean Theorem and its converse?
By using area formulas, you can prove the Pythagorean Theorem. You can also see that the converse is true by testing values for *a*, *b*, and *c* that satisfy $a^2 + b^2 = c^2$.

Applying the Pythagorean Theorem and Its Converse
Modeling

Essential question: *How can you prove the Pythagorean Theorem and its converse?*

3-9

video tutor

1 EXPLORE   Using Area to Prove the Pythagorean Theorem

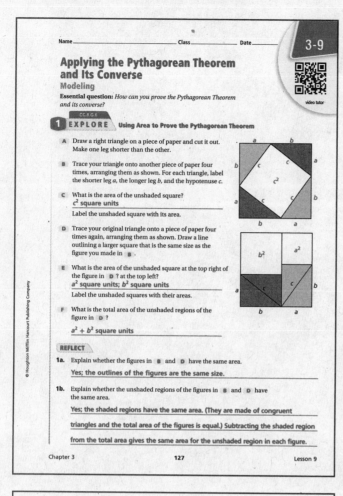

A Draw a right triangle on a piece of paper and cut it out. Make one leg shorter than the other.

B Trace your triangle onto another piece of paper four times, arranging them as shown. For each triangle, label the shorter leg *a*, the longer leg *b*, and the hypotenuse *c*.

C What is the area of the unshaded square?

c^2 square units

Label the unshaded square with its area.

D Trace your original triangle onto a piece of paper four times again, arranging them as shown. Draw a line outlining a larger square that is the same size as the figure you made in **B** .

E What is the area of the unshaded square at the top right of the figure in **D** ? at the top left?

a^2 square units; b^2 square units

Label the unshaded squares with their areas.

F What is the total area of the unshaded regions of the figure in **D** ?

$a^2 + b^2$ square units

REFLECT

1a. Explain whether the figures in **B** and **D** have the same area.

Yes; the outlines of the figures are the same size.

1b. Explain whether the unshaded regions of the figures in **B** and **D** have the same area.

Yes; the shaded regions have the same area. (They are made of congruent triangles and the total area of the figures is equal.) Subtracting the shaded region from the total area gives the same area for the unshaded region in each figure.

1c. Write an equation relating the area of the unshaded region in step B to the unshaded region in **D** .

$a^2 + b^2 = c^2$

The Pythagorean Theorem says "If a triangle is a right triangle, then $a^2 + b^2 = c^2$."

The *converse* of the Pythagorean Theorem says "If $a^2 + b^2 = c^2$, then the triangle is a right triangle."

2 EXPLORE   Testing the Converse of the Pythagorean Theorem

Decide whether the converse of the Pythagorean Theorem is true.

A Verify that the following sets of lengths make the equation $a^2 + b^2 = c^2$ true. Record your results in the table.

a	b	c	Is $a^2 + b^2 = c^2$ true?	Makes a right triangle?
3	4	5	yes	yes
5	12	13	yes	yes
7	24	25	yes	yes
8	15	17	yes	yes
20	21	29	yes	yes

B For each set of lengths in the table, cut strips of grid paper with a width of one square and lengths that correspond to the values of *a*, *b*, and *c*.

C For each set of lengths, use the strips of grid paper to try to form a right triangle. An example using the first set of lengths is shown here. Record your findings in the table.

REFLECT

2. Based on your observations, explain whether you think the converse of the Pythagorean Theorem is true.

Students should note that each set of lengths satisfies the equation $a^2 + b^2 = c^2$

and should have successfully made a right triangle with the strips of grid paper.

They should conclude that the converse of the Pythagorean Theorem is true.

Assign these pages to help your students practice and apply important lesson concepts. For additional exercises, see the Student Edition.

Answers

Additional Practice

1. yes
2. no
3. yes
4. no
5. no
6. yes
7. no
8. yes
9. 16.6 units
10. yes; $22.5^2 + 54^2 = 58.5^2$
11. yes; $6^2 + 8^2 = 10^2$

Problem Solving

1. yes; $1.2^2 + 1.6^2 = 2^2$
2. 8.1 m
3. 20.1 units
4. 13 ft
5. C
6. J
7. B
8. F

Name_____ Class_____ Date_____ | 3-9

Additional Practice

Tell whether the given side lengths form a right triangle.

1. 7, 24, 25 _____

2. 30, 40, 45 _____

3. 21.6, 28.8, 36 _____

4. 10, 15, 18 _____

5. 10.5, 36, 50 _____

6. 2.5, 6, 6.5 _____

7. 50, 64, 80 _____

8. 1.2, 1.6, 2 _____

9. A map is placed on a coordinate grid. Cincinnati is located at (5, 4) and San Diego is located at (−10, −3). How far apart is Cincinnati from San Diego on the map? Round your answer to the nearest tenth.

_____

10. Katie, Ralph, and Juan are tossing a football. Katie is 22.5 feet away from Ralph. Ralph is 58.5 feet away from Juan. Juan is 54 feet away from Katie. Do the distances between Katie, Ralph, and Juan form a right triangle? Explain.

_____

11. A rectangular picture frame has dimensions 6 inches by 8 inches. The diagonal of the frame is 10 inches. Do the sides of the frame meet at a right angle? Explain.

_____

© Houghton Mifflin Harcourt Publishing Company

Problem Solving

Solve each problem.

1. Linda made triangular flags for the spirit club to wave. The sides of each flag were 1.2 feet, 1.6 feet, and 2 feet. Are the flags that Linda made in the shape of a right triangle? Explain.

_____

2. A wheelchair ramp starts 8 meters from the base of a staircase. The staircase is 1 meter high. What is the length of the wheelchair ramp? Round to the nearest tenth of a meter.

_____

3. The city of Chicago is located at (4, 8) on a grid. The city of Memphis is located at (6, −12) on the grid. How many units apart are Chicago and Memphis on the grid? Round to the nearest tenth of a unit.

_____

4. Tony needs to use a ladder to get onto the roof. The height of the house is about 11 feet. The ladder will be placed 6 feet from the house. What is the minimum height, to the nearest foot, that the ladder can be to safely reach the roof of the house?

_____

Solve each problem.

5. An airplane is 33 miles due south and 56 miles due west of its destination airport. How far is the plane from the destination airport?

   A 9.4 miles   C 65 miles

   B 89 miles   D 4,225 miles

6. The location of a post office is marked at (2, 2) on a coordinate grid. Which point is about 18 units from the location of the post office?

   F L(−12, 9)   H M(12, 9)

   G N(12, −9)   J P(−12, −9)

7. A rectangular tabletop has a length of 3.3 feet and a width of 8.8 feet. Which is the length of its diagonal to the nearest tenth?

   A 88.33 feet   C 29.04 feet

   B 9.4 feet   D 3.5 feet

8. The location of three ships are shown on a coordinate grid by the following points: X(0, 7), Y(−5, −3), and Z(4, −1). Which ships are farthest apart?

   F X and Y   H X and Z

   G Y and Z   J Z and Y

© Houghton Mifflin Harcourt Publishing Company

© Houghton Mifflin Harcourt Publishing Company

COMMON CORE **Standards for Mathematical Content**

CC.8.EE.1 Know and apply the properties of integer exponents to generate equivalent numerical expressions.

CC.8.EE.3 Use numbers expressed in the form of a single-digit times an integer power of 10 to estimate very large or very small quantities and to express how many times as much one is than the other.

CC.8.EE.4 Perform operations with numbers expressed in scientific notation, including problems where both the decimal and scientific notation are used...

Materials
Scientific calculators

INTRODUCE

Ask students: Can you estimate the world's population and express it in scientific notation? Do you think all of the Earth's population could live on the moon? Explain to students that this project will help them answer these questions by comparing the world's population to the population that could live on the moon.

TEACH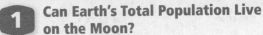

1 Can Earth's Total Population Live on the Moon?

Questioning Strategies

- Why do you need to convert the continents' populations to have the same power of 10? To add the multipliers.

- Is the sum of the multipliers times 10^7 expressed in scientific notation? Explain. No, the sum of multipliers is 903.7901, which is not greater than or equal to 1 and is not less than 10.

Avoid Common Errors

Students might get confused about which direction to move the decimal point when converting the multipliers to go with 10^8. Review with students that if the exponent of 10 is decreasing, then the decimal moves to the right. If the exponent of 10 is increasing, then the decimal moves to the left. Remind students that they can convert back to standard notation to verify their answers.

2 Can the Population of Each Continent Live on the Moon?

Questioning Strategies

- How can you determine if the population of a single continent could live on the moon? Change the continent's population to a multiplier with a power of 9 and compare with the population that can live on the moon.

- How can you compare continent populations with the moon in terms of how many times greater or smaller the population that could live on the moon is? Use division, with the population that could live on the moon as the numerator.

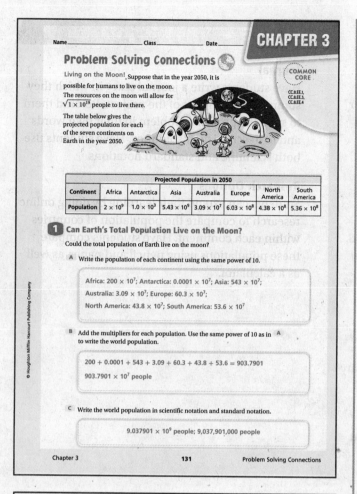

Name_____ Class_____ Date_____

Problem Solving Connections

CHAPTER 3

Living on the Moon! Suppose that in the year 2050, it is possible for humans to live on the moon. The resources on the moon will allow for $\sqrt{1 \times 10^{19}}$ people to live there.

The table below gives the projected population for each of the seven continents on Earth in the year 2050.

COMMON CORE
CC.8.EE.1,
CC.8.EE.3,
CC.8.EE.4

Projected Population in 2050							
Continent	Africa	Antarctica	Asia	Australia	Europe	North America	South America
Population	2×10^9	1.0×10^3	5.43×10^9	3.09×10^7	6.03×10^8	4.38×10^8	5.36×10^8

1 Can Earth's Total Population Live on the Moon?

Could the total population of Earth live on the moon?

A Write the population of each continent using the same power of 10.

> Africa: 200×10^7; Antarctica: 0.0001×10^7; Asia: 543×10^7;
> Australia: 3.09×10^7; Europe: 60.3×10^7;
> North America: 43.8×10^7; South America: 53.6×10^7

B Add the multipliers for each population. Use the same power of 10 as in **A** to write the world population.

> $200 + 0.0001 + 543 + 3.09 + 60.3 + 43.8 + 53.6 = 903.7901$
> 903.7901×10^7 people

C Write the world population in scientific notation and standard notation.

> 9.037901×10^9 people; $9,037,901,000$ people

D Find the number of people who could live on the moon. Use a calculator to find $\sqrt{1 \times 10^{19}}$. Write your answer in standard notation and scientific notation.

> $3,162,277,660$ people; 3.162277660×10^9 people

E Can the total population of Earth live on the moon? Use your answers from **C** and **D** to perform a calculation and explain how the result justifies your answer.

> The total population of Earth cannot live on the moon.
>
> Sample calculations:
>
> By subtraction: $9.037901 \times 10^9 - 3.162277660 \times 10^9 = 5.875623340 \times 10^9$;
> There are approximately 6 billion more people on Earth than can live on the moon.
>
> By division: $\dfrac{9.037901 \times 10^9}{3.162277660 \times 10^9} \approx 2.86$; There are about 3 times as many people on Earth than can live on the moon.

2 Can the Population of Each Continent Live on the Moon?

The projected population of Antarctica is 1.0×10^3 people. That's just 1000 people on the continent. By comparing this population to the possible population of the moon, you can determine that the entire population of Antarctica could live on the moon. Could the entire population of each of the other continents live on the moon?

A Use subtraction with numbers in scientific notation to compare the populations of Africa, Asia, and Australia to the possible population of the moon. Explain whether the entire population of each these continents could live on the moon.

Africa:

> $3.162277660 \times 10^9 - 2 \times 10^9 = 1.162277660 \times 10^9$; yes, the population of Africa is less than the possible moon population.

Asia:

> $3.162277660 \times 10^9 - 5.43 \times 10^9 = -2.267722340 \times 10^9$; no, the population of Asia is greater than the possible moon population.

Teaching Strategies

Students may have difficulty knowing when to compare with subtraction and when to compare with division. Remind students to look for the words "how much greater" or "how much smaller" to indicate subtraction, and to look for the words "how many times as..." to indicate division.

What is the Population Density on the Moon?

Questioning Strategies

- What does population density measure? **The average number of people per area unit of land, such as 500 people per square mile. It tells how densely populated a place is.**

- What assumption is made when you use only land area rather than total area to find the population density of Earth? **It assumes that people do not live in the ocean.**

- How can you explain why the population density of Earth is less than the population density of most major cities? **Population density is an average, and Earth has many land areas that are not heavily populated as well as many land areas that are. Most major cities do not have much land area that is not heavily populated.**

Technology

You may wish to allow students to use calculators to find and compare population densities. Comparing population densities of nearby communities, cities, and states is good practice and can be motivating for students.

CLOSE

Journal

Have students write a journal entry in which they summarize each part of the project. Remind them to state the project's problem in their own words and to describe their solutions. Have students use both scientific and standard notations.

Research Options

Students can extend their learning by doing online research to compare the population of countries within each continent. Have students compare these populations using pencil and paper, as well as a calculator.

Australia:

$3.162277660 \times 10^9 - 0.0309 \times 10^9 = 3.131377660 \times 10^9$; yes, the population of Australia is less than the possible moon population.

B   Use division with numbers in scientific notation to compare the populations of Europe, North America, and South America to the possible population of the moon. Explain whether the entire population of each these continents could live on the moon.

Europe:

$\dfrac{3.162277660 \times 10^9}{6.03 \times 10^8} \approx 5.24$; yes, the possible moon population is more than 5 times the population of Europe.

North America:

$\dfrac{3.162277660 \times 10^9}{4.38 \times 10^8} \approx 7.22$; yes, the possible moon population is more than 7 times the population of North America.

South America:

$\dfrac{3.162277660 \times 10^9}{5.36 \times 10^8} \approx 5.9$; yes, the possible moon population is almost 6 times the population of South America.

C   Name the continent(s) for which the entire population could live on the moon.

Africa, Antarctica, Australia, Europe, North America, South America
_____
_____

---

3   What is the Population Density on the Moon?

Population density is a measure of the number of people per a given area. For example, the population density of Boston, Massachusettes, is about 5,000 people per square kilometer.

The land surface area of Earth is 1.4894×10^8 square kilometers. The surface area of the moon is 3.793×10^7 square kilometers. Assume that humans are able to colonize the entire surface area of the moon. If $\sqrt{1 \times 10^{19}}$ people lived on the moon, would the population density be greater on Earth or on the moon?

A   Find the average population density of Earth by dividing the total population of Earth by the land surface area of Earth.

$$\dfrac{9.037901 \times 10^9}{1.4894 \times 10^8} \approx 60.68$$

There are about __61__ people per square kilometer on Earth.

B   Find the average population density of the moon by dividing the possible population of the moon by the surface area of the moon.

$$\dfrac{3.162277660 \times 10^9}{3.793 \times 10^7} \approx 83.37$$

There would be about __83__ people per square kilometer on the moon.

C   Use your answers from   A   and   B   to explain whether Earth or the moon would have a greater population density.

The population density on the moon would be greater.
_____

D   Extension   Make a conjecture about why the population density of a city like Boston is greater than the population density of Earth.

There are many regions of Earth that are not populated, but population

density is an average.
_____
_____
_____

This page provides students with the opportunity to apply concepts from the Common Core in real-world problem situations. There are three different levels of performance tasks:

⭐ **Novice:** These are short word problems that require students to apply the math they have learned in straightforward, real-world situations.

⭐⭐ **Apprentice:** These are more involved problems that guide students step-by-step through more complex tasks. These exercises include more complicated reasoning, writing, and open-ended elements.

⭐⭐⭐ **Expert:** These are open-ended, non-routine problems that, instead of stepping the students through, asks them to choose their own methods for solving and justify their answers and reasoning.

Sample answers

1. 2.275×10^5 bacteria

2. **a.** $\sqrt{200}$ and 8π
   b. $\sqrt{200}, 4^3 \times 2^{-2}, 8\pi, 6^2 - 2^3 + 3^{-1}, 2^3 \times 2^2$

3. Scoring Guide:

Task	Possible points
a	**1 point** for correctly finding the side length to be **8 inches.**
b	**2 points** for correctly finding the area of the paper to be **64 square inches.**
c	**2 points** for correctly finding that **16 ornament boxes will fit in the bottom layer** and **1 point** for a correct explanation, for example: **the quotient of the area of the bottom of the large box and the area of each ornament box is 16.**

Total possible points: 6

Name_____ Class_____ Date_____

CHAPTER 3

Performance Task

★1. Tiny organisms called bacteria can develop a resistance to drugs used to treat them. A scientist has a sample of 3.5×10^5 bacteria, and the scientist estimates that 35% of them are resistant to a certain drug. About how many of the bacteria are *not* resistant to the drug? Write your answer in scientific notation.

★2. Cory is making a poster of common geometric shapes. He draws a square with a side of length $4^3 \times 2^{-2}$ cm, an equilateral triangle with a height of $\sqrt{200}$ cm, a circle with a circumference of 8π cm, a rectangle with length $6^2 - 2^3 + 3^{-1}$ cm, and a parallelogram with base $2^3 \times 2^2$ cm.

   a. Which of these numbers are irrational?

   b. Write the numbers in this problem in order from smallest to largest. Use 3.14 as an approximation of π.

★3. The formula for the volume of a cube is $V = s^3$, where V is the volume and s is the length of each side. Maureen has a cubic box that has a volume of 512 cubic inches.

   a. Find the length of each side of the box.

   b. Maureen wants to line the bottom of the box with paper. How many square inches of paper does she need?

   c. Maureen has small ornament boxes with square bases of area 4 square inches. How many of these boxes can she place on the bottom of the large box? Justify your answer.

★4. From his home, Myles walked his dog north 5 blocks, east 2 blocks, and stopped at a drinking fountain. He then walked north 3 more blocks and east 4 more blocks. It started to rain so he cut through a field and walked straight home.

   a. Draw a diagram of his path.

   b. How many blocks did Myles walk in all? How much longer was his walk before it started to rain than his walk home?

4. Scoring Guide:

Task	Possible points
a	**3 points** for a correct diagram: 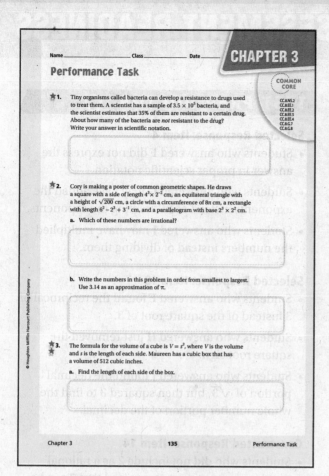
b	**2 points** for correctly calculating that the total distance was 24 blocks and **1 point** for correctly calculating that the walk before the rain started was 4 blocks longer than the walk home.

Total possible points: 6

COMMON CORE CORRELATION

Standard	Items
CC.8.EE.1	1, 2
CC.8.EE.2	7–9, 15
CC.8.EE.3	4, 6
CC.8.EE.4	3, 5
CC.8.NS.1	11, 14
CC.8.NS.2	10, 16, 17
CC.8.G.7	12–13, 18

TEST PREP DOCTOR ⊕

Selected Response: Item 4
- Students who answered **F** did not express the answer in proper scientific notation.
- Students who answered **G** may have added the exponents instead of subtracting the exponents.
- Students who answered **J** may have multiplied the numbers instead of dividing them.

Selected Response: Item 10
- Students who answered **F** found the reciprocal of 3 instead of the square root of 3.
- Students who answered **H** just removed the square root sign.
- Students who answered **J** found the decimal portion of $\sqrt{3}$, but then squared 3 to find the whole number portion of the decimal.

Constructed Response: Item 14
- Students who did not include 2 as a rational number may not have recognized that 2 can be written as the fraction $\frac{2}{1}$.
- Students who did not include $0.\overline{3}$ may not remember that rational numbers include repeating decimals.
- Students who included $\sqrt{11}$ as a rational number may not realize that only the square root of a perfect square is a rational number.

Name _____ Class _____ Date _____

SELECTED RESPONSE

1. An industrial machine creates $4^3 \cdot 4^5$ products every year. How many products does the machine create each year?

A. 4   C. 64

B. 16   (D.) 65,536

2. Simplify the expression:

$(2^2)^4 - \left(\frac{(7-1)^9}{6^2}\right) + (20-17)^3 \times 3^8$

F. $2^6 - 6^{11} + 3^{11}$ (H.) $2^8 - 6^7 + 3^{11}$

G. $4^6 - 6^{11} + 3^5$ J. $8^6 - 36^{11} + 9^{11}$

Use the table for 3 and 4.

Weights of Large Animals			
Animal	African Bush Elephant	Polar Bear	Ostrich
Weight (lb)	27,000	2,000	343.92

3. What is the weight of the ostrich written in scientific notation?

A. 0.34392×10^4 pounds

(B.) 3.4392×10^2 pounds

C. 3.4392×10^3 pounds

D. 34.392×10^4 pounds

4. How many times as great as the weight of the polar bear is the weight of the African bush elephant?

F. 0.135×10^2 pounds

G. 1.35×10^7 pounds

(H.) 1.35×10^1 pounds

J. 5.4×10^7 pounds

5. In 2009, the population of California was estimated as 3.696×10^7 people. The population of Florida was estimated as 1.854×10^7 people. What was the total estimated population for these two states?

(A) 5.550×10^7 people

B. 5.550×10^5 people

C. 1.842×10^7 people

D. 1.842×10^1 people

6. In 2009, the population of the United States was estimated as 3.07×10^8 people. The population of Maryland was estimated as 5.7×10^6 people. About how many times greater is the population of the U.S. than the population of Maryland?

F. 2 times

G. 5 times

(H.) 50 times

J. 200 times

7. A square section of a kitchen floor is made of 49 square tiles. How many tiles are on each side of the square section of the kitchen floor?

A. 4.9 tiles   C. 36 tiles

(B.) 7 tiles   D. 42 tiles

8. A sculpture of a giant cube contains 1331 cubes within it. How many smaller cubes are along each edge of the sculpture?

(F.) 11 cubes   H. 36 cubes

G. 13 cubes   J. 133 cubes

© Houghton Mifflin Harcourt Publishing Company

---

9. Chen is building a birdhouse. The bottom part is a cube with a volume of $\frac{1}{8}$ cubic foot. What is the length of each edge of the cube in feet?

(A) $\frac{1}{2}$ foot   C. $\frac{1}{64}$ foot

B. $\frac{1}{3}$ foot   D. $\frac{1}{512}$ foot

10. Which is approximately equal to $\sqrt{3}$?

F. $\frac{1}{3}$

(G.) 1.732050808...

H. 3.0

J. 9.732050808...

11. Which fraction is equivalent to $0.\overline{15}$?

A. $\frac{1}{15}$ C. $\frac{10}{15}$

(B.) $\frac{15}{99}$ D. $\frac{15}{1}$

12. One of the sails of a sailboat is in the shape of a right triangle. What is the height of the sail?

20 ft

12 ft

(F.) 16 feet   H. 32 feet

G. 23.3 feet   J. 64 feet

13. The table gives the side lengths for four triangles. Which of the triangles is a right triangle?

Triangle	Length of Sides
A	7, 9, 12
B	12, 13, 14
C	10, 23, 25
D	15, 20, 25

A. Triangle A   C. Triangle C

B. Triangle B   (D.) Triangle D

CONSTRUCTED RESPONSE

14. Explain whether each of the following numbers is rational: 2, $\frac{1}{13}$, $\sqrt{11}$, 0.3.

2 and $\frac{1}{13}$ are rational because they can be written as ratios of integers; $\sqrt{11}$ is not rational because it is not the square root of a perfect square; 0.3 is rational because it can be written as the fraction $\frac{3}{10}$.

15. Find a number greater than 1 and less than 1000 that is both a perfect square and a perfect cube. Give the principal square root and the cube root of your number.

Possible answers: 64, 8, 4; 729, 27, 9

16. Explain how you know that $\sqrt{2}$ is less than $2\sqrt{2}$ without performing any calculations.

Since $\sqrt{2}$ is positive, 2 times $\sqrt{2}$ is positive. Multiplying $\sqrt{2}$ by 2 results in a greater number.

17. Explain how you know whether $\sqrt{38}$ is closer to 6 or 7 without using a calculator.

38 is closer to 36 than to 49, so $\sqrt{38}$ is closer to 6 than to 7.

18. A 13-foot-long ladder leans against the side of a building. The bottom of the ladder is 5 feet from the base of the building. What height does the ladder reach?

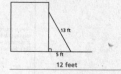

13 ft

5 ft

12 feet

© Houghton Mifflin Harcourt Publishing Company

Ratios, Proportions, and Similarity

COMMON CORE PROFESIONAL DEVELOPMENT **CC.8.G.4**

In Grade 8, the student is introduced to similarity and similar figures. Students understand that similar figures have sides that are proportional and angles with the same measure. Students will describe the sequence of transformations that will construct similar figures. They will also describe the scale factor and recognize that a scale factor greater than one is an enlargement in size and a scale factor less than one is a reduction in size.

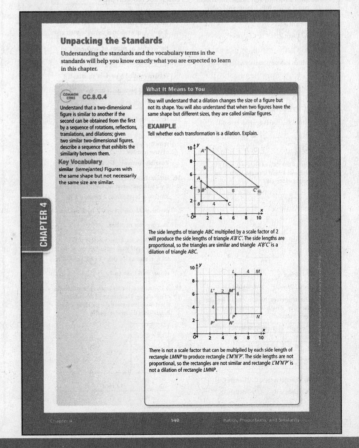

CHAPTER 4

Ratios, Proportions, and Similarity

Chapter Focus

You will find and compare unit rates. You will use tables to identify and describe proportional relationships. Two triangles are similar if their corresponding angles are congruent and the lengths of their corresponding sides are proportional. You will determine if two triangles are similar. Finally, you will use coordinates to describe the results of a dilation.

COMMON CORE

Chapter at a Glance

Lesson	Standards for Mathematical Content
4-1 Ratios, Rates, and Unit Rates	PREP FOR CC.8.EE.5
4-2 Solving Proportions	PREP FOR CC.8.EE.5
4-3 Similar Figures	CC.8.G.5
4-4 Dilations	CC.8.G.3
Problem Solving Connections	
Performance Task	
Assessment Readiness	

Chapter 4   139   Ratios, Proportions, and Similarity

Unpacking the Standards

Understanding the standards and the vocabulary terms in the standards will help you know exactly what you are expected to learn in this chapter.

COMMON CORE **CC.8.G.4**

Understand that a two-dimensional figure is similar to another if the second can be obtained from the first by a sequence of rotations, reflections, translations, and dilations; given two similar two-dimensional figures, describe a sequence that exhibits the similarity between them.

Key Vocabulary
similar *(semejantes)* Figures with the same shape but not necessarily the same size are similar.

What It Means to You

You will understand that a dilation changes the size of a figure but not its shape. You will also understand that when two figures have the same shape but different sizes, they are called similar figures.

EXAMPLE

Tell whether each transformation is a dilation. Explain.

The side lengths of triangle *ABC* multiplied by a scale factor of 2 will produce the side lengths of triangle *A'B'C'*. The side lengths are proportional, so the triangles are similar and triangle *A'B'C'* is a dilation of triangle *ABC*.

There is not a scale factor that can be multiplied by each side length of rectangle *LMNP* to produce rectangle *L'M'N'P'*. The side lengths are not proportional, so the rectangles are not similar and rectangle *L'M'N'P'* is not a dilation of rectangle *LMNP*.

Chapter 4   140   Ratios, Proportions, and Similarity

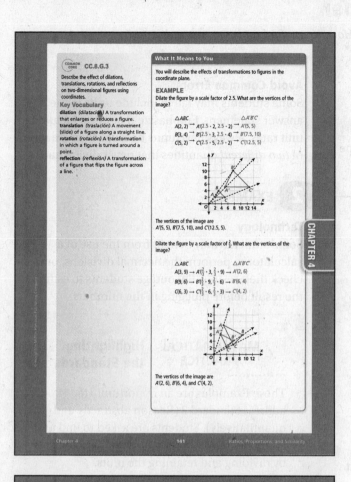

CC.8.G.3
Describe the effect of dilations, translations, rotations, and reflections on two-dimensional figures using coordinates.

Key Vocabulary
dilation *(dilatación)* A transformation that enlarges or reduces a figure.
translation *(traslación)* A movement (slide) of a figure along a straight line.
rotation *(rotación)* A transformation in which a figure is turned around a point.
reflection *(reflexión)* A transformation of a figure that flips the figure across a line.

What It Means to You
You will describe the effects of transformations to figures in the coordinate plane.

EXAMPLE
Dilate the figure by a scale factor of 2.5. What are the vertices of the image?

$\triangle ABC$ $\qquad$ $\triangle A'B'C'$
$A(2, 2) \rightarrow A'(2.5 \cdot 2, 2.5 \cdot 2) \rightarrow A'(5, 5)$
$B(3, 4) \rightarrow B'(2.5 \cdot 3, 2.5 \cdot 4) \rightarrow B'(7.5, 10)$
$C(5, 2) \rightarrow C'(2.5 \cdot 5, 2.5 \cdot 2) \rightarrow C'(12.5, 5)$

The vertices of the image are
$A'(5, 5)$, $B'(7.5, 10)$, and $C'(12.5, 5)$.

Dilate the figure by a scale factor of $\frac{2}{3}$. What are the vertices of the image?

$\triangle ABC$ $\qquad$ $\triangle A'B'C'$
$A(3, 9) \rightarrow A'(\frac{2}{3} \cdot 3, \frac{2}{3} \cdot 9) \rightarrow A'(2, 6)$
$B(9, 6) \rightarrow B'(\frac{2}{3} \cdot 9, \frac{2}{3} \cdot 6) \rightarrow B'(6, 4)$
$C(6, 3) \rightarrow C'(\frac{2}{3} \cdot 6, \frac{2}{3} \cdot 3) \rightarrow C'(4, 2)$

The vertices of the image are
$A'(2, 6)$, $B'(6, 4)$, and $C'(4, 2)$.

COMMON CORE
PROFESIONAL
DEVELOPMENT

CC.8.G.3

Students identify resulting coordinates from translations, reflections, and rotations. They will identify the relationship between the coordinates and the transformation. For example, a translation of 4 units left and 3 units up would subtract 4 from the *x*-coordinate and add 3 to the *y*-coordinate. In a dilation from the origin, students will identify the relationship between the coordinates of the preimage, the image, and the scale factor.

Key Vocabulary

center of dilation *(centro de una dilatación)* The point of intersection of lines through each pair of corresponding vertices in a dilation.

dilation *(dilatación)* A transformation that enlarges or reduces a figure.

proportion *(proporción)* An equation that states that two ratios are equivalent.

proportional relationship *(relación proporcional)* A relationship between two quantities in which the ratio of one quantity to the other quantity is constant.

scale factor *(factor de escala)* The ratio used to enlarge or reduce similar figures.

unit rate *(tasa unitaria)* A rate in which the second quantity in the comparison is one unit.

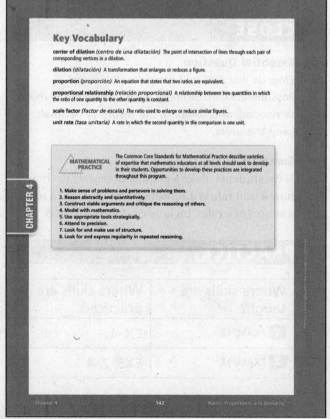

MATHEMATICAL PRACTICE

The Common Core Standards for Mathematical Practice describe varieties of expertise that mathematics educators at all levels should seek to develop in their students. Opportunities to develop these practices are integrated throughout this program.

1. Make sense of problems and persevere in solving them.
2. Reason abstractly and quantitatively.
3. Construct viable arguments and critique the reasoning of others.
4. Model with mathematics.
5. Use appropriate tools strategically.
6. Attend to precision.
7. Look for and make use of structure.
8. Look for and express regularity in repeated reasoning.

4-1 Ratios, Rates, and Unit Rates
Going Deeper

Essential question: *How do you find and compare unit rates?*

© Houghton Mifflin Harcourt Publishing Company

COMMON CORE **Standards for Mathematical Content**

Prep for CC.8.EE.5 Graph proportional relationships, interpreting the unit rate as the slope of the graph. Compare two different proportional relationships represented in different ways.

Vocabulary
unit rate

Prerequisites
Ratios

Rates

Math Background
A *ratio* compares two quantities, with or without units. A *rate* is a ratio in which two quantities are measured in different units. Both a ratio and rate can be stated in the form of a fraction, and sometimes they can be expressed as whole numbers because the denominator is assumed to be one (as in $\frac{6}{1} = 6$ or 60 mph). A rate whose denominator is 1 is called a *unit rate*, or per 1 unit.

INTRODUCE

Connect to prior learning by asking students to give examples of common rates, such as typing rates in words per minute and postage shipping rates in dollars per pound. Emphasize that "per" refers to division and that each rate is a ratio of different units that do not divide out.

TEACH

 1 EXAMPLE

Questioning Strategies
- What was done to rewrite $\frac{45}{2.5}$ as 18? **Divide 45 by 2.5, as you would any fraction.**

- You can write many equivalent rates, but can you write more than one equivalent *unit* rate? **No, unit rates are simplified rates with a denominator of 1.**

Avoid Common Errors
Some students may fail to include units in the answer statement. Emphasize that rates, including unit rates, always have units because they are ratios of *two different* quantities that never divide out.

2 EXAMPLE

Technology
Some students may benefit from the use of a calculator to perform the decimal divisions, or to check their results. Encourage students to estimate the result before plugging in the numbers.

MATHEMATICAL PRACTICE **Highlighting the Standards**

These Examples are an opportunity to address Standard 2 (Reason abstractly and quantitatively). Students are asked to find and compare unit rates for real-world problems, by dividing and retaining the units.

CLOSE

Essential Question
How do you find and compare unit rates?
Possible answer: Simplify each rate, using division as needed, and compare the resulting decimals; keep the units.

Summarize
Have students make a graphic organizer to show how a unit rate is a subset of a rate, which in turn is a subset of a ratio. Include examples for each.

PRACTICE

Where skills are taught	Where skills are practiced
1 EXAMPLE	EX. 1
2 EXAMPLE	EXS. 2–4

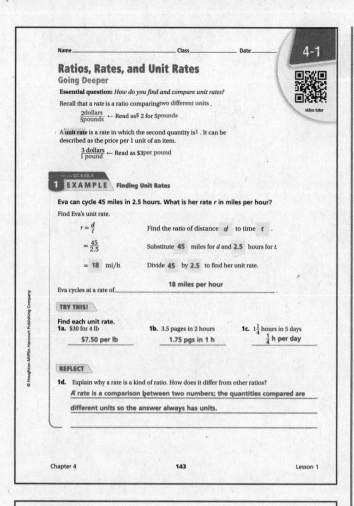

Ratios, Rates, and Unit Rates
Going Deeper

4-1

Essential question: *How do you find and compare unit rates?*

Recall that a *rate* is a ratio comparing two different units .

$$\frac{2\ dollars}{5\ pounds}$$ ← Read as $ 2 for 5 pounds

A **unit rate** is a rate in which the second quantity is 1 . It can be described as the price per 1 unit of an item.

$$\frac{3\ dollars}{1\ pound}$$ ← Read as $3 per pound

1 EXAMPLE CC.6.EE.5 Finding Unit Rates

Eva can cycle 45 miles in 2.5 hours. What is her rate *r* in miles per hour?

Find Eva's unit rate.

$r = \dfrac{d}{t}$ Find the *ratio* of distance *d* to time *t* .

$= \dfrac{45}{2.5}$ Substitute 45 miles for *d* and 2.5 hours for *t*.

$= 18$ mi/h   Divide 45 by 2.5 to find her unit rate.

Eva cycles at a rate of _____ 18 miles per hour _____

TRY THIS!

Find each unit rate.
1a. $30 for 4 lb   **1b.** 3.5 pages in 2 hours   **1c.** $1\frac{1}{4}$ hours in 5 days

   $7.50 per lb   1.75 pgs in 1 h $\frac{1}{4}$ h per day

REFLECT

1d. Explain why a rate is a kind of ratio. How does it differ from other ratios?

A rate is a comparison between two numbers; the quantities compared are

different units so the answer always has units.

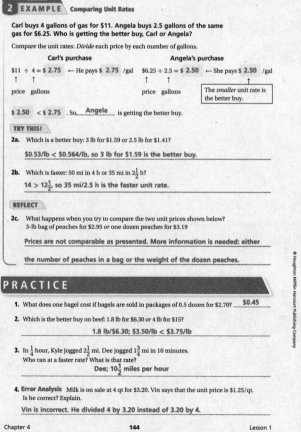

2 EXAMPLE CC.6.EE.5 Comparing Unit Rates

Carl buys 4 gallons of gas for $11. Angela buys 2.5 gallons of the same gas for $6.25. Who is getting the better buy, Carl or Angela?

Compare the unit rates: *Divide* each price by each number of gallons.

Carl's purchase	Angela's purchase

$11 ÷ 4 = $ 2.75 ← He pays $ 2.75 /gal $6.25 ÷ 2.5 = $ 2.50 ← She pays $ 2.50 /gal
↑   ↑   ↑   ↑
price   gallons   price   gallons

The *smaller* unit rate is the better buy.

$ 2.50 < $ 2.75 . So, ___ Angela ___ is getting the better buy.

TRY THIS!

2a. Which is a better buy: 3 lb for $1.59 or 2.5 lb for $1.41?

$0.53/lb < $0.564/lb, so 3 lb for $1.59 is the better buy.

2b. Which is faster: 50 mi in 4 h or 35 mi in $2\frac{1}{2}$ h?

$14 > 12\frac{1}{2}$, so 35 mi/2.5 h is the faster unit rate.

REFLECT

2c. What happens when you try to compare the two unit prices shown below?
3-lb bag of peaches for $2.95 *or* one dozen peaches for $3.19

Prices are not comparable as presented. More information is needed: either

the number of peaches in a bag or the weight of the dozen peaches.

PRACTICE

1. What does one bagel cost if bagels are sold in packages of 0.5 dozen for $2.70? ___ $0.45 ___

2. Which is the better buy on beef: 1.8 lb for $6.30 or 4 lb for $15?

   1.8 lb/$6.30; $3.50/lb < $3.75/lb

3. In $\frac{1}{4}$ hour, Kyle jogged $2\frac{1}{2}$ mi. Dee jogged $1\frac{3}{4}$ mi in 10 minutes.
Who ran at a faster rate? What is that rate?

   Dee; $10\frac{1}{2}$ miles per hour

4. Error Analysis Milk is on sale at 4 qt for $3.20. Vin says that the unit price is $1.25/qt.
Is he correct? Explain.

   Vin is incorrect. He divided 4 by 3.20 instead of 3.20 by 4.

© Houghton Mifflin Harcourt Publishing Company

ADDITIONAL PRACTICE

Assign these pages to help your students practice and apply important lesson concepts. For additional exercises, see the Student Edition.

Answers

Additional Practice

1. $\frac{8960 \text{ kg}}{\text{m}^3}$
2. 120 calories
3. $22.50
4. 61 mi/h
5. 58.125 mi/h
6. 222.2 ft/sec
7. 8.2 oz for $2.99
8. 3 lb bag for $2.99
9. 20 oz bottle for $1.55
10. $1.25

Problem Solving

1. hippo, horse, elephant, dog, cat, human, small birds
2. small birds
3. elephant and horse; cat & dog
4. B
5. H
6. C
7. G
8. A
9. J

Additional Practice

Name_____ Class_____ Date_____

1. Copper weighing 4480 kilograms has a volume of 0.5 cubic meters. What is the density of copper?

_____

2. Yoshi's yogurt contains 15 calories per ounce. How many calories are in an 8-ounce container of Yoshi's yogurt?

_____

3. Emily earns $7.50 per hour. How much does she earn in 3 hours?

_____

4. An antelope can run 152.5 miles in 2.5 hours. What is average speed of the antelope?

_____

5. Bob and Marquis went on a trip. The first day, they drove 465 miles in 8 hours. What is their average speed for the first day of their trip?

_____

6. A racecar was attempting to set a record. The racecar went 1000 feet in 4.5 seconds. To the nearest tenth, what is the average speed of the racecar?

_____

Tell which is the better buy.

7. 8.2 oz of toothpaste for $2.99 or 6.4 oz of toothpaste for $2.49

_____

8. a 3 lb bag of apples for $2.99 or a 5 lb bag of apples for $4.99

_____

9. 16 oz bottle of soda for $1.25 or 20 oz bottle of soda for $1.55

_____

10. Mavis rides the bus every day. She bought a bus pass good for the month of October for $38.75. How much was Mavis charged per day for the bus pass?

_____

Problem Solving

Scientists have researched the ratio of brain weight to body size in different animals. The results are in the table below.

1. Order the animals by their brain weight to body weight ratio, from smallest to largest.

_____

2. It has been hypothesized that the higher the brain weight to body weight ratio, the more intelligent the animal is. By this measure, which animals listed are the most intelligent?

3. Name two sets of animals that have approximately the same brain weight to body weight ratio.

Animal	Brain Weight / Body Weight
Cat	$\frac{1}{100}$
Dog	$\frac{1}{125}$
Elephant	$\frac{1}{560}$
Hippo	$\frac{1}{2789}$
Horse	$\frac{1}{600}$
Human	$\frac{1}{40}$
Small birds	$\frac{1}{12}$

Find the unit rate. Round to the nearest hundredth.

4. A 64-ounce bottle of apple juice costs $1.35.

A $0.01/oz   C $0.47/oz
B $0.02/oz   D $47.4/oz

5. Find the unit rate for a 2 lb package of hamburger that costs $3.45.

F $0.58/lb   H $1.73/lb
G $1.25/b   J $2.28/b

6. 12 slices of pizza cost $9.00.

A $0.45/slice   C $0.75/slice
B $0.50/slice   D $1.33/slice

7. John is selling 5 comic books for $6.00.

F $0.83/book   H $1.02/book
G $1.20/book   J $1.45/book

8. There are 64 beats in 4 measures of music.

A 16 beats/measure
B 12 beats/measure
C 4 beats/measure
D 0.06 beats/measure

9. The average price of a 30 second commercial for the 2002 Super Bowl was $1,900,000.

F $120.82/sec
G $1,242.50/sec
H $5,839.02/sec
J $63,333.33/sec

4-2 Solving Proportions
Going Deeper

Essential question: *How can you use tables to identify and describe proportional relationships?*

Standards for Mathematical Content

Prep for CC.8.EE.5 Graph proportional relationships, interpreting the unit rate as the slope of the graph. Compare two different proportional relationships represented in different ways.

Vocabulary
proportional relationship

proportion

Prerequisites
Ratios

Rates

Unit Rates

INTRODUCE

Connect to prior learning by asking students to distinguish between *ratios* and *rates*. Emphasize that both provide a comparison of any two quantities by division; but a rate is a special kind of ratio that compares two quantities that each have different units. Then ask students to suggest some common ratios such as speed, which is a distance divided by a time.

TEACH

1 EXPLORE

Questioning Strategies
- What quantity is in the numerator of each ratio? The denominator? **Distance in miles; time in minutes**
- Will exchanging the numerator and denominator in a proportional relationship always result in a constant ratio? **Yes, the inverse (reciprocal) of a constant number is always a constant number.**

2 EXAMPLE

Questioning Strategies
- What patterns can you use to help you fill in the table? **As gallons increase by 1, the distance increases by 32.**
- In the table, how is the distance related to gallons? **The distance is always gallons multiplied by 32.**

TRY THIS

To remind students that each rate must have units and that each quantity has an order in the ratio, ask students to identify the units for each Try This before they determine whether the relationship is proportional.

 MATHEMATICAL PRACTICE | **Highlighting the Standards**

The Explore and Example are an opportunity to address Standard 8 (Look for and express regularity in repeated reasoning). Students are asked to identify proportional relationships in tables by writing and simplifying ratios. Students then determine if the ratio is constant and apply this pattern to find unknown quantities for corresponding given values.

CLOSE

Essential Question

How can you use tables to identify and describe proportional relationships? **Possible answer: If each of the corresponding ratios in a table is the same, the relationship between the two quantities forms a proportional relationship.**

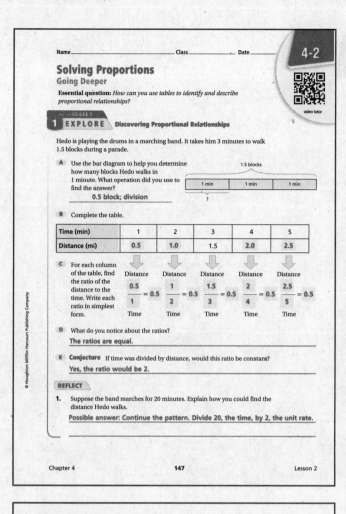

Solving Proportions
Going Deeper

Essential question: *How can you use tables to identify and describe proportional relationships?*

1 EXPLORE Discovering Proportional Relationships

Hedo is playing the drums in a marching band. It takes him 3 minutes to walk 1.5 blocks during a parade.

A Use the bar diagram to help you determine how many blocks Hedo walks in 1 minute. What operation did you use to find the answer?

0.5 block; division

B Complete the table.

Time (min)	1	2	3	4	5
Distance (mi)	0.5	1.0	1.5	2.0	2.5

C For each column of the table, find the ratio of the distance to the time. Write each ratio in simplest form.

$\dfrac{\text{Distance}}{\text{Time}} \quad \dfrac{0.5}{1} = 0.5 \quad \dfrac{1}{2} = 0.5 \quad \dfrac{1.5}{3} = 0.5 \quad \dfrac{2}{4} = 0.5 \quad \dfrac{2.5}{5} = 0.5$

D What do you notice about the ratios?

The ratios are equal.

E **Conjecture** If time was divided by distance, would this ratio be constant?

Yes, the ratio would be 2.

REFLECT

1. Suppose the band marches for 20 minutes. Explain how you could find the distance Hedo walks.

Possible answer: Continue the pattern. Divide 20, the time, by 2, the unit rate.

Chapter 4   147   Lesson 2

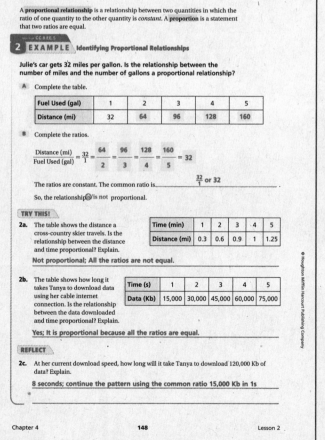

A **proportional relationship** is a relationship between two quantities in which the ratio of one quantity to the other quantity is *constant*. A **proportion** is a statement that two ratios are equal.

2 EXAMPLE Identifying Proportional Relationships

Julie's car gets 32 miles per gallon. Is the relationship between the number of miles and the number of gallons a proportional relationship?

A Complete the table.

Fuel Used (gal)	1	2	3	4	5
Distance (mi)	32	64	96	128	160

B Complete the ratios.

$\dfrac{\text{Distance (mi)}}{\text{Fuel Used (gal)}} = \dfrac{32}{1} = \dfrac{64}{2} = \dfrac{96}{3} = \dfrac{128}{4} = \dfrac{160}{5} = 32$

The ratios are constant. The common ratio is $\dfrac{32}{1}$ or 32.

So, the relationship is not proportional.

TRY THIS!

2a. The table shows the distance a cross-country skier travels. Is the relationship between the distance and time proportional? Explain.

Time (min)	1	2	3	4	5
Distance (mi)	0.3	0.6	0.9	1	1.25

Not proportional; All the ratios are not equal.

2b. The table shows how long it takes Tanya to download data using her cable internet connection. Is the relationship between the data downloaded and time proportional? Explain.

Time (s)	1	2	3	4	5
Data (Kb)	15,000	30,000	45,000	60,000	75,000

Yes; It is proportional because all the ratios are equal.

REFLECT

2c. At her current download speed, how long will it take Tanya to download 120,000 Kb of data? Explain.

8 seconds; continue the pattern using the common ratio 15,000 Kb in 1s

Chapter 4   148   Lesson 2

Assign these pages to help your students practice and apply important lesson concepts. For additional exercises, see the Student Edition.

Answers

Additional Practice

1. yes
2. yes
3. no
4. yes
5. no
6. yes
7. no
8. no
9. Yes; $\frac{6}{9} = \frac{8}{12}$
10. $3.70
11. 79.2 minutes
12. 52 cats
13. 18 teachers
14. 99 minutes

Problem Solving

1. arm span
2. 65 inches
3. 72.3 inches
4. 6 feet
5. 1.8 feet
6. 0.6 feet
7. C
8. F
9. B
10. J

Name_____ Class_____ Date_____

Additional Practice

Tell whether the ratios are proportional.

1. $\frac{3}{4} \stackrel{?}{=} \frac{9}{12}$ 2. $\frac{9}{24} \stackrel{?}{=} \frac{18}{48}$ 3. $\frac{16}{24} \stackrel{?}{=} \frac{10}{18}$ 4. $\frac{13}{25} \stackrel{?}{=} \frac{26}{50}$

5. $\frac{10}{32} \stackrel{?}{=} \frac{16}{38}$ 6. $\frac{20}{36} \stackrel{?}{=} \frac{50}{90}$ 7. $\frac{20}{28} \stackrel{?}{=} \frac{28}{36}$ 8. $\frac{14}{42} \stackrel{?}{=} \frac{16}{36}$

9. A karate team had 6 girls and 9 boys. Then 2 more girls and 3 more boys joined the team. Did the ratio of girls to boys stay the same? Explain.

10. Janessa bought 4 stamps for $1.48. At this rate, how much would 10 stamps cost?

11. Janelle can mow 5 lawns in 36 minutes. At this rate, how long will it take her to mow 11 lawns?

12. An animal shelter wants their ratio of dogs to cats to be 3:2. If the animal shelter has 78 dogs, how many cats should they have?

13. On a field trip, the ratio of teachers to students must be 2:9. If there are 81 students on the field trip, how many teachers must there be?

14. A gallery owner is hanging up 444 pictures for an art exhibit. She has put up 37 pictures in 9 minutes. If she continues at the same rate how many more minutes will it take her to hang the rest of the pictures?

Problem Solving

Use the ratios in the table to answer each question. Round to the nearest tenth.

Body Part	Body Part / Height
Femur	$\frac{1}{4}$
Tibia	$\frac{1}{5}$
Hand span	$\frac{2}{17}$
Arm span	$\frac{1}{1}$
Head circumference	$\frac{1}{3}$

1. Which body part is the same length as the person's height?

2. If a person's tibia is 13 inches, how tall would you expect the person to be?

3. If a person's hand span is 8.5 inches, about how tall would you expect the person to be?

4. If a femur is 18 inches long, how many feet tall would you expect the person to be?

5. What would you expect the head circumference to be of a person who is 5.5 feet tall?

6. What would you expect the hand span to be of a person who is 5 feet tall?

Choose the letter for the best answer.

7. Five milliliters of a children's medicine contains 400 mg of the drug amoxicillin. How many mg of amoxicillin does 25 mL contain?

  A 0.3 mg   C 2000 mg
  B 80 mg   D 2500 mg

8. A basketball player for the Seattle Supersonics averages about 2 three-pointers for every 5 he shoots. If he attempts 10 three-pointers in a game, how many would you expect him to make?

  F 4   H 8
  G 5   J 25

9. In 2002, a 30-second commercial during the Super Bowl cost an average of $1,900,000. At this rate, how much would a 45-second commercial cost?

  A $1,266,666   C $3,500,000
  B $2,850,000   D $4,000,000

10. A medicine for dogs indicates that the medicine should be administered in the ratio 2 teaspoons per 5 lb, based on the weight of the dog. How much should be given to a 70 lb dog?

  F 5 teaspoons   H 14 teaspoons
  G 12 teaspoons   J 28 teaspoons

Similar Figures
Going Deeper: Similar Triangles

Essential question: *How can you determine when two triangles are similar?*

© Houghton Mifflin Harcourt Publishing Company

COMMON CORE Standards for Mathematical Content

CC.8.G.5 Use informal arguments to establish facts about the angle sum and exterior angle of triangles, about the angles created when parallel lines are cut by a transversal, and the angle-angle criterion for similarity of triangles.

Prerequisites

Writing and solving proportions.

Math Background

Similar figures have the same shape, but they may have different sizes. Two figures are similar if there exists a sequence of transformations including dilation that transforms one figure onto the other. The corresponding angles of similar triangles are congruent, and corresponding side lengths of similar triangles are proportional. If all three corresponding sides of two triangles are proportional in length, then the triangles are similar. If two angles of two triangles are congruent, then the triangles are similar.

INTRODUCE

Students have learned that any two geometric figures are similar if there is some sequence of transformations that transforms one figure onto the other. Students also know that similar triangles have congruent corresponding angle measures and proportional corresponding side lengths. Review these concepts with students, and tell them that in this lesson they will use geometric properties to show that triangles are similar.

TEACH

1 EXPLORE

Questioning Strategies

- What do you expect the third angle to measure? **The third angle will measure 75° because of the Triangle Sum Theorem.**

- Are all of the triangles drawn the same size? **No, all have the same three angle measures and all are the same shape, but they are different sizes.**

2 EXAMPLE

Questioning Strategies

- What do you need to show in order to prove the triangles are similar? **To prove the two triangles are similar, show that at least two pairs of corresponding angles are congruent.**

- How can you find the measure of the third angle in a triangle? **Use the Triangle Sum Theorem to subtract the two given angle measures from 180°.**

3 EXAMPLE

Questioning Strategies

- How can you tell which parts of the triangles are corresponding parts from the given names of the triangles? **Corresponding parts of the triangles are listed in the same order in similarity statements.**

- Can you use two pairs of corresponding sides to show that two triangles are similar? Explain. **No, two pairs of corresponding sides is not enough. If the angle measures between the two corresponding sides are different, then the third pair of corresponding sides would not form an equivalent ratio with the other two pairs.**

Name_____ Class_____ Date_____

4-3

Similar Figures
Going Deeper: Similar Triangles

Essential question: *How can you determine when two triangles are similar?*

Recall that similar figures have the same shape, but may have different sizes. Two triangles are similar if their corresponding angles are congruent and the lengths of their corresponding sides are proportional.

CC.8.G.5

1 EXPLORE Discovering Angle-Angle Similarity

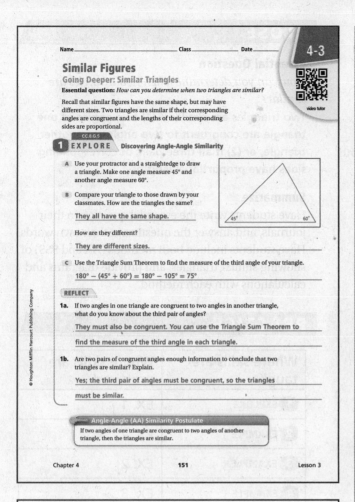

A Use your protractor and a straightedge to draw a triangle. Make one angle measure 45° and another angle measure 60°.

B Compare your triangle to those drawn by your classmates. How are the triangles the same?

__They all have the same shape.__

How are they different?

__They are different sizes.__

C Use the Triangle Sum Theorem to find the measure of the third angle of your triangle.

__180° − (45° + 60°) = 180° − 105° = 75°__

REFLECT

1a. If two angles in one triangle are congruent to two angles in another triangle, what do you know about the third pair of angles?

__They must also be congruent. You can use the Triangle Sum Theorem to__

__find the measure of the third angle in each triangle.__

1b. Are two pairs of congruent angles enough information to conclude that two triangles are similar? Explain.

__Yes; the third pair of angles must be congruent, so the triangles__

__must be similar.__

> **Angle-Angle (AA) Similarity Postulate**
> If two angles of one triangle are congruent to two angles of another triangle, then the triangles are similar.

Chapter 4   151   Lesson 3

© Houghton Mifflin Harcourt Publishing Company

CC.8.G.5

2 EXAMPLE Using the AA Similarity Postulate

Explain whether the triangles are similar.

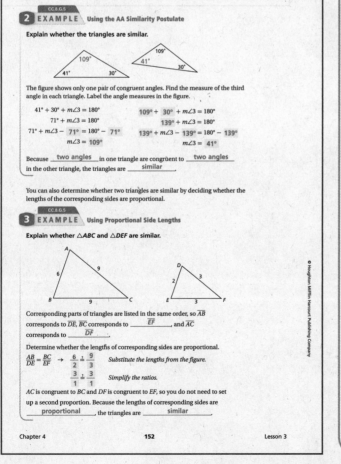

The figure shows only one pair of congruent angles. Find the measure of the third angle in each triangle. Label the angle measures in the figure.

$41° + 30° + m\angle 3 = 180°$ $109° + 30° + m\angle 3 = 180°$

$71° + m\angle 3 = 180°$ $139° + m\angle 3 = 180°$

$71° + m\angle 3 - 71° = 180° - 71°$ $139° + m\angle 3 - 139° = 180° - 139°$

$m\angle 3 = 109°$ $m\angle 3 = 41°$

Because __two angles__ in one triangle are congruent to __two angles__ in the other triangle, the triangles are __similar__.

You can also determine whether two triangles are similar by deciding whether the lengths of the corresponding sides are proportional.

CC.8.G.5

3 EXAMPLE Using Proportional Side Lengths

Explain whether △ABC and △DEF are similar.

Corresponding parts of triangles are listed in the same order, so $\overline{AB}$ corresponds to $\overline{DE}$, $\overline{BC}$ corresponds to ___$\overline{EF}$___, and $\overline{AC}$ corresponds to ___$\overline{DF}$___.

Determine whether the lengths of corresponding sides are proportional.

$\frac{AB}{DE} = \frac{BC}{EF} \rightarrow \frac{6}{2} \stackrel{?}{=} \frac{9}{3}$ *Substitute the lengths from the figure.*

$\frac{3}{1} \stackrel{?}{=} \frac{3}{1}$ *Simplify the ratios.*

AC is congruent to *BC* and *DF* is congruent to *EF*, so you do not need to set up a second proportion. Because the lengths of corresponding sides are __proportional__, the triangles are __similar__.

Chapter 4   152   Lesson 3

© Houghton Mifflin Harcourt Publishing Company

Questioning Strategies

- Which triangles in the diagram do you need to show are similar? **triangles *ABC* and *ADE***

- What corresponding parts can you use to show that the triangles are similar? **Angle *A* is congruent to itself. Angles *ABC* and *ADE* are both right angles, so they are congruent. By the AA postulate, they are similar triangles.**

- How can you use triangle similarity to find the height of the ball? **The corresponding sides are proportional in length. You can then use ratios to find *h*.**

MATHEMATICAL PRACTICE   Highlighting the Standards

This Lesson is an opportunity to address Standard 2 (Reason abstractly and quantitatively). Students examine triangles to find ways to show that they are similar. Then students use the properties of similar triangles to solve problems. In order to interpret information given and determine the information needed to apply the properties, students have to use abstract reasoning. Then students reason quantitatively to write and solve proportions to answer the question.

CLOSE

Essential Question

How can you determine when two triangles are similar?

Two triangles are similar if (1) two angles of one triangle are congruent to two angles of another triangle, or (2) if all three pairs of corresponding sides have proportional lengths.

Summarize

Have students write the essential question in their journals, and answer the question in their own words. Have students include both methods (AA and SSS) of showing similar triangles, and provide diagrams and calculations with each method.

PRACTICE

Where skills are taught	Where skills are practiced
1 EXPLORE	EX. 1
2 EXAMPLE	EX. 2
3 EXAMPLE	EX. 2
4 EXAMPLE	EX. 3

4 **E X A M P L E** CC.8.G.5 **Finding Missing Measures in Similar Triangles**

While playing tennis, Matt is 12 meters from the net that is 0.9 meter high. He needs to hit the ball so that it just clears the net and lands 6 meters beyond the base of the net. At what height in meters should Matt hit the tennis ball?

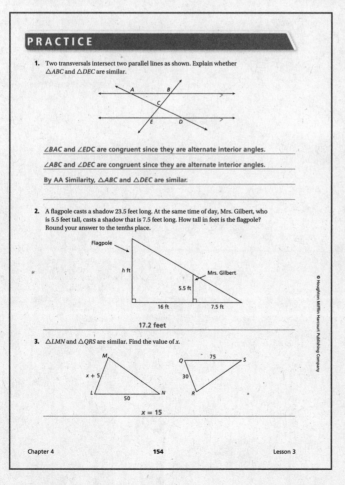

A Both triangles contain $\angle A$; $\angle A$ in $\triangle ABC$ is congruent to ____$\angle A$____ in $\triangle ADE$.

The net ($\overline{BC}$) is perpendicular to the ground ($\overline{AB}$), so $\angle ABC$ is a right angle. The line representing the height of the ball ($\overline{DE}$) is perpendicular to the ground ($\overline{AD}$), so $\angle ADE$ is a __right angle__.

There are two pairs of __congruent__ angles, so $\triangle ABC$ and $\triangle ADE$ are __similar__.

B In similar triangles, corresponding side lengths are proportional.

$\dfrac{AD}{AB} = \dfrac{DE}{BC}$ → $\dfrac{6+12}{6} = \dfrac{h}{0.9}$ *Substitute the lengths from the figure.*

$0.9 \times \dfrac{18}{6} = \dfrac{h}{0.9} \times 0.9$ *Use properties of equality to get h by itself.*

$0.9 \times 3 = h$ *Simplify.*

$2.7 = h$ *Multiply.*

Matt should hit the ball at a height of ____2.7____ meter(s).

TRY THIS!

4. What if you set up a proportion so that each ratio compares parts of one triangle?

height of $\triangle ABC$ → $\dfrac{BC}{AB} = \dfrac{DE}{AD}$ ← height of $\triangle ADE$
base of $\triangle ABC$ → $\phantom{\dfrac{BC}{AB}}$ ← base of $\triangle ADE$

Show that this proportion leads to the same value for h as in **B**.

$\dfrac{0.9}{6} = \dfrac{h}{18}$
$18 \times 0.15 = h$
$2.7 = h$

© Houghton Mifflin Harcourt Publishing Company

PRACTICE

1. Two transversals intersect two parallel lines as shown. Explain whether $\triangle ABC$ and $\triangle DEC$ are similar.

$\angle BAC$ and $\angle EDC$ are congruent since they are alternate interior angles.

$\angle ABC$ and $\angle DEC$ are congruent since they are alternate interior angles.

By AA Similarity, $\triangle ABC$ and $\triangle DEC$ are similar.

2. A flagpole casts a shadow 23.5 feet long. At the same time of day, Mrs. Gilbert, who is 5.5 feet tall, casts a shadow that is 7.5 feet long. How tall in feet is the flagpole? Round your answer to the tenths place.

Flagpole

h ft

Mrs. Gilbert

5.5 ft

16 ft   7.5 ft

____17.2 feet____

3. $\triangle LMN$ and $\triangle QRS$ are similar. Find the value of x.

M

$x+5$

L 50 N

Q 75 S

30

R

____$x = 15$____

© Houghton Mifflin Harcourt Publishing Company

ADDITIONAL PRACTICE

Assign these pages to help your students practice and apply important lesson concepts. For additional exercises, see the Student Edition.

Answers

Additional Practice

1. $\triangle QRS \sim \triangle XZY$
2. The measure of angle B is 72°, and the measure of angle D is 70°. Because two angles of one triangle are congruent to two angles of the other triangle, the triangles are similar.
3. 90 cm
4. Angle A in triangle ABC is congruent to angle A in triangle ADE, and Angle B in triangle ABC is congruent to angle D in triangle ADE. Because two angles of one triangle are congruent to two angles of the other triangle, the triangles are similar. $CE = 9.75$ cm

Problem Solving

1. 68 feet tall
2. The third pair of angles are congruent.
3. 15 in.
4. B
5. G

Name_____ Class_____ Date_____

Additional Practice

1. Which triangles are similar?

2. Explain whether the triangles are similar.

_____

_____

3. An isosceles triangle has a base of 20 cm and legs measuring 36 cm. How long are the legs of a similar triangle with base measuring 50 cm?

4. Explain why $\triangle ABC$ and $\triangle ADE$ are similar. Then find CE.

_____

_____

Problem Solving

Write the correct answer.

1. Mr. Hernstrom stands next to the Illinois Centennial Monument at Logan Square in Chicago and casts a shadow that is 18 feet long. The shadow of the monument is 204 feet long. If Mr. Hernstrom is 6 feet tall, how tall is the monument?

_____

2. If two angles in one triangle are congruent to two angles in another triangle, what do you know about the third pair of angles?

_____

3. The two shortest sides of a right triangle are 10 in. and 24 in. long. What is the length of the shortest side of a similar right triangle whose two longest sides are 36 in. and 39 in.?

_____

Choose the letter for the best answer.

4. A 9-foot street sign casts a shadow that is 12 feet long. The lamppost next to it casts a shadow that is 24 feet long. How tall is the lamppost?

 A 15 feet

 B 18 feet

 C 24 feet

 D 36 feet

5. Two tables shaped like triangles are similar. The measure of one of the larger table's angles is 38°, and another angle is half that size. What are the measures of all the angles in the smaller table?

 F 19°, 9.5°, and 61.5°

 G 38°, 19°, and 123°

 H 38°, 38°, and 104°

 J 76°, 38°, and 246°

Dilations
Going Deeper

Essential question: *How can you use coordinates to describe the result of a dilation?*

CC.8.G.3 Describe the effect of dilations on two-dimensional figures using coordinates.

Vocabulary

dilation

center of dilation

scale factor

Prerequisites

Graphing in the coordinate plane (four quadrants)

Math Background

Unlike translations, reflections, and rotations, the image of a figure after a dilation can have a different size than the pre-image. Though a dilation can change the size of a figure, it does not change its shape. The image of a rectangle after being dilated is still a rectangle. Dilations can enlarge or reduce the size of a figure. If the scale factor of the dilation is greater than 1, the image will be larger than its pre-image. If the scale factor is less than 1, the image will be smaller than its pre-image. If the scale factor is 1, the size will not change.

INTRODUCE

Ask students to imagine that they are creating a logo for their new dog-walking business. The logo is drawn as the correct size for business cards, but is too small for an advertising flyer. Tell students that in this lesson, they will learn about transformations that change the size of a figure, but not its shape.

TEACH

1 EXPLORE

Questioning Strategies

- In part D, how does each vertex in the image compare to the corresponding vertex in the pre-image? **Each vertex in the image lies on the same axis as the vertex in the pre-image, but the vertex in the image is twice as far from the origin.**

- How does the figure in part F compare to the original square and to the figure in part C? **The figure in part F is smaller, but has the same shape.**

MATHEMATICAL PRACTICE Highlighting the Standards

This Explore provides an opportunity to address Standard 7 (Look for and make use of structure). Working through the Explore should lead students to see that the relationship between the coordinates of the vertices of the pre-image and image under a dilation can be written symbolically as $(x, y) \rightarrow (kx, ky)$. Students should also notice that if they multiply each coordinate by a number greater than 1 ($k > 1$), the figure gets bigger, and if they multiply by a positive number less than 1 ($0 < k < 1$), the figure gets smaller.

---

2 EXAMPLE

Questioning Strategies

- For a dilation with a scale factor of 3, will the image be larger or smaller than its pre-image? Why? **Larger; each coordinate is multiplied by 3, so each point will be 3 times farther from the origin.**

Name_____ Class_____ Date_____

4-4

video tutor

Dilations
Going Deeper

Essential question: *How can you use coordinates to describe the result of a dilation?*

A **dilation** is a transformation that changes the size, but not the shape, of a geometric figure. The center of the figure is known as the **center of dilation**. When dilating in the coordinate plane, the center of dilation is usually the origin.

CC.8.G.3
1 EXPLORE   Applying Dilations

The square is the preimage (input). The center of dilation is the origin.

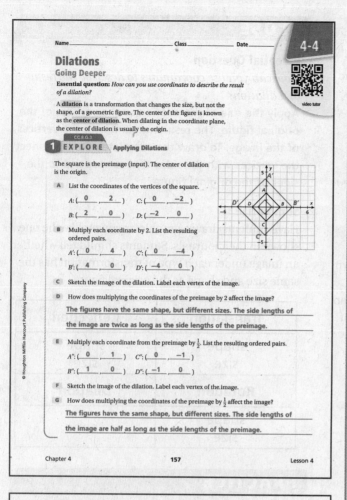

A List the coordinates of the vertices of the square.

A: (__0__ , __2__) C: (__0__ , __−2__)

B: (__2__ , __0__) D: (__−2__ , __0__)

B Multiply each coordinate by 2. List the resulting ordered pairs.

A': (__0__ , __4__) C': (__0__ , __−4__)

B': (__4__ , __0__) D': (__−4__ , __0__)

C Sketch the image of the dilation. Label each vertex of the image.

D How does multiplying the coordinates of the preimage by 2 affect the image?

The figures have the same shape, but different sizes. The side lengths of

the image are twice as long as the side lengths of the preimage.

E Multiply each coordinate from the preimage by $\frac{1}{2}$. List the resulting ordered pairs.

A'': (__0__ , __1__) C'': (__0__ , __−1__)

B'': (__1__ , __0__) D'': (__−1__ , __0__)

F Sketch the image of the dilation. Label each vertex of the image.

G How does multiplying the coordinates of the preimage by $\frac{1}{2}$ affect the image?

The figures have the same shape, but different sizes. The side lengths of

the image are half as long as the side lengths of the preimage.

© Houghton Mifflin Harcourt Publishing Company

Chapter 4   157   Lesson 4

A **scale factor** describes how much larger or smaller the image of a dilation is than the preimage.

> **Rule for Dilation**
>
> For a dilation centered at the origin with scale factor k, the image of point $P(x, y)$ is found by multiplying each coordinate by k.
>
> $$(x, y) \rightarrow (kx, ky)$$
>
> • If $k > 1$, then the image is larger than the preimage.
> • If $0 < k < 1$, then the image is smaller than the preimage.

CC.8.G.3
2 EXAMPLE   Enlargements

The figure is the preimage. The center of dilation is the origin.

A List the coordinates of the vertices of the preimage in the first column of the table.

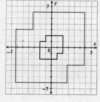

Preimage	Image
(2, 2)	(6, 6)
(2, −1)	(6, −3)
(1, −1)	(3, −3)
(1, −2)	(3, −6)
(−2, −2)	(−6, −6)
(−2, 1)	(−6, 3)
(−1, 1)	(−3, 3)
(−1, 2)	(−3, 6)

B What is the scale factor for the dilation $(x, y) \rightarrow (3x, 3y)$? __3__

C Apply the dilation to the preimage and write the coordinates of the vertices of the image in the second column of the table.

D Sketch the image under the dilation on the coordinate grid.

REFLECT

2a. How does the dilation affect the length of line segments?

Each line segment in the image is three times longer than the

corresponding line segment in the preimage.

2b. How does the dilation affect angle measures?

The dilation does not change the angle measures.

© Houghton Mifflin Harcourt Publishing Company

Chapter 4   158   Lesson 4

© Houghton Mifflin Harcourt Publishing Company

Questioning Strategies

- After plotting the points in the image, what is the next step in sketching the image? **Reference the pre-image and connect the corresponding vertices in the image.**

- How can you check that your sketch is correct? **The image should have the same shape and relative dimensions as the initial figure. It should be half the size of the pre-image.**

Teaching Strategies

Divide students into two groups. The groups will take turns providing each other with a figure drawn in the coordinate plane and a rule for its dilation. The other group must tell whether the dilation is an enlargement or a reduction and draw the image of the figure.

CLOSE

Essential Question

How can you use coordinates to describe the result of a dilation?

Apply the rule of the dilation to the vertices of the original figure. The resulting points are the vertices of the image. To draw the complete image, connect the vertices with the sides that correspond to the sides of the original figure.

Summarize

Have students draw a graphic organizer like the one shown in their journals. Students should tell whether an image under each type of transformation has the same size and shape as the original figure.

Translation	Reflection
shape size	shape size
Rotation	Dilation
shape size	shape

PRACTICE

Where skills are taught	Where skills are practiced
1 EXPLORE	EX. 1
2 EXAMPLE	EX. 2
3 EXAMPLE	EXS. 3, 4, 5

3 EXAMPLE Reductions

The arrow is the preimage. The center of dilation is the origin.

A   List the coordinates of the vertices of the preimage in the first column of the table.

Preimage	Image
(4, 2)	(2, 1)
(0, 5)	(0, 2.5)
(−4, 2)	(−2, 1)
(−2, 2)	(−1, 1)
(−2, −4)	(−1, −2)
(2, −4)	(1, −2)
(2, 2)	(1, 1)

B   What is the scale factor for the dilation $(x, y) \rightarrow \left(\frac{1}{2}x, \frac{1}{2}y\right)$? $\frac{1}{2}$

C   Apply the dilation to the preimage and write the coordinates of the vertices of the image in the second column of the table.

D   Sketch the image under the dilation on the coordinate grid.

REFLECT

3a. How does the dilation affect the length of line segments?

Each line segment in the image is half as long as the corresponding line

segment in the preimage.

3b. How would a dilation with scale factor 1 affect the preimage?

There would be no change. The image would be the same size and

shape as the preimage.

TRY THIS!

3c. Identify the scale factor of the dilation shown.

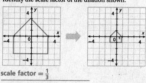

scale factor = $\frac{1}{3}$

Chapter 4   159   Lesson 4

PRACTICE

1. The square is the preimage. The center of dilation is the origin. Write the coordinates of the vertices of the preimage in the first column of the table. Then apply the dilation $(x, y) \rightarrow \left(\frac{3}{2}x, \frac{3}{2}y\right)$ and write the coordinates of the vertices of the image in the second column. Sketch the image of the figure under the dilation.

Preimage	Image
(2, 0)	(3, 0)
(0, 2)	(0, 3)
(−2, 0)	(−3, 0)
(0, −2)	(0, −3)

Sketch the image of the figure under the given dilation.

2. $(x, y) \rightarrow (2x, 2y)$

3. $(x, y) \rightarrow \left(\frac{2}{3}x, \frac{2}{3}y\right)$

Identify the scale factor of the dilation shown.

4. scale factor = $\frac{1}{4}$

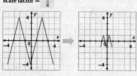

5. scale factor = $\frac{1}{2}$

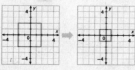

Chapter 4   160   Lesson 4

Assign these pages to help your students practice and apply important lesson concepts. For additional exercises, see the Student Edition.

Answers

Additional Practice

1. not a dilation

2. dilation

3.

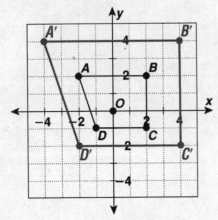

$A'(-4, 4), B'(4, 4), C'(4, -2), D'(-2,-2)$

4.

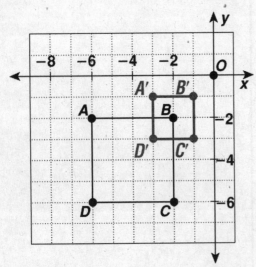

$A'(-3, -1), B'(-1, -1), C'(-1, -3), D'(-3, -3)$

Problem Solving

1. yes

2. yes; 1

3. $37\frac{1}{3}$

4. 14 in.

5. B

6. F

7. C

Name_____ Class_____ Date_____

Additional Practice

Tell whether each transformation is a dilation.

1.

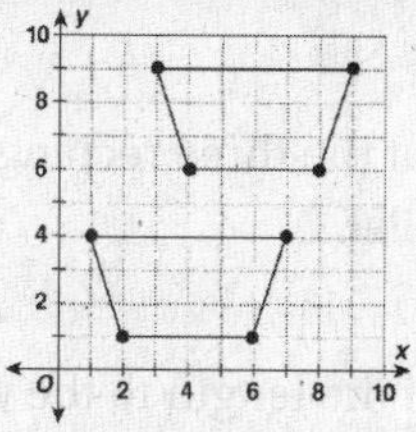

2.

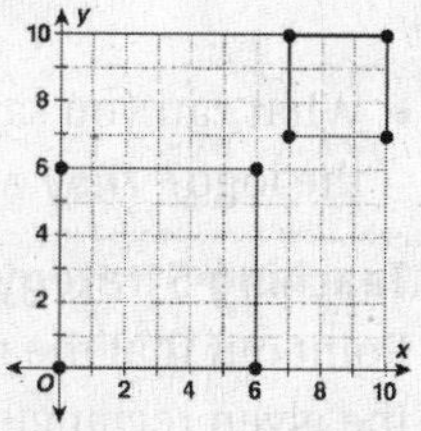

_____

_____

Dilate each figure by the given scale factor with the origin as the center of dilation. What are the vertices of the image?

3. scale factor of 2

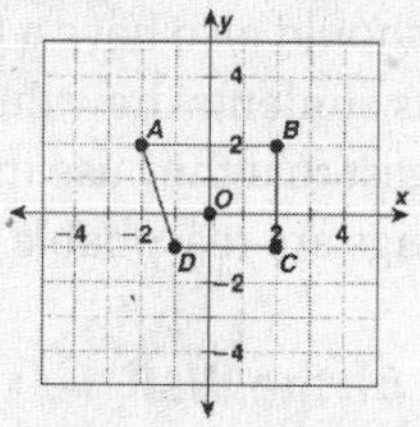

4. scale factor of $\frac{1}{2}$

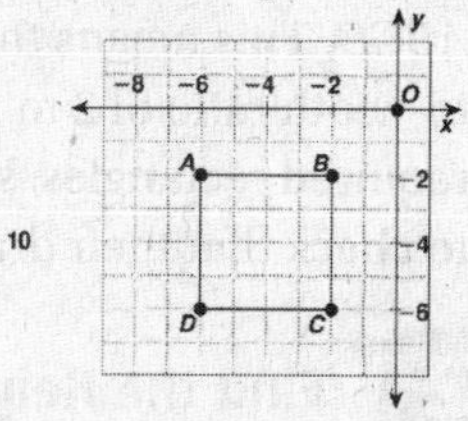

_____

_____

_____

_____

Problem Solving

Write the correct answer.

1. When you enlarge something on a photocopy machine, is the image a dilation?

2. When you make a photocopy that is the same size, is the image a dilation? If so, what is the scale factor?

3. In the movie *Honey, I Blew Up the Kid*, a two-year-old boy is enlarged to a height of 112 feet. If the average height of a two-year old boy is 3 feet, what is the scale factor of this enlargement?

4. In the movie *Honey, I Shrunk the Kids*, an inventor shrinks his kids by a scale factor of about $\frac{1}{240}$. If his kids were about 5 feet tall, how many inches tall were they after they were shrunk?

Use the coordinate plane for Exercises 5–6. Round to the nearest tenth. Choose the letter for the best answer.

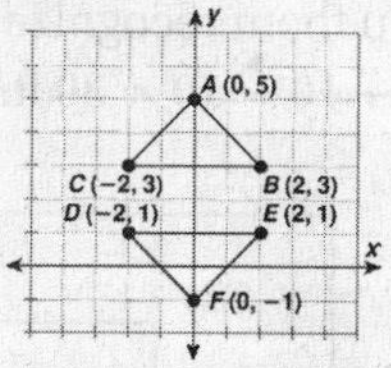

5. What will be the coordinates of A', B' and C' after $\triangle ABC$ is dilated by a factor of 5?

   A $A'(5, 10)$, $B'(7, 8)$, $C'(3, 8)$

   B $A'(0, 25)$, $B'(10, 15)$, $C'(-10, 15)$

   C $A'(0, 5)$, $B'(10, 3)$, $C'(-10, 3)$

   D $A'(0, 15)$, $B'(2, 15)$, $C'(-2, 15)$

6. What will be the coordinates of D', E' and F' after $\triangle DEF$ is dilated by a factor of 5?

   F $D'(-10, 5)$, $E'(10, 5)$, $F'(0, -5)$

   G $D'(10, 5)$, $E'(5, 5)$, $F'(0, 5)$

   H $D'(10, 0)$, $E'(5, 0)$, $F'(-5, 0)$

   J $D'(10, 5)$, $E'(5, 5)$, $F'(-10, 0)$

7. The projection of a movie onto a screen is a dilation. The universally accepted film size for movies has a width of 35 mm. If a movie screen is 12 m wide, what is the dilation factor?

   A 420   C 342.9

   B 0.3   D 2916.7

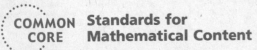

COMMON CORE **Standards for Mathematical Content**

CC.8.G.3 Describe the effect of dilations, translations, rotations, and reflections on two-dimensional figures using coordinates.

CC.8.G.4 Understand that a two-dimensional figure is similar to another if the second can be obtained from the first by a sequence of rotations, reflections, translations, and dilations; given two similar two-dimensional figures, describe a sequence that exhibits the similarity between them.

INTRODUCE

Ask students if they have seen neon signs and ask them what makes these signs unique. If necessary, help students understand that neon signs are made from glass tubing that is bent to create words or images. Ask students what they think might determine the cost of a neon sign. Students should recognize that the cost is at least partially based on the length of glass tubing that is required. Tell students that they will have a chance to use what they have learned about proportional relationships, similar figures, and dilations to design a simple neon sign and determine its cost.

TEACH

1 **Draw the Logo**

Questioning Strategies

- What is the center of dilation when you dilate on the coordinate plane? the origin
- How can you use the scale factor to find the vertices of rectangle $A'B'C'D'$? Multiply each coordinate of the vertices of rectangle *ABCD* by $\frac{3}{2}$ to find the coordinates of the vertices of rectangle $A'B'C'D'$.
- In part D, what is the scale factor of the dilation? $\frac{1}{3}$
- Do you expect rectangle $A'B'C'D'$ to be an enlargement or reduction of rectangle $A'B'C'D'$? Why? Reduction; the scale factor is less than 1.

- What can you say about the three rectangles in the logo? They are similar.

Teaching Strategy

Point out that the ratio of the length to the width of the given rectangle, rectangle *ABCD*, is 2 to 1. Since a dilation produces an image that is similar to the preimage, rectangles $A'B'C'D'$ and $A''B''C''D''$ should both be similar to rectangle *ABCD*. This means they should also have a length-to-width ratio of 2 to 1. As students draw the required rectangles, suggest that they use this fact to check that their drawings are reasonable.

2 **Find the Height of the Wall**

Questioning Strategies

- What type of triangles appear in the figure? right triangles
- Which segment represents Tyler's shadow? Which segment represents the shadow of the wall? $\overline{MN}$; $\overline{KN}$
- How do you use similar triangles to write a proportion? Use the fact that the lengths of corresponding sides are proportional.
- How do you solve the proportion? Isolate the variable by using properties of equality.

Differentiated Instruction

When finding the overall height of the neon sign, it may be helpful for visual learners to make a simple sketch of the wall and the sign. Have students label the sketch with the known dimensions. This can help them recognize that the height of the sign is $50 - 10 - 10 = 30$ ft.

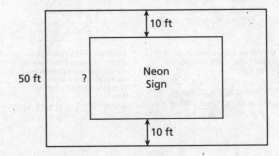

Name_____ Class_____ Date_____

Problem Solving Connections

Sign Design Tyler has been hired by the owner of a 3-D movie theater to create a neon sign for the theater. The owner asks Tyler to design a logo and then turn it into a large neon sign that covers most of an outside wall. How much will it cost to produce the neon sign?

COMMON CORE

CC.8.G.5
CC.8.G.4

1 Draw the Logo

Because the theater shows 3-D movies, Tyler decides that the logo should look like three rectangular movie screens.

A Tyler begins by drawing a rectangle, as shown. Write the coordinates of the vertices of the rectangle.

$A(-4, 2)$; $B(4, 2)$; $C(4, -2)$; $D(-4, -2)$

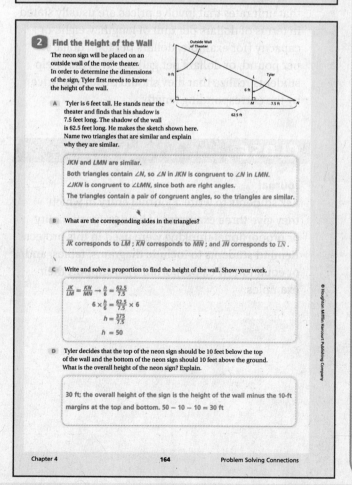

B To draw the second rectangle, Tyler dilates rectangle $ABCD$ using a dilation with scale factor $\frac{3}{2}$. Sketch the image and label the vertices A', B', C', and D'. Then write the coordinates of the vertices of the image.

$A'(-6, 3)$; $B'(6, 3)$; $C'(6, -3)$; $D'(-6, -3)$

C Write the dilation using the notation $(x, y) \rightarrow (kx, ky)$. Then use the value of k to explain whether the dilation is an enlargement or a reduction.

$(x, y) \rightarrow (\frac{3}{2}x, \frac{3}{2}y)$

Since $k > 1$, the dilation is an enlargement.

D To draw the third rectangle, Tyler dilates rectangle $A'B'C'D'$ using the dilation $(x,y) \rightarrow (\frac{1}{3}x, \frac{1}{3}y)$. Sketch the image and label the vertices A'', B'', C'', and D''. Then write the coordinates of the vertices of the image.

$A''(-2, 1)$; $B''(2, 1)$; $C''(2, -1)$; $D''(-2, -1)$

© Houghton Mifflin Harcourt Publishing Company

2 Find the Height of the Wall

The neon sign will be placed on an outside wall of the movie theater. In order to determine the dimensions of the sign, Tyler first needs to know the height of the wall.

A Tyler is 6 feet tall. He stands near the theater and finds that his shadow is 7.5 feet long. The shadow of the wall is 62.5 feet long. He makes the sketch shown here. Name two triangles that are similar and explain why they are similar.

JKN and LMN are similar.

Both triangles contain $\angle N$, so $\angle N$ in JKN is congruent to $\angle N$ in LMN.

$\angle JKN$ is congruent to $\angle LMN$, since both are right angles.

The triangles contain a pair of congruent angles, so the triangles are similar.

B What are the corresponding sides in the triangles?

$\overline{JK}$ corresponds to $\overline{LM}$; $\overline{KN}$ corresponds to $\overline{MN}$; and $\overline{JN}$ corresponds to $\overline{LN}$.

C Write and solve a proportion to find the height of the wall. Show your work.

$\frac{JK}{LM} = \frac{KN}{MN} \rightarrow \frac{h}{6} = \frac{62.5}{7.5}$

$6 \times \frac{h}{6} = \frac{62.5}{7.5} \times 6$

$h = \frac{375}{7.5}$

$h = 50$

D Tyler decides that the top of the neon sign should be 10 feet below the top of the wall and the bottom of the neon sign should be 10 feet above the ground. What is the overall height of the neon sign? Explain.

30 ft; the overall height of the sign is the height of the wall minus the 10-ft margins at the top and bottom. $50 - 10 - 10 = 30$ ft

© Houghton Mifflin Harcourt Publishing Company

3 Find the Dimensions of the Sign

Questioning Strategies

- What is meant by a "unit" on the coordinate plane? It is the distance between consecutive horizontal lines or consecutive vertical lines.

- In part C, what patterns do you see in the completed table? Possible answers: The length on the neon sign is always 5 times the length on the coordinate plane; the length on the neon sign increases by 5 as you move from one column to the next.

- What should you do in order to decide whether the relationship in the table is a proportional relationship? Check whether the ratio of the length on the neon sign to the corresponding length on the coordinate plane is constant.

MATHEMATICAL PRACTICE   Highlighting the Standards

This project is closely related to Standard 1 (Make sense of problems and persevere in solving them). According to the standard, mathematically proficient students work back and forth among multiple representations, including verbal descriptions, tables, equations, and diagrams. As students find the dimensions of the neon sign, encourage them to consider all of the mathematical representations at their disposal. For instance, the sketch on the coordinate plane shows that the outermost rectangle is 3 times as long as the innermost rectangle. Students can "carry over" this verbal description to help them mark the relevant dimensions of the neon sign in the figure. Students can also use equations in the form of proportions to help them determine the required dimensions.

4 Answer the Question

Questioning Strategies

- How can you find the perimeter of the outermost rectangle of the neon sign? Find the sum of twice the length and twice the height: $2(60) + 2(30) = 180$ ft.

- What should you do in order to determine which table shows a proportional relationship? Check to see if the ratio of price to length is constant.

- Do you need to check every pair of values in a table? Once you find two pairs of values for which the ratio is not the same you can conclude that the relationship is not a proportional relationship.

- How do you find the unit rate (or unit price) for A-Plus Neon? Divide any price in the table by the corresponding length: $\$7.50 \div 3 = \$2.50$ per foot.

Avoid Common Errors

When students find the unit rate for A-Plus Neon, they might divide the length by the corresponding price to find a unit rate of 0.4 feet per dollar. Although this is a correct ratio, remind students that unit rates that involve prices are usually stated in terms of dollars per unit of length, weight, or capacity (for example, dollars per foot, dollars per pound, or dollars per gallon). This may help students realize that they should divide the price by the corresponding length.

CLOSE

Journal

Ask students to write a journal entry in which they give three examples of how proportionality or proportional thinking were used in this project. Remind students to include diagrams, tables, and/or equations (i.e., proportions) to support their examples.

© Houghton Mifflin Harcourt Publishing Company

3 Find the Dimensions of the Sign

The neon sign will be an enlargement of the logo that Tyler designed. Tyler needs to know the dimensions of the logo when it is enlarged.

A Tyler has already determined the overall height of the neon sign. In his drawing of the logo, this height is represented by the height of the outer rectangle, rectangle A′B′C′D′. Look back at your work to complete the following.

Overall height of the neon sign: _____30_____ feet

Height of rectangle A′B′C′D′ on coordinate plane: _____6_____ units

B What length on the neon sign is represented by one unit on the coordinate plane? Explain.

> 5 ft; Since 30 ft on the neon sign are represented by 6 units on the
> coordinate plane, each unit of the coordinate plane represents 30 ÷ 6 = 5 ft.

C Complete the table.

Length on the Coordinate Plane (units)	1	2	3	4	5	6
Length on the Neon Sign (ft)	5	10	15	20	25	30

D Is the relationship in the table a proportional relationship? Why or why not?

> Yes; the ratio of the length on the neon sign to the length on the
> coordinate plane is constant.

E Use your drawing of the logo on a coordinate plane and the above table to help you find the height and width of each rectangle in the neon sign.

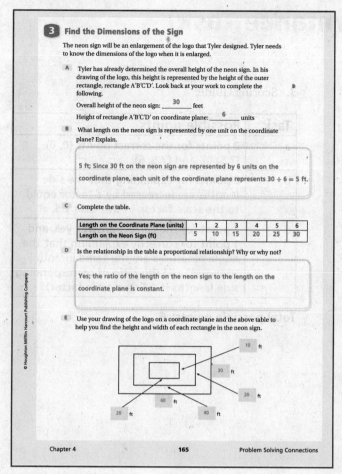

10 ft
30 ft
20 ft
60 ft
20 ft
40 ft

4 Answer the Question

Neon signs are made from glass tubing that is bent into the desired shapes. The cost of a sign depends upon the length of the tubing.

A What is the total length of the tubing that will be needed to make the neon sign for the movie theater? Explain.

> 360 ft; add the perimeters of the three rectangles.
> 60 ft + 120 ft + 180 ft = 360 ft

B Tyler gathers pricing information from two different companies that make neon signs. The prices are shown in the tables. For which company is the relationship between price and length a proportional relationship? Why?

Nancy's Neon					
Length of Tubing (ft)	4	8	12	16	20
Price of Sign ($)	14.00	24.00	42.00	52.00	60.00

A-Plus Neon					
Length of Tubing (ft)	3	6	9	12	15
Price of Sign ($)	7.50	15.00	22.50	30.00	37.50

> A-Plus Neon; the ratio of the price to the length is constant.

C Which company seems to offer a better deal on neon signs? Why?

> A-Plus Neon
> The unit rate (unit price) is $2.50 per foot. At Nancy's Neon, the ratio of the
> price to the length varies, but it is always greater than $2.50 per foot.

D Tyler chooses the company that offers a better deal. Show how he can use a proportion to find the total cost of the neon sign for the movie theater.

> $\text{Price (\$)} \rightarrow \dfrac{2.50}{1} = \dfrac{x}{360}$
> Price (ft)
>
> $360 \times \dfrac{2.50}{1} = \dfrac{x}{360} \times 360$
>
> $900 = x$
>
> The total cost of the sign is $900.

Notes

This page provides students with the opportunity to apply concepts from the Common Core in real-world problem situations. There are three different levels of performance tasks:

⭐ **Novice:** These are short word problems that require students to apply the math they have learned in straightforward, real-world situations.

⭐⭐ **Apprentice:** These are more involved problems that guide students step-by-step through more complex tasks. These exercises include more complicated reasoning, writing, and open-ended elements.

⭐⭐⭐ **Expert:** These are open-ended, non-routine problems that, instead of stepping the students through, asks them to choose their own methods for solving and justify their answers and reasoning.

Sample answers

1. **a.** $d = \frac{1}{6}t$
   b. Tim's graph would also start at (0, 0) but would have a smaller slope. Janelle runs at a faster rate, because $\frac{1}{6} > \frac{1}{8}$.
2. **a.** No; the angles have different measures.
   b. No; a dilation would result in similar figures.

3. Scoring Guide:

Task	Possible points
a	**2 points** for the correct points (0, 0), (7.5, 0), and (7.5, 6).
b	**2 points** for explaining that the side lengths are increased by a factor equal to the scale factor, in this case 1.5.
c	**1 point** for the correct answer yes, and **1 point** for correctly explaining that the angle measures are the same in both triangles, and the ratio of corresponding side lengths is 1.5 (the scale factor).

Total possible points: 6

CHAPTER 4

Performance Task

COMMON CORE

CC.8.EE.5
CC.8.G.3
CC.8.G.4

⭐ 1. Janelle runs a steady pace from the parking lot down a 5-mile trail. She makes the graph shown to describe her run. Tim jogs the same 5-mile trail, but writes the equation $d = \frac{1}{8}t$ to describe his distance d miles after jogging t minutes.

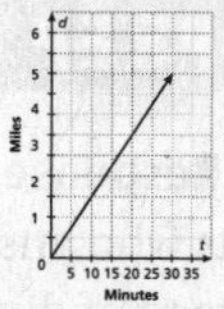

a. Write an equation to represent Janelle's graph.

b. How would Tim's graph compare to Janelle's graph? Who runs at a faster average rate? Explain.

⭐ 2. Peggy holds a rubber band between her thumb and index finger, then pulls from one point to form a triangle. When she pulls harder, the triangle gets bigger. She drew the triangles on the coordinate plane as shown.

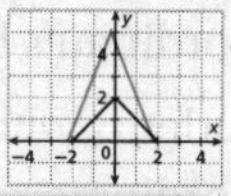

a. Are the triangles similar? How do you know?

b. Is this an example of a dilation? Explain.

⭐ 3. A triangle on the coordinate plane has vertices (0, 0), (5, 0), and (5, 4).

⭐ a. The figure is dilated by a scale factor of 1.5 with the origin as the center of dilation. Find the coordinates of the dilated figure.

b. What is the effect of the dilation on the side lengths of the figure?

c. Are the triangles similar? Explain.

⭐ 4. Fernando has a fence represented by rectangle LMNP on the coordinate plane. He asks for a new fence to enclose 6 times as much area as the current fence. He would also like the shape enclosed by the fence to be similar to shape enclosed by the current fence. The contractors construct the fence shown by the rectangle L'M'N'P'.

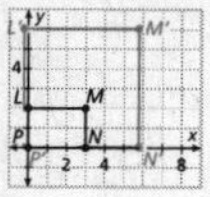

a. Did the contractors increase the area by the amount Fernando wanted? Explain.

b. Does the new fence enclose a shape similar to the old shape? How do you know?

4. Scoring Guide:

Task	Possible points
a	**1 point** for the correct answer yes, and **2 points** for correctly explaining that the original area was 2 • 3 = 6 square units, and the new area is 6 • 6 = 36 square units, which is 6 times larger than the original area.
b	**1 point** for the correct answer no, and **2 points** for a correct explanation, for example: The corresponding side lengths are not in proportion. $\frac{LP}{L'P'} = \frac{1}{3}$, but $\frac{NP}{N'P'} = \frac{1}{2}$.

Total possible points: 6

COMMON CORE CORRELATION

Standard	Items
Prep for CC.8.EE.5	1–9
CC.8.G.3	11–14, 13–15
CC.8.G.4	10, 11–12, 15, 17

TEST PREP DOCTOR ⊕

Selected Response: Item 4
- Students who answered **G** subtracted 15 from 150 instead of dividing 150 by 15.
- Students who answered **H** incorrectly set up the proportion as minutes per package.

Selected Response: Item 11
- Students who answered **A** divided by 3 instead of multiplying by 3.
- Students who answered **B** did not multiply both coordinates by 3.
- Students who answered **C** did not multiply both coordinates by 3.

Constructed Response: Item 14
- Students who listed vertices as $(0,10)$, $(2, -10)$, and $(-2, -10)$ only multiplied the y-coordinate by the scale factor of 2.5.
- Students who listed vertices as $(0,4)$, $(5, -4)$, and $(-5, -4)$ only multiplied the x-coordinate by the scale factor of 2.5.

CHAPTER 4 COMMON CORE ASSESSMENT READINESS

Name _____ Class _____ Date _____

SELECTED RESPONSE

1. Temperatures were taken after every 10 minutes for 4 experiments.

Experiment 1	52°	26°	13°
Experiment 2	28°	56°	84°
Experiment 3	14°	28°	56°
Experiment 4	67°	54°	41°

Which of the experiments' temperatures have a proportional relationship with time?

A. Experiment 1
(B.) Experiment 2
C. Experiment 3
D. Experiment 4

2. Which value would complete the table to make the relationship between the two quantities proportional?

x	y
1	22.4
2	44.8
3	?
4	89.6
5	112

F. 44.8   H. 89.6
(G.) 67.2   J. 56

3. Determine whether the ratios $\frac{8}{12}$ and $\frac{10}{18}$ are proportional.

(A.) not proportional   B. proportional

4. A factory worker can package 150 games in 15 minutes. How many games can he package per minute?

F. 20   H. 8.33
G. 135   (J.) 10

5. Sarah's pay for two weeks was $158.16. If she worked 8 hours the first week and 4 hours the second, what was her rate of pay?

A. $3.23 per hr   C. $22.60 per hr
(B.) $13.18 per hr   D. $31.64 per hr

6. Which of these is a lower unit price than 8 for $15?

F. 3 for $7   H. 10 for $20
(G.) 5 for $9   J. 12 for $25

7. Which of these prices is a lower unit price than 5 for $9.00?

A. 3 for $6.00   (C.) 6 for $10.00
B. 8 for $16.00   D. 10 for $19.00

8. Ignacio is going on vacation. He needs to drive 520 miles in 8 hours. What is his average speed in miles per hour?

F. 63 miles per hour
(G.) 65 miles per hour
H. 67 miles per hour
J. 69 miles per hour

9. Three pounds of ground beef costs $2.00. What is the unit rate?

A. $0.50/pound   C. $1.50/pound
(B.) $0.67/pound   D. $2.00/pound

---

10. Triangle *ABC* is similar to triangle *DEF*. What is the value of *x*?

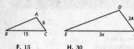

F. 15   H. 30
(G.) 20   J. 60

11. A figure is dilated by a scale factor of 3. If the origin is the center of dilation, what is the image of a vertex located at (3, 4)?

A. $(1, 1\frac{1}{2})$ C. (9, 4)
B. (3, 12)   (D.) (9, 12)

CONSTRUCTED RESPONSE

12. Dilate the figure by a scale factor of 2.5 with the origin as the center of dilation. Graph the new figure on the coordinate plane, and list the vertices of the image. Show your work.

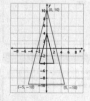

$(0, 4) \rightarrow (0 \cdot 2.5, 4 \cdot 2.5,) \rightarrow (0, 10)$

$(2, -4) \rightarrow (2 \cdot 2.5, -4 \cdot 2.5,) \rightarrow (5, -10)$

$(-2, -4) \rightarrow (-2 \cdot 2.5, -4 \cdot 2.5,) \rightarrow (-5, -10)$

13. A figure is dilated by a scale factor of 2. If the origin is the center of dilation, what are the coordinates in the original figure of a vertex located at (12, 8) in the enlarged figure?

(6, 4)

14. Su, who is 5 feet tall, is standing at point *D* in the drawing. The top of her head is at point *E*. A tree in the yard is at point *B* with the top of the tree at point *C*. Su stands so her shadow meets the end of the tree's shadow at point *A*.

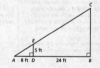

a. Which triangles are similar? How do you know?

$\triangle ABC \sim \triangle ADE$; The triangles are similar because all corresponding angles are congruent.

b. What is the ratio of the triangles?

$\frac{4}{1}$

c. Find the height of the tree.

20 feet

© Houghton Mifflin Harcourt Publishing Company

CHAPTER 5

Geometric Relationships

COMMON CORE PROFESIONAL DEVELOPMENT **CC.8.G.5**

In Grade 8, students will use explorations and deductive reasoning to establish the relationships about angles in triangles, parallel lines cut by a transversal, and angles in similar triangles.

From Grade 7, students recognize vertical angles, adjacent angles, and supplementary angles when parallel lines are cut by a transversal. They will expand on these relationships to identify other pairs of congruent angles. Using these relationships and deductive reasoning, students will find measures of missing angles.

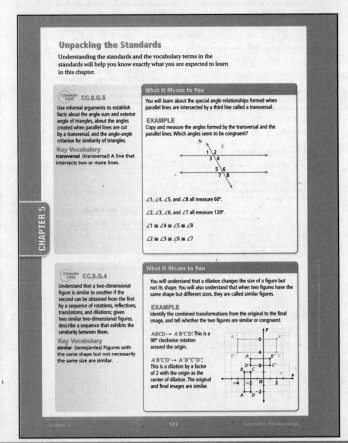

CHAPTER 5

Geometric Relationships

Chapter Focus

You will use angle pairs to solve problems. You will explore angles formed by parallel lines that are cut by a transversal and the measures of the angles in a triangle. A dilation is a transformation in which a figure and its image are similar. You will use coordinates to find the scale factor used in a dilation and to describe the result of a translation, reflection, or rotation. You will also consider what properties of a figure are preserved under a translation, reflection, or rotation. The Side-Side-Side Postulate and the Side-Angle-Side Postulate will be used to prove that two triangles are congruent. Finally, you will explore the connection between transformations and congruent figures and transformations and similar figures.

Chapter at a Glance

COMMON CORE

Lesson	Standards for Mathematical Content
5-1 Angle Relationships	PREP FOR CC.8.G.1
5-2 Parallel and Perpendicular Lines	CC.8.G.5
5-3 Triangles	CC.8.G.5
5-4 Coordinate Geometry	PREP FOR CC.8.G.3
5-5 Congruence	PREP FOR CC.8.G.2
5-6 Transformations	CC.8.G.3
5-7 Similarity and Congruence Transformations	CC.8.G.1
5-8 Identifying Combined Transformations	CC.8.G.2, CC.8.G.4
Problem Solving Connections	
Performance Task	
Assessment Readiness	

Unpacking the Standards

Understanding the standards and the vocabulary terms in the standards will help you know exactly what you are expected to learn in this chapter.

COMMON CORE CC.8.G.5

Use informal arguments to establish facts about the angle sum and exterior angle of triangles, about the angles created when parallel lines are cut by a transversal, and the angle-angle criterion for similarity of triangles.

Key Vocabulary
transversal *(transversal)* A line that intersects two or more lines.

What It Means to You

You will learn about the special angle relationships formed when parallel lines are intersected by a third line called a transversal.

EXAMPLE
Copy and measure the angles formed by the transversal and the parallel lines. Which angles seem to be congruent?

∠1, ∠4, ∠5, and ∠8 all measure 60°.

∠2, ∠3, ∠6, and ∠7 all measure 120°.

∠1 ≅ ∠4 ≅ ∠5 ≅ ∠8

∠2 ≅ ∠3 ≅ ∠6 ≅ ∠7

COMMON CORE CC.8.G.4

Understand that a two-dimensional figure is similar to another if the second can be obtained from the first by a sequence of rotations, reflections, translations, and dilations; given two similar two-dimensional figures, describe a sequence that exhibits the similarity between them.

Key Vocabulary
similar *(semejantes)* Figures with the same shape but not necessarily the same size are similar.

What It Means to You

You will understand that a dilation changes the size of a figure but not its shape. You will also understand that when two figures have the same shape but different sizes, they are called similar figures.

EXAMPLE
Identify the combined transformations from the original to the final image, and tell whether the two figures are similar or congruent.

ABCD → A′B′C′D′: This is a 90° clockwise rotation around the origin.

A′B′C′D′ → A″B″C″D″: This is a dilation by a factor of 2 with the origin as the center of dilation. The original and final images are similar.

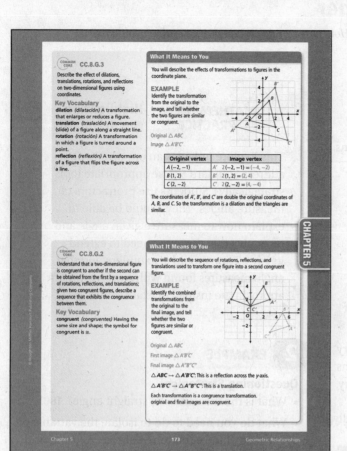

CC.8.G.3

Describe the effect of dilations, translations, rotations, and reflections on two-dimensional figures using coordinates.

Key Vocabulary
dilation *(dilatación)* A transformation that enlarges or reduces a figure.
translation *(traslación)* A movement (slide) of a figure along a straight line.
rotation *(rotación)* A transformation in which a figure is turned around a point.
reflection *(reflexión)* A transformation of a figure that flips the figure across a line.

What It Means to You
You will describe the effects of transformations to figures in the coordinate plane.

EXAMPLE
Identify the transformation from the original to the image, and tell whether the two figures are similar or congruent.

Original △ *ABC*
Image △ *A'B'C'*

Original vertex	Image vertex
A (−2, −1)	*A'* 2(−2, −1) = (−4, −2)
B (1, 2)	*B'* 2(1, 2) = (2, 4)
C (2, −2)	*C'* 2(2, −2) = (4, −4)

The coordinates of *A'*, *B'*, and *C'* are double the original coordinates of *A*, *B*, and *C*. So the transformation is a dilation and the triangles are similar.

CC.8.G.2

Understand that a two-dimensional figure is congruent to another if the second can be obtained from the first by a sequence of rotations, reflections, and translations; given two congruent figures, describe a sequence that exhibits the congruence between them.

Key Vocabulary
congruent *(congruentes)* Having the same size and shape; the symbol for congruent is ≅.

What It Means to You
You will describe the sequence of rotations, reflections, and translations used to transform one figure into a second congruent figure.

EXAMPLE
Identify the combined transformations from the original to the final image, and tell whether the two figures are similar or congruent.

Original △ *ABC*
First image △ *A'B'C'*
Final image △ *A"B"C"*

△ *ABC* → △ *A'B'C'*: This is a reflection across the y-axis.

△ *A'B'C'* → △ *A"B"C"*: This is a translation.

Each transformation is a congruence transformation. original and final images are congruent.

COMMON CORE PROFESIONAL DEVELOPMENT **CC.8.G.2**

In Grade 8, students are introduced to congruency. Students examine two figures to determine congruency by identifying the rigid transformation(s) that produced the figures. A rigid transformation is one in which the preimage and the image both have exactly the same size and shape since the corresponding angles and corresponding line segments are congruent. Students will use the symbol for congruency (≅) to write statements of congruency.

CHAPTER 5

Key Vocabulary

adjacent angles *(ángulos adyacentes)* Angles in the same plane that have a common vertex and a common side.

alternate exterior angles *(ángulos alternos externos)* For two lines intersected by a transversal, a pair of angles that lie on opposite sides of the transversal and outside the other two lines.

alternate interior angles *(ángulos alternos internos)* For two lines intersected by a transversal, a pair of nonadjacent angles that lie on opposite sides of the transversal and between the other two lines.

complementary angles *(ángulos complementarios)* Two angles whose measures add to 90°.

congruent *(congruentes)* Having the same size and shape; the symbol for congruent is ≅.

corresponding angles *(ángulos correspondientes)* For two lines intersected by a transversal, a pair of angles that lie on the same side of the transversal and on the same sides of the other two lines.

dilation *(dilatación)* A transformation that enlarges or reduces a figure.

exterior angle *(ángulo exterior)* An angle formed by one side of a polygon and the extension of an adjacent side.

image *(imagen)* A figure resulting from a transformation.

interior angles *(ángulos internos)* Angles on the inner sides of two lines cut by a transversal.

line of reflection *(línea de reflexión)* A line that a figure is flipped across to create a mirror image of the original figure.

reflection *(reflexión)* A transformation of a figure that flips the figure across a line.

remote interior angle *(ángulo interior remoto)* An interior angle that is not adjacent to the exterior angle.

rotation *(rotación)* A transformation in which a figure is turned around a point.

same-side interior angles *(ángulo de interior del mismo lado)* For two lines intersected by a transversal, a pair of angles that lie on the same side of the transversal, between the parallel lines.

scale factor *(factor de escala)* The ratio used to enlarge or reduce similar figures.

similar *(semejantes)* Figures with the same shape but not necessarily the same size are similar.

supplementary angles *(ángulos suplementarios)* Two angles whose measures have a sum of 180°.

transformation *(transformación)* A change in the size or position of a figure.

translation *(traslación)* A movement (slide) of a figure along a straight line.

transversal *(transversal)* A line that intersects two or more lines.

vertical angles *(ángulos verticales)* A pair of opposite congruent angles formed by intersecting lines.

CHAPTER 5

Angle Relationships
Going Deeper

Essential question: *How can you use angle pairs to solve problems?*

COMMON CORE

Standards for Mathematical Content

Prep for CC.8.G.1 Verify experimentally the properties of rotations, reflections, and translations.

Vocabulary
vertical angles
adjacent angles
supplementary angles
complementary angles

Prerequisites
Vertex

Math Background
Supplementary angles add to 180°. *Complementary angles* add to 90°. Students often confuse the terms supplementary and complementary. One memory device is to notice that *c* comes before *s* in the alphabet, just as 90° comes before 180° numerically.

INTRODUCE

Tell students that in this lesson they will investigate the angles formed when two lines intersect. Ask students how they measure angles. Review how to read a protractor. Emphasize how to correctly align the protractor with the vertex of the angle and how to read the two different scales based on whether the angle is acute (> 0° and < 90°) or obtuse (> 90° and < 180°).

TEACH

 EXPLORE

Materials
Straightedge
Protractor

Questioning Strategies
• What does it mean when an 'm' is placed directly in front of the angle symbol '∠'? **This refers to the angle measure (in degrees).**

• What does the word *adjacent* mean in an everyday context? **next to or adjoining**

MATHEMATICAL PRACTICE
Highlighting the Standards

This Explore provides an opportunity to address Standard 5 (Use appropriate tools strategically). Students use protractors to measure angles. They should be able to explain how to measure a given angle and recognize that they may need to extend its rays. They should also understand that angle measures found with a protractor are approximate instead of exact values.

2 EXAMPLE

Questioning Strategies
• What is the measure of a straight angle? **180°**

• What do you need to do to isolate the variable on one side of the equation? **Subtract 52 from both sides.**

CLOSE

Essential Question
How can you use angle pairs to solve problems?
Possible answer: Use angle pairs to write equations that you can solve to find the measures of unknown angles.

PRACTICE

Where skills are taught	Where skills are practiced
1 EXPLORE	EXS. 1–4, 8
2 EXAMPLE	EXS. 5–7

5-1

Angle Relationships
Going Deeper
Essential question: *How can you use angle pairs to solve problems?*

CC.8.G.1

1 EXPLORE   Measuring and Describing Angles

A When lines intersect, several angles are formed. Use a ruler or straightedge to draw a pair of intersecting lines. Label each angle in order clockwise from 1 to 4.

Possible drawing:

B Use a protractor to find each angle measure.

Angle	Angle Measure
1	same as m∠3
2	same as m∠4
3	same as m∠1
4	same as m∠2

C What can you say about m∠1 and m∠3? <u>They are the same.</u>

Angles 1 and 3 are **vertical angles**. They are *opposite* one another. Vertical angles have equal measures, *no* sides in common, and *no* common interior points.

What is the other pair of vertical angles in A ? <u>∠2 and ∠4</u>

D What can you say about m∠1 and m∠2? About m∠2 and m∠3?

<u>Possible answer: They are next to each other; they share a side.</u>

Angles 1 and 2 and angles 2 and 3 are **adjacent angles**. They share a common vertex and a common side.

What are the two other pairs of adjacent angles in the figure?

<u>∠3 and ∠4; ∠4 and ∠1</u>

E What can you say about the sum of the degree measures of each pair of adjacent angles? <u>The sum is 180°.</u>

Two angles whose measures add up to **180°** are called **supplementary angles**.

Each pair of adjacent angles in the figure you made are <u>supplementary</u> angles.

Two angles whose measures add up to **90°** are called **complementary angles**.

REFLECT

1. Angles *A* and *B* are supplementary. m∠A = 80°. m∠B = <u>100°</u>

CC.8.G.1

2 EXAMPLE   Finding Angle Measures

Find the measure of ∠EHF.

∠EHF and <u>∠FHG</u> are <u>supplementary</u> angles.

The sum of their measures is <u>180°</u>

Write and solve an equation to find m∠EHF.

$2x + 52 = 180$

$2x = 128$

m∠EHF = <u>128°</u>

TRY THIS!

2. Write and solve an equation to find the value of 3x and m∠JML.

$3x + 75 = 180$

$3x = 105$

m∠JML = 3x = <u>105°</u>

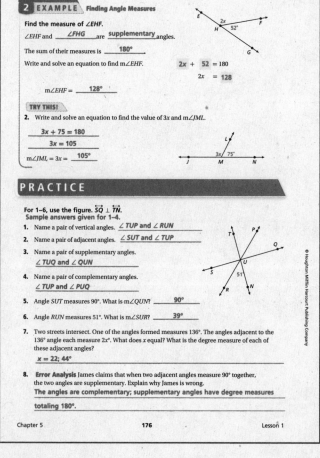

PRACTICE

For 1–6, use the figure. $\overleftrightarrow{SQ} \perp \overleftrightarrow{TN}$.
Sample answers given for 1–4.

1. Name a pair of vertical angles. <u>∠ TUP and ∠ RUN</u>

2. Name a pair of adjacent angles. <u>∠ SUT and ∠ TUP</u>

3. Name a pair of supplementary angles.
<u>∠ TUQ and ∠ QUN</u>

4. Name a pair of complementary angles.
<u>∠ TUP and ∠ PUQ</u>

5. Angle *SUT* measures 90°. What is m∠QUN? <u>90°</u>

6. Angle *RUN* measures 51°. What is m∠SUR? <u>39°</u>

7. Two streets intersect. One of the angles formed measures 136°. The angles adjacent to the 136° angle each measure 2x°. What does x equal? What is the degree measure of each of these adjacent angles?
<u>x = 22; 44°</u>

8. **Error Analysis** James claims that when two adjacent angles measure 90° together, the two angles are supplementary. Explain why James is wrong.
<u>The angles are complementary; supplementary angles have degree measures</u>
<u>totaling 180°.</u>

© Houghton Mifflin Harcourt Publishing Company

Assign these pages to help your students practice and apply important lesson concepts. For additional exercises, see the Student Edition.

Answers

Additional Practice

1. ∠*NXP*, ∠*MXR*, ∠*MXN*, or ∠*RXP*

2. ∠*MXS* and ∠*RXS*

3. ∠*NXS* and ∠*PXS*

4. ∠*RXS* and ∠*SXM*

5. Possible answer: ∠*NXP* and ∠*MXN*, ∠*RXM* and ∠*MXN*, ∠*RXP*, and ∠*PXN*

6. m∠4 = 110°　　7.　m∠3 = *n*°

8. m∠*ECD* = 150°

Problem Solving

1. Possible answer: ∠*DAB*

2. Possible answers: ∠*DAE*, ∠*EAB*

3. Possible answers: ∠*AED*, ∠*DAE*

4. Possible answers: ∠*DGI*, ∠*IGE*

5. C　　　　　　6.　F

7. C　　　　　　8.　H

9. C　　　　　10.　J

5-1

Name _____ Class _____ Date _____

Additional Practice

Use the diagram to name each figure.

1. a right angle

_____

2. two acute angles

_____

3. two obtuse angles

_____

4. a pair of complementary angles

_____

_____

5. three pairs of supplementary angles

_____

_____

_____

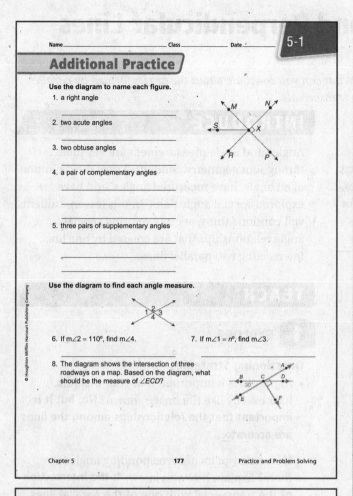

Use the diagram to find each angle measure.

6. If m∠2 = 110°, find m∠4.   7. If m∠1 = n°, find m∠3.

8. The diagram shows the intersection of three
   roadways on a map. Based on the diagram, what
   should be the measure of ∠ECD?

Problem Solving

Use the flag of the Bahamas to solve the problems.

1. Name a right angle in the flag.

_____

2. Name a pair of complementary
   angles in the flag.

_____

3. Name two acute angles in the flag.

_____

4. Name a pair of supplementary
   angles in the flag.

_____

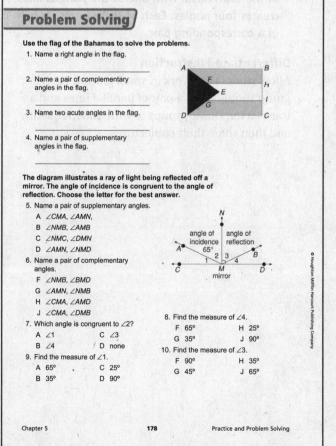

**The diagram illustrates a ray of light being reflected off a
mirror. The angle of incidence is congruent to the angle of
reflection. Choose the letter for the best answer.**

5. Name a pair of supplementary angles.

   A ∠CMA, ∠AMN,

   B ∠NMB, ∠AMB

   C ∠NMC, ∠DMN

   D ∠AMN, ∠NMD

6. Name a pair of complementary
   angles.

   F ∠NMB, ∠BMD

   G ∠AMN, ∠NMB

   H ∠CMA, ∠AMD

   J ∠CMA, ∠DMB

7. Which angle is congruent to ∠2?

   A ∠1   C ∠3

   B ∠4   D none

9. Find the measure of ∠1.

   A 65°   C 25°

   B 35°   D 90°

8. Find the measure of ∠4.

   F 65°   H 25°

   G 35°   J 90°

10. Find the measure of ∠3.

   F 90°   H 35°

   G 45°   J 65°

Parallel and Perpendicular Lines
Going Deeper

Essential question: *What can you conclude about the angles formed by parallel lines that are cut by a transversal?*

COMMON CORE

Standards for Mathematical Content

CC.8.G.5 Use informal arguments to establish facts about the angle sum and exterior angle of triangles, about the angles created when parallel lines are cut by a transversal, and the angle-angle criterion for similarity of triangles.

Vocabulary

transversal

corresponding angles

alternate interior angles

alternate exterior angles

same-side interior angles

Prerequisites

Parallel lines

Translations

Solving equations

Math Background

If t is a line that intersects lines ℓ_1 and ℓ_2 then t is a transversal. In this lesson, students discover the angle relationships that result from a transversal intersecting two parallel lines. They learn that when a transversal intersects parallel lines, corresponding angles are congruent, alternate interior angles are congruent, alternate exterior angles are congruent, and same-side interior angles are supplementary. Knowing these angle relationships allows students to solve for missing angle measures in a diagram.

INTRODUCE

Angles and angle measurement are key ideas throughout geometry. Students know the definition of an angle, have measured angles, and have explored special angle pairs. In this lesson, students will continue this work by exploring special angle relationships that are created by one line intersecting two parallel lines.

TEACH

1 EXPLORE

Questioning Strategies

- In part C, is it important that your diagram look exactly like the image shown? **No; but it is important that the relationships among the lines are accurate.**

- How many pairs of corresponding angles are there? Explain how you know. **4; the intersection of the transversal with one of the parallel lines creates four angles. Each of these angles is half of a corresponding pair.**

Differentiated Instruction

Allow students to work in small groups. Each group should draw a pair of parallel lines and a transversal. Guide groups to work independently and then share their conjectures.

Name _____ **Class** _____ **Date** _____

Parallel and Perpendicular Lines
Going Deeper

Essential question: *What can you conclude about the angles formed by parallel lines that are cut by a transversal?*

A **transversal** is a line that intersects two lines in the same plane at two different points. Transversal *t* and lines *a* and *b* form eight angles.

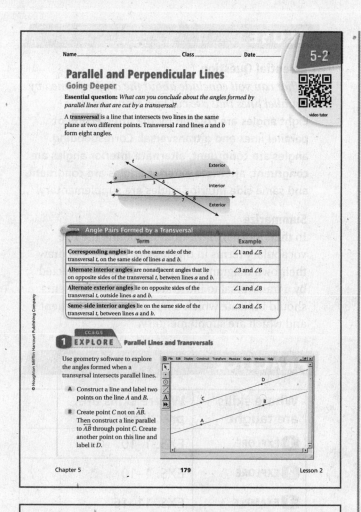

Angle Pairs Formed by a Transversal

Term	Example
Corresponding angles lie on the same side of the transversal *t*, on the same side of lines *a* and *b*.	∠1 and ∠5
Alternate interior angles are nonadjacent angles that lie on opposite sides of the transversal *t*, between lines *a* and *b*.	∠3 and ∠6
Alternate exterior angles lie on opposite sides of the transversal *t*, outside lines *a* and *b*.	∠1 and ∠8
Same-side interior angles lie on the same side of the transversal *t*, between lines *a* and *b*.	∠3 and ∠5

1 EXPLORE Parallel Lines and Transversals

Use geometry software to explore the angles formed when a transversal intersects parallel lines.

A Construct a line and label two points on the line *A* and *B*.

B Create point *C* not on $\overrightarrow{AB}$. Then construct a line parallel to $\overrightarrow{AB}$ through point *C*. Create another point on this line and label it *D*.

C Create two points outside the two parallel lines and label them *E* and *F*. Construct transversal $\overleftrightarrow{EF}$. Label the points of intersection *G* and *H*.

D Measure the angles formed by the parallel lines and the transversal. Write the angle measures in the table below.

E Drag point *E* or point *F* to a different position record the new angle measures in the table.

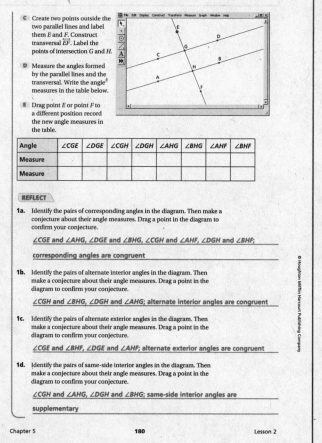

Angle	∠CGE	∠DGE	∠CGH	∠DGH	∠AHG	∠BHG	∠AHF	∠BHF
Measure								
Measure								

REFLECT

1a. Identify the pairs of corresponding angles in the diagram. Then make a conjecture about their angle measures. Drag a point in the diagram to confirm your conjecture.

∠CGE and ∠AHG, ∠DGE and ∠BHG, ∠CGH and ∠AHF, ∠DGH and ∠BHF;

corresponding angles are congruent

1b. Identify the pairs of alternate interior angles in the diagram. Then make a conjecture about their angle measures. Drag a point in the diagram to confirm your conjecture.

∠CGH and ∠BHG, ∠DGH and ∠AHG; alternate interior angles are congruent

1c. Identify the pairs of alternate exterior angles in the diagram. Then make a conjecture about their angle measures. Drag a point in the diagram to confirm your conjecture.

∠CGE and ∠BHF, ∠DGE and ∠AHF; alternate exterior angles are congruent

1d. Identify the pairs of same-side interior angles in the diagram. Then make a conjecture about their angle measures. Drag a point in the diagram to confirm your conjecture.

∠CGH and ∠AHG, ∠DGH and ∠BHG; same-side interior angles are

supplementary

© Houghton Mifflin Harcourt Publishing Company

2 EXPLORE

Questioning Strategies

- Along what line do you translate ∠2? **line t**

- After the translation, which angle does ∠2 align with? **∠2 aligns with ∠6.**

3 EXAMPLE

- In part A, what are the measures of the other numbered angles? **m∠1 = m∠8 = 55°; m∠2 = m∠3 = m∠6 = m∠7 = 125°**

- In part B, if you are given the measure of one angle (m∠SVW), can you determine the measure of the other angles? **Yes; you can use the relationships among the remaining angles to find each measure.**

MATHEMATICAL PRACTICE   **Highlighting the Standards**

This Lesson is an opportunity to address Standard 7 (Look for and make use of structure). Students should recognize the clear structure created by the intersection of parallel lines by a transversal. By understanding the relationships among the angles created, students will be able to solve a variety of problems.

CLOSE

Essential Question

What can you conclude about the angles formed by parallel lines that are cut by a transversal?
Eight angles are created by the intersection of parallel lines and a transversal. Corresponding angles are congruent, alternate interior angles are congruent, alternate exterior angles are congruent, and same-side interior angles are supplementary.

Summarize

In their journal, have students define the five vocabulary terms in this lesson. Have them draw their own diagram with parallel lines intersected by a transversal to illustrate each term. Students should indicate which angle pairs are congruent and which are supplementary.

PRACTICE

Where skills are taught	Where skills are practiced
1 EXPLORE	EXS. 1–10
2 EXPLORE	EXS. 1–10
3 EXAMPLE	EXS. 11–16

© Houghton Mifflin Harcourt Publishing Company

You can use your knowledge of transformations to informally justify the angle relationships formed by parallel lines and a transversal.

2 EXPLORE CC.8.G.5 Justifying Angle Relationships

Lines *a* and *b* are parallel. (The blue arrows on the diagram indicate parallel lines.)

A Trace line *a* and line *t* on a piece of paper. Label ∠1. Translate your traced angle down so that line *a* aligns with line *b* and line *t* aligns with itself. Which angle does ∠1 align with? **∠5**

B Because there is a translation that transforms ∠1 to **∠5**, ∠1 and **∠5** are congruent.

> **TRY THIS!**
>
> **2.** Name a pair of alternate interior angles. What transformation(s) could you use to show that that those angles are congruent?
>
> Sample answer: ∠3 and ∠6; rotate ∠3 about the intersection point of line *a* and line *t*, then translate along line *t* to align with ∠6

3 EXAMPLE CC.8.G.5 Finding Unknown Angle Measures

Find each angle measure.

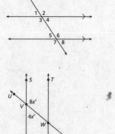

A m∠5 when m∠4 = 55°

∠4 is congruent to ∠5 because they are **alternate interior angles**

m∠5 = **55** °

B m∠SVW

∠SVW is **supplementary** to ∠YVW because they are a linear pair.

∠SVW + ∠YVW = 180°

4x° + **8x** ° = 180°

12 x = 180°

$\dfrac{12\,x}{12} = \dfrac{180}{12}$

x = **15**

∠SVW = ∠8x° = (8 · **15**)° = **120** °

PRACTICE

Use the figure for 1–4.

1. Name a pair of corresponding angles.
Sample answer: ∠1 and ∠5

2. Name a pair of alternate exterior angles.
Sample answer: ∠2 and ∠7

3. Name the relationship between ∠3 and ∠6.
alternate interior angles

4. Name the relationship between ∠4 and ∠6.
same-side interior angles

For parallel lines intersected by a transversal, tell whether each type of angle pair is congruent or supplementary.

5. alternate interior angles
congruent

6. linear pair
supplementary

7. corresponding angles
congruent

8. same-side interior angles
supplementary

9. vertical angles
congruent

10. alternate exterior angles
congruent

Find each angle measure.

11. m∠2 when m∠1 = 30°
150°

12. m∠6 when m∠1 = 30°
150°

13. m∠7 when m∠3 = 150°
150°

14. m∠EGB
100°

15. m∠AGH
100°

16. m∠DHF
80°

Notes

Assign these pages to help your students practice and apply important lesson concepts. For additional exercises, see the Student Edition.

Answers

Additional Practice

1. $\angle 1 \cong \angle 4 \cong \angle 5 \cong \angle 8$ and $\angle 2 \cong \angle 3 \cong \angle 6 \cong \angle 7$

2. 38°; $\angle 1$ and the 142° angle are supplementary angles

3. 142°; $\angle 2$ and the 142° angle are vertical angles

4. 38°; $\angle 1$ and $\angle 5$ are corresponding angles

5. 142°; $\angle 5$ and $\angle 6$ are supplementary angles

6. 142°; $\angle 8$ and the 142° angle are alternate exterior angles

7. 38°; $\angle 6$ and $\angle 7$ are supplementary angles

8. 43°; $\angle 6$ and the 137° are supplementary and $\angle 6$ and $\angle 2$ are alternate interior angles

9. 137°; $\angle 5$ and the 137° angle are vertical angles

10. 43°; $\angle 5$ and $\angle 6$ are supplementary angles

11. 43°; $\angle 7$ and the 137° angle are supplementary angles

12. 43°; $\angle 4$ and $\angle 6$ are corresponding angles

13. 137°; $\angle 3$ and $\angle 5$ are alternate interior angles

14. $\angle 4, \angle 6, \angle 8$ 15. line t

Problem Solving

1. $\angle 3, \angle 5, \angle 7, \angle 9$

2. $\angle 4, \angle 6, \angle 8, \angle 10$

3. Possible answer: $\angle 1, \angle 2$

4. $m\angle 3 = m\angle 5 = m\angle 7 = m\angle 9$ $= 75°, m\angle 2 = m\angle 4 = m\angle 6$ $= m\angle 8 = m\angle 10 = 105°$

5. Possible answer: $\angle 2, \angle 8$

6. Possible answer: $\overline{AB}, \overline{CD}, \overline{EF}$

7. B   8.   H

9. B   10.   H

11. B   12.   H

13. B

Name _____ Class _____ Date _____

Additional Practice

1. Measure the angles formed by the transversal and the parallel lines. Which angles seem to be congruent?

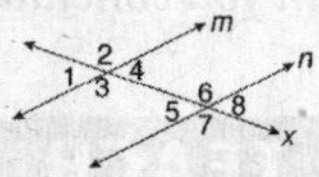

_____

_____

In the figure, line *m* ∥ line *n*. Find the measure of each angle. Justify your answer.

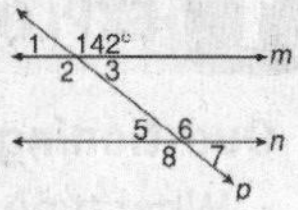

2. ∠1 _____   3. ∠2 _____

4. ∠5 _____   5. ∠6 _____

6. ∠8 _____   7. ∠7 _____

In the figure, line *a* ∥ line *b*. Find the measure of each angle. Justify your answer.

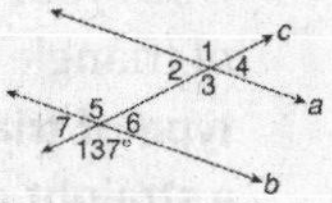

8. ∠2 _____   9. ∠5 _____

10. ∠6 _____   11. ∠7 _____

12. ∠4 _____   13. ∠3 _____

In the figure, line *r* ∥ line *s*.

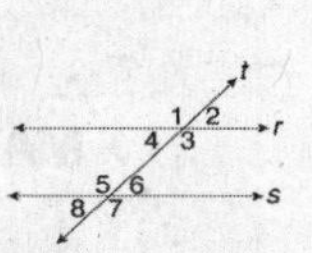

14. Name all angles congruent to ∠2.

_____

15. Which line is the transversal?

_____

Problem Solving

The figure shows the layout of parking spaces in a parking lot.
$\overline{AB} \parallel \overline{CD} \parallel \overline{EF}$

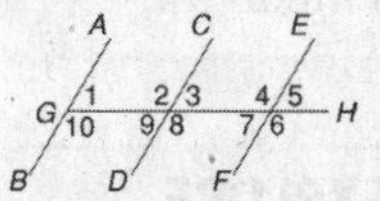

1. Name all angles congruent to ∠1.

_____

2. Name all angles congruent to ∠2.

_____

3. Name a pair of supplementary angles.

_____

4. If m∠1 = 75°, find the measures of the other angles.

_____

_____

5. Name a pair of vertical angles.

_____

6. If m∠1 = 90°, then $\overline{GH}$ is perpendicular to _____

The figure shows a board that will be cut along parallel segments *GB* and *CF*. $\overline{AD} \parallel \overline{HE}$. Choose the letter for the best answer.

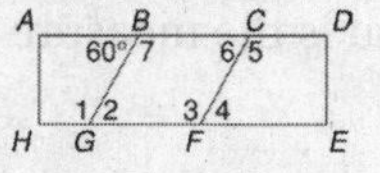

7. Find the measure of ∠1.
   A 45°   C 60°
   B 120°   D 90°

8. Find the measure of ∠2.
   F 30°   H 60°
   G 120°   J 90°

9. Find the measure of ∠3.
   A 30°   C 60°
   B 120°   D 90°

10. Find the measure of ∠4.
    F 45°   H 60°
    G 120°   J 90°

11. Find the measure of ∠5.
    A 30°   C 60°
    B 120°   D 90°

12. Find the measure of ∠6.
    F 30°   H 60°
    G 120°   J 90°

13. Find the measure of ∠7.
    A 45°   C 60°
    B 120°   D 90°

Triangles
Going Deeper: Triangle Angle Theorems

Essential question: *What can you conclude about the measures of the angles of a triangle?*

COMMON **Standards for**
CORE **Mathematical Content**

CC.8.G.5 Use informal arguments to establish facts about the angle sum and exterior angle of triangles, about the angles created when parallel lines are cut by a transversal, and the angle-angle criterion for similarity of triangles.

Vocabulary

interior angle

exterior angle

remote interior angle

Prerequisites

Triangles

Solving equations

Math Background

The sum of the measures of the interior angles of a triangle is *always* 180°. This is true for any triangle in the plane. In later geometry studies, students may extend this knowledge to find that the sum of the interior angle measures of a quadrilateral always equals 360°. Further investigation may lead students to the general formula for the sum of the interior angle measures of any polygon with n sides: $(n-2)180°$.

INTRODUCE

Tell students that in this lesson they will continue their study of special angle relationships. This time they will consider the interior and exterior angle measures of a triangle. Ask each student to draw a triangle. Have them estimate the measure of each angle of the triangle. Then have them estimate the sum of the angle measures. Compare students' estimates to look for values that cluster around 180°.

TEACH

1 EXPLORE

Questioning Strategies

- What type of triangle do you plan to sketch? **Answers will vary. Encourage students to test a wide variety of sizes and shapes.**

- Does your answer in part D depend on the type of triangle you sketched? **No; regardless of the type of triangle, the three vertices will form a straight angle.**

> **MATHEMATICAL PRACTICE** **Highlighting the Standards**
>
> This Lesson is an opportunity to address Standard 7 (Look for and make use of structure). The Triangle Sum Theorem provides structure for finding missing angle measures in many geometry diagrams. Students will strengthen their understanding of the term "structure" as it relates to mathematics when they discover and prove this theorem.

2 EXPLORE

Questioning Strategies

- How do you know that ∠4 and ∠2 are alternate interior angles? **Line *t* intersects parallel lines *a* and *b*; ∠4 and ∠2 are nonadjacent angles on opposite sides of *t*, between lines *a* and *b*.**

- What is the measure of a straight angle? **180°**

© Houghton Mifflin Harcourt Publishing Company

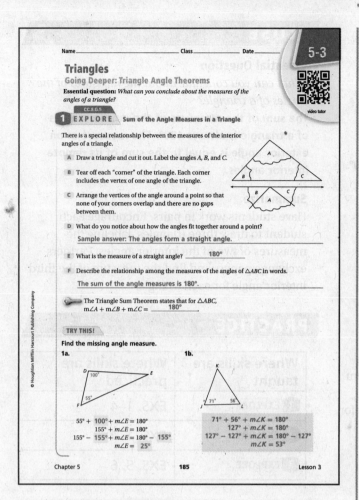

Name_____ Class_____ Date_____

5-3

Triangles

Going Deeper: Triangle Angle Theorems

Essential question: *What can you conclude about the measures of the angles of a triangle?*

CC.8.G.5

1 EXPLORE Sum of the Angle Measures in a Triangle

There is a special relationship between the measures of the interior angles of a triangle.

A Draw a triangle and cut it out. Label the angles *A*, *B*, and *C*.

B Tear off each "corner" of the triangle. Each corner includes the vertex of one angle of the triangle.

C Arrange the vertices of the angle around a point so that none of your corners overlap and there are no gaps between them.

D What do you notice about how the angles fit together around a point?

Sample answer: The angles form a straight angle.

E What is the measure of a straight angle? _____180°_____

F Describe the relationship among the measures of the angles of △*ABC* in words.

The sum of the angle measures is 180°.

The Triangle Sum Theorem states that for △*ABC*,
$m\angle A + m\angle B + m\angle C = $ _____180°_____

TRY THIS!

Find the missing angle measure.

1a.

1b.

$$55° + 100° + m\angle E = 180°$$
$$155° + m\angle E = 180°$$
$$155° - 155° + m\angle E = 180° - 155°$$
$$m\angle E = 25°$$

$$71° + 56° + m\angle K = 180°$$
$$127° + m\angle K = 180°$$
$$127° - 127° + m\angle K = 180° - 127°$$
$$m\angle K = 53°$$

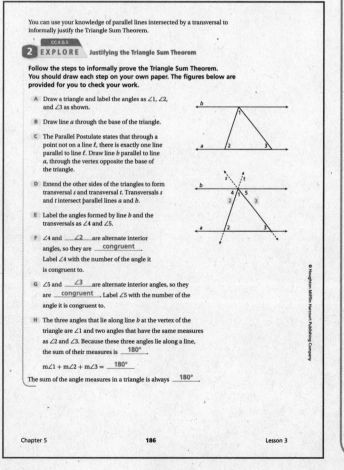

You can use your knowledge of parallel lines intersected by a transversal to informally justify the Triangle Sum Theorem.

CC.8.G.5

2 EXPLORE Justifying the Triangle Sum Theorem

Follow the steps to informally prove the Triangle Sum Theorem. You should draw each step on your own paper. The figures below are provided for you to check your work.

A Draw a triangle and label the angles as ∠1, ∠2, and ∠3 as shown.

B Draw line *a* through the base of the triangle.

C The Parallel Postulate states that through a point not on a line ℓ, there is exactly one line parallel to line ℓ. Draw line *b* parallel to line *a*, through the vertex opposite the base of the triangle.

D Extend the other sides of the triangles to form transversal *s* and transversal *t*. Transversals *s* and *t* intersect parallel lines *a* and *b*.

E Label the angles formed by line *b* and the transversals as ∠4 and ∠5.

F ∠4 and ___∠2___ are alternate interior angles, so they are ___congruent___.

Label ∠4 with the number of the angle it is congruent to.

G ∠5 and ___∠3___ are alternate interior angles, so they are ___congruent___. Label ∠5 with the number of the angle it is congruent to.

H The three angles that lie along line *b* at the vertex of the triangle are ∠1 and two angles that have the same measures as ∠2 and ∠3. Because these three angles lie along a line, the sum of their measures is ___180°___

$$m\angle 1 + m\angle 2 + m\angle 3 = \underline{\quad 180° \quad}$$

The sum of the angle measures in a triangle is always ___180°___

Questioning Strategies

- Suppose $m\angle 1 = 80°$ and $m\angle 4 = 140°$. How can you determine the measures of $\angle 2$ and $\angle 3$? $\angle 4$ and $\angle 3$ form a linear pair, so they are supplementary: $m\angle 4 + m\angle 3 = 140° + m\angle 3 = 180°$, so $m\angle 3 = 40°$; $m\angle 1 + m\angle 2 + m\angle 3 = 80° + m\angle 2 + 40° = 180°$, so $m\angle 2 = 60°$.

- Look at the triangle and exterior angles in Reflect 3a. Do you see any special relationship among the exterior angles of the triangle? **When two angles are exterior angles at the same vertex, they are congruent. They form vertical angles.**

Teaching Strategies

Before beginning the Practice problems, invite students to sketch triangles on the board and practice finding the measures of all interior and exterior angles. Work through at least one problem which gives measures for two angles and at least one problem that provides algebraic expressions for the angle measures.

CLOSE

Essential Question

What can you conclude about the measures of the angles of a triangle?

The sum of the measures of the interior angles of a triangle is always 180°. The measure of an exterior angle is equal to the sum of its remote interior angles.

Summarize

Have students work in pairs. Encourage each student to draw three triangles, labeling the measures of two of the interior angles. Partners exchange papers and find the measure of the third interior angle for each triangle.

PRACTICE

Where skills are taught	Where skills are practiced
1 EXPLORE	EXS. 1–4
2 EXPLORE	EXS. 1–4
3 EXPLORE	EXS. 5, 6

An **interior angle** of a triangle is formed by two sides of the triangle. An **exterior angle** of a triangle is formed by one side of the triangle and the extension of an adjacent side. Each exterior angle has two *remote interior angles*. A **remote interior angle** is an interior angle that is not adjacent to the exterior angle.

- ∠1, ∠2, and ∠3 are interior angles.
- ∠4 is an exterior angle.
- ∠1 and ∠2 are remote interior angles to ∠4.

3 EXPLORE   CC.8.G.5   Exterior Angles and Remote Interior Angles

There is a special relationship between the measure of an exterior angle and the measures of its remote interior angles.

A   Extend the base of the triangle and label the exterior angle as ∠4.

B   The Triangle Sum Theorem states:

m∠1 + m∠2 + m∠3 = __180°__

C   ∠3 and ∠4 form a __linear pair or straight angle__,

so m∠3 + m∠4 = __180°__.

D   Use the equations in B and C to complete the following equation:

m∠1 + m∠2 + __m∠3__ = __m∠3__ + m∠4

E   Use properties of equality to simplify the equation in D :

__m∠1 + m∠2 = m∠4__

The Exterior Angle Theorem states that the measure of an __exterior__ angle is equal to the sum of its __remote interior__ angles.

REFLECT

3a. Sketch a triangle and draw all of its exterior angles. How many exterior angles does a triangle have at each vertex?

__2__

3b. How many total exterior angles does a triangle have?

__6__

PRACTICE

Find the missing angle measure.

1.

m∠M = _____71°_____

2.

m∠Q = _____30°_____

Use the Triangle Sum Theorem to find the measure of each angle in degrees.

3.

m∠T = _____88°_____
m∠U = _____29°_____
m∠V = _____63°_____

4.

X $n°$ Y $\left(\frac{1}{2}n\right)°$
Z $\left(\frac{1}{2}n\right)°$

m∠X = _____90°_____
m∠Y = _____45°_____
m∠Z = _____45°_____

Use the Exterior Angles Theorem to find the measure of each angle in degrees.

5.

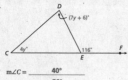

m∠C = _____40°_____
m∠D = _____76°_____
m∠DEC = _____64°_____

6.

m∠L = _____129°_____
m∠MKL = _____19°_____
m∠MKJ = _____161°_____

Assign these pages to help your students practice and apply important lesson concepts. For additional exercises, see the Student Edition.

Answers

Additional Practice

1. 41°
2. 91°
3. 74°
4. 68°
5. 65°
6. 53°
7. 58°
8. 60°
9. 62°
10. Possible answer: 30°, 60°, 90°

Problem Solving

1. right
2. isosceles
3. $x = 45°$
4. $y = 45°$
5. B
6. H
7. C
8. F
9. C

5-3

Name_____ Class_____ Date_____

Additional Practice

1. Find $x°$ in the right triangle.

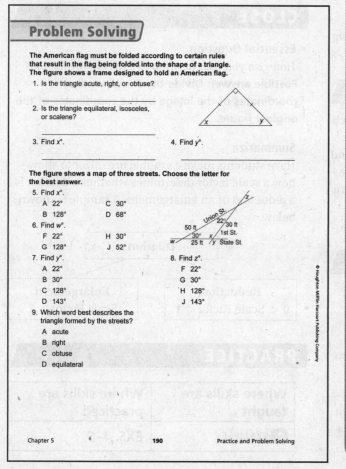

2. Find $y°$ in the obtuse triangle.

43° 46°

3. Find $m°$ in the acute triangle.

59°
$m°$ 47°

4. Find $w°$ in the acute triangle.

63° 49°

5. Find $t°$ in the scalene triangle.

78° 37°

6. Find $n°$ in the scalene triangle.

85°
42°

7. Find $x°$ in the isosceles triangle.

$x°$ $x°$
64°

8. Find y in the equilateral triangle.

$y°$
$y°$ $y°$

9. Find r in the isosceles triangle.

$r°$ $r°$
56°

10. The second angle in a triangle is one third as large as the first. The third angle is two thirds as large as the first angle. Find the angle measures. Draw a possible picture of the triangle.

_____

Problem Solving

The American flag must be folded according to certain rules that result in the flag being folded into the shape of a triangle. The figure shows a frame designed to hold an American flag.

1. Is the triangle acute, right, or obtuse?

_____

2. Is the triangle equilateral, isosceles, or scalene?

_____

x y

3. Find $x°$.   4. Find $y°$.

_____   _____

The figure shows a map of three streets. Choose the letter for the best answer.

5. Find $x°$.
   A 22°   C 30°
   B 128°   D 68°

6. Find $w°$.
   F 22°   H 30°
   G 128°   J 52°

7. Find $y°$.
   A 22°
   B 30°
   C 128°
   D 143°

8. Find $z°$.
   F 22°
   G 30°
   H 128°
   J 143°

Union St.

z

50 ft   22° 30 ft
           30°   1st St.
w 25 ft y x State St.

9. Which word best describes the triangle formed by the streets?
   A acute
   B right
   C obtuse
   D equilateral

Coordinate Geometry
Going Deeper

Essential question: *How can you use coordinates to find scale factors?*

COMMON CORE

Standards for Mathematical Content

Prep for CC.8.G.3 Describe the effect of dilations, translations, rotations, and reflections on two-dimensional figures using coordinates.

Vocabulary
dilation
scale factor

Math Background
Unlike translations, reflections, and rotations, a *dilation* is a *non-rigid* transformation, which means the size of the image can be different than the size of the original figure. Dilations can enlarge (scale factor > 1) or reduce (scale factor < 1 and > 0) the size of a figure, but do not change its shape. If the scale factor is 1, the size does not change. To perform a dilation, you must also know the center point for the dilation. In this lesson, the center is (0, 0), so that students can focus on scale factors. Using a different center of dilation does not alter the size of the figure, but it may change its resulting location on the coordinate plane.

INTRODUCE

Ask students if they have had an eye exam in which they had their eyes dilated. Explain that the black circular opening on their eye is called the pupil and drops are used to open the pupil to better observe the eye. Tell them that in this lesson, they will learn about a transformation that changes the size of a figure, but not its shape, called a dilation.

TEACH

  EXAMPLE

Questioning Strategies
• Are the distances between *B* and *B′* and between *C* and *C′* the same? **No, the distance between *B* and *B′* appears larger.**

• What is the same between *B* and *B′* and between *C* and *C′*? **The coordinates for each image vertex (*B′* and *C′*) are $\frac{3}{2}$ times the original coordinates (*B* and *C*).**

Differentiated Instruction
Help students understand that the resulting figure after an enlargement or reduction is the same shape, just larger or smaller, respectively. Point out that students can check that their sketches are correct by verifying that the image and original figure have the same shape.

> **MATHEMATICAL PRACTICE**   **Highlighting the Standards**
>
> This Example provides an opportunity to address Standard 7 (Look for and make use of structure). Working through the Example, students should recognize that each coordinate of a point must be multiplied by the scale factor, and that an enlargement and a reduction both involve the same procedure.

CLOSE

Essential Question
How can you use coordinates to find scale factors?
Possible answer: Divide the corresponding coordinates of the image by the coordinates of the original figure.

Summarize
Have students make a graphic organizer to show how a scale factor determines whether a dilation is a reduction or an enlargement. A sample is shown below.

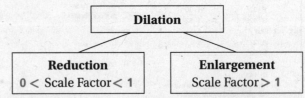

PRACTICE

Where skills are taught	Where skills are practiced
1 EXAMPLE	EXS. 1–5

© Houghton Mifflin Harcourt Publishing Company

Name_____ Class_____ Date_____ | 5-4

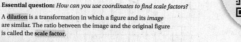

Coordinate Geometry
Going Deeper

Essential question: *How can you use coordinates to find scale factors?*

A **dilation** is a transformation in which a figure and its *image* are similar. The ratio between the image and the original figure is called the **scale factor**.

1 EXAMPLE | Finding and Graphing a Dilation

The vertices of quadrilateral *ABCD* are *A*(–4, –2), *B*(–2, 2), *C*(1, 2), and *D*(2, –2).

A   Plot points *A*, *B*, *C*, and *D*. Connect them in order to graph this polygon on the coordinate plane.

B   Quadrilateral *A′B′C′D′* is an image of quadrilateral *ABCD*. Vertex *A′* in *A′B′C′D′* has coordinates (–6, –3).

Find the scale factor: Divide the *x*- and *y*-coordinates of Vertex *A′* by the *x*- and *y*-coordinates of Vertex *A*.

x-coordinates   y-coordinates

$$\frac{image \rightarrow A'}{original \rightarrow A} \quad \frac{-6}{-4}=\frac{3}{2} \quad \frac{-3}{-2}=\frac{3}{2} \qquad \text{The scale factor is } \frac{3}{2}.$$

C   Use the scale factor to find the *x*- and *y*-coordinates of vertices *B′*, *C′*, and *D′*.

$$B(-2,2) \rightarrow B'\left(\frac{3}{2}\times -2, \frac{3}{2}\times 2\right) = (-3, 3)$$

$$C(1,2) \rightarrow C'\left(\frac{3}{2}\times 1, \frac{3}{2}\times 2\right)=\left(\frac{3}{2}, 3\right)$$

$$D(2,-2) \rightarrow D'\left(\frac{3}{2}\times 2, \frac{3}{2}\times -2\right)=(3, -3)$$

D   On the coordinate plane in   A , graph quadrilateral *A′B′C′D′*.

REFLECT

1a. Describe the figures you have graphed. What kind of quadrilateral is each one? How are they related?

Both figures are trapezoids; *A′B′C′D′* is the image of *ABCD* after a dilation with a scale factor of $\frac{3}{2}$.

© Houghton Mifflin Harcourt Publishing Company

Chapter 5   191   Lesson 4

TRY THIS!

1b. What are the coordinates of the image of quadrilateral *EFGH* after a dilation with a scale factor of $\frac{1}{2}$?

$$E(-2,0) \rightarrow E'\left(\frac{1}{2}\times -2, \frac{1}{2}\times 0\right)=(-1, 0)$$

$$F(1, 4) \rightarrow F'\left(\frac{1}{2}\times 1, \frac{1}{2}\times 4\right)=\left(\frac{1}{2}, 2\right)$$

$$G(6, 0) \rightarrow G'\left(\frac{1}{2}\times 6, \frac{1}{2}\times 0\right)=(3, 0)$$

$$H(1, -4) \rightarrow H'\left(\frac{1}{2}\times 1, \frac{1}{2}\times -4\right)=\left(\frac{1}{2}, -2\right)$$

1c. Graph *E′F′G′H′* on the coordinate plane. What kind of quadrilateral have you drawn? __kite__

PRACTICE

Use the diagram for Exercises 1–3.

1. *Q′R′S′T′* is the image of *QRST*. Find the scale factor.

$$\frac{image \rightarrow Q'}{original \rightarrow Q} \quad \frac{1}{4}$$

2. *Y′* is the image of *Y* in a dilation of △*XYZ*. Find the scale factor.

$$\frac{image \rightarrow Y'}{original \rightarrow Y} \quad \frac{1}{3}$$

3. Use the scale factor to graph △*X′Y′Z′*.

$$X(3, -1) \rightarrow X'\left(1, -\frac{1}{3}\right) \qquad Z(6, 3) \rightarrow Z'(2, 1)$$

4. Given quadrilateral *MNOP* with vertices *M*(–2, –1), *N*(2, 0), *O*(2, 2), and *P*(–1, 2), find the coordinates of its image after a dilation with a scale factor of 2.

M′(–4, –2), *N′*(4, 0), *O′*(4, 4), *P′*(–2, 4)

5. In triangle *ABC*, *AB* = 7 cm, *BC* = 6 cm, and *CD* = 10 cm. After a dilation, the length of *A′B′* = 21 cm. What is the scale factor of the dilation? What is the perimeter of *A′B′C′*?

3; 69 cm

© Houghton Mifflin Harcourt Publishing Company

Chapter 5   192   Lesson 4

Assign these pages to help your students practice and apply important lesson concepts. For additional exercises, see the Student Edition.

Answers

Additional Practice

1.

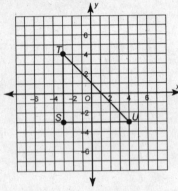

$S'(-6, -6), T'(-6, 8), U'(8, -6)$

2.

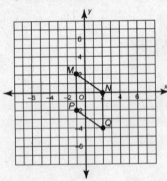

$M'(-2, 4), N'(4, 0), Q'(4, -8), P'(-2, -4)$

3. $(4, -5); J'(-1.5, 1), K'(2, 1), L'(2, -2.5),$
$M'(-1.5, -2.5)$

4. scale factor $= \frac{1}{2}; G'(4, 4), H'(6, 2)$

Problem Solving

1.

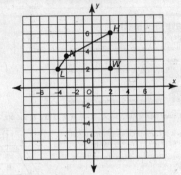

quadrilateral

2. scale factor $= 3; L'(-12, 6), W'(6, 6), H'(6, 18)$

3. $A'(-2, 0), B'(2, 0), C'(2, -1), D'(-2, -1)$

4. B

5. J

Name _____ Class _____ Date _____   5-4

Additional Practice

Graph the polygons with the given vertices. What are the coordinates of the image after a dilation with a scale factor of 2?

1. $S(-3, -3)$, $T(-3, 4)$, $U(4, -3)$

2. $M(-1, 2)$, $N(2, 0)$, $Q(2, -4)$, $P(-1, -2)$

_____   _____

3. Quadrilateral *JKLM* is a square. Find the coordinates of the missing vertex. Then find the coordinates of the image after a dilation with a scale factor of $\frac{1}{2}$.

_____

4. The vertices of triangle *FGH* are $F(4, 6)$, $G(8, 8)$, and $H(12, 4)$. Triangle *F'G'H'* is an image of triangle *FGH*. Vertex *F'* has coordinates $(2, 3)$. What is the scale factor of the dilation? What are the coordinates of vertices *G'* and *H'*?

_____

_____

Problem Solving

Nguyen and his family went to Washington D.C. Nguyen graphed the sites he and his family visited on a coordinate grid.

1. On Saturday, Nguyen and his family visited the Lincoln Memorial (*L*), the Washington Monument (*W*), the White House (*H*), and the National Academy of Sciences (*N*) The coordinates for each site are $L(-4, 2)$, $W(2, 2)$, $H(2, 6)$ and $N(-3, 3\frac{1}{2})$. Graph and label the coordinates.

Connect the vertices. Give the most specific name for the polygon formed.

_____

2. Polygon *L'W'H'N'* is the image of the polygon graphed above after a dilation. Vertex *N'* has coordinates $(-9, 10\frac{1}{2})$. What is the scale factor of the dilation? What are the coordinates of the remaining vertices of *L'W'H'N'*?

_____

_____

_____

3. Rectangle *ABCD* has vertices $A(-6, 0)$, $B(6, 0)$, $C(6, -3)$, $D(-6, -3)$. Find the coordinates of the image after a dilation with a scale factor of $\frac{1}{3}$.

_____

Choose the letter for the best answer.

4. An architect is trying to draw an isosceles right triangle on a grid to use in his next blueprint. He has a point at $(6, 3)$ and a point at $(-2, 3)$. What could the third point be?

   A $(-2, 0)$ C $(2, -2)$

   B $(6, -5)$ D $(6, 8)$

5. Triangle *QRS* has vertices $Q(-7, 3)$, $R(9, 8)$, and $S(2, 16)$. What is the scale factor if the vertices after a dilation are $Q'(-10.5, 4.5)$, $R'(13.5, 12)$, and $S(3, 24)$?

   F $\frac{1}{3}$ H $\frac{2}{3}$

   G $\frac{1}{2}$ J $\frac{3}{2}$

Congruence
Going Deeper

Essential question: *How can you prove that two triangles are congruent?*

COMMON CORE **Standards for Mathematical Content**

Prep for CC.8.G.2 Understand that a two-dimensional figure is congruent to another if the second can be obtained from the first by a sequence of rotations, reflections, and translations; given two congruent figures, describe a sequence that exhibits the congruence between them.

Math Background

Congruent triangles have the same size and shape, meaning corresponding sides and angles are congruent. So, if you know that two triangles are congruent, you can use the fact that corresponding parts are congruent to find unknown parts.

INTRODUCE

Remind students that they have studied congruent segments and angles. Ask students to find the simplest closed figure they can create using segments and angles. Students should recognize it is a triangle with 3 angles and 3 sides. Then inform students that they will learn two different ways of proving two triangles congruent.

TEACH

1 EXPLORE

Materials
Compass
Paper
Scissors
Straightedge (or ruler)

Questioning Strategies
- Are the sides of $\triangle ABC$ congruent? No, each side appears to be a different length.
- How many pairs of corresponding parts do two triangles have? 6, 3 angles and 3 sides

Avoid Common Errors

Direct students to the Side-Side-Side Postulate rule box. Emphasize that the order in which the letters are listed for each triangle is important—they must be in the corresponding order. So, $\triangle ABC \cong \triangle DEF$ means:

Corresponding sides: $\overline{AB} \cong \overline{DE}$, $\overline{BC} \cong \overline{EF}$, $\overline{AC} \cong \overline{DF}$
Corresponding angles: $\angle A \cong \angle D$, $\angle B \cong \angle E$, $\angle C \cong \angle F$

Then point out how the tick marks on the corresponding segments indicate their congruence.

2 EXPLORE

Materials
Paper
Protractor
Ruler

Questioning Strategies
- What are the corresponding sides of $\triangle RST$ and $\triangle XYZ$? $\overline{RS} \cong \overline{XY}$, $\overline{ST} \cong \overline{YZ}$, and $\overline{RT} \cong \overline{XZ}$
- What do you need to prove that two triangles are congruent using SAS? That two corresponding pairs of sides and a pair of included angles are congruent.

Differentiated Instructions

Have students label and color the angle between the given sides. Inform them that this angle is sometimes called the *included angle.*

CLOSE

Essential Question

How can you prove that two triangles are congruent?
Possible answer: By showing either SSS (3 pairs of corresponding sides are congruent) or SAS (two corresponding pairs of sides and a pair of included angles are congruent).

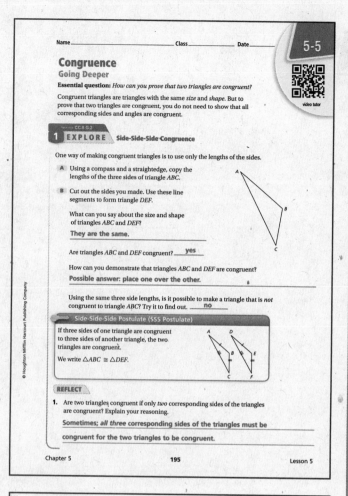

Name_____ Class_____ Date_____

5-5

video tutor

Congruence
Going Deeper

Essential question: *How can you prove that two triangles are congruent?*

Congruent triangles are triangles with the same *size* and *shape*. But to prove that two triangles are congruent, you do not need to show that all corresponding sides and angles are congruent.

1 EXPLORE   Side-Side-Side Congruence

One way of making congruent triangles is to use only the lengths of the sides.

A Using a compass and a straightedge, copy the lengths of the three sides of triangle *ABC*.

B Cut out the sides you made. Use these line segments to form triangle *DEF*.

What can you say about the size and shape of triangles *ABC* and *DEF*?

____They are the same.____

Are triangles *ABC* and *DEF* congruent? __yes__

How can you demonstrate that triangles *ABC* and *DEF* are congruent?

__Possible answer: place one over the other.__

Using the same three side lengths, is it possible to make a triangle that is *not* congruent to triangle *ABC*? Try it to find out. __no__

Side-Side-Side Postulate (SSS Postulate)

If three sides of one triangle are congruent to three sides of another triangle, the two triangles are congruent.

We write $\triangle ABC \cong \triangle DEF$.

REFLECT

1. Are two triangles congruent if only *two* corresponding sides of the triangles are congruent? Explain your reasoning.

__Sometimes; *all three* corresponding sides of the triangles must be__

__congruent for the two triangles to be congruent.__

© Houghton Mifflin Harcourt Publishing Company

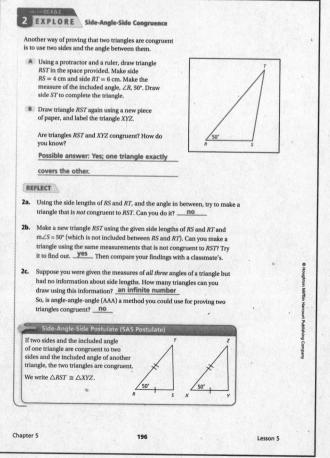

2 EXPLORE   Side-Angle-Side Congruence

Another way of proving that two triangles are congruent is to use two sides and the angle between them.

A Using a protractor and a ruler, draw triangle *RST* in the space provided. Make side *RS* = 4 cm and side *RT* = 6 cm. Make the measure of the included angle, ∠*R*, 50°. Draw side *ST* to complete the triangle.

B Draw triangle *RST* again using a new piece of paper, and label the triangle *XYZ*.

Are triangles *RST* and *XYZ* congruent? How do you know?

__Possible answer: Yes; one triangle exactly__

__covers the other.__

REFLECT

2a. Using the side lengths of *RS* and *RT*, and the angle in between, try to make a triangle that is *not* congruent to *RST*. Can you do it? __no__

2b. Make a new triangle *RST* using the given side lengths of *RS* and *RT* and m∠*S* = 50° (which is not included between *RS* and *RT*). Can you make a triangle using the same measurements that is not congruent to *RST*? Try it to find out. __yes__ Then compare your findings with a classmate's.

2c. Suppose you were given the measures of *all three* angles of a triangle but had no information about side lengths. How many triangles can you draw using this information? __an infinite number__

So, is angle-angle-angle (AAA) a method you could use for proving two triangles congruent? __no__

Side-Angle-Side Postulate (SAS Postulate)

If two sides and the included angle of one triangle are congruent to two sides and the included angle of another triangle, the two triangles are congruent.

We write $\triangle RST \cong \triangle XYZ$.

© Houghton Mifflin Harcourt Publishing Company

Assign these pages to help your students practice and apply important lesson concepts. For additional exercises, see the Student Edition.

Answers

Additional Practice

1. triangle $JKL \cong$ triangle TQP

2. 4   3. 9

4. 10   5. 10°

6. 105°   7. 15°

Problem Solving

1. 45°   2. 4 inches

3. 6 inches   4. 90°

5. 4 inches   6. B

7. G   8. D

9. J   10. C

11. J   12. C

Notes

Additional Practice

Write a congruence statement for the pair of congruent triangles.

1.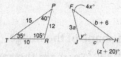

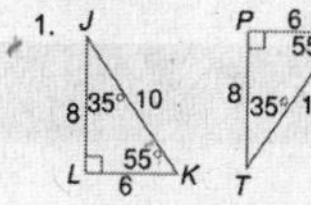

_____

In the figure, triangle $PRT \cong$ triangle FJH.

2. Find a.

_____

3. Find b.

_____

4. Find c.

_____

5. Find x.

_____

6. Find y.

_____

7. Find z.

_____

© Houghton Mifflin Harcourt Publishing Company

Problem Solving

Use the American patchwork quilt block design called Carnival to answer the questions. Triangle $AIH \cong$ Triangle AIB, Triangle $ACJ \cong$ Triangle AGJ, Triangle $GFJ \cong$ Triangle CDJ.

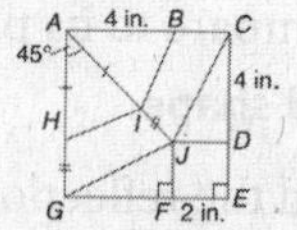

1. What is the measure of $\angle IAB$?

_____

2. What is the measure of $\overline{AH}$?

_____

3. What is the measure of $\overline{AG}$?

_____

4. What is the measure of $\angle JDC$?   5. What is the measure of $\overline{FG}$?

The sketch is part of a bridge. Trapezoid $ABEF \cong$ Trapezoid $DEBC$. Choose the letter for the best answer.

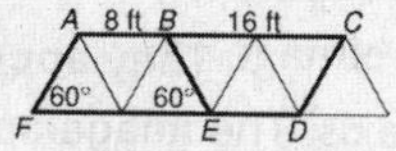

6. What is the measure of $\overline{DE}$?
   A 4 feet
   B 8 feet
   C 16 feet
   D Cannot be determined

7. What is the measure of $\overline{FE}$?
   F 4 feet   H 8 feet
   G 16 feet   J 24 feet

8. What is the measure of $\angle FAB$?
   A 45°   C 60°
   B 90°   D 120°

9. What is the measure of $\angle ABE$?
   F 45°   H 60°
   G 90°   J 120°

10. What is the measure of $\angle EBC$?
    A 45°   C 60°
    B 90°   D 120°

11. What is the measure of $\angle BED$?
    F 45°   H 60°
    G 90°   J 120°

12. What is the measure of $\angle BCD$?
    A 45°   C 60°
    B 90°   D 120°

© Houghton Mifflin Harcourt Publishing Company

Transformations
Modeling

Essential question: *How can you use coordinates to describe the result of a translation, reflection, or rotation?*

© Houghton Mifflin Harcourt Publishing Company

COMMON CORE Standards for Mathematical Content

CC.8.G.3 Describe the effect of dilations, translations, rotations, and reflections on two-dimensional figures using coordinates.

Vocabulary

transformation
preimage
image
translation
reflection
line of reflection
rotation

Prerequisites

Graphing in the coordinate plane (four quadrants)

Math Background

When a transformation is applied to a geometric figure, the vertices of the original figure are mapped to corresponding vertices in the image. In translations, reflections, and rotations, line segments are also preserved. Suppose point A is mapped to point A' and B is mapped to B'. If a line segment connects A and B in the original figure, then a corresponding line segment connects A' and B' in the transformed image.

INTRODUCE

Discuss with students some real-world examples of transformations. Translations are often found in tile or textile patterns. The image of a tree on a lake exemplifies a reflection. A pinwheel illustrates rotation. Ask students for other examples of these types of transformations.

TEACH

1 EXPLORE

Questioning Strategies

- How does the size and shape of the image compare with its preimage? They are the same size and shape.

- Did the translation change the orientation of the triangle? no

Kinesthetic/Modeling

Clear a large area on the floor and use masking tape to mark off a coordinate grid. Have students stand at different points to represent the vertices of a geometric figure. Students can stretch yarn from person to person to model the sides of the figure. Invite classmates to suggest a translation that the students on the grid can demonstrate. Ask the class to compare the preimage (initial position) to the image (final position) after the translation.

2 EXPLORE

Questioning Strategies

- How does the size and shape of the image compare to its preimage? They are the same size and shape.

- Did the reflection change the orientation of the triangle? Yes, the image "flipped" across the axis. The image appears upside down when compared to the original triangle.

- Compare the locations of the image and the preimage. They appear on opposite sides of the x-axis. The image appears below the preimage, but it did not move left or right.

Name _____ Class _____ Date _____

5-6

Transformations
Modeling

Essential question: *How can you use coordinates to describe the result of a translation, reflection, or rotation?*

You learned that a function is a rule that assigns exactly one output to each input. A **transformation** is a type of function that describes a change in the position or size of a figure. The input of a transformation is called the **preimage**, and the output of a transformation is called the **image**.

A **translation** is a transformation that slides a figure along a straight line. The image has the same size and shape as the preimage.

1 EXPLORE CC.8.G.3 **Applying Translations**

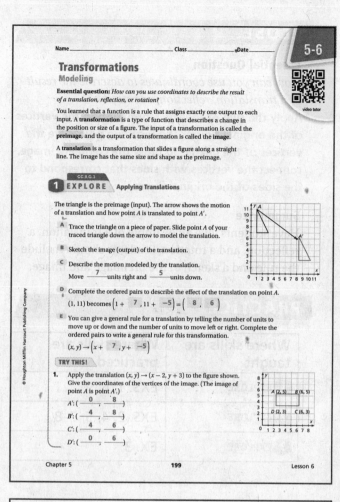

The triangle is the preimage (input). The arrow shows the motion of a translation and how point *A* is translated to point *A'*.

A Trace the triangle on a piece of paper. Slide point *A* of your traced triangle down the arrow to model the translation.

B Sketch the image (output) of the translation.

C Describe the motion modeled by the translation.
Move ___7___ units right and ___5___ units down.

D Complete the ordered pairs to describe the effect of the translation on point *A*.
$(1, 11)$ becomes $\left(1 + \underline{\ 7\ }, 11 + \underline{\ -5\ }\right) = \left(\underline{\ 8\ }, \underline{\ 6\ }\right)$

E You can give a general rule for a translation by telling the number of units to move up or down and the number of units to move left or right. Complete the ordered pairs to write a general rule for this transformation.
$(x, y) \rightarrow \left(x + \underline{\ 7\ }, y + \underline{\ -5\ }\right)$

TRY THIS!

1. Apply the translation $(x, y) \rightarrow (x - 2, y + 3)$ to the figure shown. Give the coordinates of the vertices of the image. (The image of point *A* is point *A'*.)

$A':\ (\ \underline{0}\ ,\ \underline{8}\ )$
$B':\ (\ \underline{4}\ ,\ \underline{8}\ )$
$C':\ (\ \underline{4}\ ,\ \underline{6}\ )$
$D':\ (\ \underline{0}\ ,\ \underline{6}\ )$

A **reflection** is a transformation that flips a figure across a line called the **line of reflection**. Each point and its image are the same distance from the line of reflection. The image has the same size and shape as the preimage.

2 EXPLORE CC.8.G.3 **Applying Reflections**

The triangle is the preimage. You will use the *x*- or *y*-axis as the line of reflection.

Reflection across the *x*-axis:

A Trace the triangle and the *x*- and *y*-axes on a piece of paper. Fold your paper along the *x*-axis and trace the image of the triangle on the opposite side of the *x*-axis.

B Sketch the image of the reflection. Label each vertex of the image. (The image of point *E* is point *E'*.)

C Complete the table.

Preimage	(2, 4)	(2, 1)	(5, 1)
Image	(2, −4)	(2, −1)	(5, −1)

D How does reflecting the figure across the *x*-axis change the *x*-coordinates? How does it change the *y*-coordinates?
The *x*-coordinates do not change. The *y*-coordinates are opposites.

E Complete the ordered pair to write a general rule for reflection across the *x*-axis. $(x, y) \rightarrow \left(x, y \times \underline{\ -1\ }\right)$

Reflection across the *y*-axis:

F Fold your traced image along the *y*-axis and trace the image of the triangle on the opposite side of the *y*-axis.

G Sketch the image of the reflection. Label each vertex of the image. (For clarity, label the image of point *E* as point *E''*.)

H Complete the table.

Preimage	(2, 4)	(2, 1)	(5, 1)
Image	(−2, 4)	(−2, 1)	(−5, 1)

I How does reflecting the figure across the *y*-axis change the *x*-coordinates? How does it change the *y*-coordinates?
The *x*-coordinates are opposites. The *y*-coordinates do not change.

J Complete the ordered pair to write a general rule for reflection across the *y*-axis. $(x, y) \rightarrow \left(\underline{\ x \cdot (-1)\ },\ \underline{\ y\ }\right)$

- How does the size and shape of the image compare to the preimage? They are the same size and shape.

- Did the rotation change the orientation of the triangle? Yes, the image "turned" around a point (the origin).

- Compare the locations of the image and the preimage. The vertex at the origin did not move. The other vertices moved in a circular path around the origin.

MATHEMATICAL PRACTICE — Highlighting the Standards

This Explore provides an opportunity to address Standard 4 (Model with mathematics). Transformations are functions that describe the movement of figures. Students are asked to physically move objects around the coordinate plane to model the transformation of a geometric figure. Then students compare the physical movement to the verbal and algebraic representations of the transformations being discussed. This lesson provides an excellent opportunity to deepen students' understanding of the concept of mathematical modeling.

CLOSE

Essential Question
How can you use coordinates to describe the result of a translation, reflection, or rotation?
Apply the rule of the transformation to the vertices of the original figure. The resulting points are the vertices of the image. To draw the complete image, connect the vertices with sides that correspond to the sides of the original figure.

Summarize
Have students give an example of a translation, a reflection, and a rotation. Students should include the rule and a sketch of the preimage and image.

PRACTICE

Where skills are taught	Where skills are practiced
1 EXPLORE	EXS. 1, 6, 9
2 EXPLORE	EXS. 2, 4, 5, 7–8
3 EXPLORE	EX. 3

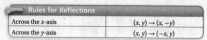

Rules for Reflections	
Across the *x*-axis	$(x, y) \rightarrow (x, -y)$
Across the *y*-axis	$(x, y) \rightarrow (-x, y)$

A **rotation** is a transformation that turns a figure around a given point called the center of rotation. The image has the same size and shape as the preimage.

CC.8.G.3

3 EXPLORE Applying Rotations

The triangle is the preimage. You will use the origin as the center of rotation.

A Trace the triangle on a piece of paper. Rotate the triangle 90° counterclockwise about the origin. The side of the triangle that lies along the *x*-axis should now lie along the *y*-axis.

B Sketch the image of the rotation. Label each vertex of the image. (The image of point *H* is point *H'*.)

C Give the coordinates of the vertices of the image.

H': (__0__ , __0__)

J': (__0__ , __3__)

K': (__−3__ , __3__)

TRY THIS!

3a. Rotate the original triangle 180° counterclockwise about the origin. Sketch the result on the coordinate grid above. Label each vertex of the image. (For clarity, label the image of point *H* as point *H''*.)

3b. Give the coordinates of the vertices of the image.

H'': (__0__ , __0__)

J'': (__−3__ , __0__)

K'': (__−3__ , __−3__)

REFLECT

3c. Compare the image of a counterclockwise rotation of 180° about the origin to the image of a clockwise rotation of 180° about the origin.

The image is the same.

3d. Through how many degrees would you need to rotate a figure for the image to coincide with the preimage? Explain.

360°; A rotation of 360° will bring the image exactly into alignment with the preimage.

Chapter 5　　　　201　　　　Lesson 6

PRACTICE

Sketch the image of the figure after the given transformation. Label each vertex.

1. Translation: $(x, y) \rightarrow (x - 3, y + 1)$

2. Reflection: $(x, y) \rightarrow (x, -y)$

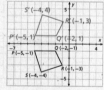

3. Rotation: 90° clockwise about the origin

4. Reflection: $(x, y) \rightarrow (-x, y)$

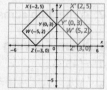

Apply each transformation to the vertices of the original rectangle, and give the coordinates of each vertex of the image.

Vertices of Rectangle	(2, 2)	(2, 4)	(−3, 4)	(−3, 2)
5. $(x, y) \rightarrow (x, -y)$	(2, −2)	(2, −4)	(−3, −4)	(−3, −2)
6. $(x, y) \rightarrow (x + 2, y - 5)$	(4, −3)	(4, −1)	(−1, −1)	(−1, −3)
7. $(x, y) \rightarrow (-x, y)$	(−2, 2)	(−2, 4)	(3, 4)	(3, 2)
8. $(x, y) \rightarrow (-x, -y)$	(−2, −2)	(−2, −4)	(3, −4)	(3, −2)
9. $(x, y) \rightarrow (x - 3, y + 1)$	(−1, 3)	(−1, 5)	(−6, 5)	(−6, 3)

Chapter 5　　　　202　　　　Lesson 6

Assign these pages to help your students practice and apply important lesson concepts. For additional exercises, see the Student Edition.

Answers

Additional Practice

1.
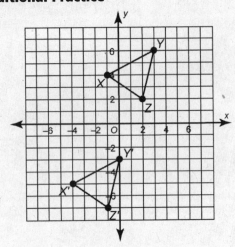

2.
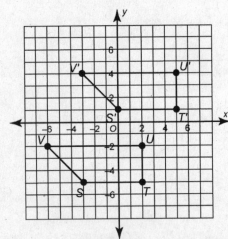

3.
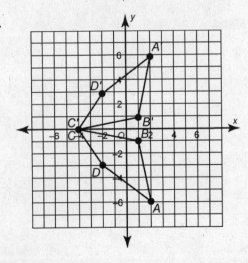

4.
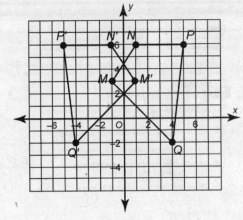

5.
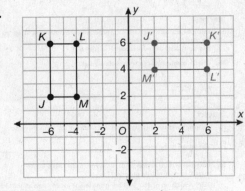

6.
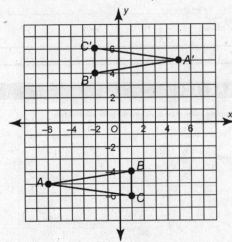

7. reflection across the *y*-axis

Problem Solving

1. (−5, −1)

2. (−2, −1)

3. (4, 4)

4. (1, 4)

5. B

6. F

7. D

8. G

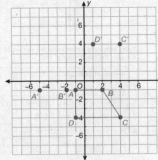

Additional Practice

Name_____ Class_____ Date_____

5-6

Graph each translation.

1. 3 units left and 9 units down

2. 3 units right and 6 units up

Graph each reflection.

3. across the *x*-axis

4. across the *y*-axis

Graph each rotation around the origin.

5. 90° clockwise

6. 180°

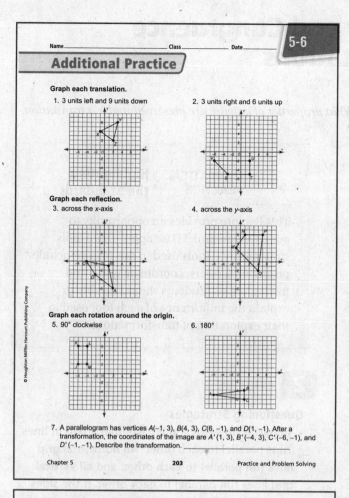

7. A parallelogram has vertices $A(-1, 3)$, $B(4, 3)$, $C(6, -1)$, and $D(1, -1)$. After a transformation, the coordinates of the image are $A'(1, 3)$, $B'(-4, 3)$, $C'(-6, -1)$, and $D'(-1, -1)$. Describe the transformation. _____

Problem Solving

Drew is going to hang a flag in his bedroom that is in the shape of a trapezoid. The grid below represents Drew's wall. The flag, a trapezoid *ABCD*, has vertices $A(-1, -1)$, $B(2, -1)$, $C(4, -4)$, and $D(-1, -4)$. Graph the transformations that Drew performs to find the right place on his wall to answer the questions.

1. What are the coordinates of Point *A* after a translation 4 units left? _____

2. What are the coordinates of Point *B* after a reflection across the *y*-axis?

   _____

3. What are the coordinates of Point *C* after a 90° counterclockwise rotation around the origin?

   _____

4. What are the coordinates of Point *D* after a 180° clockwise rotation around the origin?

   _____

A blueprint of a sailboat has a sail in the shape of a right triangle, *RST*. On the blueprint the vertices are $R(-4, 6)$, $S(-4, 2)$ and $T(1, 2)$. Use the rules to find the coordinates of the vertices of the sailboat as it changes position. Choose the letter for the best answer.

5. What are the coordinates of the sail after a reflection over the *x*-axis?

   A $R(-4, 6)$, $S(-4, 2)$, $T(1, 2)$

   B $R(-4, -6)$, $S(-4, -2)$, $T(1, -2)$

   C $R(6, -4)$, $S(2, -4)$, $T(2, 1)$

   D $R(-6, -4)$, $S(-2, -4)$, $T(2, 1)$

6. What are the coordinates of the sail after a translation left 3 units and a reflection over the *y*-axis?

   F $R(7, 6)$, $S(7, 2)$, $T(2, 2)$

   G $R(7, -6)$, $S(7, -2)$, $T(2, -2)$

   H $R(-7, -2)$, $S(-7, -2)$, $T(-2, -2)$

   J $R(-6, -7)$, $S(-2, -7)$, $T(-2, -2)$

7. What are the coordinates of Point *R* after a translation 1 unit left and a 90° clockwise rotation about (0, 0)?

   A $R(5, 6)$ C $R(-5, 6)$

   B $R(-6, -5)$ D $R(6, 5)$

8. What are the coordinates of Point *S* after a translation 4 units to the right and 5 units down?

   F $S(-3, 0)$ H $S(0, 3)$

   G $S(0, -3)$ J $S(3, 0)$

Similarity and Congruence Transformations
Reasoning

Essential question: *What properties of a figure are preserved under a translation, reflection, or rotation?*

COMMON CORE **Standards for Mathematical Content**

CC.8.G.1 Verify experimentally the properties of rotations, reflections, and translations.

CC.8.G.1.a Lines are taken to lines, and line segments to line segments of the same length.

CC.8.G.1.b Angles are taken to angles of the same measure.

CC.8.G.1.c Parallel lines are taken to parallel lines.

Prerequisites
Translations, reflections, and rotations

Math Background
It is important for students to understand how transformations act on geometric figures. When a translation, reflection, or rotation is applied to a figure, that figure does not change in size or shape. Translations, reflections, and rotations are sometimes called rigid transformations because segment lengths and angle measurements are preserved under the transformation. Encourage students to use the mathematical vocabulary of translation, reflection, and rotation instead of the more familiar terms of slide, flip, and turn.

INTRODUCE

Ask students whether they think the length of line segments changes when a figure is translated, reflected, or rotated. Tell students that in this lesson, they will investigate what happens to line segments and angles under translations, reflections, and rotations.

TEACH

1 EXPLORE

Questioning Strategies
- In part D, what is another way to measure $\overline{AD}$? **Count grid squares along the segment.**

- In part E, the figures are very small. How could you make the angles easier to measure? **Extend the rays for each angle until they are long enough to extend past the edge of the protractor.**

MATHEMATICAL PRACTICE	Highlighting the Standards

This Explore provides an opportunity to address Standard 5 (Use appropriate tools strategically). Tools used in this lesson include protractors, rulers, coordinate grids, and tracing paper. Students should be able to explain the importance of each tool used in their exploration of transformations.

2 EXPLORE

Questioning Strategies
- In part F, how can you tell whether a pair of lines runs parallel to each other? **All horizontal grid lines run parallel to each other, and all vertical grid lines run parallel to each other. If the sides of the figure lie along grid lines, you know that they are horizontal or vertical and run parallel to other horizontal or vertical line segments.**

Avoid Common Errors
After reflecting a rectangle, students may label the vertices of the image in the same orientation as the preimage. Guide students to carefully consider which vertex of the image corresponds to each vertex of the preimage. (After one reflection across a line, the top left vertex of the image will not correspond to the top left vertex of the preimage.)

CLOSE

Essential Question
What properties of a figure are preserved under a translation, reflection, or rotation?
The size and shape of a figure are preserved under translations, reflections, and rotations. The image has the same number of sides and angles as the pre-image. Each side of the image has the same length as its corresponding side in the preimage. Each angle in the image has the same measure as its corresponding angle in the preimage.

Name_____ Class_____ Date_____

Similarity and Congruence Transformations
Reasoning

Essential question: *What properties of a figure are preserved under a translation, reflection, or rotation?*

CC.8.G.1

1 EXPLORE Properties of Translations

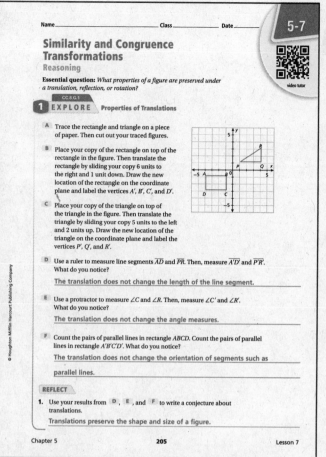

A Trace the rectangle and triangle on a piece of paper. Then cut out your traced figures.

B Place your copy of the rectangle on top of the rectangle in the figure. Then translate the rectangle by sliding your copy 6 units to the right and 1 unit down. Draw the new location of the rectangle on the coordinate plane and label the vertices A', B', C', and D'.

C Place your copy of the triangle on top of the triangle in the figure. Then translate the triangle by sliding your copy 5 units to the left and 2 units up. Draw the new location of the triangle on the coordinate plane and label the vertices P', Q', and R'.

D Use a ruler to measure line segments $\overline{AD}$ and $\overline{PR}$. Then, measure $\overline{A'D'}$ and $\overline{P'R'}$. What do you notice?

The translation does not change the length of the line segment.

E Use a protractor to measure $\angle C$ and $\angle R$. Then, measure $\angle C'$ and $\angle R'$. What do you notice?

The translation does not change the angle measures.

F Count the pairs of parallel lines in rectangle $ABCD$. Count the pairs of parallel lines in rectangle $A'B'C'D'$. What do you notice?

The translation does not change the orientation of segments such as

parallel lines.

REFLECT

1. Use your results from **D**, **E**, and **F** to write a conjecture about translations.

Translations preserve the shape and size of a figure.

Chapter 5   205   Lesson 7

© Houghton Mifflin Harcourt Publishing Company

CC.8.G.1

2 EXPLORE Properties of Reflections

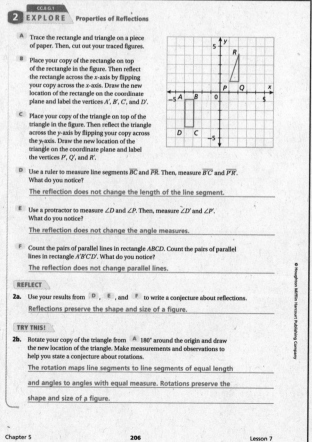

A Trace the rectangle and triangle on a piece of paper. Then, cut out your traced figures.

B Place your copy of the rectangle on top of the rectangle in the figure. Then reflect the rectangle across the *x*-axis by flipping your copy across the *x*-axis. Draw the new location of the rectangle on the coordinate plane and label the vertices A', B', C', and D'.

C Place your copy of the triangle on top of the triangle in the figure. Then reflect the triangle across the *y*-axis by flipping your copy across the *y*-axis. Draw the new location of the triangle on the coordinate plane and label the vertices P', Q', and R'.

D Use a ruler to measure line segments $\overline{BC}$ and $\overline{PR}$. Then, measure $\overline{B'C'}$ and $\overline{P'R'}$. What do you notice?

The reflection does not change the length of the line segment.

E Use a protractor to measure $\angle D$ and $\angle P$. Then, measure $\angle D'$ and $\angle P'$. What do you notice?

The reflection does not change the angle measures.

F Count the pairs of parallel lines in rectangle $ABCD$. Count the pairs of parallel lines in rectangle $A'B'C'D'$. What do you notice?

The reflection does not change parallel lines.

REFLECT

2a. Use your results from **D**, **E**, and **F** to write a conjecture about reflections.

Reflections preserve the shape and size of a figure.

TRY THIS!

2b. Rotate your copy of the triangle from **A** 180° around the origin and draw the new location of the triangle. Make measurements and observations to help you state a conjecture about rotations.

The rotation maps line segments to line segments of equal length

and angles to angles with equal measure. Rotations preserve the

shape and size of a figure.

Chapter 5   206   Lesson 7

© Houghton Mifflin Harcourt Publishing Company

Assign these pages to help your students practice and apply important lesson concepts. For additional exercises, see the Student Edition.

Answers

Additional Practice

1. Rotation 180° around origin; congruent; The rotation preserves the shape and size of the figure.

2. Translation 5 units right and 1 unit down; congruent; The translation preserves the shape and size of the figure.

3. Dilation by scale factor of 3; not congruent; The dilation does not preserve the size of the figure.

4. Reflection across the x-axis; congruent; The reflection preserves the shape and size of the figure.

Problem Solving

1. Reflection across the y-axis; congruent; The reflection preserves the shape and size of the figure.

2. Translation of 3 units left and 3 units up; congruent; The translation preserves the shape and size of the figure.

3. B

4. J

5. C

6. J

Name _____ Class _____ Date _____

Additional Practice

Identify each transformation from the original to the image, and tell whether the two figures are congruent. Justify your answer.

1. Original: $A(0, 2)$, $B(3, 4)$, $C(7, -2)$, $D(4, -4)$

   Image: $A'(0, -2)$, $B'(-3, -4)$, $C'(-7, 2)$, $D'(-4, 4)$

   _____

   _____

   _____

2. Original: $A(-3, -4)$, $B(-1, -2)$, $C(1, -4)$, $D(0, -7)$, $E(-2, -7)$

   Image: $A'(2, -5)$, $B'(4, -3)$, $C'(6, -5)$, $D'(5, -8)$, $E'(3, -8)$

   _____

   _____

   _____

3. Original: $A(-3, -3)$, $B(-2, 3)$, $C(2, -2)$

   Image: $A'(-9, -9)$, $B'(-6, 6)$, $C'(6, -6)$

   _____

   _____

   _____

4. Original: $A(-4, 8)$, $B(4, 7)$, $C(-4, 6)$

   Image: $A'(-4, -8)$, $B'(4, -7)$, $C'(-4, -6)$

   _____

   _____

   _____

Problem Solving

Identify each transformation and tell whether the two figures are congruent. Justify your answer.

1. Original: $A(-5, 6)$, $B(3, 6)$, $C(-3, 2)$

   Image: $A'(5, 6)$, $B'(-3, 6)$, $C'(3, 2)$

   _____

   _____

2. Original: $A(4, -2)$, $B(7, -1)$, $C(4, -7)$

   Image: $A'(1, 1)$, $B'(4, 2)$, $C'(1, -4)$

   _____

   _____

Choose the letter for the best answer.

3. A figure is transformed. Which best describes the transformation of the figure?

   Original: $A(7, 3)$, $B(5, -3)$, $C(3, 0)$

   Image: $A'(-7, 3)$, $B'(-5, -3)$, $C'(-3, 0)$

   A   rotation

   B   reflection

   C   translation

   D   dilation

4. A figure is transformed. Which best describes the transformation of the figure?

   Original: $A(4, 8)$, $B(6, 4)$, $C(0, 2)$

   Image: $A'(3, 6)$, $B'(4.5, 3)$, $C'(0, 1.5)$

   F   rotation

   G   reflection

   H   translation

   J   dilation

5. Which coordinate map describes a 90° counterclockwise rotation?

   A $(x, y) \rightarrow (x, -y)$

   B $(x, y) \rightarrow (y, -x)$

   C $(x, y) \rightarrow (-y, x)$

   D $(x, y) \rightarrow (-x, y)$

6. Which transformation would not necessarily result in a congruent figure?

   F   rotation

   G   reflection

   H   translation

   J   dilation

Identifying Combined Transformations
Going Deeper

Essential question: *What is the connection between transformations and congruent figures and transformations and similar figures?*

COMMON CORE Standards for Mathematical Content

CC.8.G.2 Understand that a two-dimensional figure is congruent to another if the second can be obtained from the first by a sequence of rotations, reflections, and translations; given two congruent figures, describe a sequence that exhibits the congruence between them.

CC.8.G.4 Understand that a two-dimensional figure is simiar to another if the second can be obtained from the first by a sequence of rotations, reflections, translations, and dilations; given two similar two-dimensional figures, describe a sequence that exhibits the similarity between them.

Vocabulary

congruent

similar

Prerequisites

Translations, reflections, rotations, and dilations

Math Background

If there exists a sequence of translations, reflections, and/or rotations that will transform one figure into the other, the two figures are congruent. Note that dilations are not included in this list of transformations. While dilations preserve the shape of a figure, they do not preserve the size when the scale factor does not equal one.

INTRODUCE

Show students two geometric figures in the coordinate plane. The figures should be congruent, but have different orientations. Ask students how they could verify that the two figures are congruent. Tell students that in this lesson, they will learn how to use transformations to determine whether two shapes are identical in shape and size.

TEACH

1 EXPLORE

Questioning Strategies

- Compare the original figure to the image after the transformation in part A in terms of shape, size, location, and orientation. The figures have the same shape and size. The image has a different location and is flipped upside down compared to the pre-image.

- What type of transformation is given in part B? translation

Avoid Common Errors

When applying the transformation in part E, students should make sure to rotate clockwise. Also remind students that, because the rotation is around the origin, the vertex at the origin does not move.

Teaching Strategies

Point out that to translate a figure in a coordinate plane, students can change the coordinates of the figure's points by using the guidelines below, assuming *a* and *b* are positive.

Slide right *a* units	$x \rightarrow x + a$
Slide left *a* units	$x \rightarrow x - a$
Slide up *b* units	$y \rightarrow y + b$
Slide down *b* units	$y \rightarrow y - b$

2 EXAMPLE

Questioning Strategies

- How is figure *A* different from figure *B*? One is a mirror image of the other.

- Which type of transformation results in a mirror image? reflection

- Will reflecting figure *A* across the *y*-axis result in figure *B*? no What other transformation do you need to perform to result in figure *B*? Translate left 1 unit.

Name_____ Class_____ Date_____

5-8

Identifying Combined Transformations
Going Deeper

Essential question: *What is the connection between transformations and congruent figures and transformations and similar figures?*

video tutor

CC.8.G.2

1 EXPLORE Combining Transformations

Apply the indicated series of transformations to the triangle. Each transformation is applied to the image of the previous translation, not the original figure. Label each image with the letter of the transformation applied.

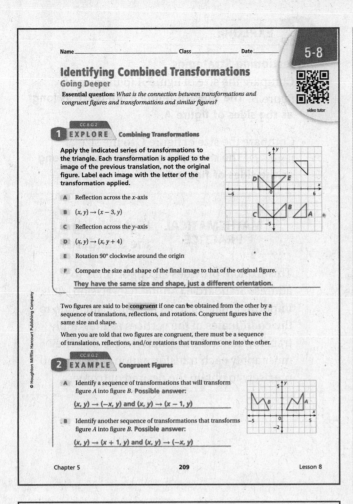

A Reflection across the *x*-axis

B $(x, y) \rightarrow (x - 3, y)$

C Reflection across the *y*-axis

D $(x, y) \rightarrow (x, y + 4)$

E Rotation 90° clockwise around the origin

F Compare the size and shape of the final image to that of the original figure.

<u>They have the same size and shape, just a different orientation.</u>

Two figures are said to be **congruent** if one can be obtained from the other by a sequence of translations, reflections, and rotations. Congruent figures have the same size and shape.

When you are told that two figures are congruent, there must be a sequence of translations, reflections, and/or rotations that transforms one into the other.

CC.8.G.2

2 EXAMPLE Congruent Figures

A Identify a sequence of transformations that will transform figure *A* into figure *B*. **Possible answer:**

$(x, y) \rightarrow (-x, y)$ and $(x, y) \rightarrow (x - 1, y)$

B Identify another sequence of transformations that transforms figure *A* into figure *B*. **Possible answer:**

$(x, y) \rightarrow (x + 1, y)$ and $(x, y) \rightarrow (-x, y)$

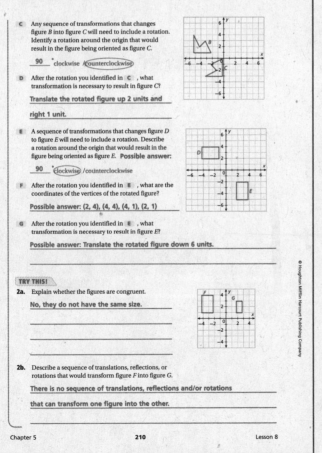

C Any sequence of transformations that changes figure *B* into figure *C* will need to include a rotation. Identify a rotation around the origin that would result in the figure being oriented as figure *C*.

___90___ ° clockwise /~~counterclockwise~~

D After the rotation you identified in **C**, what transformation is necessary to result in figure *C*?

<u>Translate the rotated figure up 2 units and</u>

<u>right 1 unit.</u>

E A sequence of transformations that changes figure *D* to figure *E* will need to include a rotation. Describe a rotation around the origin that would result in the figure being oriented as figure *E*. **Possible answer:**

___90___ ° ~~clockwise~~ /counterclockwise

F After the rotation you identified in **E**, what are the coordinates of the vertices of the rotated figure?

<u>Possible answer: (2, 4), (4, 4), (4, 1), (2, 1)</u>

G After the rotation you identified in **E**, what transformation is necessary to result in figure *E*?

<u>Possible answer: Translate the rotated figure down 6 units.</u>

TRY THIS!

2a. Explain whether the figures are congruent.

<u>No, they do not have the same size.</u>

2b. Describe a sequence of translations, reflections, or rotations that would transform figure *F* into figure *G*.

<u>There is no sequence of translations, reflections and/or rotations</u>

<u>that can transform one figure into the other.</u>

Teaching Strategies

Point out that to reflect a point in the x-axis, multiply its y-coordinate by -1.

$$(x, y) \rightarrow (x, -y)$$

To reflect a point in the y-axis, multiply its x-coordinate by -1.

$$(x, y) \rightarrow (-x, y)$$

3 **EXPLORE**

Questioning Strategies

• How does the transformation in part A affect the original figure? **It moves the figure 7 units to the right and 2 units down.**

• Which of the resulting figures are congruent to the original figure? Which are not? **The images from parts A, B, C, and D are congruent to the original figure. The image from part E is not.**

Teaching Strategies

Point out that to dilate a polygon, multiply the coordinates of each vertex by the scale factor k.

$$(x, y) \rightarrow (kx, ky)$$

4 **EXPLORE**

Questioning Strategies

• Compare the size of figure A to the size of figure B. **The sides of figure B are twice as long as the sides of figure A.**

• Compare the size of figure C to the size of figure D. **The sides of figure D are half as long as the sides of figure C.**

> **MATHEMATICAL PRACTICE** **Highlighting the Standards**
>
> This Explore provides an opportunity to address Standard 6 (Attend to precision). It is important that students pay close attention to the coordinates of the vertices as they apply transformations and graph the results. They must apply each transformation carefully and precisely to obtain the desired outcome.

---

3 EXPLORE CC.8.G.4 Combining Transformations with Dilations

Apply the indicated series of transformations to the rectangle. Each transformation is applied to the image of the previous transformation, not to the original figure. Label each image with the letter of the transformation applied.

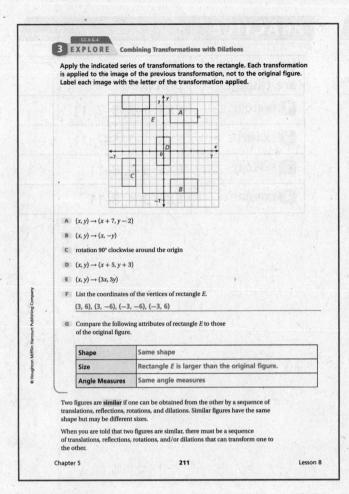

A $(x, y) \rightarrow (x + 7, y - 2)$

B $(x, y) \rightarrow (x, -y)$

C rotation 90° clockwise around the origin

D $(x, y) \rightarrow (x + 5, y + 3)$

E $(x, y) \rightarrow (3x, 3y)$

F List the coordinates of the vertices of rectangle E.

(3, 6), (3, −6), (−3, −6), (−3, 6)

G Compare the following attributes of rectangle E to those of the original figure.

Shape	Same shape
Size	Rectangle E is larger than the original figure.
Angle Measures	Same angle measures

Two figures are **similar** if one can be obtained from the other by a sequence of translations, reflections, rotations, and dilations. Similar figures have the same shape but may be different sizes.

When you are told that two figures are similar, there must be a sequence of translations, reflections, rotations, and/or dilations that can transform one to the other.

Chapter 5   211   Lesson 8

4 EXPLORE CC.8.G.4 Similar Figures

A Identify a sequence of transformations that will transform figure A into figure B.

dilation by scale factor 2 with center at origin

and $(x, y) \rightarrow (x + 4, y + 6)$

B What happens if you reverse the order of the sequence you defined in A ?

If you translate the figure first, the center

of the dilation will not be the origin.

C Tell whether figures A and B are congruent. Tell whether they are similar.

They are not congruent. They are similar.

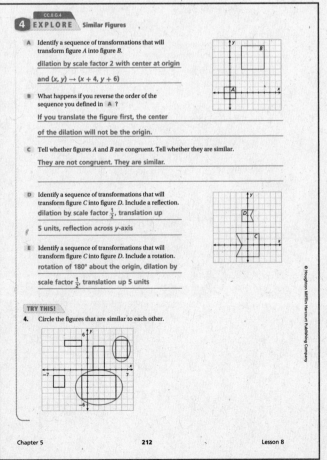

D Identify a sequence of transformations that will transform figure C into figure D. Include a reflection.

dilation by scale factor $\frac{1}{2}$, translation up

5 units, reflection across y-axis

E Identify a sequence of transformations that will transform figure C into figure D. Include a rotation.

rotation of 180° about the origin, dilation by

scale factor $\frac{1}{2}$, translation up 5 units

TRY THIS!

4. Circle the figures that are similar to each other.

Chapter 5   212   Lesson 8

Essential Question

What is the connection between transformations and congruent figures and transformations and similar figures?

If two figures have the same shape and size (are congruent), then there exists a sequence of translations, reflections, and/or rotations that transforms one onto the other.

If two figures are similar, then there exists a sequence of translations, reflections, rotations, and/or dilations that transforms one figure onto the other.

Summarize

Draw a figure in a coordinate plane and have students describe two or more transformations. Perform the combined transformation and then have students determine a transformation or a combined transformation that will map the image back onto the original figure.

Where skills are taught	Where skills are practiced
1 EXPLORE	EXS. 1–2, 5–7, 11
2 EXAMPLE	EXS. 1–2, 5–7, 11
3 EXPLORE	EXS. 3–4, 8–11
4 EXPLORE	EXS. 3–4, 8–11

PRACTICE

Use the diagram for Exercises 1 and 2.

1. Describe a sequence of translations, reflections, or rotations that would transform figure *E* into figure *F*.

   descriptions of transformations will

   vary; sample answer: rotate figure *E* 90°

   clockwise about the origin, then translate

   it 2 units to the right

2. Are figures *F* and *E* congruent or similar? Explain.

   congruent; same size, same shape

Use the diagram for Exercises 3 and 4.

3. Describe a sequence of translations, reflections, or rotations that would transform figure *G* into figure *H*.

   descriptions of transformations will vary;

   sample answer: reflect figure *G* across the

   x-axis, translate it 7 units right and 1 down, and

   then dilate it using a scale factor of one-half

4. Are figures *H* and *G* congruent or similar? Explain.

   similar; different size, same shape

Use the diagram for Exercises 5 and 6.

5. Describe a sequence of translations, reflections, or rotations that would transform figure *J* into figure *K*.

   descriptions of transformations will vary;

   sample answer: reflect figure *J* across the

   x-axis, then translate it 7 units right

6. Are figures *K* and *J* congruent or similar? Explain.

   congruent; same size, same shape

7. **Error Analysis** Sidney drew figure *A*, with vertices (−4, −1), (−1, 3), and (−1, −2). Then she drew its image, figure *A′*, with vertices (1, −1), (4, 3), and (4, −2). She described the transformation as a translation across the *x*-axis, and she described the change using the rule $(x, y) \rightarrow (x, y + 5)$. Is she correct? Explain.

   No; it is a translation across the *y*-axis, described by the rule $(x, y) \rightarrow (x + 5, y)$.

Use the coordinate plane for Exercises 8–10.

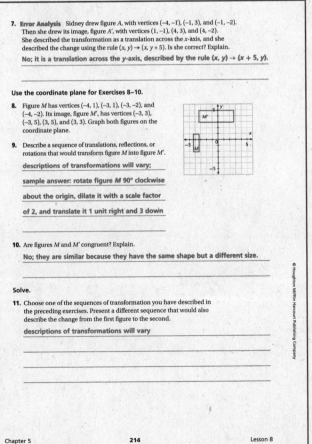

8. Figure *M* has vertices (−4, 1), (−3, 1), (−3, −2), and (−4, −2). Its image, figure *M′*, has vertices (−3, 5), (3, 5), and (3, 3). Graph both figures on the coordinate plane.

9. Describe a sequence of translations, reflections, or rotations that would transform figure *M* into figure *M′*.

   descriptions of transformations will vary;

   sample answer: rotate figure *M* 90° clockwise

   about the origin, dilate it with a scale factor

   of 2, and translate it 1 unit right and 3 down

10. Are figures *M* and *M′* congruent? Explain.

    No; they are similar because they have the same shape but a different size.

Solve.

11. Choose one of the sequences of transformation you have described in the preceding exercises. Present a different sequence that would also describe the change from the first figure to the second.

    descriptions of transformations will vary

© Houghton Mifflin Harcourt Publishing Company

Assign these pages to help your students practice and apply important lesson concepts. For additional exercises, see the Student Edition.

Answers

Additional Practice

1. Reflect across the x-axis: $(x, y) \rightarrow (x, -y)$. Then 180° rotation: $(x, y) \rightarrow (-x, -y)$. The figures are congruent.

2. Translation: $(x, y) \rightarrow (x - 5, y + 3)$. Then dilation with a scale factor of 2: $(x, y) \rightarrow (2x, 2y)$. The figures are similar.

3. Possible answer: 90° counterclockwise rotation: $(x, y) \rightarrow (-y, x)$. Then translation: $(x, y) \rightarrow (x - 4, y - 3)$. The figures are congruent.

4. Possible answer: Dilation with a scale factor of 4: $(x, y) \rightarrow (4x, 4y)$. Then reflection across the x-axis: $(x, y) \rightarrow (x, -y)$. The figures are similar.

Problem Solving

1. Final Image: $A''B''C''$ with $A''(1, -3)$, $B''(5, -1)$, $C''(1, 1)$. The figures are congruent.

2. Final Image: $A''B''C''D''$ with $A''(3, 1\frac{1}{2})$, $B''(1, -1)$, $C''(\frac{1}{2}, 1)$, $D''(2\frac{1}{2}, \frac{1}{2})$. The figures are similar.

3. Possible answer: Translation: $(x, y) \rightarrow (x - 4, y + 2)$ followed by a 90° counterclockwise rotation: $(x, y) \rightarrow (-y, x)$. The figures are congruent.

4. Possible answer: Reflection across the y-axis: $(x, y) \rightarrow (-x, y)$ followed by a translation: $(x, y) \rightarrow (x + 4, y - 5)$. The figures are congruent.

5. Possible answer: Reflection across the y-axis: $(x, y) \rightarrow (-x, y)$ followed by a translation: $(x, y) \rightarrow (x + 2, y + 1)$. The figures are congruent.

6. Possible answer: Dilation by a factor of 1.5: $(x, y) \rightarrow (1.5x, 1.5y)$ followed by a 90° clockwise rotation: $(x, y) \rightarrow (y, -x)$. The figures are similar.

7. B

8. F

Name_____ Class_____ Date_____ **5-8**

Additional Practice

Identify the combined transformations from the original to the final image, and tell whether the two figures are similar or congruent.

1.

2.

Find a sequence of at least two combined transformations for transforming the original to the final image. Justify your answer.

3.

4.

_____

_____

Problem Solving

For each sequence of transformations, find the coordinates of the final image and state whether the two figures are similar or congruent.

1. Original *ABC*: *A*(−3, 1), *B*(−1, 5), *C*(1, 1)

   A reflection across the *y*-axis, followed by a 90° clockwise rotation around the origin.

   _____

2. Original *ABCD*: *A*(6, −3), *B*(2, −2), *C*(−1, −2), *D*(−5, −1)

   A 180° rotation around the origin, followed by a dilation by a scale factor of 0.5, with the origin as the center of dilation.

   _____

Identify the combined transformations from the original to the final image. Tell whether the two figures are similar or congruent. Justify your answer.

3. Original *ABCDE* with *A*(−2, 2), *B*(0, 3), *C*(1, 2), *D*(1, 0), *E*(−1, 1)

   Final Image: *A″B″C″D″E″* with *A″*(−4, −6), *B″*(−5, −4), *C″*(−4, −3), *D″*(−2, −3), *E″*(−3, −5)

   _____

4. Original *ABC* with *A*(−6, −4), *B*(3, 6), *C*(3, −4)

   Final Image: *A″B″C″* with *A″*(10, −9), *B″*(1, 1), *C″*(1, −9)

   _____

5. Original *ABCD* with *A*(0, 1), *B*(1, 2), *C*(3, 0), *D*(2, −1)

   Final Image: *A″B″C″D″* with *A″*(2, 2), *B″*(1, 3), *C″*(−1, 3), *D″*(0, 0)

   _____

6. Original *ABCD* with *A*(0, 1), *B*(2, 1), *C*(2, −4), *D*(0, −4)

   Final Image: *A″B″C″D″* with *A″*(1.5, 0), *B″*(1.5, −3), *C″*(−6, −3), *D″*(−6, 0)

   _____

Choose the letter for the best answer.

7. What are the coordinates of the image of the point (2, −4) after a reflection across the *x*-axis followed by a rotation of 90° counter-clockwise around the origin?

   A (−4, −2)

   B (−4, 2)

   C (4, −2)

   D (4, 2)

8. What are the coordinates of the image of the point (−2, 1) after being dilated by a scale factor of 3 with the origin set as the center of dilation and then translated 2 units left and 3 units up?

   F (−3, 1)

   G (−6, 3)

   H (−4, 0)

   J (−1, 7)

Problem Solving Connections
Stitch Perfect

© Houghton Mifflin Harcourt Publishing Company

CC.8.G.1 Verify experimentally the properties of rotations, reflections, and translations: (a) Lines are taken to lines, and line segments to line segments of the same length. (b) Angles are taken to angles of the same measure. (c) Parallel lines are taken to parallel lines.

CC.8.G.2 Understand that a two-dimensional figure is congruent to another if the second figure can be obtained from the first by a sequence of rotations, reflections, and translations; given two congruent figures, describe a sequence that exhibits the congruence between them.

CC.8.G.3 Describe the effect of dilations, translations, rotations, and reflections on two-dimensional figures using coordinates.

CC.8.G.4 Understand that a two-dimensional figure is similar to another if the second figure can be obtained from the first by a sequence of rotations, reflections, translations, and dilations; given two similar two-dimensional figures, describe a sequence that exhibits the similarity between them.

INTRODUCE

Mathematical modeling is the process of using numbers, algebra, geometry, or other mathematical disciplines to describe and analyze the real world. Transformations are a powerful modeling tool that can be used to describe objects from real life, including nature and art. In this lesson, you will combine nature, art, and mathematics to create a cross-stitch pattern using transformations.

TEACH

1 Making the Body and Wings

Questioning Strategies

• Is the upper wing congruent to the lower wing? Explain. **No; the upper wing is a polygon with 5 sides, and the lower wing has 6 sides.**

• Why do you think Ellie would use reflections to create the second upper wing and the second lower wing? **In nature, a butterfly appears to be symmetric on each side of its body. The line of symmetry in a reflection mimics the symmetry of a real butterfly.**

Teaching Strategies

Give students an extra grid so that they can plot the pieces of the pattern as they work. This can act as their "rough draft" as they work. Once students have completed the pattern, they can transfer a neat sketch to the final answer grid.

2 Designing the Upper-Wing Pattern

Questioning Strategies

• Why do the instructions in part A describe the position of the square as "centered at the origin"? **The dilation in part B only provides the scale factor, which implies that the center of dilation is the origin.**

• Explain how the four squares in the upper wings are related. **The two larger squares are congruent to each other. The two smaller squares are also congruent to each other. Each square is similar to the others.**

Name_____ Class_____ Date_____

CHAPTER 5

COMMON CORE
CC.8.G.1
CC.8.G.2
CC.8.G.3
CC.8.G.4

Problem Solving Connections 🌐

Stitch Perfect Ellie is making a cross-stitch pattern for a butterfly. She uses translations, reflection, rotations, and dilations to design the parts of the butterfly. Perform the transformations as described. Then, draw the images on the final answer grid on the last page of the Problem Solving Connections.

1 Making the Body and Wings

A The coordinates of the vertices of the rectangle that represents the body of the butterfly are $(-1, 7)$, $(1, 7)$, $(1, -7)$, $(-1, -7)$. Draw the body on the final answer grid.

B What would the body of the butterfly look like if it were rotated clockwise by 180°?

It would look the same; a 180° rotation would align with the

original figure.

C Ellie draws one upper wing of the butterfly. The coordinates of the vertices of the wing are given in the table. Draw the wing on the final answer grid.

First Upper Wing	(−10, 9)	(−4, 9)	(−1, 5)	(−1, 0)	(−10, 2)
Image	(10, 9)	(4, 9)	(1, 5)	(1, 0)	(10, 2)

To find the coordinates of the other upper wing, perform a reflection across the *y*-axis. Draw the image of the first wing on the final answer grid.

D Ellie draws one lower wing of the butterfly. The coordinates of the vertices of the wing are given in the table. Draw the wing on the final answer grid.

First Lower Wing	(1, 0)	(5, 0)	(9, −2)	(10, −9)	(5, −9)	(1, −2)
Image	(−1, 0)	(−5, 0)	(−9, −2)	(−10, −9)	(−5, −9)	(−1, −2)

To find the coordinates of the other lower wing, perform a reflection across the *y*-axis. Draw the image of the first wing on the final answer grid.

E Is the first upper wing congruent to its image? Is the first lower wing congruent to its image? Explain how you know.

Yes; there is a sequence of transformations (reflection across the

y-axis) that would transform the first wing to its image.

© Houghton Mifflin Harcourt Publishing Company

---

2 Designing the Upper-Wing Pattern

A On the grid below, draw a square centered at the origin, with side lengths of 6 units.

B Ellie transforms the figure from **A** under the dilation $(x, y) \rightarrow \left(\frac{1}{3}x, \frac{1}{3}y\right)$. Write the coordinates of the image. Then, draw the image on the grid below.

$(-1, 1)$, $(1, 1)$, $(1, -1)$, $(-1, -1)$

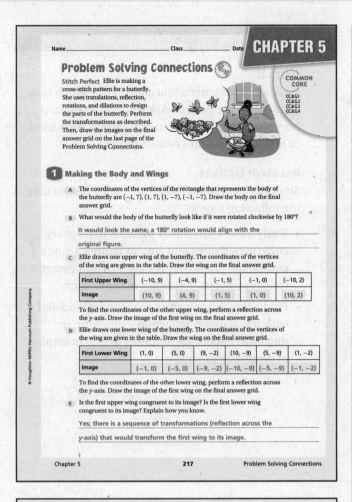

C Ellie transforms the figure from **B** under the translation $(x, y) \rightarrow (x + 5, y + 4)$. Write the coordinates of the image. Then, draw the image on the final answer grid.

$(4, 5)$, $(6, 5)$, $(6, 3)$, $(4, 3)$

D Ellie transforms the figure from **C** by reflecting it across the *y*-axis. Write the coordinates of the image. Then, draw the image on the final answer grid.

$(-4, 5)$, $(-6, 5)$, $(-6, 3)$, $(-4, 3)$

E On the final answer grid, there is a black square. Ellie reflects the square across the *y*-axis. Write the coordinates of the image. Then, draw the image on the final answer grid.

$(-9, 8)$, $(-6, 8)$, $(-6, 5)$, $(-9, 5)$

© Houghton Mifflin Harcourt Publishing Company

Designing the Lower-Wing Pattern

Questioning Strategies

- Explain how the four triangles in the lower wings are related. **All the triangles are congruent. Each one was created from the original figure using a sequence of translations, reflections, and rotations.**

- How can you double-check your algebraic work? **If a figure is out of place in the design on the final answer grid, you know that you have made an error.**

4 Final Answer Grid

Questioning Strategies

- What is the difference between two figures being congruent and two figures being similar? **Both congruent figures and similar figures are characterized by the same shape and congruent corresponding angle measures. In congruent figures, corresponding side lengths are congruent. While in similar figures, corresponding side lengths are proportional.**

MATHEMATICAL PRACTICE · **Highlighting the Standards**

This Project provides an opportunity to address Standard 4 (Model with mathematics). As students work through the lesson, they should discover the structure behind the final image. This will lead to an understanding of how mathematics can be used to describe, or model, real-life objects.

CLOSE

Journal

Have students write a journal entry in which they summarize the project. Ask students to explain how different types of transformations were used to make the final cross-stitch pattern.

Research Options

Students can extend their learning by researching the following topics:

- Study other cross-stitch patterns to discover congruent figures and similar figures. Draw a coordinate plane over the pattern and describe transformations that result in the design.

- Find examples in nature that can be modeled with translations, reflections, rotations, or dilations. Encourage students to find examples of symmetry in nature.

3 **Designing the Lower-Wing Pattern**

A On the final answer grid, there is a black triangle. Ellie reflects the triangle across the *y*-axis. Write the coordinates of the image. Then, draw the image on the final answer grid.

(8, −5), (9, −8), (6, −8)

B Ellie rotates the original triangle by 180° about the origin. Write the coordinates of the image. Then, draw the image on the grid below.

(8, 5), (9, 8), (6, 8)

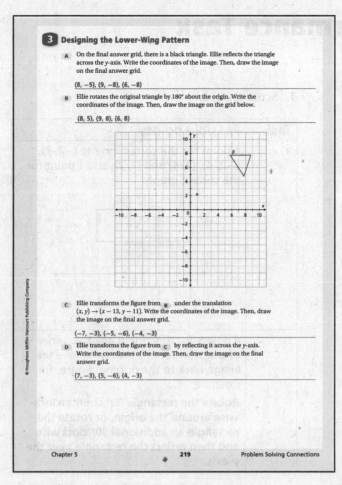

C Ellie transforms the figure from **B** under the translation
$(x, y) \rightarrow (x − 13, y − 11)$. Write the coordinates of the image. Then, draw the image on the final answer grid.

(−7, −3), (−5, −6), (−4, −3)

D Ellie transforms the figure from **C** by reflecting it across the *y*-axis. Write the coordinates of the image. Then, draw the image on the final answer grid.

(7, −3), (5, −6), (4, −3)

4 **Final Answer Grid**

Use this final answer grid to draw Ellie's completed butterfly design.

Are there any similar figures (that are not congruent) in Ellie's butterfly design? Use what you know about transformations and similarity to justify your answer. (If there are similar figures in the design, describe a sequence of transformations that would transform one of the similar figures to the other.)

Yes, the two squares in the upper-right wing are similar. Translate the smaller square down 4 units and left 5 units so that it is centered at the origin. Then dilate the figure by a scale factor of $\frac{3}{2}$. Then translate the result 6.5 units up and 7.5 units right. There is a sequence of transformations that are applied to one figure to result in the other, so the squares are similar.

This page provides students with the opportunity to apply concepts from the Common Core in real-world problem situations. There are three different levels of performance tasks:

⭐ **Novice:** These are short word problems that require students to apply the math they have learned in straightforward, real-world situations.

⭐⭐ **Apprentice:** These are more involved problems that guide students step-by-step through more complex tasks. These exercises include more complicated reasoning, writing, and open-ended elements.

⭐⭐⭐ **Expert:** These are open-ended, non-routine problems that, instead of stepping the students through, asks them to choose their own methods for solving and justify their answers and reasoning.

Sample answers

1. **a.** 72º, 72º, 36º; the exterior angle of the triangle is supplementary to the adjacent angle of the triangle, so it measures 72º. Since the triangle is isosceles, the other base angle has a measure of 72º. There are 180 degrees in a triangle, so the last angle measure is 180º − 72º − 72º = 36º.
   b. The angle measures stay the same.

2. **a.** No; it is a translation 6 units right.
   b. Yes; possible explanation: Because the gray triangle can be obtained from the black triangle by a translation, the figures are congruent.

3. Scoring Guide:

Task	Possible points
a	**1 point** for the correct points (−2, 2), (−2, 4), (2, 4) and (2, 2), and **1 point** for the correct graph: 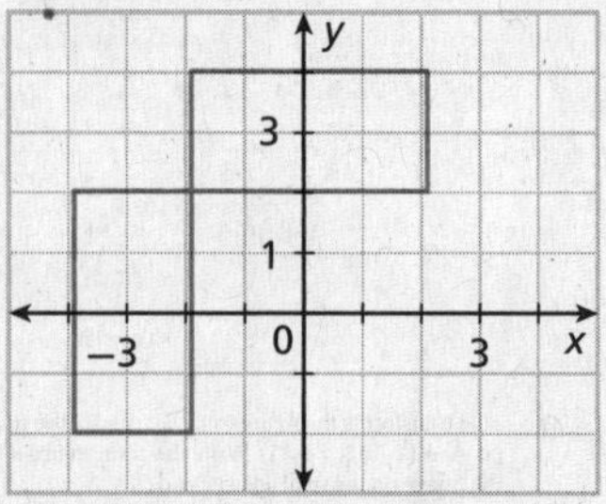
b	**4 points** for describing any two series of transformations that will move the image back to the original figure, for example: Rotate the rectangle 90° counterclockwise around the origin, or rotate the rectangle an additional 90° clockwise and then reflect the rectangle over the y-axis.

Total possible points: 6

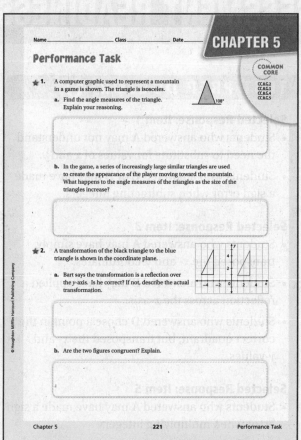

CHAPTER 5

COMMON
CORE
CC.8.G.2
CC.8.G.3
CC.8.G.4
CC.8.G.5

Performance Task

⭐ **1.** A computer graphic used to represent a mountain in a game is shown. The triangle is isosceles.

108°

    a. Find the angle measures of the triangle. Explain your reasoning.

    b. In the game, a series of increasingly large similar triangles are used to create the appearance of the player moving toward the mountain. What happens to the angle measures of the triangles as the size of the triangles increase?

⭐ **2.** A transformation of the black triangle to the blue triangle is shown in the coordinate plane.

    a. Bart says the transformation is a reflection over the *y*-axis. Is he correct? If not, describe the actual transformation.

    b. Are the two figures congruent? Explain.

---

4. Scoring Guide:

Task	Possible points
a	**1 point** for the correct answer (−6, −4) and **2 points** for correctly showing the steps: (−2, 2) → (2, −2), 180° rotation about origin, (2, −2) → (−3, −2), translation 5 units left, and (−3, −2) → (−6, −4), dilation by a scale factor of 2.
b	**3 points** for any correct series of transformations, for example: reflect over the *x*-axis, reflect over the *y*-axis, dilate by a factor of 2, and translate 10 units to the left.

Total possible points: 6

⭐⭐ **3.** A rectangle is shown in the coordinate plane.

    a. The figure is rotated 90° clockwise about the origin. Give the coordinates of the image of the rectangle. Then draw its image in the coordinate plane.

    b. Describe two ways you could use transformations that would move the image from part back to the original figure. One or both ways can involve more than one transformation if you want.

⭐⭐⭐ **4.** A pentagon is drawn on the coordinate plane. It is then rotated 180° about the origin, translated 5 units left, and dilated by a factor of 2.

    a. A vertex of the original figure was at (−2, 2). Where is this vertex after the three transformations? Describe each step.

    b. Describe a different series of transformations that would lead to the same final image. Use two reflections, a dilation, and finally a translation.

© Houghton Mifflin Harcourt Publishing Company

COMMON CORE CORRELATION

Standard	Items
CC.8.G.1	11
CC.8.G.2	4
CC.8.G.3	1–3, 5, 6, 11–13
CC.8.G.4	4, 14
CC.8.G.5	7–10

TEST PREP DOCTOR ✚

Selected Response: Item 1
- Students who answered **A** may not understand the need to substitute for values of x and y.
- Students who answered **C** or **D** may have made a sign error when subtracting integers.

Selected Response: Item 3
- Students who answered **A** may have simply transposed the x- and y-coordinates.
- Students who answered **B** may have applied a reflection across the x-axis.
- Students who answered **D** chose a point in the correct quadrant, but transposed the x- and y-values.

Selected Response: Item 5
- Students who answered **A** may have made a sign error when multiplying integers.
- Students who answered **B** or **C** may have divided, instead of multiplying, when applying the dilation.

Constructed Response: Item 12
- A triangle with an incorrect orientation may be the result of a mistake in applying the rotation. If a student's triangle is in an incorrect position, the mistake may have occurred when applying the translation.

Constructed Response: Item 14
- Students may reverse the order of the transformations from Item 13. There are many possible correct responses. Students should NOT, however, include a dilation.

© Houghton Mifflin Harcourt Publishing Company

CHAPTER 5 COMMON CORE ASSESSMENT READINESS

Name _____ Class _____ Date _____

SELECTED RESPONSE

1. Which is the image of (2, 3) under the translation $(x, y) \rightarrow (x - 5, y - 2)$?

A. (−5, −2) C. (3, 5)

B. (−3, 1) D. (3, −1)

2. Which is the image of (2, 3) under a reflection across the y-axis?

F. (2, 3) H. (2, −3)

G. (−2, 3) J. (−2, −3)

3. Which is the image of (2, 3) under a 180° rotation about the origin?

A. (3, 2) C. (−2, −3)

B. (2, −3) D. (−3, −2)

4. Which sequence of translations, reflections, rotations, and/or dilations transforms figure A into figure B?

F. 180° rotation; reflection across y-axis

G. dilation with center at origin with scale factor of 2; translation 6 units left

H. reflection across the y-axis; translation 2 units right

J. reflection across the x-axis; dilation with center as origin with scale factor of $\frac{1}{2}$

Use the figure to answer 5 and 6.

5. Which is the image of point A under a dilation centered at the origin described by the rule $(x, y) \rightarrow (4x, 4y)$?

A. (8, 4) C. $\left(-\frac{1}{2}, -\frac{1}{4}\right)$

B. $\left(\frac{1}{2}, \frac{1}{4}\right)$ D. (−8, −4)

6. Which is the image of point B under a dilation centered at the origin with scale factor $\frac{1}{3}$?

F. $\left(\frac{1}{3}, -\frac{2}{3}\right)$ H. $\left(\frac{4}{3}, -\frac{5}{3}\right)$

G. (3, −6) J. (−3, 6)

7. What is the measure of angle x?

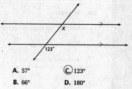

A. 57° C. 123°

B. 66° D. 180°

---

8. What is the value of x?

F. 30° H. 87°

G. 63° J. 93°

CONSTRUCTED RESPONSE

Use the figure for 9 and 10.

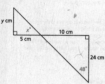

9. Explain how to find the value of x.

The third angle of the triangle on the right measures 180° − (90° + 48°) = 42°.

This angle and the angle marked x° are vertical angles, so x = 42.

10. Explain how to find the value of y.

The triangles are similar by AA, so you can solve the proportion $\frac{5}{10} = \frac{y}{24}$ to find that y = 12.

Use the figure for 11 through 14.

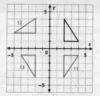

11. Sketch the image of the triangle under a reflection across the x-axis.

12. Sketch the image of the triangle after a rotation 90° counterclockwise about the origin followed by a translation left 1 unit.

13. Sketch the image of the triangle after a reflection across the y-axis followed by a reflection across the x-axis.

14. Identify another transformation or sequence of transformations that results in the same image as the result of Problem 13.

Possible answer: Rotate 180° about the origin.

CHAPTER 6

Measurement and Geometry

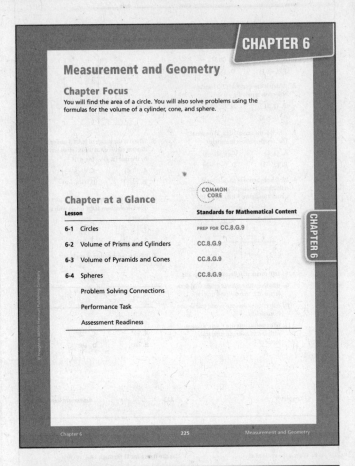

CHAPTER 6

Measurement and Geometry

Chapter Focus
You will find the area of a circle. You will also solve problems using the formulas for the volume of a cylinder, cone, and sphere.

Chapter at a Glance

COMMON CORE

Lesson	Standards for Mathematical Content
6-1 Circles	PREP FOR CC.8.G.9
6-2 Volume of Prisms and Cylinders	CC.8.G.9
6-3 Volume of Pyramids and Cones	CC.8.G.9
6-4 Spheres	CC.8.G.9
Problem Solving Connections	
Performance Task	
Assessment Readiness	

COMMON CORE PROFESIONAL DEVELOPMENT **CC.8.G.9**

In Grade 8, students will use their understanding of circles and volumes developed in Grade 7 as the foundation to develop the formulas for the volume of cylinders, cones, and spheres. Students will recognize the relationship between the volumes of cylinders and cones. They will also recognize the relationship between the volumes of cylinders and spheres.

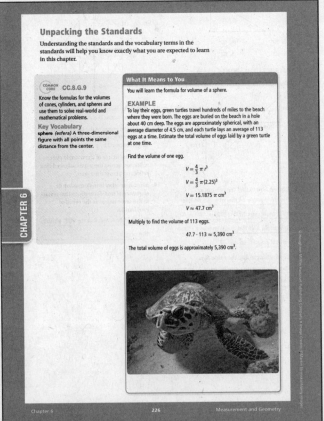

Unpacking the Standards
Understanding the standards and the vocabulary terms in the standards will help you know exactly what you are expected to learn in this chapter.

COMMON CORE **CC.8.G.9**
Know the formulas for the volumes of cones, cylinders, and spheres and use them to solve real-world and mathematical problems.

Key Vocabulary
sphere *(esfera)* A three-dimensional figure with all points the same distance from the center.

What It Means to You

You will learn the formula for volume of a sphere.

EXAMPLE
To lay their eggs, green turtles travel hundreds of miles to the beach where they were born. The eggs are buried on the beach in a hole about 40 cm deep. The eggs are approximately spherical, with an average diameter of 4.5 cm, and each turtle lays an average of 113 eggs at a time. Estimate the total volume of eggs laid by a green turtle at one time.

Find the volume of one egg.

$$V = \frac{4}{3}\pi r^3$$
$$V = \frac{4}{3}\pi (2.25)^3$$
$$V = 15.1875\,\pi \text{ cm}^3$$
$$V \approx 47.7 \text{ cm}^3$$

Multiply to find the volume of 113 eggs.

$$47.7 \cdot 113 \approx 5{,}390 \text{ cm}^3$$

The total volume of eggs is approximately 5,390 cm³.

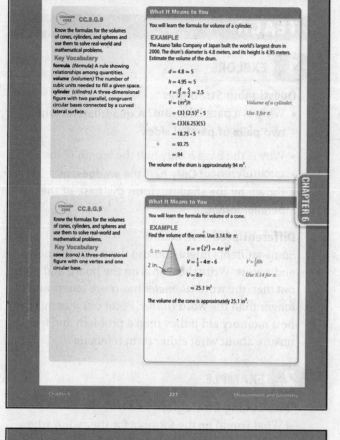

COMMON CORE **CC.8.G.9**

Know the formulas for the volumes of cones, cylinders, and spheres and use them to solve real-world and mathematical problems.

Key Vocabulary

formula *(fórmula)* A rule showing relationships among quantities.

volume *(volumen)* The number of cubic units needed to fill a given space.

cylinder *(cilindro)* A three-dimensional figure with two parallel, congruent circular bases connected by a curved lateral surface.

What It Means to You

You will learn the formula for volume of a cylinder.

EXAMPLE

The Asano Taiko Company of Japan built the world's largest drum in 2000. The drum's diameter is 4.8 meters, and its height is 4.95 meters. Estimate the volume of the drum.

$$d = 4.8 \approx 5$$
$$h = 4.95 \approx 5$$
$$r = \frac{d}{2} = \frac{5}{2} = 2.5$$
$$V = (\pi r^2)h \qquad \text{Volume of a cylinder.}$$
$$= (3)(2.5)^2 \cdot 5 \qquad \text{Use 3 for } \pi.$$
$$= (3)(6.25)(5)$$
$$= 18.75 \cdot 5$$
$$= 93.75$$
$$\approx 94$$

The volume of the drum is approximately 94 m³.

COMMON CORE **CC.8.G.9**

Know the formulas for the volumes of cones, cylinders, and spheres and use them to solve real-world and mathematical problems.

Key Vocabulary

cone *(cono)* A three-dimensional figure with one vertex and one circular base.

What It Means to You

You will learn the formula for volume of a cone.

EXAMPLE

Find the volume of the cone. Use 3.14 for π.

$$B = \pi (2^2) = 4\pi \text{ in}^2$$
$$V = \frac{1}{3} \cdot 4\pi \cdot 6 \qquad V = \frac{1}{3}Bh$$
$$V = 8\pi \qquad \text{Use 3.14 for } \pi.$$
$$\approx 25.1 \text{ in}^3$$

The volume of the cone is approximately 25.1 in³.

CHAPTER 6

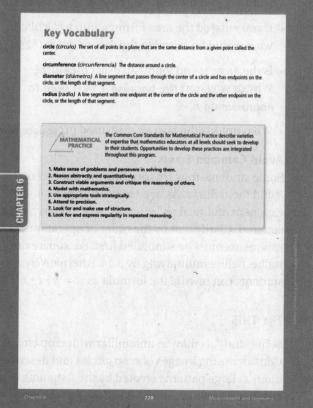

Key Vocabulary

circle *(círculo)* The set of all points in a plane that are the same distance from a given point called the center.

circumference *(circunferencia)* The distance around a circle.

diameter *(diámetro)* A line segment that passes through the center of a circle and has endpoints on the circle, or the length of that segment.

radius *(radio)* A line segment with one endpoint at the center of the circle and the other endpoint on the circle, or the length of that segment.

MATHEMATICAL PRACTICE

The Common Core Standards for Mathematical Practice describe varieties of expertise that mathematics educators at all levels should seek to develop in their students. Opportunities to develop these practices are integrated throughout this program.

1. Make sense of problems and persevere in solving them.
2. Reason abstractly and quantitatively.
3. Construct viable arguments and critique the reasoning of others.
4. Model with mathematics.
5. Use appropriate tools strategically.
6. Attend to precision.
7. Look for and make use of structure.
8. Look for and express regularity in repeated reasoning.

© Houghton Mifflin Harcourt Publishing Company

CHAPTER 6

6-1

Circles
Going Deeper

Essential question: How do you find the area of a circle?

COMMON CORE
Standards for Mathematical Content

Prep for CC.8.G.9 Know the formulas for the volumes of cones, cylinders, and spheres and use them to solve real-world and mathematical problems.

Vocabulary
circle
circumference
radius
diameter

Prerequisites
Area

Math Background
The circumference of a circle is similar to the perimeter of a polygon. The ratio of the distance around a circle (circumference) to the distance across it (diameter) is a constant named π. The ratio $\pi = \frac{C}{d}$ is an irrational number—so it cannot be expressed exactly as the ratio of two integers. This text uses the approximate value 3.14 for π, so students should understand that answers are not exact and should include *about* or *approximately*. Circumference is measured in linear units, but the area of a circle is measured in square units and is found using the formula $A = \pi r^2$.

INTRODUCE

Begin by reviewing the vocabulary related to circles. Verify that students understand each term by having them point to or draw examples of center, radius, and diameter. Students can trace the circumference of a circle and color to shade its area. Then have students discuss how the area is measured in square units. Contrast this with circumference, which is measured in linear units. To illustrate the difference, roll a coin and point out that the distance it rolls is a linear measure and related to the circumference of the circle. When the coin stops, it covers a surface that is measured in square units.

TEACH

1 EXPLORE

Questioning Strategies
- What is a parallelogram? **A quadrilateral with two pairs of parallel sides**
- Why is the base b only half the length of the circumference? **Only half the wedges, as shown by the shading, form the base of the parallelogram.**

Differentiated Instruction
Some students might confuse the terms diameter and radius. Write the words on the board and point out that the word *diameter* has more letters and is longer than the word *radius*. Point out that this can be a memory aid if they read a problem and feel unsure about what either term refers to.

2 EXAMPLE

Questioning Strategies
- What would be the formula for the radius when you are given the diameter? $r = \frac{d}{2}$
- If you entered the area formula into a calculator, what would be raised to the second power? **25**
- Is the answer you found an exact measure? Why or why not? **No, because 3.14 is used to approximate π.**
- What units is the answer measured in? **square feet**

Avoid Common Errors
Some students may try squaring the product of π and the radius r. As needed, clarify that 2 is an exponent and read as "squared" so r^2 means radius squared. Clarify that by the order of operations, exponents must be simplified first. So, square the radius before multiplying by 3.14. Alternatively, students can rewrite the formula as $A = \pi \cdot r \cdot r$.

TRY THIS

Some students may be unfamiliar with crop circles. Consider using images of crop circles and describe them as large patterns created by the flattening of a crop such as wheat.

Name_____ Class_____ Date_____

6-1

Circles
Going Deeper

Essential question: *How do you find the area of a circle?*

A **circle** is a set of points in a plane that are a fixed distance from a given point, called the center.

The **circumference** of a circle is the distance around it.

A **radius** is a line segment that connects the center of a circle to any point on the circle.

A **diameter** is a line segment that connects two points on the circle and passes through the center.

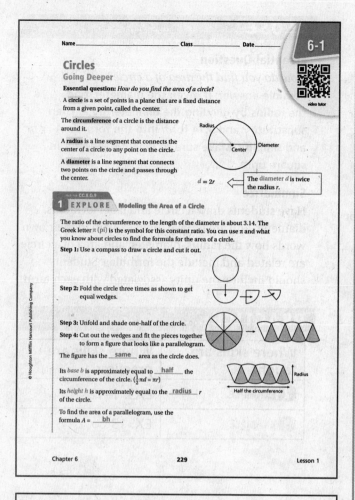

$d = 2r$

The **diameter** d is twice the radius r.

---

1 EXPLORE   **Modeling the Area of a Circle**

The ratio of the circumference to the length of the diameter is about 3.14. The Greek letter π (pi) is the symbol for this constant ratio. You can use π and what you know about circles to find the formula for the area of a circle.

Step 1: Use a compass to draw a circle and cut it out.

Step 2: Fold the circle three times as shown to get equal wedges.

Step 3: Unfold and shade one-half of the circle.

Step 4: Cut out the wedges and fit the pieces together to form a figure that looks like a parallelogram.

The figure has the ___same___ area as the circle does.

Its *base b* is approximately equal to ___half___ the circumference of the circle. ($\frac{1}{2}\pi d = \pi r$)

Its *height h* is approximately equal to the ___radius___ r of the circle.

Radius

Half the circumference

To find the area of a parallelogram, use the formula $A =$ ___bh___.

Chapter 6   229   Lesson 1

To find the area of a circle, substitute for b and h in the area formula.

$A = bh$

$A = \pi r h$ *Substitute πr for b.*

$A = \pi r \cdot r$ *Substitute r for h.*

$A = \pi r^2$ $r \cdot r = r^2$

So, the area of a circle is equal to π times the radius squared: $A = \pi r^2$

REFLECT

1. Explain why your answer will be an approximation when you use 3.14 for pi to find the area of a circle.

   Pi is an irrational number; 3.14 is pi rounded to the nearest hundredth.

---

2 EXAMPLE   **Finding the Area of a Circle**

The Anasazi of the American Southwest built underground circular rooms called kivas. The Great Kiva at Chetro Ketl in Chaco Canyon in New Mexico has a diameter of about 50 feet. What is its approximate area?

Step 1: First find the radius. $d = 2r$

$50 = 2r$ *Substitute 50 for the diameter d.*

$\frac{50}{2} = \frac{2r}{2}$ *Divide both sides by 2 to isolate r.*

$25 = r$

Step 2: Next find the diameter. $A = \pi r^2$

$\approx 3.14 \cdot 25 \cdot 25$ *Substitute 25 for the radius r. Use 3.14 for π.*

$\approx 3.14 \cdot 625$ *Simplify.*

$\approx 1,962.5$

The area of the Great Kiva is about ___1,962.5___ ft².

REFLECT

2a. Does the answer make sense? Explain.

   Yes; by rounding the factors to 3 and 600, you can see that 1962.5 is a reasonable product.

TRY THIS!

2b. The radius of a crop circle is 52 feet. What is the area of the crop circle?

   about 8,490.56 ft²

Chapter 6   230   Lesson 1

Questioning Strategies

- What are you looking for to solve this problem?
  The diameter of the plate

- Can you estimate the diameter given the area of the plate? Possible answer: No, not directly since the area formula uses the radius and not the diameter.

Differentiated Instruction

Some students may benefit from using a calculator to perform the calculations or to check their answers. Caution students to use 3.14 and not the π key on the calculator.

MATHEMATICAL PRACTICE — Highlighting the Standards

This Example is an opportunity to address Standard 1 (Make sense of problems and persevere in solving them). Students need to read the problem and create a solution plan that has two distinct steps: finding the radius from the area of a circle formula, and then finding the diameter. Students then make sense of the answer in the context by comparing the diameter they found to the length of the fork to answer the question.

CLOSE

Essential Question

How do you find the area of a circle?

Possible answer: If given the diameter, find the radius by dividing the diameter by 2. Then substitute r and 3.14 for π into the formula $A = \pi r^2$ and simplify. Make sure to label the answer in square units.

Summarize

Have students draw a circle and label its radius, diameter, and area. Have them explain in their own words how the radius, diameter, and area of a circle are related and include the formulas. Students should include the units associated with each term.

PRACTICE

Where skills are taught	Where skills are practiced
2 EXAMPLE	EXS. 1–12
3 EXAMPLE	EX. 13

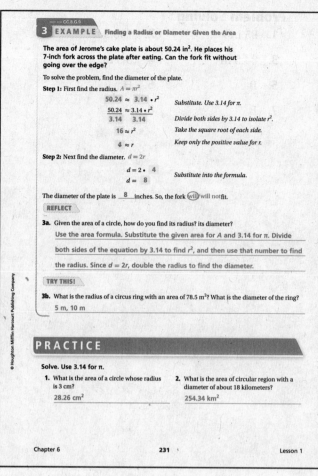

3 EXAMPLE Finding a Radius or Diameter Given the Area

The area of Jerome's cake plate is about 50.24 in². He places his 7-inch fork across the plate after eating. Can the fork fit without going over the edge?

To solve the problem, find the diameter of the plate.

Step 1: First find the radius. $A = \pi r^2$

$$50.24 \approx 3.14 \cdot r^2 \qquad \text{Substitute. Use 3.14 for } \pi.$$

$$\frac{50.24}{3.14} \approx \frac{3.14 \cdot r^2}{3.14} \qquad \text{Divide both sides by 3.14 to isolate } r^2.$$

$$16 \approx r^2 \qquad \text{Take the square root of each side.}$$

$$4 \approx r \qquad \text{Keep only the positive value for } r.$$

Step 2: Next find the diameter. $d = 2r$

$$d = 2 \cdot 4$$
$$d = 8 \qquad \text{Substitute into the formula.}$$

The diameter of the plate is __8__ inches. So, the fork (will) will not fit.

REFLECT

3a. Given the area of a circle, how do you find its radius? its diameter?

Use the area formula. Substitute the given area for A and 3.14 for π. Divide both sides of the equation by 3.14 to find r², and then use that number to find the radius. Since d = 2r, double the radius to find the diameter.

TRY THIS!

3b. What is the radius of a circus ring with an area of 78.5 m²? What is the diameter of the ring?

5 m, 10 m

PRACTICE

Solve. Use 3.14 for π.

1. What is the area of a circle whose radius is 3 cm?

28.26 cm²

2. What is the area of circular region with a diameter of about 18 kilometers?

254.34 km²

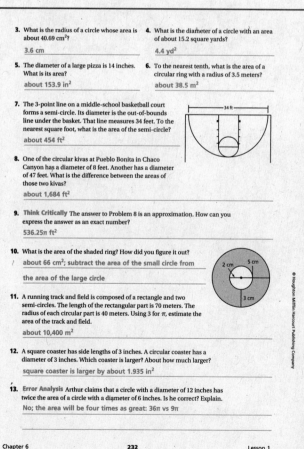

3. What is the radius of a circle whose area is about 40.69 cm²?

3.6 cm

4. What is the diameter of a circle with an area of about 15.2 square yards?

4.4 yd²

5. The diameter of a large pizza is 14 inches. What is its area?

about 153.9 in²

6. To the nearest tenth, what is the area of a circular ring with a radius of 3.5 meters?

about 38.5 m²

7. The 3-point line on a middle-school basketball court forms a semi-circle. Its diameter is the out-of-bounds line under the basket. That line measures 34 feet. To the nearest square foot, what is the area of the semi-circle?

about 454 ft²

8. One of the circular kivas at Pueblo Bonita in Chaco Canyon has a diameter of 8 feet. Another has a diameter of 47 feet. What is the difference between the areas of those two kivas?

about 1,684 ft²

9. Think Critically The answer to Problem 8 is an approximation. How can you express the answer as an exact number?

536.25π ft²

10. What is the area of the shaded ring? How did you figure it out?

about 66 cm²; subtract the area of the small circle from the area of the large circle

11. A running track and field is composed of a rectangle and two semi-circles. The length of the rectangular part is 70 meters. The radius of each circular part is 40 meters. Using 3 for π, estimate the area of the track and field.

about 10,400 m²

12. A square coaster has side lengths of 3 inches. A circular coaster has a diameter of 3 inches. Which coaster is larger? About how much larger?

square coaster is larger by about 1.935 in²

13. Error Analysis Arthur claims that a circle with a diameter of 12 inches has twice the area of a circle with a diameter of 6 inches. Is he correct? Explain.

No; the area will be four times as great: 36π vs 9π

Notes

Assign these pages to help your students practice and apply important lesson concepts. For additional exercises, see the Student Edition.

Answers

Additional Practice

1. 81π in² or 254.3 in²

2. 49π cm² or 153.9 cm²

3. 400π ft² or 1256 ft²

4. 72.3π m² or 226.9 m²

5. 59.3π m² or 186.2 m²

6. 484π yd² or 1519.8 yd²

7. 3 in.

8. 12 cm

9. 4069.44 in²

10. $A = 9\pi$ units² or 28.3 units²;

    $C = 6\pi$ units or 18.8 units

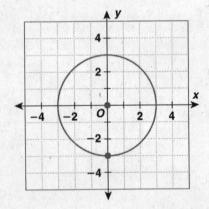

Problem Solving

1. 95 in²

2. 706.5 ft²

3. 34.5 in²

4. 6.3 in.

5. B

6. H

7. B

8. F

Additional Practice

Find the area of each circle, both in terms of π and to the nearest tenth. Use 3.14 for π.

1. circle with radius 9 in.

_____

2. circle with diameter 14 cm

_____

3. circle with radius 20 ft

_____

4. circle with diameter 17 m

_____

5. circle with diameter 15.4 m

_____

6. circle with radius 22 yd

_____

Solve. Use 3.14 for π.

7. A circle has an area of about 28.26 in². What is the radius of the circle?

_____

8. What is the diameter of a circle whose area is about 113.04 cm²?

_____

9. A round tablecloth has a radius of 36 inches. What is the area of the tablecloth?

_____

10. Graph a circle with center (0, 0) that passes through (0, –3). Find the area and circumference, both in terms of π and to the nearest tenth. Use 3.14 for π.

_____

_____

Problem Solving

Round to the nearest tenth. Use π for π. Write the correct answer.

1. A frying pan has a diameter of 11 inches. What is the area to the nearest square inch of the smallest cover that will fit on top of the pan?

2. A dog is on a 15-foot chain that is anchored to the ground. How much area can the dog cover while he is on the chain?

3. A small pizza has a diameter of 10 inches, and a medium has a diameter of 12 inches. How much more pizza do you get with the medium pizza?

4. How much more crust do you get with a medium pizza with a diameter of 12 inches than a small pizza with a 10 inch diameter?

Round to the nearest tenth. Use π for π. Choose the letter for the best answer.

5. The wrestling mat for college NCAA competition has a wrestling circle with a diameter of 32 feet, while a high school mat has a diameter of 28 feet. How much more area is there in a college wrestling mat than a high school mat?

  A 12.6 ft²

  B 188.4 ft²

  C 234.8 ft²

  D 753.6 ft²

6. A round dining table has a radius of 24 inches. A round tablecloth has a diameter of 60 inches. What is the area to the nearest tenth of an inch of the part of the tablecloth that will hang down the side of the table?

  F 19 in²

  G 113 in²

  H 1017 in²

  J 9495 in²

7. In men's Olympic discus throwing competition, an athlete throws a discus with a diameter of 8.625 inches. What is the circumference of the discus?

  A 13.5 in.

  B 27.1 in.

  C 58.4 in.

  D 233.6 in.

8. An athlete in a discus competition throws from a circle that is approximately 8.2 feet in diameter. What is the area of the discus throwing circle?

  F 52.8 ft²

  G 25.7 ft²

  H 12.9 ft²

  J 211.1 ft²

6-2 Volume of Prisms and Cylinders
Going Deeper

Essential question: *How can you solve problems using the formula for the volume of a cylinder?*

COMMON CORE Standards for Mathematical Content

CC.8.G.9 Know the formulas for the volumes of cones, cylinders, and spheres and use them to solve real-world and mathematical problems.

Prerequisites
Circumference and area of a circle
Volume

Math Background
Students have worked with circles in two dimensions (area and circumference). The volume of a cylinder is found using the same general formula for the volume of a prism: $V = Bh$, where B is the area of a circular base instead of the area of a polygon. The volume of a cylinder can also be written as $V = \pi r^2 h$ where πr^2 is the area of the circular base with radius r.

INTRODUCE

Using models of a rectangular prism and a cylinder, review how to find the volume of a prism as a product of the area of the base times the height. Then ask students to suggest ways to find the volume of the cylinder. Students should recognize it is similar to a prism, base area times height. Then discuss what is different between finding the volume of a prism and the volume of a cylinder. Students should recognize that finding the area of the base would be different.

TEACH

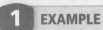 **EXAMPLE**

Questioning Strategies
• What is a reasonable estimate for part A? **270 in³**

• What types of units are used to describe volume?
When calculated using length dimensions, volume is expressed in cubic units such as m³ or in³.

• How can you find the area of the base B of a cylinder? **The base is a circle, so use $A = \pi r^2$.**

Differentiated Instruction
Use cubes to form the base layer of a rectangular prism. Show how the number of layers, each stacked on top of the base layer, gives the prism's height. Then build a cylinder using circular chips. Discuss how the total volume of the cylinder is the volume of one chip multiplied by the number of stacked chips.

> **MATHEMATICAL PRACTICE** **Highlighting the Standards**
>
> This Example is an opportunity to address Standard 6 (Attend to precision). Students perform computations using 3.14 for π. So, each solution step after this substitution uses the approximately equal sign. In the final answer statement, students use the word *about* to indicate an approximate value for the volume.

CLOSE

Essential Question
How can you solve problems using the formula for the volume of a cylinder?
Possible answer: If given the diameter, find the radius by dividing the diameter by 2. Then substitute the given values into the formula $V = Bh$ or $V = \pi r^2 h$ and simplify. Make sure to label the answer in cubic units.

Summarize
Have students draw a rectangular prism and a cylinder and write the formulas for the volume of each solid. Then discuss how the formulas are alike and different.

PRACTICE

Where skills are taught	Where skills are practiced
1 EXAMPLE	EXS. 1–11

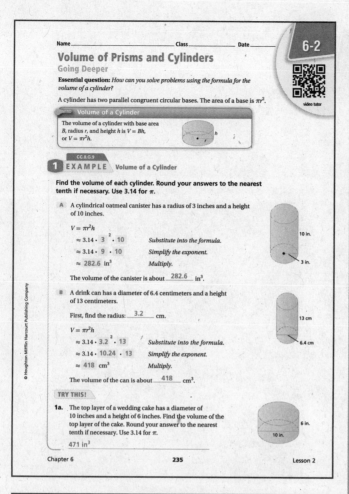

Name_____ Class_____ Date_____

6-2

Volume of Prisms and Cylinders
Going Deeper

Essential question: *How can you solve problems using the formula for the volume of a cylinder?*

A cylinder has two parallel congruent circular bases. The area of a base is πr^2.

Volume of a Cylinder

The volume of a cylinder with base area B, radius r, and height h is $V = Bh$, or $V = \pi r^2 h$.

CC.8.G.9

1 EXAMPLE   Volume of a Cylinder

Find the volume of each cylinder. Round your answers to the nearest tenth if necessary. Use 3.14 for π.

A A cylindrical oatmeal canister has a radius of 3 inches and a height of 10 inches.

$V = \pi r^2 h$

$\approx 3.14 \cdot 3^2 \cdot 10$ *Substitute into the formula.*

$\approx 3.14 \cdot 9 \cdot 10$ *Simplify the exponent.*

≈ 282.6 in³   *Multiply.*

The volume of the canister is about ___282.6___ in³.

10 in.
3 in.

B A drink can has a diameter of 6.4 centimeters and a height of 13 centimeters.

First, find the radius: ___3.2___ cm.

$V = \pi r^2 h$

$\approx 3.14 \cdot 3.2^2 \cdot 13$ *Substitute into the formula.*

$\approx 3.14 \cdot 10.24 \cdot 13$ *Simplify the exponent.*

≈ 418 cm³   *Multiply.*

The volume of the can is about ___418___ cm³.

13 cm
6.4 cm

TRY THIS!

1a. The top layer of a wedding cake has a diameter of 10 inches and a height of 6 inches. Find the volume of the top layer of the cake. Round your answer to the nearest tenth if necessary. Use 3.14 for π.

___471 in³___

6 in.
10 in.

PRACTICE

Find the volume of each figure. Round your answers to the nearest tenth if necessary. Use 3.14 for π.

1.
13 ft
10 ft

___4,082 ft³___

2.
12 ft
4 ft

___602.9 ft³___

3. The area of the circular base of a can of dog food is 12.5 in². The can is 6 inches high. What is its volume?

___75 in³___

4. A can of soup has a volume of 2,797.74 cm³. It is 11 cm high. What is the length of the radius of its base?

___9 cm___

5. A cookie container is in the shape of a cylinder. Its diameter is 9 inches and its height is 3 inches. To the nearest cubic inch, what is its volume?

___191 in³___

6. The volume of a rooftop cylindrical water tank is 1,493 ft³. The tank is 30 feet high. To the nearest square foot, what is the area of its base?

___50 ft²___

7. A cake has three cylindrical layers, and each layer is 5 inches tall. The top layer has a 12-inch diameter. Each of the other layers has a diameter 2 inches greater than the layer above it. To the nearest cubic inch, what is the cake's volume?

___2,339 in³___

8. How is finding the volume of a cylinder like finding the volume of a prism? How is it different?

The volume of a cylinder, like the volume of a prism, is found by multiplying the area of the base, B, by the height of the figure. The only difference is in the formula used to find B.

9. A cylinder and a prism both have the same base area and height. Which has the greater volume?

They have the same volume.

10. Which gives a cylinder greater volume: a radius of 16 cm and a height of 20 cm, or a radius of 20 cm and a height of 16 cm? Explain.

radius of 20 cm, height of 16 cm, because 20,096 cm³ > 16,076.8 cm³

11. **Error Analysis** Diane says that tripling the diameter of the base of a can of soup will increase its volume by a factor of 6. Is she correct? Explain.

No. Tripling the diameter increases the volume by a factor of 3², or 9.

Assign these pages to help your students practice and apply important lesson concepts. For additional exercises, see the Student Edition.

Answers

Additional Practice

1. 2122.6 cm^3
2. 22,608 cm^3
3. 376.8 mm^3
4. 1243.4 in^3
5. 2009.6 ft^3
6. 803.8 m^3
7. 3818.2 cm^3
8. Possible answer: The original cylinder has a volume of 2826 ft^3. If you triple the height the volume is 8478 ft^3, which is triple the original volume.

Problem Solving

1. Cylinder
2. 0.1 in^3
3. B
4. G
5. B
6. J

Additional Practice

Find the volume of each figure to the nearest tenth.
Use 3.14 for π.

1.
6.5 cm

16 cm

2.
15 cm
32 cm

3.
4 mm

7.5 mm

4.
11 in.   6 in.

5. A cylinder has a diameter of 8 feet and height of 40 feet.

_____

6. A cylinder has a diameter of 16 meters and height of 4 meters.

_____

7. A cylindrical paint can is 19 centimeters tall and has a radius of 8 centimeters. What is the volume of the paint can? Round your answer to the nearest tenth.

_____

8. A cylinder has a radius of 6 ft and a height of 25 ft. Explain whether tripling the height will triple the volume of the cylinder.

_____

_____

_____

Problem Solving

A rectangular box is 2 inches high, 3.5 inches wide and 4 inches long. A cylindrical box is 3.5 inches high and has a diameter of 3.2 inches. Use 3.14 for π. Round to the nearest tenth.

1. Which box has a larger volume?   2. How much bigger is the larger box?

Use 3.14 for π. Choose the letter for the best answer.

3. A can has diameter of 9.8 cm and is 13.2 cm tall. What is the capacity of the can? Round to the nearest tenth.

A 203.1 cm³

B 995.2 cm³

C 3980.7 cm³

D 959.2 cm³

4. How many cubic feet of air are in a room that is 15 feet long, 10 feet wide and 8 feet high?

F 33 ft³

G 1200 ft³

H 1500 ft³

J 3768 ft³

5. How many gallons of water will the water trough hold? Round to the nearest gallon. (Hint: 1 cubic foot of water is approximately 7.5 gallons.)

2 ft

6 ft

A 19 gallons

B 71 gallons

C 141 gallons

D 565 gallons

6. A child's wading pool has a diameter of 5 feet and a height of 1 foot. How much water would it take to fill the pool? Round to the nearest gallon. (Hint: 1 cubic foot of water is approximately 7.5 gallons.)

F 79 gallons

G 589 gallons

H 59 gallons

J 147 gallons

Notes

Volume of Pyramids and Cones
Going Deeper

Essential question: *How can you solve problems using the formula for the volume of a cone?*

COMMON **Standards for**
CORE **Mathematical Content**

CC.8.G.9 Know the formulas for the volumes of cones, cylinders, and spheres and use them to solve real-world and mathematical problems.

Prerequisites

Circumference and area of a circle

Math Background

For a prism and a pyramid that have congruent bases and the same height, the volume of the prism will be three times the volume of the pyramid. Likewise, for a cylinder and a cone that have congruent bases and the same height, the volume of the cylinder will be three times the volume of the matching cone. The volume of a cone is found using the same general formula as for the volume of a pyramid, $V = \frac{1}{3}Bh$, where the base area for a cone is the area of a circle instead of a polygon, resulting in the formula $V = \frac{1}{3}\pi r^2 h$.

INTRODUCE

Have students give their own definition of volume. Then ask them to give examples of items/products that use cones, such as ice cream cones, party hats, sport or traffic cones, and so on. Finally, review the meanings of each variable in the volume formula.

TEACH

 EXAMPLE

Questioning Strategies

- Would you expect the volume of a cone to be greater than or less than the volume of a cylinder with the same dimensions? Explain. **Less than; the volume of a cone is one-third that of a cylinder with the same dimensions.**

- How can you estimate the volume of a cone? **Use 3 for π and multiply by $\frac{1}{3}$ to find the product 1. Then you can estimate the volume of a cone using r^2h. In part A, you could estimate 32 in³. In part B, you could estimate 144 ft³.**

Differentiated Instruction

Using models, demonstrate how a cone would fit inside a cylinder with the same base area. (Note that the same can be done for a pyramid and its corresponding prism –however, the condition must be stated as congruent bases or bases with the same dimensions because 'same area' is not satisfactory.) If your models permit, show how exactly three cones full of water or rice exactly fill the corresponding cylinder.

> ⚠ MATHEMATICAL **Highlighting**
> PRACTICE **the Standards**
>
> This Example is an opportunity to address Standard 6 (Attend to precision). Students must perform computations using the order of operations by first squaring the radius. They also need to round their final answer to the nearest tenth.

CLOSE

Essential Question

How can you solve problems using the formula for the volume of a cone?

Possible answer: If given the diameter, find the radius by dividing the diameter by 2. Then substitute the given values into the formula $V = \frac{1}{3}Bh$ or $V = \frac{1}{3}\pi r^2 h$ and simplify. Make sure to label the answer in cubic units.

Summarize

Have students write the formulas for the volume of a cylinder and the volume of a cone. Then ask them to describe how the formulas are alike and different.

PRACTICE

Where skills are taught	Where skills are practiced
1 EXAMPLE	EXS. 1–10

Name _____ Class _____ Date _____

Volume of Pyramids and Cones
Going Deeper

Essential question: *How can you solve problems using the formula for the volume of a cone?*

A cone has one circular base. The area of the base is πr^2.

Volume of a Cone

The volume of a cone with base area B, radius r, and height h is $V = \frac{1}{3} Bh$, or $V = \frac{1}{3} \pi r^2 h$.

CC.8.G.9

1 EXAMPLE Volume of a Cone

Find the volume of each cone. Round your answers to the nearest tenth if necessary. Use 3.14 for π.

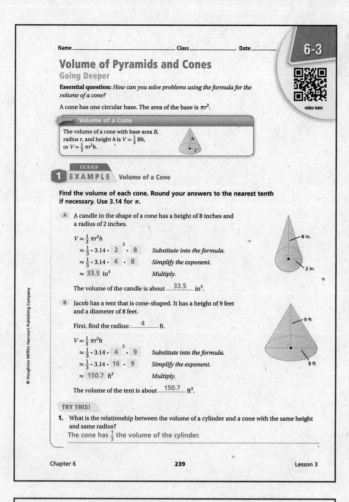

A A candle in the shape of a cone has a height of 8 inches and a radius of 2 inches.

$V = \frac{1}{3} \pi r^2 h$

$\approx \frac{1}{3} \cdot 3.14 \cdot \underline{2}^2 \cdot \underline{8}$ *Substitute into the formula.*

$\approx \frac{1}{3} \cdot 3.14 \cdot \underline{4} \cdot \underline{8}$ *Simplify the exponent.*

$\approx \underline{33.5}$ in³   *Multiply.*

The volume of the candle is about ___33.5___ in³.

8 in.

2 in.

B Jacob has a tent that is cone-shaped. It has a height of 9 feet and a diameter of 8 feet.

First, find the radius: ___4___ ft.

$V = \frac{1}{3} \pi r^2 h$

$\approx \frac{1}{3} \cdot 3.14 \cdot \underline{4}^2 \cdot \underline{9}$ *Substitute into the formula.*

$\approx \frac{1}{3} \cdot 3.14 \cdot \underline{16} \cdot \underline{9}$ *Simplify the exponent.*

$\approx \underline{150.7}$ ft³   *Multiply.*

The volume of the tent is about ___150.7___ ft³.

9 ft

8 ft

TRY THIS!

1. What is the relationship between the volume of a cylinder and a cone with the same height and same radius?
   The cone has $\frac{1}{3}$ the volume of the cylinder.

PRACTICE

Find the volume of each figure. Round your answers to the nearest tenth if necessary. Use 3.14 for π.

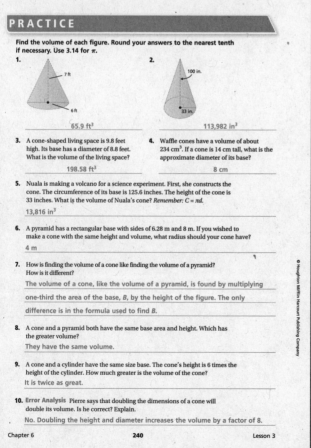

1.

7 ft

6 ft

___65.9 ft³___

2.

100 in.

33 in.

___113,982 in³___

3. A cone-shaped living space is 9.8 feet high. Its base has a diameter of 8.8 feet. What is the volume of the living space?
   ___198.58 ft³___

4. Waffle cones have a volume of about 234 cm³. If a cone is 14 cm tall, what is the approximate diameter of its base?
   ___8 cm___

5. Nuala is making a volcano for a science experiment. First, she constructs the cone. The circumference of its base is 125.6 inches. The height of the cone is 33 inches. What is the volume of Nuala's cone? *Remember: $C = \pi d$.*
   ___13,816 in³___

6. A pyramid has a rectangular base with sides of 6.28 m and 8 m. If you wished to make a cone with the same height and volume, what radius should your cone have?
   ___4 m___

7. How is finding the volume of a cone like finding the volume of a pyramid? How is it different?
   The volume of a cone, like the volume of a pyramid, is found by multiplying one-third the area of the base, B, by the height of the figure. The only difference is in the formula used to find B.

8. A cone and a pyramid both have the same base area and height. Which has the greater volume?
   They have the same volume.

9. A cone and a cylinder have the same size base. The cone's height is 6 times the height of the cylinder. How much greater is the volume of the cone?
   It is twice as great.

10. **Error Analysis** Pierre says that doubling the dimensions of a cone will double its volume. Is he correct? Explain.
   No. Doubling the height and diameter increases the volume by a factor of 8.

Assign these pages to help your students practice and apply important lesson concepts. For additional exercises, see the Student Edition.

Answers

Additional Practice

1. 6358.5 in^3
2. 3299.2 m^3
3. 29.3 ft^3
4. 1138.8 cm^3
5. 9454.2 cm^3
6. 339.29 in^3
7. 108.3 ft^3

Problem Solving

1. 25.1 in^3
2. less
3. $27,321.7 \text{ m}^3$
4. 35.9 times larger
5. C
6. J
7. A

Additional Practice

Find the volume of each figure to the nearest tenth. Use 3.14 for π.

1.
15 in.
27 in.

2.
20.5 m
12.4 m

_____   _____

3.
7 ft
4 ft

4.
17 cm
16 cm

_____   _____

5. The radius of a cone is 19.4 cm and its height is 24 cm. Find the volume of the cone to the nearest tenth.

_____

6. A funnel has a diameter of 9 in. and is 16 in. deep. Use a calculator to find the volume of the funnel to the nearest hundredth.

_____

7. A cone has a diameter of 6 ft and a height of 11.5 ft. Find the volume of the cone. Round your answer to the nearest tenth.

_____

Problem Solving

Round to the nearest tenth. Use π. Write the correct answer.

1. An oil funnel is in the shape of a cone. It has a diameter of 4 inches and a height of 6 inches. If the end of the funnel is plugged, how much oil can the funnel hold before it overflows?

2. One quart of oil has a volume of approximately 57.6 in³. Does the oil funnel in exercise 3 hold more or less than 1 quart of oil?

3. The Feathered Serpent Pyramid is located in Teotihuacan, Mexico. Its base is a square that measures 65 m on each side. The pyramid is 19.4 m high. What is the volume of the Feathered Serpent Pyramid?

4. The Sun Pyramid in Teotihuacan, Mexico, is larger than the Feathered Serpent Pyramid. The sides of the square base and the height are each about 3.3 times larger than the Feathered Serpent Pyramid. How many times larger is the volume of the Sun Pyramid than the Feathered Serpent Pyramid?

Round to the nearest tenth. Use π. Choose the letter for the best answer.

5. An ice cream cone has a diameter of 4.2 cm and a height of 11.5 cm. What is the volume of the cone?

A 18.7 cm³

B 25.3 cm³

C 53.1 cm³

D 212.3 cm³

6. When decorating a cake, the frosting is put into a cone-shaped bag and then squeezed out a hole at the tip of the cone. How much frosting is in a bag that has a radius of 1.5 inches and a height of 8.5 inches?

F 5.0 in³   H 15.2 in³

G 13.3 in³   J 20.0 in³

7. What is the volume of the hourglass at the right?

A 13.1 in³

B 26.2 in³

C 52.3 in³

D 102.8 in³

8 in.
2.5 in.

Spheres
Going Deeper

Essential question: *How can you solve problems using the formula for the volume of a sphere?*

© Houghton Mifflin Harcourt Publishing Company

COMMON CORE **Standards for Mathematical Content**

CC.8.G.9 Know the formulas for the volumes of cones, cylinders, and spheres and use them to solve real-world and mathematical problems.

Prerequisites
Volume

Math Background
A sphere can be divided into two equal halves called *hemispheres*. Using a cone that fits exactly into one of the hemispheres (with height *h* equal to the radius of the hemisphere and base area the same as the area of a circular cross-section that goes through the center of the sphere), it can be shown that the contents of 2 such cones will exactly fill the hemisphere. Thus, $4\left(\frac{1}{3}\pi r^2 \cdot r\right) = \frac{4}{3}\pi r^3$ can be shown to be the volume of a sphere.

INTRODUCE

Discuss that if you cut through the center of a sphere with a plane, the intersection of the plane and the sphere (called a cross-section) would be a circle (called a *great circle*). Elicit from students that the radius of that circle is the same as the radius of the sphere. Furthermore, the 'height' of the sphere is twice the radius, or the diameter, of the sphere.

TEACH

Questioning Strategies
- What information do you need in order to find the volume of a sphere? **the length of the radius**

- Why is the radius length cubed when finding the volume of a sphere and squared when finding the area of a circle? **Area is a two-dimensional measurement; volume is a three-dimensional measurement.**

- How can you estimate the volume of a sphere? **Use 3 for π and multiply with $\frac{4}{3}$ to find the product 4. Then you can estimate the volume of a sphere using $4r^3$. In part A, you could estimate the volume to be $4 \cdot 2^3$ or $32\ cm^3$.**

MATHEMATICAL PRACTICE **Highlighting the Standards**

This Example is an opportunity to address Standard 4 (Model with mathematics). In Reflect 1b, students are asked to find the volume of a hemisphere by dividing the volume of its corresponding sphere in half. You can extend this question by asking students to find the volume of 3 tennis balls from part B.

CLOSE

Essential Question
How can you solve problems using the formula for the volume of a sphere?
Possible answer: If given the diameter, find the radius by dividing the diameter by 2. Then substitute the given values into the formula $V = \frac{4}{3}\pi r^2 h$ and simplify. Make sure to label the answer in cubic units.

Summarize
Have students draw a cone and sphere and write the formulas for the volume of each solid. Then discuss how the formulas are alike and different.

Cone: $V = \frac{1}{3}\pi r^2 h$ **Sphere:** $V = \frac{4}{3}\pi r^3$

For instance, both use π, *r*, and a fraction with a denominator of 3. Also, both products result in cubic units. However, the cone formula uses $\frac{1}{3}$ and a height *h*, while the sphere formula uses $\frac{4}{3}$ and only the radius. Also, the cone formula uses the square of the radius while the sphere formula uses the cube of the radius.

PRACTICE

Where skills are taught	Where skills are practiced
1 EXAMPLE	EXS. 1–9

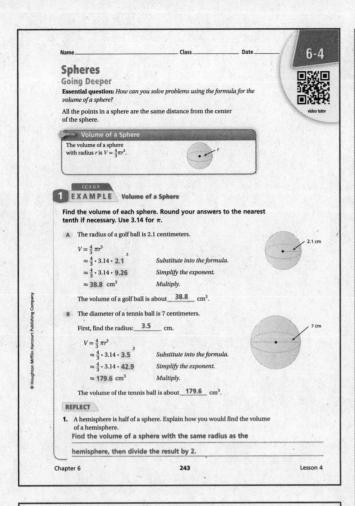

Name_____ Class_____ Date_____

6-4

video tutor

Spheres
Going Deeper

Essential question: *How can you solve problems using the formula for the volume of a sphere?*

All the points in a sphere are the same distance from the center of the sphere.

Volume of a Sphere

The volume of a sphere with radius r is $V = \frac{4}{3}\pi r^3$.

---

1 EXAMPLE CC.8.G.9 **Volume of a Sphere**

Find the volume of each sphere. Round your answers to the nearest tenth if necessary. Use 3.14 for π.

A The radius of a golf ball is 2.1 centimeters.

2.1 cm

$$V = \frac{4}{3}\pi r^3$$
$$\approx \frac{4}{3} \cdot 3.14 \cdot 2.1^3 \qquad \textit{Substitute into the formula.}$$
$$\approx \frac{4}{3} \cdot 3.14 \cdot 9.26 \qquad \textit{Simplify the exponent.}$$
$$\approx 38.8 \ \text{cm}^3 \qquad \textit{Multiply.}$$

The volume of a golf ball is about __38.8__ cm³.

B The diameter of a tennis ball is 7 centimeters.

First, find the radius: __3.5__ cm.

7 cm

$$V = \frac{4}{3}\pi r^3$$
$$\approx \frac{4}{3} \cdot 3.14 \cdot 3.5^3 \qquad \textit{Substitute into the formula.}$$
$$\approx \frac{4}{3} \cdot 3.14 \cdot 42.9 \qquad \textit{Simplify the exponent.}$$
$$\approx 179.6 \ \text{cm}^3 \qquad \textit{Multiply.}$$

The volume of the tennis ball is about __179.6__ cm³.

REFLECT

1. A hemisphere is half of a sphere. Explain how you would find the volume of a hemisphere.

Find the volume of a sphere with the same radius as the

hemisphere, then divide the result by 2.

© Houghton Mifflin Harcourt Publishing Company

PRACTICE

Solve. Use 3.14 for π.

1. A ball has a diameter of 20 inches. What is the volume of the ball? Give your answer to the nearest cubic inch.

about 4,187 in³

2. The radius of a soccer ball is 11 cm. What is the volume of the ball? Give your answer to the nearest cubic centimeter.

about 5,572 cm³

3. An enormous spherical structure houses a planetarium. The diameter of the building is 60 yards. To the nearest cubic yard, what is the volume of the structure?

about 113,040 yd³

4. A steel ball with a diameter of 4 cm is placed in a water-filled cylinder that is 10 cm high and 5 cm in diameter. What is the volume of the water the ball will displace?

about 33.5 cm³

5. The diameter of an official squash ball ranges from 39.5 mm to 40.5 mm. What is the approximate difference in volume between the largest and smallest official squash ball?

about 2,512 mm³

6. A sphere and a cylinder have the same diameter, and the cylinder's height is the same as its diameter. How will their volumes compare? First guess, then try a few examples to find out.

The volume of the cylinder will be 1.5 times as great as the volume of

the sphere.

7. You double the radius of a sphere. How does this affect the volume?

It will be 2^3 or 8 times as great.

8. Three tennis balls, each with a diameter of 2.6 inches, are packaged in a cylindrical container.

a. What is the total volume of the balls, to the nearest cubic inch?

about 28 in³

b. What is the volume of the container to the nearest cubic inch, assuming that the balls touch its sides, top, and bottom?

about 41 in³

9. Error Analysis Curtis claims that the volume of this ball is about 1,436.03 in³. Is he correct? If not, what was his error?

7 in.

No. He made an error using the formula; he used the

diameter rather than the radius.

© Houghton Mifflin Harcourt Publishing Company

Assign these pages to help your students practice and apply important lesson concepts. For additional exercises, see the Student Edition.

Answers

Additional Practice

1. 972π ft^3 $\approx$ 3052.1 ft^3

2. $12{,}348\pi$ m^3 $\approx$ 38,772.7 m^3

3. 4500π cm^3 $\approx$ 14,130 cm^3

4. 2304π cm^3 $\approx$ 7234.6 cm^3

5. 4869.7π in^3 $\approx$ 15,290.8 in^3

6. 5471.6π ft^3 $\approx$ 17,180.8 ft^3

7. 997.8 ft^3

8. 4186.7 cm^3

9. 7234.6 in^3

10. 12.8 in^3

11. 807.7 in^3

Problem Solving

1. 2.48 in^3

2. decrease

3. C

4. G

5. B

6. H

6-4

Name_____ Class_____ Date_____

Additional Practice

Find the volume of each sphere, both in terms of π and to the nearest tenth. Use 3.14 for π.

1. $r = 9$ ft

2. $r = 21$ m

3. $d = 30$ cm

_____   _____   _____

4. $d = 24$ cm

5. $r = 15.4$ in.

6. $r = 16.01$ ft

_____   _____   _____

Find the volume of each sphere. Round your answers to the nearest tenth. Use 3.14 for π.

7.

6.2 ft

8.

10 cm

9.

12 in.

_____   _____   _____

10. A baseball has a diameter of 2.9 inches. Find the volume of the baseball. Round your answer to the nearest tenth. Use 3.14 for π.

11. A ball with a diameter of 10 inches is placed in a box that is 11 inches by 11 inches by 11 inches. What is the volume of the box that is not filled by the ball? Round your answer to the nearest tenth. Use 3.14 for π.

Problem Solving

Early golf balls were smooth spheres. Later it was discovered that golf balls flew better when they were dimpled. On January 1, 1932, the United States Golf Association set standards for the weight and size of a golf ball. The minimum diameter of a regulation golf ball is 1.680 inches. Use 3.14 for π. Round to the nearest hundredth.

1. Find the volume of a smooth golf ball with the minimum diameter allowed by the United States Golf Association.

_____

2. Would the dimples on a golf ball increase or decrease the volume of the ball?

_____

Use 3.14 for π. Use the following information for Exercises 3–4. A track and field expert recommends changes to the size of a shot put. One recommendation is that a shot put should have a diameter between 90 and 110 mm. Choose the letter for the best answer.

3. Find the volume of a shot put with a diameter of 90 mm.

   A 25,434 mm³

   B 101,736 mm³

   C 381,510 mm³

   D 3,052,080 mm³

4. Find the volume of a shot put with diameter 110 mm.

   F 37,994 mm³

   G 696,557 mm³

   H 2,089,670 mm³

   J 5,572,453 mm³

5. Find the volume of the earth if the average diameter of the earth is 7926 miles.

   A 2.0×10^{8} mi³

   B 2.6×10^{11} mi³

   C 7.9×10^{8} mi³

   D 2.1×10^{12} mi³

6. An ice cream cone has a diameter of 4.2 cm and a height of 11.5 cm. One spherical scoop of ice cream is put on the cone that has a diameter of 5.6 cm. If the ice cream were to melt in the cone, how much of it would overflow the cone? Round to the nearest tenth.

   F 0 cm³   H 38.8 cm³

   G 12.3 cm³   J 54.3 cm³

Problem Solving Connections
Where in the Park is Xander?

COMMON Standards for
CORE Mathematical Content

CC.8.EE.6 Use similar triangles to explain why the slope m is the same between any two distinct points on a non-vertical line in the coordinate plane; derive the equation $y = mx$ for a line through the origin and the equation $y = mx + b$ for a line intercepting the vertical axis at b.

CC.8.G.5 Use informal arguments to establish facts about the angle sum and exterior angle of triangles, about the angles created when parallel lines are cut by a transversal, and the angle-angle criterion for similarity of triangles.

CC.8.G.6 Explain a proof of the Pythagorean theorem and its converse.

CC.8.G.7 Apply the Pythagorean theorem to determine unknown side lengths in right triangles in real-world and mathematical problems in two and three dimensions.

CC.8.G.8 Apply the Pythagorean theorem to find the distance between two points in a coordinate system.

CC.8.G.9 Know the formulas for the volumes of cones, cylinders, and spheres and use them to solve real-world and mathematical problems.

INTRODUCE

Discuss with students what it would be like to get lost in the woods. Ask students if they believe that geometry could really help them find the way again. Tell students that in this exploration, you will look at ways that geometric formulas and properties can be useful—even in the great outdoors!

TEACH

1 Packing for the Trip

Questioning Strategies

- In what units are the general daily water recommendations given? ounces

- In what units are the suggestions from the hiking resources given? liters

- In what units are the dimensions of Xander's water bottle given? centimeters

- How can you convert length units of centimeters to capacity units of liters? Use the equivalent measures to form conversion factors: $\frac{1 \text{ cm}^3}{1 \text{ mL}}$ and $\frac{1000 \text{ mL}}{1 \text{ L}}$, or combined $\frac{1000 \text{ cm}^3}{1 \text{ L}}$.

2 Following the Map

Questioning Strategies

- How can you find the measures of the other angles? Identify angle pairs formed by two parallel lines and a transversal and the given information that one angle measures 120° to find the other measures: 60° or 120°.

- What type of angle pair is described by "northeast corner" and "southwest corner"? vertical angles

Teaching Strategies

Have students copy the diagram and label it with the measures of all angles created by the transversal (Crossover Trail) and the parallel trails (North Rim and South Springs). Encourage them to suggest as many angle relationships as possible to help them find the correct trail.

Name_____ Class_____ Date_____

CHAPTER 6

Problem Solving Connections

Where in the Park is Xander? Xander plans a hiking trip in a national park. Instead of obtaining an accurate trail map from the National Park Service, he downloaded *Bob's Hiking Guide* from a website. Xander's hiking guide eventually gets him lost. Can you help find Xander?

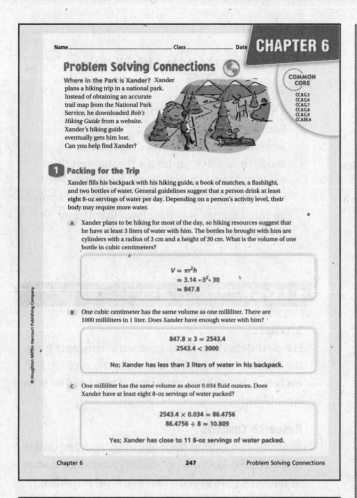

COMMON CORE
CC.8.G.5
CC.8.G.6
CC.8.G.7
CC.8.G.8
CC.8.G.9
CC.8.EE.6

1 Packing for the Trip

Xander fills his backpack with his hiking guide, a book of matches, a flashlight, and two bottles of water. General guidelines suggest that a person drink at least eight 8-oz servings of water per day. Depending on a person's activity level, their body may require more water.

A Xander plans to be hiking for most of the day, so hiking resources suggest that he have at least 3 liters of water with him. The bottles he brought with him are cylinders with a radius of 3 cm and a height of 30 cm. What is the volume of one bottle in cubic centimeters?

$$V = \pi r^2 h$$
$$\approx 3.14 \cdot 3^2 \cdot 30$$
$$\approx 847.8$$

B One cubic centimeter has the same volume as one milliliter. There are 1000 milliliters in 1 liter. Does Xander have enough water with him?

$$847.8 \times 3 = 2543.4$$
$$2543.4 < 3000$$

No; Xander has less than 3 liters of water in his backpack.

C One milliliter has the same volume as about 0.034 fluid ounces. Does Xander have at least eight 8-oz servings of water packed?

$$2543.4 \times 0.034 = 86.4756$$
$$86.4756 \div 8 \approx 10.809$$

Yes; Xander has close to 11 8-oz servings of water packed.

2 Following the Map

Xander follows the maps in *Bob's Hiking Guide* and starts out on South Springs Trail.

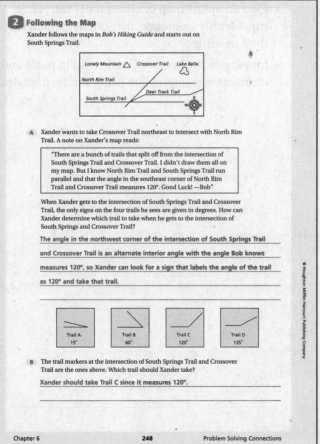

A Xander wants to take Crossover Trail northeast to intersect with North Rim Trail. A note on Xander's map reads:

> "There are a bunch of trails that split off from the intersection of South Springs Trail and Crossover Trail. I didn't draw them all on my map. But I know North Rim Trail and South Springs Trail run parallel and that the angle in the southeast corner of North Rim Trail and Crossover Trail measures 120°. Good Luck! —Bob"

When Xander gets to the intersection of South Springs Trail and Crossover Trail, the only signs on the four trails he sees are given in degrees. How can Xander determine which trail to take when he gets to the intersection of South Springs and Crossover Trail?

The angle in the northwest corner of the intersection of South Springs Trail and Crossover Trail is an alternate interior angle with the angle Bob knows measures 120°, so Xander can look for a sign that labels the angle of the trail as 120° and take that trail.

Trail A 15°	Trail B 60°	Trail C 120°	Trail D 135°

B The trail markers at the intersection of South Springs Trail and Crossover Trail are the ones above. Which trail should Xander take?

Xander should take Trail C since it measures 120°.

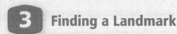

3 Finding a Landmark

Questioning Strategies

- How can you use similar triangles to find Xander's distance from the base of the mountain? A line of sight from Xander to the top of the mountain will be the hypotenuse. A 15-ft tree 50 ft in front of Xander forms a smaller right triangle with the line of sight. Using properties of similar triangles, solve a proportion to find the height of Lonely Mountain.

Teaching Strategies

Point out to students that there is more than one way to show that the triangles are similar by AA Similarity: (1) use the congruent right angles and the shared angle, or (2) use the congruent right angles and the parallel vertical sides to identify corresponding angles.

4 Finding Xander

Questioning Strategies

- What information does Xander have before making the 911 call? He knows the triangles are similar; the height of the tree is about 15 ft; and his distance from the tree is about 50 ft.

- What information does the ranger contribute? The ranger knows that the mountain is 3000 ft high.

- How can you use classify the triangle in part B by angle measures? Use the Triangle Sum Theorem to find the missing angle measure of 90° and classify the triangle as right.

- How can you use the Pythagorean theorem to find the lengths of the legs? Because the legs are the same length and $a = b$, you can use $2a^2 = c^2$ or $2b^2 = c^2$.

This project is an opportunity to address Standard 4 (Model with mathematics). Students draw geometric diagrams to model and solve problems throughout this project. Models can help students visualize relationships so they can recognize and apply geometric concepts they have learned in this unit.

CLOSE

Journal

Have students list all the geometric concepts from the chapter that they have used in the project. For each one, have them write how it was used to solve a problem.

Research Options

Students can extend their learning by doing online research. For example, students can choose a state or national park and do the following activities:

- Find an online map of hiking trails and plan a trip. Identify landmarks that can help them keep their bearings.

- Investigate the height of landmarks in parks and create their own problem using similar triangles.

3 Finding a Landmark

Xander makes a mistake and takes the trail marked 60°. After hiking for a while, he realizes that he is lost and his cell phone battery is almost dead.

A Xander stands 50 feet in front of a young tree and looks up across the top of the tree to the top of a mountain in the distance. Xander estimates the height of the tree as 15 feet. Draw a diagram involving similar triangles that shows the relationship between the tree and the mountain from Xander's perspective.

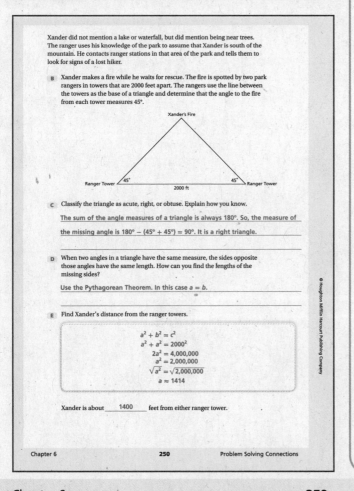

Lonely
Mountain

Xander 15 ft
50 ft

B Explain how you know that the triangles in your diagram are similar triangles.

The large triangle has a right triangle formed by the mountain and the ground;

the smaller triangle has a right angle formed by the tree and the ground. Both

triangles include the angle formed by Xander's line of sight and the ground. The

triangles are similar by AA Similarity.

C How can the diagram help Xander?

Corresponding sides of similar triangles are proportional. If Xander knows the

height of the mountain, he could calculate his distance from the mountain.

4 Finding Xander

Xander's cell phone battery has just enough life to make a brief call to 911. He quickly tells the dispatcher about the mountain and the tree. The dispatcher tells Xander to stay in the same spot and then Xander's phone dies.

A The dispatcher contacts a ranger at the National Park Service. The ranger knows that the height of the mountain is 3000 feet. Use the height of the mountain and your diagram to find Xander's distance from the mountain.

$$\frac{x}{50} = \frac{3000}{15}$$

$$x = \frac{3000}{15}(50)$$

$$x = 10{,}000$$

Xander is about ____10,000____ feet from the mountain.

Performance Task

This page provides students with the opportunity to apply concepts from the Common Core in real-world problem situations. There are three different levels of performance tasks:

⭐ **Novice:** These are short word problems that require students to apply the math they have learned in straightforward, real-world situations.

⭐⭐ **Apprentice:** These are more involved problems that guide students step-by-step through more complex tasks. These exercises include more complicated reasoning, writing, and open-ended elements.

⭐⭐⭐ **Expert:** These are open-ended, non-routine problems that, instead of stepping the students through, asks them to choose their own methods for solving and justify their answers and reasoning.

Sample answers

1. No; the volume of the paraffin block is $4\cdot6\cdot8$, or 192 cm^3, and the volume of the candle is $\frac{1}{3}\pi(2.5)^2(25)$, or about 163.5 cm^3. The volume of the candle is less than the volume of the block of paraffin.

2. 16 in.; the volume of the sphere is
$\frac{4}{3}\pi(12)^3 = 7{,}234.56$ in.^{3}.
So, $7{,}234.56 = 3.14\cdot12^2 h$,
and $h = \frac{7{,}234.56}{3.14\cdot12^2} = 16$.

3. Scoring Guide:

Task	Possible points
a	**1 point** for correctly finding the interior height to be **13.75 in.**, **1 point** for finding diameter to be **7.5 in.**, and **1 point** for correct explanation that **the diameter of the interior is the diameter of the vase shortened by 0.5 in., and the height is shortened by 0.25 in.**
b	**2 points** for correctly using the dimensions from part **a** to find the interior volume: $V = 3.14 \cdot 3.75^2 \cdot 13.75 \approx 607$ in.^{3}
c	**1 point** for correctly calculating the volume of the vase with thicker sides and stating that it has a smaller volume.

Total possible points: 6

© Houghton Mifflin Harcourt Publishing Company

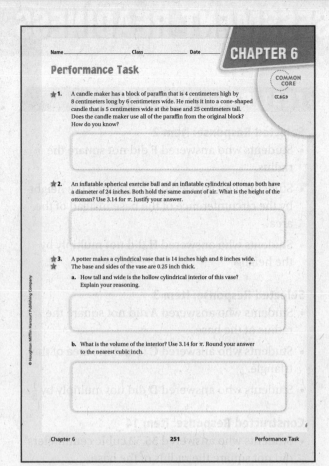

Performance Task

COMMON CORE
CC.8.G.9

★**1.** A candle maker has a block of paraffin that is 4 centimeters high by 8 centimeters long by 6 centimeters wide. He melts it into a cone-shaped candle that is 5 centimeters wide at the base and 25 centimeters tall. Does the candle maker use all of the paraffin from the original block? How do you know?

★**2.** An inflatable spherical exercise ball and an inflatable cylindrical ottoman both have a diameter of 24 inches. Both hold the same amount of air. What is the height of the ottoman? Use 3.14 for π. Justify your answer.

★**3.** A potter makes a cylindrical vase that is 14 inches high and 8 inches wide. ★ The base and sides of the vase are 0.25 inch thick.

  a. How tall and wide is the hollow cylindrical interior of this vase? Explain your reasoning.

  b. What is the volume of the interior? Use 3.14 for π. Round your answer to the nearest cubic inch.

© Houghton Mifflin Harcourt Publishing Company

Chapter 6   **251**   Performance Task

  c. Another vase having the same outside dimensions has thicker sides. Choose a side thickness and calculate the volume. Is the inside volume of this vase greater or less than the volume of the original vase?

★**4.** A company makes snow globes. Each snow globe is in the shape of a sphere, ★ and the diameter of the sphere is 8 centimeters. ★

  a. One cubic centimeter of water has a mass of about 1 gram. If the snow globe is filled with water, what is the total mass of the water in the snow globe? Explain how you found your answer. Use 3.14 for π and round to the nearest whole gram.

  b. The company has another snow globe with a diameter of 9 centimeters and a mass of 934 grams. The plastic shell, decorations, and base make up 454 grams of that mass. Is the snow globe filled with water? Explain your reasoning.

© Houghton Mifflin Harcourt Publishing Company

Chapter 6   **252**   Performance Task

4. Scoring Guide:

Task	Possible points
a	**1 point** for correctly finding a mass of 268 grams, and **1 point** for explaining that they found the volume of the sphere, and then multiplied that amount by 1 gram/cm³ to find the mass.
b	**1 point** for correctly answering that it is not water, and **3 points** for giving an explanation, for example: The mass of the liquid is $934 - 454 = 480$ g. The volume of the liquid inside the globe is about 381 g/cm³. The liquid weighs more than 1 g/cm³, so it is probably not water.

Total possible points: 6

COMMON CORE CORRELATION

Standard	Items
CC.8.G.9	1–15

TEST PREP DOCTOR ⊕

Selected Response: Item 2
- Students who answered **F** did not square the radius.
- Students who answered **G** multiplied the height by the circumference of the base instead of the area.
- Students who answered **H** did not multiply by the height.

Selected Response: Item 3
- Students who answered **A** did not square the radius of the base.
- Students who answered **C** found the area of the triangle.
- Students who answered **D** did not multiply by $\frac{1}{3}$.

Constructed Response: Item 14
- Students who answered 56.52 cubic centimeters did not square the radius of the base.
- Students who answered 113.04 cubic centimeters multiplied the height by the circumference of the base instead of the area.
- Students who answered 56.52 cubic centimeters found the area of a cone.

CHAPTER 6 (COMMON CORE) ASSESSMENT READINESS

Name _____ Class _____ Date _____

SELECTED RESPONSE

1. Find the area of the circle to the nearest tenth. Use 3.14 for π.

A. 114 m²   C. 145.2 m²
B. 36.3 m²   D. 21.4 m²

2. Find the volume of the cylinder. Round your answer to the nearest tenth.

7 mm
4 mm

F. 87.9 mm³   H. 153.9 mm³
G. 175.8 mm³   J. 615.4 mm³

3. Find the volume of the figure. Use 3.14 for π. If necessary, round your answer to the nearest tenth.

18 ft
8.5 ft

A. 160.1 ft³   C. 75.6 ft³
B. 1361.2 ft³   D. 4083.6 ft³

4. A county has constructed a conical building to store sand. The cone has a height of 195 ft and a diameter of 307 ft. Find the volume of this building to the nearest hundredth.

F. 1,531,546.25 ft³   H. 31,329.35 ft³
G. 14,427,165.67 ft³   J. 4,809,055.23 ft³

5. To the nearest tenth, find the volume of a sphere with a diameter of 10 cm. Use 3.14 for π.

A. 314.2 cm³   C. 1256.6 cm³
B. 523.3 cm³   D. 4188.8 cm³

6. Find the volume of a sphere with a radius of 6 cm to the nearest tenth. Use 3.14 for π.

F. 37.7 cm³   H. 904.3 cm³
G. 452.2 cm³   J. 226.1 cm³

7. A cylinder is 5 centimeters tall and has a radius of 2.1 centimeters. Find the volume to the nearest tenth. Use 3.14 for π.

A. 33.0 cm³   C. 65.9 cm³
B. 61.2 cm³   D. 69.2 cm³

8. The diameter of the base of a cylinder is 10 cm and the height is 20 cm. What is the volume of the cylinder? Use 3.14 for π.

F. 628 cm³   H. 1,570 cm³
G. 1,256 cm³   J. 6,280 cm³

9. Find the area of a circle with diameter 31.6 cm, both in terms of π and to the nearest tenth. Use 3.14 for π.

A. $A = 249.64\pi$ cm² ≈ 783.9 cm²
B. $A = 63.2\pi$ cm² ≈ 198.4 cm²
C. $A = 31.6\pi$ cm² ≈ 99.2 cm²
D. $A = 998.56\pi$ cm² ≈ 3135.5 cm²

10. The diameter of an ice-hockey puck is 3.0 inches. To the nearest tenth, what is the area of the flat upper surface? Use 3.14 for π.

F. 3.5 in²   H. 7.1 in²
G. 9.4 in²   J. 28.3 in²

---

11. Riggoletto's Portraits specializes in making circular portraits of people. A large portrait is 78 in. in diameter. A medium portrait is 26 in. in diameter. Estimate the difference between the areas of the two sizes of portraits. Use 3.14 for π. Round your answer to the nearest whole number.

A. about 82 in²   C. about 16981 in²
B. about 4245 in²   D. about 163 in²

12. A farmer is building a new silo. The circular silo is 27 meters tall and has a radius of 14 meters. What is the area of the base of the silo? Round your answer to the nearest tenth. Use 3.14 for π.

F. 615.4 m²   H. 2,461.8 m²
G. 1,230.9 m²   J. 16,616.9 m²

Constructed Response

13. Your soccer club wants to sell frozen yogurt to raise money for new uniforms. The club has the choice of the two different size containers shown. Each container costs the club the same amount. The club plans to charge customers $2.50. Which container should the club buy? Explain.

5.5 cm
6 cm
6 cm
5.5 cm

Possible answer: Volumes: Using 3.14 for π, cylinder is 155.43 cm³, cone is 51.81 cm². The soccer club would make more money using the cone-shaped container because its volume is smaller.

14. Find the volume of the cylinder to the nearest hundredth. Use 3.14 for π.

3 cm
6 cm

169.56 cubic centimeters

15. A new movie theater is going to sell popcorn. The manager has the choice of the three different size containers shown. The manager plans to charge $4.75 for a container of popcorn.

9 cm
21 cm
9 cm
9 cm
21 cm
9 cm
21 cm
9 cm
9 cm

Which container would you choose as the manager of the movie theater? Explain.

Possible answer: Volumes: Using 3.14 for π, cylinder is 1335.29 cm³, the cone is 445.10 cm³, the prism is 736.55 cm³. The cone has the smallest volume, so it would use the least popcorn.

CHAPTER 7

Multi-Step Equations

COMMON CORE PROFESIONAL DEVELOPMENT   **CC.8.EE.7a**

In Grade 8, students will solve one-variable equations with variables on both sides of the equals sign. Students will interpret the results to determine if the equation has one solution, infinitely many solutions, or no solutions.

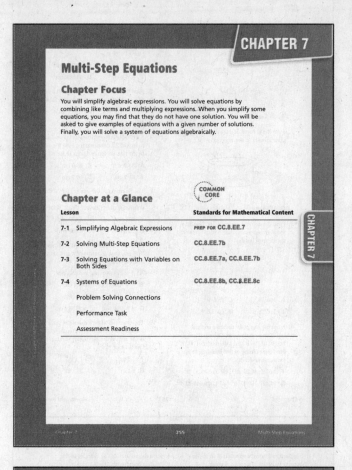

CHAPTER 7

Multi-Step Equations

Chapter Focus

You will simplify algebraic expressions. You will solve equations by combining like terms and multiplying expressions. When you simplify some equations, you may find that they do not have one solution. You will be asked to give examples of equations with a given number of solutions. Finally, you will solve a system of equations algebraically.

Chapter at a Glance

COMMON CORE

Lesson		Standards for Mathematical Content
7-1	Simplifying Algebraic Expressions	PREP FOR CC.8.EE.7
7-2	Solving Multi-Step Equations	CC.8.EE.7b
7-3	Solving Equations with Variables on Both Sides	CC.8.EE.7a, CC.8.EE.7b
7-4	Systems of Equations	CC.8.EE.8b, CC.8.EE.8c
	Problem Solving Connections	
	Performance Task	
	Assessment Readiness	

CHAPTER 7

Chapter 7   255   Multi-Step Equations

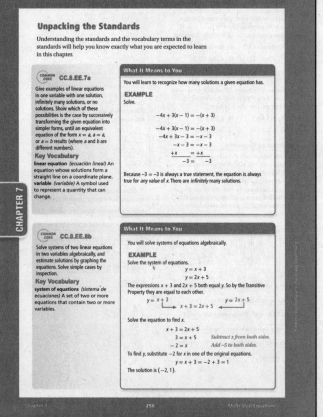

Unpacking the Standards

Understanding the standards and the vocabulary terms in the standards will help you know exactly what you are expected to learn in this chapter.

COMMON CORE   **CC.8.EE.7a**

Give examples of linear equations in one variable with one solution, infinitely many solutions, or no solutions. Show which of these possibilities is the case by successively transforming the given equation into simpler forms, until an equivalent equation of the form $x = a$, $a = a$, or $a = b$ results (where a and b are different numbers).

Key Vocabulary

linear equation *(ecuación lineal)* An equation whose solutions form a straight line on a coordinate plane.

variable *(variable)* A symbol used to represent a quantity that can change.

What It Means to You

You will learn to recognize how many solutions a given equation has.

EXAMPLE

Solve.

$$-4x + 3(x - 1) = -(x + 3)$$

$$-4x + 3(x - 1) = -(x + 3)$$
$$-4x + 3x - 3 = -x - 3$$
$$-x - 3 = -x - 3$$
$$\underline{+x \qquad = +x}$$
$$-3 = -3$$

Because $-3 = -3$ is always a true statement, the equation is always true for *any* value of *x*. There are *infinitely* many solutions.

COMMON CORE   **CC.8.EE.8b**

Solve systems of two linear equations in two variables algebraically, and estimate solutions by graphing the equations. Solve simple cases by inspection.

Key Vocabulary

system of equations *(sistema de ecuaciones)* A set of two or more equations that contain two or more variables.

What It Means to You

You will solve systems of equations algebraically.

EXAMPLE

Solve the system of equations.

$$y = x + 3$$
$$y = 2x + 5$$

The expressions $x + 3$ and $2x + 5$ both equal y. So by the Transitive Property they are equal to each other.

$$y = x + 3 \qquad\qquad y = 2x + 5$$
$$x + 3 = 2x + 5$$

Solve the equation to find *x*.

$$x + 3 = 2x + 5$$
$$3 = x + 5 \qquad \textit{Subtract x from both sides.}$$
$$-2 = x \qquad \textit{Add −5 to both sides.}$$

To find *y*, substitute -2 for *x* in one of the original equations.

$$y = x + 3 = -2 + 3 = 1$$

The solution is $(-2, 1)$.

Chapter 7   256   Multi-Step Equations

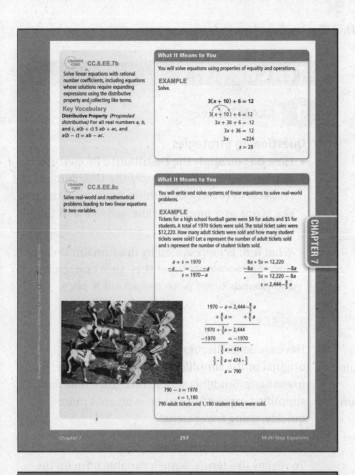

CC.8.EE.7b

Solve linear equations with rational number coefficients, including equations whose solutions require expanding expressions using the distributive property and collecting like terms.

Key Vocabulary

Distributive Property *(Propiedad distributiva)* For all real numbers a, b, and c, $a(b + c) 5 ab + ac$, and $a(b - c) = ab - ac$.

What It Means to You

You will solve equations using properties of equality and operations.

EXAMPLE

Solve.

$$3(x + 10) + 6 = 12$$

$$3(x + 10) + 6 = 12$$
$$3x + 30 + 6 = 12$$
$$3x + 36 = 12$$
$$3x = 224$$
$$x = 28$$

CC.8.EE.8c

Solve real-world and mathematical problems leading to two linear equations in two variables.

What It Means to You

You will write and solve systems of linear equations to solve real-world problems.

EXAMPLE

Tickets for a high school football game were $8 for adults and $5 for students. A total of 1970 tickets were sold. The total ticket sales were $12,220. How many adult tickets were sold and how many student tickets were sold? Let a represent the number of adult tickets sold and s represent the number of student tickets sold.

$$a + s = 1970$$
$$-a \quad = \quad -a$$
$$s = 1970 - a$$

$$8a + 5s = 12,220$$
$$-8a \qquad = \qquad -8a$$
$$5s = 12,220 - 8a$$
$$s = 2,444 - \tfrac{8}{5}a$$

$$1970 - a = 2,444 - \tfrac{8}{5}a$$
$$+ \tfrac{8}{5}a = \quad + \tfrac{8}{5}a$$
$$1970 + \tfrac{3}{5}a = 2,444$$
$$-1970 \qquad = -1970$$
$$\tfrac{3}{5}a = 474$$
$$\tfrac{5}{3} \cdot \tfrac{3}{5}a = 474 \cdot \tfrac{5}{3}$$
$$a = 790$$

$$790 - s = 1970$$
$$s = 1,180$$
790 adult tickets and 1,180 student tickets were sold.

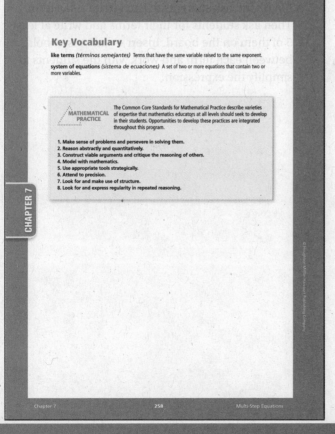

Key Vocabulary

like terms *(términos semejantes)* Terms that have the same variable raised to the same exponent.

system of equations *(sistema de ecuaciones)* A set of two or more equations that contain two or more variables.

MATHEMATICAL PRACTICE

The Common Core Standards for Mathematical Practice describe varieties of expertise that mathematics educators at all levels should seek to develop in their students. Opportunities to develop these practices are integrated throughout this program.

1. Make sense of problems and persevere in solving them.
2. Reason abstractly and quantitatively.
3. Construct viable arguments and critique the reasoning of others.
4. Model with mathematics.
5. Use appropriate tools strategically.
6. Attend to precision.
7. Look for and make use of structure.
8. Look for and express regularity in repeated reasoning.

COMMON CORE PROFESIONAL DEVELOPMENT

CC.8.EE.7b

Based on work with multi-step equations in Grade 7, students by Grade 8 have the tools to solve one-variable equations with variables on both sides of the equals sign. Students understand that the solution to the equation is the value(s) of the variable, which make a true equality when substituted back into the equation. In Grade 8, equations will include rational numbers, the Distributive Property, and combining like terms.

Simplifying Algebraic Expressions
Going Deeper

Essential question: *How do you simplify algebraic expressions?*

© Houghton Mifflin Harcourt Publishing Company

COMMON CORE Standards for Mathematical Content

Prep for CC.8.EE.7 Solve linear equations in one variable.

Prep for CC.8.EE.7b Solve linear equations with rational number coefficients, including equations whose solutions require expanding expressions using the distributive property and collecting like terms.

Vocabulary
like terms

Prerequisites
Algebraic expressions

Math Background
In this lesson, students write, simplify, and evaluate *algebraic expressions*. An algebraic expression includes one or more variables and has one or more *terms* that are separated by + or − symbols. An expression has *like terms* if two or more terms have the same variable raised to the same exponent. We can *combine,* or *collect*, like terms by applying the Distributive Property in reverse to simplify an expression.

INTRODUCE

Review how an algebraic expression includes at least one variable and one term. As needed, clarify the meaning of *term* and review *like terms* that can be combined. Consider guiding students to observe that the number of + and/or − symbols in an algebraic expression is always one less than the number of terms that it contains.

TEACH

1 EXAMPLE

Questioning Strategies
- How do you apply the Distributive Property to add the two like terms? Apply the Distributive Property in reverse by writing the sum of the two like terms as a product of the variable and the sum of the two numbers.

- What unit is represented by the sum $6p$? Dollars, since $6p$ represents what they spent on apples and pounds times price per pound is price.

REFLECT

Have students discuss which expression, the original or the simplified one, they would prefer to evaluate. Students should recognize how the simplified expression can be evaluated more quickly, using fewer steps.

Differentiated Instruction
To review like terms, write a variable term on the board and ask students to each write a like term. Then ask students for their terms and write at least 5 of them on the board. Insert + and − symbols between each term and work with the students to simplify the expression.

Name_____ Class_____ Date_____

7-1

video tutor

Simplifying Algebraic Expressions
Going Deeper

Essential question: *How do you simplify algebraic expressions?*

Like terms, such as 3*t* and 4*t*, or 3*m*³ and 2.5*m*³, have the *same* variables raised to the *same* exponents.

To simplify an expression means to combine, or collect, its like terms to form an equivalent expression with as few terms as possible. You can use number properties to combine like terms.

CC.8.EE.7

1 EXAMPLE   Writing and Simplifying Single-Variable Expressions

Alex bought 2.5 pounds of apples and Derrick bought 3.5 pounds of apples. Write and simplify an expression that represents how much they spent on apples.

A   Write expressions for how much Alex and Derrick spent on apples.
Let *p* represent the price of apples per pound.

Alex: **2.5** *p*   Derrick: **3.5** *p*

B   Add both expressions to represent the total amount they spent.

$2.5\ p + 3.5\ p = \left(2.5 + 3.5\right)p$ Use the ___Distributive___ Property.

$= 6p$ *Add within the parentheses.*

The expression ___6p___ represents how much they spent on apples.

REFLECT

1a. Suppose that apples sold for $0.90 per pound. Evaluate the original expression to find how much Alex and Derrick spent on apples. Then evaluate the simplified expression. Are the amounts the same?

2.5(0.90) + 3.5(0.90) = $2.25 + $3.15 = $5.40; 6(0.90) = $5.40; $5.40 = $5.40.

Yes, the amounts are the same.

TRY THIS!

1b. Simplify $2(n-5) + 7.4n$.

$2(n-5) + 7.4n = 2n - 10 + 7.4\ n$ ___Distributive___ Property

$= 2n + 7.4\ n - 10$ ___Commutative___ Property

$= \left(2n + 7.4n\right) - 10$ ___Associative___ Property

$= \left(2 + 7.4\right)n - 10$ ___Distributive___ Property

$= 9.4\ n - 10$ *Simplify.*

Chapter 7   259   Lesson 1

CC.8.EE.7

2 EXAMPLE   Writing and Simplifying Two-Variable Expressions

Devin bought $2\frac{1}{2}$ pounds of mixed nuts and $1\frac{3}{4}$ pounds of cheese for the class party. At the same store, Kim bought $1\frac{1}{2}$ pounds of cheese and $1\frac{1}{4}$ pounds of mixed nuts. Write and simplify an expression that represents how much they spent in all.

A   Write expressions for how much Devin and Kim spent.
Let *m* represent the cost per pound for mixed nuts. Let *c* represent the cost per pound for cheese.

Devin: $2\frac{1}{2}\ m + 1\frac{3}{4}\ c$ Kim: $1\frac{1}{2}\ c + 1\frac{1}{4}\ m$

B   Add both expressions to represent the total amount they spent.

$2\frac{1}{2}\ m + 1\frac{3}{4}\ c + 1\frac{1}{2}\ c + 1\frac{1}{4}\ m$

$\left(2\frac{1}{2}m + 1\frac{1}{4}\ m\right) + \left(1\frac{3}{4}c + 1\frac{1}{2}\ c\right)$ ___Commutative___ and ___Associative___ Properties

$\left(2\frac{1}{2} + 1\frac{1}{4}\right)m + \left(1\frac{3}{4} + 1\frac{1}{2}\right)c$ ___Distributive___ Property

$\left(\frac{5}{2} + \frac{5}{4}\right)m + \left(\frac{7}{4} + \frac{3}{2}\right)c$ *Write mixed numbers as improper fractions.*

$\left(\frac{5}{2}\cdot\frac{2}{2} + \frac{5}{4}\right)m + \left(\frac{7}{4} + \frac{3}{2}\cdot\frac{2}{2}\right)c$ *Multiply by fractions equal to 1.*

$\left(\frac{10}{4} + \frac{5}{4}\right)m + \left(\frac{7}{4} + \frac{6}{4}\right)c$ *Rewrite with a common denominator.*

$\frac{15}{4}\ m + \frac{13}{4}\ c$ *Simplify.*

The expression ___$\frac{15}{4}m + \frac{13}{4}c$___ represents how much Devin and Kim spent on mixed nuts and cheese.

REFLECT

2a. What are the advantages of the simplified expression over the original expression? Of the original expression over the simplified expression?

Possible answer: The simplified expression is easier to evaluate for given

values of *m* and *s*. The original expression shows what each individual bought.

2b. How is simplifying expressions with *two or more* variables like simplifying expressions with *one* variable?

Possible answer: In both instances, the task is to use the Commutative,

Associative, and Distributive properties to combine like terms.

Chapter 7   260   Lesson 1

© Houghton Mifflin Harcourt Publishing Company

Questioning Strategies

- How many terms are in the original expression? In the simplified expression? **4 terms, 2 terms**

- In which order do you write the terms in a simplified algebraic expression with two (or more) variables? **In alphabetical order**

Differentiated Instruction

Have students identify *like terms* by marking them using colors or shapes. For instance, they could circle the terms with *m* and draw a square around terms with *c*. Students can then recognize that they have two distinct sets of like terms, and they can more easily apply the Commutative and Associative properties to combine each pair of like terms.

MATHEMATICAL PRACTICE   **Highlighting the Standards**

This Example is an opportunity to address Standard 2 (Reason abstractly and quantitatively). Students are asked to write and simplify an algebraic expression with two variables. They identify like terms and combine them using the Distributive, Associative, and Commutative properties. In the Reflect question, students are guided to see that the same simplification process applies for one-variable and two-variable expressions.

Essential Question

How do you simplify algebraic expressions?
Possible answer: Apply the Distributive, Commutative, and Associative properties to transform an expression into a simpler equivalent expression in which no further operations can be performed.

Summarize

Have students make a graphic organizer to reinforce the distinction between one- and two-variable expressions. Students should include examples for one-, two-, and three-term expressions. Use the graphic to clarify the meaning of *terms* and that expressions may or may not include *like terms*.

Algebraic Expressions	
One Variable	**Two Variables**
One Term: $3y$	One Term: xy
Two Terms: $2x + 1$	Two Terms: $2x + y$
Three Terms: $5 - m^2 + 9m^2$	Three Terms: $5 - m^2 - 4n$

PRACTICE

Where skills are taught	Where skills are practiced
1 EXAMPLE	EXS. 1, 4, 6–8, 11
2 EXAMPLE	EXS. 2–3, 5, 9–10, 12–19

TRY THIS!

2c. Simplify $5(x + 2\frac{1}{2}y) + 3y - \frac{3}{4}x$. Tell what properties you used.

$4\frac{1}{4}x + 14y$; Distributive, Commutative, and Associative properties

PRACTICE

Simplify each algebraic expression.

1. $4w + 5 - 1.5w$

$2.5w + 5$

2. $7b + 5 - 9b + c$

$-2b + c + 5$

3. $x + 2.3(x - y)$

$3.3x - 2.3y$

4. $3(n + 4) - \frac{2}{3}n$

$2\frac{1}{3}n + 12$

5. $\frac{3}{8}(k + 24) + 2(r - \frac{1}{4})$

$\frac{3}{8}k + 2r + 8\frac{1}{2}$

6. $5.2(3 - x) - 3x$

$-8.2x + 15.6$

7. $4.2y + 8.1y + 1.8y + 3(y + 0.5)$

$17.1y + 1.5$

8. $9w + 6 - 2.5w$

$6.5w + 6$

Read each description. Then define and use variables to write and simplify an algebraic expression that represents it. Sample answers given; variables used may differ.

9. Krin buys 3 headbands and 2 wristbands. His brother Clay buys 4 headbands and 1 wristband. What is the total cost?

$7h + 3w$

10. Lemons cost x¢ per pound and limes cost y¢ each. Ellie buys 3.5 pounds of lemons and a dozen limes. What is the total cost?

$3.5x + 12y$

11. Jerome and Claire make the same hourly rate. Jerome worked for three-quarters of an hour on Tuesday and for one and one-half hours on Wednesday. On Tuesday, Claire worked twice as long as Jerome did. On Wednesday she worked for one-third of an hour. What is their total income?

$4\frac{1}{12}h$

12. Mara bought $2\frac{1}{2}$ pounds of sliced turkey and half a pound of roast beef. Leah bought 2 pounds of roast beef, $1\frac{3}{4}$ pounds of sliced turkey, and half a pound of coleslaw. What the total cost of the food?

$4\frac{1}{4}t + 2\frac{1}{2}r + \frac{1}{2}c$

13. The length of a rectangular field is 5 yards less than twice its width.

expression for perimeter: $6w - 10$

expression for area: $2w^2 - 5w$

Use the table to write a simplified expression for each purchase. Include a 10% tip. *Think*: The expression will be an amount of money.

PAT'S PIZZA EXPRESS		
Pie	**Topping**	**Drink**
Small...................$11.00	Mushrooms...........$2.50	Small.....................$1.50
Medium...............$15.50	Onions..................$2.25	Medium.................$2.25
Large $18.25	Peppers $2.50	Large $4.00
Gargantuan $22.00	Pineapple..............$3.50	Enormous..............$5.50

14. two small pies with no toppings and two medium pies with mushrooms

$63.80

15. a small pie with peppers, a large pie with all toppings, and four small drinks

$53.35

16. two large pies with mushrooms and peppers, one gargantuan pie with pineapple, and three enormous drinks

$97.35

17. six enormous drinks, two medium pies with all toppings, and two large pies with all toppings

$157.85

18. Error Analysis Ira says that to simplify $3(2.5n + 3p)$ you would apply the Distributive Property as follows: $3 + 2.5n + 3 + 3p$ and then combine like terms to form $2.5n + 3p + 6$. Explain his error.

He did not distribute the multiplication over the addition. $3(2.5n + 3p)$ correctly

simplifies to $3(2.5n) + 3(3p) = 7.5n + 9p$

19. Simplify $9(a + 1\frac{2}{9}b) + 8(b - 1\frac{3}{4}a)$. Tell what properties you used.

$-3\frac{4}{5}a + 20\frac{3}{5}b$; Distributive, Commutative, and Associative properties.

Assign these pages to help your students practice and apply important lesson concepts. For additional exercises, see the Student Edition.

Answers

Additional Practice

1. $3a^3$

2. $19g$

3. $11a + 6$

4. $11x + 3y$

5. $7k + 5h$

6. $17p^6 - 7q$

7. $5k^2 + 10k$

8. $5c + 12d - 6$

9. $8 + 10b$

10. $11f + 4$

11. $4x^3 + 8y$

12. $n + 7$

13. $4x + 7$

14. $42 + 11x$

15. $15 + 5x$

16. $y = 2$

17. $b = 7$

18. $q = 4$

19. $q + p + 4q + 8p; 5q + 9p$

20. 165 coins

Problem Solving

1. $x + 0.05x; 1.05x$

2. $d - 0.2d; 0.8d$

3. 10, 11, 12

4. 16, 18, 20

5. B

6. J

7. A

8. F

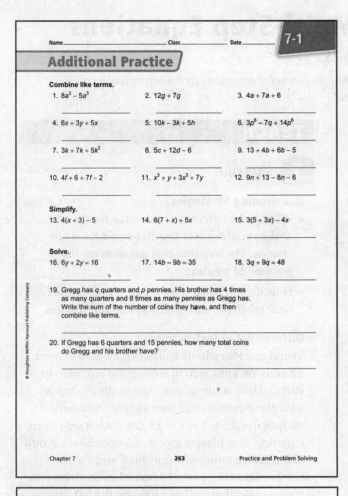

Name _____ Class _____ Date _____   **7-1**

Additional Practice

Combine like terms.

1. $8a^3 - 5a^3$

2. $12g + 7g$

3. $4a + 7a + 6$

4. $6x + 3y + 5x$

5. $10k - 3k + 5h$

6. $3p^6 - 7q + 14p^6$

7. $3k + 7k + 5k^2$

8. $5c + 12d - 6$

9. $13 + 4b + 6b - 5$

10. $4f + 6 + 7f - 2$

11. $x^3 + y + 3x^3 + 7y$

12. $9n + 13 - 8n - 6$

Simplify.

13. $4(x + 3) - 5$

14. $6(7 + x) + 5x$

15. $3(5 + 3x) - 4x$

Solve.

16. $6y + 2y = 16$

17. $14b - 9b = 35$

18. $3q + 9q = 48$

19. Gregg has q quarters and p pennies. His brother has 4 times as many quarters and 8 times as many pennies as Gregg has. Write the sum of the number of coins they have, and then combine like terms.

20. If Gregg has 6 quarters and 15 pennies, how many total coins do Gregg and his brother have?

Chapter 7   263   Practice and Problem Solving

Problem Solving

Write the correct answer.

1. An item costs x dollars. The tax rate is 5% of the cost of the item, or $0.05x$. Write and simplify an expression to find the total cost of the item with tax.

2. A sweater costs d dollars at regular price. The sweater is reduced by 20%, or $0.2d$. Write and simplify an expression to find the cost of the sweater before tax.

3. Consecutive integers are integers that differ by one. You can represent consecutive integers as x, $x + 1$, $x + 2$ and so on. Write an equation and solve to find three consecutive integers whose sum is 33.

4. Consecutive even integers can be represented by x, $x + 2$, $x + 4$ and so on. Write an equation and solve to find three consecutive even integers whose sum is 54.

Choose the letter for the best answer.

5. In Super Bowl XXXV, the total number of points scored was 41. The winning team outscored the losing team by 27 points. What was the final score of the game?

   A 33 to 8
   B 34 to 7
   C 22 to 2
   D 18 to 6

6. A high school basketball court is 34 feet longer than it is wide. If the perimeter of the court is 268, what are the dimensions of the court?

   F 234 ft by 34 ft
   G 67 ft by 67 ft
   H 70 ft by 36 ft
   J 84 ft by 50 ft

7. Julia ordered 2 hamburgers and Steven ordered 3 hamburgers. If their total bill before tax was $7.50, how much did each hamburger cost?

   A $1.50
   B $1.25
   C $1.15
   D $1.02

8. On three tests, a student scored a total of 258 points. If the student improved his performance on each test by 5 points, what was the score on each test?

   F 81, 86, 91
   G 80, 85, 90
   H 75, 80, 85
   J 70, 75, 80

Chapter 7   264   Practice and Problem Solving

Solving Multi-Step Equations
Going Deeper

Essential question: *How do you solve equations by collecting like terms and multiplying expressions?*

COMMON CORE **Standards for Mathematical Content**

CC.8.EE.7b Solve linear equations with rational number coefficients, including equations whose solutions require expanding expressions using the distributive property and collecting like terms.

Prerequisites

Identifying and combining like terms

Solving equations in one variable

Math Background

Solving equations involves finding the value of a variable that makes the equation a true statement. This is accomplished by isolating the variable on one side of the equation and simplifying the expression on the other side. To solve some equations, you need to combine, or collect, like terms. This means to add or subtract terms that have the same variable raised to the same exponent. For example, $2x + 3x$ can be simplified as $5x$. Other equations require you to expand an expression using the Distributive Property. For example, $2(x + 3) = 2(x) + 2(3) = 2x + 6$.

INTRODUCE

Connect to prior learning by asking students to identify like terms such as $5x$, $-3x$, and $2.5x$. Ask students to explain how to use the Distributive Property to show that $2(3 + 4) = 14$. Explain that equations can be used to represent real-world situations. For example, an equation may be used to calculate the cost of a cell phone bill. Constants and variables in equations represent fixed and variable amounts, such as a flat fee per month plus the cost per minute over a certain number of minutes. In this lesson, students will solve equations by collecting like terms and using the Distributive Property.

TEACH

1 EXPLORE

Questioning Strategies

- What is the difference between a fixed cost and a variable cost? **The fixed cost does not change. The variable cost depends on the number of trophies.**

- How do you know what value to use for the Club's total cost? **The club spent $97.50 on trophies.**

Differentiated Instruction

Visual and kinesthetic learners may benefit from a hands-on approach to solving the equation in Part D. Have students use algebra tiles to model a similar equation that uses simpler numbers, such as $3 + 2x + 4 + x = 13$. On the left side of an equation mat, place a group of 3 unit-tiles, a group of 2 x-tiles, a group of 4 unit-tiles, and 1 x-tile. On the right side, place 13 unit-tiles. Students can model collecting the like terms on the left side before performing operations on both sides of the equation to solve for x.

2 EXPLORE

Questioning Strategies

- What does the variable x represent in this situation? **Carla's number**

- What key words can help you write an equation? **subtract, multiply, quantity, add, result**

- How do you use the Distributive Property to simplify an expression? **Multiply the term outside the parentheses by each term inside the parentheses. Then collect like terms.**

Teaching Strategies

Help students translate the keywords in the problem. For example, *multiply* means multiplication, *quantity* probably means there is an expression inside parentheses, and *result* means the value on the other side of the equal sign. Verify that students write the equation as $4(x - 5) + 7 = 35$.

Name_____ Class_____ Date_____

7-2

Solving Multi-Step Equations
Going Deeper

Essential question: *How do you solve equations by collecting like terms and multiplying expressions?*

CC.8.EE.7b

1 EXPLORE Solving Equations by Collecting Like Terms

A soccer club spent $97.50 on trophies from a custom trophy company. The cost of manufacturing x custom trophies is $18.50 for the setup cost, plus $12.50 per trophy. To ship the trophies, the company charges a standard fee of $4 per order plus $2.50 per trophy. How many trophies did the soccer club order?

A Write an expression representing the **cost of manufacturing**.

Setup cost	+	Cost for x trophies
18.50	+	12.50x

B Write an expression representing the **cost of shipping**.

Standard fee	+	Cost for x trophies
4.00	+	2.50x

C Write an equation that can be solved to find the number of trophies the soccer club ordered.

Cost of manufacturing	+	Cost of shipping	=	Club's total cost
18.50 + 12.50x	+	4.00 + 2.50x	=	97.50

D Solve your equation for x.

$$18.50 + 12.50x + 4.00 + 2.50x = 97.50$$
$$22.50 + 15x = 97.50$$
$$\underline{-22.50} \qquad \underline{-22.50}$$
$$15x = 75$$
$$\frac{15x}{15} = \frac{75}{15}$$
$$x = 5$$

The soccer club ordered ____5____ trophies.

TRY THIS!

Solve each equation.

1a. $14x + 6 - 10x + 30 = 64$

$$4x + 36 = 64$$
$$4x = 28$$
$$x = 7$$

1b. $2\frac{1}{3}x + 10 + 5\frac{2}{3}x - 9\frac{1}{2} = 12\frac{1}{2}$

$$8x + \frac{1}{2} = 12\frac{1}{2}$$
$$8x = 12$$
$$x = 1\frac{1}{2}$$

© Houghton Mifflin Harcourt Publishing Company

Chapter 7   265   Lesson 2

CC.8.EE.7b

2 EXPLORE Solving Equations by Using the Distributive Property

Carla chose a number between 1 and 50 and then described to Henry how he could determine the number she chose.

Carla says, "If you subtract 5 from my number, multiply that quantity by 4, and then add 7 to the result, you get 35."

Write an equation that Henry can solve to find Carla's number.

A First write an expression for "subtract 5 from my number."

$x - 5$

B Use your answer to **A** to write an expression for "multiply that quantity by 4."

$4(x - 5)$

C Now use your answer to **B** to write an expression for "then add 7 to the result."

$4(x - 5) + 7$

D Use your answer to **C** and the rest of Carla's description to write an equation that you can solve to find Carla's number.

$4(x - 5) + 7 = 35$

E Solve the equation for x. Use the Distributive Property to simplify one side of the equation before collecting like terms.

$$4(x - 5) + 7 = 35$$
$$4x - 20 + 7 = 35$$
$$4x - 13 = 35$$
$$4x - 13 + 13 = 35 + 13$$
$$4x = 48$$
$$\frac{4x}{4} = \frac{48}{4}$$
$$x = 12$$

Carla's number is ____12____.

TRY THIS!

Solve each equation.

2a. $3(x + 2) + 4 = 31$

$$3x + 6 + 4 = 31$$
$$3x = 21$$
$$x = 7$$

2b. $4 - 3(x + 2) - 2(x - 4) + 8 = -1$

$$4 - 3x - 6 - 2x + 8 + 8 = -1$$
$$-5x + 14 = -1$$
$$-5x = -15$$
$$x = 3$$

© Houghton Mifflin Harcourt Publishing Company

Chapter 7   266   Lesson 2

Essential Question

How do you solve equations by collecting like terms and multiplying expressions?

Possible answer: Collecting like terms can help you isolate the variable on one side of the equation. Multiplying expressions by using the Distributive Property may help you remove parentheses. Then you can use properties of equality and the order of operations to solve the equation.

Summarize

Have students respond to the following in their journals: Think of a real-world situation that can be modeled by an equation. Write an equation to model your situation and solve it. Interpret the solution in the context of your situation.

PRACTICE

Where skills are taught	Where skills are practiced
1 EXPLORE	EXS. 1–4, 11–14, 17–22
2 EXPLORE	EXS. 5–10, 15–16

PRACTICE

Solve each equation.

1. $3x + 4 + 2x + 5 = 34$

$x = 5$

2. $2.5x - 5 + 3x + 8 = 19.5$

$x = 3$

3. $\frac{1}{2}x + 6 - 2x + \frac{1}{2} = \frac{7}{2}$

$x = 2$

4. $-10x - 3 - 2.5x + 20 = 67$

$x = -4$

5. $2(x + 1) + 4 = 12$

$x = 3$

6. $-3(x + 4) + 15 = -12$

$x = 5$

7. $15 - 3(x - 1) = 12$

$x = 2$

8. $3(x - 2) + 2(x + 1) = -14$

$x = -2$

9. $\frac{1}{2}(x + 8) - 15 = -3$

$x = 16$

10. $2.5(x + 2) + 4.5 + 1.5(x - 3) = 15$

$x = 2.5$

Solve by writing and solving an equation.

11. The perimeter of a rectangular garden is 4.8 meters. Its length is twice its width. How wide is the garden?

$2(2w) + 2w = 4.8$; 0.8 meter

12. Willy and Freddie spent a total of $17.50 on lunch. Willy spent 4 times as much as Freddie did. How much did Freddie spend?

$f + 4f = 17.50$; $3.50

13. Half a number plus 2.5 times that number equals 18. What is the number?

$0.5n + 2.5n = 18$; 6

14. Jason is 6 years older than his sister. Their mother is 15 years older than the sum of their ages. If their mother is 39, how old is Jason?

$j + (j - 6) + 15 = 39$; 15

15. Tanya has a certain amount of money in her savings account. Each month, for 6 months, she deposits $50 less than her original savings amount. After 6 months, she has a total of $750 in the account. How much money did she have in the account when she began adding money to it?

$m + 6(m - 50) = 750$; $150

16. A class of 24 students hopes to collect 1,200 plastic bottles per week. In the first week, the students collected 34 bottles each. This was not enough. How many more bottles per student must the class collect to meet the weekly goal of 1,200?

$24(34 + b) = 1,200$; 16 more bottles per student

17. Six times a number increased by 12 plus 3 times the number increased by 6 is equal to 58.5. What is the number?

$6n + 12 + 3n + 6 = 58.5$; 4.5

18. The larger of two numbers is three times the smaller. The sum of the two numbers is 6. What are the numbers?

$n + 3n = 6$; $1\frac{1}{2}$ and $4\frac{1}{2}$

19. Consecutive integers are 1 apart. The sum of three consecutive integers is 54. What are the integers?

$n + (n + 1) + (n + 2) = 54$; 17, 18, 19

20. Find the mystery number: When you multiply a number by -4 and then add 3 times the number to the product, the result is 4. What is the number?

$-4n + 3n = 4$; -4

21. Jake and Abigail worked on a job together. Jake earned three-fourths of what Abigail did. Together, they earned $140. How much did each earn?

$a + 0.75a = 140$; Jake: $60, Abigail: $80

22. **Error Analysis** Five dollars more than half the price of a sweater comes to $45.49. A student wrote the following equation to find the sweater price: $\frac{n}{2 + 5} = \$45.49$. What should the correct equation be? What does the sweater cost?

$\frac{n}{2} + 5 = \$45.49$; $80.98

ADDITIONAL PRACTICE

Assign these pages to help your students practice and apply important lesson concepts. For additional exercises, see the Student Edition.

Answers

Additional Practice

1. $x = 3$ **2.** $y = 5$

3. $w = 3$ **4.** $b = -7$

5. $t = 3$ **6.** $x = 3$

7. $m = 1$ **8.** $n = -5$

9. $a = -5$ **10.** $x = -8$

11. $m = -4$ **12.** $x = 7$

13. $k = 2$ **14.** $y = -6$

15. $a = -1$

16. angle $= 59°$; complement $= 31°$

17. angle $= 127°$; supplement $= 53°$

18. $AC = 25$ units; $BC = 50$ units

$AB = 51$ units

19. $36°$; $72°$; $72°$

Problem Solving

1. 20 miles   **2.** 28 miles

3. 4 years   **4.** $37,500

5. B   **6.** G

7. C   **8.** J

Name_____ Class_____ Date_____

Additional Practice

Solve.

1. $2x + 5x + 4 = 25$

_____

2. $9 + 3y - 2y = 14$

_____

3. $16 = 2(2w + w - 1)$

_____

4. $26 = 3b - 2 - 7b$

_____

5. $31 + 4t - t = 40$

_____

6. $2(7 - x) + 4x = 20$

_____

7. $\frac{5m}{8} - \frac{6}{8} + \frac{3m}{8} = \frac{2}{8}$

_____

8. $-4\frac{2}{3} = \frac{2n}{3} + \frac{1}{3} + \frac{n}{3}$

_____

9. $7a + 16 - 3a = -4$

_____

10. $\frac{x}{2} + 1 + \frac{3x}{4} = -9$

_____

11. $7m + 3 - 4m = -9$

_____

12. $\frac{2x}{5} + 3 - \frac{4x}{5} = \frac{1}{5}$

_____

13. $\frac{7k}{8} - \frac{3}{4} - \frac{5k}{16} = \frac{3}{8}$

_____

14. $3(2y + 3) - 4y = -3$

_____

15. $\frac{5a}{6} - \frac{7}{12} + \frac{3a}{4} = -2\frac{1}{6}$

_____

16. The measure of an angle is 28° greater than its complement. Find the measure of each angle.

_____

17. The measure of an angle is 21° more than twice its supplement. Find the measure of each angle.

_____

18. The perimeter of the triangle is 126 units. Find the measure of each side.

_____

19. The base angles of an isosceles triangle are congruent. If the measure of each of the base angles is twice the measure of the third angle, find the measure of all three angles.

_____

Problem Solving

A taxi company charges $2.25 for the first mile and then $0.20 per mile for each mile after the first, or $F = \$2.25 + \$0.20(m - 1)$ where F is the fare and m is the number of miles.

1. If Juan's taxi fare was $6.05, how many miles did he travel in the taxi?

_____

2. If Juan's taxi fare was $7.65, how many miles did he travel in the taxi?

_____

A new car loses 20% of its original value when you buy it and then 8% of its original value per year, or $D = 0.8V - 0.08Vy$ where D is the value after y years with an original value V.

3. If a vehicle that was valued at $20,000 new is now worth $9,600, how old is the car?

4. A 6-year old vehicle is worth $12,000. What was the original value of the car?

The equation used to estimate typing speed is $S = \frac{1}{5}(w - 10e)$,

where S is the accurate typing speed, w is the number of words typed in 5 minutes and e is the number of errors. Choose the letter of the best answer.

5. Jane can type 55 words per minute (wpm). In 5 minutes, she types 285 words. How many errors would you expect her to make?

　A 0　　　　C 2
　B 1　　　　D 5

6. If Alex types 300 words in 5 minutes with 5 errors, what is his typing speed?

　F 48 wpm　　H 59 wpm
　G 50 wpm　　J 60 wpm

7. Johanna receives a report that says her typing speed is 65 words per minute. She knows that she made 4 errors in the 5-minute test. How many words did she type in 5 minutes?

　A 285　　　　C 365
　B 329　　　　D 1825

8. Cecil can type 35 words per minute. In 5 minutes, she types 255 words. How many errors would you expect her to make?

　F 2　　　　H 6
　G 4　　　　J 8

© Houghton Mifflin Harcourt Publishing Company

Solving Equations with Variables on Both Sides
Going Deeper

Essential question: How can you give examples of equations with a given number of solutions?

Standards for Mathematical Content

CC.8.EE.7a Give examples of linear equations in one variable with one solution, infinitely many solutions, or no solutions. Show which of these possibilities is the case by successively transforming the given equation into simpler forms, until an equivalent equation of the form $x = a$, $a = a$, or $a = b$ results (where a and b are different numbers).

CC.8.EE.7b Solve linear equations with rational number coefficients, including equations whose solutions require expanding expressions using the distributive property and collecting like terms.

Prerequisites
Solving multi-step equations

Math Background
Linear equations assume many forms. In this lesson, students work with linear equations in one variable. The standard form of a linear equation in one variable is $ax + b = c$, though not every linear equation is presented in the standard form.

Every linear equation in one variable can be simplified to one of three forms: $x = a$, $a = a$, or $a = b$ (for $a \neq b$). When an equation simplifies to $x = a$, the equation is true only when the variable assumes the value a, and the equation has only one solution. When an equation simplifies to $a = a$, there are infinitely many solutions because this statement is true for any value of the variable. When an equation simplifies to $a = b$ (for $a \neq b$), the equation has no solutions because there is no value of the variable that will make a equal to b.

INTRODUCE

In your everyday life, some questions have exactly one answer: "Who is your homeroom teacher?". Other questions have many right answers: "Who is your friend?". Tell students that in this lesson, they will learn to analyze linear equations to determine whether they have one solution, many solutions, or no solution at all.

TEACH

1 EXPLORE

Questioning Strategies
- How would you begin to simplify the equation in Part A? **Use properties of equality to get the variable terms on one side of the equation and the constant terms on the other side.**

- Why isn't the final equation in Part C in the form $x = a$? **When you used the properties of equality, the variable terms simplified to 0.**

2 EXPLORE

Questioning Strategies
- Why do you start with a false statement? **There are no values of the variable that make the statement true, which means there are no solutions.**

- What statement could you start with if you wanted to write a linear equation that has many solutions? **Any statement in the form $a = a$, such as $2 = 2$.**

© Houghton Mifflin Harcourt Publishing Company

7-3

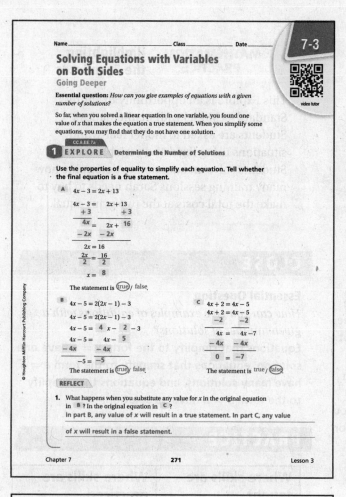

Name_____ Class_____ Date_____

Solving Equations with Variables on Both Sides
Going Deeper

Essential question: *How can you give examples of equations with a given number of solutions?*

So far, when you solved a linear equation in one variable, you found one value of x that makes the equation a true statement. When you simplify some equations, you may find that they do not have one solution.

CC.8.EE.7a
1 EXPLORE Determining the Number of Solutions

Use the properties of equality to simplify each equation. Tell whether the final equation is a true statement.

A
$$4x - 3 = 2x + 13$$

$$\frac{\begin{array}{ll} 4x - 3 = & 2x + 13 \\ +3 & +3 \end{array}}{4x = \ \ 2x + 16}$$
$$\frac{-2x \ \ -2x}{2x = 16}$$
$$\frac{2x}{2} = \frac{16}{2}$$
$$x = 8$$

The statement is (true) / false.

B
$$4x - 5 = 2(2x - 1) - 3$$
$$4x - 5 = 2(2x - 1) - 3$$
$$4x - 5 = \ \ 4x - 2 \ \ - 3$$
$$\frac{4x - 5 = \ \ 4x - 5}{-4x \quad -4x}$$
$$\frac{}{-5 = -5}$$

The statement is (true) / false.

C
$$4x + 2 = 4x - 5$$
$$4x + 2 = 4x - 5$$
$$\frac{-2 \quad -2}{4x = \ \ 4x - 7}$$
$$\frac{-4x \quad -4x}{0 = -7}$$

The statement is true / (false).

REFLECT

1. What happens when you substitute any value for x in the original equation in **B** ? In the original equation in **C** ?
   In part B, any value of x will result in a true statement. In part C, any value
   of x will result in a false statement.

When you simplify an equation using the properties of equality, you will find one of three results.

Result	What does this mean?	How many solutions?
$x = a$	When the value of x is a, the equation is a true statement.	1
$a = a$	Any value of x makes the equation a true statement.	Infinitely many
$a = b$	There is no value of x that makes the equation a true statement.	0

CC.8.EE.7a
2 EXPLORE Writing Equations with a Given Number of Solutions

Write a linear equation in one variable that has no solutions.

You can use the strategy of working backward:

A Start with a false statement such as $3 = 5$. Add the same variable term to both sides.
Sample answer: (add x to both sides) $3 + x = 5 + x$

B Next, add the same constant to both sides and combine like terms on each side of the equation.
Sample answer: (add 7 to both sides) $10 + x = 12 + x$

C Verify that your equation has no solutions by using properties of equality to simplify your equation. Sample answer:
$$\frac{\begin{array}{l} 10 + x = 12 + x \\ -x \quad\quad -x \end{array}}{10 = 12}$$

REFLECT

2a. Explain why the result of the process above is an equation with no solutions.
   You started with a false statement and performed balanced operations
   on both sides of the equation. This does not change the true or false
   nature of the original statement.

TRY THIS!   Sample answer given for 2d.

Tell whether each equation has one, zero, or infinitely many solutions.

2b. $6 + 3x = x - 8$
   one solution

2c. $8x + 4 = 4(2x + 1)$
   infinitely many solutions

Complete each equation so that it has the indicated number of solutions.

2d. No solutions: $3x + 1 = 3x +$ 6   **2e.** Infinitely many: $2x - 4 = 2x -$ 4

3 EXPLORE

Questioning Strategies

- For each gym, identify the fixed amount and the variable amount. **The fixed amount is the flat fee per month for membership. The variable amount is the cost for x training sessions.**

- What keyword or phrase in the original problem tells you how to set up the equation for Part D? **The phrase "cost at the two gyms equal" tells you to write an equation that sets the expressions for total cost at each gym equal to each other.**

Avoid Common Errors

Show students that the variable amount (cost for x training sessions) depends on the number of training sessions (x). The cost for training sessions is greater when the number of training sessions is greater.

CLOSE

Essential Question

How can you give examples of equations with a given number of solutions?

Equations that simplify to the form $x = a$ have one solution, equations that simplify to the form $a = a$ have many solutions, and equations that simplify to the form $a = b$ have no solution.

PRACTICE

Where skills are taught	Where skills are practiced
1 EXPLORE	EXS. 1–4
2 EXPLORE	EXS. 5–6
3 EXPLORE	EXS. 7–11

3 EXPLORE | GC.8.EE.7b | Solving Equations with Variables on Both Sides

At Silver Gym, membership is $25 per month, and personal training sessions are $30 each. At Fit Factor, membership is $65 per month, and personal training sessions are $20 each. In one month, how many personal training sessions would Sarah have to buy to make the total cost at the two gyms equal?

A Write an expression representing the **total monthly cost at Silver Gym**.

Monthly membership	+	Cost for x training sessions
25	+	30x

B Write an expression representing the **total monthly cost at Fit Factor**.

Monthly membership	+	Cost for x training sessions
65	+	20x

C How can you find the number of personal training sessions in one month that would make the total costs of the gyms equal?

Set the expressions equal to each other and solve for x.

D Write an equation that can be solved to find the number of training sessions in one month that makes the total costs equal.

Total cost at Silver Gym = Total cost at Fit Factor

$25 + 30x$ = $65 + 20x$

E Solve the equation for x. Use inverse operations to get all variable terms on one side of the equation and all constants on the other side.

$$\begin{array}{rcl} 25 + 30x &=& 65 + 20x \\ -25 & & -25 \\ \hline 30x &=& 40 + 20x \\ -20x & & -20x \\ \hline 10x &=& 40 \\ \dfrac{10x}{10} &=& \dfrac{40}{10} \\ x &=& 4 \end{array}$$

Sarah would have to buy ___4___ personal training sessions to make the total cost at the two gyms equal.

TRY THIS!

Solve each equation.

3a. $10x + 5 = 20 - 20x$

$$\begin{array}{rcl} 10x + 5 &=& 20 - 20x \\ 30x &=& 15 \\ x &=& \frac{1}{2} \end{array}$$

3b. $\frac{1}{4}x + 4 = \frac{3}{4}x - 8$

$$\begin{array}{rcl} \frac{1}{4}x + 4 &=& \frac{3}{4}x - 8 \\ -\frac{1}{2}x &=& -12 \\ x &=& 24 \end{array}$$

PRACTICE

Tell whether each equation has one, zero, or infinitely many solutions.

1. $4 + 5y = y - 8$

one solution

2. $4.5n + 3 = 4.5(n + 3)$

zero solutions

3. $3.1n = 2(1.55n)$

infinitely many solutions

4. $\frac{3}{8}w + 5 = 9w$

one solution

Complete each equation so that it has the indicated number of solutions.

5. No solutions: $5k + 2 = 5k +$ any number but 2

6. Infinitely many: $2b - 3 = 2b - $ 3

Solve by writing and solving an equation.

7. When 15 is added to twice a number, the result is the same as when 3 is added to 5 times the number. What is the number?

$2n + 15 = 5n + 3$; 4

8. Albert's father is 24 years older than Albert is. In 8 years, his father will be twice as old as Albert. How old is Albert now? How old is his father?

$2(a + 8) = (a + 8) + 24$; Albert is 16 and his father is 40.

9. Cal's Carriage Rides charges $20 plus $4.50 an hour for rides in the park. Hal's Horse & Buggy charges $30 plus $2.50 an hour for the same service. For how many hours would you pay the same total fee for a ride? What is that fee?

$20 + 4.5h = 30 + 2.5h$; At 5 hours; $42.50

10. Mr. Guerrero left his house and drove north at an average speed of 40 mph. Two hours later, his daughter Miranda left the house and drove the same route as her father, but at an average speed of 48 mph. How far from home were they when Miranda overtook her father?

$40t = 48(t - 2)$; 480 miles

11. Error Analysis A student solved an equation as shown. Explain the error the student made. Then solve the equation correctly.

$$\begin{array}{rcl} 3n + 4 - n &=& 12 + n \\ 3n + 4 &=& 12 \\ 3n &=& 8 \\ n &=& \frac{8}{3} \end{array}$$

The student subtracted n from the right side, but added it to the left. The correct answer is $n = 8$.

Assign these pages to help your students practice and apply important lesson concepts. For additional exercises, see the Student Edition.

Answers

Additional Practice

1. $x = -2$

2. $a = 3$

3. $t = -2.5$

4. $y = 88$

5. $k = -300$

6. $x = 3$

7. $y = -0.4$

8. $w = 40$

9. $x = 7$

10. $d = \dfrac{3}{4}$

11. $y = 84$

12. $x = 3$

13. 11

14. 12 units

15. $B = \dfrac{3V}{h}$

Problem Solving

1. 250 minutes

2. 224 minutes

3. 198 minutes

4. C

5. H

6. D

7. H

Additional Practice

Solve.

1. $7x - 11 = -19 + 3x$

2. $11a + 9 = 4a + 30$

3. $4t + 14 = \frac{6t}{5} + 7$

4. $\frac{3y}{8} - 9 = 13 + \frac{y}{8}$

5. $\frac{3k}{5} + 44 = \frac{12k}{25} + 8$

6. $15 - x = 2(x + 3)$

7. $15y + 14 = 2(5y + 6)$

8. $14 - \frac{w}{8} = \frac{3w}{4} - 21$

9. $\frac{1}{2}(6x - 4) = 4x - 9$

10. $4(3d - 2) = 8d - 5$

11. $\frac{y}{3} + 11 = \frac{y}{2} - 3$

12. $\frac{2x - 9}{3} = 8 - 3x$

13. Forty-eight decreased by a number is the same as the difference of four times the number and seven. Find the number.

14. The square and the equilateral triangle at the right have the same perimeter. Find the length of the sides of the triangle.

15. The equation $V = \frac{1}{3} Bh$ gives the volume V of a pyramid, where B is the area of the base and h is the height. Solve this equation for B.

© Houghton Mifflin Harcourt Publishing Company

Problem Solving

The chart below describes three long-distance calling plans. Round to the nearest minute. Write the correct answer.

1. For what number of minutes will plan A and plan B cost the same?

Long-Distance Plans

Plan	Monthly Access Fee	Charge per minute
A	$3.95	$0.08
B	$8.95	$0.06
C	$0	$0.10

2. For what number of minutes per month will plan B and plan C cost the same?

3. For what number of minutes will plan A and plan C cost the same?

Choose the letter for the best answer.

4. Carpet Plus installs carpet for $100 plus $8 per square yard of carpet. Carpet World charges $75 for installation and $10 per square yard of carpet. Find the number of square yards of carpet for which the cost including carpet and installation is the same.

A 1.4 yd^2
B 9.7 yd^2
C 12.5 yd^2
D 87.5 yd^2

5. One shuttle service charges $10 for pickup and $0.10 per mile. The other shuttle service has no pickup fee but charges $0.35 per mile. Find the number of miles for which the cost of the shuttle services is the same.

F 2.5 miles
G 22 miles
H 40 miles
J 48 miles

6. Joshua can purchase tile at one store for $0.99 per tile, but he will have to rent a tile saw for $25. At another store he can buy tile for $1.50 per tile and borrow a tile saw for free. Find the number of tiles for which the cost is the same. Round to the nearest tile.

A 10 tiles
B 13 tiles
C 25 tiles
D 49 tiles

7. One plumber charges a fee of $75 per service call plus $15 per hour. Another plumber has no flat fee, but charges $25 per hour. Find the number of hours for which the cost of the two plumbers is the same.

F 2.1 hours
G 7 hours
H 7.5 hours
J 7.8 hours

© Houghton Mifflin Harcourt Publishing Company

Systems of Equations
Going Deeper

Essential question: *How can you solve a system of equations algebraically?*

COMMON CORE **Standards for Mathematical Content**

CC.8.EE.8b Solve systems of two linear equations in two variables algebraically, and estimate solutions by graphing the equations. Solve simple cases by inspection.

CC.8.EE.8c Solve real-world and mathematical problems leading to two linear equations in two variables.

Vocabulary

system of equations

Prerequisites

Solving systems of equations graphically

Slope-intercept form

Math Background

It may be difficult to use a graph to solve equations with very large values or when the solution has non-integer coordinates. Sometimes an approximate solution is sufficient. For instance, when comparing prices from two different companies, a graph might clearly show that when buying fewer than about 30 items, Company A has lower prices than Company B. This may be enough information for you to make a decision. In other situations, an exact solution is needed. In these cases, you will need to solve the system algebraically.

INTRODUCE

Sketch the graph of a system of equations with decimal solutions on the board. For example, graph $2x - y = 6$ and $3x + y = 10$. Invite students to try solving the system using the graphs. Check students' solutions by substituting values for the variables in the equations. Discuss why solving this system graphically is difficult.

TEACH

1 EXAMPLE

Questioning Strategies

- Why are the properties of equality important when solving equations? **The properties of equality maintain balance on each side of the equation. Each equation in the solution process has the same solution set.**

- How is the system in Part B different from the one in Part A? **In Part A, the variable y was already isolated. In Part B, you must solve for y in one of the equations before you can substitute.**

Teaching Strategies

Invite students to present their work on the board. Ask them to justify their reasoning at each step. If students are reluctant to present an entire problem, you might ask several students to present only one or two steps at a time.

2 EXAMPLE

Questioning Strategies

- In Part C, what is the first step in solving the system algebraically? **Solve one of the equations for one of the variables.**

- Which variable should you solve for? Which equation should you use? **The coefficient of x in the first equation is 1, so it is easy to solve that equation for x.**

- Suppose your algebraic solution is $\left(-\frac{11}{5}, \frac{24}{5}\right)$. How do you know immediately that you have made a mistake? **The graph shows that the solution lies in Quadrant III. This solution is in Quadrant II.**

Name_____ Class_____ Date_____

7-4

Systems of Equations
Going Deeper

Essential question: *How can you solve a system of equations algebraically?*

A **system of equations** is a set of equations that have the same variables. An ordered pair is a solution of a system if it satisfies every equation in the system.

CC.8.EE.8b

1 EXAMPLE Solving Systems Algebraically

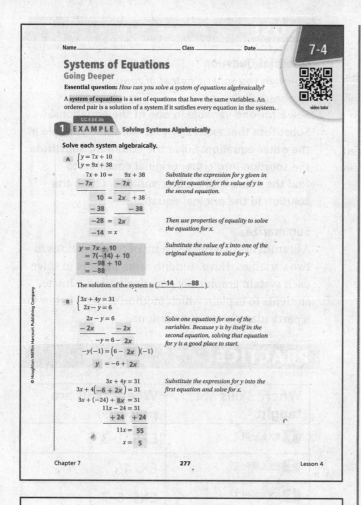

Solve each system algebraically.

A $\begin{cases} y = 7x + 10 \\ y = 9x + 38 \end{cases}$

$$7x + 10 = 9x + 38$$
$$\underline{-7x} \qquad \underline{-7x}$$
$$10 = 2x + 38$$
$$\underline{-38} \qquad \underline{-38}$$
$$-28 = 2x$$
$$-14 = x$$

Substitute the expression for y given in the first equation for the value of y in the second equation.

Then use properties of equality to solve the equation for x.

$$y = 7x + 10$$
$$= 7(-14) + 10$$
$$= -98 + 10$$
$$= -88$$

Substitute the value of x into one of the original equations to solve for y.

The solution of the system is (__−14__ , __−88__).

B $\begin{cases} 3x + 4y = 31 \\ 2x - y = 6 \end{cases}$

$$2x - y = 6$$
$$\underline{-2x} \qquad \underline{-2x}$$
$$-y = 6 - 2x$$
$$-y(-1) = (6 - 2x)(-1)$$
$$y = -6 + 2x$$

Solve one equation for one of the variables. Because y is by itself in the second equation, solving that equation for y is a good place to start.

$$3x + 4y = 31$$
$$3x + 4(-6 + 2x) = 31$$
$$3x + (-24) + 8x = 31$$
$$11x - 24 = 31$$
$$\underline{+24} \quad \underline{+24}$$
$$11x = 55$$
$$x = 5$$

Substitute the expression for y into the first equation and solve for x.

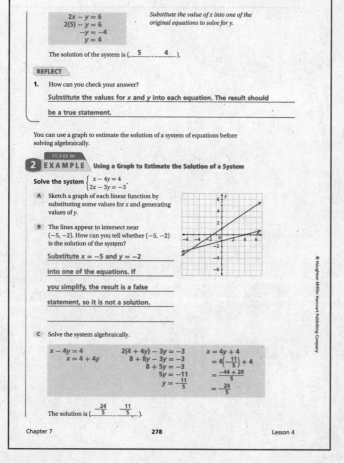

$$2x - y = 6$$
$$2(5) - y = 6$$
$$-y = -4$$
$$y = 4$$

Substitute the value of x into one of the original equations to solve for y.

The solution of the system is (__5__ , __4__).

REFLECT

1. How can you check your answer?

Substitute the values for *x* and *y* into each equation. The result should

be a true statement.

You can use a graph to estimate the solution of a system of equations before solving algebraically.

CC.8.EE.8b

2 EXAMPLE Using a Graph to Estimate the Solution of a System

Solve the system $\begin{cases} x - 4y = 4 \\ 2x - 3y = -3 \end{cases}$

A Sketch a graph of each linear function by substituting some values for *x* and generating values of *y*.

B The lines appear to intersect near (−5, −2). How can you tell whether (−5, −2) is the solution of the system?

Substitute x = −5 and y = −2

into one of the equations. If

you simplify, the result is a false

statement, so it is not a solution.

C Solve the system algebraically.

$$x - 4y = 4$$
$$x = 4 + 4y$$

$$2(4 + 4y) - 3y = -3$$
$$8 + 8y - 3y = -3$$
$$8 + 5y = -3$$
$$5y = -11$$
$$y = -\frac{11}{5}$$

$$x = 4y + 4$$
$$= 4\left(-\frac{11}{5}\right) + 4$$
$$= \frac{-44 + 20}{5}$$
$$= -\frac{24}{5}$$

The solution is (__−$\frac{24}{5}$__ , __−$\frac{11}{5}$__).

Questioning Strategies

- How do you find the slope of a line? Calculate the ratio of the change in y to the change in x.

- How do you write an equation in slope-intercept form? Start with the general form $y = mx + b$. Then substitute the coordinates of a known point for x and y and the slope for m. Solve for b. Then return to the general form and substitute for m and b.

Avoid Common Errors

Students may calculate the slope for an incorrect combination of points (for example, the slope of the lines connecting A with C and B with D). They should double-check their work. Students can check their work by comparing their calculated slopes to the lines on the graph. The graph shows that one slope is positive and one is negative.

MATHEMATICAL PRACTICE   **Highlighting the Standards**

This Example is an opportunity to address Standard 5 (Use appropriate tools strategically). Students must choose when to solve a system graphically and when to solve a system algebraically. Students need to think strategically to solve the problem in the most efficient manner. Present several problem-solving situations to students and ask them to determine the best approach to solving the problem. Ask students why they prefer one method over another.

CLOSE

Essential Question

How can you solve a system of equations algebraically?

Solve for one variable in one of the equations. Substitute that expression for the same variable in the other equation. Solve the equation. Substitute the solution into either original equation to find the value of the other variable. Check the solution in the original equations.

Summarize

Ask students to write a system of two equations in two variables. Have students work in pairs to solve each system graphically and algebraically. Invite students to explain which method worked better for a particular system of equations.

PRACTICE

Where skills are taught	Where skills are practiced
1 EXAMPLE	EXS. 1–3, 5
2 EXAMPLE	EX. 4
3 EXAMPLE	EXS. 6–7

D Use the estimate you made using the graph to judge the reasonableness of your solution.

$-\frac{24}{5}$ is close to the estimate of -5, and $-\frac{11}{5}$ is close to the estimate of -2, so the solution seems reasonable.

REFLECT

2. How can you determine that the system $\begin{cases} 5x - 2y = 8 \\ 5x - 2y = -3 \end{cases}$ has no solution without graphing or using algebraic methods?

The expression $5x - 2y$ cannot equal both 8 and -3.

3 EXAMPLE Problem Solving with Systems of Equations

Aaargh! There's pirate treasure to be found,
So search on the island, all around.
Draw a line through A and B.
Then a second line through C and D.
Dance a jig, "X" marks the spot,
If the lines intersect, that's the treasure's plot!

A Give the coordinates of each point and find the slope of the line through each pair of points.

$A: (\underline{-2}, \underline{-1})$ $C: (\underline{-1}, \underline{4})$

$B: (\underline{2}, \underline{5})$ $D: (\underline{1}, \underline{-4})$

Slope:

$\dfrac{5 - (-1)}{2 - (-2)} = \dfrac{6}{4}$

$= \dfrac{3}{2}$

Slope:

$\dfrac{-4 - 4}{1 - (-1)} = \dfrac{-8}{2}$

$= -4$

B Use the slopes of the lines to determine whether they will intersect.

The slopes are different, so the lines are not parallel and are not the same line. The lines do intersect.

C Write equations in slope-intercept form describing the line through points A and B and the line through points C and D.

Line through A and B:

$5 = \left(\dfrac{3}{2}\right)2 + b$
$b = 2$
$y = \dfrac{3}{2}x + 2$

Line through C and D:

$4 = -4(-1) + b$
$b = 0$
$y = -4x$

D Solve the system algebraically.

$\dfrac{3}{2}x + 2 = -4x$ $y = -4\left(-\dfrac{4}{11}\right) = \dfrac{16}{11}$

$\dfrac{11}{2}x = -2$

$x = -\dfrac{4}{11}$

The solution is $(\underline{-\dfrac{4}{11}}, \underline{\dfrac{16}{11}})$.

PRACTICE

Solve each system of equations algebraically.

1. $\begin{cases} y = \frac{2}{3}x - 5 \\ y = -x + 10 \end{cases}$ **2.** $\begin{cases} 3x + 2y = 9 \\ y = 4x - 1 \end{cases}$ **3.** $\begin{cases} 5x - 2y = 4 \\ 2x - y = 1 \end{cases}$

$(9, 1)$ $(1, 3)$ $(2, 3)$

4. **Error Analysis** Zach solves the system $\begin{cases} x + y = -3 \\ x - y = 1 \end{cases}$ and finds the solution $(1, -2)$.

Use a graph to explain whether Zach's solution is reasonable.

The graph shows that the x-coordinate of the solution is negative, so Zach's solution is not reasonable.

5. **Error Analysis** Angelica solves the system $\begin{cases} 3x - y = 0 \\ \frac{1}{4}x + \frac{3}{4}y = \frac{5}{2} \end{cases}$

and finds the solution $(1, 3)$. Use substitution to explain whether Angelica's solution is correct.

Substituting 1 for x and 3 for y in each equation results in a true statement, so Angelica's solution is correct.

Angelo bought apples and bananas at the fruit stand. He bought 20 pieces of fruit and spent $11.50. Apples cost $0.50 and bananas cost $0.75 each.

6. Write a system of equations to model the problem. (Hint: One equation will represent the number of pieces of fruit. A second equation will represent the money spent on the fruit.)

$\begin{cases} x + y = 20 \\ 0.50x + 0.75y = 11.50 \end{cases}$

7. Solve the system algebraically. Tell how many apples and bananas Angelo bought.

14 apples and 6 bananas

Assign these pages to help your students practice and apply important lesson concepts. For additional exercises, see the Student Edition.

Answers

Additional Practice

1. $(3, 2)$ **2.** $(4, 6)$

3. $(-1, -3)$ **4.** $(4, 8)$

5. no solution   **6.** $(1, 2)$

7. $(-1, 1)$ **8.** $(3, 2)$

9. infinite number   **10.** $(-3, -4)$

11. $x + y = 24; y = x - 6; (15, 9)$

12. $x + y = 18; x + 4 = y; (7, 11)$; Luke biked 7 miles, and Kerry biked 11 miles

Problem Solving

1. $y = 20{,}000 + 2500x$

2. $y = 25{,}000 + 2000x$

3. no   **4.** $(10, 45{,}000)$

5. Job B   **6.** D

7. F   **8.** C

Notes

Name_____ Class_____ Date_____

Additional Practice

Solve each system of equations.

1. $y = 2x - 4$
$y = x - 1$

_____

2. $y = -x + 10$
$y = x + 2$

_____

3. $y = 2x - 1$
$y = -3x - 6$

_____

4. $y = 2x$
$y = 12 - x$

_____

5. $y = 2x - 3$
$y = 2x + 1$

_____

6. $y = 3x - 1$
$y = x + 1$

_____

7. $x + y = 0$
$5x + 2y = -3$

_____

8. $2x - 3y = 0$
$2x + y = 8$

_____

9. $2x + 3y = 6$
$4x + 6y = 12$

_____

10. $6x - y = -14$
$2x - 3y = 6$

_____

11. The sum of two numbers is 24. The second number is 6 less than the first. Write a system of equations and solve it to find the number.

_____

12. Kerry and Luke biked a total of 18 miles in one weekend. Kerry biked 4 miles more than Luke. Write a system of equations and solve it to find how far each boy biked.

_____

© Houghton Mifflin Harcourt Publishing Company

Problem Solving

After college, Julia is offered two different jobs. The table summarizes the pay offered with each job. Write the correct answer.

1. Write an equation that shows the pay y of Job A after x years.

_____

Job	Yearly Salary	Yearly Increase
A	$20,000	$2500
B	$25,000	$2000

2. Write an equation that shows the pay y of Job B after x years.

_____

3. Is (8, 35,000) a solution to the system of equations in Exercises 1 and 2?

_____

4. Solve the system of equations in Exercises 1 and 2.

_____

5. If Julia plans to stay at this job only a few years and pay is the only consideration, which job should she choose?

_____

A travel agency is offering two Orlando trip plans that include hotel accommodations and pairs of tickets to theme parks. Use the table below. Choose the letter for the best answer.

6. Find an equation about trip A where x represents the hotel cost per night and y represents the cost per pair of theme park tickets.

A $5x + 2y = 415$ C $8x + 6y = 415$
B $2x + 3y = 415$ D $3x + 2y = 415$

Trip	Number of nights	Pairs of theme park tickets	Cost
A	3	2	$415
B	5	4	$725

7. Find an equation about trip B where x represents the hotel cost per night and y represents the cost per pair of theme park tickets.

F $5x + 4y = 725$
G $4x + 5y = 725$
H $8x + 6y = 725$
J $3x + 4y = 725$

8. Solve the system of equations to find the nightly hotel cost and the cost for each pair of theme park tickets.

A ($50, $105)
B ($125, $20)
C ($105, $50)
D ($115, $35)

© Houghton Mifflin Harcourt Publishing Company

© Houghton Mifflin Harcourt Publishing Company

© Houghton Mifflin Harcourt Publishing Company

 COMMON CORE Standards for Mathematical Content

CC.8.EE.7a Give examples of linear equations in one variable with one solution, infinitely many solutions, or no solutions. Show which of these possibilities is the case by successively transforming the given equation into simpler forms, until an equivalent equation of the form $x = a$, $a = a$, or $a = b$ results (where a and b are different numbers).

CC.8.EE.7b Solve linear equations with rational number coefficients, including equations whose solutions require expanding expressions using the distributive property and collecting like terms.

CC.8.EE.8b Solve systems of two linear equations in two variables algebraically, and estimate solutions by graphing the equations. Solve simple cases by inspection.

CC.8.EE.8c Solve real-world and mathematical problems leading to two linear equations in two variables.

INTRODUCE

Ask students if they have ever participated in a school fundraiser such as a bake sale or car wash. Have students explain what they did to raise money and ask them to describe any costs that were associated with the fundraiser. Ask the class how to determine the total amount of money that was raised for the school. Be sure students understand that the amount of money raised for the school is the total amount of income or revenue minus the total costs. Tell students they will have a chance to apply these ideas, as well as everything they have learned about solving equations, to solve a multi-part problem about a school fundraiser.

TEACH

1 Order the Shirts

Questioning Strategies
- For each company, which costs do not depend on the number of shirts ordered? **The Shirt Shoppe: setup fee and shipping fee; Tee Town: setup fee**

- What should you do to simplify the expression that represents the total cost of ordering x t-shirts from Tee Town? **combine like terms**

Avoid Common Errors
When students solve the equation $0.8(5.50x + 33.50) = 150$, they may incorrectly apply the Distributive Property to the left side of the equation and write $4.40x + 33.50 = 150$. Remind students that the 0.8 must be distributed to both terms inside the parentheses.

2 Order Gift Bags

Questioning Strategies
- In part A, how are the two expressions you wrote similar? How are they different? **When simplified, both contain the term 1.05b; the constant terms are different.**

- In part B, how do you know that the equation has no solution? **When you use properties of equality to transform the equation you eventually end up with the false statement $0 = 3$. Since no value of x makes this true, the equation has no solution.**

- Which type of bag is less expensive? Why? **Regular paper; for any value of b, the expression $1.05b + 5.00$ is \$3 less than the expression $1.05b + 8.00$**

- How do you find the cost of 30 bags made from regular paper? **Substitute $b = 30$ in the expression $1.05b + 5.00$.**

Technology
Students can use their graphing calculators to explore this situation more deeply. Have them enter $1.05X + 5.00$ as **Y1** and $0.95X + 8.00 + 0.10X$ as **Y2**. Graphing these functions shows that the graphs are parallel lines. Because the graphs do not intersect, the related system of equations has no solution. Student can also view a table of values for the two functions. Scrolling up and down in the table shows that for any number of bags, the cost of bags made from heavy paper is exactly \$3 more than the cost of bags made from regular paper.

Name_____ Class_____ Date_____

CHAPTER 7

Problem Solving Connections

COMMON CORE
CC.8.EE.7a
CC.8.EE.7b
CC.8.EE.8b
CC.8.EE.8c

Shirts for Sale! Emerson Middle School is having its annual spring fair. A group of students have decided to sell t-shirts at the fair to raise money for the school. The students plan to sell tie-dyed shirts and hand-painted shirts. How many of each type of shirt should they make, and how much money will they raise?

1 Order the Shirts

Mikiko is in charge of ordering the t-shirts that will be dyed and painted. She plans to spend $150 on plain white shirts that are printed with the name of the school. She gathers pricing information from two companies that make custom shirts.

Company Name	Price per Shirt	Setup Fee	Shipping Fee
The Shirt Shoppe	$4.25	$16.75	$5.75
Tee Town	$4.75	$25.50	$8 plus $0.75 per shirt

A Write and simplify an expression that represents the total cost of ordering x t-shirts from The Shirt Shoppe.

$4.25x + 16.75 + 5.75 = 4.25x + 22.50$

B Write and solve an equation to find the number of t-shirts Mikiko can order from The Shirt Shoppe.

$4.25x + 22.50 = 150; x = 30$

She can order 30 shirts.

C Write and simplify an expression that represents the total cost of ordering x t-shirts from Tee Town.

$4.75x + 25.50 + 8 + 0.75x = 5.50x + 33.50$

D Mikiko has a coupon for 20% off the total cost of her order at Tee Town. What percent of the total cost does Mikiko pay? How do you write this as a decimal?

80%; 0.8

E Write an expression that represents the final cost of ordering x t-shirts at Tee Town after the discount is taken.

$0.8(5.50x + 33.50)$

© Houghton Mifflin Harcourt Publishing Company

F Write and solve an equation to find the number of t-shirts Mikiko can order from Tee Town. Show the steps in solving the equation.

$$0.8(5.50x + 33.50) = 150$$
$$4.40x + 26.80 = 150$$
$$\underline{-26.80 \quad -26.80}$$
$$4.40x = 123.20$$
$$\frac{4.40x}{4.40} = \frac{123.20}{4.40}$$
$$x = 28$$

G Mikiko wants to get the greatest number of shirts possible. Which company should she choose and how many shirts should she order?

The Shirt Shoppe; 30 shirts

2 Order Gift Bags

The group decides to package the t-shirts in gift bags that are printed with the name of the school. Jamal is in charge of ordering the bags. He gets pricing information from a company that prints custom bags.

Type of Bag	Price per Bag	Shipping Fee
Regular Paper	$1.05	$5
Heavy Paper	$0.95	$8 plus $0.10 per bag

A Write expressions that represent the total cost of ordering b bags made from regular paper and the total cost of ordering b bags made from heavy paper.

Regular paper: $1.05b + 5.00$

Heavy paper: $0.95b + 8.00 + 0.10b$

B Jamal wants to compare the cost of regular paper versus heavy paper. He decides to find out how many bags he would have to order so that the costs are equal. Show how to write and solve an equation to find this number of bags.

$$1.05b + 5.00 = 0.95b + 8.00 + 0.10b$$
$$1.05b + 5.00 = 1.05b + 8.00$$
$$\underline{\quad -5.00 = \quad -5.00}$$
$$1.05b = 1.05b + 3.00$$
$$\underline{-1.05b \quad -1.05b}$$
$$0 = 3.00$$

The equation has no solution.

© Houghton Mifflin Harcourt Publishing Company

3 Determine the Number of Each Type of Shirt

Questioning Strategies

- What expression represents the total number of shirts sold? **$t + h$**

- What expression represents the total income from selling tie-dyed shirts? **$15t$**

- What expression represents the total income from selling hand-painted shirts? **$20h$**

- What expression represents the total income from sales of the shirts? **$15t + 20h$**

- In part C, how can you check your solution? **The total number of shirts is $10 + 20 = 30$ and the total income from sales of the shirts is $10(\$15) + 20(\$20) = \$550$, so the solution is correct.**

> ⊹ **MATHEMATICAL** **Highlighting**
> **PRACTICE** **the Standards**
>
> This project offers several opportunities to make connections to Standard 7 (Look for and make use of structure). The standard describes how mathematically proficient students are able to "see complicated things, such as some algebraic expressions, as single objects or as composed of several objects." For example, students should recognize that the expression $15t + 20h$ is a single entity that represents the amount of money the group makes from sales of t-shirts. As such, the expression, as a whole, must be equal to $550. On the other hand, students should understand that the expression is made up of components that have their own meanings. In particular, the term $15t$ is the total income from tie-dyed shirts and the term $20h$ is the total income from hand-painted shirts.

4 Answer the Question

Questioning Strategies

- What expression represents the total cost of supplies for tie-dyed shirts in 2010? for hand-painted shirts? **$4x$; $2y$**

- What expression represents the total cost of supplies in 2010? **$4x + 2y$**

- Why should you only draw the graphs of the equations in the first quadrant? **The variables represent costs, which must be nonnegative.**

- How do you use the graph to estimate the solution of the system of equations? **Find the approximate coordinates of the point where the two lines intersect.**

Teaching Strategy

If students have difficulty calculating the total amount of money the group will raise, suggest that they organize their work in a table. Students can use positive numbers to represent income and negative numbers to represent costs. In this case, the amount of money the group will raise is simply the sum of the items in the table, as shown below.

Income from t-shirt sales	+$550.00
Cost of t-shirts	−$150.00
Cost of gift bags	−$36.50
Cost of supplies	−$62.50
TOTAL	+$301.00

CLOSE

Journal

Ask students to write a journal entry in which they summarize the main steps of the project. Ask them to include an example of how they solved a multi-step equation, an example of how they solved an equation with no solution, and an example of how they solved a system of equations.

© Houghton Mifflin Harcourt Publishing Company

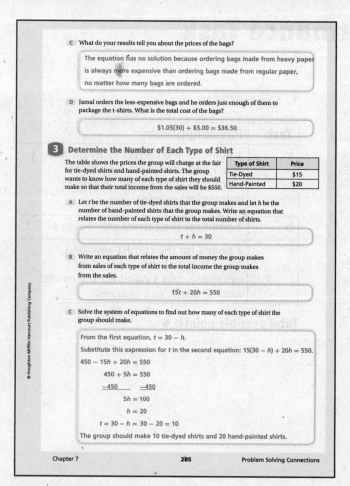

C What do your results tell you about the prices of the bags?

The equation has no solution because ordering bags made from heavy paper is always more expensive than ordering bags made from regular paper, no matter how many bags are ordered.

D Jamal orders the less-expensive bags and he orders just enough of them to package the t-shirts. What is the total cost of the bags?

$1.05(30) + $5.00 = $36.50

3 Determine the Number of Each Type of Shirt

The table shows the prices the group will charge at the fair for tie-dyed shirts and hand-painted shirts. The group wants to know how many of each type of shirt they should make so that their total income from the sales will be $550.

Type of Shirt	Price
Tie-Dyed	$15
Hand-Painted	$20

A Let *t* be the number of tie-dyed shirts that the group makes and let *h* be the number of hand-painted shirts that the group makes. Write an equation that relates the number of each type of shirt to the total number of shirts.

$t + h = 30$

B Write an equation that relates the amount of money the group makes from sales of each type of shirt to the total income the group makes from the sales.

$15t + 20h = 550$

C Solve the system of equations to find out how many of each type of shirt the group should make.

From the first equation, $t = 30 - h$.

Substitute this expression for *t* in the second equation: $15(30 - h) + 20h = 550$.

$450 - 15h + 20h = 550$

$450 + 5h = 550$

$\underline{-450 \qquad -450}$

$5h = 100$

$h = 20$

$t = 30 - h = 30 - 20 = 10$

The group should make 10 tie-dyed shirts and 20 hand-painted shirts.

4 Answer the Question

In previous years, other groups of students sold t-shirts at the fair. Emma looks up information about the cost of supplies, such as dye and paint, in those years so that she can estimate costs for this year. The table shows her findings.

Year	Number of Tie-Dyed Shirts	Number of Hand-Painted Shirts	Total Cost of Supplies
2010	4	2	$10
2011	6	1	$10

A Let *x* represent the cost of supplies for making one tie-dyed shirt and let *y* represent the cost of supplies for making one hand-painted shirt. Use the data in the table to write a system of equations for *x* and *y*.

$4x + 2y = 10$

$6x + y = 10$

B Sketch a graph of each equation in the system by substituting some values of *x* and generating values of *y*. Make the graphs on the coordinate plane at right.

C Use your graph to estimate the solution of the system of equations

Possible answer: $x \approx 1.25$; $y \approx 2.5$

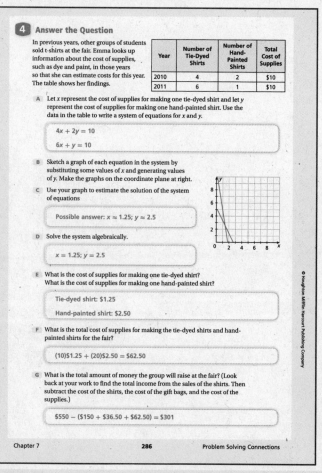

D Solve the system algebraically.

$x = 1.25$; $y = 2.5$

E What is the cost of supplies for making one tie-dyed shirt? What is the cost of supplies for making one hand-painted shirt?

Tie-dyed shirt: $1.25

Hand-painted shirt: $2.50

F What is the total cost of supplies for making the tie-dyed shirts and hand-painted shirts for the fair?

(10)1.25 + (20)$2.50 = 62.50

G What is the total amount of money the group will raise at the fair? (Look back at your work to find the total income from the sales of the shirts. Then subtract the cost of the shirts, the cost of the gift bags, and the cost of the supplies.)

$550 - ($150 + $36.50 + $62.50) = 301

Notes

This page provides students with the opportunity to apply concepts from the Common Core in real-world problem situations. There are three different levels of performance tasks:

⭐Novice: These are short word problems that require students to apply the math they have learned in straightforward, real-world situations.

⭐⭐Apprentice: These are more involved problems that guide students step-by-step through more complex tasks. These exercises include more complicated reasoning, writing, and open-ended elements.

⭐⭐⭐Expert: These are open-ended, non-routine problems that, instead of stepping the students through, asks them to choose their own methods for solving and justify their answers and reasoning.

Sample answers

1. **a.** Pete's Pizza: $13(2) + 1.5x$;
   Mama's House: $15(2) + x$
   b. $13(2) + 1.5x = 15(2) + x; x = 8$;
   the cost for 2 pizzas and 8 sodas is the same at each restaurant.

2. **a.** Let s be the price of one shirt and p be the price of one pair of pants; $4s + 2p = 126$, $3s + p = 81$
   b. $s = 18, p = 27$;
   shirts are $18 and pants are $27.

3. Scoring Guide:

Task	Possible points
a	**1 point** for the correct expression $x + 3$, and **1 point** for explaining that x represents the number of perfect quizzes last quarter.
b	**1 point** for the correct expression $3x$.
c	**2 points** for the correct equation $2(x + 3) = 3x$ (or an equivalent equation), and **1 point** for the correct answer, $x = 6$, or 6 quizzes.

Total possible points: 6

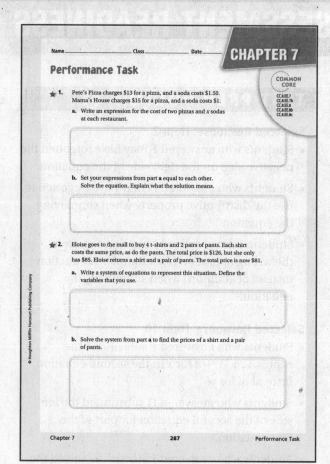

CHAPTER 7

COMMON
CORE
CC.8.EE.7
CC.8.EE.7b
CC.8.EE.8
CC.8.EE.8
CC.8.EE.8b
CC.8.EE.8c

Performance Task

⭐ **1.** Pete's Pizza charges $13 for a pizza, and a soda costs $1.50.
Mama's House charges $15 for a pizza, and a soda costs $1.

    a. Write an expression for the cost of two pizzas and *x* sodas
at each restaurant.

    b. Set your expressions from part **a** equal to each other.
Solve the equation. Explain what the solution means.

⭐ **2.** Eloise goes to the mall to buy 4 t-shirts and 2 pairs of pants. Each shirt
costs the same price, as do the pants. The total price is $126, but she only
has $85. Eloise returns a shirt and a pair of pants. The total price is now $81.

    a. Write a system of equations to represent this situation. Define the
variables that you use.

    b. Solve the system from part **a** to find the prices of a shirt and a pair
of pants.

© Houghton Mifflin Harcourt Publishing Company

⭐⭐ **3.** Hannah got a perfect score on 3 more spelling quizzes this quarter than last quarter.
If she doubles the number of perfect quizzes she had this quarter, she will tie the
school record. The record is 3 times the number of spelling quizzes Hannah scored
perfectly on last quarter.

    a. Write an expression for the number of perfect spelling quizzes Hannah
had this quarter. What does your variable represent?

    b. Write an expression for the record number of perfect spelling quizzes.

    c. Use your expressions from parts a and b to write and solve an equation
to find the number of perfect spelling quizzes Hannah had last quarter.

⭐⭐⭐ **4.** A coin purse has only nickels and quarters in it. The total value of the coins is $1.05.

    a. Millie claims that there are 10 coins in the purse. Write and solve a system
of equations for this situation.

    b. Is Millie's claim correct? Explain how you know.

© Houghton Mifflin Harcourt Publishing Company

© Houghton Mifflin Harcourt Publishing Company

---

4. Scoring Guide:

Task	Possible points
a	**2 points** for the correct answer of $q + n = 10$, $0.25q + 0.05n = 1.05$ (or an equivalent system) and **1 point** for the correct answer of $q = 2.75$, $n = 7.25$
b	**1 point** for the correct answer that Millie is not correct, and **2 points** for explaining that the solutions to the system are not whole numbers, which means that there are no possible numbers of nickels and quarters that add up to 10 and have a value of $1.05, OR an equivalent explanation.

Total possible points: 6

COMMON CORE CORRELATION

Standard	Items
CC.8.EE.7a	3, 4, 8, 9
CC.8.EE.7b	1, 2, 5–6 ,14
CC.8.EE.8a	13
CC.8.EE.8b	10, 12, 13
CC.8.EE.8c	7, 11

TEST PREP DOCTOR ⊕

Selected Response: Item 2

- Students who answered **F** may have forgotten the negative sign on the right side of the equation.
- Students who answered **H** may have forgotten to use the distributive property when simplifying the equation.
- Students who answered **J** may have chosen the wrong operation (for example, subtraction instead of addition) when simplifying the equation.

Selected Response: Item 10

- Students who answered **F** substituted the expression $4x + 3$ for x in the second equation instead of for y.
- Students who answered **H** substituted the left side of the second equation for part of the first equation.
- Students who answered **J** incorrectly solved the second equation for a variable and substituted this incorrect expression into the first equation.

Constructed Response: Item 13

- Students who answered **no** may have substituted or simplified incorrectly when checking the solution.

Name _____ Class _____ Date _____

SELECTED RESPONSE

1. Which value of x makes the equation
   $5(x - 2) - 4 = 6$ true?

   A. 2   C. 4
   B. 3   D. 5

2. Which has the same solution as
   $2(x + 4) = -7 - 3x$?

   F. $5x = 15$
   G. $-5x = 15$
   H. $-x = 11$
   J. $x = 15$

3. How many solutions does the equation
   $2(x - 5) = 2x + 3$ have?

   A. 0   C. 2
   B. 1   D. infinitely many

4. How many solutions does the equation
   $4x + 28 = 4(x + 3) + 16$ have?

   F. 0   H. 2
   G. 1   J. infinitely many

5. Solve.
   $3(9 - 8x - 4x) + 8(3x + 4) = 11$

   A. $x = 3$ C. $x = 24$
   B. $x = 4$ D. $x = 5$

6. Solve $2d - 7 = 8 - 3d$.

   F. $d = -\frac{1}{5}$
   G. $d = \frac{1}{5}$
   H. $d = 3$
   J. $d = -15$

7. A hockey season ticket holder pays $72.48 for her tickets plus $6.00 for a program each game. A second person pays $18.08 for a ticket to every game, but doesn't buy programs. In how many games will they have paid the same amount?

   A. 5   C. 13
   B. 4   D. 6

8. Which of the following equations has infinitely many solutions?

   F. $b + 2 = b + 2$
   G. $b = -b + 2$
   H. $b + 2 = b - 2$
   J. $b + b = 2$

9. Which of the following equations has only one solution?

   A. $c + 2 = c + 2$
   B. $c = -c + 2$
   C. $c + 2 = c - 2$
   D. $c - c = 2$

---

10. Which equation can you use to solve the system of equations shown?

    $$\begin{cases} -4x + y = 3 \\ 11x - 5y = 16 \end{cases}$$

    F. $11(4x + 3) - 5y = 16$
    G. $11x - 5(4x + 3) = 16$
    H. $-4(11x - 5y) = 3$
    J. $-4x + 16 - 11x = 3$

11. Students from Thornebrooke Elementary are going on a field trip to an amusement park. Those who have annual passes will pay $10. Other students will pay $35. The school collected $1,375 for 50 students.

    Which system of linear equations models this situation?

    A. $\begin{cases} 10x + 35y = 50 \\ x + y = 1{,}375 \end{cases}$

    B. $\begin{cases} 10x + 35y = 1{,}375 \\ x + y = 50 \end{cases}$

    C. $\begin{cases} 10x + y = 50 \\ 35x + y = 1{,}375 \end{cases}$

    D. $\begin{cases} 10x + y = 1{,}375 \\ x + 35y = 50 \end{cases}$

12. Which ordered pair is a solution of the system shown?

    $$\begin{cases} -4x + 5y = 14 \\ 7x + 3y = -1 \end{cases}$$

    F. $(1, 2)$
    G. $(1, -2)$
    H. $(-1, 2)$
    J. $(-1, -2)$

CONSTRUCTED RESPONSE

13. Dani solves the system of equations shown graphically and finds that the solution is $(2, 7)$. Explain whether Dani is correct.

    $$\begin{cases} 7x - y = 7 \\ -3x + 2y = 8 \end{cases}$$

    Yes, (2, 7) is where the lines intersect.

    Both are true statements for the

    ordered pair (2, 7).

    _____

    _____

14. Solve the equation $5(x - 2) + 3 = 7x - 9$.

    $5(x - 2) + 3 = 7x - 9$
    $5x - 10 + 3 = 7x - 9$
    $5x - 7 = 7x - 9$
    $-7 = 2x - 9$
    $2 = 2x$
    $1 = x$

CHAPTER 8

Graphing Lines

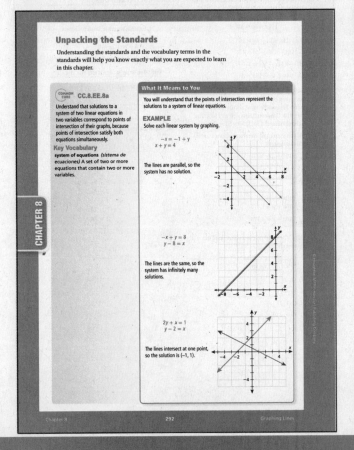

COMMON CORE PROFESIONAL DEVELOPMENT **CC.8.EE.8a**

Students will solve a system of two linear equations graphically. They will recognize the relationship between the lines graphed and the solution to the system.

Two lines intersect   1 solution

Two lines parallel   no solution

Two lines coincide   infinitely many solutions

Building on their understanding that the graph of an equation in two variables represents all ordered pairs that are solutions of the related equation, students will be able to draw the conclusion that the point of intersection of two lines is a solution of both related equations.

Inset page 291 (Chapter at a Glance)

CHAPTER 8

Graphing Lines

Chapter Focus

You will find a rate of change and show that the slope of a line is the same between any two points on the line. You will use slopes and intercepts to write and graph linear equations. The slope-intercept form and point-slope form of an equation will be developed. You will learn to identify a direct variation, and finally, you will solve a system of equations by graphing.

Chapter at a Glance

COMMON CORE

Lesson	Standards for Mathematical Content
8-1 Graphing Linear Equations	CC.8.F.4
8-2 Slope of a Line	CC.8.EE.6
8-3 Using Slopes and Intercepts	CC.8.EE.6, CC.8.F.3, CC.8.F.4
8-4 Point-Slope Form	CC.8.F.4
8-5 Direct Variation	CC.8.EE.5
8-6 Solving Systems of Linear Equations by Graphing	CC.8.EE.8a, CC.8.EE.8c
Problem Solving Connections	
Performance Task	
Assessment Readiness	

Inset page 292 (Unpacking the Standards)

Unpacking the Standards

Understanding the standards and the vocabulary terms in the standards will help you know exactly what you are expected to learn in this chapter.

COMMON CORE **CC.8.EE.8a**

Understand that solutions to a system of two linear equations in two variables correspond to points of intersection of their graphs, because points of intersection satisfy both equations simultaneously.

Key Vocabulary

system of equations (sistema de ecuaciones) A set of two or more equations that contain two or more variables.

What It Means to You

You will understand that the points of intersection represent the solutions to a system of linear equations.

EXAMPLE

Solve each linear system by graphing.

$$-x = -1 + y$$
$$x + y = 4$$

The lines are parallel, so the system has no solution.

$$-x + y = 8$$
$$y - 8 = x$$

The lines are the same, so the system has infinitely many solutions.

$$2y + x = 1$$
$$y - 2 = x$$

The lines intersect at one point, so the solution is (–1, 1).

CC.8.F.4

Construct a function to model a linear relationship between two quantities. Determine the rate of change and initial value of the function from a description of a relationship or from two (x, y) values, including reading these from a table or from a graph. Interpret the rate of change and initial value of a linear function in terms of its situation it models, and in terms of its graph or a table of values.

Key Vocabulary
linear function (*función lineal*) A function whose graph is a straight line.

What It Means to You

You will learn to identify the slope of a line and the y-intercept.

EXAMPLE
The cash register deducts $2.50 from a $25 Java Café gift card for every medium coffee the customer buys. The linear equation $y = -2.50x + 25$ represents the number of dollars y on the card after x medium coffees have been purchased. Explain the meaning of the slope and the y-intercept.

The slope represents the rate of change, −$2.50 per medium coffee.

The y-intercept represents the initial amount on the card, $25.

CC.8.EE.5

Graph proportional relationships, interpreting the unit rate as the slope of the graph. Compare two different proportional relationships represented in different ways.

Key Vocabulary
unit rate (*tasa unitaria*) A rate in which the second quantity in the comparison is one unit.
slope (*pendiente*) A measure of the steepness of a line on a graph; the rise divided by the run.

What It Means to You

You will recognize constant rates and apply your understanding of rates to analyzing real-world situations.

EXAMPLE
The table shows the volume of water released by Hoover Dam over a certain period of time. Use the data to make a graph. Find the slope of the line and explain what it shows.

Water Released from Hoover Dam	
Time (s)	Volume of Water (m³)
5	75,000
10	150,000
15	225,000
20	300,000

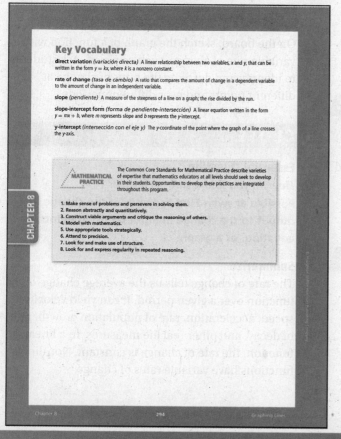

Water Released from Hoover Dam

The slope of the line is 15,000. This means that for every second that passed, 15,000 m³ of water was released from Hoover Dam.

Key Vocabulary

direct variation (*variación directa*) A linear relationship between two variables, x and y, that can be written in the form $y = kx$, where k is a nonzero constant.

rate of change (*tasa de cambio*) A ratio that compares the amount of change in a dependent variable to the amount of change in an independent variable.

slope (*pendiente*) A measure of the steepness of a line on a graph; the rise divided by the run.

slope-intercept form (*forma de pendiente-intersección*) A linear equation written in the form $y = mx + b$, where m represents slope and b represents the y-intercept.

y-intercept (*intersección con el eje y*) The y-coordinate of the point where the graph of a line crosses the y-axis.

MATHEMATICAL PRACTICE
The Common Core Standards for Mathematical Practice describe varieties of expertise that mathematics educators at all levels should seek to develop in their students. Opportunities to develop these practices are integrated throughout this program.

1. Make sense of problems and persevere in solving them.
2. Reason abstractly and quantitatively.
3. Construct viable arguments and critique the reasoning of others.
4. Model with mathematics.
5. Use appropriate tools strategically.
6. Attend to precision.
7. Look for and make use of structure.
8. Look for and express regularity in repeated reasoning.

COMMON CORE PROFESIONAL DEVELOPMENT **CC.8.F.4**

Students will identify the initial value (*y*-intercept) and the rate of change (slope) from tables, graphs, equations, or verbal descriptions.

From a table, students recognize that the y-intercept is the y-value when x is equal to 0. They can determine the slope by finding the ratio $\frac{y}{x}$ between the change in two y-values and the change between the two corresponding x-values.

From a graph, students will identify the y-intercept as the point where the line intersects the y-axis and the slope as $\frac{rise}{run}$.

From a linear equation, students will recognize the coefficient of x as the slope and the constant as the y-intercept. Linear equations need to be stated in forms other than the slope intercept form $y = mx + b$, such as $y = b + mx$ which is often the format from contextual situations. In Grade 8, point-slope form and standard forms are not expectations.

CHAPTER 8

....
COMMON **Standards for**
 CORE **Mathematical Content**
....

CC.8.F.4 Construct a function to model a linear relationship between two quantities. Determine the rate of change and initial value of the function from a description of a relationship or from two (x, y) values, including reading these from a table or from a graph. Interpret the rate of change and initial value of a linear function in terms of the situation it models, and in terms of its graph or a table of values.

Vocabulary
rate of change

Prerequisites
Ordered pairs
Graphing on a coordinate plane

Math Background
Velocity, acceleration, growth, speed, and decay are all rates of change, but not all constant rates of change. A linear relationship expresses a *constant* rate of change. A proportional relationship expresses a constant rate of change in which an input of 0 results in the output 0. Proportional relationships are a special type of linear relationship.

INTRODUCE

Be sure students realize that the word *variable* is used in two different ways in this lesson. In the terms *input variable* and *output variable*, the word *variable* refers to a letter or symbol that is used to represent a value. When referring to the rate of change, the word *variable* means "changing."

TEACH

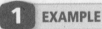
1 EXAMPLE

Questioning Strategies
• How can you tell which row in the table represents the input value? **Possible answer: The amount Eve earns will change based on the number of lawns she mows. The quantity of payment depends on the quantity of work.**

• Compare the table in the example with the table in Try This. How are the rates of change different? **Possible answer: The example table represents a constant rate of change, or a linear relationship. The table in Try This does not represent a constant rate of change.**

Avoid Common Errors
In the table in Try This, students may see that the input of 0 results in an output of 0 and quickly assume that it is a proportional relationship. Remind students a linear relationship must have a constant rate of change.

2 EXPLORE

Questioning Strategies
• How can you use rate of change to explain to someone how to move from point (2, 8) to point (3, 6)? **Tell them the number of units to move vertically and then the number of units to move horizontally. In this case, move 2 units down from 8 to 6 and one unit right from 2 to 3.**

REFLECT

On the board, sketch the graph of a function with a variable rate of change, such as $y = x^2$. Ask students to identify and describe the rates of change at different points and over different periods.

CLOSE

Essential Question
How do you find a rate of change?
Possible answer: Find the ratio of the change in output to the change in input by using points, an equation, or a graph.

Summarize
The rate of change tells us the average change of the function over a given period. It can yield velocity, speed, acceleration, rate of population growth, rate of decay, and other real life measures. In a linear function, the rate of change is constant. Non-linear functions have variable rates of change.

Name_____ Class_____ Date_____

8-1

Graphing Linear Equations
Reasoning: Rates of Change

Essential question: *How do you find a rate of change?*

A **rate of change** is a ratio of the amount of change in the output to the amount of change in the input.

1 EXAMPLE Investigating Rates of Change
CC.8.F.4

Eve keeps a record of the number of lawns she mows and the money she earns.

	Day 1	Day 2	Day 3	Day 4	Day 5
Number of Lawns	1	3	6	8	13
Amount Earned ($)	15	45	90	120	195

Input variable: number of lawns   Output variable: amount earned

Find the rates of change:

Day 1 to Day 2 $\frac{\text{change in \$}}{\text{change in lawns}} = \frac{45-15}{3-1} = \frac{30}{2} = 15$

Day 2 to Day 3 $\frac{\text{change in \$}}{\text{change in lawns}} = \frac{90-45}{6-3} = \frac{45}{3} = 15$

Day 3 to Day 4 $\frac{\text{change in \$}}{\text{change in lawns}} = \frac{120-90}{8-6} = \frac{30}{2} = 15$

Day 4 to Day 5 $\frac{\text{change in \$}}{\text{change in lawns}} = \frac{195-120}{13-8} = \frac{75}{5} = 15$

The rates of change are (constant)/ variable.

TRY THIS!

1. The table shows the approximate height of a football after it is kicked.

Time (s)	0	0.5	1.5	2
Height (ft)	0	18	31	26

Input variable: time   Output variable: height

Find the rates of change:

$\frac{18-0}{0.5-0} = 36;\ \frac{31-18}{1.5-0.5} = 13;\ \frac{26-31}{2-1.5} = -10$

The rates of change are constant /(variable).

© Houghton Mifflin Harcourt Publishing Company

Chapter 8   295   Lesson 1

You can also use a graph to find rates of change.

2 EXPLORE Using Graphs to Find Rates of Change
CC.8.F.4

The graph shows the distance Nathan bicycled over time. What is Nathan's rate of change?

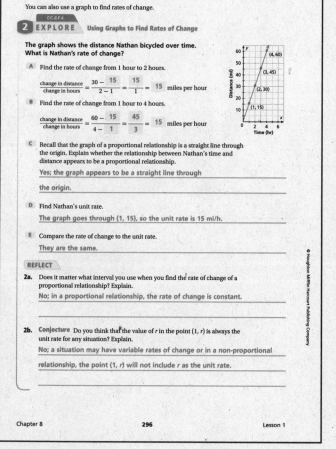

A Find the rate of change from 1 hour to 2 hours.

$\frac{\text{change in distance}}{\text{change in hours}} = \frac{30-15}{2-1} = \frac{15}{1} = 15$ miles per hour

B Find the rate of change from 1 hour to 4 hours.

$\frac{\text{change in distance}}{\text{change in hours}} = \frac{60-15}{4-1} = \frac{45}{3} = 15$ miles per hour

C Recall that the graph of a proportional relationship is a straight line through the origin. Explain whether the relationship between Nathan's time and distance appears to be a proportional relationship.

Yes; the graph appears to be a straight line through

the origin.

D Find Nathan's unit rate.

The graph goes through (1, 15), so the unit rate is 15 mi/h.

E Compare the rate of change to the unit rate.

They are the same.

REFLECT

2a. Does it matter what interval you use when you find the rate of change of a proportional relationship? Explain.

No; in a proportional relationship, the rate of change is constant.

2b. **Conjecture** Do you think that the value of *r* in the point (1, *r*) is always the unit rate for any situation? Explain.

No; a situation may have variable rates of change or in a non-proportional

relationship, the point (1, *r*) will not include *r* as the unit rate.

© Houghton Mifflin Harcourt Publishing Company

Chapter 8   296   Lesson 1

Assign these pages to help your students practice and apply important lesson concepts. For additional exercises, see the Student Edition.

Answers

Additional Practice

1. variable

2. constant

3. 0.06

4. No; the graph does not go through the origin.

5. $ 0.06 of commission per $1 in sales, or $60 of commission per $1000 in sales

Problem Solving

1. 50 miles per hour

2. Yes; the graph appears to be a straight line through the origin.

3. C   4. F

5. B   6. J

8-1

Name_____ Class_____ Date_____

Additional Practice

Determine whether the rates of change are constant or variable.

1.

x	0	1	2	4	5
y	3	4	5	6	7

_____

2.

x	2	4	6	8	12
y	7	9	11	13	17

_____

The graph shows the commission a real estate agent earns based on his total sales.

3. What is the rate of change of the real estate agent's commission?

_____

4. Explain whether the relationship between sales and commissions is proportional.

_____

_____

5. Find the unit rate of the real estate agent's commission.

_____

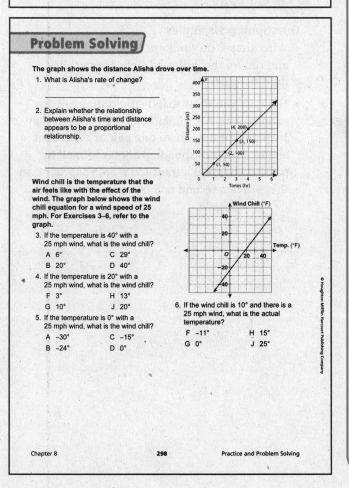

© Houghton Mifflin Harcourt Publishing Company

Chapter 8   297   Practice and Problem Solving

Problem Solving

The graph shows the distance Alisha drove over time.

1. What is Alisha's rate of change?

_____

2. Explain whether the relationship between Alisha's time and distance appears to be a proportional relationship.

Wind chill is the temperature that the air feels like with the effect of the wind. The graph below shows the wind chill equation for a wind speed of 25 mph. For Exercises 3–6, refer to the graph.

3. If the temperature is 40° with a 25 mph wind, what is the wind chill?

   A 6°   C 29°

   B 20°   D 40°

4. If the temperature is 20° with a 25 mph wind, what is the wind chill?

   F 3°   H 13°

   G 10°   J 20°

5. If the temperature is 0° with a 25 mph wind, what is the wind chill?

   A −30°   C −15°

   B −24°   D 0°

6. If the wind chill is 10° and there is a 25 mph wind, what is the actual temperature?

   F −11°   H 15°

   G 0°   J 25°

© Houghton Mifflin Harcourt Publishing Company

Chapter 8   298   Practice and Problem Solving

© Houghton Mifflin Harcourt Publishing Company

Slope of a Line
Reasoning

Essential question: *How can you show that the slope of a line is the same between any two points on the line?*

Standards for Mathematical Content

CC.8.EE.6 Use similar triangles to explain why the slope m is the same between any two distinct points on a non-vertical line in the coordinate plane; derive the equation $y = mx$ for a line through the origin and the equation $y = mx + b$ for a line intercepting the vertical axis at b.

Vocabulary
slope

Math Background
Slope is a ratio of vertical change (change in y-values) to horizontal change (change in x-values). Equivalent slope ratios indicate a constant rate of change, and a constant rate of change indicates a linear relationship. Equivalent ratios and constant rates both relate to lines in the coordinate plane. Using any two pairs of points on a line in the coordinate plane, you can form a similar right triangle by connecting the horizontal and vertical segments that connect the two points. The legs of these right triangles represent the change in y and the change in x that make the constant slope ratio.

INTRODUCE

Review with students how to graph equivalent ratios and how to use the slope formula (rise over run) to find the slope of a line in a coordinate plane. Tell students that in this lesson, they will apply what they have learned about parallel lines and transversals and similar triangles to the slope of a line.

TEACH

1 EXPLORE

Questioning Strategies
- How do you use two points to calculate the slope of the line? **Find the difference in their y-values divided by the difference in their corresponding x-values.**
- What do you find when you calculated the slope using different points? **The slope is the same value for all pairs of points.**

Avoid Common Errors
Students should be careful to use the slope formula properly. Remind students to subtract the y-values and the x-values in the same order, and to watch negative signs carefully when subtracting integers.

2 EXPLORE

Questioning Strategies
- What shapes do you form by drawing the rise and run for the indicated slopes in part B? **right triangles**
- How can you show that the right triangles are similar using AA Similarity? **They are both right triangles, so they share one pair of congruent angles. The corresponding angles formed by parallel lines and a transversal are congruent, so they share a second pair of congruent angles.**

Name _____ Class _____ Date _____

8-2

video tutor

Slope of a Line
Reasoning

Essential question: *How can you show that the slope of a line is the same between any two points on the line?*

CC.8.EE.6

1 EXPLORE Investigating Slope

The graph shows the linear function $y = -\frac{2}{3}x + 4$.

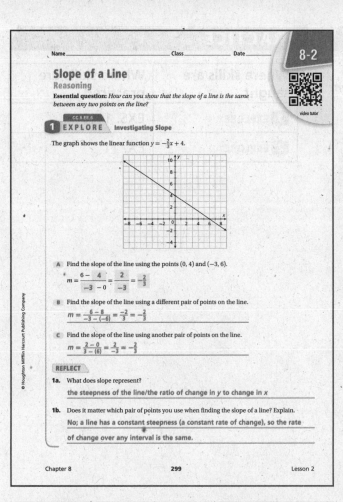

A Find the slope of the line using the points $(0, 4)$ and $(-3, 6)$.

$$m = \frac{6 - 4}{-3 - 0} = \frac{2}{-3} = -\frac{2}{3}$$

B Find the slope of the line using a different pair of points on the line.

$$m = \frac{6 - 8}{-3 - (-6)} = \frac{-2}{3} = -\frac{2}{3}$$

C Find the slope of the line using another pair of points on the line.

$$m = \frac{2 - 0}{3 - (6)} = \frac{2}{-3} = -\frac{2}{3}$$

REFLECT

1a. What does slope represent?

the steepness of the line/the ratio of change in *y* to change in *x*

1b. Does it matter which pair of points you use when finding the slope of a line? Explain.

No; a line has a constant steepness (a constant rate of change), so the rate

of change over any interval is the same.

The **slope** of a line is the ratio of the change in
y-values (rise) for a segment of the graph to the
corresponding change in *x*-values (run).

2 EXPLORE Using Similar Triangles to Explain Slope

Use similar triangles to show that the slope of a line is constant.
Use this space to make your drawing:

A Draw line ℓ that is not a horizontal line. Label four points on the line as
A, B, C, and *D*.

You need to show that the slope between points *A* and *B* is the same as the
slope between points *C* and *D*.

B Draw the rise and run for the slope between points *A* and *B*. Label the
intersection as point *E*. Draw the rise and run for the slope between
points *C* and *D*. Label the intersection as point *F*.

C Write expressions for the slope between *A* and *B* and between *C* and *D*.

Slope between *A* and *B*: $\dfrac{BE}{AE}$

Slope between *C* and *D*: $\dfrac{DF}{CF}$

D Extend $\overleftrightarrow{AE}$ and $\overleftrightarrow{CF}$ across your drawing. $\overleftrightarrow{AE}$ and $\overleftrightarrow{CF}$ are both horizontal
lines, so they are parallel. Line ℓ is a transversal that intersects parallel lines.

E Complete the following statements:

$\angle BAE$ and $\underline{\angle DCF}$ are corresponding angles and are $\underline{\text{congruent}}$

$\angle BEA$ and $\underline{\angle DFC}$ are right angles and are $\underline{\text{congruent}}$

Essential Question

How can you show that the slope of a line is the same between any two points on the line?

You can calculate the slope of a line for different pairs of points and see that the slope is the same for each pair of points. To show that the slope of a line is constant between *any* two points, you need to use the properties of similar triangles to show that the ratios of the change in *y* over the change in *x* are always equal.

Where skills are taught	Where skills are practiced
1 EXPLORE	EXS. 1–10
2 EXPLORE	EX. 11

F By Angle-Angle Similarity, △ABE and △CDF are similar triangles.

G Use the fact that the lengths of corresponding sides of similar triangles are proportional to complete the following ratios: $\frac{BE}{DF} = \frac{AE}{CF}$.

H Recall that you can also write the proportion so that the ratios compare parts of the same triangle: $\frac{BE}{AE} = \frac{DF}{CF}$.

I The proportion you wrote in step **H** shows that the ratios you wrote in **C** are equal. So, the slope of the line is constant.

PRACTICE

The graph shows how gas in the fuel tank in Ed's car changes in relation to how far he drives. Use the graph for Questions 1–6.

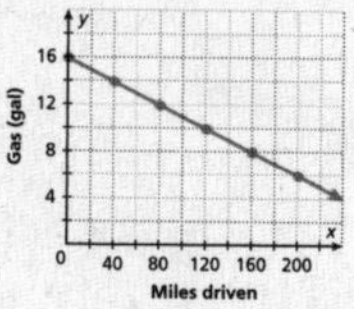

1. Is the slope of the line positive or negative? How do you know?

   negative; it falls from left to right

2. To find the slope of the line, you would choose the coordinates of two points along it, and then divide the change in the __y__ values by the change in the __x__ values. Another way to describe the process is to divide the __rise__ by the __run__.

3. Will the choice of points affect the slope you find for the line? Explain.

   No; the steepness of a line is constant, so you can use any two points along the line to calculate slope.

4. What is the slope of the line? __$\frac{1}{20}$__

5. So, the amount of gas decreases by 1 gallon for every __20__ miles driven.

6. If the slope of the line were 0 or positive, would it make sense as a way of describing this real-world situation? Why?

   No; the amount of gas in a fuel tank decreases as a car is driven.

© Houghton Mifflin Harcourt Publishing Company

Solve.

7. Which roof is steeper: one with a rise of 8 and a run of 4, or one with a rise of 12 and a run of 7? Explain.

   Rise of 8, run of 4 because the slope, 8 ÷ 4, or 2, is greater than 12 ÷ 7, or $1\frac{5}{7}$.

8. How would you describe a line that has a slope of 0? A line that has *no* slope?

   slope of 0: horizontal line; no slope: vertical line

9. Which hill is steeper: one with a rise of 5 and a run of 4, or one with a rise of 4 and a run of 5? Explain.

   Rise of 5, run of 4 because the slope, 1.25, is greater than 0.8.

10. Error Analysis A student says that the slope of a line that passes through the points (1, 3) and (7, 5) is 3. What error did the student make? What is the correct slope?

   The student divided the change in x-values by the change in y-values.

   The correct slope is $\frac{1}{3}$.

11. Right triangle ABC has coordinates A(0, 4), B(6, 10), and C(6, 4). Similar right triangle ADE has coordinates A(0, 4), D(3, 7), and E(3, 4). What can you say about the slopes of the hypotenuses of the two triangles?

   They are both 1.

© Houghton Mifflin Harcourt Publishing Company

© Houghton Mifflin Harcourt Publishing Company

Assign these pages to help your students practice and apply important lesson concepts. For additional exercises, see the Student Edition.

Answers

Additional Practice

1. 2

2. $-\dfrac{2}{3}$

3. 4

4. 2

5. 0

6. -2

7. $-\dfrac{4}{3}$

8. 2

9. undefined

10. $-\dfrac{5}{7}$

11. The slope is $\dfrac{3}{4}$, which means that for every 4 minutes Ms. Long drives, she travels 3 miles.

She is driving 45 mph.

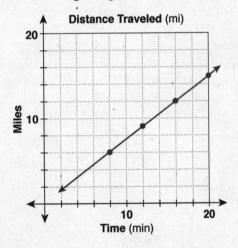

Problem Solving

1. about -0.0015

2. $\dfrac{19.4}{32.5}$

3. 7%

4. $\dfrac{1}{4}$

5. C

6. F

7. A

8. H

Name_____ Class_____ Date_____ 8-2

Additional Practice

Find the slope of each line.

1.

2.

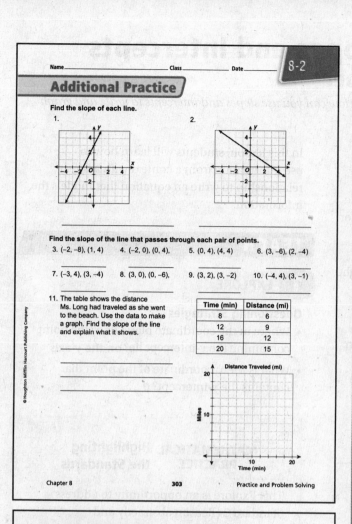

_____   _____

Find the slope of the line that passes through each pair of points.

3. (-2, -8), (1, 4)   4. (-2, 0), (0, 4),   5. (0, 4), (4, 4)   6. (3, -6), (2, -4)

_____   _____   _____   _____

7. (-3, 4), (3, -4)   8. (3, 0), (0, -6),   9. (3, 2), (3, -2)   10. (-4, 4), (3, -1)

_____   _____   _____   _____

11. The table shows the distance Ms. Long had traveled as she went to the beach. Use the data to make a graph. Find the slope of the line and explain what it shows.

Time (min)	Distance (mi)
8	6
12	9
16	12
20	15

_____

_____

_____

Distance Traveled (mi)

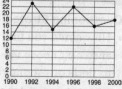

Miles

Time (min)

Chapter 8   303   Practice and Problem Solving

Problem Solving

Write the correct answer.

1. The state of Kansas has a fairly steady slope from the east to the west. At the eastern side, the elevation is 771 ft. At the western edge, 413 miles across the state, the elevation is 4039 ft. What is the approximate slope of Kansas?

2. The Feathered Serpent Pyramid in Teotihuacan, Mexico, has a square base. From the center of the base to the center of an edge of the pyramid is 32.5 m. The pyramid is 19.4 m high. What is the slope of each triangular face of the pyramid?

3. On a highway, a 6% grade means a slope of 0.06. If a highway covers a horizontal distance of 0.5 miles and the elevation change is 184.8 feet, what is the grade of the road? (Hint: 5280 feet = 1 mile.)

4. The roof of a house rises vertically 3 feet for every 12 feet of horizontal distance. What is the slope, or pitch of the roof?

Use the graph for Exercises 5–8.

5. Find the slope of the line between 1990 and 1992.

A $\frac{2}{11}$ C $\frac{11}{2}$

B $\frac{35}{3982}$ D $\frac{11}{1992}$

6. Find the slope of the line between 1994 and 1996.

F $\frac{7}{2}$ H $\frac{2}{7}$

G $\frac{37}{3990}$ J $\frac{7}{1996}$

7. Find the slope of the line between 1998 and 2000.

A 1   C $\frac{1}{1000}$

B $\frac{1}{999}$ D 2

Number of Earthquakes Worldwide with a Magnitude of 7.0 or Greater

8. What does it mean when the slope is negative?

F The number of earthquakes stayed the same.

G The number of earthquakes increased.

H The number of earthquakes decreased.

J It means nothing.

Chapter 8   304   Practice and Problem Solving

Using Slopes and Intercepts
Going Deeper

Essential question: *How can you use slopes and intercepts to write and graph linear equations?*

COMMON CORE **Standards for Mathematical Content**

CC.8.EE.6 ... derive the equation $y = mx$ for a line through the origin and the equation $y = mx + b$ for a line intercepting the vertical axis at b.

CC.8.F.3 Interpret the equation $y = mx + b$ as defining a linear function, whose graph is a straight line

CC.8.F.4 Construct a function to model a linear relationship between two quantities. Determine the rate of change and initial value of the function from a description of a relationship or from two (x, y) values, including reading these from a table or from a graph. Interpret the rate of change and initial value of a linear function in terms of the situation it models, and in terms of its graph or a table of values.

Vocabulary

y-intercept

slope-intercept form

Prerequisites

Slope formula

Linear functions

Math Background

The slope-intercept form of a linear equation provides all the information needed to define a unique line at-a-glance. There are other forms of linear equations that students will learn, too, but the slope-intercept form is the most commonly used form for graphing. The slope and *y*-intercept define a unique line. In other words, there is exactly one line for any given slope and *y*-intercept.

INTRODUCE

Suppose you plan a road trip. You know that during most of the trip you will be traveling a constant rate of 60 miles per hour. When will you reach your destination? How long will your trip take? How far away is your destination at the beginning of the trip? You can use the graph of a linear equation to answer all these questions.

In this lesson, students will learn how to use information from a context with a linear relationship to write an equation that models the information.

TEACH

1 EXPLORE

Questioning Strategies

- Where in the coordinate plane does the point containing the *y*-intercept lie? **on the *y*-axis**

- What is the *x*-coordinate of the point that contains the *y*-intercept? **0**

> **MATHEMATICAL PRACTICE** **Highlighting the Standards**
>
> This Explore is an opportunity to address Standard 2 (Reason abstractly and quantitatively). Students reason abstractly when they solve equations with only variables for one of the variables. Students use the slope formula to write the relationship between the *y*-intercept and another point. By using properties of equality students transform the slope between the *y*-intercept and another point into an equation in slope-intercept form. This reasoning and justification develops students' abstract reasoning abilities.

2 EXAMPLE

Questioning Strategies

- How could you find other points to plot? **Possible answer: Choose values of *x* and use the equation to find corresponding values for *y*.**

- Why is it helpful to graph three points when only two points are needed to define a line? **By plotting a third point, you can confirm the line defined by the first two points.**

© Houghton Mifflin Harcourt Publishing Company

Name_____ Class_____ Date_____

8-3

Using Slopes and Intercepts
Going Deeper

Essential question: *How can you use slopes and intercepts to write and graph linear equations?*

The graph of every non-vertical line crosses the y-axis. The **y-intercept** is the y-coordinate of the point where the graph intersects the y-axis. The x-coordinate of this point is always 0.

To write the equation of a line or to graph a line, you just need to know its slope and y-intercept.

CC.8.EE.6

1 EXPLORE   Deriving the Slope-Intercept Formula

A Let L be a line with slope m and y-intercept b. Circle the point that must be on the line. Justify your choice.

$(b, 0)$ $(0, b)$ $(0, m)$ $(m, 0)$

The value of x is 0 at the point that includes the y-intercept.

Let (x, y) be a point on line L other than the point containing the y-intercept.

B Write an expression for the change in y values between the point that includes the y-intercept and the point (x, y). $y - b$

C Write an expression for the change in x values between the point that includes the y-intercept and the point (x, y). $x - 0$

D Recall that slope is the ratio of change in y to change in x. Complete the equation for the slope m of the line. $m = \dfrac{y - b}{x - 0}$

E In an equation of a line, we often want y by itself on one side of the equation. Solve the equation from **D** for y.

$m = \dfrac{y - b}{x}$ *Simplify the denominator.*

$m \cdot x = \dfrac{y - b}{x} \cdot x$ *Multiply both sides of the equation by* x

$m\,x = y - b$

$mx + b = y - b + b$ *Add* b *to both sides of the equation.*

$mx + b = y$

$y = mx + b$ *Write the equation with y on the left side.*

REFLECT

1. Write the equation of a line with slope m that passes through the origin.

The y-intercept is 0, so the equation is $y = mx$.

Chapter 8   305   Lesson 3

The equation $y = mx + b$ is called the **slope-intercept form** of the equation of a line. In this form, it is easy to see the slope and the y-intercept. When the equation of a line is in slope-intercept form, you can quickly graph the line.

CC.8.F.3

2 EXAMPLE   Using Slope-Intercept Form to Graph a Line

Graph $y = -2x + 5$.

Step 1 Identify the slope and the y-intercept.

slope: $m = -2 = \dfrac{-2}{1}$

y-intercept: $b = 5$

Step 2 The point that contains the y-intercept is $(0, 5)$. Plot this point.

Step 3 Use the slope to find a second point on the line. Count down 2 unit(s) and right 1 unit(s). Plot this point.

Step 4 Draw a line connecting the two points.

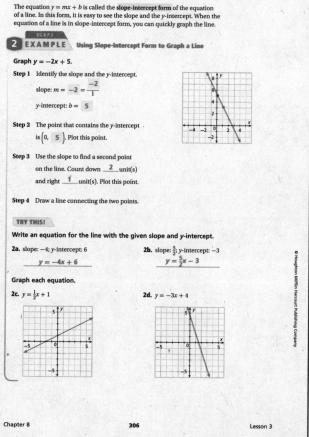

TRY THIS!

Write an equation for the line with the given slope and y-intercept.

2a. slope: -4; y-intercept: 6

$y = -4x + 6$

2b. slope: $\frac{5}{2}$; y-intercept: -3

$y = \frac{5}{2}x - 3$

Graph each equation.

2c. $y = \frac{1}{2}x + 1$

2d. $y = -3x + 4$

Chapter 8   306   Lesson 3

3 EXPLORE

Questioning Strategies

- How can you tell that the rate of change is constant in the table? **The input and output values are both increasing at regular intervals.**

- What strategy can you use to find the *y*-intercept? **Substitute the slope and one point from the table into the linear equation $y = mx + b$, and solve for *b*.**

- Which number represents the base price regardless of minutes used? **the *y*-intercept**

- Which number represents the cost per minute? **the slope**

4 EXPLORE

Questioning Strategies

- How can you use the graph to determine the slope of the line? **Find two points on the line, and find the slope.**

- What does a negative slope indicate in this situation? **As Katie drives longer, the distance to the beach decreases.**

Differentiated Instruction

With students working together in groups, give each group a graph to analyze and write a linear function to represent. Have each group present their graph and results to the rest of the class, explaining how they found the information to write the function.

© Houghton Mifflin Harcourt Publishing Company

3 EXPLORE CC.8.F.4 · Writing an Equation for a Function from a Table

Elizabeth can choose from several monthly cell phone plans. The cost of each plan is a linear function of the number of minutes that are included in the plan. Write an equation in slope-intercept form that represents the function.

Minutes Included, x	100	200	300	400	500
Cost of Plan ($), y	18	28	38	48	58

A Choose any two ordered pairs from the table to find the slope.

$m = \dfrac{y_2 - y_1}{x_2 - x_1} = \dfrac{28 - 18}{200 - 100} = \dfrac{10}{100} = 0.10$ Sample calculations shown.

B Use the equation $y = mx + b$ and any point from the table. Substitute values for y, m, and x into the equation and solve for b.

$y = mx + b$

$18 = 0.10 \cdot 100 + b$ *Substitute for y, m, and x.*

$18 = 10 + b$ *Simplify on the right side.*

$-10 \quad -10$ *Subtract the number that is added to b from both sides.*

$8 = b$

C Use the slope and y-intercept values to write an equation in slope-intercept form.

$y = 0.10\,x + 8$

REFLECT

3a. Use the equation to predict the cost of a cell phone plan that includes 175 minutes.

$y = 0.10(175) + 8 = 25.5$; $25.50

3b. What is the base price for any cell phone plan, regardless of how many minutes are included?

$8; There is an $8 fee included in each plan's cost.

TRY THIS!

3c. **What If?** Elizabeth's cell phone company changed the prices for each of their plans. Write an equation in slope-intercept form that represents the function.

Minutes Included, x	100	200	300	400	500
Cost of Plan ($), y	30	35	40	45	50

$y = 0.05x + 25$

Chapter 8   307   Lesson 3

---

4 EXPLORE CC.8.F.4 · Writing an Equation for a Function from a Graph

Kate is planning a trip to the beach. She used an estimated average speed to make a graph showing the progress she expects to make on her trip. Write an equation in slope-intercept form that represents the function.

A Choose two points on the graph to find the slope. Sample calculations shown.

$m = \dfrac{y_2 - y_1}{x_2 - x_1} = \dfrac{0 - 300}{5 - 0} = \dfrac{-300}{5} = -60$

B Read the y-intercept from the graph.

$b = 300$

C Use your slope and y-intercept values to write an equation in slope-intercept form.

$y = -60x + 300$

REFLECT

4a. What does the value of the slope represent in this context?

Kate expects to travel at an average speed of 60 mi/h.

4b. Is the slope positive or negative? What does the sign of the slope mean in this context?

Negative; Slope is negative because Kate is decreasing her distance to the beach.

4c. Describe the meaning of the y-intercept.

When time is 0 hours, Kate is 300 miles from the beach. This means Kate starts her trip 300 miles away from her destination.

TRY THIS!

The graph shows the distance Norma skateboarded over a period of time.

4d. Write an equation in slope-intercept form that represents the function.

$y = 12x$

4e. Describe the meaning of the y-intercept.

When time is 0 hours, Norma has skateboarded 0 kilometers.

Chapter 8   308   Lesson 3

Questioning Strategies

- How can you find the slope of this function when you don't have a rule or a graph? **Write the information as two ordered pairs (temperature, chirps): (59, 76) and (65, 100).**

- Does it matter which point you use to solve for *b*? **No, either point will give the same answer.**

Teaching Strategies

Ask students to suggest situations that could be modeled with a linear function. Use their descriptions to create mathematical models. Prepare a couple of examples to get things started.

> ⚹ **MATHEMATICAL PRACTICE** **Highlighting the Standards**
>
> This Explore provides an opportunity to address Standard 7 (Look for and make use of structure). Students are asked to identify a linear relationship in tables, graphs, and real-world situations, and write a function to model the linear relationship. The structure of a linear function is the same regardless of how it is presented. Students learn to translate the information they are given into the information that is needed in order to write the linear function model.

CLOSE

Essential Question

How can you use slopes and intercepts to write and graph linear equations?

Possible answer: Find the slope, or rate of change, and the *y*-intercept. When working with a description, you must use key words to identify the rate. You can identify the *y*-intercept by looking for initial values or base rates. Use the slope-intercept formula to write the equation of the linear function.

Summarize

Information is presented to us in a variety of ways. A mathematical model is a tool that helps us analyze the information. We should be able to model information with an equation whether the information is presented in the form of a table, a graph, or a description.

PRACTICE

Where skills are taught	Where skills are practiced
3 EXPLORE	EXS. 1–4
4 EXPLORE	EXS. 5–7
5 EXPLORE	EXS. 8–9

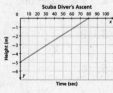

Notes

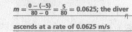

5 EXPLORE Writing an Equation for a Function from a Description

The rate at which crickets chirp is a linear function of temperature. At 59 °F, they chirp 76 times per minute, and at 65 °F, they chirp 100 times per minute. Write an equation in slope-intercept form that represents the function.

A Identify the input and output variables in this relationship.

Input variable: ___temperature___   Output variable: ___chirps per minute___

B Write the information given in the problem as ordered pairs.

At 59 °F, crickets chirp 76 times per minute: $\left(\underline{59}, \underline{76} \right)$

At 65 °F, crickets chirp 100 times per minute: $\left(\underline{65}, \underline{100} \right)$

C Find the slope.

$$m = \frac{y_2 - y_1}{x_2 - x_1} = \frac{100 - 76}{65 - 59} = \frac{24}{6} = 4$$

D Use the equation $y = mx + b$ and one of the ordered pairs.
Substitute values for y, m, and x into the equation and solve for b.

$y = mx + b$

$100 = \underline{4} \cdot \underline{65} + b$ Substitute for y, m, and x.

$100 = \underline{260} + b$ Simplify on the right side.

$\underline{-260} \quad \underline{-260}$ Subtract the number that is added
                                                to b from both sides.

$-160 = \qquad b$

E Write an equation in slope-intercept form.

$y = 4x - 160$

REFLECT

5a. Predict the number of chirps per minute when the temperature is 72 °F.

$y = 4(72) - 160 = 128$

5b. Without graphing, tell whether the graph of this function rises or falls from left to right. What does the sign of the slope mean in this context?

Slope is positive, so the graph rises from left to right. This means that crickets

chirp at faster rates as the temperature increases.

Chapter 8   309   Lesson 3

PRACTICE

The table shows the temperature at different altitudes. The temperature is a linear function of the altitude.

Altitude (ft), x	0	2,000	4,000	6,000	8,000	10,000	12,000
Temperature (°F), y	59	51	43	35	27	19	11

1. Find the slope of the function.

$m = \frac{51 - 59}{2,000 - 0} = \frac{-8}{2,000} = -0.004$

2. Find the y-intercept of the function.

$b = 59$

3. Write an equation in slope-intercept form that represents the function.

$y = -0.004x + 59$

4. Use your equation to determine the temperature at an altitude of 5,000 feet.

$y = -0.004(5000) + 59 = 39$ °F

The graph shows a scuba diver's ascent over time.

5. Use the graph to find the slope of the line. Tell what the slope means in this context.

$m = \frac{0 - (-5)}{80 - 0} = \frac{5}{80} = 0.0625$; the diver

ascends at a rate of 0.0625 m/s

Scuba Diver's Ascent

(graph with Height (m) on y-axis from −6 to 0, Time (sec) on x-axis from 0 to 100)

6. Identify the y-intercept. Tell what the y-intercept means in this context.

−5; the diver starts 5 meters below the water's surface.

7. Write an equation in slope-intercept form that represents the function.

$y = 0.0625x - 5$

The formula for converting Celsius temperatures to Fahrenheit temperatures is a linear function. Water freezes at 0 °C, or 32 °F, and it boils at 100 °C, or 212 °F.

8. Find the slope and y-intercept. Then write an equation in slope-intercept form that represents the function.

$m = \frac{212 - 32}{100 - 0} = \frac{180}{100} = \frac{9}{5}$, $b = 32$; $y = \frac{9}{5}x + 32$ where $y = $ °F and $x = $ °C

9. Average human body temperature is 37 °C. What is this temperature in degrees Fahrenheit?

$y = \frac{9}{5}x + 32 = \frac{9}{5}(37) + 32 = 98.6$; 98.6 °F

Chapter 8   310   Lesson 3

© Houghton Mifflin Harcourt Publishing Company

Assign these pages to help your students practice and apply important lesson concepts. For additional exercises, see the Student Edition.

Answers

Additional Practice

1.

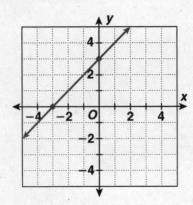

x-intercept is -3;

y-intercept is 3

2.

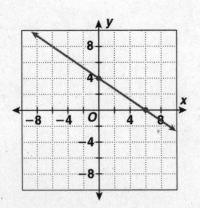

x-intercept is 6;

y-intercept is 4

3. $y = -3x$; $m = -3$; $b = 0$

4. $y = 2x + 15$; $m = 2$; $b = 15$

5. $y = \frac{1}{5}x - 2$; $m = \frac{1}{5}$; $b = -2$

6. $y = 2x - 2$ 7. $y = -3x - 4$

8. $y = \frac{5}{3}x - 5$

9. The y-intercept represents the cost of a pizza with no toppings. The slope represents the rate of change ($2 per topping).

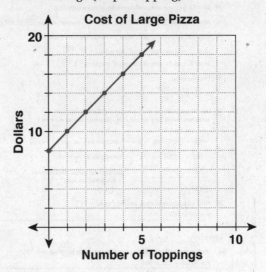

Problem Solving

1. x-intercept $= 16$, y-intercept $= 20$, slope $= -1.25$

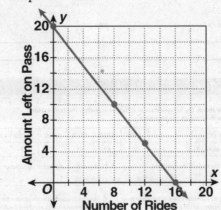

2. $y = \frac{4}{3}x - 50$

3. B   4. F

5. C   6. G

Name_____ Class_____ Date_____ 8-3

Additional Practice

Find the x-intercept and y-intercept of each line.
Use the intercepts to graph the equation.

1. $x - y = -3$

2. $2x + 3y = 12$

_____ _____

Write each equation in slope-intercept form, and then find the slope and y-intercept.

3. $3x + y = 0$

4. $2x - y = -15$

5. $x - 5y = 10$

_____ _____ _____

Write the equation of the line that passes through each pair of points in slope-intercept form.

6. (3, 4), (4, 6)

7. (−1, −1), (2, −10)

8. (6, 5), (−9, −20)

_____ _____ _____

9. A pizzeria charges $8 for a large cheese pizza, plus $2 for each topping. The total cost for a large pizza is given by the equation $C = 2t + 8$, where t is the number of toppings. Graph the equation for t between 0 and 5 toppings, and explain the meaning of the slope and y-intercept.

Cost of Large Pizza

_____

_____

Problem Solving

Write the correct answer.

1. Jaime purchased a $20 bus pass. Each time she rides the bus, $1.25 is deducted from the pass. The linear equation $y = -1.25x + 20$ represents the amount of money on the bus pass after x rides. Identify the slope and the x- and y-intercepts. Graph the equation at the right.

_____

2. The rent charged for space in an office building is related to the size of the space rented. The rent for 600 square feet of floor space is $750, while the rent for 900 square feet is $1150. Write an equation for the rent y based on the square footage of the floor space x.

Choose the letter of the correct answer.

3. A limousine charges $35 plus $2 per mile. Which equation shows the total cost of a ride in the limousine?

A $y = 35x + 2$
B $y = 2x + 35$
C $y = 2x - 35$
D $2x + 35y = 2$

4. A newspaper delivery person earns $75 each day plus $0.10 per paper delivered. Which equation shows the daily earnings of a delivery person?

F $y = 0.1x + 75$
G $y = 75x + 0.1$
H $x + 0.1y = 75$
J $0.1x + y = 75$

5. A friend gave Ms. Morris a $50 gift card for a local car wash. If each car wash costs $6, which equation shows the number of dollars left on the card?

A $50x + 6y = 1$
B $y = 6x + 50$
C $y = -6x + 50$
D $y = 6x - 50$

6. Antonio's weekly allowance is given by the equation $A = 0.5c + 10$, where c is the number of chores he does. If he received $16 in allowance one week, how many chores did he do?

F 10
G 12
H 14
J 15

© Houghton Mifflin Harcourt Publishing Company

Point-Slope Form
Going Deeper

Essential question: *How can you develop the point-slope form of an equation of a line?*

Standards for Mathematical Content

CC.8.F.4 Construct a function to model a linear relationship between two quantities. Determine the rate of change and initial value of the function from a description of a relationship or from two (x, y) values, including reading these from a table or from a graph. Interpret the rate of change and initial value of a linear function in terms of the situation it models, and in terms of its graph or a table of values.

Prerequisites
Slope

Math Background
The definition of slope can be used to derive the *point-slope form* of a linear equation. Note that this derivation assumes that the line is a nonvertical line, because division by zero (if $x - x_1 = 0$) is not allowed.

INTRODUCE

Inform students that they will learn a new way to find the equation of a line given its slope and a point on the line. Consider using an alternate presentation by using numbers instead of variables for the point and slope. You can graph the line and even transform the equation into the slope-intercept form to show how both forms describe the same line.

TEACH

 **EXPLORE**

Questioning Strategies
• What does the slope of a line refer to? **Rise over run or the change in *y*-values divided by the change in *x*-values**

• Can you quickly identify the slope of a line from the point-slope form? **Yes, because the slope *m* is outside of the parentheses on the side with the *x* variable.**

Error Prevention
Watch for students who confuse the signs in the point-slope form. Some students benefit from using the form: $y + (-y_1) = m[x + (-x_1)]$.

> **MATHEMATICAL PRACTICE** **Highlighting the Standards**
>
> This Explore is an opportunity to address Standard 7 (Look for and make use of structure). Students transform the slope equation into the point-slope form of a linear equation. By the end of this lesson, students will have learned three distinct forms for a linear equation and will recognize that each form can describe the same relationship between two variables.

CLOSE

Essential Question
How can you develop the point-slope form of an equation of a line?
Possible answer: Transform the equation for the slope of a line so that $y - y_1$ is isolated on one side of the equation.

Summarize
Have students create the table shown by filling in the right column with each of the forms of a linear equation that they have learned.

Linear Equations	
Standard Form	$Ax + By = C$
Slope-Intercept Form	$y = mx + b$
Point-Slope Form	$y - y_1 = m(x - x_1)$

PRACTICE

Where skills are taught	Where skills are practiced
1 EXPLORE	EXS. 1–13

Name_____ Class_____ Date_____

8-4

Point-Slope Form
Going Deeper

Essential question: *How can you develop the point-slope form of an equation of a line?*

CC.8.F.4

1 EXPLORE Developing the Point-Slope Form

A Let L be a line with slope m that passes through the points (x, y) and (x_1, y_1).

Recall that slope is the ratio of change in y to change in x. Complete the equation for the slope m of the line.

$$\frac{y - y_1}{x - x_1} = m \qquad \text{Use the formula for slope.}$$

$$(x - x_1)\left(\frac{y - y_1}{x - x_1}\right) = m(x - x_1) \qquad \text{Multiply both sides by } \underline{x - x_1}.$$

$$y - y_1 = m\left(\underline{x - x_1}\right) \qquad \text{Point-slope form of an equation}$$

B What is the point-slope form of the equation of a line with $m = 5$ that passes through $(4, 2)$?

If you know the slope of a line and a point on the line, you can use substitution to write the point-slope form of the equation for that line.

$$y - y_1 = m(x - x_1) \qquad \text{Write the point-slope form.}$$

$$y - \underline{2} = \underline{5}\,(x - \underline{4}) \qquad \text{Substitute } \underline{2} \text{ for } y_1, \ \underline{5} \text{ for m, and } \underline{4} \text{ for } x_1.$$

The point-slope form of a line with $m = 5$ that passes through $(4, 2)$ is $\underline{y - 2 = 5(x - 4)}$.

REFLECT

1. How would you contrast the point-slope form of the equation for a line with the slope-intercept form of the equation for a line?

Sample answer: The point-slope form includes the slope of a line and the coordinates of a point along the line. The slope-intercept form includes the slope of a line and the point at which the line crosses the y-axis.

© Houghton Mifflin Harcourt Publishing Company

Chapter 8   313   Lesson 4

PRACTICE

Write the point-slope form of the equation of a line with the given slope that passes through the indicated point.

1. the line with slope 5 passing through $(4, -2)$
$$y + 2 = 5(x - 4)$$

2. the line with slope 3 passing through $(2, -3)$
$$y + 3 = 3(x - 2)$$

3. the line with slope 2.5 passing through $(1, -3)$
$$y + 3 = 2.5(x - 1)$$

4. the line with slope -2 passing through $(-3, -5)$
$$y + 5 = -2(x + 3)$$

5. the line with slope -1 passing through $(6, 4)$
$$y - 4 = -1(x - 6)$$

6. the line with slope 3.5 passing through $(2, 2)$
$$y - 2 = 3.5(x - 2)$$

Use the point-slope form of each equation to identify a point the line passes through and the slope of the line.

7. $y + 2.5 = 2(x - 3.5)$
$$(3.5, -2.5), 2$$

8. $y - 4 = 2.2(x + 3.1)$
$$(-3.1, 4), 2.2$$

9. $y - 1 = -4(x + 4)$
$$(-4, 1), -4$$

10. $y + 1.8 = 0.7(x - 2.4)$
$$(2.4, -1.8), 0.7$$

Solve.

11. A stretch of highway has a 4% uphill grade. This means that the road rises 1 foot for every 25 feet of horizontal distance. The beginning of the highway $(x = 0)$ has an elevation of 2,225 feet. Write an equation for this stretch of roadway in point-slope form.
$$y - 2225 = 0.04x$$

12. What is the highway's elevation a mile from its beginning? Explain how to find that elevation.

2,436.2 ft; divide 5,280, the number of feet in a mile, by 25. Then add that quotient to the beginning elevation, 2,225 ft.

13. Write the point-slope form of an equation with $m = 2$ that passes through the point $(2, 5)$. Then graph the equation on the coordinate plane.

$$y - 5 = 2(x - 2)$$

© Houghton Mifflin Harcourt Publishing Company

Chapter 8   314   Lesson 4

Assign these pages to help your students practice and apply important lesson concepts. For additional exercises, see the Student Edition.

Answers

Additional Practice

1. $m = 4; (x_1, y_1) = (1, 2)$

2. $m = 2; (x_1, y_1) = (3, -1)$

3. $m = -3; (x_1, y_1) = (-1, 4)$

4. $m = -2; (x_1, y_1) = (-6, -5)$

5. $m = -9; (x_1, y_1) = (-3, -4)$

6. $m = -7; (x_1, y_1) = (7, 7)$

7. $m = 6; (x_1, y_1) = (8, 10)$

8. $m = 2.5; (x_1, y_1) = (-4, -12)$

9. $m = \frac{1}{2}; (x_1, y_1) = (3, -8)$

10. $y - 5 = -1(x - 2)$

11. $y - 4 = 2(x + 1)$

12. $y + 2 = 4(x + 3)$

13. $y + 6 = 3(x - 7)$

14. $y - 4 = -3(x + 6)$

15. $y - 1 = -2(x - 5)$

16. $y - 84 = 60(x - 1)$; highway marker for 114 miles

Problem Solving

1. $y - 102{,}000 = 43.41(x - 1600)$

2. $y = 43.41x + 32{,}544$

3. $y - 29 = 1.337(x - 40)$

4. $-24.48\ ^\circ F$

5. C **6.** G

7. D **8.** G

Name _____ Class _____ Date _____

Additional Practice

Use the point-slope form of each equation to identify a point the line passes through and the slope of the line.

1. $y - 2 = 4(x - 1)$

2. $y + 1 = 2(x - 3)$

3. $y - 4 = -3(x + 1)$

_____

4. $y + 5 = -2(x + 6)$

5. $y + 4 = -9(x + 3)$

6. $y - 7 = -7(x - 7)$

_____

7. $y - 10 = 6(x - 8)$

8. $y + 12 = 2.5(x + 4)$

9. $y + 8 = \frac{1}{2}(x - 3)$

_____

Write the point-slope form of the equation with the given slope that passes through the indicated point.

10. the line with slope –1 passing through (2, 5)

11. the line with slope 2 passing through (–1, 4)

12. the line with slope 4 passing through (–3, –2)

13. the line with slope 3 passing through (7, –6)

14. the line with slope –3 passing through (–6, 4)

15. the line with slope –2 passing through (5, 1)

16. Michael was driving at a constant speed of 60 mph when he crossed the Sandy River. After 1 hour, he passed a highway marker for mile 84. Write an equation in point-slope form, and find which highway marker he will pass 90 minutes after crossing the Sandy River.

_____

Problem Solving

Write the correct answer.

1. A 1600 square foot home in City A will sell for about $102,000. The price increases about $43.41 per square foot. Write an equation that describes the price y of a house in City A, based on the square footage x.

2. Write the equation in Exercise 1 in slope-intercept form.

3. Wind chill is a measure of what temperature feels like with the wind. With a 25 mph wind, 40 °F will feel like 29 °F. Write an equation in point-slope form that describes the wind chill y based on the temperature x, if the slope of the line is 1.337.

4. With a 25 mph wind, what does a temperature of 0 °F feel like?

From 2 to 13 years, the growth rate for children is generally linear. Choose the letter of the correct answer.

5. The average height of a 2-year old boy is 36 inches, and the average growth rate per year is 2.2 inches. Write an equation in point-slope form that describes the height of a boy y based on his age x.

   A $y - 36 = 2(x - 2.2)$

   B $y - 2 = 2.2(x - 36)$

   C $y - 36 = 2.2(x - 2)$

   D $y - 2.2 = 2(x - 36)$

6. The average height of a 5-year old girl is 44 inches, and the average growth rate per year is 2.4 inches. Write an equation in point-slope form that describes the height of a girl y based on her age x.

   F $y - 2.4 = 44(x - 5)$

   G $y - 44 = 2.4(x - 5)$

   H $y - 44 = 5(x - 2.4)$

   J $y - 5 = 2.4(x - 44)$

7. Write the equation from Exercise 6 in slope-intercept form.

   A $y = 2.4x - 100.6$

   B $y = 44x - 217.6$

   C $y = 5x + 32$

   D $y = 2.4x + 32$

8. Use the equation in Exercise 6 to find the average height of a 13-year old girl.

   F 56.3 in.

   G 63.2 in.

   H 69.4 in.

   J 97 in.

Direct Variation
Going Deeper

Essential question: *How can you identify a direct variation?*

© Houghton Mifflin Harcourt Publishing Company

COMMON CORE Standards for Mathematical Content

CC.8.EE.5 Graph proportional relationships, interpreting the unit rate as the slope of the graph. Compare two different proportional relationships represented in different ways.

Vocabulary
direct variation

Prerequisites
Linear functions

Math Background
Two variables vary *directly* with each other when one variable is directly proportional to another. This relationship can be expressed in a number of ways: the equation $y = kx$, the graph of a straight line with slope of k that passess through the origin, and a table where the ratios of y to x are the constant k, called the *constant of variation*.

INTRODUCE

Review linear functions and how they can be represented by function rules, graphs, and tables. Tell students that they will learn about a special kind of linear function in which two variables vary *directly*, meaning as one variables doubles, so does the other variable.

TEACH

1 EXAMPLE

Questioning Strategies
- What is the difference in the equations in part A and part B? **In part A, $C = 0$ or the y-intercept is 0. In part B, $C = 2$ or the y-intercept is 2.**
- What is the same and what is different in the graphs in part A and part B? **Both are lines that have a slope of 3; the y-intercept for part A is 0 while the y-intercept for part B is 2.**

Error Prevention
Some students may be confused that they are not calculating the *change* in a pair of y-values divided by the *change* in a pair of x-values, and are instead finding $\frac{y}{x}$. Point out that the ratio they are finding comes from $y = kx \rightarrow \frac{y}{x} = k$.

> **MATHEMATICAL PRACTICE** Highlighting the Standards
>
> This Example is an opportunity to address Standard 4 (Model with mathematics). Students compare two linear relationships side-by-side to see how a direct variation relationship is similar to and different from other linear relationships. Students transform equations into $y =$ format, make a table of data and compare the ratio $\frac{y}{x}$, and graph the data.

CLOSE

Essential Question
How can you identify a direct variation?
Possible answer: As a table, the ratios of y-values to x-values is a constant k; as a graph, the relationship is a line through the origin with slope k; and as an equation, the relationship can be written as $y = kx$.

Summarize
Have students create the table shown below by filling in how to identify a direct variation relationship from a table, a graph, and an equation (or function rule).

Direct Variation	
Table	Ratios of y to x are constant k
Graph	Line through origin with slope k
Equation	$y = kx$

PRACTICE

Where skills are taught	Where skills are practiced
1 EXAMPLE	EXS. 1–8

Name_____ Class_____ Date_____

8-5

Direct Variation
Going Deeper

Essential question: How can you identify a direct variation?

A *direct variation* is a linear function that has an equation of the form $y = kx$, in which k is a fixed nonzero constant called the *constant of variation*.

CC.8.EE.5

1 EXAMPLE Identifying Direct Variations

Does each equation represent a direct variation between x and y?

A $-3x + y = 0$

Write the equation in $y = kx$ form, if possible.

$$\begin{aligned} -3x + y &= 0 \\ \underline{+3x \quad\quad +3x} \\ y &= 3x \end{aligned}$$

Make a table of values. Then find the ratios of y to x.

x	−1	1	2	3
y	−3	3	6	9

$$\frac{-3}{-1} = \frac{3}{1} = \frac{6}{2} = \frac{9}{3} = 3$$

Graph the equation.

Can $-3x + y = 0$ be written as $y = kx$? __yes__

Do the ratios of y to x form a constant? __yes__

Is the graph a straight line passing through the origin? __yes__

Does $-3x + y = 0$ represent a direct variation between x and y? __yes__

The constant of variation is __3__.

B $-3x + y = 2$

Write the equation in $y = kx$ form, if possible.

$$\begin{aligned} -3x + y &= 2 \\ \underline{+3x \quad\quad +3x} \\ y &= 3x + 2 \end{aligned}$$

Make a table of values. Then find the ratios of y to x.

x	−1	1	2	3
y	−1	5	8	11

$$\frac{-1}{-1} \neq \frac{5}{1} \neq \frac{8}{2} \neq \frac{11}{3}$$

Graph the equation.

Can $-3x + y = 2$ be written as $y = kx$? __no__

Do the ratios of y to x form a constant? __no__

Is the graph a straight line passing through the origin? __no__

Does $-3x + y = 2$ represent a direct variation between x and y? __no__

© Houghton Mifflin Harcourt Publishing Company

REFLECT

1a. Does the equation $2.5x - y = 0$ represent a direct variation between x and y? If so, what is the constant of variation? What is the slope of the line?

yes; 2.5; 2.5

1b. Is the equation for finding the perimeter of a square P given the length of a side s an example of direct variation? Explain.

Yes, $P = 4s$. The perimeter of a square is always found by multiplying the length of a side by 4; 4 is the constant of variation.

PRACTICE

Tell whether the function represented by each table is or is not a direct variation. Explain your reasoning.

1.

x	1	2	3	4
y	−3	−6	−9	−12

Yes; the equation shows a direction variation between x and y: $y = -3x$

2.

x	1	2	3	4
y	4	5	6	7

No; the equation $y = x + 3$ does not show a direction variation between x and y.

Use the graph for 3–5.

3. Does the graph represent a direct variation between x and y? __yes__

4. Write an equation for the graph. __$y = 5x$__

5. What is the value of y when $x = 6$? __30__

6. The circumference of a circle varies directly with the length of its diameter. How would you describe the relationship between circumference C and diameter d? What equation can you write to show this relationship?

Possible answer: a direct variation; $C = \pi d$ or $C \approx 3.14d$

7. Explain how the constant of variation k affects the appearance of the graph of an equation that is a direct variation.

Possible answer: As k increases, the slope of the graph increases.

8. **Error Analysis** A classmate claims that the score you'll get on a test varies directly with the amount of time you spend studying. What do you think?

Possible answer: Although studying can help increase scores, the score and amount of time you study are not necessarily proportionally related.

© Houghton Mifflin Harcourt Publishing Company

© Houghton Mifflin Harcourt Publishing Company

Assign these pages to help your students practice and apply important lesson concepts. For additional exercises, see the Student Edition.

Answers

Additional Practice

1.

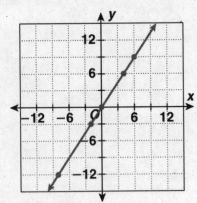

The data sets show direct variation.

2. $y = 1.5x$ or $y = \dfrac{3}{2}x$

3. $y = 8x$ 4. $y = \dfrac{1}{2}x$

5. $y = -9x$ 6. $y = \dfrac{4}{5}x$

7. $y = 3.5x$ 8. $y = \dfrac{1}{3}x$

9. There is direct variation between the lengths and widths of the flags. $y = 1.9x$, where y is the length, x is the width, and 1.9 is the constant of proportionality

Problem Solving

1. No direct variation

2. Direct variation; $R = 3.14t$

3. Direct variation; $L = \left(\dfrac{1}{50}\right)H$

4. No direct variation

5. A   6. H

7. B

Additional Practice

Name _____ Class _____ Date _____

Determine whether the data sets show direct variation.

1.

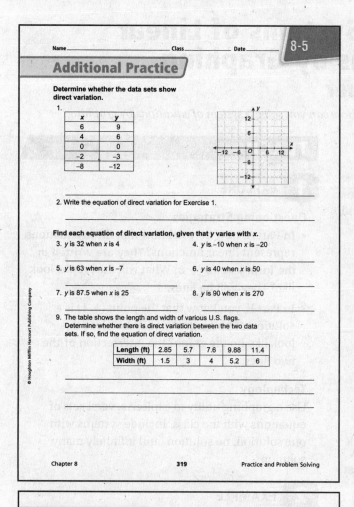

x	y
6	9
4	6
0	0
–2	–3
–8	–12

2. Write the equation of direct variation for Exercise 1.

_____

Find each equation of direct variation, given that y varies with x.

3. y is 32 when x is 4

4. y is –10 when x is –20

5. y is 63 when x is –7

6. y is 40 when x is 50

7. y is 87.5 when x is 25

8. y is 90 when x is 270

9. The table shows the length and width of various U.S. flags. Determine whether there is direct variation between the two data sets. If so, find the equation of direct variation.

Length (ft)	2.85	5.7	7.6	9.88	11.4
Width (ft)	1.5	3	4	5.2	6

Problem Solving

Determine whether the data sets show direct variation. If so, find the equation of direct variation.

1. The table shows the distance in feet traveled by a falling object in certain times.

Time (s)	0	0.5	1	1.5	2	2.5	3
Distance (ft)	0	4	16	36	64	100	144

2. The R-value of insulation gives the material's resistance to heat flow. The table shows the R-value for different thicknesses of fiberglass insulation.

Thickness (in.)	1	2	3	4	5	6
R-value	3.14	6.28	9.42	12.56	157	18.84

3. The table shows the lifting power of hot air.

Hot Air (ft³)	50	100	500	1000	2000	3000
Lift (lb)	1	2	10	20	40	60

4. The table shows the relationship between degrees Celsius and degrees Fahrenheit.

° Celsius	–10	–5	0	5	10	20	30
° Fahrenheit	14	23	32	41	50	68	86

Your weight on Earth varies directly with your weights on other planetary bodies. The table below shows how much a person who weighs 100 lb on Earth would weigh on the moon and different planets.

5. Find the equation of direct variation for the weight on earth e and on the moon m.

A m = 0.166e   C m = 6.02e

B m = 16.6e   D m = 1660e

Planetary Bodies	Weight (lb)
Moon	16.6
Jupiter	236.4
Pluto	6.7

6. How much would a 150 lb person weigh on Jupiter?

F 63.5 lb   H 354.6 lb

G 286.4 lb   J 483.7 lb

7. How much would a 150 lb person weigh on Pluto?

A 5.8 lb   C 12.3 lb

B 10.05 lb   D 2238.8 lb

Solving Systems of Linear Equations by Graphing
Going Deeper

Essential question: *How can you solve a system of equations by graphing?*

Standards for Mathematical Content

CC.8.EE.8a Understand that solutions to a system of two linear equations in two variables correspond to points of intersection of their graphs, because points of intersection satisfy both equations simultaneously.

CC.8.EE.8c Solve real-world and mathematical problems leading to two linear equations in two variables.

Prerequisites

Solving equations

Graphing in the coordinate plane

Math Background

The graph of a function is a picture of all the ordered pairs that are solutions of the equation. A system of linear equations is a set of equations that have the same variables. Graphing the solutions of the equations results in a set of lines in the coordinate plane. If the lines intersect at a single point, then that point represents the one ordered pair that satisfies each equation. This point is a solution of the system. If the graphs coincide, then every point on the line is a solution of the system. Systems with no solution will have no point of intersection.

INTRODUCE

Real-life situations can be affected by limits, or constraints. Give students the following example: You have $20 to buy snacks for 10 people. Sweet snacks and salty snacks have different prices. Tell students that they will need to use more than one equation to model situations like this. In this lesson, students will learn how to graph systems of equations to solve problems.

TEACH

1 EXPLORE

Questioning Strategies

- In Part A, how do you know that these equations represent linear functions? They are written in the form $y = mx + b$. What will the graphs look like? They will be lines.

- In Part E, you know that the point (1, 1) is a solution of both equations. What does this look like on the graph? the intersection of the two lines

Technology

Use a graphing utility to explore several sets of equations with the class. Include systems with one solution, no solution, and infinitely many solutions.

2 EXAMPLE

Questioning Strategies

- In Part A, how can you tell that the system has one solution by looking at the equations? One equation has positive slope, and one has negative slope. Since the slopes are different, the equations cannot represent the same line or parallel lines.

- In Part B, how can you tell that the system has no solutions by looking at the equations? The equations have the same slope but different y-intercepts. They are parallel lines, but not the same line.

- Why is it helpful to analyze the equations in a system before you begin graphing? You can anticipate the solution. It is helpful to analyze equations to recognize algebraic mistakes.

Name_____ Class_____ Date_____

8-6

Solving Systems of Linear Equations by Graphing
Going Deeper

Essential question: *How can you solve a system of equations by graphing?*

CC.8.EE.8a

1 EXPLORE · Investigating Systems of Equations

A   Graph the system of linear functions: $\begin{cases} y = 3x - 2 \\ y = -2x + 3 \end{cases}$

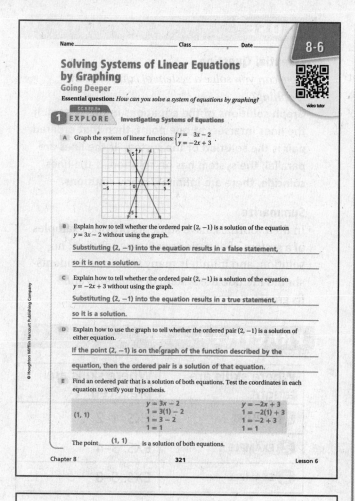

B   Explain how to tell whether the ordered pair $(2, -1)$ is a solution of the equation $y = 3x - 2$ without using the graph.

Substituting $(2, -1)$ into the equation results in a false statement,

so it is not a solution.

C   Explain how to tell whether the ordered pair $(2, -1)$ is a solution of the equation $y = -2x + 3$ without using the graph.

Substituting $(2, -1)$ into the equation results in a true statement,

so it is a solution.

D   Explain how to use the graph to tell whether the ordered pair $(2, -1)$ is a solution of either equation.

If the point $(2, -1)$ is on the graph of the function described by the

equation, then the ordered pair is a solution of that equation.

E   Find an ordered pair that is a solution of both equations. Test the coordinates in each equation to verify your hypothesis.

$(1, 1)$	$y = 3x - 2$ $1 = 3(1) - 2$ $1 = 3 - 2$ $1 = 1$	$y = -2x + 3$ $1 = -2(1) + 3$ $1 = -2 + 3$ $1 = 1$

The point ___$(1, 1)$___ is a solution of both equations.

Chapter 8   **321**   Lesson 6

© Houghton Mifflin Harcourt Publishing Company

An ordered pair (x, y) is a solution of an equation in two variables if substituting the x- and y-values into the equation results in a true statement. Recall that *a system of equations* is a set of equations that have the same variables. An ordered pair is a solution of a system if it is a solution of every equation in the system.

Since the graph of a function represents all ordered pairs that are solutions of the related equation, if a point lies on the graphs of two functions, the point is a solution of both related equations.

CC.8.EE.8a

2 EXAMPLE · Solving Systems Graphically

Solve each system by graphing.

A $\begin{cases} y = -x + 4 \\ y = 3x \end{cases}$

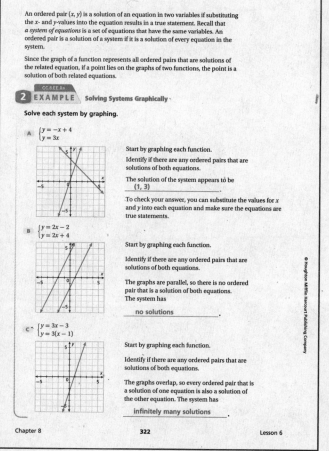

Start by graphing each function.

Identify if there are any ordered pairs that are solutions of both equations.

The solution of the system appears to be
  $(1, 3)$

To check your answer, you can substitute the values for x and y into each equation and make sure the equations are true statements.

B $\begin{cases} y = 2x - 2 \\ y = 2x + 4 \end{cases}$

Start by graphing each function.

Identify if there are any ordered pairs that are solutions of both equations.

The graphs are parallel, so there is no ordered pair that is a solution of both equations. The system has

  no solutions

C $\begin{cases} y = 3x - 3 \\ y = 3(x - 1) \end{cases}$

Start by graphing each function.

Identify if there are any ordered pairs that are solutions of both equations.

The graphs overlap, so every ordered pair that is a solution of one equation is also a solution of the other equation. The system has

  infinitely many solutions

Chapter 8   **322**   Lesson 6

© Houghton Mifflin Harcourt Publishing Company

Questioning Strategies

- How do you decide what the variables represent? The variables represent the information you are looking for: how many hot dogs and how many drinks.

- In Part B, why do you rewrite the equations? Slope-intercept form makes it easy to sketch a graph of the solutions.

- How can you use the graph in Part C to tell how many solutions the system has? The lines intersect at one point, so there is one solution.

- In Part D, why is it important to check your solution by substituting the solution into each original equation? You might have made a mistake when sketching the graphs.

MATHEMATICAL PRACTICE   Highlighting the Standards

This Example is an opportunity to address Standard 2 (Reason abstractly and quantitatively). Students must reason quantitatively to correctly sketch the graphs described by a system of equations. They must reason abstractly to analyze the graphs and draw conclusions about the solution(s) of the system. Quantitative reasoning is required to write equations that define a system. Abstract reasoning is needed to analyze the solution in order to determine whether or not it makes sense in the context of the problem.

CLOSE

Essential Question

How can you solve a system of equations by graphing?
Graph solutions of the equations in the system. If the lines intersect at one point, then that ordered pair is the solution of the system. If the lines are parallel, the system has no solution. If the lines coincide, there are infinitely many solutions.

Summarize

In their journals, have students provide examples of a system of equations with one solution, no solution, and infinitely many solutions. Students should include the system of equations and its graph.

PRACTICE

Where skills are taught	Where skills are practiced
1 EXPLORE	EXS. 1–2
2 EXAMPLE	EXS. 3–4
3 EXAMPLE	EXS. 5–8

3 EXAMPLE Solving a Real-World Problem by Graphing

Keisha and her friends visit the concession stand at a football game. The stand charges $2 for a hot dog and $1 for a drink. The friends buy a total of 8 items for $11. Tell how many hot dogs and how many drinks they bought.

A Let x represent the number of hot dogs they bought and y represent the number of drinks they bought.

Write an equation representing the **number of items they purchased**.

Number of hot dogs	+	Number of drinks	=	Total items
x	+	y	=	8

Write an equation representing the **money spent on the items**.

Cost of 1 hot dog times number of hot dogs	+	Cost of 1 drink times number of drinks	=	Total cost
$2x$	+	$1y$	=	11

B Write your equations in slope-intercept form.

$y = -x + 8; y = -2x + 11$

C Graph the solutions of both equations.

D Use the graph to identify the solution of the system of equations. Check your answer by substituting the ordered pair into both equations.

$(3, 5)$	$x + y = 8$ $3 + 5 = 8$	$2x + y = 11$ $2(3) + 5 = 11$ $6 + 5 = 11$

The point ___(3, 5)___ is a solution of both equations.

E Interpret the solution in the original context.

Keisha and her friends bought ___3___ hot dog(s) and ___5___ drink(s).

REFLECT

3. **Conjecture** Why do you think the graph is limited to the first quadrant?

It would not make sense to buy a negative number of items or to spend

a negative amount of money.

PRACTICE

Solve each system by graphing.

1. $\begin{cases} 2x - 4y = 10 \\ x + y = 2 \end{cases}$ _____ $(3, -1)$

2. $\begin{cases} 2x - y = 0 \\ x + y = -6 \end{cases}$ _____ $(-2, -4)$

Graph each system and tell how many solutions the system has.

3. $\begin{cases} x - 3y = 2 \\ -3x + 9y = -6 \end{cases}$

___infinitely many___ solutions

4. $\begin{cases} 2x - y = 5 \\ 2x - y = -1 \end{cases}$

___0___ solutions

Mrs. Morales wrote a test with 15 questions covering spelling and vocabulary. Spelling questions (x) are worth 5 points and vocabulary questions (y) are worth 10 points. The maximum number of points possible on the test is 100.

5. Write an equation in slope-intercept form to represent the number of questions on the test.

$y = -x + 15$

6. Write an equation in slope-intercept form to represent the total points on the test.

$y = -0.5x + 10$

7. Graph the solutions of both equations.

8. Use your graph to tell how many of each question type are on the test.

___10___ spelling questions; ___5___ vocabulary questions

Assign these pages to help your students practice and apply important lesson concepts. For additional exercises, see the Student Edition.

Answers

Additional Practice

1.

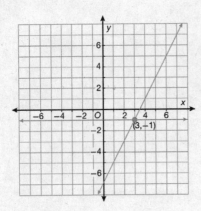

$(3, -1)$

2.

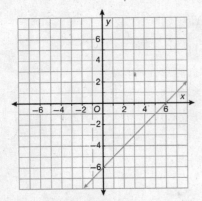

infinitely many solutions

3.

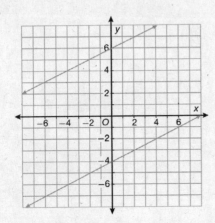

no solutions

4.

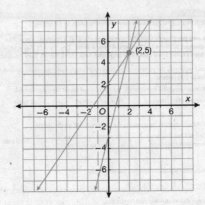

$(2, 5)$

5.

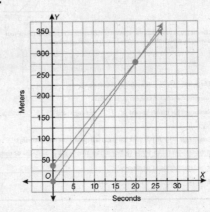

20 seconds

Problem Solving

1.

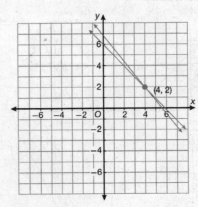

$x + y = 6$

2. $5x + 4y = 28$

3. x represents the number of chicken salads and y represents the number of egg salads

4. $(4, 2)$; 4 chicken salads and 2 egg salads

5. D   **6.** G

7. C   **8.** G

Name_____ Class_____ Date_____

Additional Practice

Solve each linear system by graphing. Check your answer.

1. $y = -1$
   $y = 2x - 7$

2. $x - y = 6$
   $2x = 12 + 2y$

3. $\frac{1}{2}x - y = 4$
   $2y = x + 6$

4. $y = 4x - 3$
   $2y - 3x = -4$

5. Two skaters are racing toward the finish line of a race. The first skater has a 40 meter lead and is traveling at a rate of 12 meters per second. The second skater is traveling at a rate of 14 meters per second. How long will it take for the second skater to pass the first skater?

Problem Solving

Write the equations for each system. Graph the system to solve each problem.

Kelly needs to order lunch for the 6 people at a business meeting. Her menu choices are chicken salad for a cost of $5 per person and egg salad for a cost of $4 per person. She only has $28 to spend. More people want chicken salad. How many of each lunch can she order?

1. Write one equation in a system for this situation. _____

2. Write a second equation in the system. _____

3. What do x and y represent?
   _____
   _____

4. How many of each type of lunch can she order?
   _____

Solve each problem.

5. How many solutions does this system have?

   $y = -3x + 6$
   $9x + 3y = 18$

   A 0   C 2
   B 1   D infinite

6. How many solutions does this system have?

   $5x - y = 1$
   $2x = 3y$

   F 0   H 2
   G 1   J infinite

7. For which system is the ordered pair $(2, -2)$ a solution?

   A $\begin{array}{l} y = x \\ y = \frac{1}{2}x - 3 \end{array}$

   C $\begin{array}{l} y = -x \\ y = \frac{1}{2}x - 3 \end{array}$

   B $\begin{array}{l} y = -\frac{1}{2}x \\ y = 2x - 4 \end{array}$

   D $\begin{array}{l} 2y = -x \\ 2y = 2x \end{array}$

8. Which is the best description for the graph of this system of equations?
   $x + y = 4$
   $4x + 4y = 8$

   F same line
   G parallel lines
   H intersecting lines
   J coinciding lines

Problem Solving Connections
Is the Price Right?

© Houghton Mifflin Harcourt Publishing Company

 COMMON CORE **Standards for Mathematical Content**

CC.8.EE.7a Give examples of linear equations in one variable with one solution, infinitely many solutions, or no solutions. Show which of these possibilities is the case by successively transforming the given equation into simpler forms, until an equivalent equation of the form $x = a$, $a = a$, or $a = b$ results (where a and b are different numbers).

CC.8.EE.7b Solve linear equations with rational number coefficients, including equations whose solutions require expanding expressions using the distributive property and collecting like terms.

CC.8.EE.8a Understand that solutions to a system of two linear equations in two variables correspond to points of intersection of their graphs, because points of intersection satisfy both equations simultaneously.

CC.8.EE.8b Solve systems of two linear equations in two variables algebraically, and estimate solutions by graphing the equations. Solve simple cases by inspection.

CC.8.EE.8c Solve real-world and mathematical problems leading to two linear equations in two variables.

INTRODUCE

When planning a vacation, there are many decisions to make including where to go, how to get there, how to get around once you arrive, and where to stay. Analyzing the situation and your options helps you make the best choices for your family.

TEACH

1 Writing Equations

Questioning Strategies

- In Part A, how is the initial fee represented in the equation? **by the *y*-intercept** How is the per mile charge represented? **by the rate of change, or slope**

- How do the equations for the taxi fare differ in Part B and Part C? **In Part C, you have to add the extra charge for Jackie's friends. The slope and initial charge do not change.**

Teaching Strategy
Have students work in small groups initially. Encourage students to discuss their reasoning and justify their strategies to each other. Ask groups to compare responses and resolve any differences.

2 Graphing a System

Questioning Strategies

- In Part C, why are there restrictions on the variables? **When an equation represents a real-world situation, you must think about which values of the variables make sense in the context. For example, for variables that represent distance, a negative value does not usually make sense.**

Teaching Strategy
Have students sketch the graphs by hand before checking their work with a graphing utility.

Name_____ Class_____ Date_____

Problem Solving Connections 🌎

Is the Price Right? Travelers who arrive at an airport usually have transportation options for getting to their next destination. Most travelers can choose between taxi or shuttle services to get to their hotels.

COMMON CORE

CC.8.EE.7a,
CC.8.EE.7b,
CC.8.EE.8a,
CC.8.EE.8b,
CC.8.EE.8c

1 Writing Equations

Jackie just arrived at the Orlando International Airport. There are two routes from the airport to Jackie's hotel:

- If the driver uses city streets, the distance to the hotel is 29 miles.
- If the driver takes the expressway, the distance is only 23 miles, but Jackie will pay an additional $2.75 in toll charges.

A The first taxi company Jackie talks to charges an initial fee of $2.00 plus $2.40 for each mile. Write an equation to show the total charge y for traveling x miles.

$y = 2 + 2.4x$

B Calculate the total cost to travel to Jackie's hotel taking each route.

Streets:
$y = 2 + 2.4x$
$= 2 + 2.4(29)$
$= 2 + 69.6$
$= 71.6$

Expressway:
$y = 2 + 2.4x + 2.75$
$= 4.75 + 2.4(23)$
$= 4.75 + 55.2$
$= 59.95$

Which route should Jackie instruct the driver to take? Why?

The expressway; the total cost is less than taking city streets.

C Jackie learns that the taxi can transport up to 4 people to the same destination at the rates given above. There is a $3 charge for each additional person. A shuttle bus company offers transportation to the hotel for $15 per person. Jackie is traveling with 3 friends. Calculate the total cost for Jackie and her friends to take the taxi along the expressway and the shuttle.

Taxi:
$59.95 + 3(3) = 68.95$

Shuttle:
$15 \times 4 = 60$

Should Jackie and her friends choose the taxi or the shuttle? Explain.
The shuttle; the total cost is less for 4 people to take the shuttle.

2 Graphing a System

Chuck and his family are also vacationing in Florida. He researches taxi rates before they leave home. There are 5 people in Chuck's family (including Chuck).

Company 1: $2 initial fee, plus $2.40 per mile for 1 to 2 passengers and $3 per person for each additional person.

Company 2: $3.75 initial fee, plus $2.00 per mile for 1 to 2 passengers and $1.50 per person for each additional person.

Company 3: $3.85 initial fee, plus $2.20 per mile for up to 5 passengers.

A Write equations in slope-intercept form to model each company's fare y for traveling x miles with 5 passengers.

Company 1:
$y = 2 + 2.4x + 3(3)$
$= 2.4x + 11$

Company 2:
$y = 3.75 + 2x + 3(1.5)$
$= 2x + 8.25$

Company 3:
$y = 2.2x + 3.85$

B Sketch a graph of the system.

C Explain any restrictions that should be placed on the values of x and y.

Both x and y should be restricted to values greater than or equal to 0 because it would not make sense to drive a negative number of miles or to pay a negative amount of money.

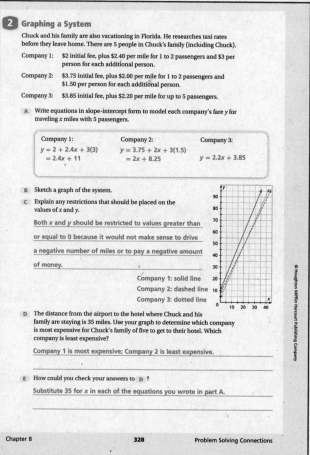

Company 1: solid line
Company 2: dashed line
Company 3: dotted line

D The distance from the airport to the hotel where Chuck and his family are staying is 35 miles. Use your graph to determine which company is most expensive for Chuck's family of five to get to their hotel. Which company is least expensive?

Company 1 is most expensive; Company 2 is least expensive.

E How could you check your answers to **D**?

Substitute 35 for x in each of the equations you wrote in part A.

Notes

3 Solving a System of Equations Algebraically

Questioning Strategies

- Why do you need to solve the system algebraically? **The graph does not show a clear point of intersection with integer coordinates. The graph gives an estimate, but you need to solve algebraically to find the exact solution.**

- How do you determine which company provides the better value? **To the right of the point of intersection, the graph corresponding to Company 3 has greater y-values (prices).**

4 Looking Back at the Context

Questioning Strategies

- In Part B and Part C, how is the rate per mile reflected in the graph? **Slope; a higher rate per mile will result in a steeper line.**

- How is the initial fee reflected in the graph?
- **y-intercept; a higher initial fee results in a greater starting y-value.**

 MATHEMATICAL PRACTICE

Highlighting the Standards

This project is an opportunity to address Standard 1 (Make sense of problems and persevere in solving them). The question posed does not have an immediate answer. In fact, as the situation changes, the mathematical model changes. Students must be flexible in their approach to the problem. Looking back at the context gives students a chance to draw general conclusions and develop reasoning skills that will help them solve future problems.

CLOSE

Journal

Have students write a journal entry in which they summarize the project. Remind them to state the project's problem in their own words and to describe their solution. Also, ask students to outline the main steps they used in order to reach their solution. Ask students to summarize what these conclusions mean to them, personally.

Research Options

Students can extend their learning by doing online research to find costs associated with transportation in a variety of cities. In addition to private transportation like a shuttle or taxi, students can investigate the costs associated with renting a car or the options for public transportation.

© Houghton Mifflin Harcourt Publishing Company

3 Solving a System of Equations Algebraically

Chuck's family decides to change their hotel reservation. They also learn that taxi company 1 will not be in operation on they day they need transportation.

A Chuck has not yet determined the distance between the airport and his family's new hotel. Explain how to use the graph from ❷ to help Chuck's family choose the best value.

The graph shows that for a distance less than about 20 miles, Company 3 is

less expensive. For distances greater than about 20 miles, Company 2 is

less expensive.

B Can you use the graph to determine which company is less expensive for a distance of 23 miles? If not, what method can you use?

It is not clear from the graph. You will need to solve the system

of equations algebraically.

C Use algebraic methods to solve the system of equations representing fares for company 2 and company 3.

$$\begin{cases} y = 2x + 8.25 \\ y = 2.2x + 3.85 \end{cases}$$
$$2.2x + 3.85 = 2x + 8.25$$
$$2.2x + 3.85 - 2x = 2x - 2x + 8.25$$
$$0.2x + 3.85 = 8.25$$
$$0.2x = 4.4$$
$$x = 22$$

D Explain what your solution means in the context of the problem.

For distances less than 22 miles, company 3 is less expensive. For distances

greater than 22 miles, company 2 is less expensive.

E Which company should Chuck's family choose to travel 23 miles to their new hotel?

company 2

4 Looking Back at the Context

A What factors do you need to consider when analyzing transportation costs?

distance of trip; toll expenses; fees for additional passengers; initial fee

from company

B Suppose two companies have the same rate per mile but different initial fees. Describe what the graph representing their fares would look like. What is the solution of the system of equations representing the fares? Which company has the lower fare?

Since the companies have the same rate per mile, the lines have the same slope.

This means the graph would show parallel lines that never intersect. Because

the lines will never intersect, the system of equations has no solution. The

company with the lower initial fee will always have the lower fare.

C Suppose two companies have the same initial fees but different rates per mile. Describe what the graph representing their fares would look like. What is the solution of the system of equations representing the fares? Which company has the lower fare?

Since the companies have the same initial fee, the graphs would have the same

y-intercept. Because the companies have different rates per mile, the lines

would have different slopes. The lines intersect when $x = 0$, so the solution of

the system is (0, initial fee). For distances greater than 0 miles, the company

with the lower rate per mile will always have the lower fare.

D Why is it important to put restrictions on the values of x and y in a real-world problem?

Without restricting the values of x and y to non-negative values, a solution

might represent an unreasonable situation when put in context. For instance,

negative values throughout these problems about transportation would have

meant negative distance traveled or negative money spent.

Notes

This page provides students with the opportunity to apply concepts from the Common Core in real-world problem situations. There are three different levels of performance tasks:

⭐ **Novice:** These are short word problems that require students to apply the math they have learned in straightforward, real-world situations.

⭐⭐ **Apprentice:** These are more involved problems that guide students step-by-step through more complex tasks. These exercises include more complicated reasoning, writing, and open-ended elements.

⭐⭐⭐ **Expert:** These are open-ended, non-routine problems that, instead of stepping the students through, asks them to choose their own methods for solving and justify their answers and reasoning.

3. Scoring Guide:

Task	Possible points
a	**1 point** for the correct answer of **10 minutes**, and **1 point** for correctly explaining that **m stays at zero until t = 10**.
b	**1 point** for the correct answer of **0.6 miles per minute**, and **1 point** for correctly explaining that **during the steepest part of the graph Frank bicycled 3 miles in 5 minutes**.
c	**2 points** for correctly explaining that **a positive slope represents bicycling away from home, a zero slope represents being stationary, and a negative slope represents bicycling toward home.**

Total possible points: 6

Sample answers

1. **a.** 1.6 yards/second

   b. $d = 1.6t$

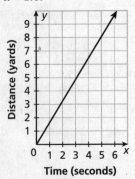
Distance (yards) vs Time (seconds)

2. **a.**

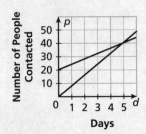
Number of People Contacted vs Days

   b. They have contacted the same number of people after 6 days ($d = 5$). Possible explanation: $d = 5$ is where the two graphs intersect.

Name_____ Class_____ Date_____

Performance Task

★ **1.** Ed begins walking home from the library. After 3 minutes, he has walked 288 yards.

    a. Use the points (0, 0) and (3, 288) to find the rate Ed is walking. Write your final answer in yards per second.

    b. Write and graph a function that gives the distance d in yards Ed walks after t seconds.

★ **2.** Han and James are telling people about their new website. Han e-mails 8 people every day for one week. James calls 20 friends on the first day, and then calls 4 friends every following day for the same week.

    a. Draw graphs that represent the total number of people p Han and James have told about the website after d days. Let the first day be $d = 0$, and the last day be $d = 6$.

    b. After how many days have Han and James contacted the same number of people? How do you know?

© Houghton Mifflin Harcourt Publishing Company

★★ **3.** The graph shows the number of miles m that Frank is from home, t minutes after starting to prepare for a bike ride.

    a. How long is it before Frank actually starts biking? How do you know?

    b. What is the fastest that Frank bicycles? Explain.

    c. Describe in your own words the significance of the sign of the slope for the 3 different segments of Frank's ride.

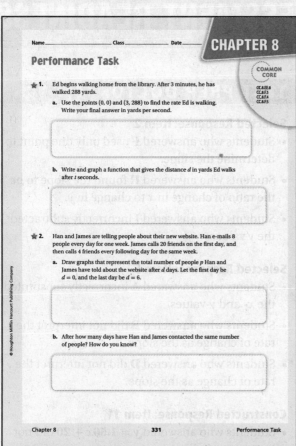

★★★ **4.** A farm sells peaches for $2 per pound. If you're a member of the farm co-op, you get 25% off per pound, but you also have to pay a one-time $10 membership fee.

    a. If you're a member, how many pounds of peaches do you have to buy before you start saving money over the regular price? Write your answer as an inequality. Explain your reasoning, and show any graphs or equations you use.

    b. The farm is considering adding another membership plan that has a $20 fee but offers a bigger discount. Choose a discount and write an equation for the plan.

© Houghton Mifflin Harcourt Publishing Company

---

4. Scoring Guide:

Task	Possible points
a	**1 point** for a correct answer of $x > 20$, where x is the number of pounds of peaches, OR equivalent, and **2 points** for an appropriate explanation, including solving the system $y = 2x$ and $y = 1.5x + 10$. Check students' graphs as appropriate.
b	**1 point** for choosing a percent discount that is larger than 25%, and **2 points** for writing an equation $y = px + 20$ where p is the discount price based on the students' discount, OR equivalent.

Total possible points: 6

© Houghton Mifflin Harcourt Publishing Company

COMMON CORE CORRELATION

Standard	Items
CC.8.EE.5	7–8, 13
CC.8.EE.6	2
CC.8.EE.8a	9
CC.8.EE.8c	9
CC.8.F.3	10–11
CC.8.F.4	1, 3–6, 10–12

TEST PREP DOCTOR ⊕

Selected Response: Item 2
- Students who answered **F** used only one point to determine the slope.
- Students who answered **H** found the slope to be the ratio of change in x to change in y.
- Students who answered **J** incorrectly subtracted the y values.

Selected Response: Item 5
- Students who answered **A** incorrectly substituted the x- and y-values.
- Students who answered **B** did not interpret the rate of change as the slope.
- Students who answered **D** did not interpret the rate of change as the slope.

Constructed Response: Item 11
- Students who answered $y = 1.50x + 20$ did not interpret a deduction as a negative rate of change (slope).
- Students who answered $y = 20x + 1.50$ did not recognize $1.50 as the rate of change.

Name _____ Class _____ Date _____

SELECTED RESPONSE

1. Determine whether the rates of change are constant or variable.

x	−5	−3	2	4
y	13	5	−15	−23

A. variable **(B.)** constant

2. Find the slope of the line.

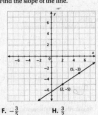

F. $-\frac{3}{5}$ **H.** $\frac{3}{2}$

(G.) $\frac{2}{3}$ **J.** $-\frac{2}{3}$

3. Write the equation of the line that passes through (7, 4) and (4, 8) in slope-intercept form.

A. $y = -\frac{4}{3}x + \frac{3}{40}$ **C.** $y = -\frac{3}{4}x + \frac{40}{3}$

(B.) $y = -\frac{4}{3}x + \frac{40}{3}$ **D.** $y = \frac{4}{3}x + \frac{40}{3}$

4. After it is planted, a tree grows at a rate of 0.3 meters per year. After 4 years the tree is 1.7 meters tall. Write the equation in point-slope form that models the situation. Then, predict the height of the tree after 7 years.

F. $y - 4 = 0.3(x - 1.7)$; 5.59 meters

G. $y - 0.3 = 1.7(x - 4)$; 5.4 meters

(H.) $y - 1.7 = 0.3(x - 4)$; 2.6 meters

J. $y - 1.7 = 4(x - 0.3)$; 28.5 meters

5. Write the point-slope form of the equation of the line with slope $\frac{2}{3}$ that passes through the point (2, −9).

A. $y - 9 = \frac{2}{3}(x + 2)$ **(C.)** $y + 9 = \frac{2}{3}(x - 2)$

B. $y + 2 = \frac{2}{3}(x - 9)$ **D.** $x - 2 = \frac{2}{3}(y + 9)$

6. A remote-control airplane descends at a rate of 2 feet per second. After 3 seconds it is 67 feet above the ground. Write the equation in point-slope form that models the situation. Then, find the height of the plane after 8 seconds.

(F.) $y - 67 = -2(x - 3)$; 57 feet

G. $y - 67 = -3(x - 2)$; 49 feet

H. $y - 3 = -2(x - 67)$; 121 feet

J. $y - 2 = 67(x - 3)$; 337 feet

7. Determine whether the data sets show direct variation.

Number of Baskets	Cost
4	$12
5	$15
7	$21
8	$24
9	$27

(A.) yes   **B.** no

8. At a summer camp there is one counselor for every 5 campers. Determine whether there is a direct variation between the number of campers, y, and the number of counselors, x. If so, find the equation of direct variation.

(F.) direct variation; $y = 5x$

G. direct variation; $x = 5y$

H. direct variation; $y = 5x + 5$

J. no direct variation

© Houghton Mifflin Harcourt Publishing Company

---

9. Solve the system by graphing.

$y = 5x + 3$
$-5x + y = 8$

A. This system has infinitely many solutions.

B. $\left(\frac{1}{2}, \frac{11}{2}\right)$

C. $\left(-\frac{1}{2}, \frac{1}{2}\right)$

(D.) This system has no solutions.

CONSTRUCTED RESPONSE

10. A plane taking off follows the path given by the equation $y = 0.5x + 2$. Graph this equation.

11. A subway pass costs $20.00 and $1.50 is deducted from the balance on the pass every time you use it. Write the equation to represent this situation, and graph it.

$y = -1.50x + 20$

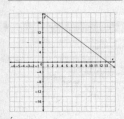

12. The altitude on a ski trail drops 2 feet for every 5 feet of horizontal distance traveled. The end of the trail has an altitude of 4,000 feet and is a horizontal distance of 2000 feet from the start.

a. Write an equation in point-slope form that represents this situation, and graph the equation.

$y - y_1 = m(x - x_1)$

$y - 4000 = -\frac{2}{5}(x - 2000)$

b. Use the graph to find the altitude at the start of the trail.

b. The altitude at the start of the slope is the y-intercept. From the graph, the value is 4800. Check by substituting the point (0, 4800) into the equation.

13. A fast-food restaurant has four sizes of cups as listed in the table below.

Size	Small, 8 oz	Medium, 12 oz	Large, 16 oz	Super, 24 oz
Cost	$0.90	$1.35	$1.80	$2.25

Do the sizes and costs of the beverages show a direct variation? If so, write the equation of variation. If not, explain why not.

No, the ratio of cost to size for the super size is different from the ratio for the other sizes.

© Houghton Mifflin Harcourt Publishing Company

CHAPTER 9

Data, Prediction, and Linear Functions

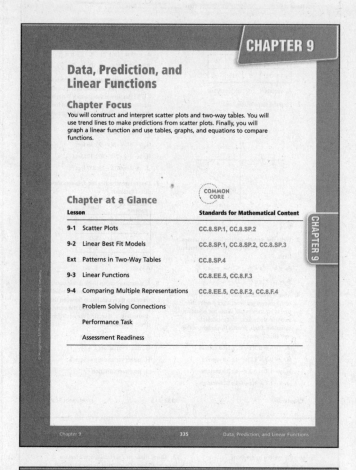

Data, Prediction, and Linear Functions

Chapter Focus
You will construct and interpret scatter plots and two-way tables. You will use trend lines to make predictions from scatter plots. Finally, you will graph a linear function and use tables, graphs, and equations to compare functions.

Chapter at a Glance

COMMON CORE

Lesson		Standards for Mathematical Content
9-1	Scatter Plots	CC.8.SP.1, CC.8.SP.2
9-2	Linear Best Fit Models	CC.8.SP.1, CC.8.SP.2, CC.8.SP.3
Ext	Patterns in Two-Way Tables	CC.8.SP.4
9-3	Linear Functions	CC.8.EE.5, CC.8.F.3
9-4	Comparing Multiple Representations	CC.8.EE.5, CC.8.F.2, CC.8.F.4
	Problem Solving Connections	
	Performance Task	
	Assessment Readiness	

COMMON CORE PROFESIONAL DEVELOPMENT   **CC.8.SP.1**

Bivariate data records the relationship between two-variable data. Students will represent this relationship as a scatter plot which consists of points in the coordinate plane. From the graph, students will recognizing patterns of clustering, outliers, and association.

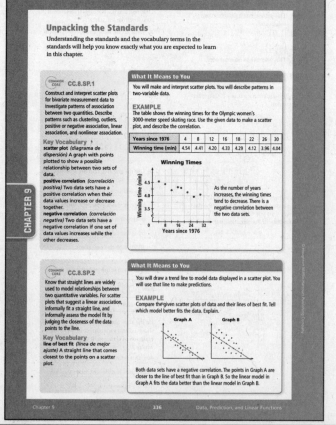

Unpacking the Standards
Understanding the standards and the vocabulary terms in the standards will help you know exactly what you are expected to learn in this chapter.

COMMON CORE   CC.8.SP.1

Construct and interpret scatter plots for bivariate measurement data to investigate patterns of association between two quantities. Describe patterns such as clustering, outliers, positive or negative association, linear association, and nonlinear association.

Key Vocabulary
scatter plot *(diagrama de dispersión)* A graph with points plotted to show a possible relationship between two sets of data.
positive correlation *(correlación positiva)* Two data sets have a positive correlation when their data values increase or decrease together.
negative correlation *(correlación negativa)* Two data sets have a negative correlation if one set of data values increases while the other decreases.

What It Means to You
You will make and interpret scatter plots. You will describe patterns in two-variable data.

EXAMPLE
The table shows the winning times for the Olympic women's 3000-meter speed skating race. Use the given data to make a scatter plot, and describe the correlation.

Years since 1976	4	8	12	16	18	22	26	30
Winning time (min)	4.54	4.41	4.20	4.33	4.29	4.12	3.96	4.04

Winning Times

As the number of years increases, the winning times tend to decrease. There is a negative correlation between the two data sets.

What It Means to You

COMMON CORE   CC.8.SP.2
Know that straight lines are widely used to model relationships between two quantitative variables. For scatter plots that suggest a linear association, informally fit a straight line, and informally assess the model fit by judging the closeness of the data points to the line.

Key Vocabulary
line of best fit *(línea de mejor ajuste)* A straight line that comes closest to the points on a scatter plot.

You will draw a trend line to model data displayed in a scatter plot. You will use that line to make predictions.

EXAMPLE
Compare the given scatter plots of data and their lines of best fit. Tell which model better fits the data. Explain.

Graph A   **Graph B**

Both data sets have a negative correlation. The points in Graph A are closer to the line of best fit than in Graph B. So the linear model in Graph A fits the data better than the linear model in Graph B.

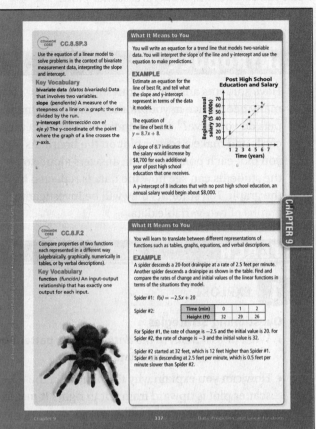

CC.8.SP.3

COMMON CORE | CC.8.SP.3

Use the equation of a linear model to solve problems in the context of bivariate measurement data, interpreting the slope and intercept.

Key Vocabulary

bivariate data *(datos bivariado)* Data that involves two variables.

slope *(pendiente)* A measure of the steepness of a line on a graph; the rise divided by the run.

y-intercept *(intersección con el eje y)* The y-coordinate of the point where the graph of a line crosses the y-axis.

What It Means to You

You will write an equation for a trend line that models two-variable data. You will interpret the slope of the line and y-intercept and use the equation to make predictions.

EXAMPLE

Estimate an equation for the line of best fit, and tell what the slope and y-intercept represent in terms of the data it models.

The equation of the line of best fit is $y = 8.7x + 8$.

A slope of 8.7 indicates that the salary would increase by $8,700 for each additional year of post high school education that one receives.

A y-intercept of 8 indicates that with no post high school education, an annual salary would begin about $8,000.

Post High School Education and Salary

(graph: Beginning annual salary ($ 1000s) vs Time (years))

COMMON CORE | CC.8.F.2

Compare properties of two functions each represented in a different way (algebraically, graphically, numerically in tables, or by verbal descriptions).

Key Vocabulary

function *(función)* An input-output relationship that has exactly one output for each input.

What It Means to You

You will learn to translate between different representations of functions such as tables, graphs, equations, and verbal descriptions.

EXAMPLE

A spider descends a 20-foot drainpipe at a rate of 2.5 feet per minute. Another spider descends a drainpipe as shown in the table. Find and compare the rates of change and initial values of the linear functions in terms of the situations they model.

Spider #1: $f(x) = -2.5x + 20$

Spider #2:

Time (min)	0	1	2
Height (ft)	32	29	26

For Spider #1, the rate of change is −2.5 and the initial value is 20. For Spider #2, the rate of change is −3 and the initial value is 32.

Spider #2 started at 32 feet, which is 12 feet higher than Spider #1. Spider #1 is descending at 2.5 feet per minute, which is 0.5 feet per minute slower than Spider #2.

CHAPTER 9

COMMON CORE PROFESIONAL DEVELOPMENT | CC.8.SP.3

Extending their understanding of positive and negative association of bivariate data in a scatter plot, students will represent the data with an equation. In Grade 8, the relationship of the bivariate data will be a linear model. In the context of the problem, students will interpret the slope and *y*-intercept to the relationship of the two-variable data.

CHAPTER 9

Key Vocabulary

bivariate data *(datos bivariado)* A data set involving two variables.

clustering *(arracimando)* A condition that occurs when data points in a scatter plot are grouped more in one part of the graph than another.

frequency *(frecuencia)* The number of times the value appears in the data set.

linear equation *(ecuación lineal)* An equation whose solutions form a straight line on a coordinate plane.

linear function *(función lineal)* A function whose graph is a straight line.

relative frequency *(frecuencia relativa)* The frequency of a specific data value divided by the total number of data values in the set.

scatter plot *(diagrama de dispersión)* A graph with points plotted to show a possible relationship between two sets of data.

trend line *(línea de tendencia)* A straight line that comes closest to the points on a scatter plot.

two-way table *(tabla de doble entrada)* A table that displays two-variable data by organizing it into rows and columns.

MATHEMATICAL PRACTICE

The Common Core Standards for Mathematical Practice describe varieties of expertise that mathematics educators at all levels should seek to develop in their students. Opportunities to develop these practices are integrated throughout this program.

1. Make sense of problems and persevere in solving them.
2. Reason abstractly and quantitatively.
3. Construct viable arguments and critique the reasoning of others.
4. Model with mathematics.
5. Use appropriate tools strategically.
6. Attend to precision.
7. Look for and make use of structure.
8. Look for and express regularity in repeated reasoning.

CHAPTER 9

Scatter Plots

Essential question: *How can you construct and interpret scatter plots?*

COMMON CORE **Standards for Mathematical Content**

CC.8.SP.1 Construct and interpret scatter plots for bivariate measurement data to investigate patterns of association between two quantities. Describe patterns such as clustering, outliers, positive or negative association, linear association, and nonlinear association.

CC.8.SP.2 Know that straight lines are widely used to model relationships between two quantitative variables. For scatter plots that suggest a linear association, informally fit a straight line, and informally assess the model fit by judging the closeness of the data points to the line.

Vocabulary

bivariate data

scatter plot

association

trend line

outlier

Prerequisites

Graphing in the coordinate plane

Math Background

Bivariate data records the relationship between two variables. This relationship can be displayed as a scatter plot which consists of points in the coordinate plane. When the values of each variable increase together, the relationship between the variables is positive. When the values of one variable increase while the other decreases, the relationship is negative.

INTRODUCE

Have students answer two questions, such as "How many people live in your home?" and "How many pets do you have?" on one index card. Collect the cards and make a scatter plot on the board. As you plot each point, read the answers aloud so the students can see how the data is reflected in the graph. Tell students they will be investigating graphs of two-variable data.

TEACH

1 EXPLORE

Questioning Strategies

- What does a *trend in the data* mean? **a pattern or a relationship between data points**

- How can you explain why the pattern in the scatter plot is upward from left to right? **It makes sense that test grades will increase as time studying increases. A downward trend would indicate that grades decrease as students study more, which is very unlikely.**

Differentiated Instruction

You can have students use centimeter cubes on a large coordinate plane to make a scatter plot. Students can plot the points and check one another's graphs before plotting the points on paper.

Name_____ Class_____ Date_____

9-1

Scatter Plots
Going Deeper

Essential question: *How can you construct and interpret scatter plots?*

A set of **bivariate data** involves two variables. Bivariate data are used to explore the relationship between two variables. You can graph bivariate data on a *scatter plot*. A **scatter plot** is a graph with points plotted to show the relationship between two sets of data.

CC.8.SP.1

1 EXPLORE Making a Scatter Plot

The final question on a math test reads, "How many hours did you spend studying for this test?" The teacher records the number of hours each student studied and the grade the student received on the test.

A Make a prediction about the relationship between the number of hours spent studying and test grades.

Sample answer: A greater number of study

hours should correlate to higher test grades.

Hours Spent Studying	Test Grade
0	75
0.5	80
1	80
1	85
1.5	85
1.5	95
2	90
3	100
4	90

B Make a scatter plot. Graph hours spent studying as the independent variable and test grade as the dependent variable.

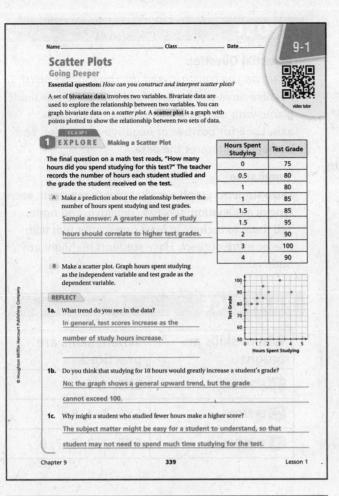

REFLECT

1a. What trend do you see in the data?

In general, test scores increase as the

number of study hours increase.

1b. Do you think that studying for 10 hours would greatly increase a student's grade?

No; the graph shows a general upward trend, but the grade

cannot exceed 100.

1c. Why might a student who studied fewer hours make a higher score?

The subject matter might be easy for a student to understand, so that

student may not need to spend much time studying for the test.

© Houghton Mifflin Harcourt Publishing Company

Association tells you how sets of data are related. A positive association means that both data sets increase together. A negative association means that as one data set increases, the other decreases. No association means that changes in one data set do not affect the other data set.

Positive Association

Negative Association

No Association

When data shows a positive or negative association and falls along a line, there is a linear association. When data shows a positive or negative relationship, but does not fall along a line, there is a nonlinear association.

CC.8.SP.1

2 EXPLORE Determining Association

Susan surveyed 20 people about the price of a cleaning product she developed. She asked each person whether they would buy the cleaner at different prices. A person may answer yes or no to more than one price. Susan's results are shown in the table.

A Make a scatter plot of the data.

Price ($)	Buyers
2	20
4	19
6	17
8	13
10	8
12	2

B Describe the type(s) of association you see between price and number of people who would buy at that price. Explain.

There is a negative association. As the price increases, the number of people

who would buy the product decreases. The data appears to be nonlinear.

© Houghton Mifflin Harcourt Publishing Company

Questioning Strategies

- **How are slope and association alike?** As a positive or negative slope increases or decreases, respectively, from left to right, so does a positive and negative association. *No slope* and *no association* are not alike.

- **How can you describe what it means for bivariate data to have *no association*?** It means that changes in the values of one variable have little or no effect on the values of the other variable.

MATHEMATICAL PRACTICE — Highlighting the Standards

This Explore is an opportunity to address Standard 4 (Model with mathematics). Students use scatter plots to model relationships between two-variable data. Using the scatter plot, students analyze mathematical relationships and draw conclusions about the data.

---

3 EXPLORE

Questioning Strategies

- **Why do you disregard outliers when drawing a trend line?** because they do not fit the trend

- **Do you think it is possible to draw a trend line for a scatter plot with no association? Explain.** No; it does not show a trend.

Technology

Show students how to enter two-variable data into lists in a graphing calculator, display a scatter plot, and graph a trend line, or *line of best fit*. Explain that the calculator graphs the best trend line possible based on calculations involving the minimum distance possible between data points and the trend line.

CLOSE

Essential Question

How can you construct and interpret scatter plots?
Possible answer: Plot bivariate data on a coordinate plane, with one variable represented by each axis. Look for positive or negative association and outliers to interpret the data.

Summarize

Have students graph a scatter plot to represent each type of association: positive, negative, and none. Tell them to include at least one scatter plot with one or more outliers. Have students highlight any outliers.

PRACTICE

Where skills are taught	Where skills are practiced
1 EXPLORE	EXS. 1, 6
2 EXPLORE	EXS. 3–4, 8
3 EXPLORE	EXS. 2–3, 5, 7, 9

When a scatter plot shows a linear association, you can use a line to model the relationship between the variables. A **trend line** is a straight line that comes closest to the points on a scatter plot. When drawing a trend line, ignore any *outliers*. An **outlier** is a data point that is very different from the rest of the data in the set.

 3 EXPLORE Drawing a Trend Line

Joyce is training for a 10K race. For some of her training runs, she records the distance she ran and how many minutes she ran.

Distance (mi)	Time (min)
4	38
2	25
1	7
2	16
3	26
5	55
2	20
4	45
3	31

A Make a scatter plot of Joyce's running data.

B To draw a trend line, use a straight edge to draw a line that has about the same number of points above and below it. Ignore any outliers.

C Use your trend line to predict how long it would take Joyce to run 4.5 miles.

about 45 minutes

REFLECT

3a. How well does your trend line fit the data?

All the data points are close to the line. The data shows a strong linear

association, so the line should fit very well.

3b. Do you think you can use a scatter plot that shows no association to make a prediction? Explain your answer.

No; no association means that there is no relationship between the

variables and the scatter plot shows no pattern.

PRACTICE

The table shows softball game results.

Hits	8	7	4	11	2	8	5	1
Runs	6	6	2	9	1	8	4	0

1. Use the data table to make a scatter plot.

2. Draw a trend line using a straightedge.

3. Describe the trend your line shows. Is it positive or negative, or is there no trend? How do you know?
    Positive; the line rises from left to right

4. What does your scatter plot show about the relationship between hits and runs scored for this team?
    There is a positive relationship between hits and runs scored.
    As the number of hits increases, the number of runs scored increases.

5. Predict how many runs the softball team would score if its players got 9 hits. What if they got 3 hits?
    Sample answer: about 7 or 8; about 1 or 2

The table shows age and sleep times for some people.

Age (yr)	6	1	5	15	19	12	3	20
Sleep (h)	9.5	15	11	8.5	7	9.25	12	7

6. Use the data in the table to make a scatter plot.

7. Draw a trend line using a straightedge.

8. What does your scatter plot show about the relationship between age and hours of sleep for this group of people?
    In general, the older one gets, the less one sleeps.

9. Predict how many hours of sleep an 18-year old might get nightly. How many hours of sleep might a 4-year old get?
    Sample answer: about 8; about 11 or 12

Assign these pages to help your students practice and apply important lesson concepts. For additional exercises, see the Student Edition.

Answers

Additional Practice

1.

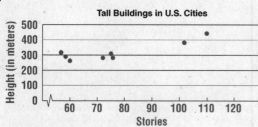

a positive correlation

2.

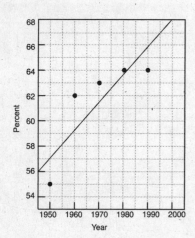

58.5%

Problem Solving

1.

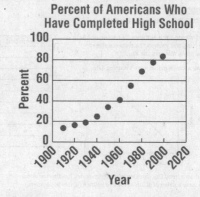

2. positive

3. about 90%

4. B

5. H

Additional Practice

1. Use the given data to make a scatter plot, and describe the correlation.

Tall Buildings in U.S. Cities

Building	City	Stories	Height (meters)
Sears Tower	Chicago	110	442
Empire State Building	New York	102	381
Bank of America Plaza	Atlanta	55	312
Library Tower	Los Angeles	75	310
Key Tower	Cleveland	57	290
Columbia Seafirst Center	Seattle	76	287
NationsBank Plaza	Dallas	72	281
NationsBank Corporate Center	Charlotte	60	265

Tall Buildings in U.S. Cities

2. Make a scatter plot of the data, and draw a line of best fit. Then use the data to predict the percentage of American homeowners in 1955.

Percent of Americans Owning Homes

Year	1950	1960	1970	1980	1990
Percent	55.0%	61.9%	62.9%	64.4%	64.2%

© Houghton Mifflin Harcourt Publishing Company

Problem Solving

Use the data given at the right.

1. Make a scatter plot of the data.

Percent of Americans Who Have Completed High School

Year	Percent
1910	13.5
1920	16.4
1930	19.1
1940	24.5
1950	34.3
1960	41.1
1970	55.2
1980	68.6
1990	77.6
1999	83.4

2. Does the data show a positive, negative or no correlation?

3. Use the scatter plot to predict the percent of Americans who will complete high school in 2010.

Choose the letter for the best answer.

4. Which data sets have a positive correlation?

  A The length of the lines at amusement park rides and the number of rides you can ride in a day

  B The temperature on a summer day and the number of visitors at a swimming pool

  C The square miles of a state and the population of the state in the 2000 census

  D The length of time spent studying and doing homework and the length of time spent doing other activities

5. Which data sets have a negative correlation?

  F The number of visitors at an amusement park and the length of the lines for the rides

  G The amount of speed over the speed limit when you get a speeding ticket and the amount of the fine for speeding

  H The temperature and the number of people wearing coats

  J The distance you live from school and the amount of time it takes to get to school

© Houghton Mifflin Harcourt Publishing Company

9-2

Linear Best Fit Models
Going Deeper

Essential question: *How can you use a trend line to make a prediction from a scatter plot?*

© Houghton Mifflin Harcourt Publishing Company

COMMON CORE Standards for Mathematical Content

CC.8.SP.1 Construct and interpret scatter plots for bivariate measurement data to investigate patterns of association between two quantities. Describe patterns such as clustering, outliers, positive or negative association, linear association, and nonlinear association.

CC.8.SP.2 Know that straight lines are widely used to model relationships between two quantitative variables. For scatter plots that suggest a linear association, informally fit a straight line, and informally assess the model fit by judging the closeness of the data points to the line.

CC.8.SP.3 Use the equation of a linear model to solve problems in the context of bivariate measurement data, interpreting the slope and intercept.

Vocabulary
cluster

Prerequisites
Scatter plots and association

Math Background
When you graph bivariate data in a scatter plot and you notice that the data have a positive or negative association, you can use a trend line to make predictions about the values that are not graphed. The accuracy of predictions made by using a trend line can be judged by how closely the line fits the data. The equation of the trend line serves as a model of the data, and properties of the trend line have meanings associated with the data.

INTRODUCE

Briefly review with students scatter plots that have positive, negative, and no association. Tell students that in this lesson they will use scatter plots to write equation models for situations involving two-variable data and use the models to make predictions.

TEACH

1 EXAMPLE

Questioning Strategies

- What are some reasons that there might be clusters in the data? **When the variability of data is small, it tends to cluster.**

- How can you identify an outlier in a scatter plot? **An outlier can be identified in a scatter plot as a point that greatly diverges from the trend shown by the majority of data points.**

Teaching Strategies
As students work through examples and exercises, have them circle clusters that they see in the data and highlight any outliers.

2 EXAMPLE

Questioning Strategies

- What is the first step in writing an equation of a trend line? **Choose two points that the trend line will go through, and use them to find the slope.**

- How can you use the slope to write an equation in the form $y = mx + b$ for the trend line? **Substitute the slope value for m and the coordinates of one of the points on the line for x and y into $y = mx + b$. Solve for b. Write the equation in the form $y = mx + b$, where x is the slope and b is the y-intercept.**

- If the chapters were on the vertical axis and the pages were on the horizontal axis, what would be the value of the slope and what would it represent? **The slope of the line would be $\frac{1}{10}$, representing a rate of $\frac{1}{10}$, or 0.1, of a chapter per page.**

9-2

Name_____ Class_____ Date_____

Linear Best Fit Models
Going Deeper

Essential question: *How can you use a trend line to make a prediction from a scatter plot?*

A **cluster** is a set of closely grouped data. Data may cluster around a point or along a line.

CC.8.SP.1

1 EXAMPLE Interpreting Clusters and Outliers

A scientist gathers information about the eruptions of Old Faithful, a geyser in Yellowstone National Park. She uses the data to create a scatter plot. The data shows the length of time between eruptions (interval) and how long the eruption lasts (duration).

A Describe any clusters you see in the scatter plot.

    There are clusters around the 50-minute

    and 80-minute intervals.

B What do the clusters tell you about eruptions of Old Faithful?

    There are short wait times followed by short eruptions and longer wait

    times followed by longer eruptions.

C Describe any outliers you see in the scatter plot.

    The point near (55, 3) appears to be an outlier because it does not fall

    into either cluster.

REFLECT

1a. Suppose the geyser erupts for 2.2 minutes after a 75-minute interval. Would this point lie in one of the clusters? Would it be an outlier? Explain your answer.

    It would not lie in either cluster because the interval was too long for the first

    cluster, and the duration was too short for the second. It might be considered

    an outlier because it is not very close to the rest of the data.

1b. Suppose the geyser erupts after an 80-minute interval. Give a range of possible duration times for which the point on the scatter plot would not be considered an outlier.

    Possible range: 3 to 5 minutes.

CC.8.SP.3

2 EXAMPLE Finding the Equation of a Trend Line

The scatter plot shows the relationship between the number of chapters and the total number of pages for several books. Draw a trend line, write an equation for the trend line, and describe the meanings of the slope and *y*-intercept.

A Draw a trend line. It will be easier to write an equation for the line if it goes through two of the data points. (Hint: Use (5, 50) as one of the points.)

Identify another point that the trend line goes through:
$\left(\boxed{17}, \boxed{170} \right)$ Answers may vary based on the second point selected.

B What type(s) of association does the scatter plot show?

    positive; linear

C Do you expect the slope of the line to be positive or negative?

    positive

D Find the slope of the trend line.

$$m = \frac{170 - 50}{17 - 5} = \frac{120}{12} = 10$$

E Use the equation $y = mx + b$, the slope, and the point (5, 50). Substitute values for *y*, *m*, and *x* into the equation and solve for *b*.

$y = mx + b$

$50 = 10 \cdot 5 + b$	*Substitute for y, m, and x.*
$50 = 50 + b$	*Simplify on the right side.*
$50 = 50 + b$	*Subtract the number that is added to b from both sides.*
$-50 \quad -50$	
$0 = b$	

Use your slope and *y*-intercept values to write an equation in slope-intercept form.

$y = 10 x + 0$

F What is the meaning of the slope in this situation?

    There is an average of 10 pages per chapter; an additional chapter is

    associated with 10 additional pages.

G What is the meaning of the *y*-intercept in this situation?

    the number of pages in a book with 0 chapters (0)

Questioning Strategies

- How can you use the equation of a trend line to make predictions? **You can substitute a value for either *x* or *y*, and solve for the value of the other variable. Then interpret the meaning for the context.**

- What is the difference between interpolation and extrapolation? **Interpolation involves the prediction of values by using data points from within the boundaries of the data used to write the trend line. Extrapolation involves the prediction of values by using data points that lie beyond those boundaries.**

⟋ **MATHEMATICAL PRACTICE**   **Highlighting the Standards**

This Explore is an opportunity to address Standard 1 (Make sense of problems and persevere in solving them). Students use scatter plots and trend lines to interpret situations involving two unknowns, to examine for possible associations between the variables, and to help them make predictions for the data in the scatter plot when there is a reasonably strong association. This multi-step process allows students to practice perseverance in problem solving.

Essential Question

How can you use a trend line to make a prediction from a scatter plot?

When a scatter plot shows a reasonably strong positive or negative association between two variables, draw a trend line as closely fitting as possible through the points. Then write an equation for that line, and use it to make predictions by substituting and solving.

Summarize

Have students make a flow chart in their journals to show the steps for using the equation of a trend line to make a prediction from a scatter plot.

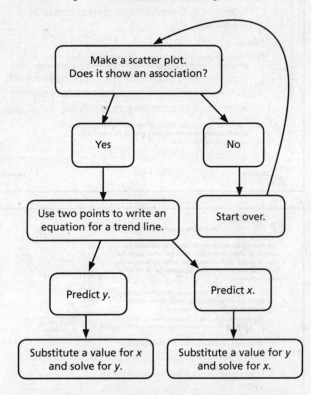

PRACTICE

Where skills are taught	Where skills are practiced
1 EXAMPLE	EXS. 1–3
2 EXAMPLE	EXS. 4–7
3 EXPLORE	EX. 8

When you use a trend line or its equation to predict a value between data points that you already know, you *interpolate* the predicted value. When you make a prediction that is outside the data that you know, you *extrapolate* the predicted value.

3 EXPLORE CC.8.SP.2 **Making Predictions** — Answers may vary depending on the equation found in the previous Example.

Refer to the scatter plot and trend line in **2**.

A Use the equation of the trend line to predict how many pages would be in a book with 26 chapters.

Is this prediction an example of interpolation or extrapolation?

extrapolation

$y =$ **10x** — *Write the equation for your trend line.*

$y =$ **10(26)** — *Substitute the number of chapters for x.*

$y =$ **260** — *Simplify.*

I predict that a book with 26 chapters would have **260** pages.

B Use the equation of the trend line to predict how many pages would be in a book with 14 chapters.

Is this prediction an example of interpolation or extrapolation?

interpolation

$y =$ **10x** — *Write the equation for your trend line.*

$y =$ **10(14)** — *Substitute the number of chapters for x.*

$y =$ **140** — *Simplify.*

I predict that a book with 14 chapters would have **140** pages.

REFLECT

3a. How well do your new points fit the original data?

They fall close to the original data, so they fit well.

3b. Do you think that extrapolation or interpolation is more accurate? Explain.

Possible answer: Interpolation is more accurate because the predicted value fits between known points where the trend is known. There is no guarantee that a trend will continue beyond the known data points.

PRACTICE

Twenty-five runners between the ages of 6 and 18 were timed in a mile run. The scatter plot shows the results.

1. In what range of running times does the data appear to cluster?

Possible answer: 6 to 10 minutes

2. What running times are outliers?

Sample answer: approximately 13.5 min for one 10-year old runner and approximately 4.5 min for one 13-year old runner

3. Suppose that Juan, who is 17, was timed at 9.5 minutes. Would his time be an outlier? Explain.

Yes; runners from ages 15 to 18 have times between 6 and 7 minutes.

The scatter plot shows the circumference and height of a variety of trees.

4. How would you describe the association between circumference and height that the scatter plot shows? Explain.

Possible answer: A positive correlation because the data rises from left to right.

5. Using (150, 80) as one of the points, draw a trend line using a straightedge. What is the slope of the line? How did you find it?

Check students' lines. Possible answer: Find the slope by choosing another point along the trend line and using the slope formula. The slope is 0.5.

6. What is the equation for your trend line? Possible answer: $y = 0.5x + 0.8$

7. Why might your classmates' equations for trend lines vary?

Students may draw the lines differently or may interpret the *y*-intercept differently.

8. **Error Analysis** A student used points (150, 80) and (50, 30) but wrote the equation $y = 5x + 0.5$. What mistake did the student make?

The student confused the *y*-intercept with the slope of the line in the linear equation.

Answers

Additional Practice

1. Linear

2. There is no clustering.

3. There are no outliers.

4. Possible answer: $y = \frac{3}{4}x + 8$

5. The slope represents the pay increase per year.

6. The y-intercept represents the pay for someone starting at the job.

Problem Solving

1. Linear

2. Positive

3. No outliers

4. B

5. H

6. A

© Houghton Mifflin Harcourt Publishing Company

9-2

Name_____ Class_____ Date_____

Additional Practice

Use the scatter plot for Exercises 1–6.

Years Worked and Hourly Wage

1. Does the pattern of association between year and pay per hour appear to be linear or nonlinear?

_____

2. Identify any clustering.

_____

3. Identify any possible outliers.

_____

4. Write an equation for the line of best fit.

_____

5. What does the slope in the scatter plot represent?

_____

6. What does the y-intercept in the scatter plot represent?

_____

Chapter 9   349   Practice and Problem Solving

Problem Solving

Use the scatter plot for Exercises 1–3.

1. Does the pattern of association between time studied and score appear to be linear or nonlinear?

2. Describe the correlation between the time studied and the scores as positive, negative, or no correlation.

_____

3. Identify any possible outliers.

_____

Studying and Scores

Choose the letter for the best answer. Use the scatter plot for Exercises 4–6.

4. What does the point (0, 400) represent in this scatter plot?

A the temperature at an elevation of 0 feet

B the elevation at a temperature of 58°F

C the elevation at a temperature of 0°F

D the temperature at an elevation of 500 feet

5. Which best describes the correlation between the temperatures and the elevations in the scatter plot?

F strong positive

G weak positive

H strong negative

J weak negative

Temperatures and Elevation

6. Which equation best represents the line of best fit?

A $y = -16x + 400$

B $y = -15x + 300$

C $y = 15x - 300$

D $y = 16x - 400$

Chapter 9   350   Practice and Problem Solving

Patterns in Two-Way Tables
Going Deeper

Essential question: *How can you construct and interpret two-way tables?*

COMMON CORE Standards for Mathematical Content

CC.8.SP.4 Understand that patterns of association can also be seen in bivariate categorical data by displaying frequencies and relative frequencies in a two-way table. Construct and interpret a two-way table summarizing data on two categorical variables collected from the same subjects. Use relative frequencies calculated for rows or columns to describe possible association between the two variables.

Vocabulary

frequency

two-way table

relative frequency

Prerequisites

Percents

Math Background

Two-way tables are used to show frequencies of data that is categorized two ways. The columns represent one categorization for the population and the rows represent a different categorization for the population. You can use relative frequencies in two-way tables to draw conclusions about whether or not there is an association between the two categories.

INTRODUCE

Present to students the following scenario:
A car dealership has four categories of automobiles (SUV, car, truck, or minivan) and five color categories (black, white, brown, red, and other). Have students think of ways to visually organize this data. Explain that in this lesson they will learn how to organize this type of data.

TEACH

1 EXPLORE

Questioning Strategies

- If 40% of the people own a bike, what percent of the people do not own a bike? **60% of the people do not own a bike.**

- How do you find the numbers to put in the table? **Use the percents to calculate numbers that belong in each cell of the table.**

- What does the vertical *Total* column represent? The horizontal *Total* row? **The *Total* column represents the total numbers of people who own a bike, people who do not own a bike, and people polled. The *Total* row represents the total numbers of people who shop at the farmer's market, people who do not shop at the farmer's market, and people polled.**

Teaching Strategies

Review operations with percents if necessary. Remind students that the entire population is 100%. Point out that the last row and the last column should have the same total in the shared cell.

2 EXAMPLE

Questioning Strategies

- How are frequency and relative frequency alike and how are they different? **Frequency is the number of times an event occurs. Relative frequency is the ratio of the frequency of an event to the total number of frequencies.**

- How can you determine from a two-way table whether there is an association between the two variables? **If the relative frequency of an event to the whole population is different than the relative frequency within a sub-population, then there is an association.**

© Houghton Mifflin Harcourt Publishing Company

Name_____ Class_____ Date_____

Patterns in Two-Way Tables
Going Deeper

Essential question: *How can you construct and interpret two-way tables?*

The **frequency** is the number of times an event occurs. A **two-way table** shows the frequencies of data that is categorized two ways. The rows indicate one categorization and the columns indicate another.

1 EXPLORE Making a Two-Way Table

CC.8.SP.4

A poll of 120 town residents found that 40% own a bike. Of those who own a bike, 75% shop at the town's farmer's market. Of those who do not own a bike, 25% shop at the town's farmer's market.

	Farmer's Market	No Farmer's Market	TOTAL
Bike	36	12	48
No Bike	18	54	72
TOTAL	54	66	120

A Start in the bottom right cell of the table. Enter the total number of people polled.

B **Fill in the right column.** 40% of those polled own a bike.

40% of 120 is ___48___

The remaining people polled do not own a bike. The number who do not own a bike is 120 − ___48___ = ___72___

C **Fill in the top row.** 75% of those who own a bike also shop at the market.

75% of ___48___ is ___36___

The remaining bike owners do not shop at the market. The number of bike owners who do not shop at the market is ___12___

D **Fill in the second row.** 25% of those who do not own a bike shop at the market.

25% of ___72___ is ___18___

The remaining people without bikes do not shop at the market. The number without a bike who do not shop at the market is ___54___

E **Fill in the last row.** In each column, add the numbers in the first two rows to find the total number of people who shop at the farmer's market and who do not shop at the farmer's market.

Chapter 9 351 Extension

F What percent of all the residents polled shop at the farmer's market?

$\frac{54}{120}$ = 0.45

___45___ % of people polled shop at the farmer's market.

REFLECT

1. How can you check that your table is completed correctly?

The last number in each row or column should be the sum of the other

numbers in that row or column.

Relative frequency is the ratio of the number of times an event occurs to the total number of events. In , the relative frequency of bike owners who shop at the market is $\frac{36}{120}$ = 0.30 = 30%. You can use relative frequencies to decide if there is an association between two variables or events.

2 EXAMPLE Deciding Whether There is an Association

CC.8.SP.4

Determine whether there is an association between the events.

A One hundred teens were polled about whether they are required to do chores and whether they have a curfew. Is there an association between having a curfew and having to do chores?

	Curfew	No Curfew	TOTAL
Chores	16	4	20
No Chores	16	64	80
TOTAL	32	68	100

Find the relative frequency of having to do chores.

Total who have to do chores → 20
Total number of teens polled → 100 = 0.20 = 20 %

Find the relative frequency of having to do chores among those who have a curfew.

Number with a curfew who have to do chores → 16
Total number with a curfew → 32 = 0.50 = 50 %

Compare the relative frequencies. Students who have a curfew are less likely / more likely to have to do chores than the general population.

Is there an association between having a curfew and having to do chores? Explain.

Yes; the relative frequencies show that having a curfew makes it more likely

that a student will have to do chores.

Chapter 9 352 Extension

- How can you find the relative frequency for international flights being late? Find the total number of all international flights: 50. Find the number of international flights that are late: 10. The relative frequency is 10 out of 50, or 20%.

Teaching Strategies

Have students highlight the cells with which they are working. Choose different colored highlighters to represent the whole population and the sub-population relative frequencies. This may help students focus on the correct numbers in the table.

MATHEMATICAL PRACTICE   **Highlighting the Standards**

This Example is an opportunity to address Standard 6 (Attend to precision). When constructing two-way tables, students need to be accurate with their computations and precise in their recording of the data. The row elements and column elements must be correctly placed in order for the totals to be calculated correctly.

CLOSE

Essential Question

How can you construct and interpret two-way tables?
Possible answer: Make a two-way table in which columns represent one set of categories for the population and the rows represent a different set of categories for the population. You can analyze data in two-way tables to see if there is an association between categories by comparing their relative frequencies.

Summarize

Have students collect data and make their own categories for a two-way table in their journals. Tell them to compare the relative frequencies and to draw any possible conclusions about associations between two categories.

PRACTICE

Where skills are taught	Where skills are practiced
1 EXPLORE	EX. 1
2 EXAMPLE	EXS. 2–7

8 Data from 200 flights was collected. The flights were categorized as domestic or international and late or not late. Is there an association between international flights and a flight being late?

	Late	Not Late	TOTAL
Domestic	30	120	150
International	10	40	50
TOTAL	40	160	200

Find the relative frequency of a flight being late.

Total flights that are late → $\dfrac{40}{200}$ = 0.20 = 20 %
Total number of flights →

Find the relative frequency of a flight being late among international flights.

Number of international flights that are late → $\dfrac{10}{50}$ = 0.20 = 20 %
Total number of international flights →

Compare the relative frequencies. International flights are less likely/ equally likely/ more likely to be late than flights in general.

Is there an association between international flights and a flight being late? Explain.

No; the relative frequencies show that international flights are just as likely to be late as any other flight.

REFLECT

3a. Compare the relative frequency of having a curfew and having chores to the relative frequency of not having a curfew and having chores. Does this comparison help you draw a conclusion about whether there is an association between having a curfew and having chores? Explain.

The relative frequency of having a curfew and having chores $\left(\frac{16}{32} = 50\%\right)$ is greater than the relative frequency of not having a curfew and having chores $\left(\frac{4}{68} \approx 6\%\right)$, so there seems to be an association between the two events.

3b. Compare the relative frequency of domestic flights being late to the relative frequency of international flights being late. Does this comparison help you draw a conclusion about whether there is an association between international flights and being late? Explain.

The relative frequency of late domestic flights $\left(\frac{30}{150} = 20\%\right)$ is equal to the relative frequency of late international flights $\left(\frac{10}{50} = 20\%\right)$, so there seems to be no association between the two events.

PRACTICE

Karen asked 150 students at her school if they played sports. She also recorded whether the student was a boy or girl. Of the 150 students, 20% did not play sports, 60% of the total were girls, and 70% of the girls played sports.

	Sports	No Sports	TOTAL
Boys	57	3	60
Girls	63	27	90
TOTAL	120	30	150

1. Complete the two-way table.

2. What is the relative frequency of a student playing sports? **80%**

3. What is the relative frequency of a boy playing sports? **95%**

4. Is there an association between being a boy and playing sports at Karen's school? Explain.

Yes; the relative frequency of being a boy and playing sports is greater than the relative frequency of total students who play sports, so there is an association between being a boy and playing sports.

Aiden collected data from 80 students about whether they have siblings and whether they have pets.

	Siblings	No Siblings	TOTAL
Pets	49	21	70
No Pets	7	3	10
TOTAL	56	24	80

5. What is the relative frequency of a student having pets? **87.5%**

6. What is the relative frequency of a student with siblings having pets? **87.5%**

7. Is there an association between having siblings and having pets? Explain.

No; the relative frequency of having pets is the same for students with siblings as for the general student, so there is no association between having siblings and having pets.

Linear Functions
Going Deeper

Essential question: *How do you graph a linear function?*

© Houghton Mifflin Harcourt Publishing Company

COMMON CORE Standards for Mathematical Content

CC.8.EE.5 Graph proportional relationships, interpreting the unit rate as the slope of the graph. Compare two different proportional relationships represented in different ways.

CC.8.F.3 Interpret the equation $y = mx + b$ as defining a linear function, whose graph is a straight line; give examples of functions that are not linear.

Vocabulary
linear function
linear equation

Prerequisites
Ordered pairs
Graphing on a coordinate plane

Math Background
A function with a constant rate of change across its domain (the set of all input values) is called a *linear function*. The graph of a linear function is a line. Any function whose rate of change is variable is a non-linear function. A line is uniquely determined by its y-intercept, b, and rate of change (slope), m. Given these two values, an equation can be written that describes the line: $y = mx + b$. If the equation of a function cannot be written in this form, then the function is non-linear.

INTRODUCE

Compare the movements of a car on the highway to a car on a city street. In the city, a car may slow down and speed up as it navigates through its course. On a highway, however, a car may reach a certain speed and maintain that speed. Ideally with cruise control, it can travel at a constant rate for long distances. In this lesson, we learn to describe and graph functions that maintain constant rates.

TEACH

1 EXPLORE

Questioning Strategies
- How do you find the values to complete the table? Multiply the time values by the rate 1.5 cm/h to get the total amounts of rain in cm.
- Why are the time values on the horizontal axis? Time is the input for this function.
- Why do the points lie along a straight line? because the rate of change is constant

REFLECT

In 1a, students consider values of the function that are not in the table. Be sure students understand that all possible (x, y) values of the function will be contained by this same line. In 1b, students consider how the constant of the function affects the slant or steepness of the graph.

2 EXAMPLE

Questioning Strategies
- How do you find values for the calories to complete the table? Substitute the given weights (input) for x in the equation, and evaluate for y.

MATHEMATICAL PRACTICE **Highlighting the Standards**

This Example is an opportunity to address Standard 4 (Model with mathematics). Students model function relationships with multiple representations. Students write equations to model a function, complete tables of values to model a function, and graph corresponding values from the table as ordered pairs to model functions with graphs.

Name_____ Class_____ Date_____

9-3

Linear Functions
Going Deeper

Essential question: *How do you graph a linear function?*

video tutor

1 EXPLORE CC.8.EE.5 Investigating Change

The U.S. Department of Agriculture defines heavy rain as rain that falls at a rate of 1.5 centimeters per hour.

A The table shows the total amount of rain that falls in various amounts of time during a heavy rain. Complete the table.

Time (h)	0	1	2	3	4	5
Total Amount of Rain (cm)	0	1.5	3	4.5	6	7.5

B Plot the ordered pairs from the table on the coordinate plane at the right.

C How much rain falls in 3.5 hours?

5.25 cm

D Plot the point corresponding to 3.5 hours of heavy rain.

E What do you notice about all of the points you plotted?

All of the points lie along a straight line.

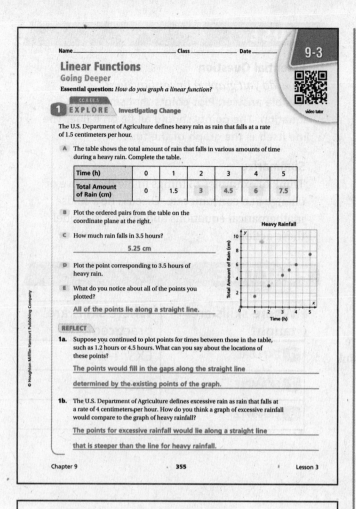

Heavy Rainfall

REFLECT

1a. Suppose you continued to plot points for times between those in the table, such as 1.2 hours or 4.5 hours. What can you say about the locations of these points?

The points would fill in the gaps along the straight line

determined by the existing points of the graph.

1b. The U.S. Department of Agriculture defines excessive rain as rain that falls at a rate of 4 centimeters per hour. How do you think a graph of excessive rainfall would compare to the graph of heavy rainfall?

The points for excessive rainfall would lie along a straight line

that is steeper than the line for heavy rainfall.

Chapter 9　355　Lesson 3

© Houghton Mifflin Harcourt Publishing Company

A **linear function** is a function whose graph is a nonvertical straight line. The function describing heavy rainfall in **1** is a linear function because its graph is a set of points that form a straight line.

A **linear equation** is an equation that represents a linear function. The solutions of a linear equation are ordered pairs that form a straight line on the coordinate plane.

2 EXAMPLE CC.8.F.3 Graphing a Linear Equation

Experts recommend that adult dogs have a daily intake of 50 calories per kilogram of the dog's weight plus 100 calories. Write an equation that gives the recommended number of daily calories y for a dog that weighs x kilograms. Then show that the equation is a linear equation.

Write an equation.

Daily calories equals 50 times weight plus 100.

| y | $=$ | $50x$ | $+$ | 100 |

Complete the table to find some solutions of the equation.

Weight (kg), x	6	8	10	12	14
Calories, y	400	500	600	700	800

Plot the points, then draw a line through the points to represent all the possible x-values and their corresponding y-values.

The equation is a linear equation because
the graph of the solutions is a straight line.

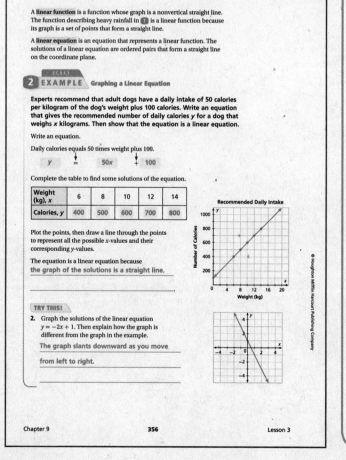

Recommended Daily Intake

TRY THIS!

2. Graph the solutions of the linear equation $y = -2x + 1$. Then explain how the graph is different from the graph in the example.

The graph slants downward as you move

from left to right.

Chapter 9　356　Lesson 3

© Houghton Mifflin Harcourt Publishing Company

Questioning Strategies

- How is the relationship between x and y in the table of values in this example different from the relationship between x and y in Example 1? **In Example 1, each input value is multiplied by the same number to get the corresponding output value. In Example 3, each input value is multiplied by a different number to get the corresponding output value.**

- Why doesn't the graph fall on a line? **It is not a linear function because there is not a constant rate of change.**

Technology

Use a graphing calculator to explore functions that do and do not have a constant rate of change to explore linear and nonlinear functions. To prepare them for Exercise 7, ask students whether they think $y = 5$ is a linear function.

CLOSE

Essential Question
How do you graph a linear function?
Possible answer: Plot points that satisfy the equation. The points should all lie on a line. The line itself is the graph of the function.

Summarize
Think of examples of things in life that move or change at a constant rate. Discuss how to use mathematical equations and graphs to model these actions.

PRACTICE

Where skills are taught	Where skills are practiced
1 EXPLORE	EXS. 1–4
2 EXAMPLE	EXS. 3–4
3 EXAMPLE	EXS. 1–7

The linear equation in has the form $y = mx + b$, where m and b are real numbers. Every equation in the form $y = mx + b$ is a linear equation. Equations that cannot be written in this form are not linear equations.

3 EXAMPLE Determining Whether an Equation is Linear

A square tile has a side length of x inches. The equation $y = x^2$ gives the area y of the tile in square inches. Determine whether the equation $y = x^2$ is a linear equation.

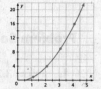

Complete the table.

Side Length, x	1	2	3	4
Area, y	1	4	9	16

Plot the points, then draw a curve through the points to represent all the possible x-values and their corresponding y-values.

Decide whether the equation $y = x^2$ a linear equation. Explain your reasoning.

No; the equation is not a linear equation because

the graph of its solutions is not a straight line.

REFLECT

3a. How is the equation $y = x^2$ different from the linear equations you have graphed?

The variable x is squared in this equation.

3b. Explain whether you think the equation $y = 2x^2 + 4$ is a linear equation.

No; the variable x is squared.

3c. Error Analysis A student graphed several solutions of $y = -2x$ as shown. The student concluded that the equation is not a linear equation. Explain the student's error.

$(-1, -2)$ and $(-2, -4)$ are not solutions of the

equation. The correct solutions all lie on a line,

so the equation is a linear equation.

PRACTICE

Graph solutions of each equation and tell whether the equation is linear or non-linear.

1. $y = 5 - 2x$

Input, x	−1	1	3	5
Output, y	7	3	−1	−5

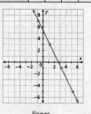

linear

2. $y = 2 - x^2$

Input, x	−2	−1	0	1	2
Output, y	−2	1	2	1	−2

non-linear

3. Olivia measured several rooms in her house in feet. She wants to express the measurements in inches. Write an equation relating feet x and inches y. Tell whether the equation is linear or non-linear.

$y = 12x$; linear

4. Seth receives $100 from his grandmother for his birthday. He also saves $20 every month. Write an equation relating months x and total savings y. Tell whether the equation is linear or non-linear.

$y = 20x + 100$; linear

Explain whether each equation is a linear equation.

5. $y = x^2 - 1$

No; the equation cannot be written in the form $y = mx + b$, and the graph of the solutions is not a straight line.

6. $y = 1 - x$

Yes; the equation can be written in the form $y = mx + b$, and the graph of the solutions is a straight line.

7. Error Analysis A student claims that the equation $y = 7$ is not a linear equation because it does not have the form $y = mx + b$. Do you agree or disagree? Why?

Disagree; the equation can be written in the form $y = mx + b$ where m is 0, and the graph of the solutions is a horizontal line.

ADDITIONAL PRACTICE

Assign these pages to help your students practice and apply important lesson concepts. For additional exercises, see the Student Edition.

Answers

Additional Practice

1. linear; −3; 2

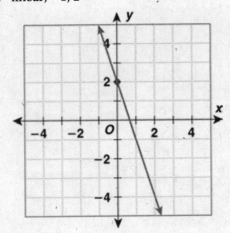

2. not linear

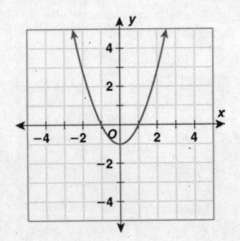

3. $f(x) = -\dfrac{1}{3}x - 1$

4. $f(x) = -2x + 10$

5. $f(x) = 1.2x + 8$, where x is the wholesale cost of the sweater.

$f(24.50) = 1.2 \cdot 24.5 + 8 = \$37.40$

Problem Solving

1. $f(x) = 3.2x$

2. 48 inches

3. $f(x) = 228(75 - x)$

4. 7980 feet

5. B

6. F

7. C

Name_____ Class_____ Date_____

Additional Practice

Determine whether each function is linear. If so, give the slope and y-intercept of the function's graph.

1. $f(x) = -3x + 2$

2. $f(x) = x^2 - 1$

Write a rule for each linear function.

3.

4.

x	y
-3	16
-1	12
3	4
7	-4

5. At the Sweater Store, the price of a sweater is 20% more than the wholesale cost, plus a markup of $8. Find a rule for a linear function that describes the price of sweaters at the Sweater Store. Use it to determine the price of a sweater with a wholesale cost of $24.50.

_____

Problem Solving

Write the correct answer.

1. On April 14–15, 1921 in Silver Lake, Colorado, 76 inches of snow fell in 24 hours, at an average rate of 3.2 inches per hour. Find a rule for the linear function that describes the amount of snow after x hours at the average rate.

2. At the average rate of snowfall from Exercise 1, how much snow had fallen in 15 hours?

3. The altitude of clouds in feet can be found by multiplying the difference between the temperature and the dew point by 228. If the temperature is 75°, find a rule for the linear function that describes the height of the clouds with dew point x.

4. If the temperature is 75° and the dew point is 40°, what is the height of the clouds?

For Exercises 5–7, refer to the table below, which shows the relationship between the number of times a cricket chirps in a minute and temperature.

5. Find a rule for the linear function that describes the temperature based on x, the number of cricket chirps in a minute based on temperature.

A $f(x) = x + 5$

B $f(x) = \dfrac{x}{4} + 40$

C $f(x) = x - 20$

D $f(x) = \dfrac{x}{2} + 20$

Cricket Chirps/min	Temperature (°F)
80	60
100	65
120	70
140	75

6. What is the temperature if a cricket chirps 150 times in a minute?

F 77.5 °F

G 95 °F

H 130 °F

J 155 °F

7. If the temperature is 85 °F, how many times will a cricket chirp in a minute?

A 61

B 105

C 180

D 200

© Houghton Mifflin Harcourt Publishing Company

Comparing Multiple Representations
Going Deeper

Essential question: How can you use tables, graphs, and equations to compare functions?

© Houghton Mifflin Harcourt Publishing Company

COMMON CORE Standards for Mathematical Content

CC.8.EE.5 Graph proportional relationships, interpreting the unit rate as the slope of the graph. Compare two different proportional relationships represented in different ways.

CC.8.F.2 Compare properties of two functions each represented in a different way (algebraically, graphically, numerically in tables, or by verbal descriptions).

CC.8.F.4 Construct a function to model a linear relationship between two quantities. Determine the rate of change and initial value of the function from a description of a relationship or from two (x, y) values, including reading these from a table or from a graph. Interpret the rate of change and initial value of a linear function in terms of the situation it models, and in terms of its graph or a table of values.

Prerequisites

Linear functions
Slope-intercept form

Math Background

Comparing functions requires that we first write them in common terms, such as in slope-intercept form. Then we need to be able to interpret the like terms and different terms in relation to the context. Parallel lines represent situations with the same constant rate of change. Lines that intersect share the same input and output values at the intersection point only.

INTRODUCE

Suppose you want to subscribe to a music download service. Different services have different monthly fees and different rates for each downloaded song. How do you compare the options and choose the plan that's best for you? In this lesson you learn to compare these two types of situations.

TEACH

1 EXPLORE

Questioning Strategies

- How can you find the rates of change for the functions? **Use two points.**

- How can you find the unit rates? **Write the slope ratios with a denominator of 1.**

- How can you tell which relationship has the greater rate of change? **Compare their unit rates: 15 wpm < 20 wpm**

2 EXPLORE

Questioning Strategies

- How can you tell that Josh pays a $10 fee each month? **The *y*-intercept is 10. That means if he downloads 0 songs, the monthly cost will still be $10.**

- What does it mean when the *y*-intercept is 0? **There is no monthly fee in addition to the per-song download charge.**

REFLECT

Discuss with students which plan would be a better choice if you do not download many songs per month and which plan would be a better choice if you do download many songs per month.

> ### MATHEMATICAL PRACTICE   Highlighting the Standards
>
> This Lesson is an opportunity to address Standard 4 (Model with mathematics). Students will learn to compare linear relationships whether they are modeled with equations or graphs. By creating an effective model, it is possible to analyze the outcome of a situation in different real-world settings. Students will learn to use the mathematical model as an effective problem-solving tool.

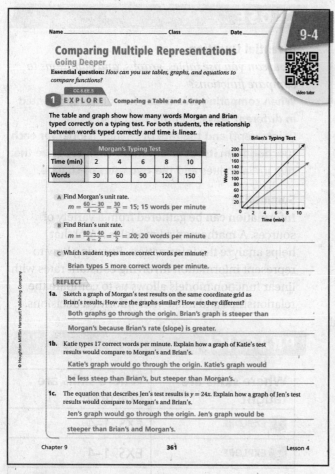

Name _____ Class _____ Date _____

9-4

Comparing Multiple Representations
Going Deeper

Essential question: How can you use tables, graphs, and equations to compare functions?

CC.8.EE.5

1 EXPLORE Comparing a Table and a Graph

The table and graph show how many words Morgan and Brian typed correctly on a typing test. For both students, the relationship between words typed correctly and time is linear.

Morgan's Typing Test					
Time (min)	2	4	6	8	10
Words	30	60	90	120	150

Brian's Typing Test

A Find Morgan's unit rate.

$m = \frac{60 - 30}{4 - 2} = \frac{30}{2} = 15$; 15 words per minute

B Find Brian's unit rate.

$m = \frac{80 - 40}{4 - 2} = \frac{40}{2} = 20$; 20 words per minute

C Which student types more correct words per minute?

Brian types 5 more correct words per minute.

REFLECT

1a. Sketch a graph of Morgan's test results on the same coordinate grid as Brian's results. How are the graphs similar? How are they different?

Both graphs go through the origin. Brian's graph is steeper than

Morgan's because Brian's rate (slope) is greater.

1b. Katie types 17 correct words per minute. Explain how a graph of Katie's test results would compare to Morgan's and Brian's.

Katie's graph would go through the origin. Katie's graph would

be less steep than Brian's, but steeper than Morgan's.

1c. The equation that describes Jen's test results is $y = 24x$. Explain how a graph of Jen's test results would compare to Morgan's and Brian's.

Jen's graph would go through the origin. Jen's graph would be

steeper than Brian's and Morgan's.

© Houghton Mifflin Harcourt Publishing Company

Chapter 9   361   Lesson 4

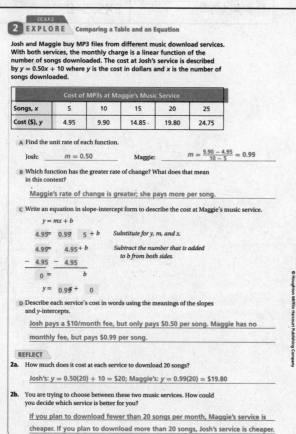

CC.8.F.2

2 EXPLORE Comparing a Table and an Equation

Josh and Maggie buy MP3 files from different music download services. With both services, the monthly charge is a linear function of the number of songs downloaded. The cost at Josh's service is described by $y = 0.50x + 10$ where y is the cost in dollars and x is the number of songs downloaded.

Cost of MP3s at Maggie's Music Service					
Songs, x	5	10	15	20	25
Cost ($), y	4.95	9.90	14.85	19.80	24.75

A Find the unit rate of each function.

Josh: $m = 0.50$ Maggie: $m = \frac{9.90 - 4.95}{10 - 5} = 0.99$

B Which function has the greater rate of change? What does that mean in this context?

Maggie's rate of change is greater; she pays more per song.

C Write an equation in slope-intercept form to describe the cost at Maggie's music service.

$y = mx + b$

$4.95 = 0.99 \cdot 5 + b$ *Substitute for y, m, and x.*

$4.95 = 4.95 + b$ *Subtract the number that is added*
$- 4.95 \quad - 4.95$ *to b from both sides.*

$0 = b$

$y = 0.99x + 0$

D Describe each service's cost in words using the meanings of the slopes and y-intercepts.

Josh pays a $10/month fee, but only pays $0.50 per song. Maggie has no

monthly fee, but pays $0.99 per song.

REFLECT

2a. How much does it cost at each service to download 20 songs?

Josh's: $y = 0.50(20) + 10 = 20; Maggie's: $y = 0.99(20) = 19.80

2b. You are trying to choose between these two music services. How could you decide which service is better for you?

If you plan to download fewer than 20 songs per month, Maggie's service is

cheaper. If you plan to download more than 20 songs, Josh's service is cheaper.

© Houghton Mifflin Harcourt Publishing Company

Chapter 9   362   Lesson 4

© Houghton Mifflin Harcourt Publishing Company

Questioning Strategies

- How can you determine the equation by looking at the graph? **Because 100 is the *y*-intercept, we know that $b = 100$. The slope shows 10 units ($) down for each 1 unit (mo) right, or $\frac{-10}{1}$, so the slope is -10. The equation is $y = -10x + 100$.**

- How can you determine the equation by reading the words? **An initial payment of $60 indicates a *y*-intercept of 60. Weekly payments of $20 indicate a slope of $\frac{-20}{1}$, or -20.**

Teaching Strategies

Present students with different functions and/or situations modeled with graphs, equations, tables, and descriptions. Have students work in groups to compare and contrast the linear functions. Ask them to make decisions based on the functions and real-world parameters.

CLOSE

Essential Question

How can you use tables, graphs, and equations to compare functions?

When comparing two linear functions represented in different ways, identify the initial value (*y*-intercept) and the rate of change (slope) for each function from its representation. Then compare the two initial values and the two rates of change.

Summarize

Information can be gathered from a variety of sources. A mathematical model is a tool that helps analyze the information. Knowing how to represent information involving constant rates with linear function models allows us to compare the relationships and make well-informed decisions.

PRACTICE

Where skills are taught	Where skills are practiced
1 EXPLORE	EXS. 1–4
2 EXPLORE	EXS. 1–4
3 EXPLORE	EXS. 5–8

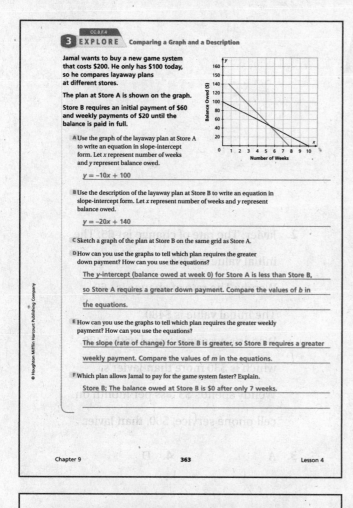

3 EXPLORE CC.8.F.4 Comparing a Graph and a Description

Jamal wants to buy a new game system that costs $200. He only has $100 today, so he compares layaway plans at different stores.

The plan at Store A is shown on the graph.

Store B requires an initial payment of $60 and weekly payments of $20 until the balance is paid in full.

A Use the graph of the layaway plan at Store A to write an equation in slope-intercept form. Let x represent number of weeks and y represent balance owed.

$y = -10x + 100$

B Use the description of the layaway plan at Store B to write an equation in slope-intercept form. Let x represent number of weeks and y represent balance owed.

$y = -20x + 140$

C Sketch a graph of the plan at Store B on the same grid as Store A.

D How can you use the graphs to tell which plan requires the greater down payment? How can you use the equations?

The y-intercept (balance owed at week 0) for Store A is less than Store B, so Store A requires a greater down payment. Compare the values of b in the equations.

E How can you use the graphs to tell which plan requires the greater weekly payment? How can you use the equations?

The slope (rate of change) for Store B is greater, so Store B requires a greater weekly payment. Compare the values of m in the equations.

F Which plan allows Jamal to pay for the game system faster? Explain.

Store B; The balance owed at Store B is $0 after only 7 weeks.

Chapter 9   363   Lesson 4

PRACTICE

The table and the graph display two different linear functions.

Input, x	Output, y
−3	5
−1	1
2	−5
3	−7
6	−13

1. Find the slope of each function.

Table: $m = \dfrac{1-5}{-1-(-3)} = \dfrac{-4}{2} = -2$

Graph: $m = \dfrac{\text{rise}}{\text{run}} = -\dfrac{2}{3}$

2. Without graphing the function represented in the table, tell which function's graph is steeper.

The function in the table has a steeper graph because the absolute value of its slope is greater.

3. Write an equation for each function.

Table: $y = -2x - 1$

Graph: $y = -\dfrac{2}{3}x + 1$

4. Use the equations from **3** to tell which function has the greater y-intercept.

The function represented on the graph.

Aisha runs a tutoring business. Students may choose to pay $15 per hour or they may follow the plan shown on the graph.

5. Describe the plan shown on the graph.

Students pay a $40 fee and $5/hr.

6. Sketch a graph showing the $15 per hour option.

7. What does the intersection of the two graphs mean?

With both options, it costs $60 for 4 hours of tutoring.

8. If you wanted to hire Aisha for tutoring, how can you decide which payment option is better for you?

If you want fewer than 4 hours of tutoring, choose the $15/hr option.

If you want more than 4 hours of tutoring, choose the other option.

Chapter 9   364   Lesson 4

© Houghton Mifflin Harcourt Publishing Company

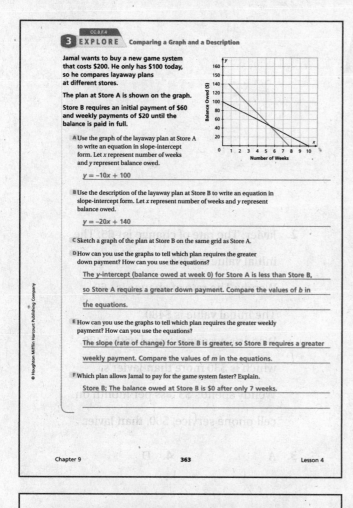

Assign these pages to help your students practice and apply important lesson concepts. For additional exercises, see the Student Edition.

Answers

Additional Practice

1. slope of f: $\frac{1}{2}$

   slope of g: $\frac{1}{4}$

   The slope of f is $\frac{1}{4}$ greater than the slope of g.

2. y-intercept of f: -2

   y-intercept of g: -1

   The y-intercept of g is 1 greater than the y-intercept of f.

3. Sheila started at 242 feet above the canyon floor, which is 42 feet higher than where Connor started. Connor climbed down the canyon wall at a rate of 10 feet per minute, which is 2 feet per minute faster than Sheila.

Problem Solving

1. Dan: The rate of change is 0.5. The initial value is 3.

   Keri: The rate of change is 0.75. The initial value is 4.

   Keri has assembled 4 bicycles, which is 1 more than Dan. She is assembling bicycles at a rate of 0.75 per hour, which is 0.25 more bicycles per hour than Dan.

2. Javier: The rate of change is -65. The initial value is $450.

   Wendy: The rate of change is -60. The initial value is $480.

   Wendy's account started with $480, which is $30 more than Javier's. Wendy spends $5 less per month on cell phone service, $60, than Javier.

3. A   4. D

Additional Practice

1. Find and compare the slopes for the linear functions f and g.

$f(x) = \dfrac{1}{2}x - 4$

x	−4	0	4	8
g(x)	−3	−2	−1	0

slope of f _____ slope of g _____

Compare _____

2. Find and compare the y-intercepts for the linear functions f and g.

x	−1	0	1	2
f(x)	−7	−2	3	8

y-intercept of f _____

y-intercept of g _____

Compare _____

Connor and Sheila are in a rock-climbing club. They are climbing down a canyon wall. Connor starts from a cliff that is 200 feet above the canyon floor and climbs down at an average speed of 10 feet per minute. Sheila climbs down the canyon wall as shown in the table.

Time (min)	0	1	2	3
Sheila's height (ft)	242	234	226	218

3. Interpret the rates of change and initial values of the linear functions in terms of the situations they model.

Connor

Initial value _____

Rate of change _____

Compare _____

Sheila

Initial value _____

Rate of change _____

© Houghton Mifflin Harcourt Publishing Company

Problem Solving

Find and compare the rates of change and initial values of the linear functions in terms of the situations they model.

1. Dan and Keri assemble bicycles. So far today, Dan has assembled 3 bikes. He works at a rate of 0.5 bikes per hour. Keri has assembled 4 bikes, so far today, and assembles bicycles as shown in the table.

Time (hr)	0	1	2	3
Bikes Keri Assembled	4	4.75	5.5	6.25

_____

_____

2. Javier and Wendy pay for their cell phone service from their checking accounts according to the equation and graph shown.
Javier: $f(x) = -65x + 450$
Wendy

Use the table and the graph for Exercises 3 and 4. Choose the letter for the best answer.

Jane and Alex each start driving from their homes, which are different distances from the warehouse where they both work, to a meeting out of town.

Jane

Time (hr)	2	3	4	5
Distance (mi)	185	240	295	350

Alex

3. How much farther from the warehouse was Jane than Alex when she started driving today?

A 50 miles C 75 miles

B 60 miles D 200 miles

4. How much faster is Jane driving than Alex?

A 55 miles per hour

B 50 miles per hour

C 25 miles per hour

D 5 miles per hour

© Houghton Mifflin Harcourt Publishing Company

CHAPTER 9 Problem Solving Connections
Give me a T!

COMMON CORE Standards for Mathematical Content

CC.8.SP.1 Construct and interpret scatter plots for bivariate measurement data to investigate patterns of association between two quantities. Describe patterns such as clustering, outliers, positive or negative association, linear association, and nonlinear association.

CC.8.SP.2 Know that straight lines are widely used to model relationships between two quantitative variables. For scatter plots that suggest a linear association, informally fit a straight line, and informally assess the model fit by judging the closeness of the data points to the line.

CC.8.SP.3 Use the equation of a linear model to solve problems in the context of bivariate measurement data, interpreting the slope and intercept.

CC.8.SP.4 Understand that patterns of association can also be seen in bivariate categorical data by displaying frequencies and relative frequencies in a two-way table. Construct and interpret a two-way table summarizing data on two categorical variables collected from the same subjects. Use relative frequencies calculated for rows or columns to describe possible association between the two variables.

INTRODUCE

Discuss with students some common variables that you might assume have either a positive or negative association. Some examples may be:

Positive
- Amount of sleep vs. Amount of energy
- Amount of sunshine vs. Amount of plant growth

Negative
- Amount of sleep vs. Amount of fatigue
- Amount of sunshine vs. Amount of rain

Tell students they will use given data to determine the association between and make predictions about the variables *height* and *arm span*.

TEACH

1 Making Scatter Plots

Questioning Strategies
- Do you see an association? If so, what kind? Explain. **Yes, the arm spans and heights seem to increase together or decrease together. It has a positive association.**
- Do you see any clusters? Do you see any outliers? Explain. **There may be slight clustering between 60 and 65 inches, which is likely due to the ages of Annika's classmates. There is an outlier at about (50, 62), which is possibly due to error in measurement.**

Avoid Common Errors
Students may confuse which variable goes on which axis. Although it does not matter in this example which variable is graphed on which axis, students must make sure they label the axes and graph each point according to the same labels.

2 Finding a Trend Line

Questioning Strategies
- What points can you choose to sketch a trend line? **Possible answer: (55, 55) and (65, 65)**
- About what arm span would you predict for a 72-in. tall person? Is this interpolation or extrapolation? Explain. **72 in.; extrapolation; 72 in. is greater than the maximum in the data.**
- About what arm span would you predict for a 57-in. tall person? Is this interpolation or extrapolation? Explain. **57 in.; interpolation; 57 in. is between the minimum and maximum in the data.**

Technology
Have students use their calculators to display and compare the scatter plot and trend line for this data in two different ways: (1) with height on the *x*-axis and arm span on the *y*-axis, and (2) with arm span on the *x*-axis and height on the *y*-axis. Lead students to the conclusion that the results are the same both ways.

Name_____ Class_____ Date_____

Problem Solving Connections

Give me a T! Annika asks several of her classmates to make a T with their bodies by standing up straight and putting their arms straight out to their sides. She measures their arm spans and their heights in inches. What associations can be made from the data she collects?

COMMON CORE
CC&SP.1
CC&SP.2
CC&SP.3
CC&SP.4

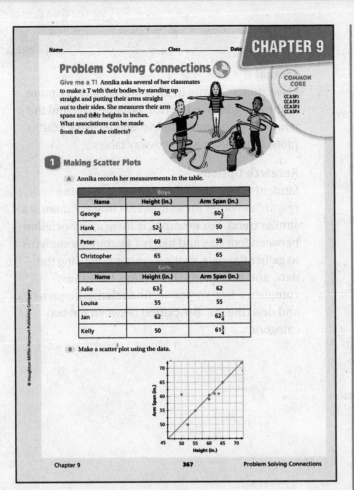

1 Making Scatter Plots

A Annika records her measurements in the table.

Boys		
Name	Height (in.)	Arm Span (in.)
George	60	$60\frac{1}{2}$
Hank	$52\frac{1}{4}$	50
Peter	60	59
Christopher	65	65

Girls		
Name	Height (in.)	Arm Span (in.)
Julie	$63\frac{1}{2}$	62
Louisa	55	55
Jan	62	$62\frac{1}{4}$
Kelly	50	$61\frac{3}{4}$

B Make a scatter plot using the data.

C What overall trends do you see in the scatter plot?

Arm span and height are approximately equal; there is a positive association

between arm span and height; the data appears to have a linear association.

D Do you see any outliers? Why might there be an outlier?

(50, $61\frac{3}{4}$) is an outlier; Annika may have made a mistake when she measured

that person's height or arm span or both.

2 Finding a Trend line

A Sketch a trend line on the scatter plot. (Hint: Because you will need to write an equation for the line later, it is a good idea to draw your line through data points, if possible.)

B How well does your trend line fit the data?

Sample answer: It matches well because most of the points are close to

the line.

C Measure your height in inches. Use the trend line to predict your arm span.

Answers will vary. For most students, arm span should be equal to (or close to)

the student's height.

D Identify two data points that your trend line goes through.

Answers will vary. Students may have drawn the trend line through

(55, 55) and (65, 65). These two points represent equal height and

arm span.

E Calculate the slope of your trend line.

$$m = \frac{65-55}{65-55} = \frac{10}{10} = 1$$

F Write an equation for the trend line in slope-intercept form.

$$y = mx + b$$
$$55 = 1(55) + b$$
$$0 = b$$
$$y = 1x + 0$$
$$y = x$$

Notes

Questioning Strategies

- With the given row and column heads, what should be the row totals and column totals? **Row totals top to bottom should be 4, 4, 8. Column totals left to right should be 2, 6, 8.**

- What are some conclusions you can make from the data displayed in the two-way table? **Possible answer: More people in the study have arm spans and heights that are not equal; there were an equal number of boys and girls surveyed.**

Teaching Strategies

Discuss with students what Annika could have done differently that would have changed the data and the resulting conclusions. For example, she could have taken multiple measures of the same person and recorded the average in order to achieve greater accuracy in measurements. She could have included more people in her sample in order to achieve a more representative sample.

 Answer the Question

Questioning Strategies

- What conclusion can be drawn from the data? **A person's arm span and height are approximately equal in length.**

Are the results the same for both boys and girls? **Yes, both boys and girls appear to have equal height and arm span.**

> **MATHEMATICAL PRACTICE** **Highlighting the Standards**
>
> This problem-solving activity addresses Standard 4 (Model with mathematics). Students model a sample of data of arm span and height in a scatter plot, with a trend line, and in a two-way table. Then students use each of these models to analyze the data and make conclusions or predictions about the general population.

CLOSE

Journal

Have students write in their journal a description of the categories in the two-variable data and the conclusions or predictions made by using scatter plots, trend lines, and two-way tables.

Research Options

Students can extend their learning by doing research of other measurements to see if there is a similar trend. For example, is there an association between foot size and height? Encourage students to gather the data, make a scatter plot using the data, and find a trend line. Then, have them complete a two-way table, find relative frequencies, and describe the association between the two categories.

G Use your trend line to interpolate how wide someone's arm span is if the individual is 58 inches tall.

$$y = x$$
$$y = 58$$

H Choose a height for which you would have to extrapolate, and use your trend line to predict what the arm span would be.

Check students' answers. Height should a reasonable height for a person and be greater than 65 inches or less than 50 inches. Arm span should equal height.

I Under what circumstances might this trend line not be a good predictor of arm span?

Babies and children do not have the same ratio of height to arm span.

When a person is having a growth spurt, their proportions may be

different.

3 Making a Two-Way Table

A Complete the two-way table using Annika's data.

	Arm Span Equal to Height	Arm Span Not Equal to Height	TOTAL
Boys	1	3	4
Girls	1	3	4
TOTAL	2	6	8

B How can you check that you completed the table correctly?

The values in each total column or row should be the sum of the other

numbers in that column or row.

© Houghton Mifflin Harcourt Publishing Company

C What is the relative frequency of boys?

Number of boys → 4
Total number of students → 8 = 0.50 = 50%

D What is the relative frequency of equal height and arm span for all students?

Total number with equal height and arm span → 2
Total number of students → 8 = 0.25 = 25%

E What is the relative frequency of equal height and arm span among boys?

Boys with equal height and arm span → 1
Total number of boys → 4 = 0.25 = 25%

4 Answer the Question

A Does there appear to be an association between being a boy and having equal height and arm span? Explain.

No; the relative frequency of boys with equal height and arm span is equal to

the relative frequency of all students with equal height and arm span, so there

is no association between being a boy and having equal height and arm span.

B Why might this data set be misleading?

Sample answers: The sample is small (only 8 students). The students may all be

the same age, so the conclusions may only be true for people at that age.

C What conclusions can Annika draw from her data?

Annika can conclude that, in general, a person's height and arm span are

approximately equal. She can also conclude that this relationship is true for

girls and boys.

© Houghton Mifflin Harcourt Publishing Company

This page provides students with the opportunity to apply concepts from the Common Core in real-world problem situations. There are three different levels of performance tasks:

⭐ **Novice:** These are short word problems that require students to apply the math they have learned in straightforward, real-world situations.

⭐⭐ **Apprentice:** These are more involved problems that guide students step-by-step through more complex tasks. These exercises include more complicated reasoning, writing, and open-ended elements.

⭐⭐⭐ **Expert:** These are open-ended, non-routine problems that, instead of stepping the students through, asks them to choose their own methods for solving and justify their answers and reasoning.

Sample answers

1. **a.** Nonlinear; the data points rise and then drop.
    b. Yes; the data points are more closely grouped around July.

2. **a.** neighbor: $C = 0.25e$; 12-pack: $C = 0.19e$; 18-pack: $C = 0.18e$
    b. The 18-pack function has the smallest slope; this is the best deal for price per egg.

3. Scoring Guide:

Task	Possible points
a	**1 point** for a reasonable line, such as: 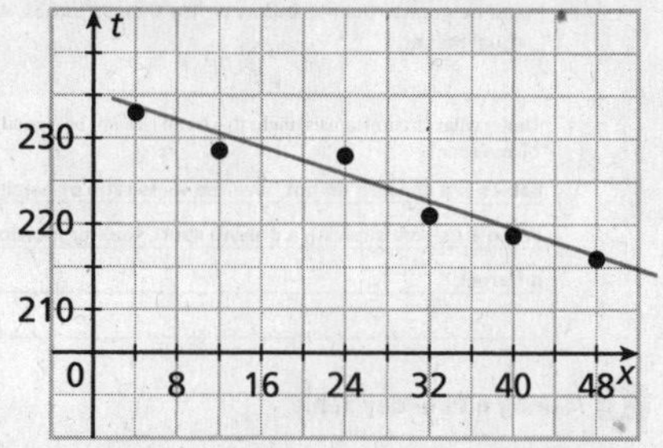 **1 point** for finding a slope around −0.4.
b	**2 points** for an equation that matches students' lines of best fit. The line shown in the graph for part **a** is approximately $y = -0.4x + 235$.
c	**1 point** for finding the time based on their answers to parts **a** and parts **b**, and **1 point** for appropriate work. $x = 2016 - 1924 = 92$, and substituting the value for x into the equation in part **b** results in a time of about 198 seconds.

Total possible points: 6

© Houghton Mifflin Harcourt Publishing Company

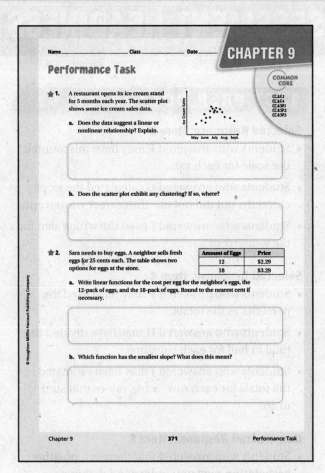

CHAPTER 9

Performance Task

COMMON CORE
CC.8.F.2
CC.8.F.4
CC.8.SP.1
CC.8.SP.2
CC.8.SP.3

⭐ 1. A restaurant opens its ice cream stand for 5 months each year. The scatter plot shows some ice cream sales data.

a. Does the data suggest a linear or nonlinear relationship? Explain.

b. Does the scatter plot exhibit any clustering? If so, where?

⭐ 2. Sara needs to buy eggs. A neighbor sells fresh eggs for 25 cents each. The table shows two options for eggs at the store.

Amount of Eggs	Price
12	$2.29
18	$3.29

a. Write linear functions for the cost per egg for the neighbor's eggs, the 12-pack of eggs, and the 18-pack of eggs. Round to the nearest cent if necessary.

b. Which function has the smallest slope? What does this mean?

⭐ 3. The scatter plot shows times for the men's 1500-meter Olympic gold medalists for certain years. The times are given in seconds, and $x = 0$ represents 1924.

a. Draw a line of best fit and estimate its slope.

b. Write an equation for the line of best fit that you drew.

c. What does your equation predict for a time for 2016? Show your work.

⭐ 4. The function $C(m) = 7 + 0.20(m - 3)$ gives the cost C for a ride of m miles in Toni's Taxi. A different company, Cozy Cab, has the sign shown.

Cozy Cab
0–5 miles: $7
More than 5 miles: $7 plus $0.15 for every mile after 5 miles

a. Compare the rates of the companies for rides that are 0 to 5 miles. For what distance are the costs the same? For what distance(s) is one company cheaper than the other?

b. Write a linear function for a ride over 5 miles using Cozy Cab. Compare the rates of the companies for rides over 5 miles, and justify your conclusions.

4. Scoring Guide:

Task	Possible points
a	**1 point** for correctly explaining that for 3 miles, the cost is the same, **1 point** for explaining that Toni's is less for rides less than 3 miles, and **1 point** explaining that Cozy is less for rides between 3 and 5 miles.
b	**1 point** for the function $F(m) = 0.15(m - 5) + 7$ or $F(m) = 0.15m + 6.25$, and **1 point** for noting that Cozy Cab is cheaper for all rides over 5 miles, and **1 point** for appropriate reasoning, using a graph, algebra, or other appropriate method to note that $C(m) < F(m)$ for all values of m.

Total possible points: 6

COMMON CORE CORRELATION

Standard	Items
CC.8.SP.1	7–9
CC.8.SP.2	2, 9
CC.8.SP.3	1, 3
CC.8.SP.4	4, 5
CC.8.F.2	6

TEST PREP DOCTOR ⊕

Selected Response: Item 2

- Students who answered **F** may have miscounted the scale for each axis.
- Students who answered **G** calculated the slope correctly, but did not use the correct y-intercept.
- Students who answered **J** used the wrong sign for the y-intercept.

Selected Response: Item 4

- Students who answered **F** may have used the percents as the totals.
- Students who answered **H** may have divided the total in half for each category.
- Students who answered **J** may have estimated the totals for each row, using values that sum to 50.

Constructed Response: Item 8

- Students who answered that there is a **positive association** may not understand that in a positive association, data points should increase from left to right.
- Students who answered **no association** may not understand that *no association* is not the same as *negative association*.

CHAPTER 9 COMMON CORE ASSESSMENT READINESS

Name _____ Class _____ Date _____

SELECTED RESPONSE

Rebecca played several games of cards with her brother. She made a scatter plot showing how many minutes each game lasted and how many points she scored during that game. Use the scatter plot for 1–3.

1. Using the trend line, how many points can Rebecca expect to score if the game lasts 25 minutes?

- A. 25
- B. 45
- Ⓒ 70
- D. 100

2. What is the equation for the trend line?

- F. $y = 2x$
- G. $y = 3x$
- Ⓗ $y = 3x - 5$
- J. $y = 3x + 5$

3. Using the equation for the trend line, how many points might Rebecca score in a game that lasts 100 minutes?

- A. 95
- B. 200
- C. 205
- Ⓓ 295

A survey of 50 adults asked whether the person had children and whether they had a cat. Use the table for 4–5.

	Cat	No cat	TOTAL
Children	5	27	
No children	16	2	
TOTAL	21	29	50

4. Of those surveyed, 64% said they do have children. Which values complete the last column of the table?

- F. Children: 64
  No children: 36
- Ⓖ Children: 32
  No children: 18
- H. Children: 25
  No children: 25
- J. Children: 30
  No children: 20

5. Which conclusion can be drawn?

- Ⓐ There appears to be an association between having no children and having a cat.
- B. The total number of people with cats is 32.
- C. There is no association between having children and having a cat.
- D. The relative frequency of people with no children is 18%.

6. Mr. Radmanovic and Mrs. Chin both fill up their cars with gasoline at the beginning of the week. The equation compares the number of miles driven, x, to the amount of gasoline in the tank, $f(x)$.

Find and compare the y-intercepts for the models and interpret their real-world meanings.

Mr. Radmanovic's Car

$f(x) = -\frac{1}{20}x + 13.6$

Mrs. Chin's Car

Miles Driven	0	8
Gasoline Remaining (gallons)	13.2	13

- F. The y-intercept for Mr. Radmanovic's car is 20. The y-intercept for Mrs. Chin's car is 13.2. Mr. Radmanovic's car has a larger gasoline tank than Mrs. Chin's car does.
- Ⓖ The y-intercept for Mr. Radmanovic's car is 13.6. The y-intercept for Mrs. Chin's car is 13.2. Mr. Radmanovic's car has a larger gasoline tank than Mrs. Chin's car does.
- H. The y-intercept for Mr. Radmanovic's car is 13.6. The y-intercept for Mrs. Chin's car is 13. Mr. Radmanovic's car has a larger gasoline tank than Mrs. Chin's car does.
- J. The y-intercept for Mr. Radmanovic's car is 20. The y-intercept for Mrs. Chin's car is 40. Mrs. Chin's car gets better gas mileage than Mr. Radmanovic's car does.

CONSTRUCTED RESPONSE

Noah researched the weekly high temperature in his city. He chose several weeks between July and December to put in a table. (The first week of July was numbered Week 1 in Noah's source material.) Use this data for Questions 7–10.

Week	High Temp (°F)	Week	High Temp (°F)
16	78	12	78
25	55	7	95
3	100	10	84
17	65	9	90
13	75	15	74
5	90	21	62

7. Use Noah's data to make a scatter plot.

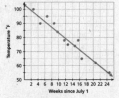

8. What type of association is shown on the scatterplot? Explain.

negative linear association; as weeks increase, temperature decreases.

9. Draw a trend line on the scatter plot.

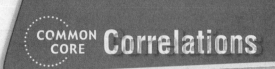

Correlation of *Explorations in Core Math* *Grade 8* to the Common Core State Standards

The Number System	Citations
CC.8.NS.1 Understand informally that every number has a decimal expansion; the rational numbers are those with decimal expansions that terminate in 0s or eventually repeat. Know that other numbers are called irrational.	pp. 5–10, 35–38, 39–40, 117–120
CC.8.NS.2 Use rational approximations of irrational numbers to compare the size of irrational numbers, locate them approximately on a number line diagram, and estimate the value of expressions (e.g., π^2).	pp. 111–116, 135–136

Expressions and Equations	Citations
CC.8.EE.1 Know and apply the properties of integer exponents to generate equivalent numerical expressions.	pp. 83–86, 87–92, 131–134, 135–136
CC.8.EE.2 Use square root and cube root symbols to represent solutions to equations of the form $x^2 = p$ and $x^3 = p$, where p is a positive rational number. Evaluate square roots of small perfect squares and cube roots of small perfect cubes. Know that $\sqrt{2}$ is irrational.	pp. 105–110, 135–136
CC.8.EE.3 Use numbers expressed in the form of a single digit times an integer power of 10 to estimate very large or very small quantities, and to express how many times as much one is than the other.	pp. 93–98, 131–134, 135–136
CC.8.EE.4 Perform operations with numbers expressed in scientific notation, including problems where both decimal and scientific notation are used. Use scientific notation and choose units of appropriate size for measurements of very large or very small quantities (e.g., use millimeters per year for seafloor spreading). Interpret scientific notation that has been generated by technology.	pp. 99–104, 131–134, 135–136
CC.8.EE.5 Graph proportional relationships, interpreting the unit rate as the slope of the graph. Compare two different proportional relationships represented in different ways.	pp. 167–168, 317–320, 355–360, 361–366
CC.8.EE.6 Use similar triangles to explain why the slope m is the same between any two distinct points on a non-vertical line in the coordinate plane; derive the equation $y = mx$ for a line through the origin and the equation $y = mx + b$ for a line intercepting the vertical axis at b.	pp. 247–250, 299–304, 305–312
CC.8.EE.7 Solve linear equations in one variable. a. Give examples of linear equations in one variable with one solution, infinitely many solutions, or no solutions. Show which of these possibilities is the case by successively transforming the given equation into simpler forms, until an equivalent equation of the form $x = a$, $a = a$, or $a = b$ results (where a and b are different numbers). b. Solve linear equations with rational number coefficients, including equations whose solutions require expanding expressions using the distributive property and collecting like terms.	pp. 23–28, 29–34, 35–38, 39–40, 265–270, 271–276, 283–286, 287–288, 327–330

CC.8.EE.8 Analyze and solve pairs of simultaneous linear equations. a. Understand that solutions to a system of two linear equations in two variables correspond to points of intersection of their graphs, because points of intersection satisfy both equations simultaneously. b. Solve systems of two linear equations in two variables algebraically, and estimate solutions by graphing the equations. Solve simple cases by inspection. c. Solve real-world and mathematical problems leading to two linear equations in two variables.	pp. 277–282, 283–286, 287–288, 321–326, 327–330, 331–332

Functions	Citations
CC.8.F.1 Understand that a function is a rule that assigns to each input exactly one output. The graph of a function is the set of ordered pairs consisting of an input and the corresponding output.	pp. 61–66, 71–74, 75–76
CC.8.F.2 Compare properties of two functions each represented in a different way (algebraically, graphically, numerically in tables, or by verbal descriptions).	pp. 75–76, 361–366, 371–372
CC.8.F.3 Interpret the equation $y = mx + b$ as defining a linear function, whose graph is a straight line; give examples of functions that are not linear.	pp. 305–312, 331–332, 355–360
CC.8.F.4 Construct a function to model a linear relationship between two quantities. Determine the rate of change and initial value of the function from a description of a relationship or from two (x, y) values, including reading these from a table or from a graph. Interpret the rate of change and initial value of a linear function in terms of the situation it models, and in terms of its graph or a table of values.	pp. 67–70, 71–74, 75–76, 295–298, 305–312, 313–316, 331–332, 361–366, 371–372
CC.8.F.5 Describe qualitatively the functional relationship between two quantities by analyzing a graph (e.g., where the function is increasing or decreasing, linear or nonlinear). Sketch a graph that exhibits the qualitative features of a function that has been described verbally.	pp. 55–60, 71–74, 75–76, 331–332

Geometry	Citations
CC.8.G.1 Verify experimentally the properties of rotations, reflections, and translations: a. Lines are taken to lines, and line segments to line segments of the same length. b. Angles are taken to angles of the same measure. c. Parallel lines are taken to parallel lines.	pp. 205–208, 217–220
CC.8.G.2 Understand that a two-dimensional figure is congruent to another if the second can be obtained from the first by a sequence of rotations, reflections, and translations; given two congruent figures, describe a sequence that exhibits the congruence between them.	pp. 209–216, 217–220, 221–222
CC.8.G.3 Describe the effect of dilations, translations, rotations, and reflections on two-dimensional figures using coordinates.	pp. 157–162, 163–166, 167–168, 199–204, 217–220, 221–222
CC.8.G.4 Understand that a two-dimensional figure is similar to another if the second can be obtained from the first by a sequence of rotations, reflections, translations, and dilations; given two similar two-dimensional figures, describe a sequence that exhibits the similarity between them.	pp. 163–166, 167–168, 209–216, 217–220, 221–222
CC.8.G.5 Use informal arguments to establish facts about the angle sum and exterior angle of triangles, about the angles created when parallel lines are cut by a transversal, and the angle-angle criterion for similarity of triangles.	pp. 151–156, 179–184, 185–190, 221–222, 247–250
CC.8.G.6 Explain a proof of the Pythagorean Theorem and its converse.	pp. 127–130, 247–250

CC.8.G.7 Apply the Pythagorean Theorem to determine unknown side lengths in right triangles in real-world and mathematical problems in two and three dimensions.	pp. 121–126, 135–136, 247–250
CC.8.G.8 Apply the Pythagorean Theorem to find the distance between two points in a coordinate system.	pp. 121–126, 135–136, 247–250
CC.8.G.9 Know the formulas for the volumes of cones, cylinders, and spheres and use them to solve real-world and mathematical problems.	pp. 235–238, 239–242, 243–246, 247–250, 253–254
Statistics and Probability	**Citations**
CC.8.SP.1 Construct and interpret scatter plots for bivariate measurement data to investigate patterns of association between two quantities. Describe patterns such as clustering, outliers, positive or negative association, linear association, and nonlinear association.	pp. 339–344, 345–350, 367–370, 371–372
CC.8.SP.2 Know that straight lines are widely used to model relationships between two quantitative variables. For scatter plots that suggest a linear association, informally fit a straight line, and informally assess the model fit by judging the closeness of the data points to the line.	pp. 339–344, 345–350, 367–370, 371–372
CC.8.SP.3 Use the equation of a linear model to solve problems in the context of bivariate measurement data, interpreting the slope and intercept.	pp. 345–350, 367–370, 371–372
CC.8.SP.4 Understand that patterns of association can also be seen in bivariate categorical data by displaying frequencies and relative frequencies in a two-way table. Construct and interpret a two-way table summarizing data on two categorical variables collected from the same subjects. Use relative frequencies calculated for rows or columns to describe possible association between the two variables.	pp. 351–354, 367–370

© Houghton Mifflin Harcourt Publishing Company